The Pity of War

NIALL FERGUSON

The Pity of War

BASIC
BOOKS

A Member of the Perseus Books Group

This book was first published in Great Britain
in 1998 by Allen Lane, The Penguin Press, The Penguin Group

Copyright © 1999 by Niall Ferguson.
"Repressions of War Experience" copyright Siegfried Sassoon,
\reproduced by permission of George Sassoon.

Published by Basic Books,
A Member of the Perseus Books Group

A CIP catalog record for this book is available from the Library of Congress.
ISBN 0-465-05711-X

99 00 01 02 /RRD   10 9 8 7 6 5 4

Contents

Figures   vi
Tables   vii
Illustrations   ix
Acknowledgements   x
Note on the illustrations   xii
Introduction   xix

1. The Myths of Militarism   1
2. Empires, Ententes and Edwardian Appeasement   31
3. Britain's War of Illusions   56
4. Arms and Men   82
5. Public Finance and National Security   105
6. The Last Days of Mankind: 28 June–4 August 1914   143
7. The August Days: The Myth of War Enthusiasm   174
8. The Press Gang   212
9. Economic Capability: The Advantage Squandered   248
10. Strategy, Tactics and the Net Body Count   282
11. 'Maximum Slaughter at Minimum Expense': War Finance   318
12. The Death Instinct: Why Men Fought   339
13. The Captor's Dilemma   367
14. How (not) to Pay for the War   395

Conclusion: Alternatives to Armageddon   433
Notes   463
Bibliography   517
Index   542

Figures

1. The peacetime strength of the German army, 1874–1914
2. The armies of the four principal European powers, 1909–1913
3. Defence expenditures of the European powers, 1890–1913
4. Defence expenditures of the two European blocs, 1890–1913
5. Estimates for total public spending as a percentage of gross national product, the five great powers, 1890–1913
6. The average monthly price of British consols, calculated on a 3 per cent coupon, 1900–1914
7. The weekly closing price of French, German and Russian bonds, all calculated on a 3 per cent coupon, 1900–1914
8. Unemployment rates in Berlin and London, July 1914–April 1915
9. The weekly closing prices in London of continental government bonds in 1914.
10. Enlistment in the British regular army and Territorial Force, August 1914–December 1915
11. The circulation of the *Daily Mail*, 1914–1918
12. The 'net body count': British casualties minus German casualties in the British sector of the Western Front, 1915–1918
13. The 'net body count': British and French soldiers permanently incapacitated minus German, August 1914–July 1918 (Western Front)
14. Exchange rates of the dollar, 1915–1918
15. Prices and trading volumes of Anglo-French 5 per cents, 1915–1918
16. The Anglo-French–American yield gap, 1915–1918
17. German prisoners taken by the British army in France, July 1917–December 1918
18. The German annual inflation rate, 1918–1923
19. The burden of reparations, 1920–1932

Tables

1. Percentages of total population enfranchised for lower chambers, 1850 and 1900
2. The socialist vote in selected European countries on the eve of war
3. Some indicators of British and German industrial strength, 1880 and 1913
4. Total foreign investments in 1913
5. International alignments, 1815–1917: an overview
6. Percentage increase in net national product, 1898–1913
7. The ratio of British to German warship tonnage, 1880–1914
8. The naval strengths of the powers in 1914
9. The military strengths of the European states in 1914
10. The military potentials of the European states in 1914
11. Total (army and naval) military personnel as a percentage of population for the five great powers, 1890–1913/14
12. Defence expenditures of the great powers, 1890–1913
13. Defence expenditures as a percentage of net national product
14. National debts in millions of national currencies (and £), 1887–1913
15. National debts as a percentage of net national product, 1887–1913
16. Major European bond prices, c. 1896–1914
17. Bond yields of the major powers, 1911–1914
18. The London acceptance market: liabilities on acceptances at year end, 1912–1914
19. The circulation of selected British newspapers, 1914–1918
20. The circulation of selected German newspapers, 1913–1918
21. The demographic imbalance
22. Estimates for real net/gross national product for four combatants, 1913–1918

23. Indices of industrial production in four combatant countries
24. Wheat production, 1914–1917
25. Average annual wartime trade deficits as a percentage of imports
26. British and German armaments production: selected statistics
27. Industrial production and real wages in Germany and Britain, 1914–1918
28. The ratio of skilled to unskilled wages in the building trade in three capital cities, 1914–1918
29. Trade union membership in Britain, France and Germany, 1913–1918
30. Strikes in Britain and Germany, 1914–1918
31. British and German food consumption as a percentage of peacetime consumption, 1917–1918
32. Total casualties in the First World War
33. Estimates for total casualties (killed, taken prisoner and wounded)
34. Manpower available in Germany, 1914–1918
35. Military deaths as percentages of manpower
36. Total expenditures, 1914–1918
37. Government deficits as a percentage of total expenditures, 1914–1918
38. National debts in millions of national currencies, 1914–1919
39. Money supply figures (broad money and currency in circulation, millions of national currency)
40. Cost-of-living indices
41. The cost of killing: war expenditure and deaths
42. Prisoners of war, 1914–1918
43. Casualties in the Russian Civil War, 1918–1922
44. Outstanding war debts and reparations liabilities in 1931
45. National debts in dollar terms, 1914 and 1922
46. The German populations of European states, c. 1919

Illustrations

First plate section

1. John Gilmour Ferguson
2. 'H.M. The King and the King of Belgium'
3. The Western Front epitomized
4. The Western Front idealized
5. The Eastern Front epitomized
6. The Eastern Front idealized
7. 'Stacks of food, etc.'
8. The life cycle of a shell, part 1
9. The life cycle of a shell, part 2
10. The life cycle of a shell, part 3
11. The life cycle of a shell, part 4
12. The life cycle of a shell, part 5
13. Images of death, 1
14. Images of death, 2
15. Images of death, 3
16. Images of death, 4
17. Images of death, 5
18. Images of death, 6

Second plate section

19. Images of death, 7
20. Comradeship, 1
21. Comradeship, 2
22. Comradeship, 3
23. Rest . . .
24. . . . and Relaxation
25. Prisoners, 1
26. Prisoners, 2
27. Prisoners, 3
28. Prisoners, 4
29. The war in the air, 1
30. The war in the air, 2
31. The war in the air, 3
32. Oh! What a lovely War, 1
33. Oh! What a lovely War, 2
34. Europe post-war

Acknowledgements

Many historians far more expert than I on the subject of the First World War have generously given encouragement and advice during the research and writing of this book. I would like to thank especially Adrian Gregory and David Stevenson, who read the first draft in its entirety and saved me from many errors. Brian Bond, John Keegan, Avner Offer, Hartmut Pogge von Strandmann, Gary Sheffield and Peter Simkins also kindly helped. Among the many others to whom I have incurred 'war debts' over the years, I should like to thank Richard Bessel, Gerry Feldman, Stig Förster, Jonathan Steinberg, Norman Stone and Jay Winter. Needless to say, none of the above bear responsibility for the arguments and opinions advanced here.

This book could not have been written without the invaluable research assistance I have received from Nick Berry, Glen O'Hara and Thomas Weber. Daniel Fattal, John Jungclaussen, Jon Thompson and Andrew Vereker also did sterling work.

Timothy Prus and Barbara Adams of the Archive of Modern Conflict, London, provided indispensable assistance with the photographs. I would also like to thank Jillian Timmis for introducing me to the Finch diaries, and the Finch family for permission to quote from them.

Over the period of this book's long gestation, I have received generous financial assistance from both the Oxford University History Faculty and Jesus College, Oxford. I am deeply grateful to both. I would also like to thank Vivien Bowyer for her help in preparing the tables and charts.

I cannot praise too highly my publishers, Penguin Press. Those who have contributed to turning my rough manuscript into a book are too numerous to name; but I hope the others will forgive me if I thank my editor Simon Winder, who started the ball rolling.

ACKNOWLEDGEMENTS

Finally, I would like to thank my family for tolerating my unreasonable working hours and irascibility.

The book is dedicated to the memory of my grandfathers, who fought for their country in the two world wars.

Note on the Illustrations

The photographs in this book are a mixture of the official and the unofficial. The latter are perhaps more interesting; they are certainly less familiar; indeed, most of the photographs taken by ordinary soldiers are reproduced here for the first time.

George Mosse has argued that 'the photographs that soldiers took themselves for their families were always realistic'; whereas the official photographs tended to perpetuate 'the Myth of the War Experience' (Mosse, *Fallen Soldiers*, pp. 150f.). To judge by these photographs, this is not quite true. Certainly, the accredited photographers whose work was published during the war tended to avoid pictures of their own side's dead; but not invariably. Indeed, it is surprising how much of the horror of war can be seen in some 'official' photography. More importantly, the soldiers' private albums are not necessarily 'realistic' — if by that one means unflinching in depicting the horrors of the trenches.

The archetype of a 'realistic' war photographer was John Heartfield. The two pictures which he captioned 'This is how a hero's death really looks' are harrowing images of dead soldiers, broken, disfigured, mud-covered. But Heartfield was an exceptionally politicized soldier. He was, in fact, German. Christened Helmut Herzfeld, he changed his name to John Heartfield in 1915 as a protest against wartime Anglophobia. He later recalled how he consciously strove to challenge the official photography while he was serving in the trenches:

Photos of the war were being used to support the policy to hold out when the war had long since been settled on the Marne and the German army had already been beaten . . . I was a soldier from very early on. Then we pasted, I pasted and quickly cut out a photo and then put one under another. Of course, that produced another counterpoint, a contradiction that expressed something different. (Pachnicke and Honnef, *John Heartfield*, p. 14)

And thus was born Weimar photomontage. However, the majority of soldiers who took cameras to the Front (and it should be remembered that British soldiers were not allowed to) were less politicized. Few strove for 'realism' in Heartfield's sense of a counterpoint to propaganda. Their photos tell us as much about the way they wanted to see the war – and the war to be seen by others – as the official photographs tell us about the objectives of government propaganda.

All pictures are courtesy of the Archive of Military Conflict, London.

For
J G F
and
T G H

For by my glee might many men have laughed,
And of my weeping something had been left,
Which must die now. I mean the truth untold,
The pity of war, the pity war distilled.

Wilfred Owen,
'Strange Meeting'

The Sinister Spirit sneered: 'It had to be!'
And again the Spirit of Pity whispered, 'Why?'

Thomas Hardy,
'And There Was a Great Calm'

Introduction

JGF

John Gilmour Ferguson had just turned sixteen when the First World War[1] broke out. The recruiting sergeant believed him—or chose to—when he lied about his age, but before the formalities of enlistment could be completed his mother arrived and dragged him home. If the boy from Fife feared at that moment that he might miss the action, however, his anxiety was unjustified. By the time he was allowed to join up the following year, any idea that the war would be a short one had been dispelled. After the usual months of training, he was sent to the trenches as a private (serial number S/22933) in the 2nd Battalion, Seaforth Highlanders, part of the 26th Brigade in the 9th Division of the British Expeditionary Force. He was one of 557,618 Scots who enlisted in the British army during the First World War. Of these, more than a quarter—26.4 per cent—lost their lives. Only the Serbian and Turkish armies sustained such severe casualties.[2]

My grandfather was one of the lucky 73.6 per cent. He was shot through the shoulder by a sniper whose bullet would certainly have killed him if it had struck a few inches lower. He survived a gas attack, though his lungs suffered permanent damage. His most vivid recollection of the war—or at least the one he related to his son—was of a German attack. As the enemy troops ran towards his trench, he and his comrades fixed bayonets and prepared for the order to go 'over the top'. At the last moment, however, the command was given to the Cameronians further down the line. So heavy were the casualties in the ensuing engagement that he felt sure he would have died if the order had been given to the Seaforths.

Not many records survive of John Ferguson's war. Like the overwhelming majority of the millions of men who fought in the First World War, he published neither poems nor memoirs. Nor have his letters home survived. His service file remains inaccessible and the regimental records offer only the barest information. It is possible, for example, that he was at the Battle of the Somme in July 1916, where—in just fourteen days' intensive fighting at Billion Wood, Carnoy and Longueuil—his battalion had seventy men killed and 381 wounded or taken prisoner out of a total strength of around 750. Perhaps he was also at Eaucourt l'Abbaye three months later, when the brigade's casualties were as high as 70 per cent in the first few minutes of the attack. Or perhaps it was at St Laurent near Arras that he received his wound. Was he lucky enough to miss Passchendaele, when his battalion lost forty-four men and a further 214 who were wounded or captured in the assault on Zeggars Cappel? Or was it there that he was gassed? Some time after he suffered these injuries, he was taken out of the front line to assist with the training of new recruits: there is a photograph of him with a large group of men seated in front of a blackboard drawing of a grenade. But his recollection of a big German attack suggests that he may conceivably have been in the trenches in the spring of 1918, when Ludendorff launched his final vain bid to win the war. The 2nd Battalion lost more than 300 men in the month of March alone as they were driven back from Gouzeaucourt.[3]

All these, however, are no more than educated guesses. Apart from his rank and serial number, the only hard evidence I have is a small box containing three medals, a tiny bible and a few photographs of him in uniform—a rather stony-faced lad in a kilt. The first of the medals, the British Medal, depicts a nude man on horseback. Behind the rider is the date 1914; at the horse's nose, the traditional terminus 1918. Under its rear hooves—apparently about to be crushed—is a skull. (Does this represent a triumph over Death or some unfortunate German?) The other side resembles nothing more than an old coin. It bears the morose regal profile and the inscription:

GEORGIVS.V.BRITTONN.REX.ET.IND.IMP

The imagery of the Victory Medal is also classical. On the front there is a winged angel bearing an olive branch in her right hand and waving her left, though it is not quite clear whether this represents British womanhood welcoming the survivor home or the angel of death waving him goodbye. The inscription on the obverse (this time in English) reads:

THE GREAT
• WAR FOR •
CIVILISATION
1914–1919[4]

My grandfather's third medal was an Iron Cross—a souvenir from a dead or captured German.

That my grandfather fought on the Western Front was, and still is, a strange source of pride. If I try to analyse that pride, I suppose it has to do with the fact that the First World War remains the worst thing the people of my country have ever had to endure. To survive it was to be mysteriously fortunate. But survival also seemed to suggest great resilience. Most impressive of all was the fact that my grandfather returned to lead a relatively stable and (at least outwardly) contented civilian life. He got a job with a small export house and was sent to sell whisky and hardware in Ecuador. That was as exotic as it got. After a couple of years he returned to Scotland, settled in Glasgow, married, set himself up as an ironmonger, had a son, lost his wife through illness, married my grandmother, and had another son: my father. The rest of his life he spent in a council house in Shettleston, an eastern suburb of Glasgow then dominated by a huge, reeking ironworks. Despite inflicting further damage on his lungs by chain-smoking (a habit probably acquired in the trenches, where tobacco was the universal drug), he had the strength to keep his small business afloat through a succession of economic storms, and lived to dandle his two grandchildren wheezily on his knee. He seems to have been able to live, in other words, quite normally. In this, of course, he resembled the great majority of men who fought in the war.

He did not talk much about it to me; after his death, however, I came to think about it a great deal. It was rather hard not to. Shortly after the war, the school my parents sent me to, the Glasgow Academy, had been formally dedicated to the memory of those who had died in the war. Between the ages of six and seventeen, therefore, I was educated literally inside a war memorial. Each morning, the first thing I saw as I approached the school was a pale, granite slab which stood at the corner of Great Western Road and Colebrooke Terrace and bore the names of former pupils of the school who had died in the war. There was a similar 'roll of honour' on the second floor of the main school building, a cavernous neo-classical edifice. Sometimes, on the way from Algebra to Latin, we walked right past it. The balcony was so narrow that we had to go in single file, and each time I had the chance to read one of the names: I seem to remember there being at least one Ferguson, though no relation of mine. And above all those dead names, in bold capitals, there was the legend which I came to know as well as the Lord's Prayer we mumbled each morning at assembly:

SAY NOT THAT THE BRAVE DIE.[5]

I think my first serious historical thought was an objection to that stern injunction. But they *did* die. Why deny it? And, as John Maynard Keynes once sarcastically remarked, in the long run we are all dead—even those with the luck to survive the First World War. Eighty years have passed since the Armistice of 11 November 1918, and—as far as it is possible to know in the absence of an official veterans' register—no more than a few hundred of those who fought in the British forces are still alive. The World War I Veterans' Association has 160 members; the Western Front Association around ninety old soldiers. Five hundred is the highest conceivable total of survivors.[6] The numbers cannot be much higher in the other combatant countries. Soon the First World War will join the Crimean War, the American Civil War and the Franco-Prussian War beyond the reach of first-hand recollection. Say not that the brave die? A schoolboy could accept, without giving it too much thought, the bald assertion that all who had died in the war had been brave. But the idea that engraving their names on a wall somehow kept them alive: that was unconvincing.

Of course, I saw a great deal more of the Second World War on television (in frequently repeated post-war films). But perhaps for that very reason the First World War always seemed to me the more serious affair; I instinctively felt this even before I knew that twice as many Britons had been killed in the earlier war.[7] The first piece of historical research I was ever asked to do, when I was barely twelve, was a 'project'. Without hesitation, I chose the subject 'Trench Warfare' and produced two bulging jotters full of pictures of the Western Front which I had cut out of magazines like *Look and Learn*, accompanied by a simple commentary, the sources of which I no longer remember (I had not yet discovered footnotes).

My English teachers encouraged this interest. Like so many schoolchildren of my generation, I was introduced at an early age (fourteen) to the poetry of Wilfred Owen—'Dulce et Decorum est' still sticks, chillingly, in the mind:

> Gas! GAS! Quick, boys! . . .
> If you could hear, at every jolt, the blood
> Come gargling from the forth-corrupted lungs,
> Obscene as cancer, bitter as cud
> Of vile, incurable sores on innocent tongues,–
> My friend, you would not tell with such high zest
> To children ardent for some desperate glory,
> The old Lie: Dulce et decorum est
> Pro patria mori.

Siegfried Sassoon's *Memoirs of a Fox-Hunting Man* was a set text in the fifth or sixth form. I also recall reading in bed Robert Graves's *Goodbye to All That* and Hemingway's *Farewell to Arms*; and watching a rather good, because understated, television adaptation of Vera Brittain's *Testament of Youth*. The small screen also introduced me to the film versions of *All Quiet on the Western Front*, which captivated me, and *Oh! What a Lovely War*, which annoyed me by its knowing anachronisms. But it was 'Dulce et Decorum est'—so unambiguously directed at schoolmasters, so unambiguously about the asphyxiation of a *boy*–that did it. I found it bizarre that we should be expected to memorize this in the morning, only to don our Cadet Force uniforms and parade around the playground that same afternoon. Despite the fact that I was born some fifty years after it broke out, the First World War has therefore had a profound influence on me–as it has on so many other Britons too young to have first-hand memories of it.

THE FORGOTTEN WAR?

To Americans, on the other hand, the First World War is the forgotten war, or so it sometimes seems to a British observer. Considering the extent of the American contribution to the war, and its effect at the time on American society, this is surprising. World War I seems almost to have fallen into an historical void between the American Civil War and World War II.

Why is this? One reason, possibly, is that to the large number of American families who immigrated to the United States after 1918 the war has no special significance; or, to those whose country of origin had been on the losing side, a purely negative significance. Yet another reason may be that, as a latecomer to the European war, the United States did not have a leading role in the conflict. Some of the greatest works of post-war American fiction convey something like an American inferiority complex on this point. In F. Scott Fitzgerald's *Tender Is the Night* (1934), for example, Dick Diver wanders obsessively and wistfully through the decaying trenches at Thiepval some six years after the war's end. He has read up about the war and is full of pretentious theories about its causes, but the key point is that he did not fight in it.[8] When the hero of Fitzgerald's earlier masterpiece *The Great Gatsby* describes his brilliant war record, nobody believes a word of it. Not even the medal he produces seems real.[9]

In *A Farewell to Arms* (1929), Ernest Hemingway wrote perhaps the most famous American novel based on personal war experience. But the novel is much further removed from autobiographical reality than, for example, the post-war novels of Siegfried Sassoon. Even in interviews, Hemingway could not resist embroidering the story of his time as Red Cross ambulance driver in Italy, enlisting retrospectively in the Italian army and promoting himself to First Lieutenant. Hemingway even claimed, quite untruthfully, to have fought in three battles. In fact, he spent most of his time in Italy in a hospital, having been hit by a stray shrapnel shell while distributing cigarettes near Piave in the summer of 1918.[10]

Does the American literature of the war testify to a genuine American detachment from—even lack of interest in—the war? Perhaps. In all, the United States mobilized around 4.3 million men to fight in the First World War. This figure should be compared with figures of 7.9 million for France, 8.4 million for the British Empire, 13.2 million for Germany and 15.8 million for Russia. Even more striking is the disparity in military participation rates: total U.S. mobilization represented around 4.3 per cent of the population; the comparable figure for France was 19.9 per cent. Mortality figures tell a similar story. Around 114,000 Americans lost their lives as a result of the war; an additional 205,000 were wounded. This was a tiny fraction of the total death toll of the war: 1.2 per cent. Moreover, the mortality rate of American troops (2.7 per cent) was the lowest of any army in the war; the figure for Scottish soldiers was almost ten times higher. Even the Indian army had a higher mortality rate than the American. Only 0.4 per cent of American men aged between 15 and 49 were killed in the conflict, compared with figures of 22.7 per cent for Serbia and 13.3 per cent for France.

Yet these figures give a misleading impression of the war's significance for the United States, for the involvement of so many American soldiers in what was at root a European war represented a watershed in American history—a first, crucial step on the road to that 'globalism' which came to characterize American foreign policy for most of the twentieth century. The personal conversion of President Woodrow Wilson from non-interventionism into an almost messianic desire to wage a war for the sake of international law and collective security was, of course, not universally experienced. But American isolationism was never again a wholly convincing doctrine. And, as we shall see, the experience of the war had all kinds of unexpected effects on American life, heavily qualifying the sacrosanctity of personal liberty for the sake of a patriotism which even by European standards was exclusive and intolerant.

Nor should we diminish the significance of those 114,000 American deaths. To be sure, the death toll of the Civil War—618,000, around a fifth of all men who were mobilized—was much higher.[11] So too was that of the Second World War (292,100). But the number of Americans who died in the much-filmed Vietnam War was 'only' 57,939, and the number killed in Korea was 33,000. Far more troops were in France in June 1918 than in Vietnam in 1969 (the peak of U.S. involvement)—a million compared with 542,000.

Moreover, in financial terms, the American contribution to the First World War was immense and arguably decisive. In terms of total expenditure, only Germany and Britain spent more on the war. Alongside U.S. government expenditure of $36.2 billion needs to be set the total value of American loans to the Entente powers (Britain, France, Russia and their allies); cash advances to these states during the war amounted to around $9.6 billion. Britain alone borrowed $4.3 billion. Much of the American money was lent to allow the combatants to import American goods, including armaments worth around $600 million. Thanks to the war, the United States went from being a net international debtor to being the world's banker, with net foreign assets of around $11 billion by the end of 1919.[12] This, and the subsequent loans to help reconstruct the European economies after the war, created enduring and uncomfortable 'golden fetters' between the New World and the Old.

TEN QUESTIONS

This book is not a narrative of the First World War; that can be found elsewhere.[13] Nor do I deal with all 'the myriad faces of war':[14] many aspects of the conflict and some theatres of war (such as East Africa and Mesopotamia) are unavoidably neglected. On the other hand, I have attempted to get out of the deeply dug trenches of academic specialization by relating economic and social history more closely than is customary to diplomatic and military history. Military historians have traditionally tended to discuss strategic and tactical issues without paying adequate attention to the economic constraints under which the generals had to labour. Economic and social historians (especially in Germany) have meanwhile tended to neglect the fighting itself, consciously or unconsciously assuming that the war was decided on the 'Home Fronts' rather than on the battlefields themselves.[15] And most historians still tend to study the war from the vantage point of a single nation-state. Nowhere is this more obvious than in books on the literary impact of the war.[16] But it is also a feature of many recent volumes of essays and conference papers.[17]

My approach is analytical. There are ten questions which I attempt to answer:

1. Was the war inevitable, whether because of militarism, imperialism, secret diplomacy or the arms race (chapters 1–4)?

2. Why did Germany's leaders gamble on war in 1914 (Chapter 5)?
3. Why did Britain's leaders decide to intervene when war broke out on the Continent (Chapter 6)?
4. Was the war, as is often asserted, really greeted with popular enthusiasm (Chapter 7)?
5. Did propaganda, and especially the press, keep the war going, as Karl Kraus believed (Chapter 8)?
6. Why did the huge economic superiority of the British Empire not suffice to inflict defeat on the Central Powers more quickly and without American intervention (chapters 9 and 11)?
7. Why did the military superiority of the German army fail to deliver victory over the British and French armies on the Western Front, as it delivered victory over Serbia, Rumania and Russia (Chapter 10)?
8. Why did men keep fighting when, as the war poets tell us, conditions on the battlefield were so wretched (Chapter 12)?
9. Why did men stop fighting (Chapter 13)?
10. Who won the peace—to be precise, who ended up paying for the war (Chapter 14)?

By way of a preamble, and to show why new answers can still be found to those questions, I wish to point out the contradictory nature of the beliefs most commonly held on the subject as it has been and is remembered. The first is that the war was horrible. The second is that it was nevertheless inevitable. It is worth asking where these ideas come from. Historians do well to remember that they owe very little indeed to the historical profession.

EVIL WAR

The persistence of the idea that the war was 'a bad thing' owes much to the genre known as 'war poetry' (usually meaning 'anti-war'), which became firmly established in British school curriculums in the 1970s.

Poems eschewing the traditional romantic, elevated diction of the Victorians, Edwardians and 'Georgians'—though not always their structural conventions—began to be written by soldiers well before the end of the war.[18] Sassoon wrote his first 'outspoken' war poem, 'In the Pink', in February 1916[19] and published a number of others in *The Old Huntsman* in May the following year; *Counter-Attack* came out in 1918, the same year as Richard Aldington's 'The Blood of the Young Men' ('We are sick of blood, of the taste and sight of it').[20] By the time of his death in 1918, Owen had written over a hundred poems, though it was only after the war that such work began to reach a wider audience.[21] Edmund Blunden's least lyrical poem—'Third Ypres'—was also published after the war,[22] as was Ivor Gurney's 'Strange Hells'.[23]

Although the influence of *fin-de-siècle* Expressionism and Symbolism on continental poetry lingered on into the war, Sassoon and Owen had their counterparts on the other side in poets like Wilhelm Klemm, Carl Zuckmeyer and the short-lived Alfred Lichtenstein, who died in the second month of the war. Indeed, Lichtenstein has a good claim to have been the first of the anti-war poets. His 'Prayer before Battle' predates Sassoon's change of style by a year and a half:

> God protect me from misfortune,
> Father, Son and Holy Ghost,
> May no high explosives hit me,
> May our enemies, the bastards,
> Never take me, never shoot me,
> May I never die in squalor
> For our well-loved fatherland.
>
> Look, I'd like to live much longer,
> Milk the cows and stuff my girl friends
> And beat up that lousy Josef,
> Get drunk on lots more occasions
> Till a blissful death o'ertakes me.
>
> Look, I'll offer heartfelt prayers,
> Say my beads seven times daily,
> If you, God, of your gracious bounty,
> Choose to kill my mate, say Huber
> Or else Meier, and let me off.
>
> But suppose I have to take it
> Don't let me get badly wounded.
> Send me just a little leg wound
> Or a slight gash on the forearm
> So I go home as a hero
> Who has got a tale to tell.

Moreover, Zuckmeyer's 1917 verses about the young soldier's lot—hunger, killing, lice, drinking, fighting and masturbation—are a good deal more brutal than anything in Owen.[24] War poetry was thus not as much of an English peculiarity as is sometimes thought:[25] the French had Guillaume Apollinaire, for example; the Italians, Giuseppe Ungaretti. One recent collection of First World War poetry includes more than fifty writers, representing nearly all the major combatants; no doubt that number could be increased.[26] As the success of this and other collections[27] shows, war poetry shows no sign of falling out of fashion in schools and universities.

Then there is the anti-war prose: the pamphlets, the war memoirs and the war novels, some of them so autobiographical as to be memoirs. It was in fact noncombatant authors who first attacked the war in prose. George Bernard Shaw spent the winter of 1914 poring over the rival powers' official works of self-justification before writing his *Common Sense about the War*, a combination of socialism and his own distinctive crankiness. This had been preceded by a newspaper article urging soldiers on both sides to 'SHOOT THEIR OFFICERS AND GO HOME'.[28] Less ludicrous was Francis Meynell's December 1914 article 'War's a Crime', which imagined vividly 'the shrieking, mutilated and stinking horrors of the battlefield' and 'the slaying and maiming and raping of innocent people'. Clive Bell's *Peace at Once* (1915) was less histrionic; Bell shared Shaw's assumption that the war would only benefit 'a few capitalists'.[29] Rather closer to the action—he watched the Battle of the Somme from an observation point—a mystified Ford Madox Ford described 'a million men moving one against the other . . . into a Hell of fear'.[30]

The first significant British attempt to voice criticism in the form of fiction was *Mr Britling Sees It Through* (1916), in which H. G. Wells posed the question: 'What have we been fighting for? What are we fighting for? Does anyone know?' After two years, Wells suggested, the war had become merely 'a monstrous strain and wasting'.[31] Two women—Agnes Hamilton and Rose Allatini—put the case against the war more strongly in 1916 and 1918 respectively.[32] Writing in 1916–17, D. H. Lawrence denounced its 'violence and injustice and destruction' and predicted that 'the deluge of iron rain will destroy the world here, utterly'. The war had 'smashed the growing tip of European civilisation'.[33]

Even propagandists changed their tune once the war was over. In *The Realities of War* (1920), the former war correspondent Philip Gibbs recanted; contrary to his own wartime reports, there had been a great carving of human flesh which was of our boyhood, while the old men directed their sacrifice, and the profiteers grew rich, and the fires of hate were stoked up at patriotic banquets and in editorial chairs . . . Modern civilization was wrecked on those fire-blasted fields . . . [There had been] a monstrous massacre of human beings who prayed to the same God, loved the same joys of life, and had no hatred of one another except as it had been lighted and inflamed by their governors, their philosophers, and their newspapers. The German soldier cursed the militarism which had plunged him into that horror. The British soldier . . . looked back on his side of the lines and saw . . . the evil of a secret diplomacy which juggled with the lives of humble men so that war might be sprung upon them without their knowledge or consent, and the evil of rulers who hated German militarism . . . because of its strength in rivalry, and the evil of a folly in the minds of men which had taught them to regard war as a glorious adventure . . . [34]

Nor was Gibbs the only repentant journalist. To Harold Begbie, the war had been 'such a mangling of butchery, such an indiscriminate anarchy of slaughter and mutilation, such a filthiness of Bedlamite carnage, as no man had witnessed from the beginning of time'.[35]

As Samuel Hynes has shown, there was an immense quantity of this kind of thing in the British fiction of the 1920s. Ford Madox Ford's Christopher Tietjens in the *Parade's End* novels personifies the decline and fall of the English elite, betrayed by the carpetbaggers at home.[36] There is a similar aristocratic casualty in Michael Arlen's *The Green Hat* (1924).[37] Virginia Woolf has yet another war victim in *Mrs Dalloway*: the suicidal ex-soldier Septimus Smith is the archetypal 'man to whom things are done', in whose eyes the war has deprived the world of meaning.[38]

The striking thing is how far the post-war gloom extended beyond Bloomsbury. Even so jingoistic a writer as John Buchan—whose wartime yarn *Greenmantle* was a harbinger of the 'Lawrence of Arabia' myth—was not immune. Buchan's *A Prince of the Captivity* (1933) has as its central character Adam Melfort, an ascetic war hero who struggles to find a use for his compulsive self-sacrificing bravery in the post-war world of cosmopolitans and proletarians.[39] By this time, Buchan was having to try hard to persuade himself that the war had not been in vain. Even writers who had been too young to play any part in the war could add to the critical mass. A crucial event in Lewis Grassic Gibbon's *A Scots Quair* (1932–4) is the execution of the heroine Chris's husband Ewan for desertion.[40] C. S. Forester's *The General* (1936) did much to propagate the stereotype of the donkey-like British commander.[41]

It has been the (often semi-fictional) testimony of the ex-soldiers, however, which has proved more influential than all these fictions. One of the earliest and most enduring novels by a British veteran, A. P. Herbert's *The Secret Battle* (1919), was based on the case of Edwin Dyett, a naval sub-lieutenant shot for cowardice: its point is that 'Harry Penrose' was a brave man whose nerves had been shattered by prolonged exposure to the terrors of combat.[42] In 1922 the *Guardian* leader-writer and war veteran C. E. Montague published his polemical memoir *Disenchantment* (surely the most influential of all post-war titles). 'Battles have no aureoles now', Montague declared, 'in the sight of the young men [who] . . . have seen the trenches full of gassed men, and the queue of their friends at the brothel-door in Béthune.' In this war, he wrote in a phrase which still resonates, 'the lions felt they had found out the asses'.[43]

By the time Montague's novel *Rough Justice* came out in 1926, it was part of a veritable wave of war writing, as if a decade had been needed for the experience to become intelligible, or at least expressible. T. E. Lawrence's *Seven Pillars of Wisdom* was published privately in 1926 and made available in an edited form as *Revolt in the Desert* the next year; 1926 also saw the publication of Herbert Read's *In Retreat*. There followed works by Max Plowman and R. H. Mottram (1927); Blunden, Sassoon and E. E. Cummings (all 1928); Richard Aldington, Charles Edmonds, Frederic Manning and Robert Graves (all 1929); and, in the bumper year 1930, Sassoon, Henry Williamson, Frederic Manning, Richard Blaker and Liam o'Flaherty.[44] Sassoon's bitter phrase that 'the war was a dirty trick which had been played on me and my generation' is one of many which might be quoted from the books of this vintage.

Such condemnations were echoed elsewhere. Henri Barbusse's *Le Feu* (1916)—which had sold 300,000 copies by the end of the war—set an early standard for French disgust with the war on the Western Front, surpassed only by the devastating early chapters of his political opposite Louis-Ferdinand Céline's *Journey to the End of the Night* (1932).[45] In 1936 Roger Martin du Gard published *The Summer of 1914*, apparently the final volume of his vast dynastic saga *The Thibaults*, in which Jacques Thibault dies trying to scatter pacifist leaflets over French and German troops in August 1914. In the year the book came out, the author wrote to a friend: 'Anything rather than war! Anything! . . . Nothing, no trial, no servitude can be compared to war . . . '[46]

Germany, of course, produced the most famous of all the anti-war novels in Erich Maria Remarque's still harrowing *All Quiet on the Western Front* (1929), which sold astonishingly well in translation in both Britain and France. But Remarque was not the only anti-war writer of the Weimar period. Similar sentiments were expressed in Ludwig Renn's *Krieg*, which had come out the year before, while Austria had Andreas Latzko's *People at War* (1917) and Arnold Zweig's *The Case of Sergeant Grischa* (1928). Vienna also produced the most coruscating critique of the war written for the stage: Kraus's *Last Days of Mankind*, which he began in 1915 and eventually published in its complete form in May 1922.[47]

Americans, too, harboured bitter memories. For the American pilot Elliott White Springs, the war was 'a grotesque comedy' and 'useless'.[48] For all his romanticizing of the man of action, even Hemingway conveyed to readers of *A Farewell to Arms* the absurdity of the Austrian–Italian war on the Isonzo Front and the cynicism of the men who fought there.

The memory of an evil war also lives on in grisly painted images. The English artist Paul Nash intended that his eerie, mud-filled landscapes like *The Menin Road* (1919) should 'bring back word from the men who are fighting to those who want to go on forever . . . and may it burn their lousy souls'.[49] Max Beckmann's brief and traumatic military career transformed his style as an artist, a change prefigured by his pathetic drawings of wounded comrades—drawings similar in style to those of a number of less well-known French *camoufleurs*.[50] The work of George Grosz was also affected by his experiences as a volunteer (he ended up in a mental hospital). His grotesque cartoon 'The Faith Healers' (dated 1918) shows a military doctor passing a skeleton as 'KV' (*kriegsdienst-verwendungsfähig*, 'fit for active service'). The war-inspired pictures of the avant garde still have the power to shock. What could be more hellish than George Leroux's *Hell* (1917–18), with its gasmasked *poilus* and half-submerged corpses, barely visible in a landscape of mud, water and dark smoke?[51] What could be more harrowing than Max Slevogt's *The Mothers*, an endless column of wailing women alongside an endless ditch full of dead men?[52]

Nothing illustrates better the persistence of the First World War's reputation as an evil war than the recent British fiction it has inspired such as Pat Barker's 1990s trilogy, *Regeneration*, *The Eye in the Door* and *The Ghost Road* and Sebastian Faulks's *Birdsong*. It is not from historians that the majority of modern readers gain their impressions of the First World War, but from books like these—and, of course, from newspapers, television, theatre and the cinema. I have already mentioned *Oh! What a Lovely War*—first performed by the Theatre Workshop in 1963—that quintessential 'message for the Sixties' that wars could always happen so long as power was in the hands of upper-class twits.[53]

Peter Weir's film *Gallipoli* has a not dissimilar theme, juxtaposing Antipodean idealism with Pom idiocy. Television documentaries have also been influential; both the twenty-six-part documentary *The Great War* (first shown on BBC2 in 1964) and the more recent KCET/BBC series *1914–1918* won large audiences. Although the earlier series was in many ways intended to explain rather than condemn the war, many viewers seem to have been almost deaf to the commentary, instead allowing the grim archive footage to reinforce their received notions about 'the horror of trench warfare' and 'the appalling and needless slaughter of innocent people'.[54] By comparison, *1914–1918* went with the grain, concentrating on the cultural history of the war as it was 'endured by millions of ordinary men and women'.[55] And so the image of a bad, futile war is endlessly replicated. Even a comedy series like Rowan Atkinson's *Blackadder Goes Forth* adds to the folk memory of donkey-like leadership.

What is more, every year thousands of people travel to the battlefields of the Western Front to 'see for themselves', a curious cross between remembrance and tourism which began almost as soon as the war ended.[56] What they see is not, of course, what the soldiers who fought there saw. They see the great, geometrical cemeteries designed by Sir Edwin Lutyens and others after the war; and the now largely healed countryside, which can be understood as tragic today only with the assistance of battlefield guidebooks.[57]

NECESSARY WAR?

One historian above all gave academic respectability to the notion of the wickedness of the Great War. A. J. P. Taylor's illustrated *The First World War*, first published in 1963, remains the most successful of all books on the subject.[58] It was one of the first adult history books I read as a boy; indeed, I think the photograph of a hideously decomposed soldier's corpse on the cover of my parents' edition was my first glimpse of a dead body. Taylor's war was study in folly and futility: 'The statesmen were overwhelmed by the magnitude of events. The generals were overwhelmed also ... All fumbled more or less helplessly ... No one asked what the war was about. The Germans had started the war in order to win; the Allies fought so as not to lose ... Winning the war was the end in itself.'[59] This pointless war was also waged ineptly and wastefully: Verdun was contested 'literally for the sake of fighting'; Third Ypres was 'the blindest slaughter of a blind war'. Taylor was anything but a sentimentalist; but precisely his acerbic—even facetious—tone complemented more emotive accounts by a number of equally readable historians who published just before him: Leon

Wolff, Barbara Tuchman, Alan Clark and Alistair Horne.[60] Writing at the time these books were appearing, Robert Kee fulminated against the 'gigantic swindle by which the top politicians and generals ... wax[ed] more powerful and prosperous ... at the expense of millions of brave men in a hell ... in some ways analogous to the concentration camps indispensable to Nazi Germany'.[61] This passion has not spent itself as the years have passed. Combining as they do the recollections of veterans and the author's own indignation, Lyn Macdonald's volumes on key phases of the war on the Western Front have tended to endorse the idea that the war was sheer hell and the soldiers its victims.[62] John Laffin continues to refer to British generals as 'butchers and bunglers'.[63]

However, it is important to recognize that these remain minority views. In fact, a surprisingly large number of historians have insisted, and continue to insist, that the First World War was not 'senseless'. If it had its evil side, then it was a necessary evil.

Of course, attempts have been made to justify the war ever since it began. The various combatant governments hastened to publish their own official explanations of the war's outbreak in books of various hues: the Belgian Grey Book, the Austrian Red Book, the Russian Black Book and the German White Book.[64] Newspapers and publishing houses also hastened to justify the war. In Britain alone, at least seven serial histories were being produced by the end of 1915: *The Times*'s and *Guardian*'s, as well as instant histories by well-established authors like John Buchan, Sir Arthur Conan Doyle, William Le Queux and even Edgar Wallace. By the end of the war, Buchan had managed to churn out no fewer than twenty-four volumes, even more than *The Times* could manage (in second place with twenty-one).[65] What all these tomes have in common is their unshakeable confidence in the rightness of the British cause.

The same can be said of the official histories published after the war. To do justice to the range and scale of these here is impossible. For Britain, the bulkiest undertaking was Sir James Edmonds's fourteen-volume account of the army's war in on the Western Front.[66] For the victors, the war was comparatively easy to justify: in the British case, Germany had posed a threat to the Empire, and the Empire had successfully met the challenge. Under the very different conditions which arose from defeat and revolution, the task was harder. Nevertheless, the Reichsarchiv's fourteen-volume *Der Weltkrieg* is doggedly proud of German operational success; significantly, its final volume was not published until after the *Second* World War.[67]

Less stridently apologetic, by their very nature, were the collections of documents published after 1918. Naturally, the Bolshevik government in Russia put its own slant on the documents it published: here the war was portrayed as an imperialist self-immolation scene.[68] Somewhat similar in political perspective was the collection of documents published by the German Social Democrat Karl Kautsky and others.[69] More ambivalent was the output of the National Assembly and Reichstag Committee of Inquiry into the Causes of the German Collapse, which gave the pre-revolutionary German leaders a chance to answer loaded questions.[70] However, the Germans set a new standard with the mighty *Grosse Politik der europäischen Kabinette* (40 volumes in 54 separate tomes, published between 1922 and 1926 and covering the entire 1871–1914 period). Initially conceived as response to the 'war guilt' clause of the Treaty of Versailles, and subtly selective to the advantage of the pre-1918 German regime, the *Grosse Politik* nevertheless was and remains the starting point for diplomatic historians.[71] Its success forced Britain and France to respond with, respectively, the eleven volumes of Foreign Office documents edited by G. P. Gooch and Harold Temperley, *British Documents on the Origins of the War, 1898–1914* (1926–1938;[72] and the less rapidly produced *Documents diplomatiques français* (1929–1959).[73]

Then there are the memoirs of those in charge; here the attempt to justify is more readily discernible. The 'top brass' were quickest off their mark with memoirs. Sir John French published *1914* a year after the Armistice. Sir Ian Hamilton's *Gallipoli Diary* appeared in 1920; while Sir William Robertson's *Soldiers and Statesmen* came six years later.[74] On the German side, Ludendorff and Tirpitz published as early as 1919, followed by Falkenhayn in 1920.[75] The American commander John J. Pershing was a relative latecomer, publishing his account only in 1931.[76] The politicians, despite having less enforced leisure than the soldiers, were also prolific. The former German Chancellor Theobald von Bethmann Hollweg had good reason to try to vindicate himself quickly: his *Reflections on the World War* were available in English as early as 1920.[77] The Kaiser was not far behind with his *Memoirs* (1922), which insisted that the Entente powers had waged a premeditated war of aggression against an innocent Germany.[78] Churchill got the first volume of *The World Crisis* out that same year; Asquith published *The Genesis of the War* in 1923, followed by *Memories and Reflections* in 1928; Sir Edward Grey (now Viscount Grey of Falloden) published *Twenty-Five Years* in 1925; and Lord Beaverbrook brought out *Politicians and the War* in 1928.[79] Lloyd George brought up the rear with his six-volume *War Memoirs* (1933–6).[80]

Few of the memoirists ventured to deny that the war had been horrible; nearly all insisted, however, that it had been inevitable. Indeed, the view most frequently expressed by British politicians was that the war had been the result of such vast historical forces that no human agency could have prevented it. 'The nations slithered over the brink into the boiling cauldron of war,' wrote Lloyd George in a famous passage in his *War Memoirs*. Nor was this the only metaphor he employed to convey the vast, impersonal forces at work. The war was a 'cataclysm', a 'typhoon' beyond the control of the statesmen. As Big Ben struck 'the most fateful hour' on 4 August, it 'echoed in our ears like the hammer of destiny ... I felt like a man standing on a planet that had been suddenly wrenched from its orbit ... and was spinning wildly into the unknown'.[81] Churchill used the same astronomical image in his *World Crisis*:

'One must think of the intercourse of nations in those days ... as prodigious organizations of forces ... which, like planetary bodies, could not approach each other in space without ... profound magnetic reactions. If they got too near the lightnings would begin to flash, and beyond a certain point they might be attracted altogether from the orbits ... they were [in] and draw each other into due collision.'[82]

Climactic images were also popular. Like Churchill, who remembered 'a strange temper in the air', Grey laid part of the blame on the 'miserable and unwholesome atmosphere'. Interestingly, an obscure German war veteran used much the same language in his memoir of the war:

... [W]hat as a boy had seemed to me a lingering disease, I now felt to be the quiet before the storm ... [T]he Balkans were immersed in that livid sultriness which customarily announces the hurricane, and from time to time a beam of brighter light flared up ... But then came the Balkan War and with it the first gust of wind swept across a Europe grown nervous. The time which now followed lay on the chests of men like a heavy nightmare, sultry as a feverish tropical heat, so that due to a constant anxiety the sense of the approaching catastrophe turned at last to longing: let Heaven at last give free rein to the fate which could no longer be thwarted. And then the first mighty lightning flash struck the earth; the storm was unleashed and with the thunder of Heaven mingled the roar of the World War batteries. [*Mein Kampf*, chapter 5][83]

To the politicians who had made the war—rather than (as in Hitler's case) having been made by it—the appeal of all these images of natural catastrophe is easy to explain. At a time when the war had come to be seen as the greatest calamity of modern times, they served to illustrate vividly the politicians' claim that it had been beyond their power to prevent it. Grey stated quite explicitly that the war had been 'inevitable'.[84] In fact, he had expressed this view as early as May 1915, when he admitted that 'one of his strongest feelings' during the July Crisis had been 'that he himself had no power to decide policy'.[85] 'I used to torture myself', he admitted in April 1918, 'by questioning whether by foresight or wisdom I could have prevented the war, but I have come to think no human individual could have prevented it.'[86] Bethmann had used similar words just two months before: 'Again and again I ask myself if it could have been avoided and what I should have done differently.'[87] Needless to say, he could think of nothing.

A few historians continue to favour the imagery of profound natural forces, propelling the great powers into the abyss. Eric Hobsbawm has likened the outbreak of war to a fire and a thunderstorm; Correlli Barnett has compared the British government to 'a man in a barrel going over Niagara Falls'; while Norman Davies has likened the war to an earthquake caused by the slipping of a continental plate.[88]

It is, of course, possible to portray the war as an inevitable calamity without recourse to such imagery. Unreconstructed Social Darwinists shared the view of the former Austrian Chief of the General Staff Franz Conrad von Hötzendorf that 'the catastrophe of the world war came almost inevitably and irresistibly' because of the 'great principle' of struggle for survival.[89] Some inter-war German historians were attracted to the geopolitical interpretation that Germany, the 'land in the middle', was peculiarly vulnerable to encirclement, and therefore condemned to choose between Bismarckian 'stopgaps' or a Wilhelmine preventive war.[90] Historians outside Germany also advanced impersonal or systemic theories. The American Sidney Fay elaborated on President Woodrow Wilson's thesis that the war was the result of flaws in the international system (secret but contractually binding alliances, and the lack of independent arbitration mechanisms).[91] Others peddled the Leninist view that the war was the consequence of imperialist economic rivalries wished upon European workers by capitalist interests—a notable reversal of the pre-war arguments by men of the Left from Karl Kautsky to J. A. Hobson that the capitalists were too shrewd to will their own self-destruction.[92] This approach—which hardened into an inflexible dogma in the historiography of the German Democratic Republic—still has a few adherents.[93]

Later, in the wake of a second global conflagration, as the world seemed poised on the brink of a third and final world war, came the argument (again popularized in Britain by A. J. P. Taylor) that the plans devised by General Staffs in response to technological change made a war 'by timetable' unstoppable after a certain point: 'All were trapped by the ingenuity of their preparations.'[94] Arno Mayer attempted to generalize from the German example to suggest that the war had been caused by domestic political pressures in all the major combatants, as aristocratic élites sought to ward off the threats of democracy and socialism by striking a Faustian pact with radical nationalism.[95] There is even a demographic explanation of the war, in which war 'did something to relieve rural overcrowding'.[96] Finally, there is the purely cultural interpretation that the war was a product of a complex of ideas: 'nationalism', 'irrationalism', 'militarism' and the like.[97] These ideas had in fact been foreshadowed by none other than Bethmann as early as August 1914: 'The imperialism, nationalism and economic materialism, which during the last generation detemined the outlines of every nation's policy, set goals which could only be pursued at the cost of a general conflagration.'[98]

For Bethmann, tormented by the question of whether or not the war 'could have been avoided', there was only one tolerable conclusion: all the nations were to blame. But he still added: 'Germany too bears a large part of the responsibility.'[99] An alternative and very influential argument has been that the First World War was inevitable precisely because of the conduct of Germany's leaders, Bethmann included.

In their memoirs most British politicians tended to argue, as they had in August 1914, that Britain had been under a moral and contractual obligation to defend the neutrality of Belgium against German aggression. As Asquith put it, adopting the idiom of the public-school playground: 'It is impossible for people of our blood and history to stand by . . . while a big bully sets to work to thrash and trample to the ground a victim who has given him no provocation.'[100] Lloyd George concurred.[101] The argument that British intervention in the war was made inevitable by the violation of Belgian neutrality has been repeated by historians ever since.[102]

However, of more importance—certainly to Grey and to Churchill—was a second argument, that Britain 'could not, for our own safety and independence, allow France to be crushed as the result of aggressive action by Germany'.[103] According to Churchill, a 'continental tyrant' was aiming at 'the dominion of the world'.[104] In his memoirs, Grey made both points. 'Our coming into the war at once and united,' he recalled, 'was due to the invasion of Belgium.'[105] 'My own instinctive feeling [however] was that . . . we ought to go to the help of France.'[106] If Britain had stood aside, 'Germany . . . would then [have been] supreme over all the Continent of Europe and Asia Minor, for the Turk would be with a victorious Germany.'[107] 'To stand aside would mean the domination of

Germany; the subordination of France and Russia; the isolation of Britain; the hatred of her by both those who had feared and those who had wished for her intervention; and ultimately that Germany would wield the whole power of the Continent.'[108] According to K. M. Wilson, this self-interested argument was more important than the fate of Belgium, which was emphasized by the government mainly to salve the consciences of wavering Cabinet ministers and to keep the Opposition out of office. More than anything else, the war was fought because it was in Britain's interests to defend France and Russia and prevent 'the consolidation of Europe under one potentially hostile regime'.[109] David French takes a similar view;[110] as do most recent syntheses,[111] as well as Paul Kennedy's *The Rise of the Anglo-German Antagonism*.[112] In Trevor Wilson's view, Germany was 'seeking a European hegemony incompatible with Britain's independence.'[113]

It is perhaps not wholly surprising that British historians have argued this way. At the time, the most commonly aired justification for the war was that it was necessary to defeat Prussian militarism and 'frightfulness', exemplified by the atrocities perpetrated by the German army against Belgian civilians. This was an argument which appealed to liberals, conservatives and socialists alike; it was also an argument which could be reconciled with aversion towards the carnage of war itself. Yet the argument that Germany had to be stopped would surely not have enjoyed as much longevity had it not received unexpected endorsement in the 1960s from German scholars too. The publication of Fritz Fischer's seminal *Griff nach der Weltmacht* in 1961 came as a profound shock to the author's more conservative contemporaries in the German historical profession, with its implication that German war aims in the First World War had been little different from those pursued by Hitler in the Second.[114] For British readers, this was merely confirmation of a very old hypothesis: that Wilhelmine Germany had indeed been bidding for 'world power', a power which could only be attained at the expense of Britain. For German historians, however, the 'continuity thesis' not only seemed to resurrect the 'war guilt' clause of the Treaty of Versailles; more seriously, it lent force to the argument that the years 1933–45, far from being an aberration in modern German history, were merely the culmination of a deep-rooted deviation from some kind of Anglo-American norm.[115] *Alles war falsch*—it had *all* been wrong, including even the Bismarckian Reich. This argument was rooted in documents Fischer saw in what were then the East German archives at Potsdam; and at first sight it seemed to some critics in the West that he was vindicating the Marxist-Leninist line. However, his research had an even greater appeal to a younger generation of historians in

West Germany, who saw in it posthumous confirmation of the ideas advanced by Eckart Kehr in the 1920s about the defects of the pre-1914 Reich. Fischer himself followed the lead of some of these younger writers by relating German's expanionist foreign policy to domestic politics: the excessive political influence of a reactionary aristocracy, the East Elbian *Junker*, and the anti-socialist industrialists of the Ruhr. Kehr had seen the errors of Wilhelmine foreign policy before 1914 as due to the primacy of these groups' narrow economic interests;[116] now it was possible to extend his thesis to the war itself.

Fischer's argument was open to criticism on a number of points of detail and intepretation. Was there, as Fischer sought to show in *War of Illusions*, a plan for war, dating back to as early as December 1912, based on the belief that British neutrality could be secured in a war of conquest against Russia and France?[117] Or was Bethmann taking some kind of 'calculated risk', gambling on a localized war to preserve the Reich's 'freedom of action'—if not to preserve the Reich itself?[118] Alternatively, was he trying to win a colonial empire in Africa by defeating France on the battlefields of Europe, hoping somehow to keep Britain neutral?[119]

The other counter-argument against the theory of German 'sole guilt' was, of course, that all the European states had their imperialist war aims and their militarist elites too. In the past decades, a series of individual studies has been produced, covering the diplomatic and military policies of the principal combatants;[120] and such studies have in turn helped others to reappraise the war's origins from an international perspective.[121] For a number of Fischer's critics, this has been a welcome shift away from the 'thesis of sole responsibility'.[122]

However, as long ago as 1965 Immanuel Geiss set out to rebut the charge that Fischer's thesis was excessively German-centred with his influential collection of documents on the July Crisis, drawn from the collections published by the former belligerents in the 1920s and after. Geiss concluded that, though its immediate causes lay in the German government's support for an Austrian punitive strike against Serbia, the war had its roots in German *Weltpolitik*, which inevitably posed a threat to Britain. 'Germany was the aggressor . . . deliberately provoking Russia. [This] drove Russia, France and Britain to the wall and into a position when they could not but react against massive German ambitions.'[123] Geiss's later synthesis, *The Long Road to Catastrophe: The Prehistory of the First World War 1815–1914*, goes even further, arguing that the First World War was the inevitable consequence of German unification nearly half a century before.[124] Germany was the 'most significant crisis-spot' in 1848, scene of the 'most extreme version' of European nationalism in the 1860s and, once united, the 'strongest power of the Continent'.[125] According to Geiss, it was 'German *Weltpolitik* which plunged Europe into the world war ... In exporting themselves world-politically ... it was the Germans themselves who created the decisive conflict which escalated into the world war.'[126] The implication is that the central mistake of German foreign policy was to spurn the possibility of *rapprochement* with England; to build a German battleship fleet 'amounted to a declaration of war against England'.[127] Admittedly, some more conservatively inclined historians now insist that this challenge to Britain was legitimate; but no one seriously disputes the reality of the challenge.[128] The Anglo-German confrontation has thus become one of the most over-determined events of modern history.

AVOIDABLE WAR?

Does this mean, then, that the war memorials are right? Did those 'many multitudes' who are commemorated by the unknown soldier buried in Westminster Abbey really die

FOR KING AND COUNTRY
FOR LOVED ONES HOME AND EMPIRE
FOR THE SACRED CAUSE OF JUSTICE AND
THE FREEDOM OF THE WORLD[?]

Did the former pupils commemorated in the memorial court at Winchester College really 'lay down their lives for mankind', to say nothing of God, their country and their school?[129] Did the Old Hamptonians really die 'to maintain all that is dear to Englishman's heart, "Our honoured word" ... for Freedom ... [and] Constitutional Liberty'?[130]

Most (though not all) of the war memorials which stand in squares, schools and churchyards all over Europe, whether they portray idealized warriors, mourning women or (as at Thiepval) merely list names on stone or bronze, insist that those who died in the war did not die in vain.[131] '*Morts pour la Patrie*' is the most frequently encountered inscription on French *monuments aux morts*, whether heroic, civic or funerary.[132] '*Deutschland muss leben, auch wenn wir sterben müssen*,' reads the legend of the Dammtor memorial I used to pass every day as a student in Hamburg: 'Germany must live, even if we must die.' Only a few memorials venture to suggest that the 'sacrifice' of those they commemorate was in vain.[133]

The fundamental question this book seeks to answer, then, is the question every visitor to Thiepval, Douaumont or any of the great monuments to the dead asks himself: what were all these deaths—more than 9 million in all—really *worth*? This seems an obvious question to ask; but in many ways it is more complex than it looks. To be precise: Was Britain truly confronted by such a threat to her security in 1914 that it was necessary to send millions of raw recruits across the Channel and beyond in order to 'wear down' Germany and her allies? What exactly was it that the German government sought to achieve by going to war? These are the questions addressed in the first six chapters, which seek to evaluate the threats each side faced, or thought they faced.

These threats tended to fade from view once the war had begun. Having started the war, as Taylor said, the leading politicians and generals became obsessed simply with winning it as an end in itself. At the same time, the combination of censorship and the spontaneous bellicosity of many newspapers tended to discourage arguments for compromise and to encourage demands for annexations and other 'war aims' which only a complete victory could achieve. An important question addressed in chapters 7 and 8 is how far the popular support for the war often cited by historians (for its initial phase at least) was a creation of the mass media.

Why did total victory prove so elusive? This is in part an economic question. Resources were finite on both sides: a country which overspent in financial and material terms to achieve short-term success on the battlefields might ultimately lose in a protracted conflict. Its supply of shells could run out. Its supply of labour—especially skilled labour—might be exhausted, or its workforce down tools. Its sources of food for army and civilians alike might dwindle. Its internal and external debts might reach unsustainable levels. Because all these factors mattered as much as what happened on the battlefield itself, the First World War remains a subject for the economic historian as well as the military historian. Yet in economic terms, the war was—or ought to have been—a foregone conclusion, so immense were the resources of the coalition led by Britain, France and Russia relative to those of Germany and her Allies. Chapter 9 considers why this advantage failed to deliver victory without direct American support, and questions the widely held view that the German war economy was inefficiently organised.

Was strategy the key to the outcome of the war? That question is addressed in Chapter 10. In some ways, the stalemate on the Western Front and the inconclusive results of the 'indirect approach' in other theatres were inevitable consequences of military technology. However, the strategy which emerged more or less by default in the absence of decisive breakthroughs—that of attrition—clearly was flawed. A common conclusion drawn by generals on both sides from the stalemate was that their objective was to kill more enemy soldiers than they themselves lost of their own men. On this basis, it possible to assess the value of human sacrifice in strictly military terms: by calculating the 'net body count' (numbers of soldiers killed on one side minus numbers killed on the other) using monthly and other detailed casualty figures, it is possible to assess military effectiveness. In effect, the value of one soldier's death can be expressed in terms of the number of enemy soldiers he notionally managed to kill, directly or indirectly, before dying. Assessing military effectiveness this way is a macabre business (indeed, some readers may even find my approach somewhat tasteless); but the logic originates in the minds of the generals and politicians at the time. Judged in these terms, it is clear that the Central Powers enjoyed a substantial superiority; the mystery now becomes why *they* lost the war. One possibility (explored in Chapter 11) is that these two measures—of economic efficiency and military effectiveness—can be combined. In other words, it is possible that what mattered was not just how many of the other side one succeeded in killing, but how much it cost to kill them. This however only deepens the mystery, for in these terms the Central Powers were even more successful.

In order to answer the question why the Germans lost, we therefore need to look beyond the net body count per dollar. We also need to consider the smaller sacrifices made by soldiers who were not killed but merely wounded or taken prisoner. The latter loom especially large in my analysis; for although their fate was, from their own point of view, preferable to those of their dead or mutilated comrades, from the generals' standpoint, a soldier captured was as much of a loss as a soldier killed. In some ways he was a more serious loss: alive, he might be able to provide the enemy with intelligence or cheap labour. In assessing the casualties one side inflicted on the other, we therefore must give more weight to men captured than to men wounded, for a substantial proportion of wounded men were able to return to fight another day. This in turn raises some fundamental questions about the motivations of individual soldiers. If conditions in the trenches were as dire as the anti-war literature suggests, why did men fight on? Why did more of them not desert, mutiny or surrender? These questions are addressed in chapters 12 and 13.

Finally, no analysis of the war can be complete without some attempt to assess the peace which followed; for many of those who expressed disenchantment in the 1920s were really disenchanted by the peace. Was the Treaty of

Versailles—and the other treaties signed by the vanquished in the suburbs of Paris—the worm in the post-war bud? This is dealt with in Chapter 14.

The reader will notice that in addressing all the above questions, I frequently refer to so-called 'counter-factual' scenarios, trying to imagine how events might have turned out if circumstances had in one way or another been different. Indeed, it is possible to read this book as an exploration of the war's many alternative outcomes. What if Britain had not appeased France and Russia on imperial and later continental issues after 1905? What if Germany had been able to achieve greater security before 1914 by increasing its defence capability, which it could have afforded to do? What if Britain had not intervened in August 1914, as the majority of Cabinet ministers would probably have preferred? What if the French army had failed to hold the Germans at the Marne which would have been understandable after the casualties it had already suffered? What if Britain had reserved the whole of the Expeditionary Force for use against Turkey and had managed the Gallipoli invasion more successfully? What if the Russians had acted rationally by making a separate peace with the Germans? What if there had been more mutinies in the British as well as the French armies in 1917? What if the Germans had not resorted to unrestricted submarine warfare; or had not risked everything on Ludendorff's 1918 offensive? And what if a harsher peace had been imposed on Germany in 1919? Or a more lenient peace? As I have argued elsewhere, such counter-factual questions help us in two ways: to recapture the uncertainty of decision-makers in the past, to whom the future was merely a set of possibilities; and to assess whether the optimal choices were made.[134] It does not give too much away about what follows to say that, on the whole, I do not think they were.

I

The Myths of Militarism

PROPHETS

It is often asserted that the First World War was caused by culture: to be precise, the culture of militarism, which is said to have prepared men so well for war that they yearned for it. Some men certainly foresaw war; but how many actually looked forward to it is doubtful.

If the First World War was caused by self-fulfilling prophecies, then one of the earliest prophets was Headon Hill, whose novel *The Spies of Wight* (1899) revolves around the sinister machinations of German spies against Britain.[1] This was the beginning of a spate of fictional anticipations of a future Anglo-German war. A. C. Curtis's *A New Trafalgar* (1902) was one of the first novels to imagine a lightning German naval strike against Britain in the absence of the Channel Squadron; fortunately, the Royal Navy has a lethal new battleship in reserve which wins the day.[2] In Erskine Childers's famous yarn *The Riddle of the Sands* (1903), the heroes Carruthers and Davies stumble across evidence of a German plan whereby

multitudes of sea-going lighters, carrying full loads of soldiers . . . should issue simultaneously in seven ordered fleets from seven shallow outlets and, under the escort of the Imperial navy, traverse the North Sea and throw themselves bodily upon English shores.[3]

Following a similar invasion, Jack Montmorency, the schoolboy hero of L. James's *The Boy Galloper* (also 1903), has to leave the Prefects' room and don his Cadet Corps uniform to take on the Germans.[4] Perhaps the most famous of all the fictional German invasions was imagined by William Le Queux in his breathless bestseller *The Invasion of 1910*, first serialized in the *Daily Mail* in 1906, which imagined a successful invasion of England by a 40,000-strong German army followed by such horrors as 'The Battle of Royston' and 'The Bombardment of London'.[5] *When the Eagle Flies Seaward* (1907) increased the invading force to 60,000, but was essentially the same story; both stories end – no doubt to the relief of British readers – with the defeat of the invaders.[6] In R. W. Cole's *The Death Trap* (1907), it is the Japanese who come to the rescue after the Kaiser's invasion force has landed.[7] It was not until A. J. Dawson's *The Message* (also 1907) that the prospect of an irretrievable British débâcle – leading to occupation, reparations and the loss of several colonies – had to be faced.

In Dawson's book, significantly, the enemy is within as well as without: while pacifists demonstrate for disarmament in Bloomsbury, a German waiter tells our hero: 'Vaire shtrong, sare, ze Sherman Armay.' It turns out that he and thousands of other German immigrants have been acting as pre-invasion intelligence-gatherers, ensuring that 'the German Army knew almost to a bale of hay what provender lay between London and the coast'.[8] E. Phillips Oppenheim's *A Maker of History* (1905) had already started this hare. As 'Captain X', the head of German intelligence in London, explains:

There are in this country 290,000 young countrymen of yours and of mine who have served their time, and who can shoot ... Clerks, waiters and hairdressers ... each have their work assigned to them. The forts which guard this great city may be impregnable from without, but from within – that is another matter.[9]

Similarly, in Walter Wood's *The Enemy in our Midst* (1906) there is a 'German Committee of Secret Preparations' covertly laying the foundation for a putsch in London. There were numerous variations on this theme: so many that the phrase 'spy fever' seems warranted. In 1909, perhaps Le Queux's most influential novel, *Spies of the Kaiser*, was published, which posited the existence of a secret network of German spies in Britain.[10] Also in 1909 came Captain Curties's *When England Slept*; here London is occupied overnight by a German army which has entered the kingdom by stealth over a period of weeks.[11]

Nor were such fantasies confined to penny-dreadful fiction. The traveller and poet Charles Doughty produced some quaintly archaic verses on the subject, notably *The Cliffs* (1909) and, three years later, *The Clouds* – bizarre works in which the imagined invaders express the ideas of Le Queux in pseudo-Chaucerian language.[12] Major Guy du Maurier's play *An Englishman's Home* (1909) translated the same fantasy on to the stage.[13] Schoolboys too had to confront the nightmare of invasion. Beginning in December 1913 the magazine *Chums* ran a serial about yet another Anglo-German war to come.[14] In 1909 the Aldeburgh Lodge school magazine rather wittily imagined how children would be taught in 1930, assuming that England by then would have become merely 'a small island off the western coast of Teutonia'.[15]

Even Saki (Hector Hugh Munro) – one of the few popular writers of the period still read with any respect – tried his hand at the genre. In *When William Came: A Story of London under the Hohenzollerns* (1913) his hero, Murrey Yeovil – 'bred and reared as a unit of a ruling race' – returns from darkest Asia to find a vanquished Britain 'incorporated within the Hohenzollern Empire . . . as a Reichsland, a sort of Alsace-Lorraine washed by the North Sea instead of the Rhine', with continental-style cafés in the 'Regentstrasse' and on-the-spot fines for walking on the grass in Hyde Park.[16] Though Yeovil yearns to resist the Teutonic occupation, he finds himself deserted by his Tory contemporaries, who have fled (along with George V) to Delhi, leaving behind a despicable crew of collaborators, including Yeovil's own amoral wife, her Bohemian friends, various petty bureaucrats and the 'ubiquitous' Jews.[17] Note here the strangely tolerable, even seductive quality of German conquest – at least, to the more decadent Britons. Ernest Oldmeadow's earlier *North Sea Bubble* (1906) also imagined the Germans wooing their new vassals with universal Christmas gifts and subsidised food. Indeed, the worst atrocities inflicted by the occupiers in Oldmeadow's German Britain are the introduction of a diet of sausages and sauerkraut, the correct spelling of Handel's name in concert programmes and Home Rule for Ireland.[18]

The Germans too had their visions of wars to come. Karl Eisenhart's *The Reckoning with England* (1900) imagines Britain, defeated in the Boer War, being attacked by France. Britain imposes a naval blockade, ignoring the rights of neutral shipping; and it is this which precipitates war between Britain and Germany. A German secret weapon (the electrically powered battleship) decides the war in the latter's favour, and the joyful Germans reap a rich harvest of British colonies, including Gibraltar.[19] In *World War – German Dreams* (1904) August Niemann imagined 'the armies and fleets of Germany, France and Russia moving together against the common enemy' – Britain – 'who with his polypus arms enfolds the globe'. The French and German navies defeat the Royal Navy and an invasion force lands at the Firth of Forth.[20] Max

Heinrichka envisaged (in *Germany's Future in 100 Years*) an Anglo-German war over Holland, culminating in another successful German invasion. As in Niemann's story, victory allows Germany to acquire the choicest parts of the Empire.[21] Not all German writers were so confident, admittedly. *Sink, Burn, Destroy: The Blow Against Germany* (1905) reversed the roles: here it is the British navy which defeats the German, and it is Hamburg which has to endure a British invasion.[22]

On the basis of such evidence, it would be easy to argue that the First World War happened at least partly because people expected it to happen. Indeed, books like these continued to be produced even after the prophecy had been fulfilled. Le Queux rushed out *The German Spy: A Present-Day Story* in late 1914 and Gaumont's previously banned film version of *The Invasion of 1910* was released under the title *If England Were Invaded*. Paul Georg Münch's *Hindenburg's March on London*, which imagined the victor of Tannenberg leading a successful cross-Channel invasion, was published in 1915.[23]

Such fantasies, however, need to be seen in a wider context. Not all prophets of war expected it to be between England and Germany. In fact, hardly any pre-1900 works in the genre concerned a German enemy. With uncanny prescience, the authors of *The Great War of 189 –*, published in 1891 in the illustrated weekly *Black and White*, began their imagined war in the Balkans with a royal assassination (an attempt on the life of Prince Ferdinand of Bulgaria, apparently by Russian agents). When Serbia seizes the moment to declare war on Bulgaria, Austria–Hungary occupies Belgrade, prompting Russia to send troops into Bulgaria. Germany honours her treaty obligations by mobilizing against Russia in support of Austria–Hungary, while France honours hers by declaring war on Germany in support of Russia. However, there is a twist in the tale. Having initially remained neutral – despite the German violation of Belgian neutrality – Britain lands troops at Trebizond in support of Turkey, prompting France and Russia to declare war on her. There follows a major engagement between the British and French navies off Sardinia and two short, decisive battles outside Paris between the French and German armies – the second won by a heroic French charge.[24] In Louis Tracy's *The Final War* (1893), Germany and France conspire to invade and conquer Britain, but at the eleventh hour the Germans defect to the British side and it is Paris which falls to Lord Roberts: a triumph for combined Anglo-Saxon

4

might.[25] Even William Le Queux had started his scaremongering career as a Francophobe and Russophobe, not a Germanophobe: his *The Poisoned Bullet* (also 1893) has the Russians and French invading Britain.[26] The later *England's Peril: A Story of the Secret Service* has as its villain the chief of the French Secret Service 'Gaston La Touche'.[27]

The Boer War precipitated a spate of similar anti-French stories: *The Campaign of Douai* (1899), *London's Peril* (1900), *The Great French War of 1901*, *The New Battle of Dorking*, *The Coming Waterloo* and Max Pemberton's *Pro Patria* (all 1901), two of which featured a French invasion launched through a Channel tunnel.[28] In Louis Tracy's *The Invaders* (1901), the invasion of Britain is a joint Franco-German venture.[29] The same fearful combination features in *A New Trafalgar* (1902) and in *The Death Trap* (1907), though the French by now show an admirably perfidious tendency to desert their German confederates. The same theme attracted French writers, like the author of *La Guerre avec l'Angleterre* (1900).[30]

There are similar variations in the German prophetic literature. Rudolf Martin's science-fiction extravaganza *Berlin–Baghdad* (1907) visualized 'The German World Empire in the Age of Airship Travel, 1910–1931'; but here the principal conflict is between Germany and a post-revolutionary Russia. An ultimatum to England – prior to the complete unification of Europe under German leadership – comes as something of an afterthought and is soon forgotten when the Russians launch an air attack on India.[31]

It should also be stressed that many contemporaries found the more febrile of the scaremongers simply laughable. In 1910 Charles Lowe, a former *Times* correspondent in Berlin, inveighed against books like Le Queux's *Spies of the Kaiser*, not because he did not believe that the German General Staff sent officers to gather information on England and other potential foes, but because the evidence adduced by writers like Le Queux was so slight.[32] In 1908 *Punch* cruelly sent up Colonel Mark Lockwood, one of the most vociferous of spy maniacs in the House of Commons.[33] A year later A. A. Milne lampooned Le Queux in 'The Secret of the Army Aeroplane', also published in *Punch*:

'Tell us the whole facts, Ray,' urged Vera Vallance, the pretty fair-haired daughter of the Admiral Sir Charles Vallance, to whom he was engaged.

'Well, dear, they are briefly as follows,' he replied, with an affectionate glance at her . . . 'Last Tuesday a man with his moustache brushed up the wrong way alighted at Basingstoke station and inquired for the refreshment-room. This leads me to believe that a dastardly attempt is about to be made to wrest the supremacy of the air from our grasp.'

'And even in the face of this the Government denies the activity of German spies in England!' I exclaimed bitterly.[34]

Perhaps the best of all these satires is P. G. Wodehouse's *The Swoop! or, How Clarence Saved England: A Tale of the Great Invasion* (1909), a wonderful *reductio ad absurdum* in which the country is simultaneously overrun (on the August Bank Holiday) by the Germans, the Russians, the Swiss, the Chinese, Monaco, Morocco and 'the Mad Mullah'. Here the idea of a German invasion has become so commonplace that a newsvendor's poster reads as follows:

SURREY

DOING

BADLY

GERMAN ARMY

LANDS IN ENGLAND

Frantically turning to the late news column, Wodehouse's Boy Scout hero finds the fateful news inserted almost invisibly between cricket scores and the late racing results. 'Fry not out, 104. Surrey 147 for 8. A German army landed in Essex this afternoon. Loamshire Handicap: Spring Chicken, 1; Salome, 2; Yip-i-addy, 3. Seven ran.'[35] Heath Robinson's eleven cartoons on the subject of German spies in *The Sketch* (1910) are almost as funny, depicting Germans disguised as birds, Germans dangling from trees in Epping Forest, Germans in bathing costumes raiding Yarmouth beach – even Germans disguised as exhibits in the Graeco-Roman galleries of the British Museum.[36]

Germans too could see the absurdity of war prophecy. There is an obviously humorous map of the world of 1907 in which the British Empire is reduced to Iceland, leaving the rest – including even 'Kgl. Preuss. Reg. Bez. Grossbritannien' – to Germany.[37] Carl Siwinna's *Guide for Fantasy Strategists* (1908) rather laboriously but effectively demolishes the war prophets on both sides of the Channel.[38]

Above all, the more bellicose prophets of war need to be set alongside those more pessimistic writers who perceptively foresaw that a major European war would be a calamity. H. G. Wells's *War in the Air* (1908) – unlike its German equivalent by Rudolf Martins – offers an airborne

apocalypse, in which European civilization is 'blown up' by bombardments from airships, leaving only 'ruins and unburied dead, and
shrunken yellow-faced survivors in a mortal apathy'.[39] One of the most
influential of all British books on the subject of future war argued that
the consequences would be so economically calamitous that war would
simply not happen: this, at least, was how many readers interpreted
Norman Angell's *The Great Illusion* (see below).

Nor were all German prophets of war unequivocal 'hawks'. In *The
Collapse of the Old World* (1906), 'Seestern' (Ferdinand Grauthoff, the
editor of the *Leipziger Neuesten Nachrichten*) predicted that a minor
clash between Britain and Germany over a colonial question such as
Samoa could lead to 'crash and ruin' and the 'annihilation' of 'peaceful
civilization'. In retaliation for the imagined Samoese spat, the Royal
Navy attacks Cuxhaven, precipitating a full-scale European war. This
proves disastrously costly to both sides. The story ends with a prescient
prophecy (delivered, intriguingly, by the former Conservative Prime
Minister Arthur Balfour):

THE DESTINY OF THE WORLD NO LONGER LIES IN THE HANDS OF THE
TWO NAVAL POWERS OF THE GERMANIC RACE, NO LONGER WITH
BRITAIN AND GERMANY, but on land it has fallen to Russia, and on sea to
the United States of America. St Petersburg and Washington have taken the
place of Berlin and London.[40]

In a similar vein, Karl Bleibtreu's *Offensive Invasion against England*
(1907) envisaged an ultimately disastrous German naval strike against
British naval bases (an inversion of the 'Copenhagen complex' of an
analogous British attack which haunted the imaginations of German
naval planners).[41] Despite inflicting heavy losses, the Germans cannot
hold out against a British blockade; the end result is once again to
weaken both sides. Thus 'every European war could only benefit the
other continents of the world . . . A naval war between the British and
the Germans would be the beginning of the end – the collapse of the
British Empire and of the European supremacy in Asia and Africa. Only
a lasting friendly union of the two great Germanic races can save
Europe.'[42] Both Grauthoff and Bleibtreu conclude with ardent and
rather modern-sounding appeals for European unity.

Obviously, the fact that so many different authors felt the need to
imagine some kind of future war tempts us to conclude that a war was
likely in the second decade of the twentieth century. But it is worth

noting that of all the authors discussed above, not one accurately foresaw what the 1914–18 war would be like. As we shall see, the idea of a German invasion of Britain, the most popular of all scenarios, was entirely divorced from strategic reality. Ninety per cent of war fiction betrayed a colossal ignorance of the technical constraints with which armies, navies and air forces on all sides had to contend. In fact, only a handful of pre-war writers can be said to have forecast with any degree of accuracy what a war would be like.

One was Marx's collaborator Friedrich Engels, who in 1887 envisaged a

world war of never before seen extension and intensity, if the system of mutual outbidding in armament, carried to the extreme, finally bears its natural fruits ... [E]ight to ten million soldiers will slaughter each other and strip Europe bare as no swarm of locusts has ever done before. The devastations of the Thirty Years War condensed into three or four years and spread all over the continent; famine, epidemics, general barbarization of armies and masses, provoked by sheer desperation; utter chaos in our trade, industry and commerce, ending in general bankruptcy; collapse of the old states and their traditional wisdom in such a way that the crowns roll in the gutter by the dozens and there will be nobody to pick them up; absolute impossibility to foresee how all this will end and who will be victors in that struggle; only one result absolutely certain: general exhaustion and the creation of circumstances for the final victory of the working class.[43]

Three years later, in his last speech to the German Reichstag, the Elder Moltke, the retired chief of the Prussian Great General Staff, conjured up a not dissimilar conflagration:

The age of cabinet war is behind us – all we have now is people's war ... Gentlemen, if the war that has been hanging over our heads now for more than ten years like the sword of Damocles – if this war breaks out, then its duration and its end will be unforeseeable. The greatest powers of Europe, armed as never before, will be going into battle with each other; not one of them can be crushed so completely in one or two campaigns that it will admit defeat, will be compelled to conclude peace under hard terms, and will not come back, even if it is a year later, to renew the struggle. Gentlemen, it may be a war of seven years' or of thirty years' duration – and woe to him who sets Europe alight, who first puts the fuse to the powder keg.[44]

The most detailed of all these more accurate forecasts of future war, however, was the work of a man who was neither a socialist nor a soldier. In *Is War Now Impossible?* (1899), the abridged and somewhat mistitled English version of his massive six-volume study, the Warsaw financier Ivan Stanislavovich Bloch argued that, for three reasons, a major European war would be unprecedented in its scale and destructiveness.[45] Firstly, military technology had transformed the nature of warfare in a way which ruled out swift victory for an attacker. 'The day of the bayonet [was] over'; cavalry charges too were obsolete. Thanks to the increased rapidity and accuracy of rifle fire, the introduction of smokeless powder, the increased penetration of bullets and the greater range and power of the breech-loading cannon, traditional set-piece battles would not occur. Instead of hand to hand combat, men caught in the open would 'simply fall and die without either seeing or hearing anything'. For this reason, 'the next war . . . [would] be a great war of entrenchments'. According to Bloch's meticulous calculations, a hundred men in a trench would be able to kill an attacking force up to four times as numerous, as the latter attempted to cross a 300-yard wide 'fire zone'. Secondly, the increase in the size of European armies meant that any war would involve as many as ten million men, with fighting 'spread over an enormous front'. Thus, although there would be very high rates of mortality (especially among officers), 'the next war [would] be a long war'.[46] Thirdly, and consequently, economic factors would be 'the dominant and decisive element in the matter'. War would mean:

entire dislocation of all industry and severing of all the sources of supply . . . the future of war [is] not fighting, but famine, not the slaying of men, but the bankruptcy of nations and the break-up of the whole social organisation.[47]

The disruption of trade would badly affect food supply in those countries reliant on imported grain and other foodstuffs. The machinery of distribution would also be disrupted. There would be colossal financial burdens, labour shortages and, finally, social instability.

All this was singularly prescient, the more so when one compares it with the rubbish written by the scaremongers. Yet even Bloch erred in a number of important respects. He was wrong, for example, to think that the next war would be between, on the one hand, Russia and France and, on the other, Germany, Austria–Hungary and Italy – though the error was entirely understandable in 1899. He was wrong too when he suggested that 'the city dweller is by no means as capable of lying out at nights in damp and exposed positions as the peasant', and that for this reason, and because of her agricultural self-sufficiency,

'Russia [would be] better able to support a war than more highly organised nations'.[48] Bloch also overrated the benefits of British naval power. A navy smaller than the British, he argued, was 'not worth having at all . . . a navy which is not supreme is only a hostage in the hands of the Power whose fleet is supreme'. This put Britain 'in a different category from all the other nations'.[49] Logically, this seems to contradict Bloch's argument about the likely stalemate on land. After all, if one power could establish unrivalled dominance on sea, could not something similar be achieved on land? Alternatively, what was to prevent another power building a navy large enough to challenge Britain's? And, of course, though he was right about how terrible a European war would be, Bloch was wrong that this would make war economically and socially unsustainable. The conclusion he drew from his analysis was ultimately too optimistic:

The war . . . in which great nations armed to the teeth . . . fling themselves with all their resources into a struggle for life and death . . . is the war that every day becomes more and more impossible . . . A war between the Triplice [Germany, Austria and Italy] and the Franco-Russian Alliance . . . has become absolutely impossible . . . The dimensions of modern armaments and the organisation of society have rendered its prosecution an economic impossibility, and . . . if any attempt were made to demonstrate the inaccuracy of my assertions by putting the matter to a test on a large scale, we should find the inevitable result in a catastrophe which would destroy all existing political organisations. Thus the great war cannot be made, and any attempt to make it would result in suicide.[50]

In fairness to Bloch – who is sometimes misrepresented as a naive idealist – he added a crucial rider: 'I do not . . . deny that it is possible for nations to plunge themselves and their neighbours into a frightful series of catastrophes which would probably result in the overturn of all civilised and ordered government.'[51] (It is a rich irony that the book received its strongest endorsement from the Russian government; it was supposedly Nicholas II's reading of 'a book by a Warsaw banker named Bloch' which inspired his 'Appeal to the Rulers' in 1898 and the subsequent Hague Peace Conference.)[52] Where Bloch erred most was in overlooking the fact that such revolutions were unlikely to happen in all the combatant states simultaneously; whichever side put off social collapse longer would win. For that reason, if a war were to break out, there would be an incentive to continue it in the hope that the other side would collapse first. And that, as we shall see, was more or less what happened after 1914.

HACKS AND SPOOKS

Those who attempted to visualize a future war generally had two motives: to sell copies of their books (or the newspapers which serialized them) to the reading public; and to advance a particular political view. Thus William Le Queux's paranoid fantasies were useful to newspaper proprietors like Lord Northcliffe (who redrew the route of his fictional German invasion so that it passed through towns with large potential *Daily Mail* readerships) and D. C. Thompson (who ran *Spies of the Kaiser* in his *Weekly News*, preceded by advertisements offering readers £10 for information about 'Foreign Spies in Britain').[53] 'What sells a newspaper?', one of Northcliffe's editors was once asked. He replied: 'The first answer is "war". War not only creates a supply of news but a demand for it. So deep rooted is the fascination in a war and all things appertaining to it that . . . a paper has only to be able to put up on its placard "A Great Battle" for its sales to go up.'[54] After the Boer War there was a shortage of real wars of interest to British readers. Le Queux and his ilk provided the press with fictional substitutes. (One has a certain sympathy with the German official who refused to issue a passport to a *Daily Mail* stringer in Berlin in 1914 'because he believed he had been largely instrumental in bringing about the war'.)[55]

The scaremongers also served to advance the political case for some form of army reform. Le Queux's *Invasion of 1910* was quite explicit in its propaganda for a system of national service, the scheme which Field-Marshal Lord Roberts had resigned his post as commander-in-chief to promote. 'Everywhere people were regretting that Lord Roberts's solemn warnings in 1906 had been unheeded, for had we adopted his scheme for universal service, such dire catastrophe would never have occurred.' These words were carefully chosen; it had in fact been Roberts who had encouraged him to write the book.[56] Others who were attracted to Le Queux included Admiral Lord Charles Beresford, who pursued a parallel campaign against Sir John Fisher's deployment of the Channel Fleet.[57] The scaremongers could also implicitly argue the case for immigration restrictions by equating foreigners and spies: 'This is what comes of making London the asylum for all the foreign scum of the earth,' exclaims the hero of Oppenheim's *A Maker of History*.[58]

Writers like Le Queux also played an extremely important role in the creation of Britain's modern intelligence service. An unholy alliance developed between hack writers and military careerists like Lieutenant-Colonel James Edmonds (later the author of the British official history of the Western Front) and Captain Vernon Kell ('Major K'). It was principally due to their combined lobbying that a new counter-espionage 'Secret Service Bureau' M O (t) (later M O 5 (g)) was set up as an offshoot of M O 5, the Special Section of the War Office's Directorate of Military Operations and Intelligence (and forerunner of MI5). It was also in large part the fault of this unholy alliance that so much British pre-war intelligence on Germany was distorted by journalistic fantasy and the wishful thinking of would-be spycatchers.[59]

This is not to say that spying was not going on. The German Admiralty certainly had a number of agents whose job it was to relay intelligence about the Royal Navy back to Berlin. Between August 1911 and the outbreak of war, M O 5 arrested some ten suspected spies, of whom six received prison sentences.[60] The spycatchers also identified a ring of twenty-two spies working for Gustav Steinhauer, the German naval officer in charge of intelligence operations in Britain; all but one were arrested on 4 August 1914, though only one was actually brought to trial.[61] As Christopher Andrew has said, Kell and his staff of eleven had 'totally defeated' the German spy menace, even if it was a 'third-rate' menace.[62] A further thirty-one alleged German spies were caught between October 1914 and September 1917, of whom nineteen were sentenced to death and ten imprisoned; and 354 aliens were 'recommended for deportation'.[63] The Germans also had a network of military agents compiling similar evidence for both their western and eastern borders in the areas where German troops would be deployed in the event of war. These proved crucial in alerting the German government to Russian mobilization in August 1914.[64]

On the other hand, Britain had its spies too. In 1907 the War Office began to make surveys of the area in Belgium, near Charleroi, where a British Expeditionary Force might have to fight in the event of a war with Germany.[65] At the same time, Edmonds was attempting to organize a network of spies for M O 5 in Germany itself.[66] From 1910 Commander Mansfield Smith-Cumming (a retired naval officer with a fondness for fast cars and planes) was formally entrusted by M O 5 with the duty of espionage abroad: this Foreign Section was the embryonic SIS (later MI6).[67] In 1910–11, his agent Max Schultz (a naturalized Southampton ship-dealer) and four German informants were arrested in Germany and imprisoned. Another agent, John Herbert-Spottiswood, was also arrested, as were two enthusiastic officers not under MO5's orders, who decided on their own initiative to inspect German coastal defences while on leave; and a madcap Old Etonian lawyer who unsuccessfully attempted to become a double agent.[68] There were also British spies in Rotterdam, Brussels and St Petersburg.[69] Regrettably, the Foreign Section's files remain closed, so it is hard to be sure how well informed Britain was about German war planning. (Not well, if the British Expeditionary Force's difficulties in finding the enemy in 1914 give any indication.) In fact, most of the intelligence gathered by British agents seems to have concerned submarines and Zeppelins. No one, however, thought it worthwhile (or sporting) to crack the codes in which foreign military signals were transmitted – a grave omission.

The extraordinary point is how seriously the scaremongers' allegations were taken by senior British officials and ministers. In a report submitted to the Committee of Imperial Defence in 1903, Colonel William Robertson of the War Office's Intelligence Department argued that, in the event of a war against Britain, Germany's 'best, if not only, chance of bringing the contest to a favourable conclusion would be to strike a blow at the heart of the British Empire before the British Navy could exert its full strength and throw her upon the defensive, blockade her fleet, destroy her mercantile trade and render her huge army useless'. Although Robertson acknowledged 'that oversea invasions are very difficult enterprises under any circumstances; that the adversary is bound to receive warning, since he cannot be kept wholly in ignorance of the preliminary preparations; and that, even if the sea were crossed in safety, a force invading England would eventually find its communications severed', he nevertheless insisted that the Germans were capable of landing 'a force of 150,000 to 300,000 men . . . upon the British eastern coast':

[T]he invading force, once landed, could live upon the country and maintain itself unsupported for several weeks. In the meantime it would be hoped that the moral effect produced on the densely-crowded population of England, and the shock given to British credit, might lead, if not to complete submission, at least to a Treaty by which England would become a German satellite.[70]

Even Edward VII worried in 1908 that his cousin the Kaiser might have a 'plan' to 'throw a *corps d'armée* or two into England, making proclamation that he has come, not as an enemy to the King, but as the grandson of Queen Victoria, to deliver him from the Socialistic gang which is ruining the country'.[71] Senior officials at the British Foreign Office shared the same fear: the permanent under-secretary of state Sir Charles Hardinge, the German-born Eyre Crowe and the Foreign Secretary himself, Sir Edward Grey, all accepted that 'the Germans have studied and are studying the question of invasion'.[72]

Grey also had no doubt that 'a great number of German officers spend their holidays in this country at various points along the East and South coast . . . where they can be for no other reason except that of making strategical notes as to our coasts'.[73] Richard Haldane, the War Minister, also became a believer, though his views may have been coloured by the increase in the number of recruits to the Territorial Army – his creation – which followed the opening of du Maurier's play *An Englishman's Home*.[74] Although his predecessor as prime minister had publicly rubbished Le Queux's claims, in 1909 Asquith instructed a special sub-committee of the Committee of Imperial Defence to investigate his and others' allegations of foreign espionage. It was on the basis of this sub-committee's secret report that MO(t) was set up.[75] In the words of the report: 'The evidence which was produced left no doubt in the minds of the sub-committee that an extensive system of German espionage exists in this country.'[76] As Home Secretary in July 1911, during the second Moroccan crisis, Churchill ordered soldiers to be posted at the naval magazine around London, lest 'twenty determined Germans . . . arrived well armed upon the scene one night'.[77] In reality there were apparently no German military (as opposed to naval) agents in Britain, despite the efforts of Kell and his colleagues to find the feared horde.[78] In any case, most of the information which Le Queux and his associates suspected German spies of trying to obtain was readily available for a small price in the form of Ordnance Survey and Admiralty maps. In the immediate aftermath of the outbreak of war, some 8,000 suspect aliens were investigated on the basis of a list of 28,830 immigrants which had been completed the previous April; but it soon became clear that there was no military organization controlling them.[79] As late as December 1914 the Secretary to the Committee of Imperial Defence, Maurice Hankey, was still warning that '25,000 able-bodied Germans and Austrians still at large in London' might be capable of 'knocking on the head simultaneously most of the Cabinet Ministers'.[80] The secret army never materialized. Equally vain were the searches for concealed concrete platforms on which, it was claimed, the Germans would be able to position their mighty siege artillery pieces.

In Germany too bellicose writers usually had a political as well as a commercial motive for their work. The classic example of this was General Friedrich von Bernhardi, whose book *Germany and the Next War* (1912) did much to fuel British anxieties about German intentions. Bernhardi, a former cavalry general who had worked in the Historical Section of the Great General Staff before taking early retirement, had close links to August Keim, the leader of the German Army League, a lobby group which favoured increasing the size of the army. Often cited as a classic text of Prussian militarism, his book really needs to be read as Army League propaganda, attacking as it does not only the pacifism and anti-militarism of the Left, but also the German government's pusillanimity in the second Moroccan crisis and – most importantly – the arguments advanced by conservatives within the Prussian military for the maintenance of a relatively small army.[81]

THE POLITICS OF MILITARISM

Yet the important point to note is that in both Britain and in Germany the advocates of increased military preparedness enjoyed only limited success, and certainly failed to win over the majority of voters. In Britain, arguments for improving 'national efficiency' undoubtedly attracted widespread interest right across the political spectrum after the embarrassments of the Boer War.[82] Yet when concrete proposals were made for improving Britain's military preparedness – such as conscription – they proved politically unpopular. The National Service League founded by George Shee had at its peak in 1912 98,931 members and another 218,513 'supporters' (who paid just a penny). No more than 2.7 per cent of the male population aged between fifteen and forty-nine were members of the Volunteer Force.[83] Baden-Powell's Boy Scouts had 150,000 current members in 1913: a tiny proportion of the nation's male youth.[84] Conscription appealed to a curious mix of retired officers, journalists and clergymen (like the Hampshire vicar who circulated two thousand parishioners with a pamphlet entitled 'Religious Thought and National Service'). As Summers has conceded, the various patriotic leagues had virtually 'no electoral presence'.[85] Even the frequently cited

Mafeking celebrations following the relief of Mafeking in the Boer War should not be taken as unambiguous evidence of widespread working-class 'jingoism'.[86]

In France Raymond Poincaré's premiership (January 1912–January 1913) and subsequent presidency saw not only talk of a *réveil national* (symbolically, a national holiday in honour of Jeanne d'Arc was introduced) but also action. General Joseph Joffre became Chef d'état-major général, a new post which gave him supreme command of the army in wartime, and a law extending the period of military service from two to three years was passed. The Teachers' Union (Syndicat des instituteurs) was also dissolved for giving its support to an anti-militarist society, the Sou du Soldat.[87] But even this nationalist revival should not be exaggerated. It had far less to do with foreign affairs than with the internal struggles over electoral and tax reform, and in particular the need for an unlikely cross-party alliance against the Radicals on the question of proportional representation (introduced despite Radical opposition in July 1912). There was no attempt to undo the commercial treaty with Germany negotiated by Joseph Caillaux, minister of finance under Georges Clemenceau, in 1911; indeed, it was Italy not Germany which Poincaré confronted following a minor naval incident in early 1912. The most obvious choice as an anti-German premier, Théophile Delcassé, was passed over. In reality, only a minority of deputies – just over 200 out of 654 – can really be identified as supporters of the nationalist revival, and no fewer than 236 deputies failed to give their support to the Three Years Law.[88]

Inevitably, there has been a good deal more research on the German radical Right, since its components can be portrayed as harbingers of National Socialism. The work of Geoff Eley, Roger Chickering and others on the character of the radical nationalist organizations which favoured increased armaments before 1914 has certainly done much to challenge the view that these were mere ciphers of conservative élites. Even when (as in the case of the Navy League) they were established to generate public support for government policy in a way which could legitimately be described as 'manipulative', such organizations attracted supporters whose militarism so outstripped official intentions that they gradually came to constitute a kind of 'national opposition'. According to Eley, this reflected the mobilization of hitherto politically apathetic groups mainly drawn from the petty bourgeoisie – a populist element challenging the dominance of 'notables' in bourgeois associational life.[89]

This was part of that 'reshaping' of the Right which, in his view, prefigured the post-war merger of traditional conservative élites, radical nationalists, lower-middle-class economic interest groups and anti-Semites into a single political movement: Nazism.[90] Yet the idea that the plethora of political lobbying organizations involved were gradually fused into an increasingly homogeneous entity called 'the Right' understates the complexity, even ambiguity, of radical nationalism. Moreover, attempting to identify the radical Right with a specific social group – the petty bourgeoisie – is to ignore the continuing dominance of the élite *Bildungsbürgertum* not only in radical nationalist organizations, but also in the evolution of radical nationalist ideology.

At their respective peaks, the principal German radical nationalist associations claimed 540,000 members, the majority (331,900) in the Navy League.[91] However, this figure exaggerates the level of participation: some people were enthusiastic members of more than one league or association,[92] while many other members existed only on paper, having been induced merely to part with the insignificant membership fee.[93] The social composition of the Army League does not bear out the theory of a lower-middle-class mass movement. Of the twenty-eight men who were on the Executive Committee of the Stuttgart branch, eight were army officers, eight were senior bureaucrats and seven were businessmen; and as it spread to towns in Brandenburg, Saxony, the Hanseatic ports and beyond, it attracted similar 'notable' types: bureaucrats in Posen; academics in Tübingen; businessmen in Oberhausen.[94] The picture is not dissimilar in the case of the Pan-German League, two-thirds of whose members were university educated.[95]

By contrast, the one truly 'populist' nationalist association, the Veterans' Association – which anyone who had completed his military service could join – was anything but radical in its nationalism. This was the biggest of all the German leagues: with 2.8 million members in 1912 it even outnumbered the Social Democratic Party (SPD), the biggest political party in Europe. Yet, with its oaths to the crown and its Sedan Day parades, the Veterans' Association was profoundly conservative in ideology. In the words of the Prussian Minister of the Interior in 1875, it constituted 'an inestimable means . . . of keeping the loyal attitude . . . lively in the lower middle classes'.[96] This will hardly come as a revelation to anyone who has read Heinrich Mann's *Man of Straw* (1918), with its craven anti-hero Diederich Hessling.

An important point sometimes overlooked is the importance of radical forms of Protestantism in Wilhelmine radical nationalism. In Protestant sermons on the theme of war between 1870 and 1914, 'God's will' (*Gottes Fügung*) gradually evolved into 'God's leadership' (*Gottes Führung*): a very different concept. It is worth noting that militarist sentiment was by no means monopolized by orthodox pastors like Reinhold Seeberg: liberal theologians like Otto Baumgarten were especially prone to invoke '*Jesu-Patriotismus*'.[97] Faced with such competition, German Catholics felt obliged to demonstrate that, in the words of one of their leaders: 'No one can out-do us when it comes to love for Prince and Fatherland.'[98]

Such sentiments from the godly were influential. Much of the rhetoric of the Pan-German League, for example, had a distinctly eschatological quality. Heinrich Class, one of the League's most radical leaders, declared: 'War is holy to us, since it will awaken all that is great and self-sacrificing and selfless in our people and cleanse our souls of the dross of selfish pettiness.'[99] The Army League was overwhelmingly a Protestant league, set up in the Protestant enclaves of largely Catholic Württemberg by a man who had been expelled from the Navy League for attacking the Catholic Centre Party. Nor was it merely radical nationalists who reflected the tone of contemporary Protestantism. The Younger Moltke had become involved through his wife and daughter with the theosophist Rudolf Steiner, whose theories derived largely from the Book of Revelation – a stark contrast with the austere Hutterian-Pietism of his predecessor Count Alfred von Schlieffen.[100]

Nor is it without significance that Schlieffen liked to sign himself 'Dr Graf Schlieffen' in correspondence with academics: many elements of pre-war militarism and radical nationalism clearly had their roots in the universities as well as the churches. This should not be overstated, of course. German academics were far from being a homogeneous 'bodyguard of the House of Hohenzollern'; and Wilhelmine media dons, like the Pan-German Dietrich Schäfer, were in many ways exceptional in striking radical nationalist postures even in their inaugural lectures.[101] On the other hand, there were many faculties which made significant contributions to the evolution of radical nationalist ideology, not least history. Geopolitics, a derivative of geography and history, was immensely influential, particularly in giving currency to the idea of 'encirclement'. A student of philosophy like Bethmann Hollweg's private secretary, Kurt Riezler, could see the inevitable 'conflict between nations for power' in terms derived from Schopenhauer.[102] For others, racial theories provided a justification for war. Admiral Georg von Müller spoke of 'upholding the German race in opposition to Slavs and Romans', as did Moltke;[103] while it was university Germanists who held a 1913 conference on the subject of 'The extermination of the Un-German . . . and the Propagation of the Superiority of the German "Essence"'.[104] The Army League's members included archaeologists and ophthalmologists.[105] In short, when the Pan-German Otto Schmidt-Gibichenfels – writing in the *Political-Anthropological Review* – described war as 'an indispensable factor of culture' he perfectly summed up its significance for the German educated élite.[106] During the war, the Army League member von Stranz was stating something of a commonplace in such circles when he declared: 'For us it does not matter whether we win or lose a few colonies, or if our trade balance will be 20 billion . . . or 25 billion . . . What really is at issue is something spiritual . . .'[107] Thomas Mann's *Reflections of an Unpolitical Man* would become the classic wartime statement of the belief that Germany was fighting for *Kultur* against England's dreary, soapy, materialistic *Zivilisation*.[108]

This sociological fit between the educated middle class and radical nationalism explains the high degree of continuity from German National Liberalism to radical nationalism.[109] Max Weber's Freiburg inaugural lecture remains the most famous call for a new era of National Liberalism under the standard of *Weltpolitik*;[110] but there are many other such echoes. For example, an important contribution was made by the historical profession, which created a mythology of unification of enormous importance to National Liberals: Wilhelmine proponents of *Mitteleuropa* as a German-dominated customs union – later one of Germany's official war aims – consciously harked back to the Prussian *Zollverein's* role in German unification.[111] Above all, the National Liberal Party and the Army League worked closely together in the debates over the 1912 and 1913 Army Bills. Keim himself might claim that 'military issues had nothing to do with party politics', and seek to recruit Reichstag deputies in the conservative parties as well as the National Liberals; but this rhetoric of 'unpoliticism' was the stock-in-trade of German nationalists, and in practice he stood most chance of success by co-operating closely with the National Liberal leader Ernst Bassermann. The latter's slogan, 'Bismarck lives on in the people, but not in the government,' gives a flavour of the National Liberal core of 'radical nationalism'; the historian Friedrich Meinecke used similar language.[112] It was the Badenese National Liberal Edmund Rebmann who declaimed in February 1913: 'We have the weapons, and we are willing to use them', if necessary, to achieve 'the same thing as in the year 1870'.[113] There was remarkably little about German radical nationalism that was genuinely new: its core, as in the 1870s, was composed of historically minded upper-middle-class notables.

Of course, there were those whose revolutionary impulses took them significantly beyond the political pale of vintage German liberalism. With eerie foresight, Class argued that even a lost war would be welcome, since it would increase 'the present domestic fragmentation to [the point of] chaos', allowing 'a dictator's mighty will' to intercede.[114] It is hardly surprising that one or two Army League members ultimately ended up in the Nazi Party in the 1920s.[115] Even the Kaiser, when day-dreaming about the dictatorial power he did not have, chose Napoleon as his role model.[116] Viewed in this light, Modris Eksteins' impressionistic argument that the First World War represented a cultural confrontation between a revolutionary, modernist Germany and a conservative England is (whatever other reservations one may have about it) to be preferred to the old view that the war was caused by a conservative Germany's determination to uphold 'the dynastic . . . ideal of the state' against 'the modern revolutionary and national democratic principle of self-government'. That only really became true in October 1918, when President Woodrow Wilson revealed that a German revolution would be a condition of any armistice.[117] The question nevertheless remains how far radical nationalism in Germany really differed from that in other European countries before 1914. *Pace* Eksteins, there is good reason to think that the similarities outweighed the differences.[118]

ANTI-MILITARISM

Overt 'pacifism' – the word was coined in 1901 – was undeniably one of the early twentieth century's least successful political movements.[119] But to consider merely those who called themselves pacifists is to understate the extent of popular anti-militarism in Europe.

In Britain, the Liberal Party won three elections in succession in 1906 and January and December 1910 (the third admittedly with Labour and Irish Nationalist support), against a manifestly more militaristic Conservative and Unionist opposition. The Non-Conformist conscience, the Cobdenite belief in free trade and peace, the Gladstonian preference for international law to *Realpolitik*, as well as the Grand Old Man's aversion to excessive military spending and the historic dislike of a big army – these were just some of the Liberal traditions which seemed to imply a pacific policy, to which might be added the party's perennial, distracting preoccupations with Ireland and parliamentary reform.[120] To these, the 'New Liberalism' of the Edwardian period added a concern with redistributive public finance and 'social' questions, as well as a variety of influential theories such as J. A. Hobson's about the malign relationship between financial interests, imperialism and war, or H. W. Massingham's on the perils of secret diplomacy and the disingenuous doctrine of the balance of power. Such ideas were ten a penny in the Liberal press – especially in the *Manchester Guardian*, the *Speaker* and the *Nation*.[121]

Some Liberal writers were less pacifist than is sometimes thought. One of the best-known expressions of Liberal sentiment in the pre-1914 period is Norman Angell's tract *The Great Illusion* (first published under that title in 1910).[122] Superficially, Angell's book is a model of pacifist argument. War, he argues, is economically irrational: the fiscal burdens of armaments are excessive, indemnities prove difficult to collect from defeated powers, 'trade cannot be destroyed or captured by a military Power' and colonies are not a source of fiscal profit. 'What is the real guarantee of the good behaviour of one state to another?' asks Angell. 'It is the elaborate interdependence which, not only in the economic sense, but in every sense, makes an unwarrantable aggression of one state upon another react upon the interests of the aggressor.'[123] Moreover, war is also socially irrational, as the collective interests which bind nations together are less real than those which bind classes together:

The real conflict is not English against Russians at all, but the interest of all law-abiding folk – Russian and English alike – against oppression, corruption and incompetence . . . [W]e shall see at the bottom of any conflict between the armies or Governments of Germany and England lies . . . the conflict in both states between democracy and autocracy, or between Socialism and Individualism, or reaction and progress, however one's sociological sympathies may classify it.[124]

Angell also questions the argument that conscription could in any way enhance the moral health of a nation: on the contrary, conscription meant 'Germanizing England, though never a German soldier land on our soil'. That he was later a keen advocate of the League of Nations, a Labour MP and the winner of the Nobel Peace Prize in 1933: all this has served to accentuate *The Great Illusion*'s pacifist reputation.

Yet this will not quite wash. For one thing, Angell wrote the book while in the employ of the arch-scaremonger Northcliffe, editing his *Continental Daily Mail*; and a close reading of the text reveals that it is not quite the innocent pacifist tract of popular memory. Thus Part I, Chapter 2 considers 'German dreams of conquest' and concludes that the 'results of [a] defeat of British arms and [the] invasion of England' would be 'forty millions starving'. Similarly, Chapter 3 asks 'If Germany annexed Holland, would any German benefit or any Hollander?', while the fourth chapter poses the well-loaded question 'What would happen if a German invader looted the Bank of England?' In making the point in Chapter 6 that 'England ... does not own ... her self-governing colonies' and that they are not 'a source of fiscal profit', Angell also wonders: 'Could Germany hope to do better? [It is] inconceivable she could fight for the sake of making [such a] hopeless experiment'.[125] What Angell is really arguing, in other words, is that a German military challenge to Britain would be irrational.

In any case, he goes on, it is positively in the rest of the world's interest to leave the British Empire intact. 'The British Empire', Angell loftily declares, 'is made up in large part of practically independent states, over whose acts not only does Great Britain exercise no control, but concerning whom Great Britain has surrendered in advance any intention of employing force.'[126] Moreover, the Empire is the guarantor of 'trade by free consent', and hence encourages the 'operation of [economic] forces stronger than the tyranny of the cruellest tyrant who ever reigned by blood and iron'.[127] (The last phrase is carefully chosen.) Angell fully reveals his true colours when he concludes:

It is to English practice and ... experience that the world will look as a guide in this matter ... *The extension of the dominating principle of the British Empire to European society as a whole is the solution of the international problem which this book urges.* The day for progress by force has passed; it will be progress by ideas or not at all. And because these principles of free human co-operation between communities are, in a special sense, an English development, it is upon England that falls the responsibility of giving a lead ...[128]

The Great Illusion, in other words, was a Liberal Imperialist tract directed at German opinion. Written at a time of considerable Anglo-

German antagonism over the German naval programme and 'spy fever', it was designed to encourage the Germans to abandon their bid to challenge British sea power. Evidently (to judge by its enduring reputation as a pacifist tract) the book's core argument – that Germany could not defeat Britain – was so swathed in irenic language as to be invisible to many readers. But not to all. Viscount Esher – a key figure on the Committee of Imperial Defence and a man whose main 'objective' (as he noted in January 1911) was to 'maintain the overwhelming superiority of the British Imperial Navy' – enthusiastically took up Angell's ideas.[129] Admiral Fisher described *The Great Illusion* as 'heavenly manna . . . So man did eat angel's food'.[130] The *Daily Mail*'s chief leader writer and assistant editor H. W. Wilson put his finger on the mark when he remarked sneeringly to Northcliffe: 'Very clever, and it would be difficult to write a better book in defence of his particular thesis than his; let us hope that he will succeed better in fooling the Germans than in convincing me.'[131]

Further to the Left, in the Labour Party, there was more genuine anti-militarism, however. Fenner Brockway's play *The Devil's Business*, written in 1914, vividly anticipated the Asquith government's decision for war just a few months later, though it portrayed the Cabinet as mere pawns of the international arms industry.[132] The 'merchants of death' were also the targets of Henry Noel Brailsford's *The War of Steel and Gold*, published in 1914. Keir Hardie and Ramsay MacDonald were among those in the British Labour movement who backed the idea of a general strike as a way to stop an imperialist war. At the same time, MacDonald's hostility to Tsarist Russia and his strong sympathy with the German Social Democrats led him consistently to oppose Grey's Germanophobe foreign policy before 1914. The SPD, he declared in 1909, had 'never voted a brass farthing to enable their government to build up the German navy'; the party was making 'magnificent efforts . . . to establish friendship between Germany and ourselves'.[133] This kind of Germanophilia was widespread among the Fabians, who saw not only the SPD itself but also the German system of social insurance as worthy of imitation. Typically, Sidney and Beatrice Webb were about to embark on a six-month tour of Germany to study 'developments in state action and in German co-operation, trade unionism and professional organisation' when war broke out in August 1914, having spent much of July debating the merits of social insurance with G. D. H. Cole and a group of inebriated Oxonian 'guild socialists'.[134] George

Bernard Shaw, ardent Wagnerite, 'clamour[ed] for an entente with Germany' in 1912, modifying this the following year into a typically Shavian proposal for a triple alliance against war between England, France and Germany; or to be precise, a double arrangement whereby 'if France attack Germany we combine with Germany to crush France, and if Germany attack France we combine with France to crush Germany'.[135]

Nor was it only on the Left that Germanophilia flourished in pre-war Britain. The Liberal German Count Harry Kessler's appeal for an exchange of friendly letters between British and German intellectuals elicited signatures from Thomas Hardy and Edward Elgar on the British side; Siegfried Wagner was among the Germans. As this suggests, music was important: the Covent Garden spring season in 1914 featured no fewer than seventeen performances of *Parsifal*, as well as productions of *Die Meistersinger*, *Tristan und Isolde* and *Die Walküre*, and, despite the outbreak of war, the 1914 Proms continued to be dominated by German composers: Beethoven, Mozart, Mendelssohn, Strauss, Liszt and Bach.[136] Numerous English literary figures had German roots – indeed German names: think only of Siegfried Sassoon, Ford Madox Ford (christened Joseph Leopold Ford Madox Hueffer) or Robert Ranke Graves, great-nephew of the historian Leopold von Ranke.[137]

Admittedly, Graves found that at Charterhouse his mother's nationality was 'a social offence' and felt obliged to 'reject the German in me'. In the ancient universities, by contrast, there was a good deal of Germanophilia. The anti-war stance of Cambridge's wittiest philosopher, Bertrand Russell, is well known; but the experience of pre-war Oxford is often overlooked. No fewer than 335 German students matriculated at Oxford between 1899 and 1914, including thirty-three in the last year of peace, of whom around a sixth were Rhodes Scholars. Among the German Oxonians were the sons of the Prussian minister Prince Hohenlohe, Vice-Admiral Moritz von Heeringen and Chancellor Bethmann Hollweg (Balliol, class of 1908). The existence of undergraduate clubs like the Hanover Club, the German Literary Society and the Anglo-German Society, which had 300 members in 1909, testify to the belief of at least some British undergraduates in the '*Wahlverwandtschaft* [elective affinity] between German *Geist* and Oxonian *Kultur*'.[138] The majority of those who received honorary doctorates from Oxford in 1914 were Germans: Richard Strauss, Ludwig Mitteis (the Dresden classicist), Prince Lichnowsky, the ambassador, and the Duke of Saxe-

Coburg-Gotha; also the Austrian international lawyer Heinrich Lammasch.[139] In 1907 the Kaiser himself had been so honoured. The portrait which marked the occasion of his DCL *honoris causa* was restored to the walls of the Examination Schools in the 1980s after a long period in ignominious storage.[140]

The high proportion (28 per cent) of Germans at Oxford who were from the nobility also provides a reminder that links between the German and British high aristocracy – particularly the royal family and its satellites – were extremely close. The half-German Queen Victoria had married her wholly German cousin Albert of Saxe-Coburg-Gotha; among her sons-in-law were the German Kaiser Frederick III, Prince Christian of Schleswig-Holstein and Henry of Battenberg; and among her grandchildren were Kaiser William II of Germany and Prince Henry of Prussia. Similar dynastic ties joined the financial élites of the two countries: not only the Rothschilds but also the Schröders, Huths and Kleinworts were leading City banking families which had originated in Germany; the Rothschilds in particular retained links with their German relatives. Lord Rothschild was married to one of his Frankfurt-born relatives, and their son Charles married a Hungarian.[141]

In Germany, though pacifism had shallow roots and Social Democracy was susceptible to 'negative integration' (the tendency to conform in the face of state persecution),[142] the fact remains that only a minority of Germans were militarists, and a minority of them were Anglophobes. In 1906 the Chancellor, Prince Bülow, had effectively postponed the idea of a preventive war until 'a cause arose which would inspire the German people'.[143] One point to emerge from the Kaiser's so-called 'war council' of December 1912 is that all the military leaders present doubted whether Serbia was such a cause;[144] and studies of popular (as opposed to educated middle-class) opinion in 1914 suggest that the subsequent attempts to alert 'the man in the street' to Germany's interest in the Balkan question achieved little.[145] Alongside the Germany of the radical nationalist leagues, there was 'another Germany' (in the phrase of Dukes and Remak) – a Germany whose excellence-pursuing universities, boosting city councils and independent newspaper editors seem to invite comparisons with the war's last combatant, the United States.[146]

In addition, there was the Germany of the organized working class, whose leaders were among the most critical of militarism in Europe. It must never be forgotten that the most electorally successful party of the pre-war period was the SPD (which also attracted a considerable number of middle-class votes). It was consistently hostile to 'militarism' throughout the period until 1914; indeed, it won its biggest election victory in 1912 campaigning against 'dear bread for militarism', an allusion to the fact that increased defence expenditure tended to be financed by indirect taxation in Germany (see Chapter 5). In all, the SPD won 4.25 million votes in 1912 – 34.8 per cent of the total vote – compared with 13.6 per cent for the National Liberals, the party most committed to an aggressive foreign policy and increased military spending. No other party ever secured such a high proportion of the vote in the Second Reich.

Of all the SPD's theorists, Karl Liebknecht was among the most radical anti-militarists. For Liebknecht, militarism was a dual phenomenon: the German army, he argued, was at once a tool for the advancement of capitalist interests abroad and a means of controlling the German working class, directly through coercion or indirectly through military indoctrination:

Militarism . . . has the task of protecting the prevailing social order, of supporting capitalism and all reaction against the struggle of the working class for freedom . . . Prussian-German militarism has blossomed into a very special flower owing to the peculiar semi-absolutist, feudal-bureaucratic conditions in Germany.[147]

(As if to illustrate the validity of this theory, Liebknecht was murdered by soldiers when he attempted to stage a Bolshevik-style coup in Berlin in January 1919.)

The problem for historians is that the SPD's campaign against militarism, though it failed ultimately to prevent the First World War, has nevertheless been hugely influential on subsequent scholarship. Paradoxically, the anti-militarists in Wilhelmine society were so numerous and so vociferous that we have come to believe their complaints about the militarism of Germany, instead of realizing that the very volume of their complaints is proof of the reverse. Thus there is now a dauntingly large literature on German militarism, not all of which acknowledges that the term itself originates in left-wing propaganda.[148] Historians writing in the Marxist-Leninist tradition were still parroting Liebknecht's arguments as recently as 1989–90: militarism, according to Zilch, was an expression of 'the aggressive character of the bourgeoisie, allied with the Junkers' and their 'reactionary and dangerous strivings'.[149]

More influential in non-Marxist historiography has been the analysis of Eckart Kehr. A kind of German Hobson, Kehr accepted the pre-war SPD argument that there had been an alliance of agrarians and industrialists in Wilhelmine Germany which had encouraged, among other things, militaristic policies. He entered two qualifications: first, the Prussian aristocracy had the upper hand over their junior partners among industrialists and other reactionary bourgeois groups; second (and here he also resembled later Marxists like Antonio Gramsci), militarism was in part the creation of autonomous state institutions. In other words, his was an argument which left room for bureaucratic and departmental self-interest as well as class interest. Yet these qualifications do not radically differentiate Kehr from orthodox Marxists. When carried away with his own fundamental thesis – that all foreign policy decisions were subordinate to domestic socio-economic factors – Kehr was perfectly capable of writing in language scarcely different from that of his Marxist contemporaries.

Kehr's arguments, which were effectively buried by the German historical profession after his early death, were revived by Hans-Ulrich Wehler in the 1960s, and adopted by Fritz Fischer.[150] According to Wehler's classic 'Kehrite' textbook on Wilhelmine Germany, militarism served not only an economic purpose (arms contracts for industry), but was also a weapon of last resort in the struggle against Social Democracy and a rallying point for popular chauvinism, turning attention away from the Reich's 'anti-democratic' political system.[151]

To be sure, the idea that an aggressive foreign policy could help the Reich government overcome its internal political difficulties was not a figment of Kehr's (or Liebknecht's) imagination, but a real governmental strategy. The Prussian Finance Minister Johannes Miquel and Prince Bülow, Bethmann Hollweg's predecessor as Reich Chancellor, undoubtedly did engage in sabre-rattling to strengthen the position of the 'state-supporting' parties (the Conservatives and National Liberals) in the Reichstag, just as Bismarck had done before them. And there really were those in 1914 who believed that a war would 'strengthen the patriarchal order and mentality' and 'halt the advance of Social Democracy'.[152]

But there is a need for qualification. The idea that an aggressive foreign policy could weaken the domestic political challenge posed from the Left was hardly an invention of the German Right; it had become something of a cliché in Napoleon III's France and by the turn of the century was an almost universal justification for imperial policies.

Moreover, there was a good deal less agreement than has sometimes been claimed between German politicians, generals, agrarians and industrialists.[153] Typical was the fact that at least two National Liberal deputies for rural constituencies (Paasche and Dewitz) were forced to resign from the Army League by their local Agrarian League supporters, who regarded the Army League's argument for a bigger army as dangerously radical. This illustrates an important point to be returned to below: there was anti-militarism even within the ranks of Prussian conservatism itself. Nor is it persuasive to attribute decisions taken in Potsdam and Berlin during July and August 1914 to the influence of a radical 'national opposition'. As Bethmann said of the far Right, 'With these idiots one cannot conduct a foreign policy'; the memory was still fresh of the second Moroccan crisis, when the then Foreign Minister Alfred von Kiderlen-Wächter had been acutely embarrassed by the intemperate demands of the radical nationalist press.[154]

Finally, and most importantly, successive German Chancellors were well aware that militarism could backfire, particularly if it led to war. In 1908 Bülow told the Crown Prince that:

Nowadays no war can be declared unless a whole people is convinced that such a war is necessary and just. A war, lightly provoked, even if it were fought successfully, would have a bad effect on the country, while if it ended in defeat, it might entail the fall of the dynasty . . .[155]

In June 1914 his successor Bethmann Hollweg himself accurately forecast that 'a world war with its incalculable consequences would strengthen tremendously the power of Social Democracy, because they preached peace, and topple many a throne'.[156] Both men had the experience of Russia in 1905 in mind – as did the Russian Minister of the Interior Pyotr Durnovo when he warned Nicholas II in February 1914: 'A social revolution in its most extreme form will be unavoidable if war goes badly.'[157]

Militarism, then, was far from being the dominant force in European politics on the eve of the Great War. On the contrary: it was in political decline, and not least as a direct consequence of democratization. Table 1 shows how the franchise had been extended in all the key countries in the last half of the nineteenth century; on the eve of the war, as Table 2 shows, overtly anti-militarist socialist parties were in the electoral ascendant in most of the future combatant countries.

In France the April 1914 election returned a left-wing majority and

Table 1 *Percentages of total population enfranchised for lower chambers, 1850 and 1900*

	1850	1900
France	20	29
Prussia/Germany	17	22
Britain	4	18
Belgium	2	23
Serbia	0	23
Russia	0	15
Rumania	0	16
Austria	0	21
Hungary	0	6
Piedmont/Italy	n/a	8

Source: Goldstein, *Political Repression in Nineteenth Century Europe*, pp. 4f.
Note: Universal suffrage would have given around 40–50 per cent of the population the vote.

Table 2 *The socialist vote in selected European countries on the eve of war*

Country	Date	Percentage of votes	Socialist seats
Austria	1911	25.4	33
Belgium	1912	22.0	40
France	1914	16.8	103
Germany	1912	34.8	110
Italy	1913	17.6	52
Russia	1912	n/a	24
Britain	1910	6.4	42

Source: Cook and Paxton, *European Political Facts, 1900–1996*, pp. 163–267.

Poincaré had to let the socialist René Viviani form a government. (It would have been Caillaux if his wife had not taken the unusual step of killing a newspaper editor-in-chief, Gaston Calmette of the *Figaro*, to prevent the publication of some of her husband's letters to her.) Jean

Jaurès, the Germanophile socialist, was at the height of his influence. In Russia there was a three-week long strike in the Putilov works in Petrograd which after 18 July spread to Riga, Moscow and Tbilisi. Over 1.3 million workers – around 65 per cent of all Russian factory workers – were involved in strikes in 1914.[158] Even where the socialists were not especially strong, there was no militarist majority: in Belgium the dominant Catholic party strenuously resisted efforts to increase the country's readiness for war. But nowhere was the anti-militarist Left stronger than in Germany, which had one of the most democratic of all European franchises. Yet so enduring have the arguments of Germany's pre-war anti-militarists proved that one can still read them in history textbooks; with the perverse consequence that we understate the extent of that very anti-militarism at the time. The evidence is unequivocal: Europeans were not marching to war, but turning their backs on militarism.

2

Empires, Ententes and Edwardian Appeasement

IMPERIALISM: ECONOMICS AND POWER

The resolution on 'Militarism and International Conflicts', passed by the Second International of socialist parties at their Stuttgart conference in 1907, is a classic statement of the Marxist theory of the war's origins:

Wars between capitalist states are as a rule the result of their rivalry for world markets, as every state is not only concerned in consolidating its own market, but also in conquering new markets . . . Further, these wars arise out of the never-ending armament race of militarism . . . Wars are therefore inherent in the nature of capitalism; they will only cease when the capitalist economy is abolished . . .[1]

Once the First World War had begun – throwing the Second International into disarray – this argument was set in stone by the Left. The German Social Democrat Friedrich Ebert declared in January 1915:

All great capitalistic states have registered an increased expansion in their economic life during the past decade . . . The fight for markets was fought more intensively. In conjunction with the fight for markets ran the fight for territory . . . So the economic conflicts led to political conflicts, to continued gigantic armaments increases and finally to world war.[2]

According to the 'revolutionary defeatist' Lenin (one of the few socialist leaders who openly looked forward to his own country's defeat), the war was the product of imperialism. The contest between the great powers for overseas markets, spurred on by the falling rate of profit in their domestic economies, could only have ended in a suicidal war; in turn, the social consequences of the conflagration would precipitate the long-awaited international proletarian revolution and the 'civil war' against the ruling classes which Lenin urged from the moment the war began.[3]

Until the revolutions of 1989–91 undid the dubious achievements of Lenin and his comrades, historians in the Communist bloc continued to argue along these lines. In a book published a year after the fall of the Berlin Wall, the East German historian Willibald Gutsche was still claiming that, by 1914, in addition to 'mining and steel monopolists, influential representatives of large banks, electrical engineering and shipping corporations . . . [were] now inclined to pursue a non-peaceful option'.[4] His colleague Zilch criticized the 'unambiguously aggressive objectives' of the Reichsbank president Rudolf Havenstein on the eve of the war.[5]

Superficially, there is reason to think that capitalist interests stood to gain from war. The arms industry in particular could hardly fail to win huge contracts in the event of a major conflagration. The British branch of the Rothschilds' bank, which epitomized for Marxists and anti-Semites alike the malign power of international capital, had financial links with the Maxim-Nordenfelt company, whose machine-gun was famously cited by Hilaire Belloc as the key to European hegemony, and helped finance its takeover by Vickers Brothers in 1897.[6] The Austrian Rothschilds also had an interest in the arms industry: their Witkowitz ironworks was an important supplier of iron and steel to the Austrian navy and later of bullets to the Austrian army. German shipyards, to give another example, won big government contracts as a result of Grand Admiral Alfred von Tirpitz's naval programme. Altogether sixty-three out of the eighty-six naval vessels commissioned between 1898 and 1913 were built by a small group of private firms. Over a fifth of the output of the Hamburg shipbuilders Blohm & Voss, which all but monopolized the construction of large cruisers, was for the navy.[7]

Inconveniently for Marxist theory, however, there is scarcely any evidence that these interests made businessmen *want* a major European war. In London the overwhelming majority of bankers were appalled at the prospect, not least because war threatened to bankrupt most if not all of the major acceptance houses engaged in financing international trade (see Chapter 7). The Rothschilds strove vainly to avert an Anglo-German conflict, and for their pains were accused by the foreign editor of *The Times*, Henry Wickham Steed, of 'a dirty German-Jewish international financial attempt to bully us into advocating neutrality'.[8] Among the handful of German businessmen kept (partially) informed of developments during the July Crisis, neither the shipowner Albert Ballin nor the banker Max Warburg favoured war. On 21 June 1914, following a banquet in Hamburg, the Kaiser himself gave a notorious analysis of Germany's 'general situation' to Warburg at the end of which he 'hinted . . . [at] whether it would not be better to strike now [against Russia and France], rather than wait'. Warburg 'advised decidedly against' this:

[I] sketched the domestic political situation in England for him (Home Rule), the difficulties for France of maintaining the three year service period, the financial crisis in which France already found itself, and the probable unreliability of the Russian army. I strongly advised [him] to wait patiently, keeping our heads down for a few more years. 'We are growing stronger every year; our enemies are getting weaker internally.'[9]

In 1913 Karl Helfferich, a director of the Deutsche Bank, had published a book entitled *Germany's National Wealth, 1888–1913* which was intended to prove just that point. Germany's iron and steel production had overtaken Britain's; its national income was now greater than that of France. There is no evidence that Helfferich had any inkling of the impending calamity which would so disastrously stunt that growth: he was entirely preoccupied with negotiations about the Baghdad railway concession (see below).[10] Despite his interest in the question of economic mobilization, Walther Rathenau, head of the Allgemeine Elektrizitäts Gesellschaft, was unable to interest Reich officials in the idea of an 'Economic General Staff' and Bethmann simply ignored his argument against going to war on Austria's account in 1914.[11] Conversely, when Havenstein summoned eight directors of the principal joint-stock banks to the Reichsbank on 18 June 1914 to ask them to raise their reserve ratios (in order to reduce the dangers of a monetary crisis in the event of war), they politely but firmly told him to get lost.[12] The only evidence which Gutsche can provide of a capitalist appetite for war is a quotation from the distinctly unrepresentative Alfred Hugenberg, director of the Krupp armaments company. The heavy industrialist Hugo Stinnes was so uninterested in the idea of war that in 1914 he established the Union Mining Company in Doncaster, with a view to bringing German technology to the British coalfields.[13]

The Marxist interpretation of the war's origins can therefore be consigned to the rubbish bin of history, along with the regimes which most avidly fostered it. However, there remains – largely intact – another model of the role of economics in 1914. The work of Paul Kennedy, in particular, has done much to propagate the idea of economics as one of the 'realities behind diplomacy' – a determinant of power, capable of being expressed in terms of population, industrial output, iron and steel production and energy consumption. In this view, politicians have more 'free will' to attempt imperialist expansion without necessarily being subordinate to the interests of business; but their country's economic resources place the ultimate constraint on that expansion, which, beyond a certain point, becomes unsustainable.[14] In these terms, Britain in 1914 was a power in relative decline, suffering from imperial 'overstretch'; Germany was an irresistibly rising rival. Kennedy and his many followers point to indicators of economic, industrial and export growth to suggest that a confrontation between the declining Britain and the rising Germany was, if not inevitable, then at least likely.[15]

Typical of this approach is the argument advanced by Geiss that its development of 'the strongest modern industrial economy' made Germany the 'super great power of the continent':

In its enormous and still expanding power Germany was like a fast-breeder reactor without a protective shell [sic] . . . The economic sense of power magnified the self-confidence acquired since 1871 into that self-over-estimation which drove the German Reich through *Weltpolitik* into the First World War.[16]

Unification in 1870–71 had given Germany 'latent hegemony [in Europe] literally overnight . . . It was inevitable that the union of all or most Germans in a single state would become the strongest power in Europe.' The advocates of a German-dominated Europe were therefore correct, at least in theory: 'There was nothing wrong with the conclusion . . . that Germany and continental Europe west of Russia would only be able to hold their own . . . [alongside] the coming giant economic and political power blocs . . . if Europe pulled together. And a united Europe would fall almost automatically under the leadership of the strongest power – Germany.'[17] For the majority of British historians, it is axiomatic that this challenge had to be resisted.[18]

The history of Europe between 1870 and 1914 thus continues to be written as a history of economic rivalry, with Britain and Germany as the principal rivals. Yet this model of the relationship between economics and power is also deeply flawed.

It is quite true that between 1890 and 1913 German exports were growing faster than those of its European rivals and that its gross

Table 3   *Some indicators of British and German industrial strength,*
1880 and 1913

	1880		1913	
	Britain	Germany	Britain	Germany
Relative shares of world manufacturing (per cent)	22.9	8.5	13.6	14.8
Total industrial potential (Britain in 1900 = 100)	73.3	27.4	127.2	137.7
Per capita industrialization (Britain in 1900 = 100)	87.0	25.0	115.0	85.0

Source: Kennedy, *Great Powers*, pp. 256, 259.

domestic capital formation was the highest in Europe. Table 3 summarizes some of Kennedy's statistical evidence of the German challenge to Britain. Moreover, if one calculates growth rates for Germany's population (1.34 per cent per annum), gross national product (2.78 per cent) and steel production (6.54 per cent), there is no question that she was outstripping both Britain and France between 1890 and 1914.[19]

Yet in reality the most important economic factor in early twentieth-century world politics was not the growth of German economic power at all. Rather, it was the immense extent of British *financial* power.

Already by the 1850s British overseas investments totalled in the region of £200 million.[20] In the second half of the century, however, there were three great waves of capital export. Between 1861 and 1872 net foreign investment rose from just 1.4 per cent of GNP to 7.7 per cent, before dropping back down to 0.8 per cent in 1877. It then rose more or less steadily to 7.3 per cent in 1890, before once again falling down below 1 per cent in 1901. In the third upswing, foreign investment rose to an all-time peak of 9.1 per cent in 1913 – a level not subsequently surpassed until the 1990s.[21] In absolute terms, this led to a huge accumulation of foreign assets, rising more than tenfold from £370 million in 1860 to £3.9 billion in 1913 – around a third of the total stock of British wealth. No other country came close to this level of foreign investment: as Table 4 shows, the closest, France, had foreign assets worth less than half the British total, Germany just over a quarter.

Table 4 Total foreign investments in 1913

	Total (£ million)	of which in Europe (per cent)
Britain	793	5.2
France	357	51.9
Germany	230	44.0
USA	139	20.0
Other	282	n/a
Total	1,800	26.4

Source: Kindleberger, *Financial History of Western Europe*, p. 225.

Britain accounted for something like 44 per cent of total foreign investment on the eve of the First World War.[22] Moreover, as the table shows, most British foreign investment was outside Europe; a far higher proportion of German investment was within the continent. In 1910 Bethmann Hollweg referred to England as 'the decisive rival of Germany when it comes to the policy of economic expansion'.[23] This was true if by economic expansion Bethmann meant overseas investment – though not if he meant increasing exports, as Britain's policy of free trade meant that there was nothing to prevent German exporters from challenging British firms in imperial markets (and, indeed, in the home market itself). This commercial competition naturally did not go unnoticed; but it would be absurd to see the journalistic campaigns against products 'Made in Germany' as harbingers of an Anglo-German war, any more than American talk of the Japanese economic 'threat' in the 1980s presaged a military conflict.[24]

Some economic historians have argued that high levels of capital export undermined the British economy: the City of London is the favourite whipping-boy of those who see manufacturing as in some way superior to services as a generator of income and employment. The reality is that capital exports were only starving British industry of investment if it can be shown that there was a capital shortage inhibiting firms from modernizing their plant. There is little evidence to support this view.[25] Although there was certainly an inverse relationship between the cycle of foreign investment and that of domestic fixed investment, capital export was not really a 'drain' of capital from the British economy; nor should it be seen as somehow 'causing' the British trade deficit to widen.[26] In fact, the income earned on these investments more than matched the export of new capital, just as (when coupled with revenue from 'invisible' earnings) it invariably exceeded the trade deficit. In the 1890s net foreign investment amounted to 3.3 per cent of gross national product, compared with net property income from abroad of 5.6 per cent. For the next decade the figures were respectively 5.1 and 5.9.[27]

Why did the British economy behave in this way? The greater part of overseas investment was 'portfolio' rather than 'direct' in nature, in other words it was mediated by stock exchanges through sales of bonds and shares issued on behalf of foreign governments and companies. According to Edelstein, the explanation for the 'pull' of foreign securities was that, even allowing for the higher degree of risk involved, their yields were rather higher (by around 1.5 percentage points) than those of domestic securities when averaged out over the period 1870–1913. However, this averaging conceals substantial fluctuations. Analysing the accounts of 482 firms, Davis and Huttenback have shown that domestic rates of return were sometimes higher than foreign – in the 1890s, for example.[28] Their work also quantifies the importance in the eyes of investors of imperialism, as rates of return on investments in the Empire were markedly different from those on investments in foreign territories not politically controlled by Britain: as much as 67 per cent higher in the period before 1884, but 40 per cent lower thereafter.[29] Was the rising level of British investment abroad therefore an economically irrational product of imperialism – a case of capital following the flag rather than maximum profits? In fact, Davis and Huttenback show that imperial possessions were not the main destination of British investment taken as a whole: for the period between 1865 and 1914, only around a quarter of investment went to the Empire, compared with 30 per cent for the British economy itself and 45 per cent for foreign economies. Their work points to the existence of an élite of wealthy British investors with a material interest in the Empire as a mechanism for stabilizing the international capital market *as a whole*.

High levels of capital export from Britain were also an integral part of the British economy's global role as an exporter of manufactures, an importer of food and other primary products and a major 'exporter' of people: total net emigration from the United Kingdom between 1900 and 1914 was an astonishing 2.4 million.[30] The Bank of England was also the lender of last resort in the international monetary system: in

1868, only Britain and Portugal had been on the gold standard, which had taken root in Britain during the eighteenth century; by 1908 all of Europe was on gold (though the currencies of Austria–Hungary, Italy, Spain and Portugal were not fully convertible into specie).[31] In many ways, then, imperialism was the political accompaniment to economic developments in the late nineteenth century similar to those we call 'globalization' in the late twentieth century. As in our own time, globalization then was associated with the emergence of a single world superpower: today the United States of America, then Britain – with the difference that British dominance had a much more formal character. In 1860 the territorial extent of the British empire was some 9.5 million square miles; by 1909 the total had risen to 12.7 million. Some 444 million people lived under some form of British rule on the eve of the First World War, only 10 per cent in the United Kingdom itself. Nor do these figures take into account that Britannia more or less ruled the waves, thanks to the possession of the world's biggest navy (in terms of warship tonnage more than twice the size of the German in 1914), and its biggest merchant marine. It was, as J. L. Garvin put it in 1905, 'an extent and magnificence of dominion beyond the natural'. From the vantage point of other major powers this seemed unfair. 'We can't talk about conquest and grabbing,' concedes even Carruthers in *The Riddle of the Sands*. 'We've collared a fine share of the world, and they've every right to be jealous.'[32]

Yet in a period characterized by unprecedented and as yet unmatched freedom of movement of people, goods and capital, it was not immediately clear how any power could challenge the global superpower. While Britain in the two decades before the war saw rising emigration and capital export, Germany ceased to export Germans and exported a diminishing proportion of new capital formed.[33] Whether this divergence caused or was caused by the differences in the two countries' domestic economic performance is unclear, but the implications in terms of relative international power are obvious. As Offer has recently suggested, Britain's high level of emigration created bonds of kinship which ensured the loyalty of the dominions to the mother country.[34] By contrast, the declining German birth rate and a rising volume of immigration heightened German awareness of eastern Europe's superior manpower. True, Germany's growing success as an exporter appeared to pose a threat to British interests, but Germans feared that export growth (and the corollary, a continued reliance on imported raw materials) could be jeopardized by the protectionist policies of more successful colonial powers.[35] Though Britain continued to pursue a policy of free trade throughout its empire before 1914, the debate on 'imperial preference' and tariff reform sparked by Joseph Chamberlain raised a worrying possibility which other exporting economies could hardly ignore.

Finally, British and French capital exports undoubtedly increased those countries' international political leverage. In one of its earliest publications, the Pan-German League complained:

[We are] a people of fifty million, who dedicate our best strength to military service [and] who spend over half a billion every year on defence . . . Our sacrifices of blood and money would indeed be excessive if our military power enabled us . . . to secure our just rights only where we receive the gracious assent of the English.[36]

But as Bülow lamented: 'The enormous [international] influence of France . . . is to a great extent the product of her wealth of capital and liquidity.'[37] Economic historians often praise the German banks' preference for domestic industrial investment; but such investment did nothing to enhance German power overseas. Germany's international influence was therefore circumscribed: the dramatic level of industrial growth experienced since 1895 tended in some ways, paradoxically, to weaken its international bargaining position.

WARS FORGONE

If there was a war which imperialism should have caused it was the war between Britain and Russia which failed to break out in the 1870s and 1880s; or the war between Britain and France which failed to break out in the 1880s or 1890s. These three powers were, after all, the real imperial rivals, coming into repeated conflict with one another from Constantinople to Kabul (in the case of Britain and Russia), from the Sudan to Siam (in the case of Britain and France). Few contemporaries in 1895 would have predicted that they would end up fighting a war on the same side within twenty years. After all, the collective diplomatic memory of the previous century was of recurrent friction between Britain, France and Russia, as Table 5 shows.

It is easy to forget how bad relations between Britain and both Russia

Table 5   *International alignments, 1815–1917: an overview*

Period	'West'	'Middle'	'East'
1793–1815		France	<Britain + Russia + Prussia + Austria>
1820–29	(Britain)	Spain + Portugal + Naples + Greece	<Russia + Prussia + Austria + France>
1830–39	Britain + France	Belgium	<Russia + Prussia + Austria>
1840–49	Britain + Turkey	France + Piedmont + Hungary + Prussia	Russia + Austria
1850–58	<Britain + France + Austria + Turkey>	(Prussia)	Russia
1859–67	(Britain) (Russia)	France + Piedmont + Prussia	Austria
1867–71	(Britain) (Russia) (Austria)	<Germany + Italy>	France
1871–5	(Britain)	France	<Russia + Austria + Italy> <Germany + Austria + Italy>
1876–8	Britain + Turkey	<Germany + Austria + Italy>	Russia
1879–86	Britain	France	<Russia + Germany + Austria>
1887–9	<Britain + Italy + Austria>	France	<Russia + Germany> <Germany + Austria>
1890–98	Britain	<France + Russia>	<Germany + Austria + Italy>
1899–1901	Britain + Germany?	<France + Russia>	<Germany + Austria>
1902–4	<Britain + Japan>	<France + Russia>	<Germany + Austria + Italy>
1905	<Britain + Japan> <Britain + France>	<France + Russia>	Germany + Russia?
1906–14	<Britain + Japan>	Italy	<Germany + Austria>
1914–17	<Britain + France + Russia>	<Britain + France + Russia + Italy>	<Germany + Austria + Turkey>

Notes: < > formal alliance or entente; ( ) neutral

and France were in the 1880s and 1890s. The British military occupation of Egypt in 1882 had been primarily intended to (and did in fact) stabilize Egyptian finances, in the interests not only of British investors but of European investors generally. However, it was a long-standing diplomatic embarrassment. Between 1882 and 1922 Britain felt obliged to promise the other powers no fewer than sixty-six times that she would end her occupation of Egypt. It did not happen; and from the moment Egypt was occupied, Britain found herself at a diplomatic disadvantage when trying to check analogous expansion by her two main imperial rivals.

There were at least two regions where Russia could legitimately stake comparable claims: in Central Asia and the Balkans. In neither case was it entirely credible for Britain to resist. In April 1885, in the dying days of Gladstone's second ministry, an Anglo-Russian conflict threatened to break out following the Russian victory over Afghan forces at Penjdeh. It was a similar story in 1885 when the Russian government intervened to prevent the Bulgarian King Alexander from unifying Bulgaria and Eastern Rumelia on his own terms. France reacted even more aggressively to the British takeover in Egypt: indeed, in many ways it was the Anglo-French antagonism which was the most important feature of the diplomatic scene in the 1880s and 1890s. In 1886, at the time of the French expedition to Tonkin (in Indo-China), the French Rothschilds uneasily predicted to Bismarck's son Herbert 'that the next European war will be between England and France'.[38] Though some observers hoped that the return of the Liberal Earl of Rosebery as Foreign Secretary in 1892 might improve matters, it rapidly became apparent that Rosebery was inclined to continue the previous government's Francophobe policy elsewhere. He was dismayed by rumours that France intended some kind of takeover of Siam following a naval confrontation on the Mekong river in July 1893. And the following January, Rosebery responded to Austrian worries about Russian designs on the Straits by assuring the Austrian ambassador that he 'would not recoil from the danger of involving England in a war with Russia'.[39]

Predictably, it was Egypt and her southern neighbour the Sudan which proved the main cause of Anglo-French antagonism – so much so that a war between England and France seemed a real possibility in 1895. By early 1894 it was apparent that the French government intended to make some kind of bid for control of Fashoda on the Upper Nile. Fearful that French control of Fashoda would compromise the British position in Egypt, Rosebery – who became Prime Minister that March – hastily concluded an agreement with the King of the Belgians to lease the area south of Fashoda to the Belgian Congo in return for a strip of the Western Congo, with the obvious intention of blocking French access to Fashoda. In the difficult negotiations which ensued, attempts by the French Foreign Minister Gabriel Hanotaux to reach some kind of compromise over Fashoda failed; and, when an expedition led by the French explorer Marchand set off for the Upper Nile, Rosebery's parliamentary under-secretary at the Foreign Office, Sir Edward Grey, denounced it as 'an unfriendly act'. It was at this critical moment (June 1895) that Rosebery resigned, leaving Britain in a position of unprecedented diplomatic isolation. However, luckily for the incoming Salisbury government, the contemporaneous defeat of Italy by the Abyssinian forces at Adowa provided a distracting sideshow. This was an encouragement for Britain to act swiftly and, exactly a week later, the order was given to reconquer the Sudan. Nevertheless, when Hanotaux's successor Théophile Delcassé reacted to Kitchener's victory over the Sudanese dervishes at Omdurman by occupying Fashoda, war loomed large.

Fashoda is of interest here because it reminds us of a war between the great powers which did not happen, but might have. Similarly, it is important to remember that in 1895 and 1896 both Britain and Russia toyed with the idea of using their navies to force the Black Sea Straits and assert their direct control over Constantinople. In the event, neither side was sufficiently sure of its naval power to risk such a step; but, had it been attempted, there would have been at the very least a diplomatic crisis as serious as that of 1878. Here too there was an unrealized war, this time between Britain and Russia. All this goes to show that, if we are to explain why a war eventually broke out in which Britain, France and Russia fought on the same side, imperialism is unlikely to provide the answer.

It was fortunate for Britain that her two imperial rivals were not sufficiently close to one another at this stage to join forces. St Petersburg would never support Paris on African issues, any more than Paris would support St Petersburg over the Black Sea Straits. France was a republic, with one of Europe's most democratic franchises; Russia was the last of the absolutist monarchies. However, a Franco-Russian alliance made both strategic and economic sense. France and Russia had common foes: Germany between them and Britain all around them.[40] Moreover, France was a capital exporter, while industrializing Russia was hungry for foreign loans. Indeed, French diplomats and bankers began to discuss the possibility of a Franco-Russian entente based on French capital as early as 1880. Bismarck's decision to prohibit the use of Russian bonds as collateral for Reichsbank loans (the famous 'Lombardverbot') is usually seen as the catalyst for a more or less inevitable reorientation.[41]

There were also a number of non-financial reasons for closer Franco-Russian ties, not least the increasingly unfriendly attitude of the German government following the accession of William II in 1888 and the dismissal of Bismarck two years later. The assurances of William and the new Chancellor, General Leo von Caprivi, that Germany would support Austria in the event of a war with Russia and their blunt refusal to renew the secret Reinsurance Treaty made financial inducements superfluous: logically, France and Russia were likely to gravitate towards one another. Nevertheless, it is important to realize how many obstacles there were to such an alignment. There were, to begin with, financial difficulties. Recurrent instability on the Paris bourse – the Union Générale crisis of 1882 was followed by the failure of the Comptoir d'Escompte in 1889 and the Panama Canal crisis in 1893 – cast doubt on France's basic capacity to cope with large-scale Russian operations. On the Russian side too there were financial problems. It was only in 1894–7 that the rouble was finally put on the gold standard, and the French bond market remained wary of Russian bonds; it was only after sharp price falls in 1886, 1888 and 1891 that a steady appreciation set in.

The first major French loan to Russia was floated on the bourse in the autumn of 1888.[42] The following year, the Paris Rothschilds agreed to undertake two major Russian bond issues with a total face value of some £77 million, and a third £12-million issue followed the next year.[43] In 1894 a further loan worth around £16 million was issued;[44] and there was another for the same amount in 1896.[45] By that time, the rise in Russian funds was beginning to look sustainable, though the second loan was only placed with investors slowly – even with the timely assistance of a visit by the Tsar to Paris.[46] Now the German banks were being positively encouraged by the German Foreign Office to participate in the 1894 and 1896 Russian loans, precisely in order to prevent a French monopoly on Russian finance.[47] It was too late. As the new century dawned, no diplomatic relationship was more solidly founded than the Franco-Russian alliance. It remains the classic illustration of an international combination based on credit and debt. In all, French loans to Russia by 1914 totalled more than 3 billion roubles, 80 per cent of the country's total external debt.[48] Nearly 28 per cent of all French overseas investment was in Russia, nearly all of it in state bonds.

Economic historians used to be critical of the Russian government's strategy of borrowing abroad to finance industrialization at home. But it is very hard to find fault with the results. There is no question that the Russian economy industrialized with extraordinary speed in the three decades before 1914. According to Gregory's figures, net national product grew at an average annual rate of 3.3 per cent between 1885 and 1913. Annual investment rose from 8 per cent of national income to 10 per cent. Between 1890 and 1913 per capita capital formation rose 55 per cent. Industrial output grew at an annual rate of 4–5 per cent. In the period 1898–1913 pig iron production rose by more than 100 per cent; the railway network increased in size by some 57 per cent; and raw cotton consumption increased by 82 per cent.[49] In the countryside too there was progress. Between 1860 and 1914 agricultural output grew at an average annual rate of 2 per cent. That was significantly faster than the rate of growth of population (1.5 per cent per annum). The population grew by around 26 per cent between 1900 and 1913; but total national income very nearly doubled. As Table 6 shows, it was not Germany but Russia which had the fastest growing economy before 1914.

It is fashionable for historians of the 1917 revolutions in Russia to begin their accounts in the 1890s. But the economic historian sees little evidence of a coming calamity. In per capita terms Russians were on average clearly better off in 1913 than they had been 15 years before: per capita incomes rose by some 56 per cent in that period. The death rate fell from 35.7 per thousand in the late 1870s to 29.5 (1906–10), as did infant mortality (from 275 per thousand live births to 247). The literacy rate rose from 21 per cent of the population to 40 per cent between 1897 and 1914. To be sure, rapid industrialization tended to widen social cleavages in urban Russia without reducing those in land-hungry rural Russia (where 80 per cent of the population still lived). On the other hand, industrialization seemed to have the result

Table 6   Percentage increase in net national product, 1898–1913

Britain	Italy	Germany	Russia	France	Austria
40.0	82.7	84.2	96.8	59.6	90.9

Source: Hobson, 'Wary Titan', p. 505.

which Russia's leaders most fervently desired from it: increasing military power. With astonishing rapidity, the Russian Empire expanded eastwards and southwards. Between the well-known defeats of the Crimea and Tsushima, Russian generals won countless obscure victories in Central Asia and the Far East. By 1914 the Russian Empire covered 8.6 million square miles and extended from the Carpathians to the borders of China.

The remarkable (and for Britain lucky) thing is that the Franco-Russian alliance was never seriously used against the two members' principal imperial foe: Britain. The possibility was taken seriously in Britain, and not only by fantasists like William Le Queux (see Chapter 1). Reflecting in 1888 on the challenges the British army might have to face in the future, the Liberal politician Sir Charles Dilke mentioned 'only Russia and France' as potential foes. 'Between ourselves and France differences are frequent, and between ourselves and Russia war is one day almost certain.'[50] As late as 1901 the First Sea Lord, the Earl of Selborne, felt it necessary to warn that the combined battleship fleets of France and Russia would soon be equal to that of the Royal Navy.[51]

The idea of an alternative world war, with Britain fighting both France and Russia in theatres as far afield as the Mediterranean, the Bosphorus, Egypt and Afghanistan strikes us today as inconceivable. But at the time such a scenario was less implausible than the notion of British alliances with France and Russia, both of which had for years seemed impossible – 'foredoomed to failure', in Chamberlain's phrase.

THE LION AND THE EAGLE

Strong economic and political forces thus propelled France and Russia into their fateful alliance. The same cannot be said, of course, for Britain and Germany; but nor can it be claimed that there were insuperable forces generating an ultimately lethal Anglo-German antagonism. Indeed, precisely the opposite outcome seemed not only desirable but possible: an Anglo-German understanding (if not an outright alliance). After all, Dilke was not alone in thinking that Germany had 'no interests sufficiently at variance with our own to be likely to lead to a quarrel'.

There is always a strong temptation for the historian to be condescending to diplomatic initiatives that fail, by assuming that they were bound to do so. The efforts to secure some kind of understanding between

Britain and Germany in the years before the outbreak of the First World War have often been the object of such condescension. At best, the idea of an Anglo-German alliance has been seen as appealing too narrowly to the bankers of the City of London, particularly those of German and Jewish origin – a view which, of course, Germanophobe contemporaries did not hesitate to express.[52] Yet the ultimate descent of the relationship between Britain and Germany into war should not be retrospectively over-determined. In many ways, the arguments for some kind of under-standing were founded on common international interests. *A priori*, there is no obvious reason why an 'over-stretched' power (as Britain perceived herself to be) and an 'under-stretched' power (as Germany perceived herself to be) should not have co-operated diplomatically. It is simply untrue to say that 'the fundamental priorities of policy of each country were mutually exclusive'.[53] This is not to resuscitate the old argument about 'missed opportunities' in Anglo-German relations which could have averted the carnage of the trenches, a line which has all too often rested on the wisdom of hindsight and unreliable memoirs;[54] it is merely to suggest that the failure of the Anglo-German entente to develop was a more contingent than predetermined outcome.

The possibility of an Anglo-German entente had deep roots. Britain, after all, had stood aside in 1870–71, when Germany had inflicted a humiliating defeat on France. Britain's difficulties with Russia in the 1880s also had positive implications for relations with Germany. Although Bismarck's proposal of an Anglo-German alliance in 1887 came to nothing, Salisbury's secret Triple Entente with Italy and Austria to preserve the status quo in the Mediterranean and the Black Sea created an indirect link to Berlin through the German Triple Alliance, of which Italy and Austria were also members.

This partly explains why, when Germany began to make colonial demands in the 1880s, Britain put up little resistance. The German Chancellor's map of Africa was, of course, no more than a shadow of his map of Europe (and perhaps also his map of German domestic politics); nevertheless, he played up German ambitions there in order to exploit Britain's vulnerability over Egypt. Beginning in 1884, Bismarck used Egypt as the pretext for a series of audacious German interventions in the region, menacing Britain with a Franco-German 'League of Neutrals' in Africa, asserting German control over Angra Pequeña in South-West Africa and claiming all the territory between Cape Colony and Portuguese West Africa. The British response was, in effect, to appease Germany by accepting the South-West African colony and conceding further territorial acquisitions in the Cameroons and East Africa. The issue of Zanzibar raised by the German ambassador Paul von Hatzfeldt in 1886 was typical: Germany had no economic interest worth talking about in Zanzibar (and indeed exchanged it for Heligoland in the North Sea in 1890); but it was worth laying claim to it when Britain was so ready literally to give ground. The 1890 agreement between Britain and Germany gave Britain Zanzibar in return for the North Sea island of Heligoland and a narrow strip of land which gave German South-West Africa access to the Zambezi River.

It was over China that some form of Anglo-German co-operation seemed most likely to develop. As so often, this had its roots in finance. Since 1874, the date of the first foreign loan raised for Imperial China, the Chinese government's principal source of external finance had been two British firms based in Hong Kong, the Hong Kong & Shanghai Banking Corporation and Jardine, Matheson & Co.[55] The British government, in the person of Sir Robert Hart, also controlled the Imperial Maritime Customs. In March 1885, the German banker Adolph Hansemann approached the Hong Kong & Shanghai Bank with a proposal to divide Chinese government and railway finance equally between the British and German members of a new syndicate. Negotiations culminated in the creation of the Deutsch-Asiatische Bank in February 1889, a joint venture involving more than thirteen leading German banks.[56]

By raising the spectre of increased Russian influence in the Far East, the Japanese defeat of China in the war of 1894–5 created a perfect opportunity for co-operation between Berlin and London. In essence, the bankers (Hansemann and Rothschild) sought to promote a partnership between the Hong Kong & Shanghai Bank and the new Deutsch-Asiatische Bank which they hoped, if given suitable official backing by their respective governments, would prevent Russia from gaining an excessive influence over China. To be sure, the aspirations of the bankers were far from being the same as those of the diplomats and politicians. Friedrich von Holstein, the *éminence grise* at the German Foreign Office, wanted Germany to side with Russia and France rather than with Britain, and joined in their objections to the Japanese annexation of Liaotung under the treaty of Shimoneseki in April 1895. But events bore out the wisdom of the bankers' view.[57] The announcement in May that China would finance her indemnity payment to Japan with a Russian loan was a blow to both the British and German governments. The loan, of course, could not be financed by Russia herself, given that Russia was an international debtor; in effect, it was a French loan, and the benefits were divided evenly between Russia and France, the former gaining the right to extend its Trans-Siberian Railway through Manchuria, the latter securing railway concessions in China. There was even a new Russo-Chinese bank, again backed by French capital, and a formal Russo-Chinese alliance in May 1896.[58] In the wake of this reverse, Hansemann's proposal that the Hong Kong & Shanghai Bank should join forces with the Deutsch-Asiatische Bank looked more attractive, and an agreement between the two banks was signed in July 1895. The main aim of this alliance was to end competition between the great powers by putting Chinese foreign loans in the hands of a single multinational consortium, as had been done in the past for Greece and Turkey, though with an implicit Anglo-German predominance. After much diplomatic manoeuvring, this was finally achieved when a second Chinese loan was issued in 1898.

There continued to be difficulties, admittedly. Salisbury refused to give the loan a government guarantee, with the result that the British share proved embarrassingly hard to place. In November 1897 the Germans seized Kiao-Chow, the main port of the Shantung province, and this was followed by a dispute between the Hong Kong & Shanghai Bank and Hansemann over a railway concession in Shantung.[59] However, this was quickly forgotten when Russia demanded a 'lease' of Port Arthur in March 1898, prompting Britain to demand the 'consolation' of Wei-hai-wei (the harbour opposite Port Arthur).[60] At a conference of bankers and politicians in London at the beginning of September it was agreed to divide China into 'spheres of influence' for the purpose of allocating rail concessions, leaving the Yangtse Valley to the British banks, Shantung to the Germans and splitting the Tientsin–Chinkiang route.[61] Disputes about railways continued but the pattern of collaboration had been established.[62] When the Germans sent an expedition to China following the Boxer Rising and the Russian occupation of Manchuria in 1900, they assured London that 'the Russians won't risk a war', and in October Britain and Germany signed a new agreement to maintain the integrity of the Chinese Empire and an 'Open Door' trade regime.[63] This was the high water mark of Anglo-German political co-operation in China; but it is important to recognize that business co-operation continued for some years to come. Further disagreements (prompted by the intrusion of the so-called 'Peking Syndicate' into the Hoangho region) were resolved at another bankers' conference in Berlin in 1902.[64]

It was apparently in the wake of a dinner at the time of the Port Arthur crisis that Hatzfeldt raised the possibility of an Anglo-German alliance with Chamberlain. As Arthur Balfour recalled:

Joe is very impulsive: and the Cabinet discussion of the preceding days [about Port Arthur] had forced on his attention our isolated and occasionally therefore difficult diplomatic position. He certainly went far in the expression of his own personal leaning towards a German alliance; he combated the notion that our form of Parliamentary government rendered such an alliance precarious (a notion which apparently haunts the German mind), and I believe even threw out a vague suggestion as to the form which an arrangement between the two countries might take.

The response from the then German Foreign Secretary Bülow, Balfour recalled, was 'immediate':

[H]is telegraphic reply . . . dwelt again on the Parliamentary difficulty, – but also expressed with happy frankness the German view of England's position in the European system. They hold, it seems, that we are more than a match for France, but not more than a match for Russia and France combined. The issue of such a contest would be doubtful. They could not afford to see us succumb, – not because they loved us, but because they know that they would be the next victims – and so on. The whole tenor of the conversation (as represented to me) being in favour of a closer union between the countries.[65]

Further talks followed in April between Chamberlain and Baron Hermann von Eckardstein, the first secretary at the German embassy, whom the Kaiser had briefed 'to keep official sentiment in England favourable to us and *hopeful*'. Eckardstein now proposed, in the Kaiser's name, 'a possible alliance between England and Germany . . . the basis of [which] would be a guarantee by both Powers of the possessions of the other'. As part of the package, he offered Britain 'a free hand in Egypt and the Transvaal', and hinted that 'a direct defensive alliance . . . might come later'. 'Such a Treaty', minuted Chamberlain to Salisbury, 'would make for peace and might be negotiated at the present time'.[66] The idea resurfaced in a similar form in 1901.[67]

So why did the idea of an Anglo-German entente ultimately fail? One rather unsophisticated answer relates to the personalities involved.

Edward VII's Francophilia is occasionally cited, or the fundamental unseriousness of Eckardstein.[68] Certainly, Bülow and Holstein exaggerated the weakness of Britain's bargaining position.[69] But a more serious political obstacle (as the Germans divined) was probably Salisbury's fundamental lack of enthusiasm.[70] Chamberlain too contributed to the failure of his own design. Privately, he spoke of a limited 'Treaty or Arrangement between Germany and Great Britain for a term of years . . . of a defensive character based upon a mutual understanding as to policy in China and elsewhere.'[71] In public, however, he talked grandly of a 'New Triple Alliance between the Teutonic race and the two great branches of the Anglo-Saxon race' and – quite unrealistically – expected the Germans to reply in the same effusive spirit. When, in a Reichstag speech of 11 December 1899, Bülow expressed his readiness 'on the basis of full reciprocity and mutual consideration to live with [England] in peace and harmony', Chamberlain petulantly dismissed this as the 'cold shoulder'.[72] When difficulties arose, Chamberlain lost patience: 'If they are so short-sighted', he snapped, 'and cannot see that it is a question of the rise of a new constellation in the world, they are beyond help.'[73]

There were other factors, however, which arguably counted for more than personal foibles. A familiar objection is that colonial disputes militated against Anglo-German rapprochement. The historian Hans Delbrück's 1899 article is often cited, in which he declared, 'We can pursue [colonial] policy with England or without England. With England means peace; against England means – through war.'[74] But the reality was that Germany was able to pursue her colonial policy very largely *with* England (and the correct inference to be drawn from Delbrück's piece was that she would have to). Thus the protracted haggling with Portugal over the future of her African colonies (and especially the Delagoa Bay) finally produced an agreement in 1898 whereby Britain and Germany jointly lent money to Portugal secured on her colonial property, but with a secret clause dividing the Portuguese territory into spheres of influence.[75] Nor was there a conflict of interest in West Africa.[76] In the Pacific the Samoan crisis which blew up in April 1899 was resolved by the end of the year.[77] The two countries even co-operated (despite vociferous complaints in the British press) over Venezuela's external debt in 1902.[78]

Another more strategically important region where Anglo-German partnership seemed viable was the Ottoman Empire, an area of increasing interest to German business even before the Kaiser's first visit to Constantinople in 1889. So long as Russia seemed to menace the Straits, the prospects for some sort of Anglo-German co-operation in the region remained good. Thus the two countries worked closely together following the military defeat of Greece by Turkey in 1897, hammering out the details of a new financial control over Athens. A better-known opportunity for co-operation came in 1899 – a year after the Kaiser's second visit to the Bosphorus – when the Sultan agreed to the proposal for an Imperial Ottoman Baghdad Railway, the brainchild of Georg von Siemens of the Deutsche Bank (hence the 'Berlin–Baghdad Railway'). Siemens and his successor Arthur von Gwinner always intended to secure British as well as French participation in the venture; the problem was the lack of interest in the City, which had largely lost faith in the future of the Ottoman regime.[79] In March 1903, an agreement was drawn up for an extension of the line to Basra, which would have given the British members of a consortium – led by Sir Ernest Cassel and Lord Revelstoke – 25 per cent; but the fact that German investors would hold 35 per cent prompted a barrage of criticism in right-wing journals like the *Spectator* and the *National Review*, and Balfour – now Prime Minister – chose to pull out.[80]

There was one region of potential Anglo-German conflict, however: South Africa. William II's telegram after the abortive Jameson Raid, congratulating President Kruger on repelling the invaders, certainly ruffled feathers in London; and German expressions of sympathy for the Boers during the war that broke out with the Transvaal Republic in 1899 were a further cause of tension between London and Berlin. The point of the 1898 agreement with Germany over Portuguese Mozambique was partly that it was supposed to discourage the Germans from siding with Kruger, but the outbreak of war seemed to cast doubt on that arrangement. Matters were not helped by renewed German talk of a 'continental league' against Britain at the end of 1899 and the British interception of German mail steamers in South African waters in January 1900. Yet the Boer War did not do as much damage to Anglo-German relations as some had feared. German banks had no qualms about applying for a share of the post-war British Transvaal loan. Perhaps more importantly, in undermining British self-confidence the war strengthened the arguments for ending diplomatic isolation. Rhetoric about 'national efficiency' and the efforts of the militarist 'leagues' could not compensate for the anxieties the war had awakened

about the costs of maintaining Britain's vast overseas imperium –
exemplified by Balfour's hyperbolic claim that 'we were for all practical
purposes at the present moment only a third-rate power'.[81] Out of the
increasingly complex institutional framework within which imperial
strategy was made (and which the new Committee of Imperial Defence
and the Imperial General Staff did little to streamline),[82] there emerged
a consensus. Because it seemed financially and strategically impossible
for Britain simultaneously to defend its Empire and itself, isolation
could no longer be afforded – and therefore diplomatic understandings
had to be reached with one or more of Britain's imperial rivals. Indeed,
it was during the Boer War – in the early months of 1901 – that a
renewed effort was made to bring Chamberlain and the new Foreign
Secretary Lord Lansdowne into contact with German representatives
on the basis of (in Chamberlain's words) 'co-operation with Germany
and adherence to Triple Alliance'.[83]

The territory which was now brought into the discussions in earnest
– Chamberlain had first raised it in 1899 – was Morocco. Because of
later events, it is easy to assume there was something inevitable about
disagreements between Britain and Germany over Morocco; but that
seemed far from likely in 1901. Indeed, French designs in the entire
north-west African region (further advanced by a secret deal with Italy
in 1900) seemed positively to favour some sort of joint action. Britain
was already concerned by Spanish fortifications at Algeciras, which
seemed to pose a threat to Gibraltar, that vital Mediterranean gatepost.
The possibility of a joint Franco-Spanish 'liquidation' of Morocco was
a real one. The obvious alternative was to divide Morocco into British
and German spheres of influence, with Britain taking Tangier, and
Germany the Atlantic coast. This was the basic thrust of a draft
agreement discussed in May and again in December. The discussions
continued sporadically into 1902. It was in fact German *lack* of interest
in Morocco – as expressed unambiguously by both Bülow and the
Kaiser in early 1903 – which prevented any such scheme being realized.[84]

THE LOGIC OF APPEASEMENT

The real explanation for the failure of the Anglo-German alliance
project was not German strength but German *weakness*. It was, after
all, the British who killed off the alliance idea, as much as the Germans.[85]

And they did so not because Germany began to pose a threat to Britain, but, on the contrary, because they realized she did *not* pose a threat.

The primary British concern had, of course, been to reduce rather than increase the likelihood of expensive overseas conflicts. Despite German paranoia, these were in fact much more likely to be with powers which already had large empires than with a power which merely aspired to have one. For this reason, it is not surprising that rather more fruitful diplomatic approaches ended up being made to France and Russia. As the assistant under-secretary at the Foreign Office, Francis Bertie, said in November 1901, the best argument against an Anglo-German alliance was that if one were concluded 'we [should] never be on decent terms with France, our neighbour in Europe and in many parts of the world, or with Russia, whose frontiers are coterminous with ours or nearly so over a large portion of Asia'.[86] Salisbury and Selborne took a very similar view of the relative merits of France and Germany. German reluctance to support British policy in China in 1901 for fear of antagonizing Russia merely confirmed the British view: for all her bluster, Germany was weak.[87]

By comparison, France could offer a far more impressive list of imperial issues over which agreements could be reached.[88] For example, the French had a bigger and better concession to offer Britain than anything Germany might have offered: final acceptance of the British position in Egypt. After over twenty years of recurrent friction, this was a major diplomatic climb-down by Delcassé, and it is easy to see why Lansdowne hastened to commit it to paper. The price of this agreement was that France acquired the right 'to preserve order in Morocco and to provide assistance for the purpose of all administrative, economic, financial and military reforms which it may require' – a concession which the French regarded as giving them the same position of *de facto* power in Morocco as Britain had enjoyed in Egypt since 1882. In the subsequent rows about Morocco, the Germans were in fact quite often in the right; but the fact was that Britain had opted for France and so was bound to back French claims even when they went beyond the legal status quo.

The Anglo-French *Entente Cordiale* of 8 April 1904 amounted, then, to colonial barter (Siam was also settled);[89] but it proved to have two broader implications. Firstly, it demoted the importance to Britain of good relations with Germany, as became evident during the first Moroccan crisis, which began when the Kaiser landed at Tangier on

31 March 1905 and demanded an international conference to reaffirm Morocco's independence. Far from supporting the German arguments for an 'Open Door' in Morocco, Lansdowne worried that the crisis might topple Delcassé and end with a French retreat.[90]

Secondly, because of the closeness of links between Paris and St Petersburg, the Anglo-French entente implied better Anglo-Russian relations.[91] In quick succession, Britain indicated her readiness to appease Russia over Manchuria and Tibet, and to avoid unnecessary friction over the Black Sea Straits, Persia – even (to the Indian Viceroy Lord Curzon's dismay) over Afghanistan.[92] It is possible that this drive for good relations might have led sooner to a formal understanding, as it did in the case of France, had it not been for Russia's defeat by Japan. (On the other hand, if Britain had continued to feel menaced by Russia in the East – if Russia had defeated Japan in 1904, for example – then the arguments for an Anglo-German entente might have been strengthened.) But the advent of Japan as an effective counterweight to Russian ambitions in Manchuria introduced a new variable into the equation. The German government had always felt uneasy about the prospect of an arrangement with Britain which conceivably could have meant Germany fighting a war against Russia in Europe for the sake of British interests in China: this explains the assurances given by Bülow and the Kaiser in 1901 of German neutrality in the event of an Anglo-Russian conflict in the Far East. Japan, by contrast, had every reason to look for a European ally. When the Russian government refused to compromise over Manchuria, Tokyo turned readily to London, and in January 1902 a defensive alliance was concluded. It is a good indication of the rationale of British policy – appease the strong – that this alliance came to be seen as taking precedence over any colonial deal with Russia.[93]

Another example may be given of an aggressive power which posed a direct threat to Britain in the Atlantic and Pacific; a power which shared a border over three thousand miles long with one of the Empire's most prosperous territories. This was the United States.

Though the two powers had not come to blows since 1812, it is easily forgotten how many reasons they had to quarrel in the 1890s. The US took issue with Britain over the border between Venezuela and British Guiana, a dispute not settled until 1899; went to war with Spain over Cuba and in the process acquired the Philippines, Puerto Rico and Guam in 1898; annexed Hawaii in the same year; fought a bloody colonial war in the Philippines between 1899 and 1902; acquired some of the Samoan Islands in 1899; and eagerly took a hand in the economic carve-up of China. The next stage of American imperial expansion was to construct a canal across the Central American isthmus. Compared with the US, Germany was a pacific power. Once again Britain appeased the strong. The 1901 Hay-Pauncefote Treaty waived Britain's objection to American control and fortification of the projected Panama Canal; and London allowed President Theodore Roosevelt to ride roughshod over Colombian objections by assisting a Panamanian revolt in the chosen Canal Zone. In 1901–2 Selborne took the decision to wind down Britain's naval capacity for war with the United States in the Caribbean and the Atlantic.[94] This appeasement had predictable results. In 1904 the Americans established financial control over the Dominican Republic; the same thing happened in Nicaragua in 1909 (with military backing in 1912). Woodrow Wilson claimed to deplore the 'dollar diplomacy' and the 'big stick'; but it was he who sent the marines to take over Haiti in 1915 and to the Dominican Republic in 1916; and it was he who authorized military intervention in Mexico, first in 1914 to change the Mexican government and then in March 1916 to punish 'Pancho' Villa for a raid on New Mexico.[95] But no one in Britain said a word. America was powerful; so there could be no Anglo-American antagonism.

British foreign policy between 1900 and 1906, then, was to appease those powers which appeared to pose the greatest threat to her position, even at the expense of good relations with less important powers. The key point is that Germany fell into the latter category; France, Russia and the United States into the former.

3

Britain's War of Illusions

THE COMPLETE ANGLER

Such was the diplomatic legacy inherited by the Liberals following Balfour's resignation in December 1905 and their subsequent landslide election victory. It is vital to emphasize that it in no way doomed Britain to fight the First World War. Certainly, it arranged Britain's diplomatic priorities *vis-à-vis* the other great powers in the order: France, Russia, Germany. But it did not irrevocably commit Britain to the defence of France, much less Russia, in the event of a German attack on one or both. It did not, in short, make war between Britain and Germany inevitable, as a few pessimists – notably Rosebery – feared.[1] What is more, a Liberal government – particularly of the sort led by Sir Henry Campbell-Bannerman – seemed at first sight less likely to fall out with Germany or to fall in with France or Russia than its predecessor. Indeed, the new government was committed to trying (in Lloyd George's words) 'to reduce the gigantic expenditure on armaments built up by the recklessness of our predecessors'.[2] The law of unintended consequences, however, is never more likely to operate than when a government is as fundamentally divided as the Liberal government by degrees became.

As early as September 1905, Asquith, Grey and Haldane had agreed to act in concert as a Liberal League (in effect, imperialist) faction within the new administration, in order to counter the Radical tendencies feared by, among others, the King.[3] The appointment of Grey as Foreign Secretary was one of the faction's first and most important successes.

Sir Edward Grey – 3rd baronet, later Viscount Grey of Falloden – generally appears in the history books as a tragic figure. In 1908 the editor of the *Daily News* A. G. Gardiner summed him up in terms which have largely stuck:

The inflexibility of his mind, unqualified by large knowledge, swift apprehension of events of urgent passion for humanity, constitutes a peril to the future. His aims are high, his honour stainless; but the slow movement of his mind and his unquestioning faith in the honesty of those on whom he has to rely render it easy for him to drift into courses which a more imaginative sense and a swifter instinct would lead him to question and repudiate.[4]

Having entirely fulfilled Gardiner's worst fears in 1914, Grey has, perhaps not surprisingly, continued to be judged in this way. Lloyd George's posthumous portrait of Grey said similar things more nastily: Grey had 'a high intelligence but of a . . . commonplace texture'. His speeches were 'clear, correct and orderly' but 'characterised by no distinction of phrase or thought'. 'He lacked the knowledge . . . vision, imagination, breadth of mind and that high courage, bordering on audacity, which his immense task demanded.' He was 'a pilot whose hand trembled in the palsy of apprehension, unable to grip the levers and manipulate them with a firm and clear purpose . . . waiting for public opinion to decide his direction for him'.[5] And so the sad verdict echoes and re-echoes: 'Truly tragic . . . at heart a philanthropist, a man of peace'; 'as high-minded an apostle of the moral law as ever was'; 'could deal with questions that had rational answers; when faced with the inexplicable, he tended to retreat'.[6]

No doubt there was a whiff of the tragic about Grey. Within two months of becoming Foreign Secretary he lost his wife, to whom he had been devoted. His most famous utterance was a metaphor about fading illumination; by a cruel irony, he himself went almost completely blind during the war. Yet these misfortunes should not distract us from the clarity of Grey's diplomatic vision prior to the war. He had made his political mark as parliamentary under-secretary at the Foreign Office in the period of isolation which culminated at Fashoda. Yet despite his support of the Boer War and the suspicions of his critics in the Radical press, Grey was far from being an ardent imperialist. He shared the Radicals' desire 'to pursue a European policy without keeping up a great army' and welcomed the support of the Gladstonians like John Morley when trying to rein in the Government of India.[7] However, this position was merely a function of his dominant belief, from as early as 1902, that Britain should align itself against Germany. He spoke in this sense at a meeting of the cross-party 'Co-efficients' discussion group in December 1902, to the dismay of Bertrand Russell.[8] In January 1903 he told the poet Henry Newbolt: 'I have come to think that Germany is our worst enemy and our greatest danger . . . I believe the policy of Germany to be that of using us without helping us: keeping us isolated, that she may have us to fall back on.'[9] 'If any Government drags us back into the German net', he declared to the Liberal MP Ronald Munro-Ferguson in August 1905, 'I will oppose it openly at all costs.' Two months later, on the eve of coming to power, he underlined this commitment:

I am afraid the impression has been spread with some success by those interested in spreading it, that a Liberal Government would unsettle the understanding with France in order to make up to Germany. I want to do what I can to combat this.[10]

'Nothing we do in our relations with Germany', he told a City audience two days later, 'is in any way to impair our existing good relations with France.'[11]

Grey's Germanophobia and his zeal for the Entente with France were from the outset at odds with the views of the majority of the Liberal Cabinet. This division ought to have caused trouble much sooner than it did. However, Campbell-Bannerman was a prime minister with wool over at least one eye on foreign policy; while Asquith – who succeeded him in April 1908 – was adept at covering Grey's position.[12] Asquith came to be seen by admirers as a master 'in the arts of balancing one party against another'; by critics as 'combin[ing] unrivalled gifts of parliamentary leadership with a complete incapacity to face facts or to come to any decision upon them'.[13] He was both. One way of avoiding awkward facts which might unbalance the parliamentary party was to limit its influence over, and knowledge of, foreign policy; a mode of operation highly convenient to Grey and the senior officials at the FO. It was typical of Grey to complain, as he did in October 1906, about Liberal MPs having 'now acquired the art of asking questions and raising debates, and there is so much in foreign affairs which attracts attention and had much better be left alone'. When Cabinet colleagues pronounced on foreign affairs, Grey sought 'to convince them that there are such things as brick walls' against which they were merely 'run[ning] their own heads'.[14]

In this he was unquestionably aided and abetted by the Opposition's tacit approval of his policy. It must always be remembered that the Liberals' majority was steadily whittled away between 1906 and 1914.

Under such circumstances, the influence of the Opposition was bound to increase. Had the Conservative leadership disagreed with Grey's policy, they could have made life as difficult for him as they made it for Lloyd George, with whose fiscal policy they disagreed, and Asquith, whose Irish policy they abhorred. But they did not. They believed that Grey was continuing their policy. As the Tory Chief Whip Lord Balcarres put it in May 1912, his party had 'supported Grey for six years on the assumption that he continues the Anglo-French Entente which Lord Lansdowne established and the Anglo-Russian Entente Lord Lansdowne began'.[15] True, Balfour had to be careful not to offend the right of his party by appearing to 'love' the government too much.[16] Still, the fact remains that there was more agreement between Grey and the Opposition front bench than within the Cabinet itself, to say nothing of the Liberal party as a whole. Indeed, during the second Moroccan crisis in 1911 the Tory press ended up defending Grey against his Radical critics.[17] What this meant was that the detail of Grey's policy (and the devil lay there) was not subjected to close enough parliamentary scrutiny.

This gave Grey far greater freedom of action than his memoirs subsequently suggested. Nor, it should be noted, was he a man unused to freedom. A chronic underachiever at both Winchester and Balliol (he was rusticated for idleness and could only manage a Third in Jurisprudence), Grey's life-long passion was fishing for trout and salmon.[18] Fly fishing, as those readers who have attempted it will know, is not an occupation conducive to a deterministic cast of mind.[19] In his book on the subject, published in 1899, Grey waxed lyrical about its uncertain, unpredictable pleasures. One passage in particular, in which he describes landing an eight-pound salmon, deserves quotation:

There was no immediate cause for dreading catastrophe. But . . . there came on me a grim consciousness that the whole affair must be very long, and that the most difficult part of all would be at the end, not in playing the fish, but in landing it . . . It seemed as if any attempt to land the fish with [my] net would precipitate a catastrophe which I could not face. More than once I failed and each failure was horrible . . . For myself, I know nothing which equals the excitement of having hooked an unexpectedly large fish on a small rod and fine tackle.[20]

It is with this Grey in mind – the excited, anxious fisherman on the riverbank, rather than the broken self-apologist of the memoirs – that we should interpret British foreign policy between 1906 and 1914. At the risk of pushing the analogy too far, it might be said that much of the time – and especially in the July Crisis – Grey conducted himself exactly as he had on that occasion. He hoped he might land the fish, but knew the risk of 'catastrophe'. In neither case was the outcome a foregone conclusion.

In one sense, it must be said, the analogy is misleading. For in his dealings with Russia and France, it was arguably Grey who was the fish others hooked. In the case of Russia, Grey later maintained that he had effectively continued his predecessor's policy of detente, despite the distaste of the Radicals for the Tsarist regime.[21] On closer inspection, however, he went significantly further than Lansdowne. The diminution of Russian power following the defeat by Japan and the 1905 revolution made matters easy for him. Under these circumstances, he could rely on backbench support for cuts in spending on the defence of India, and so could override those at the War Office and Government of India to whom Russia remained the menace on the north-west frontier.[22] He also found (qualified) support from Colonel William Robertson of the War Office Intelligence Department, who argued against increasing Britain's military commitments in Persia or the Afghan border when Germany was the more serious military threat:

For centuries past we have thwarted . . . each and every power in turn which has aspired to continental predominance; and concurrently, and as a consequence, we have enlivened our own sphere of imperial ascendancy . . . A new preponderance is now growing, of which the centre of gravity is Berlin. Anything . . . which would assist us in opposing this new and most formidable danger would be of value to us.[23]

This gave Grey his cue to make some profound changes to British foreign policy.

The immediate deals struck on 31 August 1907 were over Tibet and Persia. The former became a buffer state; the latter was divided into spheres of influence – the north to Russia, the middle neutral and the south-east to Britain. In the words of Eyre Crowe, 'the fiction of an independent and united Persia' had to be 'sacrificed' for the sake of avoiding any 'quarrel' with Russia.[24] 'For centuries past' – to use Robertson's phrase – Britain had also sought to resist Russian expansion towards the Black Sea Straits as well as into Persia and Afghanistan. Now, for the sake of good relations with Russia, this could be dropped. 'If Asiatic things are settled favourably', Grey told the under-secretary of state Sir Arthur Nicolson, 'the Russians will not have any trouble with us about the entrance to the Black Sea.'[25] 'The old policy of closing the Straits against her, and throwing her weight against her at any conference of the Powers' would be 'abandoned' – though Grey refused to say quite when.[26] In order to reinforce Russia's role as a 'counterpoise to Germany on land', Grey even showed signs of favouring Russia's traditional ambitions in the Balkans.[27] Indeed, some of his officials were *plus russe que le Czar*; when Russia accepted the Austrian annexation of Bosnia-Hercegovina in 1909, Nicolson was quite indignant.[28] Grey sanctioned the Russian sponsorship of Balkan Slav nationalism with his eyes open, as he made clear in a letter to his ambassador in Berlin, Sir William Goschen, in November 1908:

A strong Slav feeling has arisen in Russia. Although this feeling appears to be well in hand at present, bloodshed between Austria and Servia would certainly raise the feeling to a dangerous height in Russia; and the thought that peace depends upon Servia restraining herself is not comfortable.[29]

His counterpart Sazonov was optimistic. As he noted apropos of Persia in October 1910, 'the English, in pursuing political aims of vital importance in Europe, will abandon in case of necessity certain interests in Asia simply in order to maintain the convention with us which is so important for them.'[30] But the position in London was more precarious than he knew. When Grey heard that the Russians and Germans had made a deal at Potsdam regarding the Ottoman Empire and Persia, he contemplated resigning to make way for a Germanophile Foreign Secretary who could resist Russian claims in Persia and Turkey.[31] Relations got even worse when the Russians proposed opening the Straits to Russian warships in order to balance the Italian attack on Turkey in Tripoli, and on 2 December 1911 Grey again threatened to resign. The most he was prepared to offer was the opening of the Straits to all; anything else would have incensed his own radicals.[32] On the very eve of the war the Russians once again raised the question of the Straits; indeed, unbeknown to Grey, Sazonov had already revived the old Russian dream of seizing Constantinople.[33] It is clear that Grey would not have resisted this if Russia had been able to achieve it during the war – in fact he accepted it as a legitimate Russian war aim. All this marked a clear break in British foreign policy. It is even more remarkable that the break was made by a Liberal Foreign Secretary, given the Russian government's abysmal reputation for anti-Semitism and other illiberal practices.[34] This truly was appeasement, in the pejorative sense the word later acquired.

It was much easier for a Liberal Foreign Secretary to pursue a Francophile policy than a Russophile policy, and, as we have seen, Grey had signalled his intention to pursue the former even before taking office. Again it appeared that Tory policy was being continued. But again – as he himself admitted – Grey went significantly 'further than the late Government here were required to do'.[35] In particular, he encouraged the evolution of a military 'sub-text' to the Anglo-French Entente.

Even before the Liberals came in, British military planners had begun to think seriously about British naval and military support for France in the event of a war with Germany. The plans for a naval blockade of Germany had, of course, already been formulated.[36] However, it was in September 1905 that the General Staff first began to think seriously of sending an 'expeditionary force' to the continent in the event of a Franco-German war. It was in this context that the question of Belgian neutrality came up. Although the generals considered it 'unlikely that Belgium [would] form part of the theatre of war during the first oper-ations', they nevertheless acknowledged 'that the tide of battle might bring about such a state of affairs as to make it almost imperative for one of the belligerents (more especially Germany) to disregard Belgium's neutrality'. Under these circumstances, they estimated that two army corps could be transported to Belgium within twenty-three days. This had the attraction of giving Britain a more effective and more auton-omous role than she would have if she were merely 'supply[ing] . . . a small contingent to a great [French] continental army, [which] might be unpopular in this country'.[37] Before December 1905 this was little more than thinking aloud. But within days of the new government taking office the Director of Military Operations Lieutenant-General James Grierson had meetings to discuss such an expeditionary force with the French military attaché Huguet.[38]

The timing of these discussions – at a moment when new ministers were still finding their feet – has naturally raised the suspicion that, as on the continent, the military men were trying to pull a fast one. However, those who attended the so-called Whitehall Gardens confer-ence, held simultaneously at the CID offices, were notably cautious. For example, they concluded that Britain had the 'right to intervene' in the case of violation of Belgian neutrality, not the obligation.[39] In the words of Sir Thomas Sanderson, the permanent under-secretary at the Foreign Office, the 1839 treaty was not 'a positive pledge . . . to use material force for the maintenance of the guarantee [of neutrality] *in any circumstances and at whatever risk*'. That would be, he added, 'to read into it what no government can reasonably be expected to promise'.[40] In any case, Fisher – who would remain First Sea Lord until 1910 – disliked the idea of ferrying the army across the Channel and continued to argue for a purely naval strategy in the event of war with Germany, or at most some kind of amphibious operation to land troops on the German coast.[41]

It was Grey who provided the advocates of an expeditionary force with a helpful nudge. On 9 January 1906, in the heat of the Moroccan negotiations which he took over from Lansdowne, he told the German ambassador Count Metternich that if 'France got into trouble' over Morocco, 'feeling in England and sympathy for France . . . would be so strong that it would be impossible for any Government to remain neutral'. In his report of this conversation to the Prime Minister he went on: 'The War Office . . . ought to be ready to answer the question, what could they do if we had to take part against Germany, if for instance the neutrality of Belgium was violated?'[42]

Grey was cautious: he insisted that military discussions with the French should have an unofficial character – so unofficial that Campbell-Bannerman himself was not initially informed.[43] The Foreign Secretary and his officials spoke in veiled terms of giving France 'more than . . . diplomatic support', repeatedly stating that the military discussions were not of a 'binding' nature; Eyre Crowe even claimed, nonsensically, that 'a British promise of armed assistance [would] involve no practical liability'.[44] But that Grey was prejudging the issue is clear: 'I am told that 80,000 men with good guns is [*sic*] all we can put into the field in Europe,' he informed Bertie (now ambassador in Paris) on 15 January. The next day he wrote to Lord Tweedmouth, the First Lord of the Admiralty: 'We haven't *promised* any help but it is quite right that our naval and military authorities should discuss the question in this way . . . and be prepared to give an answer when they are asked, or rather if they are asked.'[45] That hastily corrected 'when' speaks volumes. By February 1906 the Anglo-French talks were well advanced, the number of troops promised by the General Staff had risen to 105,000 and senior officers like Robertson and John Spencer Ewart, the new Director of Military Operations, were beginning to regard 'armed collision' with Germany as inevitable.[46] Grey commented:

If there is war between France and Germany it will be very difficult for us to keep out if the entente and still more the constant and emphatic demonstrations of affection (official, naval . . . commercial and municipal) . . . have created in France a belief that we should help her in war . . . [A]ll the French officers take this for granted . . . If the expectation is disappointed France will never forgive us . . . The more I review the situation the more it appears to me that we cannot [keep out of a war] without losing our good name and our friends and wrecking our policy and position in the world.[47]

In June 1906 the core members of the Committee of Imperial Defence set the seal on the new policy by ruling against Fisher and the 'navalists':

a. the dispatch of a large expeditionary force to the Baltic would be impracticable until the naval situation had cleared. Such a plan of operations could not take effect till after great battles had been fought on the frontier.
b. any military co-operation on the part of the British Army, if undertaken at the outset of war, must take the form either of an expedition to Belgium or of direct participation in the defence of the French frontier.
c. a German violation of Belgian territory would apparently necessitate the first course. The possibility of such violation taking place with the consent of the Belgian Government must not be overlooked.
d. in any case, the views of the French would have to be considered, as it is essential that any measure of co-operation on our part should harmonize with their strategic plans.
e. whichever course was adopted, a preliminary landing on the French north-western coast would be advantageous.[48]

Thus, within half a year of coming into office, Grey had presided over a transformation of the Entente with France, which had begun life as an attempt to settle extra-European quarrels, into a *de facto* defensive alliance.[49] He had conveyed to the French that Britain would be prepared to fight with them against Germany in the event of a war. And the military planners had now decided more or less exactly what form support for France should take.[50] (Grey later claimed not to have known the details of the Anglo-French military discussions; but this seems highly unlikely.)[51] Despite Fisher's continued obstructiveness and Esher's reservations about the size of the projected Expeditionary Force, the continental strategy was confirmed in 1909 by the CID sub-committee on the military needs of the Empire.[52]

Indeed, it might even be suggested – to turn Fritz Fischer on his head

– that the CID meeting of 23 August 1911 (rather than the notorious meeting between the Kaiser and his military chiefs sixteen months later) was the real 'war council' which set the course for a military confrontation between Britain and Germany. In a memorandum submitted in advance of the meeting, the General Staff dismissed the idea (advanced by Churchill among others) that the French army unassisted could hope to withstand a German attack:

In the case of our remaining neutral, Germany will fight France single handed. The armies of Germany and the fleets of Germany are much stronger than those of France, and the results of such a war can scarcely be doubted . . . [I]n a single handed war France in all probability would be defeated.[53]

If, on the other hand, 'England became the active ally of France', the combination of naval dominance and the speedy despatch of a force consisting of the entire regular army of six infantry divisions and one of cavalry could turn the tables:

[T]he actual disparity in numbers becomes less, and owing to causes which it would take too long to enumerate here, the numbers of the opposing forces at the decisive point would be so nearly equal during the opening and early actions of the war that it is possible for the allies to win some initial successes which might prove invaluable . . . [In addition], and perhaps this is the most important consideration of all, it is believed that the *morale* of the French troops and nation would be greatly strengthened by British co-operation; and there might be a corresponding decrease, or at least some decrease, in the *morale* of the Germans. It seems, therefore, that in a war between Germany and France in which England takes active part with the French, the result in the opening moves might be doubtful, but the longer the war lasted the greater the strain would be on Germany.[54]

As Asquith pointed out with perhaps a hint of scepticism, 'the question of time was all important in this scheme'; but the General Staff's case was ably defended by Henry Wilson, Ewart's successor as Director of Military Operations, who predicted that the war would be decided by a clash between the German spearhead of forty divisions passing between Maubeuge and Verdun and a French force of at most thirty-nine divisions, 'so that it was quite likely that our six divisions might prove to be the deciding factor'. Wilson 'shattered rather rudely' the suggestion (advanced by Grey) that the Russians might be able to influence the outcome and, 'after a long and . . . ineffectual talk' (Wilson's words) the general rested his case: 'First . . . we *must* join the French. Second . . . we *must* mobilize the same day as the French. Third . . . we *must* send the whole six divisions.'[55]

The senior service's *de haut en bas* criticisms of this plan (voiced by the First Sea Lord Arthur Wilson and Reginald McKenna, Tweedmouth's successor at the Admiralty) were unconvincing.[56] Worse, the Admiralty's rival plans for a close blockade of the principal German river estuaries and the landing of a division of troops on the north German coast were savaged by the Chief of the Imperial General Staff, Field Marshal Sir William Nicholson:

The truth was that this class of operation possibly had some value a century ago, when land communications were indifferent, but now, when they were excellent, they were doomed to failure . . . [Would] the Admiralty continue to press that view even if the General Staff expressed their considered opinion that the military operations on which it was proposed to employ this division were madness[?][57]

This was enough for Grey, who concluded that 'the combined operations outlined were not essential to naval success and the struggle on land would be the decisive one'; and for Asquith, who dismissed Arthur Wilson's plans as 'puerile' and 'wholly impracticable'. The politicians' only caveat was that two of the army's divisions should be kept at home.[58] Maurice Hankey was quite wrong (as he himself later acknowledged) in claiming that no decision had been reached at the meeting.[59] As Esher gloomily observed on 4 October: 'The mere fact of the War Office plan having been worked out in detail with the French General Staff has certainly committed us to fight . . .'[60]

One reason the Admiralty ultimately acquiesced in the adoption of the BEF strategy was that it was not incompatible with the navy's alternative strategy of a long-distance blockade of Germany. To be sure, not everyone in the navy believed in this – Arthur Wilson privately doubted whether a blockade could affect the outcome of a Franco-German war[61] – just as not everyone at the War Office was sure of the Expeditionary Force strategy. On the other hand, it is important to note that the former strategy had major implications for the latter. In December 1912, at another CID meeting, both Churchill and Lloyd George argued strongly that, in the event of a war, 'it would be quite impossible for the Netherlands and Belgium to maintain their neutrality . . . They must either be friends or foes.' 'This country could not afford to wait and see what these countries would do,' argued Lloyd George:

The geographical position of the Netherlands and Belgium made their attitude in a war between the British Empire in all with France and Russia against the Triple Entente [*sc.* Alliance] one of immense importance. If they are neutral, and accorded full rights of neutrals, we should be unable to bring any offensive economic pressure upon her. It was essential that we should do so.

It also worried General Sir John French, Nicholson's successor as CIGS, that the Belgians might be prepared to disregard a limited infringement of their territory. The meeting concluded that

In order to bring the greatest possible pressure to bear upon Germany, it is essential that the Netherlands and Belgium should either be entirely friendly to this country, in which case we should limit their overseas trade, or that they should be definitely hostile, in which case we should extend the blockade to their ports.[62]

In other words: if Germany had not violated Belgian neutrality in 1914, Britain would have. This puts the British government's much-vaunted moral superiority in fighting 'for Belgian neutrality' in another light.

The Belgians were not, it should be said, unconscious of these deliberations. In April 1912 Lieutenant-Colonel Bridges expressed the view that, if war had broken out over Morocco the previous year, British troops would have landed on the Belgian coast. But the Belgian view was that such intervention could only be legitimate if they appealed to the guarantors under the 1839 treaty; and the British were doubtful that such an appeal would be made – especially if, as was still considered possible, a German invasion passed through only part of the country, say to the south of Liège. When in 1910 the Dutch proposed to build a new fort at Flushing which might have given them command of the mouth of the River Scheldt, there was consternation in London, as such a fort would have threatened British naval access to Antwerp. The Belgians, however, did not express strong objections; they feared a British naval violation of their neutrality as much as the German army.[63]

The navalists were also mollified with another point: that the defence of the Mediterranean should be left to the French fleet, a division of responsibility which had been informally agreed by the two Admiralties in Fisher's day (without reference to the Foreign Secretary or Cabinet). To be sure, Churchill was unable to secure the complete withdrawal of British ships from the Mediterranean; but the decision to keep a battle fleet in that theatre 'equal to a one-power standard *excluding France*' spoke for itself. There was no public agreement, but a tacit one.[64] This was followed by secret naval conversations with Russia in 1914.[65] Thus, despite their differences, the plans of the army and navy could co-exist; and after the exhausting debates of August 1911, that was more or less what they did.

All of this makes German fears of encirclement seem less like paranoia than realism. When Bülow denounced in the Reichstag the efforts to 'encircle Germany, to build a circle of powers around Germany in order to isolate and render it impotent', he was not – as British statesmen subsequently insisted in their memoirs – fantasizing.[66] By comparison with the analogous German meetings, the British military discussions were relatively conclusive. And what, after all, had prompted the so-called 'war council' summoned by the Kaiser in December 1912? A communication from Haldane *via* the German ambassador to the effect that 'Britain could not allow Germany to become the leading power on the continent and it to be united under German leadership'. The Kaiser's inference 'that Britain would fight on the side of Germany's enemies' was not wrong; as Bethmann said, this 'merely reflected what we have known [for some time]'.[67]

THE NAPOLEON NEUROSIS

Traditionally, Grey's anti-German policy has been justified by historians because Germany's *Weltpolitik* had come to be viewed in London as a growing threat to British interests in Africa, Asia and the Near East; and, more importantly, that Germany's naval construction constituted a serious challenge to British security. Yet on close inspection, neither colonial issues nor naval issues were leading inevitably to an Anglo-German showdown before 1914.

As Churchill later put it, 'We were no enemies to German colonial expansion.'[68] Indeed, an agreement between Britain and Germany which would have opened the way to increased German influence in the former Portuguese colonies in Southern Africa came close to being concluded.[69] Grey himself said in 1911 that it did not 'matter very much whether we ha[d] Germany or France as a neighbour in Africa'. He was eager to bring about a 'division' of the 'derelict' Portuguese colonies 'as soon as possible . . . in a pro-German spirit'.[70] The deal was only scuppered in 1914 by his officials' resistance – dressed up as reluctance to renege publicly on British commitments to Portugal made sixteen years before, but in reality rooted in their compulsive Germanophobia. The German banks (notably M. M. Warburg & Co.) that had become involved had no inkling of the antagonism to the project expressed by the likes of Bertie (not to mention Henry Wilson).[71] Even where Grey inclined to give French interests primacy – in Morocco – there was not a complete impasse with respect to Germany. In 1906 Grey had been willing to consider giving Germany a naval coaling station on the country's Atlantic coast.[72] It is true that the government took an aggressive line during the second Moroccan crisis in 1911, warning Berlin not to treat Britain 'as if she were of no account in the Cabinet of Nations' (Lloyd George's phrase in his Mansion House speech of 21 July).[73] But even Grey had to accept that 'we need not and cannot be irreconcilable about the west coast of Morocco'. As he said to Bertie the day before Lloyd George's speech, 'The French have drifted into difficulties without knowing which way they really want to go . . . We are bound and prepared to give diplomatic support, but we cannot go to war in order to set aside the Algeciras Act [agreed after the first Moroccan crisis] and put France in virtual possession of Morocco.' The compromise reached – 'a deal between France and Germany based upon some concession in the French Congo' – reflected this lack of British interest, and Grey urged the French to accept it.[74]

When the German government turned its attentions to Turkey, it was even harder for Grey to take a strongly anti-German line without playing into the hands of the Russians with respect to the Black Sea Straits. In any case, Grey had no complaint about the way the Germans acted during the Balkan wars of 1912–13 and was relatively unworried by the Liman von Sanders affair (the appointment of a German general as Inspector General to the Turkish army). Relations were further improved by Germany's conciliatory response to British concerns over the Berlin–Baghdad railway.[75] Bethmann himself had said in January 1913 that 'colonial questions of the future point to co-operation with England', though the Portuguese colonies deal was never done.[76]

In this light, it was not unreasonable of the *Frankfurter Zeitung* to speak, as it did in October 1913, of *rapprochement* between Britain and Germany, 'a better understanding between the governing minds in both countries' and an 'end to the sterile years of mutual distrust'.[77] When he saw the German ambassador at Tring in March 1914, Lord Rothschild 'said most decidedly that as far as he could see and as far as he knew, there was no reason for fear of war and no complications ahead'.[78] It was just another symptom of the good financial relations then prevailing between Britain and Germany that Max Warburg was in London on three separate occasions to finalize his firm's role in the Portuguese colonies deal.[79] That summer British newspapers carried reports of the attendance of senior British naval officers at the annual Kiel regatta, quoting the German Admiral von Koester's comment that 'the relations between the British and German bluejackets were the best imaginable'.[80] The Foreign Office view as late as 27 June 1914 – the eve of the Sarajevo assassination – was that the German government was 'in peaceful mood and . . . very anxious to be on good terms with England'.[81] Warburg too heard rumours that 'mad love [eine wahnsinnige Liebe] had broken out between the Germans and the English'.[82] As late as 23 July Lloyd George pronounced Anglo-German relations 'very much better than they were a few years ago . . . The two great Empires begin to realise they can co-operate for common ends, and that the points of co-operation are greater and more numerous and more important than the points of possible controversy.'[83]

Likewise, it is quite misleading to see the naval race as a 'cause' of the First World War. There were strong arguments on both sides for a naval agreement. Both governments were finding the political conse-quences of increasing naval expenditure difficult to live with. The possibility of some kind of arms limitation agreement surfaced on numerous occasions: in December 1907, when the Germans proposed a North Sea convention with Britain and France;[84] in February 1908, when the Kaiser wrote to Lord Tweedmouth explicitly denying that Germany aimed 'to challenge British naval supremacy';[85] six months later, when he met the permanent under-secretary of state at the FO Sir Charles Hardinge at Kronberg;[86] in 1909–10, when Bethmann pro-posed to Goschen 'a naval agreement . . . as part of a scheme for a good general understanding';[87] and in March 1911, when the Kaiser called for 'a political understanding and a naval agreement tending to limit naval expenditure'.[88] The most famous opportunity came in February 1912, when, at the suggestion of the businessmen Sir Ernest Cassel and Albert Ballin, Haldane travelled to Berlin, ostensibly 'about the business of a university committee', in reality to discuss the possibility of a naval, colonial and non-aggression agreement with Bethmann, Tirpitz and the

Kaiser.[89] Churchill floated the idea of a 'naval construction holiday' in 1913[90] and a last, vain effort by Cassel and Ballin in the summer of 1914.[91]

So why was there no deal? The traditional answer is that the Germans were only willing to discuss naval issues after they had received an unconditional British pledge of neutrality in the event of a Franco-German war. Yet this is only half the story. Asquith later claimed that the German formula of neutrality would 'have precluded us from coming to the help of France should Germany on any pretext attack her'. In fact, Bethmann's draft stated:

The high contracting powers . . . will not either of them make any unprovoked attack upon the other or join in any combination or design against the other for the purpose of aggression . . . If either . . . becomes entangled in a war *in which it cannot be said to be the aggressor*, the other will at least observe towards the power so entangled a benevolent neutrality.[92]

The clause was also to be regarded as void 'in so far as it may not be reconcilable with existing agreements'. The most that Grey was willing to offer, however, was a commitment 'neither to make *nor join in* any unprovoked attack upon Germany' because, in his words, 'the word neutrality . . . would give the impression our hands were tied'.[93] This (as the Colonial Secretary Lewis Harcourt pointed out) was plainly not the sense of Bethmann's formula.

The other explanation for the failure of the Haldane mission is that Tirpitz and the Kaiser torpedoed it by introducing a new naval increase on the eve of Haldane's arrival, thereby 'ruin[ing] the relationship with England . . . for good'. According to Geiss, 'Germany's refusal to come to terms with Britain on curbing the costly arms race at sea by naval agreement blocked any kind of rapprochement'.[94] The British government said much the same at the time.[95] But this too needs to be treated with scepticism. The Germans were willing to make a naval deal in return for a neutrality statement; it was on the neutrality issue that the talks really foundered. And arguably it was the British position which was the more intransigent – not surprisingly, as it was based on unassailable strength. As Grey put it in 1913, 'If you are going to have an absolute standard superior to all the other European navies put together . . . your foreign policy is comparatively simple.'[96] His view was accordingly uncompromising: Bethmann seemed to want something in return for recognizing 'permanent [British] naval superiority' – or, as his principal private secretary William Tyrrell put it, 'the principle of our absolute supremacy at sea' – but why should Britain bargain for something she already possessed?[97] It is not difficult to see why Bethmann's proposed deal was rejected out of hand.

What is harder to understand is Grey's belief that almost *any* expression of Anglo-German *rapprochement* was out of the question. Why, if Germany posed neither a colonial nor a naval threat to Britain, was Grey so relentlessly anti-German? The simple answer is, of course, that – like his Tory predecessors – Grey cared more about good relations with France and Russia. 'Nothing we do in our relations with Germany', he had declared in October 1905, 'is in any way to impair our existing good relations with France.' 'The danger of speaking civil words in Berlin', he wrote the following January, 'is that they may be … interpreted in France as implying that we shall be lukewarm in our support of the entente.'[98] He made the point unambiguously to Goschen in April 1910: 'We cannot enter into a political understanding with Germany which would separate us from Russia and France.'[99] However, when Grey said that an understanding with Germany had to be 'consistent with the preservation of [our existing] relations and friendships with other powers', he was effectively ruling out such an understanding.[100] The archetypal Grey argument was that, because the entente with France was so 'vague', any 'agreement with Germany would necessarily tend to supersede' it and so could not be contemplated.[101] It was a view constantly endorsed by his Foreign Office officials. Any rapprochement with Germany, warned Mallet, would lead to 'estrange-[ment] from France'.[102] Nicolson opposed the idea of an agreement with Germany in 1912 mainly because it would 'seriously impair our relations [with France] – and such a result would at once react on our relations with Russia'.[103]

On close inspection, Grey's reasoning was deeply flawed. Firstly, his notion that bad relations with France and Russia might actually have led to war was preposterous. There was a big difference in this respect between his situation and that of his Tory predecessors. At the time, Grey himself acknowledged that Russia's recovery from the ravages of defeat and revolution would take a decade. Nor did he see France as a threat: as he put it to the American President Theodore Roosevelt in 1906, France was 'peaceful and neither aggressive nor restless'.[104] The original point of the ententes had been to settle overseas differences with France and Russia. This having been done, the chances of war between Britain and either power were remote. It was simply fantastic for Grey to suggest, as he did to the editor of the *Manchester Guardian*, C. P. Scott, in September 1912, 'that if France is not supported against Germany she would join with her and the rest of Europe in an attack upon us'.[105] Only slightly less chimerical was the fear that France or Russia might 'desert to the Central Powers'.[106] Yet this was a constant Foreign Office preoccupation. As early as 1905 Grey feared 'losing France and not gaining Germany, who won't want us if she can detach France from us'. If Britain did not respond to French overtures over Algeciras, Mallet warned, 'We shall . . . be looked upon as traitors by the French and . . . be despised by the Germans.'[107] Hardinge said much the same: 'If France is left in the lurch an agreement or alliance between France, Germany and Russia in the near future is certain.'[108] Typically, Nicolson argued for a formal alliance with France and Russia 'to deter Russia from moving towards Berlin . . . [and] prevent [France] from deserting to the Central Powers'.[109] Obsessively, Grey and his officials dreaded losing their 'value as friends' and ending up 'standing *alone*' – without friends'. Their recurrent nightmare was that Russia or France would succumb to 'the Teuton embrace', leaving Britain to face 'the united navies of Europe'. For this reason, they tended to see all German policy as aimed at 'smashing . . . the Triple Entente'.[110] It was typical of Grey to reason that:

if . . . by some misfortune or blunder our Entente with France is to be broken up, France will have to make her own terms with Germany. And Germany will again be in a position to keep us on bad terms with France and Russia, and to make herself predominant upon the Continent. Then, sooner or later, there will be a war between us and Germany.[111]

The analogous fear was that 'Germany [would] go to St Petersburg and propose holding Austria in if Russia will leave the Entente . . . We are sincerely afraid lest . . . Russia should emerge on the side of the Central Powers' Alliance.'[112]

Yet, in his determination to preserve the Entente with France, Grey was willing to make military commitments which made war with Germany more rather than less likely, sooner rather than later. By a completely circular process of reasoning, he wished to commit Britain to a possible war with Germany – because otherwise there might be war with Germany. Appeasement of France and Russia had once made sense; but Grey prolonged the life of the policy well after its rationale had faded.

The strongest justification for all of this, of course, was that Germany had megalomaniac ambitions which posed a threat not only to France but to Britain itself. This view was widely held by the Germanophobes. In his famous memorandum of November 1907 Eyre Crowe warned that Germany's desire to play 'on the world's stage a much larger and more dominant part than she finds allotted to herself under the present distribution of material power' might lead her 'to diminish the power of any rivals, to enhance her own [power] by extending her dominion, to hinder the co-operation of other states, and ultimately to break up and supplant the British Empire'.[113] Fundamental to Crowe's analysis was a historical parallel with the challenge which post-Revolutionary France had posed to Britain. As Nicolson put it in a letter to Grey in early 1909: 'The ultimate aims of Germany surely are, without doubt, to obtain the preponderance on the continent of Europe, and when she is strong enough, [to] enter on a contest with us for maritime supremacy.' Goschen and Tyrrell said much the same. Germany wanted 'the hegemony of Europe'.[114] By 1911 Grey himself was warning against a 'Napoleonic' threat in Europe. If Britain 'allowed France to be crushed, we should have to fight later on'. There were, he told the Canadian prime minister in 1912, 'no limits to the ambitions which might be indulged in by Germany'.[115]

Nor was this line of argument peculiar to the diplomats. When making the case for a continental expeditionary force, the General Staff employed the same analogy: 'It is a mistake', ran its 1909 memorandum to the CID sub-committee, 'to suppose that command of the sea must necessarily influence the immediate issue of a great land struggle. The battle of Trafalgar did not prevent Napoleon from winning the battles of Austerlitz and Jena and crushing Prussia and Austria.'[116] The argument was repeated two years later at the CID 'war council'. In the event of a German victory over France and Russia:

Holland and Belgium might be annexed to Germany, and a huge indemnity would be placed on France, who would also lose some of her colonies. In short, the result of such a war would be that Germany would attain to that dominant position which has already been stated to be inimical to the interests of this country.

This 'would place at [its] disposal . . . a preponderance of naval and military force which would menace the importance of the United Kingdom and the integrity of the British Empire'; in the 'long run' this would be 'fatal'.[117] Even navalists like Esher sometimes took the same line. In 1907 he wrote:

German prestige is more formidable to us than Napoleon at his *apogée*. Germany is going to contest with us the command of the sea ... She must have an outlet for her teeming population, and vast acres where Germans can live and remain. These acres only exist within the confines of our Empire. Therefore 'L'Ennemi, c'est l'Allemagne'.[118]

Without the navy, feared Churchill, Europe would pass 'after one sudden convulsion ... into the iron grip of the Teuton and of all that the Teutonic system meant'. Lloyd George remembered the same argument: 'Our fleet was as much the sole guarantor of our independence ... as in the days of Napoleon.'[119] Robertson was thus only guilty of slight exaggeration when he wrote in December 1916 that 'Germany's ambition to establish an empire stretching across Europe and the North Sea and Baltic to the Black Sea and the Aegean and perhaps even to the Persian Gulf and Indian Ocean [had] been known for the last twenty [*sic*] years or more'.[120]

If all this had been true, then it might be said that Grey was engaged in appeasing the wrong powers. The ententes with France and Russia had made sense when it was they who menaced the Empire; but if by 1912 it was clearly Germany, then the argument for an entente with Germany ought to have been taken more seriously. Yet it is a striking fact that the alarmist claims of a German Napoleonic design were at odds with much of the intelligence which was actually being received from Germany. This is a point which has hitherto been neglected by historians. True, the quality of military intelligence on Germany before 1914 remains impossible for us to assess; but Goschen was not a bad observer, while the reports from British consuls in Germany were of a high quality. A far better analysis than Crowe's of 1907 was Churchill's of November 1909, which argued – almost certainly on the basis of such reports – that Germany was in fact suffering from acute fiscal weakness (see Chapter 5). This was only one of many expert verdicts to the same effect. Why then did Grey and the most senior officials in the Foreign Office and the General Staff nevertheless conjure up a German design for Napoleonic power, posing a direct threat to Britain? The possibility arises that they were exaggerating – if not fabricating – such a threat in order to justify the military commitment to France they favoured. In other words, precisely *because* they wished to align

Britain with France and Russia, it was necessary to impute grandiose plans for European domination to the Germans.

THE CONTINENTAL NON-COMMITMENT

Nevertheless, it would be quite wrong to conclude that British diplomacy and military planning made war inevitable. For the reality was that the British continental commitment – which clearly existed at the level of diplomacy and at the level of grand strategy – did not exist at the level of parliamentary politics.

From the outset, the majority of Cabinet members (to say nothing of Parliament) had been kept in ignorance of the discussions with the French. As the permanent under-secretary Sanderson put it to Cambon, the notion of a military commitment to France 'gave rise to divergences of opinion' – 'anything of a more definite nature would have been at once rejected by the Government'. Extraordinarily, as we have seen, even the Prime Minister Campbell-Bannerman was initially kept in the dark; and, when he was told, immediately expressed anxiety that 'the stress laid upon joint preparations . . . comes very close to an honourable undertaking'. Haldane accordingly had to make it 'clear' to the Chief of the General Staff, Neville Lyttleton, 'that we were to be in no way committed by the fact of having entered into communications'.[121] The official FO line in 1908 was unequivocal: 'In the event of Germany provoking hostilities with France, the question of armed intervention by Great Britain is one *which will have to be decided by the Cabinet.*'[122] As Hardinge emphasized in his testimony before the CID sub-committee meeting of March 1909:

We had given *no assurance that we would help* [the French] on land, and . . . the only grounds upon which the French could base any *hopes* of military assistance were the *semi-official* conversations which had taken place between the French military attaché and our General Staff.

Accordingly, the sub-committee concluded that 'in the event of an attack on France by Germany, the expediency of sending a military force abroad, or of relying on naval means only, is *a matter of policy that can only be determined, when the occasion arises, by the Government of the day*'.[123] Asquith himself underlined the point when he described the CID as 'a purely advisory body' and reminded its members that the government was not 'in the least committed by any of its decisions'.[124] When questioned about the nature of the British commitment to France, Grey had to be exceedingly careful to avoid using:

words which implied the possibility of a secret engagement unknown to Parliament all these years committing us to a European war. I carefully worded the answer so as to convey that the engagement [to France] of 1904 might not [*inserted in margin*: under certain circumstances] be continued and have larger consequences than its strict letter.[125]

Such denials of a binding continental commitment grew more frequent the more Grey's conduct aroused the suspicions of the Radical press and his party colleagues. Writing in the *Guardian* in the wake of Lloyd George's 1911 Mansion House speech, the *Economist* editor F. W. Hirst anticipated the language of a later diplomatic fiasco when he described it as 'extravagant' to imagine a British minister 'asking millions of his innocent countrymen to give up their lives for a continental squabble about which they know nothing and care less'. The *Nation* accused Grey of taking the country 'to the razor-edge of strife . . . for a non-British interest' and subjecting it to 'a harassing blackmail on the part of associate powers'.[126] Similar sentiments soon began to emanate from the new Liberal Foreign Affairs backbench committee set up by Arthur Ponsonby and Noel Buxton in November that year.[127] In January 1912 the York Liberal Association – the MP Arnold Rowntree's association – wrote to Grey expressing the hope 'that all efforts may be made by the British Government to promote friendship and cordiality between' Britain and Germany, and denouncing 'the aggressive and unjustified action of Russia in Persia'.[128]

But it was in the Cabinet that Grey faced the stiffest opposition. As far as ministers knew (if they knew anything), the option of military intervention was merely being considered and its logistical implications explored. It was the Cabinet, not Grey, which would make the final decision; and the government as a whole was, in Grey's words, 'quite free'.[129] In Loreburn's eyes intervention in 'a purely French quarrel' was therefore inconceivable, because it could be done only with (as he put it to Grey) 'a majority largely composed of Conservatives and with a very large number of the Ministerial side against you . . . This would mean that the present Government could not carry on.'[130] In the wake of the CID 'war council' of August 1911, Lewis Harcourt and Sir Walter Runciman, the minister for agriculture and fisheries, agreed that the idea of sending British troops to France in the event of war would be 'criminal folly'.[131] Asquith, ever the weathervane, blew with this wind, warning Grey that military conversations with France were 'rather dangerous . . . especially the part which refers to British assistance'.[132] It was only with difficulty that Grey resisted pressure to forbid further Anglo-French military discussions.[133] At the beginning of November 1911 he was comprehensively outvoted in the Cabinet (by fifteen to five) when Viscount Morley, the Lord President, raised:

the question of . . . conversations being held or allowed between the General Staff of the War Office and the General Staff of foreign states, such as France, in regard to possible military co-operation, without the previous knowledge . . . of the Cabinet.

Asquith hastened to reassure Morley that 'all questions of policy have been and must be regarded as the decision of the Cabinet, and that it is quite outside the function of military and naval officers to prejudice such questions'; but the discussion was an uncomfortable one for Grey.[134] Although Haldane felt that he had emerged from the decisive meeting 'unhampered in any material point', that was not the way Asquith summarized the Cabinet's conclusion to the King:

No communications should take place between the General Staff and the Staffs of other countries which can, directly or indirectly, commit this country to military or naval intervention . . . Such communications, if they related to concerted action by land or sea, should not be entered into without the previous approval of the Cabinet.[135]

Humiliatingly, Grey was forced to state in the Commons: 'Such engagements as there are which really commit Parliament to anything of that kind [i.e. intervention in a continental war] are contained in treaties and agreements which have been laid before the house . . . We have not made a single secret article of any kind since we came into office.'[136] In the eyes of the Opposition, the Foreign Secretary was in 'retreat', his policy a 'wreck'.[137] Small wonder the French military attaché in Berlin assumed that, in a war with Germany, Britain would be 'but of very little assistance to us'.

Nor did the wrecking end there. In July 1912 Churchill (now at the Admiralty) had to confirm that the naval division of responsibility which concentrated the French navy in the Mediterranean and the British fleet in home waters did not 'in any way affect the full freedom of action possessed by both countries'.[138] The dispositions had been

made independently because they are the best which the separate interests of each country suggests [*sic*] . . . They do not arise from any naval agreement or convention . . . *Nothing in the naval or military arrangements ought to have the effect of exposing us. . . if, when the time comes, we decide to stand out.*[139]

There was, Harcourt told the *Daily Telegraph* in October, 'no alliance or understanding, actual or implied'; British policy was 'unfettered'.[140] On 24 March 1913, Asquith was repeating the formula in the Commons:

As has repeatedly been stated, this country is not under any obligation, not public and known to parliament, which compels it to take part in any war. In other words, if war arises between European Powers, there are no unpublished agreements which will restrict or hamper the freedom of the Government or of Parliament to decide whether or not Great Britain should participate in a war.[141]

Under these circumstances, Grey had no option but to break it gently to the French and Russian governments. Sazonov was informed that the government had 'decided to keep our hands free', though 'if Germany dominated the policy of the continent it would be disagreeable to us' (a typical Grey hint).[142] To Cambon, Grey said simply that there was no 'engagement that commits either Government . . . to co-operate in war'.[143] The Anglo-Russian naval talks implied still less of a commitment. Indeed, there was growing unease in London about the Russian appetite for unreciprocated concessions in the Near East.[144] As Grey told Cambon in May 1914, 'We could not enter into any military engagement, even of the most hypothetical kind, with Russia.' On 11 June 1914 – just days before the Sarajevo assassinations – he had to repeat his assurance to the Commons that:

if war arose between the European Powers, there were no unpublished agreements which would restrict or hamper the freedom of the Government or of Parliament to decide whether or not Great Britain should participate in a war. No such negotiations are in progress, and none are likely to be entered into as far as I can judge.[145]

Thus the sole plausible justification for Grey's strategy – that it would deter a German attack on France – fell away. 'An Entente between Russia, France and ourselves would be absolutely secure,' he had declared shortly after becoming Foreign Secretary. 'If it is necessary to check Germany it could be done.'[146] That had been the basis for his, Haldane's and even the King's statements to various German representatives in 1912 that Britain could 'under no circumstance tolerate France being crushed'.[147] These statements have often been seen by historians as categorical commitments which the Germans were fools to ignore. But the truth, as the German government could hardly fail to realize, was that the ententes were not 'absolutely secure'. Opposition to the continental commitment within his own party had made it impossible for Grey to take the step towards a formal alliance with France (and perhaps also Russia) favoured by the diplomatic hawks Mallet, Nicolson and Crowe and urged by Churchill in August 1911.[148] Yet only an alliance would have been 'absolutely secure'. Even Crowe had to concede in February 1911:

the fundamental fact ... that the Entente is not an alliance. For purposes of ultimate emergencies it *may* be found to have no substance at all. For an Entente is nothing more than a frame of mind, a view of general policy which is shared by the governments of two countries, but which *may* be, or become, so vague as to lose all content.[149]

The French might reassure themselves that 'England would be bound by her own interest to support France lest she be crushed'.[150] But politically they were relying on nothing more than Grey's *private* undertaking as a Wykehamist, a Balliol man and an angler that 'no British government would refuse [France] military and naval assistance if she were unjustly threatened and attacked'.[151] The reality was that British intervention would only happen if Grey could convert the majority of the Cabinet to his standpoint, something he had wholly failed to do in 1911. If he could not, then he and possibly the whole government would resign – hardly a cause for German trepidation.[152] It was a sign of the diplomats' frustration that Nicolson said to Paul Cambon on 10 April 1912: 'This radical-socialist Cabinet [supported by] financiers, pacifists, faddists and others ... will not last, it is done for, and, with the Conservatives, you will get something precise': a remarkable utterance for a public servant.[153]

In their memoirs, those responsible for British foreign policy between 1906 and 1914 did their best to justify this extraordinary mixture of diplomatic and strategic commitment and practical and political non-commitment.[154] Their arguments do not convince. On balance, as Steiner has argued, the uncertainty about Britain's position probably made a continental war more rather than less likely, by encouraging the Germans to consider a pre-emptive strike.[155] What British policy most certainly did not do was to make British intervention in such a war inevitable; indeed, it barely made it possible.

4

Arms and Men

A RACE TO WAR?

In early 1914 Bethmann Hollweg's secretary, Kurt Riezler, published (pseudonymously) a book entitled *Characteristics of Contemporary World Politics*. In it he argued that the unprecedented levels of armament in Europe were 'perhaps the most controversial, urgent and difficult problem of the present time'. Sir Edward Grey, always fond of explanations of the war which minimized human agency, would later agree. 'The enormous growth of armaments in Europe,' he wrote in his post-war memoirs, 'the sense of insecurity and fear caused by them – it was these that made war inevitable. This, it seems to me, is the truest reading of history . . . the real and final account of the origins of the Great War.'[1]

Historians seeking great causes for great events are naturally drawn to the pre-war arms race as a possible explanation for the First World War. As David Stevenson has put it: 'A self-reinforcing cycle of heightened military preparedness . . . was an essential element in the conjuncture that led to disaster . . . The armaments race . . . was a necessary precondition for the outbreak of hostilities'.[2] David Herrmann goes further: by creating a sense that 'windows of opportunity for victorious wars' were closing, 'the arms race did precipitate the First World War'. If the Archduke Franz Ferdinand had been assassinated in 1904 or even in 1911, Herrmann speculates, there might have been no war; it was 'the armaments race . . . and the speculation about imminent or preventive wars' which made his death in 1914 the trigger for war.[3]

Yet, as both Stevenson and Herrmann acknowledge, there is no law of history stating that all arms races end in wars. The experience of the Cold War shows that an arms race can deter two power blocs from going to war and can ultimately end in the collapse of one side without the need for a full-scale conflagration. Conversely, the 1930s illustrates the danger of *not* racing: if Britain and France had kept pace with German rearmament after 1933, Hitler would have had far greater difficulty persuading his generals to remilitarize the Rhineland or to risk war over Czechoslovakia.

The key to the arms race before 1914 is that one side lost it, or believed that it was losing it. It was this belief which persuaded its leaders to gamble on war before they fell too far behind. Riezler erred when he argued that 'the more the nations arm, the greater must be the superiority of one over the other if the calculation is to fall out in favour of war'. On the contrary: the margin of disadvantage had to be exceedingly small – perhaps, indeed, only a projected margin of disadvantage – for the side losing the arms race to risk a war. The paradox is that the power which found itself in this position of incipient defeat in the arms race was the power with the greatest reputation for excessive militarism – Germany.

DREADNOUGHT

Aside from the economic and imperial rivalries discussed in previous chapters, the German naval programme is traditionally seen by historians as the principal cause of deteriorating Anglo-German relations.[4] The British response, however, quickly demonstrated that this challenge stood little chance of succeeding. Indeed, so decisive was the British victory in the naval arms race that it is hard to regard it as in any meaningful sense a cause of the First World War.

In 1900 the First Lord of the Admiralty, the Earl of Selborne, had gloomily commented that a 'formal alliance with Germany' was 'the only alternative to an ever-increasing Navy and ever-increasing Navy estimates'.[5] Yet by 1902 he had completely changed his view, having become 'convinced that the new German Navy is being built up from the point of view of a war with us'.[6] This was an understandable conclusion. As early as 1896, Korvettenkapitän (later Admiral) Georg von Müller had summed up the aim of German *Weltpolitik* as being to break 'Britain's domination of the world and thus make available the necessary colonial property for the central European states which need to expand'.[7]

However, Tirpitz's naval programme did not necessarily mean war.

The aim was partly defensive – and far from irrational given the danger of a British naval blockade in the event of a war with Germany.[8] The projected German fleet's offensive capability was also limited. At most, Tirpitz aimed to build a navy big enough (sixty ships) to make the risk of an Anglo-German war unacceptably high to the Royal Navy. This, Tirpitz explained to the Kaiser in 1899, would make Britain 'concede to Your Majesty such a measure of maritime influence which will make it possible for Your Majesty to conduct a great overseas policy' – without a fight, in other words.[9]

What the German navy did, then, was to pose a threat to Britain's near-monopoly of naval power; or rather it would have posed a threat if it could have been completed without anyone in London noticing. While the navy was being built up, as Bülow remarked, Germany was 'like the caterpillar before it had grown into a butterfly'.[10] But the chrysalis was all too transparent (even Britain's amateurish military intelligence service could spot a battleship being constructed, especially one which had been authorized by the Reichstag).

By 1905, with the completion of Fisher's initial naval reforms, the director of Naval Intelligence could confidently describe Britain's 'maritime preponderance' over Germany as 'overwhelming'.[11] This was quite right: the number of German battleships increased from thirteen to sixteen between 1898 and 1905, whereas the British battle fleet rose from twenty-nine to forty-four ships. This did not maintain the 1889 two-power standard, but it sufficed to check a purely German threat; indeed it reminded Berlin of the British threat to Germany – hence the panic about a pre-emptive British naval strike which gripped Berlin in 1904–5.[12] Tirpitz's original target had been an approximate ratio of British to German naval strength of 1.5 to 1. As Table 7 shows, he never got near.

The campaign orchestrated by the right-wing press in Britain in 1909 made sure of that. British alarmists – those who cried 'We want eight and we won't wait' – believed the Germans were aiming to accelerate their building 'tempo' so much that within a few years they would have

Table 7   The ratio of British to German warship tonnage, 1880–1914

1880	1890	1900	1910	1914
7.4	3.6	3.7	2.3	2.1

Source: Kennedy, *Great Powers*, p. 261.

Table 8   *The naval strength of the powers in 1914*

Country	Personnel	Large naval vessels	Tonnage
Russia	54,000	4	328,000
France	68,000	10	731,000
Britain	209,000	29	2,205,000
TOTAL	331,000	43	3,264,000
Germany	79,000	17	1,019,000
Austria–Hungary	16,000	3	249,000
TOTAL	95,000	20	1,268,000

Source: Reichsarchiv, *Weltkrieg*, erster Reihe, vol. I, pp. 38f.

more dreadnoughts than the Royal Navy.[13] In fact, the German total in 1912 was nine to Britain's fifteen.[14] When war came, the Triple Entente possessed 43 of the big warships; the Central Powers just 20 (Table 8).[15]

The Germans knew they were beaten. As early as November 1908 the authoritative *Marine-Rundschau* published an anonymous article which admitted as much:

Britain could only be defeated by a power that seized permanent command of the British sea. That has to be a fleet that has not only reached the same size as the Royal Navy but is also superior in big battleships. Boxed in between France and Russia, Germany has to maintain the greatest army in the world ... It is obviously beyond the capacity of the German economy to support at the same time a fleet which could outgrow the British.[16]

Thus to Bülow's question in June 1909 as to 'when we could contemplate a war with England with confidence', Tirpitz could only respond that 'in five or six years, the danger would be completely over'. Moltke concluded from this lame answer that 'we have no chance whatever to fight out a conflict with England successfully' and therefore urged 'an honourable understanding' with England.[17] The so-called 'war council' of military chiefs summoned by the Kaiser in December 1912 was really nothing of the kind. Although Moltke argued for 'war, the sooner the better', Tirpitz asked for another eighteen months because his navy was not yet ready. The result, as Admiral Müller noted in his dairy, was 'pretty well zero'.

The preservation of Britain's maritime supremacy encouraged hubris at the Admiralty. German fears of a new Copenhagen were more than mere fantasies: Fisher assured Lord Lansdowne in April 1905 that, with French support, the navy 'could have the German fleet, the Kiel Canal and Schleswig-Holstein within a fortnight'. In the same way, Fisher had unshakeable confidence in Britain's power to impose an effective trade blockade on Germany. 'It's so very peculiar that Providence has arranged England as a sort of huge breakwater against German commerce,' Fisher remarked in April 1906. 'Such is our naval superiority that on the day of war we "mop up" 800 German merchant steamers. Fancy the "knock-down" blow to German trade and finance. Worth Paris!'[18] This belief that a war could be decided by restricting German food imports was well established in naval circles by 1907:[19] that was why there was so much opposition to the resolutions drafted at the second Hague Peace Conference that year to restrict the use of the blockade during hostilities.[20] As Sir Charles Ottley, the former head of Naval Intelligence and secretary of the CID, explained in December 1908, the Admiralty view was that:

(in a protracted war) the wheels of our sea-power (though they would grind the German population slowly perhaps) would grind them 'exceedingly small' – grass would sooner or later grow in the streets of Hamburg and wide-spread dearth and ruin would be inflicted.[21]

So overwhelming did the British superiority appear that devout navalists like Esher found it hard to imagine Germany risking a war at sea.[22] Tirpitz was well aware of the danger: in January 1907 he warned that Germany would suffer from serious shortages of food in a war which he envisaged would last as long as one and a half years.[23]

British politicians too refused to acknowledge the legitimacy of any challenge to their 'absolute supremacy' at sea. To Haldane the two-power standard seemed sacrosanct, and the rising cost of maintaining it was Germany's fault for trying to narrow the gap.[24] To Churchill the British navy was 'a necessity' on which Britain's 'existence' depended, whereas the German navy was merely 'a luxury', the purpose of which could only be 'expansion' – tremendous humbug considering Britain's blockade plans.[25] After his move to the Admiralty in October 1911, Churchill even upped the ante by aiming to maintain a new '60 per cent standard . . . in relation not only to Germany but to the rest of the world'.[26] 'The Triple Alliance is being outbuilt by the Triple Entente,' he crowed to Grey in October 1913.[27] 'Why', he asked bluntly the following month, 'should it be supposed that we should not be able to defeat [Germany]? A study of the comparative fleet strength in the line of battle will be found reassuring.'[28] By 1914, as Churchill recalled, 'naval rivalry had . . . ceased to be a cause of friction . . . We were proceeding inflexibly . . . it was certain we could not be overtaken.'[29] Even Asquith later admitted that 'the competition in naval expenditure was not in itself a likely source of immediate danger. We had quite determined to maintain our necessary predominance at sea and we were well able to make that determination effective.'[30] Lloyd George went so far as to declare the naval race over in an interview with the *Daily News* in January 1914:

Relations with Germany are infinitely more friendly now than they have been for years . . . Germany has nothing which approximates to a two-power standard . . . That is why I feel convinced that even if Germany ever had any idea of challenging our supremacy at sea, the exigencies of the present situation have put it completely out of her head.[31]

The confidence of British navalists in their superiority over Germany can also be seen in the way they assessed the threat of a German invasion – that favourite nightmare of the scaremongers. The Committee of Imperial Defence was unpersuaded by William Robertson's alarmist paper of 1903 (see Chapter 1) and a General Staff paper in 1906 was also sceptical about the feasibility of a German invasion.[32] When (in response to Lord Roberts's public endorsement of the invasion 'threat') a sub-committee of the CID was set up to investigate the subject in 1907, its report concluded unequivocally: '[T]he fundamental idea that Germany could secure command of the North Sea for a period long enough to admit of the unmolested passage of the transports must be dismissed as impracticable.'[33] When the possibility of a German invasion came up for discussion yet again in 1914, it seemed no more likely.[34] This was quite right: the Germans had in fact abandoned the idea more than ten years previously.[35]

THE CLOSING WINDOW

The Germans faced a similar disadvantage on land, especially once the Franco-Russian alliance had been agreed. Even before that, the experience of desperate French resistance after the defeat at Sedan in

1870 had persuaded the Elder Moltke that, in the event of a war against both powers, Germany 'could not hope to rid itself quickly of one enemy by a rapid and successful offensive, leaving itself free to deal with the other enemy'.[36] His pupil Colmar von der Goltz echoed this judgement in his book *The People in Arms*, arguing that 'war in the near future must lose much of the element of mobility that characterized to a large extent our last campaigns.'[37] Perhaps the most devastating warning that the days of short, limited wars were over came in 1895 from the quartermaster in the General Staff, Major General Köpke. In the event of a war on two fronts, he predicted (in a secret memorandum, the original of which is now lost):

even with the most offensive spirit . . . nothing more can be achieved than a tedious and bloody crawling forward step by step – here and there by way of an ordinary attack in siege style – in order slowly to win some advantages . . . We cannot expect rapid and decisive victories. Army and nation will have to get used to that thought early on in order to avoid alarming pessimism right at the beginning of the war . . . Positional warfare in general, the struggle surrounding long fronts of field fortifications, the siege of large fortresses, must be carried out successfully. Otherwise we will not be able to achieve successes against the French. Hopefully we will then not lack in the necessary intellectual and material preparations and we will, at the decisive moment, be well trained and equipped for this form of fighting.[38]

Köpke's analysis was substantially borne out by the use of entrenchment in the Russo-Japanese war. It was the belief that Russian fortifications were inferior to French and her mobilization slower that made Moltke and Waldersee adopt the idea of attacking Russia first if war came.[39]

As is well known, on taking over from Waldersee, Schlieffen sought to solve the problem of French defences by circumventing them, attacking France from the north. As early as 1897 he hit on the idea of a high-speed advance through Luxembourg and Belgium; by 1904–5 he had sketched the key elements of a great flanking movement, now also passing through Holland; and in December 1905, on the eve of his retirement, he completed his famous *Grosse Denkschrift*. In it he envisaged a massive offensive by around two-thirds of the German army (thirty-three and a half divisions) through Belgium and Holland and into northern France. Alsace-Lorraine and East Prussia were barely to be defended: only one division was to remain in the latter to withstand the expected Russian advance. The aim was nothing less than the 'annihilation' (*Vernichtung*) of the French army within six weeks, after which any enemy troops that had penetrated German territory would be mopped up.[40]

Yet there was from the outset until the outbreak of war in 1914 a defect in the plan: eight of the divisions which Schlieffen planned to use did not exist. Historians have long been familiar with the arguments within the military establishment against expanding the army: Kehr detailed them in the 1920s.[41] As Stig Förster has argued, there was in fact a 'double militarism' in Germany – or rather there were two militarisms: a reactionary 'traditional, Prussian, conservative' militarism 'from above', which dominated between 1890 and 1905, and a 'bourgeois' militarism 'from below', which 'tended to the radical right' and triumphed thereafter.[42] In the eyes of the former, the essential desideratum was, as Waldersee put it in 1897, 'to keep the army intact'.[43] Put simply, that meant trying to keep the percentage of officers from aristocratic families at around 60 per cent; and the percentage of NCOs and other rankers from rural areas at the same level, so as to exclude those 'democratic and other elements, unsuitable for the [military] estate' which the Prussian War Minister Karl von Einem later warned against.[44] In this, the military conservatives could make common cause with Tirpitz and the other advocates of building a big German battle fleet. Successive war ministers made no bones about accepting the army's subordination to the navy in defence budget increases and agreeing to modest growth in the army's size. Between 1877 and 1889 the German army's peacetime strength had stagnated at around 468,400. In the subsequent seven years it increased to only 557,430, despite two attempts to implement universal military service (which would have added 150,200 in 1890). Thereafter there were only the most minimal increases, so that its peacetime strength was just over 588,000 in 1904 (see figure 1). Perhaps the best proof of the limits of German militarism lies in the conservatism of the German army itself.

However, by December 1912 – nearly twenty years since the failure of Reich Chancellor Caprivi's attempt to achieve universal military service – much had changed within the army, despite the best efforts of the conservatives. To be sure, the proportion of generals who were aristocrats had fallen only slightly, and the senior ranks continued to be cluttered with von Bülows and von Arnims.[45] But the proportion of all army officers who were aristocratic had fallen from 65 per cent to just 30 per cent. The change was especially marked in the General Staff,

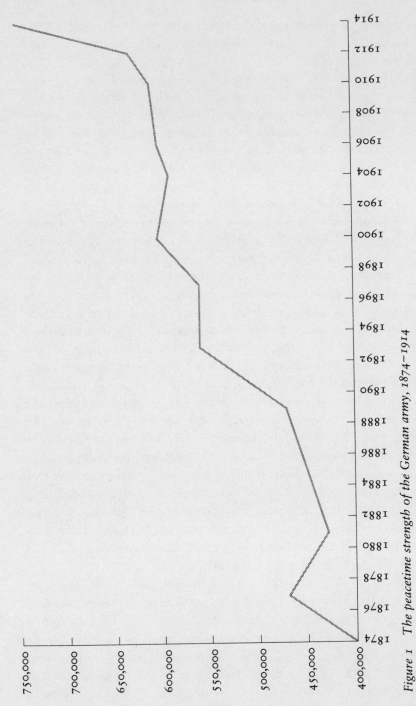

Figure 1   The peacetime strength of the German army, 1874–1914

Note: Figures do not include *Landsturm* (militia) or *Landwehr* (territorials).

Source: Förster, *Doppelte Militarismus.*

which by 1913 was 70 per cent non-aristocratic, with some departments – notably the important Railway Section – almost entirely middle class.[46] Here the spirit was technocratic rather than conservative, and the principal concern was with external rather than internal enemies – above all, with the threat posed by the French and Russian armies. The most dynamic figure of the new military 'meritocracy' was Erich Ludendorff, who as early as July 1910 had argued that 'any state which is involved in a struggle for its survival . . . must use all its forces and resources'.[47] In November 1912 he stated the case for enforcing universal service in language which harked back to the era of the Wars of Liberation: 'We must once again become the people in arms.'[48] Ludendorff's 'Great Memorandum' of December 1912 called for putting an additional 30 per cent of those eligible through military service (increasing the call-up rate from 52 per cent to 82 per cent, i.e. to the French level), a total increase of 300,000 recruits over two years.[49] Even Bethmann seemed persuaded: 'We cannot afford to leave out any recruit who can wear a helmet,' he declared.[50] To the military conservatives in the War Ministry, the radical connotations of Ludendorff's plan were clear. General Franz von Wandel retorted bluntly: 'If you carry on like this with your demands, you will bring the German people to [the point of] revolution.'[51] When the Kaiser seemed to support the idea of a new army bill at the 'war council' of December 1912, the War Minister Josias von Heeringen demurred 'because the entire structure of the army, instructors, barracks etc. could not digest more recruits'. Indeed, Heeringen explicitly went so far as to blame the 'doubts . . . about our war strength' which had arisen in 'sections of the army' on the 'agitation of the Army League and the Pan-Germans'.[52] Denouncing Ludendorff's plan as 'democratization' of the army, he secured his demotion to a regimental command in Düsseldorf and drew up an alternative army bill for an increase of just 117,000 troops.[53]

Ludendorff was right. The 1912 and 1913 bills increased the peacetime strength of the German army to 748,000. But the forces of Russia and France had grown more rapidly in the preceding years. The Russian and French armies had a total peacetime strength in 1913–14 of 2,170,000, compared with a combined German and Austrian strength of 1,242,000: a discrepancy of 928,000. In 1912, that gap had been only 794,665; while in 1904, it had been just 260,982.[54] This meant that, at its full war-time strength, the German army totalled around 2.15 million men, to which could be added 1.3 million Habsburg troops; whereas on a war footing the combined forces of Serbia, Russia, Belgium and France numbered 5.6 million (see Table 9).[55]

The growing disadvantage was equally clear in terms of total numbers called up in 1913–14: 585,000 to 383,000. According to the German General Staff, 83 per cent of those eligible for military service in France performed it; compared with 53 per cent in Germany (see Table 10).[56] It is true that only 20 per cent of the annual cohort in Russia was called up; but given the enormous absolute numbers involved, this was scant consolation for Berlin.[57] As Schlieffen himself put it in 1905, 'We keep on puffing about our high population . . . but these masses are not trained and armed to the full extent of those suitable [for military service].'[58] 'Although the German Empire contains 65,000,000 inhabitants, compared to 40,000,000 of French,' commented Bernhardi seven years later, 'this excess in population represents so much dead capital, unless a corresponding majority of recruits are annually enlisted, and unless in peacetime the necessary machinery is set up for their organization.'[59] 'I shall do what I can,' Moltke told his opposite number Baron Franz Conrad von Hötzendorf in May 1914. 'We do not have superiority over the French.'[60]

Figure 2 summarizes the problem, showing how much larger the

Table 9   The military strengths of the European states in 1914

Country	Peacetime strength	Colonial	Wartime strength	Infantry divisions	Cavalry divisions
Russia	1,445,000		3,400,000	114.5	36
Serbia	52,000		247,000	11.5	1
Montenegro	2,000				
France	827,000	157,000	1,800,000	80	10
Britain	248,000	190,000	162,000	6	1
Belgium	48,000		117,000	6	1
TOTAL	2,622,000	347,000	5,726,000	218	49
Germany	761,000	7,000	2,147,000	87.5	11
Austria–Hungary	478,000		1,338,000	49.5	11
TOTAL	1,239,000	7,000	3,485,000	137	22

Source: Reichsarchiv, Weltkrieg, erster Reihe, vol. I, pp. 38f.

Table 10   The military potentials of the European states in 1914

Country	Population	Colonial population	Men of military age	Of which trained (excluding navy)	Percentage trained
Russia	164,000,000		17,000,000	6,000,000	35
Serbia	4,000,000		440,000		
Montenegro	400,000		60,000		
France	36,600,000	57,700,000	5,940,000	5,067,000	85
Britain	46,000,000	434,000,000	6,430,000	248,000	4–8
Belgium	7,500,000	17,500,000			
TOTAL	258,500,000	509,200,000			
Germany	67,000,000	12,000,000	9,750,000	4,900,000	50
Austria–Hungary	51,000,000		6,120,000	3,000,000	49
TOTAL	118,000,000	12,000,000			

Source: Reichsarchiv, *Weltkrieg*, erster Reihe, vol. I, pp. 38f.

combined French and Russian armies were on the eve of the war than those of Germany and Austria–Hungary. In terms of divisions (a term which admittedly meant different things in different countries), it looked even worse.[61]

As Table 11 shows, the most militarized society – in the sense of the proportion of the population under arms – in pre-war Europe was undoubtedly France: 2.29 per cent of the population were in the army and navy. The Three Years Law on military service passed in July 1913 merely widened a long-standing lead.[62] Germany came next (1.33), but Britain was not far behind (1.17). These figures alone confirm that Norman Angell was right when he said that Germany was only 'reputed (quite wrongly, incidentally) to be the most military nation in Europe'.[63]

Of course, numbers are not everything. It is true that, when other factors (particularly the ratios of officers, non-commissioned officers and armaments to men) are taken into account, the discrepancy was less pronounced. Within the German military, the debate between conservatives and radicals was as much about military technology as about manpower. At issue were questions about the continued utility of cavalry, the need for improved field artillery and the need to equip

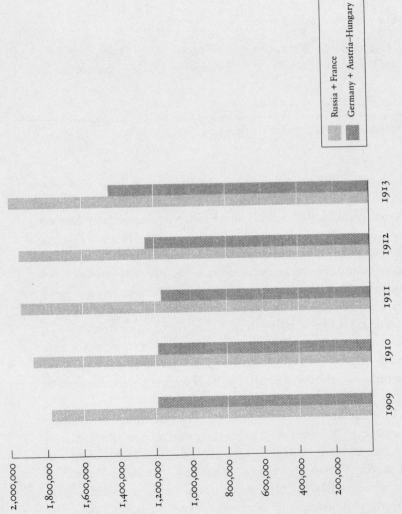

Figure 2 The armies of the four principal European powers, 1909–1913

Note: I have supplied from another source a figure for Austria–Hungary for 1913, which Herrmann's source (*von Loebells Jahresberichte*) does not provide.

Source: Herrmann, *Arming of Europe*, p. 234.

Table 11   Total (army and naval) military personnel as a percentage of population for the five great powers, 1890–1913/14

	1890	1900	1910	1913/14
Russia	0.58	0.86	0.81	0.77
France	1.42	1.84	1.95	2.29
Russia + France	0.79	1.08	1.03	1.05
Britain	1.12	1.52	1.27	1.17
Russia + France + Britain	0.85	1.16	1.08	1.07
Germany	1.02	0.94	1.08	1.33
Austria–Hungary	0.81	0.82	0.84	0.85
Germany + Austria–Hungary	0.93	0.89	0.97	1.12
Italy	0.95	0.79	0.94	0.98

Note: The population figures Kennedy gives are for 1913, the personnel figures for 1914.
Source: Kennedy, *Great Powers*, pp. 255, 261.

the army with machine-guns. In particular, the radicals within the General Staff were distinguished by their preoccupation with the role of railways.

Great strides had been made in this regard, to be sure. In 1870 it had taken twenty-seven days to mobilize the Prussian army against France; as late as 1891 German mobilization within the borders of the Reich still took place across five different time-zones. The General Staff devoted itself in the ensuing decades to improving this. Although its work included war-gaming, making maps, teaching military history and going on rural 'rides',[64] it was the General Staff's responsibility for devising and perfecting the Military Travel Plan – the crucial fifth stage of German mobilization – which was crucial. In one of the later versions of his plan, Schlieffen had taken the battle of Cannae as his model for a future 'war of annihilation' against France; but it was the technocrats like Wilhelm Groener who had to work out how to get the German army to the decisive field at the optimal moment. Here a knowledge of the classics counted for less than a knowledge of railway maps and timetables. By the eve of the war the Military Travel Plan had been reduced to a 312-hour exercise, involving 11,000 trains moving 2 million men, 600,000 horses and the necessary supplies.[65]

Yet even with this remarkable achievement of logistics the Germans could not feel satisfied. In addition to Russian numbers and Russian artillery, Russian railways were an acute source of anxiety in Berlin in 1914.[66] Such fears were given wide currency by Groener's testimony before the Reichstag Budget Committee in April 1913, in which he claimed that Germany had lagged behind both Russia and France in railway construction since 1870.[67] This was true. Between 1900 and 1914 the number of trains which could be sent westwards from Russia in a single day had been increased from 200 to 360. In September 1914 the Russians intended to introduce a new mobilization plan (Plan 20) which would have cut the time needed to put seventy-five infantry divisions into the field from thirty to eighteen days.[68]

No doubt the Germans over-estimated their enemies in some ways. The Russians were certainly numerous but woefully ill-equipped. The French, for all their military commitment, were handicapped by mad strategy: Plan XVII, the *attaque brusquée* on Alsace-Lorraine devised by Joffre and agreed in May 1913, was predicated on the assumption that the offensive (in the form of cavalry charges and close order advances with fixed bayonets) was the best form of defence.[69] In particular, the French generals' belief that, in the words of the artillery expert Hippolyte Langlois in 1904, 'the steady growth in the power of artillery always facilitates the attack,' led them to waste manpower on such a huge scale in the first months of the war that they very nearly handed victory to the Germans.[70] Even more short-sightedly, the French made no attempt to prevent the economically vital Briey area (which accounted for nearly three-quarters of French iron ore output) from falling into enemy hands.[71]

On the other hand, it is quite wrong to suggest that German fears of relative military decline were groundless. It seems increasingly evident that those in the know in the General Staff realized that the Schlieffen Plan could not be made to work as had originally been intended. In order to resist the anticipated French offensive into Lorraine, Moltke felt it necessary to divert troops away from the right wing, which was intended to encircle Paris, to channel its advance through Belgium alone, leaving Holland unscathed, and, to support the Austrians, to use the 8th Army in the opening offensive against Russia. As the plan stood in 1914, it was almost certain not to annihilate the French army, not least because no army could have marched as far and as fast as the 1st Army on the far right wing was expected to – up to 300 miles in the space of a month – without succumbing to physical exhaustion.[72] That may have been why Moltke decided to avoid Holland, so that it could continue to act as a neutral 'windpipe' for German imports. Moltke had already warned the Kaiser in January 1905 that a war with France could not be 'won in one decisive battle, but will turn into a long and tedious struggle with a country that will not give up before the strength of its entire people has been broken. Our people too will be utterly exhausted, *even if* we should be victorious.' This analysis had been confirmed by a report of the Third Department of the General Staff in May 1910. Moltke and Ludendorff had even written to the War Ministry in November 1912 warning:

We will have to be ready to fight a lengthy campaign with numerous hard, lengthy battles until we force down *one* of our enemies; the strain and consumption of resources will increase as we will have to win in several theatres in the West and the East one after another and . . . to fight with inferiority against superiority. The need for much ammunition for a long period of time will become absolutely necessary . . .[73]

This was their second request for increased stockpiling of ammunition. On 14 May 1914 Moltke explicitly warned the State Secretary for the Interior Delbrück that 'a perhaps lengthy war against two fronts can only be sustained by an economically strong people'.[74]

Historians have often wondered why Germany's military and political leaders were so pessimistic in the years before the First World War. In 1909, for example, Tirpitz feared a lightning strike against his fleet by the British Navy; while the retired Schlieffen had nightmares of 'a concentrated attack on the Central Powers' by France, Russia, Britain and Italy:

At the given moment, the drawbridges are to be let down, the doors are to be opened and the million-strong armies let loose, raving and destroying, across the Vosges, the Meuse, the Niemen, the Bug and even the Isonzo and the Tyrolean Alps. The danger seems gigantic.[75]

Moltke too was conscious of 'the Gorgon head of war grin[ning]' at him as early as 1905. 'We all live under a dull pressure which kills the joy of achievement,' he confided in his diary, 'and almost never can we begin something without hearing the inner voice say: "What for? It is all in vain!"'[76] To Moltke, even as he unleashed the German offensive, war meant 'the mutual tearing to pieces by Europe's civilized nations' and the 'destruction [of] civilization in almost all Europe for decades

97

to come'.[77] 'War', he declared dolefully after his failure and resignation in September 1914, 'demonstrates how the epochs of civilization follow one another in a progressive manner, how each nation has to fulfil its preordained role in the development of the world . . . Assuming that Germany would be annihilated in this war, this would mean the destruction of German intellectual life, on which the further development of mankind depends, and of German culture; the whole development of mankind would be set back in the most disastrous way . . .'[78] The same fatalism is detectable in the later remarks of Moltke's Austrian opposite number, Conrad.[79] Even so ardent a militarist as Bernhardi had to try to rationalize the possibility of defeat in 'the next war': 'Even defeat can bear a rich harvest.'[80] This was exactly what General Erich von Falkenhayn, the man who would succeed Moltke, said on 4 August 1914: 'Even if we are ruined by it, it was still beautiful [*Wenn wir auch darüber zugrunde gehen, schön war's doch*].'[81] Germany's military leaders on the eve of war felt weak, not strong.

And not only her military leaders. For no one felt this pessimism more strongly than Reich Chancellor Bethmann Hollweg. He was, he confessed in 1912, 'gravely distressed by our relative strength in case of war. One must have a good deal of trust in God and count on the Russian revolution as an ally in order to be able to sleep at all.'[82] In June 1913 he admitted to feeling 'sick of war, the clamour for war and the eternal armaments. It is high time that the great nations quieted down again . . . otherwise an explosion will occur which no one deserves and which will harm all.'[83] To the National Liberal leader Bassermann, he said 'with fatalistic resignation: "If there is a war with France, the last Englishman will march against us." '[84] His secretary, Kurt Riezler, recorded some of his musings in his diary for 7 July 1914:

The Chancellor expects that a war, whatever its outcome, will result in the uprooting of everything that exists. The existing [world] very antiquated, without ideas . . . Thick fog over the people. The same in all Europe. The future belongs to Russia, which grows and grows and weighs upon us as an ever heavier nightmare . . . The Chancellor very pessimistic about the intellectual condition of Germany.[85]

On 20 July Bethmann returned to his Russian theme: 'Russia's claims [are] growing [along with her] enormously explosive strength . . . In a few years no longer to be warded off, particularly when the present European constellation persists.' A week later he told Riezler that he felt 'a fate [*Fatum*] greater than human power hanging over Europe and our own people'.[86] That mood of near-despair, sometimes attributed by cultural historians to excessive exposure to the works of Nietzsche, Wagner and Schopenhauer, becomes more intelligible when the military realities of Europe in 1914 are considered.

What made the German analysis of strategic decline more compelling was the even worse predicament of their allies' armies. Conrad warned Moltke in February 1913 that if the 'enmity' between Austria–Hungary and Russia took 'the form of a racial struggle' then:

We can hardly expect our Slavs, who make up 47 per cent of the population, to show enthusiasm for the fight against their kinsmen. Now the army is still permeated by the feeling that historically it is one and is held together by the cement of discipline; whether ... this will still hold good in the future is doubtful.[87]

This was hardly reassuring. As early as January 1913 the General Staff began to contemplate the 'necessity for Germany to defend itself against France, Russia and England alone'.[88] In fact, it was Austria–Hungary which had to fight virtually unaided in the opening phase of the war, because the Schlieffen Plan deployed most of the German army in the west. In a masterpiece of Habsburg bumbling, Conrad initially sent four of his reserve of twelve divisions to Serbia, then had to recall them to Galicia when it became clear that the German 8th Army was not going to assist him against the Russians.[89]

Moreover, the incompetence of the Italian army and navy had been exposed by the less than smooth invasion of Tripoli (Libya) in 1911.[90] Even before that, British diplomats were joking that it was 'all to the good that Italy remain in the Triple Alliance and be a source of weakness'.[91] The Germans apparently had no serious expectation that the Italians would fight in 1914.[92]

There were two possible responses to this sense of diminishing military power. One was to avoid war and instead to deter the other side from attacking: that had been the final conclusion of the Elder Moltke. The other was to launch a pre-emptive war before matters got any worse. This was an argument advanced repeatedly by German generals. The Elder Moltke himself had urged Bismarck to attack France again in 1875 and twelve years later urged the same course of action against Russia.[93] His successor Waldersee was even more devoted to the idea of a first strike. Even Schlieffen urged an attack on France while Russia was distracted by war with Japan.[94] Conrad too was a devotee of the pre-emptive mentality: he proposed a strike against Italy in 1907 and 1911, and in 1913 urged that Austria 'cut off the South Slavs and the West Slavs culturally and politically from the East Slavs, to remove them from Russian influence': code for a first strike against Serbia.[95] On every occasion before 1914 the politicians dismissed these proposals. By 1914, however, the case seemed to have become unanswerable. In April 1914 the Crown Prince told the American diplomat Joseph Grew 'that Germany would fight Russia soon'.[96] The Younger Moltke put it to Conrad at Carlsbad on 12 May 1914: 'To wait any longer meant a diminishing of our chances; as far as manpower is concerned we cannot enter into a competition with Russia'; and repeated it to the German Foreign Minister Gottlieb von Jagow eight days later, as they drove from Potsdam to Berlin:

Russia will have completed her armaments in two or three years. The military superiority of our enemies would be so great that he [Moltke] did not know how we might cope with them. In his view there was no alternative to waging a preventive war in order to defeat the enemy as long as we could still *more or less* pass the test.[97]

A month later, following a banquet in Hamburg, the German Emperor William II echoed this analysis in a conversation with the banker Max Warburg:

He was worried about the Russian armaments, about the planned railway construction, and detected [in these] the preparations for a war against us in 1916. He complained about the inadequacy of the rail links that we had to the Western Front against France; and hinted . . . [at] whether it would not be better to strike now, rather than to wait.[98]

This was exactly a week before the Sarajevo assassinations. In other words, the arguments for a pre-emptive strike were already well-established in Berlin before the diplomatic crisis furnished a near-perfect pretext (a *casus belli* which Vienna would not shirk). Historians have long been aware of this; they have not always acknowledged the validity of the German General Staff's fears. Strangely, it was the British journal the *Nation* which got it right in March 1914: 'The Prussian military', it commented, 'would be less than human if it did not dream of anticipating the crushing accumulation of force.'[99] The following month Grey begged to differ; he doubted 'that Germany would make an aggressive and menacing attack upon Russia' because 'though Germany might have successes at first, Russia's resources were so great that, in the long run, Germany would be exhausted . . .'[100] But Lord Bryce, later to win fame as the author of the official British report into German atrocities in Belgium, remarked in June that Germany was 'right to arm and . . . would need every man' against Russia, which was 'rapidly becoming a menace to Europe'.[101]

The question continues to be debated: did Germany intend merely to aim for a diplomatic success in 1914 by splitting the Entente powers, or was it always intended to launch a European war, whether 'preventive' or more deliberately expansionist? In this context it is worth noting that at the time the Crown Prince made his prediction to Joseph Grew, the General Staff was mainly concerned with a new upgrading of its strategic railways; work projected to take several years to complete and not due to begin, as the Chancellor noted in April, until 1915.[102] At any event, what seems clear is that Germany's military leaders did not, contrary to the well-established legend of the 'short-war illusion', go to war in August 1914 in the expectation of celebrating Christmas in the Champs Elysées.[103]

THE UNREADY

There was only one consolation left to the Germans; and that was that some of their potential foes were significantly less prepared for war. The Belgian army, for example, was woefully unready to resist a German offensive. Its Francophone officers stood in much the same relation to its Flemish rank-and-file as Austrian officers to the Good Soldier Švejk. Contemporary calculations showed that in 1840 the Belgian army had been around one-ninth the size of Prussia's and one-fifth that of France, yet by 1912 the respective figures were one-fortieth and one-thirty-fifth. In per capita terms the Swiss spent 50 per cent more on defence; the Dutch 100 per cent more and the French four times more. In 1909, despite fierce resistance by Flemish Catholics, military service was made compulsory for one son in each family. However, the period of service was simultaneously reduced to fifteen months and the army budget remained unchanged. Finally, on 30 August 1913 the Militia Law was passed which increased the annual intake of recruits from 15,000 to 33,000 by removing the exemption for younger sons; the target was an army which could number 340,000 in the event of war. This was accompanied by a reorganization of the army's divisional structure. However, the reforms had too little time to take effect: total forces mobilized in July 1914 numbered 200,000 and between them they had just 120 machine-guns and no heavy artillery.[104]

Not much more ready was the power which pledged itself publicly to defend Belgian neutrality. Despite the experience of the Boer War, which had exposed serious deficiencies in the British army, remarkably little was done by either party before 1914 to remedy matters.[105] In Liberal eyes, conscription – recommended by three successive official inquiries – was anathema, Lord Roberts's proposals for national service merely the thin end of the wedge. As War Minister, the most Haldane could do was to create the Territorial Army, a part-time reserve force. Including them, the reservists, the navy and British soldiers in the Indian Army, that brought the number of British men 'committed to military service in peacetime' to around 750,000.[106] Beckett has argued that around 8 per cent of the male population had seen some military service, including the Yeomanry and later Territorials; and that around two-fifths of all adolescents were enrolled in quasi-military youth organisations like the Boys' Brigade or the Scouts on the eve of the war. But this could hardly be regarded as a serious reserve for the regular army, especially as only 7 per cent of Territorial soldiers were prepared to serve overseas.[107] When Eyre Crowe suggested to Henry Wilson that the Territorials might be sent to France in the event of a war, the latter exploded: 'What amazing ignorance of war! No officers, no transport, no mobility, no compulsion to go, no discipline, obsolete guns, no horses etc. Even Haldane said it would not do.'[108] The regular army, on which Britain's continental commitment depended, remained a dwarf force – just seven divisions (including one of cavalry), compared with Germany's ninety-eight and a half. As Sir Henry Wilson said to Roberts, that was 'fifty too few'. The Lord Chancellor Earl Loreburn made the same point in January 1912: 'If war came we could not prevent [France] from being overrun. If we are to continue the present policy we shall need to send not 150,000 men but at least half a million to do any good.'[109] Moreover, recruits continued to be drawn from what the German ambassador called in 1901 'the dregs of the population . . . morally degraded, idiots, undersized and pitiable beings'.[110] This was putting it too harshly, but it is undeniable that the British regular army mainly recruited semi-literate, unskilled working-class youths.[111]

Despite improvements at the General Staff, the officer corps was dominated by men whose principal accomplishment was a 'good seat' on a
hunter.[112] There was considerable resistance to the adoption of the
machine-gun, and ammunition reserves continued to be based on
the South African experience.[113] Nor was much effort made to learn
from the economic lessons of the Boer War: despite the warnings of
the Murray Committee, the War Office continued to rely on a small
'charmed circle' of contractors to supply its needs.[114] In short, scarely
anything was done to ensure that Britain would be able to make an
effective contribution on the French side in the expected Franco-German
war. Britain was quite simply 'unprepared' for war.[115] Gradually, and
despite (or perhaps because of) the efforts of Esher to chip away at the
continental commitment, the Committee of Imperial Defence ceased to
be a forum for grand strategic debate. There developed in its place a
technocratic obsession with logistics as set down in departmental 'War
Books' – with the result that the disagreements of the rival service
departments were not properly resolved until war had begun.[116]

Seen in the light of all this, Wilson's arguments at the CID 'war
council' of August 1911 had been disingenuous. Like the Kaiser, he did
not really believe the tiny BEF could make an 'appreciable difference'
in a future European war with Germany; he hoped merely to strengthen
the War Office for a future departmental war with the Admiralty.

During and after the crisis of July 1914 the French government always
argued that an equivocal statement of British support for France at an
early stage would have sufficed to deter Germany – a claim subsequently
repeated by critics of Grey, including Lloyd George and Lansdowne,
as well as the greatest chronicler of the war's immediate origins,
Albertini.[117] But the fact remains that the British Expeditionary Force
was not large enough to worry the German General Staff.[118] As J. M.
Hobson has argued, only a bigger continental commitment – in the
sense of a larger British regular army – could have deterred the Germans
from attacking France in the first place.[119] But this amounts to the
contemporary argument for conscription, and – as we shall see – can
be considered a counter-factual without political plausibility under a
Liberal government.[120] As Lloyd George said to Balfour in August
1910 (at the time of their first flirtation with the idea of a coalition
government), conscription was out of the question 'because of the
violent prejudices which would be excited even if it were supposed that
a Government contemplated the possibility of establishing anything of

the kind'.[121] As late as 25 August 1914 Churchill's arguments in Cabinet for 'the necessity of compulsory service' were dismissed by all present, including Asquith and Lloyd George, because 'the people would not listen to such proposals'.[122] British policy was therefore, as Grey said, 'to pursue a European policy without keeping up a great army'.[123] The idea that this was possible was perhaps the greatest of all British illusions.

5

Public Finance and National Security

THE BURDENS OF DEFENCE

Why, when the military experts in both Britain and Germany knew that they lacked the resources to make their war plans work, were the deficiencies not made good? The obvious answer is that domestic political considerations ruled out the kind of huge armies dreamt of by men like Erich Ludendorff and Henry Wilson. On 24 October 1898 the Marquess of Salisbury was moved by an invitation to a conference on disarmament to reflect on the opposite phenomenon:

... there has been a constant tendency on the part of almost every nation to increase its armed force, and to add to an already vast expenditure on the appliances of war. The perfection of the instruments thus brought into use, their extreme costliness, and the horrible carnage and destruction which would ensue from their employment on a large scale, have acted no doubt as a serious deterrent from war. But the burdens imposed by this process on the populations affected must, if prolonged, produce a feeling of unrest and discontent menacing both to internal and external tranquillity.[1]

But how heavy, in reality, were the 'burdens' of armament? How 'vast' the expenditure? To Sir Edward Grey, speaking in the House of Commons in March 1911, it was already 'becoming intolerable' – so intolerable that it 'must in the long run break civilization down [and] lead to war'.[2] Some historians have followed Grey in arguing that it was, above all, the intolerable level of military expenditure which prevented Germany from holding her own in the naval arms race against Britain or the land arms race against Russia and France. There is, however, an apparent paradox which requires explanation: the cost of the arms race was not in fact very high.

It is a notoriously difficult exercise to arrive at figures for military

Table 12 *Defence expenditures of the great powers, 1890–1913 (£ million)*

	Britain	France	Russia	France + Russia	Triple Entente	Germany	Austria	Italy	Germany + Austria	Triple Alliance
1894	33.4	37.6	85.8	123.4	156.8	36.2	9.6	14.0	45.8	59.8
1913	72.5	72.0	101.7	173.7	246.2	93.4	25.0	39.6	118.4	158.0
£ increase	39.1	34.4	15.9	50.3	89.4	57.2	15.4	25.6	72.6	98.2
percentage increase	117.1	91.5	18.5	40.8	57.0	158.0	160.4	182.9	158.5	164.2

Source: Hobson, 'Wary Titan', pp. 464f.

expenditure which are comparable, because of differing definitions in national budgets. To give an example: estimates of German military spending in the year 1913–14 vary from 1,664 million marks to 2,406 million marks, depending on the method of computation. The figure used below (2,095 million marks) is arrived at by excluding items of expenditure not identified in the budget as specifically military in purpose (e.g. spending on railways and canals), but counting other items not included in the army and navy budgets but nevertheless clearly defence-related.[3] Similar problems arise for every country. Attempts have been made by modern scholars, however, to sort out these problems, so that it is now possible to quantify the cost of the arms race quite precisely.[4]

Prior to around 1890 armies and navies had been relatively cheap, even for the major empire-builders like Britain. Expeditions like the one sent to Egypt by Gladstone in 1882 had been run on a shoestring. The defence budgets of the great powers were not much higher in the early 1890s than they had been in the early 1870s. As Table 12 shows, that changed in the two decades before 1914. Taking Britain, France and Russia together, total defence expenditure (expressed in sterling terms) increased by 57 per cent. For Germany and Austria together, the increase was even higher – around 160 per cent.

In the years before 1914, as Figure 3 shows, the German, French, Russian and British defence budgets were not separated by much in absolute terms (setting aside the impact of the Boer War and the Russo-Japanese war). Germany moved ahead of France between 1900 and 1907, but this was mainly due to the cost of the naval race with Britain. After 1909 there was a marked acceleration in the growth of the budgets of all the powers except Austria–Hungary. In per capita terms, however, Germany lagged behind Britain and France: defence spending per capita in 1913 was 28 marks for the Reich, compared with 31 marks for France and 32 marks for Britain. Germany also assigned a lower proportion of public spending to defence: 29 per cent in 1913, compared with figures of 43 per cent for France and Britain.[5] Even more striking is the differential if one adds together the budgets of, on the one hand, Britain, France and Russia and, on the other, Germany, Austria–Hungary and Italy (see Figure 4). Taking the period 1907–13, the Triple Entente powers between them spent on average £83 million more a year than the Triple Alliance powers.

The correct measure of the burden of defence, however, is not the absolute cash total of expenditure – or even the per capita level –

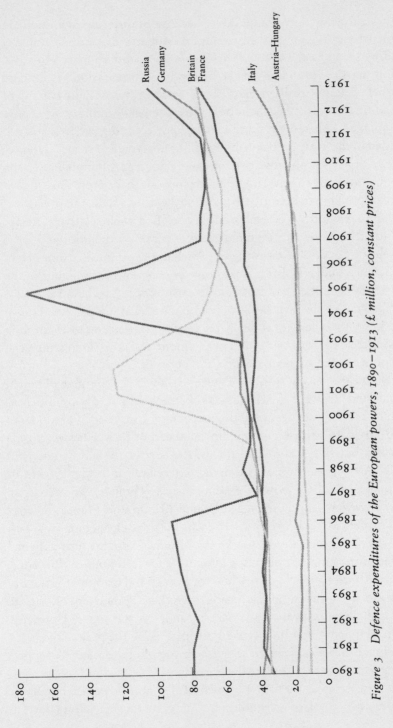

Figure 3 Defence expenditures of the European powers, 1890–1913 (£ million, constant prices)

Source: Hobson, 'Wary Titan', pp. 464f.

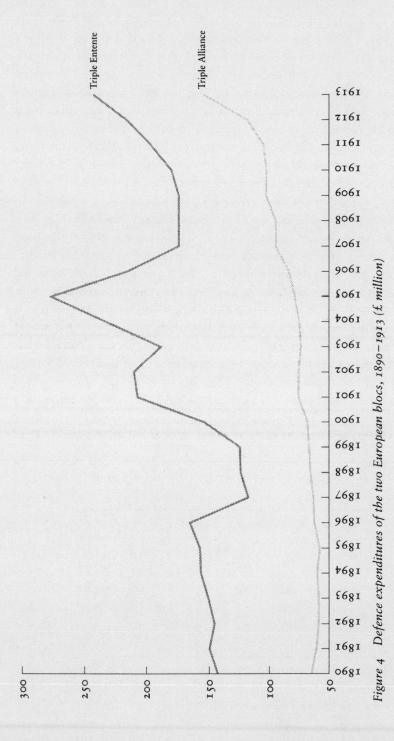

Figure 4 Defence expenditures of the two European blocs, 1890–1913 (£ million)

Source: Hobson, 'Wary Titan', pp. 464f.

but the proportion of national product spent on defence.[6] Unlike the 'externally fixed opportunities and limitations' of geography, which fascinate the more conservative among German historians, this proportion is not fixed but politically determined. In 1984, at a time of superpower confrontation, Britain spent around 5.3 per cent of gross domestic product on defence; at the time of writing, when there is no discernible foreign threat to Britain's security, the figure has fallen to around 3.7 per cent.[7] By contrast, the Soviet Union probably accelerated its own collapse by devoting over 15 per cent of total output to defence.[8] German peacetime defence spending has fluctuated widely in the past century, from 1 per cent in the Weimar years (and just 1.9 per cent in 1991) to as much as 20 per cent before the Second World War.[9]

In the period before 1914, as Table 13 shows, the military burden rose in relation to the economy as a whole in Britain, France, Russia, Germany and Italy from between 2 and 3 per cent of net national product in the period before 1893 to between 3 and 5 per cent by 1913. These figures lay to rest the idea that the British empire imposed a heavy burden on British taxpayers; in truth, Britain enjoyed world power on the cheap.[10] Haldane was quite right when he described the naval estimates as 'not an extravagant premium of insurance' for the country's immense commerce.[11] They also cast doubt on the notion that the arms race before 1914 imposed a 'vast' financial burden on any country. Perhaps the most surprising revelation of all is that in these terms Germany lagged behind both France and Russia. In 1913 – after

Table 13   Defence expenditures as a percentage of net national product, 1887–1913

	Britain	France	Russia	Germany	Austria	Italy
1873	2.0	3.1		2.4	4.8	1.9
1883	2.6	4.0		2.7	3.6	3.6
1893	2.5	4.2	4.4	3.4	3.1	3.6
1903	5.9	4.0	4.1	3.2	2.8	2.9
1913	3.2	4.8	5.1	3.9	3.2	5.1
1870–1913	3.1	4.0	–	3.2	3.1	3.3

Note: Hobson's figure is for Austria alone. My estimates for Austria–Hungary are lower.
Source: Hobson, 'Wary Titan', pp. 478f.

two major army bills – the Reich was spending 3.9 per cent of net national product on defence; more than her own ally Austria and more than Britain (3.2 per cent), but significantly less than France (4.8 per cent) and Russia (5.1 per cent). Italy also had a high military burden: as much as 5.1 per cent of net national product on the eve of the war. My attempt to calculate proportions of gross national product produce similar, though not identical differentials: Germany – 3.5 per cent; Britain – 3.1 per cent; Austria–Hungary – 2.8 per cent; France – 3.9 per cent; Russia – 4.6 per cent. To provide some sort of 'control' I also constructed a series for defence spending from the data in *The Statesman's Yearbook* from the years 1900 to 1914, which exclude British colonial spending, but include substantial expenditures on the Russo-Japanese war omitted by Gregory. For 1913, the percentages of GNP are: Germany – 3.6 per cent; Britain – 3.1 per cent; Austria–Hungary – 2.0 per cent; France – 3.7 per cent; Russia – 4.6 per cent. The higher military burden of the Triple Entente remains obvious.[12]

Historically, these burdens do not seem excessive. Indeed, if one takes the example of Britain in the eighteenth century, they seem quite low.[13] Yet financing this rising burden was one of the central political problems of the period. Symbolically, it was rising military spending which precipitated both Randolph Churchill's resignation as chancellor in 1886 and Gladstone's as prime minister in March 1894. They were among the first of many political casualties of a new 'military–financial complex' which brought to an end the era of the night-watchman state, the mid nineteenth-century idyll in which economic growth accelerated and the state contracted.

The problem of how to pay for rising military costs was compounded by the rising cost of government as a whole. The increase in public spending was seen as a universal tendency in Europe from the late nineteenth century onwards: 'the law of growing state expenditures', as Adolph Wagner called it.[14] Whether to appease politically powerful (or potentially dangerous) social groups or to increase 'national efficiency', governments began to spend increasing amounts on infrastructure, education and provision for the sick, unemployed, poor and elderly. Though by modern standards the amounts involved were trifling, the increases in expenditure, when combined with rising military costs, were generally ahead of aggregate economic growth. As Bethmann patiently explained to Baroness Spitzemberg: 'In order to build [a fleet], a lot of money [is required] which only a rich country can afford, so

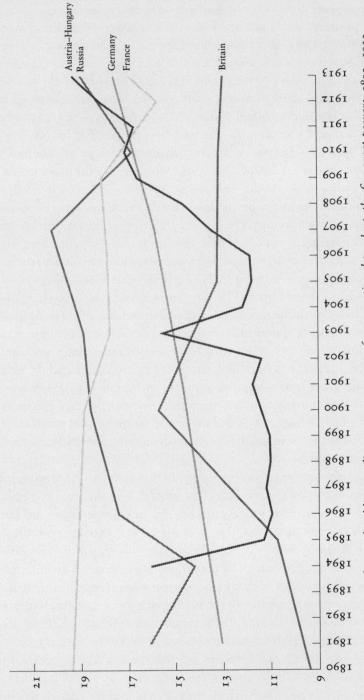

Figure 5   Estimates for total public spending as a percentage of gross national product, the five great powers, 1890–1913

Source: Ferguson, 'Public Finance', p. 159.

Germany should become rich.'[15] Germany did, as we have seen, become rich. But not even the German economy was able to grow more rapidly than the German budget (see Figure 5).

British budgets were formulated in a relatively rigorous way, in that the First Lord of the Treasury and the Chancellor of the Exchequer were generally in a position to exert effective control over the other departments of government, while fiscal policy was subject to relatively rigorous parliamentary scrutiny. Peelite doctrines of balanced budgets, sound money and remission of taxation explain why, as a proportion of GNP, gross public expenditure had tended to decline for most of the nineteenth century, and rose only slightly after 1890. However, the period after 1870 saw a steady growth of public expenditure in nominal terms from around £70 million to around £180 million on the eve of war. Total public spending rose at a rate of 3.8 per cent between 1890 and 1913, increasing as a proportion of GNP from 9.4 per cent to 13.1 per cent. This was due not only to the rising costs of imperial defence (the Boer War and the Dreadnought programme in particular) but also to the proliferation of non-military expenditures. The county councils set up by Salisbury in 1899, which went on to acquire responsibilities for housing and education; the new system of free elementary education; Irish land reform (subsidies to peasant purchasers); the system of non-contributory old-age pensions introduced in 1907–8; the subsidized system of national insurance for health and unemployment – all these represented significant increases in non-military public expenditure, particularly at the previously insignificant local level. However, central government still accounted for 55 per cent of total spending on the eve of the war, and defence spending in turn accounted for 43 per cent of total central government spending. In other words, although political pressures led to increased social spending, this was not at the expense of military spending.[16]

This explains why Winston Churchill got into such political difficulty in 1913 over his naval estimates. The Liberals had got away with reneging in 1909 on their election pledges to cut arms spending, thanks in large measure to press scaremongering.[17] By 1913, however, the German naval threat was yesterday's news: yet Churchill, despite his awareness of 'the strong feeling that exists in the Liberal Party against any increasing liabilities', demanded a figure in excess of £50 million and the laying down of four capital ships for 1914–15.[18] Churchill's announcement of the new figures provoked a full-blown revolt in the parliamentary party and the Cabinet. In his eyes, the higher figure was necessary to force the Germans to accept a 'naval understanding', in the possibility of which he stubbornly continued to believe.[19] But as Lloyd George pointed out, Churchill's demands were incompatible with those of 'education and other social services' in the absence of 'fresh taxation': money which Churchill wanted for dreadnoughts was money needed for social spending.[20] In the words of Norman Angell, the 'enormous sums that now go to armaments' were sums which could not be spent on social policy.[21] In the end a compromise was reached, but a very uneasy one, whereby Churchill promised to moderate the Admiralty's demands in 1915 and 1916. But the crisis came very close to forcing his resignation (and perhaps also that of the Sea Lords and Churchill's two junior ministers) or that of Lloyd George.[22] This was one of those turning points at which history fails to turn: for had Churchill or Lloyd George gone, as we shall see, the Cabinet might very well have acted differently in August the following year. The other possibility was a dissolution of Parliament and an election the Liberals would almost certainly have lost.[23]

In France military expenditure was generally less controversial than the means of paying for it. Of all the powers, France was the most successful in slowing the rise of public spending as a whole to just 1.9 per cent per annum between 1890 and 1913, allowing the public sector share of GNP to fall from its relatively high level of 19 per cent in 1890 to 17 per cent in 1913.[24] The only item of the budget which was not reined in was defence: between 1873 and 1913 it rose as a share of total central government expenditure from 25 per cent to 42 per cent.[25] The French fiscal system, it should be noted, was more centralized than the British. The budgets of the departments and communes were both subject to central government approval, and amounted to less than a quarter of all public spending.[26]

Of all the great powers, Russia had the most rapidly expanding fiscal system: total public spending grew at an average annual rate of 6.1 per cent between 1890 and 1913, nearly quadrupling in nominal terms from just over 1 billion to 4 billion roubles. As a percentage of national income, however, this represented a relatively modest increase from around 17 per cent to 20 per cent, reflecting the rapid growth of the Russian economy as a whole.[27] The exact extent of the military burden is hard to quantify. According to budget statistics for 1900–1913, the army and navy accounted for a mere 20.5 per cent of expenditure, but these figures take no account of various off-budget military expenditures classified as 'extraordinary'. In fact, around 33 per cent of total central government spending went on military purposes.[28] This is not significantly higher than the figures for the other great powers. The biggest difference between Russia and its immediate neighbours was the very high degree of financial centralization, which was greater even than in France. Local government accounted for just 13 per cent of total government spending.

The powers of the Triple Entente were thus, albeit to varying extents, centralized states with, for fiscal purposes, just two tiers of government. Moreover, both Britain and Russia had fought wars – and thus flexed their financial sinews – within the decade and a half prior to 1914. For Britain, the Boer War had cost an estimated £217 million, or 12 per cent of 1900 GNP; the Russo-Japanese war cost Russia around 2.6 billion roubles, or around 20 per cent of 1904 NNP.[29]

Arrangements in the Central Powers were very different, for the profoundly important reason that both Germany and Austria–Hungary were *federal* systems. As has long been recognized, Bismarck's attempt, in devising the Reich constitution, to 'stick more to the confederation of states [*Staatenbund*] [model] while in practice giving it the character of a federal state [*Bundesstaat*]',[30] left the Reich significantly less than the sum of its parts, particularly in financial terms. The states retained control in many spheres of government activity – education, police, public health, tax collection. As Figure 5 shows, in no state was the growth of public spending as steady as in Germany (from 13 per cent to 18 per cent of GNP).[31] The critical point, however, was the growth of non-military spending, which in turn reflected the balance of fiscal power in the federal system. A tradition of public entrepreneurship meant that the German states spent substantial amounts on railways and other infrastructure: such spending accounted for around half the Prussian budget in 1913. Moreover, expenditure at the state and communal level on social and educational facilities rose steadily, accounting for 28 per cent of total public spending in 1913. By contrast, defence spending actually fell as a share of total public spending from around 25 per cent to 20 per cent. This clearly reflected the states' access to more elastic sources of revenue. The ratio of direct to indirect taxation for total public revenues was around 57 to 43; but for the Reich alone only 14 per cent of revenue came from direct taxation, as a result of the inheritance tax and other minor property taxes introduced after

1903; whereas the major states were deriving between 40 and 75 per cent of their revenue from income tax by 1913.[32]

Even at the centre there were institutional problems. The Reich Treasury Office was ill equipped to control German finances: it had just fifty-five officials in 1880, was responsible for only 30 per cent of total public spending and had limited authority over the defence departments.[33] More controversially, it was not clear how much control the lower house of the Reich parliament, the Reichstag, exercised over the budgetary process. Among historians there remains a profound division between those who see the Reichstag's power as extremely limited – part of the Reich's 'sham constitutionalism' – and those who argue for a gradual process of parliamentarization before 1914 – albeit without the English system of ministerial responsibility to Parliament.[34] Certainly, it would have been odd if Bismarck, having been appointed by William I to resist 'any kind of restriction imposed on the strength of the army' by the Prussian Diet in the 1860s, had proceeded to concede unqualified control of the military budget to the Reichstag in the 1870s. But historians, following Bismarck's left–liberal critics at the time, have frequently exaggerated the effectiveness of the qualifications Bismarck was able to place on the Reichstag's budget-right. It is true that, under Article 63 of the Constitution, the Emperor 'determine[d] the peacetime strength, the structure and distribution of the army'. However, the question of financing what he determined was more complex. Between 1867 and 1874 the issue was put off, under a temporary rule that the army would be equivalent in size to 1 per cent of the Reich population; but Article 62 of the Constitution clearly stated that changes in the military budget would need the agreement of the legislature. The final decision fell far short of the Prussian monarch's ideal of an 'eternal' defence budget: separate seven-year (later five-year) military budgets, removing defence spending from the annual budget, but not from the Reichstag's control. The Reichstag thus could and did amend government finance bills; despite occasional threatening noises, the most that the executive ever did in reply was to call a general election (as in December 1906).[35] In practice, therefore, if the government wished to spend more on defence – or on its civil functions – the Reichstag's approval was needed for both the expenditure and, if it exceeded existing revenues, the means of financing it.

The fact that the Reichstag was the most democratic of imperial Germany's representative assemblies, while the separate states retained various forms of restricted franchise, created a peculiar impasse. A democratic assembly was in a position to influence the level of indirect taxes, to pay for mainly military expenditures; while more exclusive assemblies raised taxes on income and property for mainly civilian purposes. Designed to weaken liberalism on the assumption that 'below the three-thaler [franchise qualification] line nine-tenths of the population are conservative', Bismarck's decision to introduce universal male suffrage for Reichstag elections in fact benefited the parties of political Catholicism and socialism; and these increasingly made their political capital by criticizing Reich finance policy, whether by demanding special treatment for South German peasants and small businessmen,[36] or by criticizing the regressive taxation of working-class consumers.[37] Governments wishing to spend more on defence thus found themselves between the devil of particularist state governments and the deep blue – or rather black and red – sea of the most popular Reichstag parties, the Centre Party and Social Democrats. Bismarck and his successors were ingenious in devising strategies to weaken these 'anti-Reich' parties and strengthen the more 'state-supporting' conservative and National Liberal parties. But the common factor linking the construction of the navy and the acquisition of colonies – supposed 'national acts' which would awaken patriotic feelings and reduce economic discontent – with more direct electoral bribes like tax rebates and social insurance, was that they cost yet more money. Far from strengthening the government's position, the ensuing debates on increased expenditure in fact tended to underline the Centre Party's pivotal position in the Reichstag and lent credibility to the Social Democrats' election slogans, while the revenue-raising options tended to divide rather than unite the 'government' parties. Such were the contradictions of *Sammlungspolitik*.[38]

Austria–Hungary's dualist system suffered from similar problems. In essence, the 1867 settlement between Austria and Hungary created a common foreign and defence policy: indeed, this was about all that was done jointly, as the military budget accounted for around 96 per cent of the total common budget.[39] As a percentage of GNP, total state spending in both Austria and Hungary (i.e. separate and common expenditure together) rose: from around 11 per cent (1895–1902) to 19 per cent (1913) – a steady increase of around 3.2 per cent per annum. However, state spending grew much more rapidly than 'common' spending: between 1868 and 1913 the common budget increased by a factor of 4.3, but the Hungarian budget rose by a factor of 7.9 and the

Austrian by a factor of 10.6. The consequence was that military spending, as the principal item of the common budget, was held down: as we have seen, it was equivalent to just 2.8 per cent of combined GNP in 1913, despite the increased costs of naval construction and the annexation of Bosnia-Hercegovina. The proportion of the Austrian budget spent on defence fell from 24 per cent of state spending (1870) to 16 per cent (1910), whereas spending on railways rose from 4 per cent to 27 per cent. Just 12 per cent of the Hungarian budget went on defence. In May 1914, on the basis of some back-of-envelope calculations, the Austrian Socialist newspaper the *Arbeiter Zeitung* complained pointedly:

We spend half as much on armaments as Germany yet Austria's gross product is only one-sixth of Germany's. In other words, we spend proportionately three times as much on war as Kaiser Wilhelm. Must we play the great power at the cost of poverty and hunger?[40]

However, the reality was that Austria–Hungary was only just managing to play the great power. As Robert Musil put it in *The Man without Qualities*, the reality was that: 'One spent enormous sums on the army; but only just enough to assure one of remaining the second weakest among the great powers.'

TAXES

There were two ways in which this increased expenditure could be met, and each had profound political implications. One way of raising public revenue was, of course, by putting up taxation: the great question was whether this should be indirect taxation (principally in the form of duties on articles of consumption from bread to beer) or direct (taxes on higher incomes or property).

In Britain the break with protectionism had occurred earlier (1846) and proved more enduring than elsewhere. Once again taxes on imported food were rejected by the electorate in 1906, despite the efforts of Chamberlain and others to give tariffs an imperialist rationale. This inevitably put the onus on the rich: the question was what form the direct taxes should take and at what rates they should be levied (flat, differentiated or progressive). Unlike most European states, late nineteenth-century Britain already had a well established income tax –

the Younger Pitt's great innovation to finance the wars against France, which Peel had converted into a peacetime source of revenue in 1842. (The economist Gustav Schmoller was not being facetious when he observed that Germans would be 'jubilant' if they had 'so adaptable a factor of revenue'.) However, by 1892 the income tax had been reduced to just 6½d. in the pound, and the classical liberal purists (like the elderly Gladstone) were still dreaming of its disappearance. To meet the £1.9 million deficit caused mainly by the 1889 Naval Defence Bill, Goschen opted not to increase income tax but to introduce a one per cent duty on all estates above £10,000. Sir William Harcourt then formalized 'death duties' by introducing a proper inheritance tax in 1894.

It was the unexpectedly high cost of the Boer War, however, which led to the biggest pre-war increases in British direct tax. In 1907, for example, Asquith raised the tax on 'unearned' (investment) income to 1s. (12d.) in the pound, compared with 9d. for 'earned' income. Two years later, Lloyd George's 'People's Budget' aimed to raise total revenue by 8 per cent by (among other measures) levying a 'super-tax' (extra income tax) on incomes above £5,000, adding 2d. in the pound to the income tax due on unearned income and introducing a capital gains tax on land.[41] As a consequence of the budgets of 1907 and 1909–10, the share of central government income from direct taxation rose to 39 per cent. By 1913 direct taxation and customs and excise accounted for almost exactly equal shares of total government income, and income tax was bringing in over £40 million pounds a year. Lloyd George's last pre-war budget envisaged yet more increases, notably an extra 2d. in the pound on income tax, a new super-tax on incomes above £3,000, with rates rising more progressively to a top rate of 2s. 8d. in the pound, and death duties of up to 20 per cent on estates valued at more than £1 million.[42] The pre-war Liberals seemed to have devised an ingenious policy which combined both guns (in the form of dreadnoughts) and butter (in the form of more progressive taxation and some social expenditures).

Hobson has argued that, in purely fiscal terms, Britain could have afforded to create a conscript army of between 1 and 2 million men by increasing taxation.[43] Yet this is to overlook the profound political conflicts which Liberal fiscal policy unleashed. As we have already seen, the Liberals had come in pledged to cut arms spending, and could not easily sell increases in the naval estimates to their backbenchers and the radical press. Although progressive taxation was popular in those quarters, Lloyd George's budgets did much to drive richer voters back to the Conservatives: it was not only the Lords who disliked the 'People's Budget'. At the last pre-war general election of December 1910 the Liberals and Tories had won 272 seats apiece, so that the government had to rely on forty-two Labour MPs for its majority. Because the Conservatives won sixteen out of the twenty by-elections which followed, by July 1914 that majority had been reduced to just twelve, increasing the influence of the eighty or so Irish Nationalists.[44] This helps explain why the 1914 budget had to be subject to a government guillotine (with twenty-two Liberal abstentions and one vote against) and the separate Revenue Bill containing the more objectionable measures abandoned altogether. In particular, there was vociferous opposition to Lloyd George's proposal that revenue for income tax increases should be used to make grants to local authorities to compensate them for losses due to changes in local rates.[45] The most that can be said about Britain, then, is that the political conflicts generated by increased armaments expenditure were less bitter than on the continent, and that there is no evidence that a domestic political crisis (of this or any other sort) encouraged the government to opt for war in 1914.[46]

In France, by comparison, taxation remained remarkably regressive in its incidence until the very eve of the war. This partly reflected the revolutionary tradition, which protected the citizen's income and property from state scrutiny, preferring to collect so-called *contributions* on the basis of supposedly 'objective' assessments of the average ability to pay; as well as the principle of equality (of incidence), which ruled out progressive tax rates. The consequence was that the 'four old women' – the land tax, the business tax, the movable property tax and the door and window tax – yielded sums which bore less and less relation to actual incomes and wealth. The introduction of a new tax on securities in 1872 was a rare innovation: for most of the nineteenth century the French bourgeoisie was undertaxed. Pre-war expenditure was therefore financed principally by indirect taxes. On the eve of the war, tariffs (reintroduced in 1872 after just twelve years of free trade) accounted for some 18 per cent of the government tax 'take', consumption taxes (mainly on beverages, salt and tobacco, which the government monopolized) for fully a third. The second major source of income was the various forms of stamp tax paid on minor legal transactions (around a quarter of 1913 tax revenue). Direct taxes brought in just 14 per cent of total ordinary revenue in 1913.[47] Attempts to introduce a modern income tax were repeatedly defeated in the face of parliamentary opposition in 1896, in 1907 and again in 1911. It was only on the very eve of war that this opposition was overcome. In March 1914 the old revenue taxes were reformed; and in July 1914 a general comprehensive income tax was finally introduced on incomes over 7,000 francs a year. Although it had a standard 2 per cent rate, this tax was in fact progressive. In addition, five partial income taxes (*impôts cédulaires sur les revenus*) were introduced, similar in effect to the schedules of the British system (i.e. with differentiated incidence for different types of income).[48] The acceptance of this reform owed as much to Poincaré's introduction of proportional representation and the consequent weakening of the Radical Party as to the deteriorating international situation. The outbreak of war, however, meant that this tax was not imposed until January 1916.

The Russian system was even more heavily reliant on revenues from indirect taxation: only a small share of revenue (around 7 per cent between 1900 and 1913) came from direct tax. Business opposition in the Duma meant that there was no income tax. Government was therefore financed overwhelmingly from the revenues of state enterprises (net receipts from the railway network were around 270 million roubles in 1913) and from taxes on the consumption of basic essentials, such as kerosene, matches, sugar and vodka. The most important of these consumption taxes was without doubt the excise levied on vodka sales, on which the state had established a monopoly in the late 1890s. Net revenue from the vodka monopoly was roughly two and a half times higher than that from the state railways; and gross revenue from it (900 million roubles in 1913) accounted for more than a quarter of all state revenue. As the economic historian Alexander Gerschenkron rightly said, the total tax burden rose from 12.4 per cent of per capita national income in 1860 to 16.9 per cent in 1913. But he was wrong to think that this had the effect of reducing living standards; witness the rising revenue from taxes on consumption.[49]

In Germany matters were once again complicated by the federal system. The federal states enjoyed an effective monopoly on direct taxation; and attempts by Bismarck to shift the balance in favour of the Reich were constantly frustrated.[50] Indeed, in some years there were net transfers from the Reich to the states – averaging 350 million marks per annum in the 1890s. Thus, while the states (and the local communes) were able to modernize their fiscal systems by introducing income taxes,[51] the Reich in the 1890s remained almost entirely dependent (for 90 per cent of its revenue) on the old taxes on consumption and imports. As Bülow put it, echoing Bismarck, it remained 'a poor traveller, stubbornly knocking on the doors of the individual states, a wholly unwelcome guest in search of subsistence'.[52] The Reich was therefore mainly restricted to financing itself (and hence the German army and navy) from indirect taxes. The tendency was therefore for tariffs to rise as military spending rose; but popular dissatisfaction with the combination of 'dear bread' and 'militarism' was so successfully exploited by the Social Democrats that the government was soon forced to contemplate introducing property taxes at the Reich level. Contrary to the assumptions of many on the German Right, spending more on the army and navy tended to help the SPD which became, in effect, the party of those hit by regressive taxation.[53] On the Right, by contrast, economic interests cut across party lines, and coalitions based on them tended to vary from issue to issue – so that, for example, many of those business groups (such as the League of Industrialists) which favoured a direct tax in 1912 denounced the finished product as excessively progressive in 1913. More importantly, this was also a debate about constitutional ideas – between particularists and advocates of a more centralized Reich; and between defenders of royal prerogatives and proponents of increased parliamentary power. In this debate, economic interests were often exaggerated to reinforce constitutional points. Finally, it was a debate in which fundamental historical positions of the various parties – the Centre's anti-Prussianism, the SPD's anti-militarism, the National Liberals' anti-socialism and the Conservatives' pro-governmentalism – were all, almost simultaneously, compromised.

The story of German domestic politics before 1912 was therefore, in large part, a story of budgetary stalemate: the states resisting the Reich's bids for a share of direct tax revenue, the Treasury Office struggling in vain to check the rival spending departments, the government increasingly forced to debate finance with the Reichstag, and the Reichstag parties themselves at loggerheads on tax questions. The Social Democrats' resounding election victory in 1912 and the subsequent introduction of two new direct taxes to finance the 1913 Army Bill have often been interpreted by historians as the culmination of this deadlock; though opinions vary as to whether the Reich was at a 'turning point', down a 'blind alley', or in a 'latent crisis'.[54] Certainly, the atmosphere was changed by the 1912 election – revealingly described by one SPD deputy as 'a great demonstration by the people against the extension of indirect taxes.'[55] In a remarkable realignment, the National Liberals joined the Centre, the left-liberal Progressive Party and the SPD in calling for the creation of a 'general property tax' at the Reich level by April 1913 (the so-called 'Bassermann–Erzberger' resolution, named after the National Liberal and Centre Party leaders). Indeed, the National Liberals went so far as to support an SPD resolution stating that the new tax should be set annually, as well as a Progressive resolution restoring the sugar tax reduction and calling for the passage of the 1909 inheritance tax extension bill.[56] A second significant change to emerge was the new willingness of the Centre Party and the Social Democrats to support increased military spending. In the Centre's case, this was reflected in Erzberger's transformation from opponent of colonial expenditure to supporter of naval expenditure; in the case of the Social Democrats it found expression in the carefully phrased statement of 1912 that: 'We Social Democrats, as before, will not vote a single man or a single penny for militarism. But if . . . we can see to it that an indirect tax can be replaced by a direct one, then we are willing to vote for such a direct tax.' The events of 1913 can also be seen as the culmination of the battle to reduce the Reich's financial inferiority to the states. Certainly, Bethmann had no doubt that the political stakes had been raised high by the Bassermann–Erzberger resolution. The choice for the states was between accepting the Reich capital gains tax (Vermögenszuwachssteuer) now proposed by the government, or:

to cause the politics of the Reich – and thus also the federal states – to take a turn which would deepen irreparably the rift between the bourgeois parties, and could only come to a positive conclusion, if a degree of influence over the government and over its policy were conceded to the radical elements – something which would break with the political traditions of the Reich and all the individual states.

To this the Prussian Finance Minister – after consultations with the Conservative leaders – could retort that ending the states' monopoly on direct taxes would represent 'a disastrous step on the way to parliamentary government': the crucial thing was that 'Prussia should remain Prussia'. Still more adamant was the Saxon monarch Frederick Augustus, who saw the capital gains tax as the tool of 'unitarism'. When the measure was finally passed against the Saxon vote on the Bundesrat, and with National Liberal and Social Democrat votes in the Reichstag, reactions were stronger still. According to the Conservative Count Westarp, the Reich was now on course to become 'a democratically governed unitary state'. The opposition parties proclaimed 'the day of Philippi' and (with heavy irony) 'the end of the world'.[57]

It used to be argued that it was this domestic political crisis which convinced the ruling élites of the Reich of the need for war: 'flight forwards', to escape from the rising tide of Social Democracy.[58] As we have seen, this was not a factor in Bethmann's calculations. However, that is not to say that the financial wrangles of 1908–14 have no significance for the origins of the war. On closer inspection, their true importance may lie precisely in their financial insignificance; for in this respect little of substance had been achieved. The army bill had envisaged one-off costs of 996 million marks and an average annual increment of 194 million marks, with the additional burden on the 1913 budget amounting to 512 million marks. The original government bill envisaged financing this with new stamp taxes on company charters and insurance certificates (rising from 22 to 64 million marks per annum); the extension of the state's right of mortmain (5–15 million marks per annum); a one-off defence contribution – a levy of 0.5 per cent on all property worth more than 10,000 marks and 2 per cent of all incomes above 50,000 marks – to be raised in three tranches (one of 374 million marks, plus two of 324.5 million marks); and a capital gains tax levied progressively in ten bands rising from 0.6 per cent on gains of between 25,000 and 50,000 to 1.5 per cent on gains of more than a million marks (projected revenue: 82 million marks per annum). After all was said and done, this was far from being a revolution in Reich finances.[59] The debate on the Budget Committee was mainly concerned with the differentiated treatment of specific economic groups, not with absolute levels of revenue and expenditure. Moreover, the outcome was politically fudged. Rather than representing a final victory for a progressive coalition against the forces of reaction, the passage of the defence and finance bills principally revealed the extent of division within the parties.[60] If anything, the very minor political breakthrough represented by the passage of a direct Reich tax (or rather three direct Reich taxes, given that the defence contribution could in theory be repeated) seemed likely to be followed by a reaction as conservative elements regrouped – though the significance of such a regrouping has sometimes been exaggerated by historians.[61] Kehr was thus in error when he suggested that Reich revenues were growing rapidly in 1912–13 and that, if it had been put to them, the 'militarized and feudalized' members of the Reichstag would have passed Ludendorff's Great Memorandum programme.[62] It is highly doubtful that the government could have got a parliamentary majority for the higher taxes it would have required.

Austria–Hungary had similar problems to the Reich on the revenue side. The common (mainly defence) budget was financed from the joint revenues from customs and additional contributions from the separate kingdoms; while other governmental functions were financed either by the separate kingdoms, or by their subordinate states and communes. It is usually said that the Hungarians did not pay a fair share of the common expenses. This is only true to a limited degree. To begin with, the Austrian *Länder* and *Königreiche* paid around 70 per cent, while Hungarian *Länder* paid 30 per cent; but under a new agreement reached in 1907, the Austrian share fell to 63.6 per cent and the Hungarian rose to 36.4 per cent. This was not so far out of line with the two halves' relative populations (Hungary accounted for around 40 per cent of the total Austro-Hungarian population). However, the contemporary perception was that Austria was over-burdened. According to one calculation, around 14.6 per cent of the Austrian state budget went to the common treasury in 1900, but only 9.5 per cent of the Hungarian. A far more important point was the reliance of both halves, separately and together, on indirect taxation. The principal source of common revenue was customs duties, which accounted for 25 per cent of the total common income in 1913. For Austria–Hungary overall only 13 per cent of total public revenues came from direct taxation.

All continental countries, in other words, suffered from the lack of a modern income tax, and therefore had to rely on essentially regressive taxes to finance their armaments and other expenditures. In Germany and Austria–Hungary, however, the political system created more numerous obstacles to improving the system, particularly because of the tensions between central and regional government within federal systems.

DEBTS

The other way of paying for the rising costs of domestic and foreign policy was, of course, by borrowing. As Table 14 shows, this was an option favoured in some countries more than in others. Both Germany and Russia borrowed heavily in the period after 1887; however, when adjustment is made for the appreciation of the rouble in sterling terms after Russian entry into the gold standard, the debt burden in the Russian case rose by just two-thirds between 1890 and 1913 while the German debt more than doubled. In absolute terms France borrowed a lot too, though from a starting point of higher indebtedness than Germany (hence the lower percentage increase). Britain was unusual among the great powers in reducing the level of her national debt between 1887 and 1913. This achievement is all the more impressive when one remembers that the cost of the Boer War drove up government borrowing – by £132 million in total – in the years between 1900 and 1903.

Once again, these were not unsustainable burdens at a time of unprecedented economic growth. Indeed, in all four cases total debt tended to fall in relation to net national product, as Table 15 shows.

Table 14 National debts in millions of national currencies (and £), 1887–1913

	France (francs)	Britain (pounds)	Germany (marks)	Russia (roubles)
1887	23,723 (£941)	655	8,566 (£419)	4,418 (£395)
1913	32,976 (£1,308)	625	21,679 (£1,061)	8,858 (£937)
percentage increase*	39	−5	153	137

Notes: Germany = Reich plus federal states. *Increase in sterling terms.
Sources: Schremmer, 'Public Finance', p. 398; Mitchell and Deane, *British Historical Statistics*, pp. 402f; Hoffmann *et al.*, *Das Wachstum der deutschen Wirtschaft*, pp. 789f; Apostol, Bernatzky and Michelson, *Russian Public Finances*, pp. 234, 239.

Table 15 National debts as a percentage of net national product, 1887–1913

	France	Britain	Germany	Russia
1887	119.3	55.3	50.0	65.0
1913	86.5	27.6	44.4	47.3

Note: Germany = Reich plus federal states.
Sources: as Table 14 and Hobson, 'Wary Titan', pp. 505f.

The British government had a system of public borrowing with an unrivalled history of success stretching back into the eighteenth century. Unlike all the major continental countries, Britain had come through the wars which culminated at Waterloo without defaulting on its obligations to bondholders or defrauding them by inflation (that was the significance of the decision to return to the gold standard taken in 1819). For most of the century (until 1873, in fact) the British national debt had therefore been significantly higher than that of the continental powers. It amounted to more than ten times total public tax revenue; while debt charges accounted for around 50 per cent of gross expenditure from 1818 until 1855.[63] This made British politicians extremely wary of new borrowing: when it happened, as during the Boer War, they felt queasy. As the Treasury mandarin Edward Hamilton told Asquith in 1907: '[T]he state cannot raise an indefinite amount of money. We all thought so during the Boer War, but we now know that we have damaged our credit very materially by the amount we borrowed during that war.'[64]

The reality was, however, that until that point the market for 'consols' (the gilt-edged securities of the nineteenth century) had scarcely been stretched since the 1820s. So successful had Victorian politicians been in limiting public borrowing that the total nominal amount of debt had actually fallen from around £800 million in 1815 to just over £600 million a hundred years later, an almost unique achievement in nineteenth-century fiscal history. As a proportion of national income, Britain's public debt on the eve of the First World War was at a historic low: just 28 per cent, far less than the equivalent figures for the other great powers. Total debt was just over three times total revenue and debt charges accounted for a mere 10 per cent of total expenditure. In addition, Britain had the biggest and most sophisticated money market in the world, managed by the Bank of England and an informal élite of private and joint-stock banks, so that short-term borrowing was also relatively straightforward.

By modern standards France had a singularly high level of public debt, equivalent to around 86 per cent of national income in 1913, having increased by nearly 40 per cent since 1887. This was also the highest level of all the great powers, and consequently debt service accounted for the highest proportion of central government spending.[65] This reflected the tendency of the French state (regardless of political complexion) to run budget deficits; the budget was balanced in only a handful of years in the twentieth century, so that debt mounted up inexorably from the relatively low level of 1815. A big public debt also suited the appetite of French savers, who formed an attachment to *rentes perpétuelles* (the benchmark French government bond which, as its name suggests, was irredeemable) even stronger than that of the proverbial British widows and orphans to consols. Tax breaks encouraged the habit of lending long to the government in return for low but dependable interest. It is not by chance that economists still refer to those who live from their investments as *rentiers*: the species was native to nineteenth-century France.

Russia's total public debt also increased sharply in nominal terms in the second half of the nineteenth century: it doubled between 1886 and 1913 from 4.4 billion roubles to 8.8 billion. However – contrary to the argument advanced by Kahan that high levels of state borrowing to finance heavy industrial expansion lead to 'crowding out' of private sector investment – this did not constitute a crippling burden.[66] So rapid was Russian economic growth that the Russian debt burden tended to fall from around 65 per cent of national income to just 47 per cent on the eve of the war. Moreover, the ratio of total debt to tax revenue was lower in Russia (2.6:1) than in either France (6.5:1) or Britain (3.3:1). Debt service accounted for around 13 per cent of central government spending between 1900 and 1913, slightly less than in Britain.[67] There is no real evidence of crowding out: the percentage of total Russian capital market issues accounted for by government bonds fell from 88 per cent in 1893 to 78 per cent in 1914. In any case, a very substantial proportion of the state debt was funded by foreigners who would not have been prepared to invest in private Russian companies.[68]

In Germany, it was an established principle of *Finanzwissenschaft* that not only extraordinary expenditure like the costs of war but also 'productive' expenditures like investment in state enterprises should be financed by borrowing rather than out of current revenues. The belief that the peacetime construction of a German navy would 'pay interest' justified financing the Tirpitz programme in this way.[69] As naval expenditure leapt from 86 million marks per annum in the five-year period 1891–5 to 228 million marks in 1901–5, the Reich debt therefore rose too, from 1.1 billion to 2.3 billion marks.[70] Between 1901 and 1907 an average of around 15 per cent of total (ordinary and extraordinary) Reich revenues came from borrowing; in 1905 over a fifth of revenue came from this source.[71] The cost of debt service grew proportionately as a share of total Reich expenditures, prompting political complaints about the 'interest-serfdom of the masses for the sake of the state's creditors'.[72] Moreover, persistent deficits at the Reich level led to an increase in short-term borrowing as a percentage of total indebtedness from 4 to 9 per cent.

The German position was complicated because Reich borrowing coincided with an enormous increase in borrowing by the other tiers of government, the states and communes. In effect, the three tiers were in competition with one another on the capital market. In 1890 the total Reich debt stood at 1.3 billion marks, only slightly more than that of the communes (1.0 billion). The combined debt of the states was 9.2 billion marks – around two-thirds accounted for by Prussia. Here there may have been a measure of crowding out. Between 1896 and 1913, the volume of public sector bond issues rose 166 per cent, compared with just 26 per cent for private sector issues; and after 1901 public sector bond issues accounted for, on average, between 45 and 50 per cent of the nominal value of all stock market issues.[73] By 1913 the total public sector debt had grown to 32.8 billion marks, of which slightly more than half was state debt, compared with 16 per cent issued by the Reich and the remainder by the communes.[74] Unlike Britain and France, Germany required foreign assistance to finance its public sector borrowing requirement. Of the total public debt in 1913, almost 20 per cent was held by foreign investors.

Contemporaries, as we shall see, were perturbed by this. Yet it is important to put the German debt burden in perspective. The total public debt on the eve of the war was equivalent to around 60 per cent of gross national product. The rising burden of debt service accounted for 11 per cent of total public spending in 1913. If one compares the central government debts of the three Entente powers with the combined

Reich and state debts (Table 15), the latter was in fact lower than that of Russia and France.

In Austria–Hungary too there were fears of impending fiscal disaster. As Holstein reported to Berlin in the late 1880s, 'notwithstanding all the new taxes the balancing of the budget is known to be a *pium desiderium*. Meanwhile they continue to borrow merrily . . .'[75] The economist E. Böhm-Bawerk insisted that the dual monarchy was 'living beyond its means'. Needless to say, the Austrians grumbled that the Hungarians were not paying their way: their contribution to the servicing of the common debt was fixed at a flat rate of 2.9 million gulden per annum, leaving the western half of the dual monarchy to take the strain of any new borrowing. Yet once again contemporary anxieties were overdone. In fact, the total public debt was under 40 per cent of national income in 1913. Compared with the period before 1867, this was extraordinary fiscal continence. Debt service accounted for just 14 per cent of Austrian spending in 1907, as against around 33 per cent in the 1850s and 1860s.[76]

In short, the effects of the arms race on public borrowing were relatively trivial: in real terms debt burdens actually fell despite the arms race. Nevertheless, contemporaries were disturbed by the absolute increase in government borrowing. One important reason for this was that it seemed to be causing an increase in the *cost* of government borrowing, as measured by the price of (or yield on) government bonds.

In the course of the nineteenth century the international bond market had evolved into a singularly sensitive barometer of capitalist economic and political sentiment. By the early 1900s it had an immense turnover of funds for investment, largely the savings of the western world's propertied élites, and, given their still disproportionate political influence at this time, its fluctuations deserve a great deal more attention than historians have generally paid them. It was a relatively efficient market, in that the number of individuals and institutions buying and selling was by 1914 quite large, and transaction costs were relatively low. Moreover, thanks to the breakthroughs in international communications – the telegraph in particular – it was a market which responded swiftly to political news. The decline in bond prices – or rise in yields – which manifested itself after around 1890 (Table 16) was widely seen as evidence of fiscal 'over-stretch'.

The principal cause of this decline was in fact the acceleration of

Table 16   Major European bond prices, c. 1896–1914

	Peak price	Date	Trough price	Date	Percentage change
British 2.75 per cent consols*	113.50	July 1896	78.96	Dec. 1913	−30.4
French 3 per cent rentes	105.00	Aug. 1897	80.00	July 1914	−23.8
Russian 4 per cents	105.00	Aug. 1898	71.50	Aug. 1906	−31.9
German Imperial 3 per cents	99.38	Sept. 1896	73.00	July 1913	−26.5

Note: *For 1913, 2.5 per cent price recalculated on a 2.75 per cent coupon.
Source: *Economist* (weekly closing prices).

inflation, a monetary phenomenon caused by the increase in gold production and, more importantly, the rapid development of banking intermediation, which was increasing the use of paper money and cashless transaction methods (especially inter-bank clearing). Contemporaries, however, interpreted rising bond yields as a form of market protest against lax fiscal policies. This was only really true in so far as public sector bond issues were tending to push up the cost of borrowing across the board by competing with private sector claims on the capital market: that was certainly the case in Germany. Nevertheless, the accusation of fiscal incontinence was repeatedly levelled at most governments – even the British – by critics on both the Left and Right. Table 17 shows that rising yields were a universal phenomenon; of more interest, however, is the fact that there were pronounced differences or 'gaps' between the yields on the various countries' bonds. These yield gaps genuinely did express market assessments not just of fiscal policy but more generally of political stability and foreign policy, given the

Table 17   Bond yields of the major powers, 1911–1914

	British consols	French rentes	German 3 per cents	Russian 4 per cents	German– British yield gap	Russian– British yield gap
Mar 1911	3.08	3.13	3.56	4.21	0.48	1.13
July 1914	3.34	3.81	4.06	4.66	0.72	1.32
Average	3.29	3.36	3.84	4.36	0.55	1.07

Source: *Economist* (average monthly London prices).

traditionally close correlations between the perils of revolution, war and insolvency. Perhaps predictably, given the experience of 1904–5 and her more general problems of economic and political 'backwardness', Russia was regarded as the biggest credit risk among the great powers. More surprising is the wide differential between German yields and those for British and French bonds, which were remarkably similar. This cannot be explained in terms of the greater demands by the German private sector on the Berlin capital market, as these are *London* prices (and in any case investors were generally choosing between different governments' bonds, not between industrial securities or bonds). Plainly, investors believed that Wilhelmine Germany was financially less strong than its Western rivals.

The weekly and monthly bond prices published in financial journals like the *Economist* allow us to follow the fluctuations more closely. For historic reasons, the nominal interest on the bonds issued by the great powers varied: British consols paid 3 per cent for most of the nineteenth century, but this was reduced to 2.75 per cent in 1888 and 2.5 per cent in 1903. By the 1890s German and French bonds paid 3 per cent, but Russian bonds paid 4 per cent, and new issues after the 1905 Revolution paid 5 per cent. Contemporary investors were generally more interested in the yield of bonds, of course, and bid prices up and down, primarily in accordance with their expectations of the respective states' solvency. For ease of comparison, I have chosen to recalculate, using yield ratios, the bond prices of the principal powers as if they were all paying interest at 3 per cent. Figure 6 shows the average monthly price of British consols between 1900 and 1914 recalculated in this way; Figure 7 shows the weekly closing price of French, German and Russian bonds for the same period, with the Russian price similarly recalculated.

Once again, it will be noted that German bonds were priced significantly lower – on average roughly 10 per cent lower – than British and French bonds. Although technical differences may have accounted for some of this, more than anything else the bond price gap reflected the perceived riskiness of German bonds compared with British. The gap between German and Russian bond prices is also illuminating: not surprisingly, this widened considerably during the Russo-Japanese war and the subsequent revolution, but by 1910 the gap had narrowed to rather less than that between French and German paper. Nor was it only Britain and France which were regarded as a better credit risk than Germany. At one point shortly after Bülow's fall, the price of 4 per cent

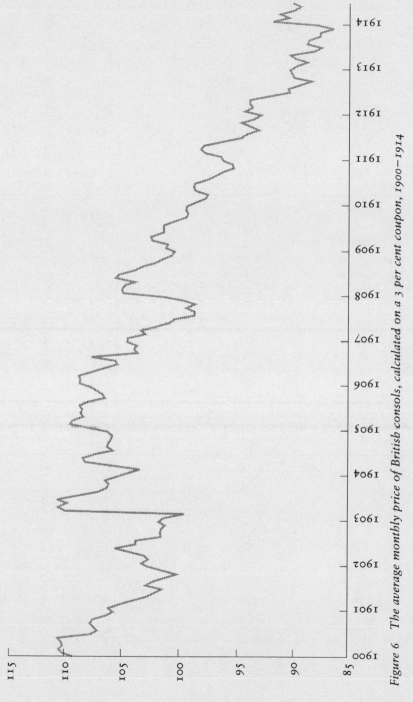

Figure 6   *The average monthly price of British consols, calculated on a 3 per cent coupon, 1900–1914*

Source: *Accounts and Papers of the House of Commons*, vols. li, xxi.

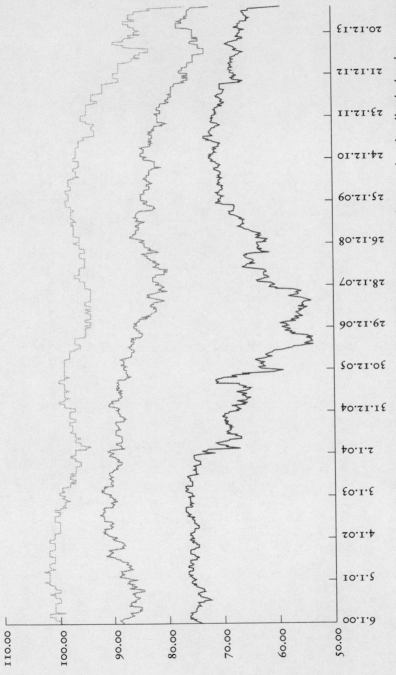

Figure 7 The weekly closing price of French (top), German (middle) and Russian (bottom) bonds, all calculated on a 3 per cent coupon, 1900–1914

Source: *Economist.*

Reich bonds actually fell below that of 3.5 per cent Italian bonds.[77]

This did not go unnoticed by contemporaries. When issues of Reich and Prussian bonds totalling 1.28 billion marks were poorly received on the bourse in 1909–10, many observers concluded with the State Secretary at the Treasury, Adolf Wermuth, that Germany's 'financial armament' did not match its 'military armament'.[78] The problem of rising German yields especially worried international bankers like Max Warburg.[79] In 1903, at the instigation of Bülow, he tried to raise the subject with the Kaiser after a dinner, only to be brushed aside by the latter's confident assurance that 'the Russians will go bust first'.[80] In 1912 Warburg wrote a paper for the General German Bankers' Congress entitled 'Suitable and Unsuitable Ways to Lift the Price of State Bonds';[81] and the following year the economist Otto Schwartz countered the Kaiser's earlier argument by asserting that Germany's finances were now weaker than Russia's.[82] It was noticed abroad too: the fact that 'German Three per Cents. [stood] at 82' while 'Belgian [stood] at 96' provided Angell with one of his better arguments against the economic rationality of militarism.[83] By the same token, the high yield of the new German loan issued in 1908 led some City commentators to suspect it of being a 'war loan'.[84]

FROM FISCAL IMPASSE TO STRATEGIC DESPAIR

The perception of relative German and Austro-Hungarian financial weakness was to have profound historical consequences because of its implications for future military expenditure. As we have seen, because of the influence of Prussian conservatives in the War Ministry, there were constraints on how rapidly the German army could expand. But even if Ludendorff had been given a free hand to implement near-universal military service, it is not clear that it would have been affordable. For the German defence budget was also constrained: by resistance within the federal system to increased fiscal centralization, by resistance within the Reichstag to increased taxation and by the impossibility of borrowing without widening the bond yield gap between Germany and her western rivals. Unable to reduce the large shares of the states and local government in total revenue; unable to raise as much in direct taxation as Britain or as much in indirect taxation as Russia; and unable to borrow as cheaply as Britain and France, the Reich seemed doomed to lose the financial arms race.

Contemporaries frequently acknowledged the problem. 'What use is an army ready for action, a navy prepared for war, if we are let down by our finances?' asked the leading authority on the Reich's financial system, Wilhelm Gerloff;[85] while Bülow spoke of the need 'to convince the German people that morally and *materially* the [financial] reform is a matter of *life and death*'.[86] The Army League journal *Die Wehr* agreed: 'If one wants to live peacefully, one must also carry burdens, pay taxes: without that it simply cannot be done.'[87] This was really the bottom line of Bernhardi's book, *Germany and the Next War*, which on close inspection turns out to be a call for financial reform timed to influence the political debates of 1912:

It would . . . be a fatal and foolish act of political weakness to disregard the military and strategic standpoint and to make the bulk of the preparations for war dependent on the financial means momentarily available. 'No expenditure without security,' runs the formula in which this policy clothes itself. It is justified only when the security is fixed by the expenditure. In a great civilized state it is the duties which must be fulfilled . . . that determine the expenditure, and the great Finance Minister is not the man who balances the national accounts by sparing the national forces, while renouncing the politically indispensable outlay . . .[88]

But it was not just military men who argued this way. The President of the Reichsbank, Havenstein, was no less explicit about the financial basis of deterrence: 'We will only be able to maintain peace', he declared on 18 June 1914, 'if we are financially as well as militarily strong.' That needs to be read not as an indication of war-readiness, but just the opposite: Havenstein's view was that Germany was not financially strong.[89]

Yet political obstacles seemed insurmountable. 'We have the people and the money,' commented the Army League leader Keim in frustration: 'We are lacking only in determination to place both at the service of the Fatherland.'[90] The same problem could be seen from a Social Democrat perspective: 'Some demand more ships, others clamour for more soldiers,' commented Daniel Stücklein. 'If only other organisations could be founded whose goals would be to create the money necessary for these demands.'[91] The government's dilemma was simple: 'The financial burdens at present [are] too enormous for the economy to bear', wrote a Prussian War Ministry official in 1913, 'and any [further] agitation would add grist to the mill of the Social Democrats.'[92] This was perhaps what Warburg had in mind when he warned in November 1908 that 'if we carry on our fiscal policy in the same way . . . [then] one fine day we will find that we can only make good the damage with the greatest possible sacrifice – if we can make it good at all.'[93] The following year, his friend Albert Ballin expressed the fear that 'a new financial reform' could lead to 'a very serious turn' in domestic politics.[94] Ironically, however, the real cause of the tax gridlock was the Prussian Conservative Party: an irony embodied by the figure of Ottomar Baron von der Osten-Sacken und vom Rhein, who on the one hand favoured universal military service; but on the other opposed the embourgeoisement of the officer corps and the taxation of the great East Elbian estates.[95]

Fiscal impasse led to strategic despair. In 1912 the *Ostdeutsche Buchdrückerei und Verlagsanstalt* published a leaflet with the revealing title: 'Is Germany Prevented by its Financial Situation from Fully Utilizing its Entire National Strength in its Army?'[96] The answer was yes. 'We just cannot afford a race in dreadnoughts against the much wealthier British,' lamented Ballin.[97] By 1909 the Kaiser too accepted that 'under the inexorable constraints of the tightness of funds . . . justified demands of the "Front" had to be left unfulfilled'.[98] Even Moltke saw the problem, commenting in December 1912: 'Our enemies are arming more vigorously than we, because we are strapped for cash.'[99] That same month, the Kaiser had declared: 'The German people [are] prepared to make any sacrifice . . . [The] people understand, that unsuccessful war is much dearer than this or that tax.' He did not doubt 'the willingness of the population to grant each and every thing [that was asked] for military purposes'.[100] It is the fundamental paradox of the Wilhelmine period that, despite all the outward signs that Germany's was a militaristic culture, he was wrong.

German financial weakness was no secret. Although the popular press in England periodically fretted about the rise of German industrial and commercial power before 1914, informed contemporaries were well aware that the Reich's *financial* power was less impressive. In November 1909 Churchill (then president of the Board of Trade) argued that 'the increasing difficulties of getting money' were 'becoming terribly effective' as 'checks upon German naval expansion'. His memorandum is such an accurate assessment of the German domestic predicament that it deserves to be quoted at length:

The overflowing expenditure of the German Empire strains and threatens every dyke by which the social and political unity of Germany is maintained. The high customs duties have been largely rendered inelastic through commercial treaties . . . The heavy duties upon food-stuffs, from which the main proportion of the customs revenue is raised, have produced a deep cleavage between the agrarians and the industrial[ist]s, and the latter deem themselves quite uncompensated for the high price of food-stuffs by the most elaborate devices of protection for manufacturers. The splendid possession of the State railways is under pressure, being constantly degraded to a mere instrument of taxation. The field of direct taxation is already largely occupied by the State and local systems. The prospective inroad by the universal suffrage Parliament of the Empire upon this depleted field unites the propertied classes, whether Imperialists or State-right men, in a common apprehension, with which the governing authorities are not unsympathetic. On the other hand, the new or increased taxation on every form of popular indulgence powerfully strengthens the parties of the Left, who are themselves the opponents of expenditure on armaments and much else besides.

Meanwhile the German Imperial debt has more than doubled in the last thirteen years of unbroken peace . . . The effect of recurrent borrowings to meet ordinary annual expenditure has checked the beneficial process of foreign investment and dissipated the illusion . . . that Berlin might supplant London as the lending centre of the world. The credit of the German Empire has fallen to the level of that of Italy . . .

These circumstances force the conclusion that a period of severe internal strain approaches in Germany.[101]

Nor was Churchill alone in discerning Germany's financial weakness. As early as April 1908 Grey himself had 'pointed out that that finance might in the course of the next few years prove a very serious difficulty to Germany and exercise a restraining influence on her'. The German ambassador in London, Count Metternich, actually drew Grey's attention to domestic 'resistance' to naval expenditure the following year.[102] Goschen, his British counterpart in Berlin, commented on public 'murmurs' against naval expenditure in 1911 and was sceptical when the Kaiser sought to refute 'the general idea abroad that Germany had no money'.[103] At the time of the 1913 Army Bill, he noted that 'each class would . . . be glad to see the financial burden thrust onto shoulders other than its own'.[104] In March 1914 Nicolson went so far as to predict that 'unless Germany is prepared to make still further financial sacrifices for military purposes, the days of her hegemony in Europe will be numbered'.[105]

Similar views were expressed by those who knew Germany well in the City of London. Lord Rothschild was quick to discern the limits of German power. '[T]he German Government is very hard up,' Rothschild noted in April 1906, as yet another Reich loan was put on the market.[106] Nor did he overlook the difficulties experienced by the Reichsbank during the international financial crisis of 1907, which were in many ways more serious than anything experienced in London and were exacerbated by short-term public sector borrowing.[107] Rothschild was especially struck by the German need to sell bonds on foreign capital markets, an expedient to which neither Britain nor France had to resort in peacetime.[108] The impression of an over-stretched Reich was further confirmed by the large Prussian bond issue in April 1908 and by the Reich budget deficit.[109] Small wonder the Rothschilds, like the Warburgs in Hamburg, expected the German government to seek some sort of agreement limiting naval construction.[110] The second Moroccan crisis in 1911 underlined the vulnerability of the Berlin market to withdrawals of foreign capital.[111] To the bankers, then, Germany seemed weak, not strong.

The American diplomat John Leishman was another foreign observer who well understood the significance of the 1913 Army Bill:

Although quite of the opinion that Germany's action was not prompted by any hidden intentions of making war on any nation, as the feeling prevails in the very highest quarters that even a successful war would put Germany back fifty years in its commercial development, the Emperor's action is certain to raise suspicious doubts in the minds of the other powers, and as the increase in the German force is sure to be followed by a relative increase in both the French and Russian armies, it is difficult to comprehend how the German government can figure on gaining an advantage at all commensurate with the enormously increased burdens, and still more difficult to understand how the already over-taxed population could so meekly submit to such a heavily increased burden.

Although Germany, on account of the position in which she finds herself, is naturally compelled to maintain a certain military strength, being surrounded on all sides by military powers, this defence or so-called insurance cannot be carried too far without great risk of serious economic disturbances . . .

However, Leishman feared that 'a powerful military party' might 'plung[e] a country into a war despite the pacific efforts of the government, and a less capable and far-seeing monarch than the present German Emperor, might, upon several occasions, have found himself unable to resist the pressure of the war party . . .'[112] In February 1914 the American ambassador Walter Page warned the State Department: 'Some government (probably Germany) will see bankruptcy staring it in the face and the easiest way out will seem a great war. Bankruptcy before a war would be ignominious; after a war it could be charged to "Glory".' His eye was caught at around this time by an article in the 'Berlin Post . . . urging an immediate war, on the ground that Germany is in a more favourable position to-day than she will be shortly'.[113]

And there was the rub. The danger – in Churchill's words – was that the German government, rather than try to 'soothe the internal situation', might 'find an escape from it in external adventure'. The Rothschilds too saw that financial constraints might positively encourage the German government to pursue an aggressive foreign policy, even at the risk of 'incur[ring] fresh military and naval expenditure on a grand scale'.[114] The Social Democrat leader August Bebel made essentially the same point in a memorable Reichstag speech in December 1911:

There will be armaments and rearmaments on all sides until one day: Rather end in horror than horror without end . . . They might also say: Listen, if we wait longer, we are the weaker side instead of the stronger . . . The twilight of the gods of the bourgeois world is in prospect.[115]

This analysis was all too shrewd. Not for nothing did Moltke argue in March 1913 that 'things must be so built up that war will be seen as a deliverance from the great armaments, the financial burdens, the political tensions'.[116]

Of course, it is no longer fashionable to speak of the domestic origins of the First World War.[117] Nevertheless, it does seem legitimate to continue speaking of the war's domestic origins (if not of the *primacy* of domestic politics) in another sense: for the domestically determined financial constraint on Germany's military capability was a – perhaps *the* – crucial factor in the calculations of the German General Staff in 1914.

LUDENDORFF'S COUNTER-FACTUAL

Could Germany have been less 'tight' with money? Two calculations suggest that, but for the political log-jam, it would have been economically possible. The 1913 Army Bill envisaged increasing the army by 117,000 men, at a cost of 1.9 billion marks over five years: with the additional burden on the 1913 budget amounting to 512 million marks. On the basis of proportionality, the Ludendorff maximum plan outlined in the Great Memorandum for an increment of 300,000 men would have cost 4.9 billion marks over five years, which, for the year 1913–14, would have represented an additional 864 million marks of military spending. This would have increased the German defence budget by around 33 per cent above the Russian in absolute terms; but in relative terms – whether as a percentage of GNP (which would have risen to 5.1 per cent) or in relation to total public expenditures – German spending would not have been significantly greater than that of other powers.

It is also possible to envisage ways in which this could have been financed. If the increase had been paid for solely by borrowing, the German debt would still have been less as a fraction of GNP than the French and Russian, and debt service less as a fraction of non-local expenditure than the French and British. Alternatively, if the *Wehrbeitrag* had been increased from 996 million marks to 2,554 million marks, and the annual yield of the capital gains tax from 100 million marks to 469 million marks – or if additional direct taxes had been devised – the increase could have been financed exclusively from direct taxation. This would merely have brought German direct tax levels into line with British as a share of GNP (3.3 per cent) and still left them lower as a percentage of public spending. In other words, although politically impossible, the increased military expenditures implied by Ludendorff's Great Memorandum were within the range of the economically possible as defined by the budgets of Germany's rivals. A further point may be added, namely that a more expansive monetary policy by the German Reichsbank could have eased the strain of financing increased arms spending in the short run. The Reichsbank was hoarding gold at a time of economic downturn; it could easily have purchased a substantial issue of treasury bills without jeopardizing its minimum reserve ratio.[118]

Such counter-factual hypotheses are not universally regarded as legitimate by historians. However, the same point can be made by considering what did in fact happen after July 1914. Once war had broken out, as we shall see, both the fiscal and the monetary constraints on defence spending were quickly broken through, revealing what the Reich might have been capable of beforehand. By 1917 total public spending had risen to more than 70 per cent of GNP, the Reich had sharply increased its share of revenue and expenditure and the Reichsbank was supporting the war effort by high levels of short-term lending to government.[119] By this time, of course, declining output and rising inflation were beginning to indicate the limits of German economic might. But the fact that the Reich had been able to sustain the cost of waging total war on three fronts for over three years suggests that it could easily have borne the much lower cost of *averting* war without difficulty. The fact that this proved politically impossible without the mood of national solidarity induced by war attests to the weakness, for practical purposes, of Wilhelmine Germany's much criticized militarism. The paradoxical conclusion is that higher German military spending before July 1914 – in other words, a *more* militaristic Germany – far from causing the First World War, might have averted it.

6

The Last Days of Mankind: 28 June–4 August 1914

WHY BOSNIA?

For the diplomatic historian, 1914 was the most explosive of all the answers to that favourite poser of statesmen and examiners alike: the 'Eastern Question',[1] the protracted struggle, involving both great power rivalry and Balkan nationalism, to drive the Ottoman Empire out of Europe. The question was: After the Turk, who? It was a struggle in which, for most of the nineteenth century, Russia had been the most aggressive power and Austria its perennial but much distracted rival, with Britain and France tending to line up against Russia. The 'Near East' (unlike the 'Middle' and 'Far' variants, the phrase has fallen into disuse) was also a convenient place for naval war – nothing was easier for the British fleet than to chug along from Gibraltar to the Dardanelles – though an unhealthy place for soldiering, as all concerned discovered at Sebastopol in 1854–5 and again at Gallipoli sixty years later. The Russians also experienced the problem in 1877, when their advance towards Constantinople was checked at Plevna, thereby reducing the risk of a second Crimean War.

Throughout the nineteenth century Prussia and then Germany played almost no part in this drama. Bismarck wisely preserved the bones of his Pomeranian grenadiers for use in more northerly climes. At the turn of the century, however, there was a realignment. In the absence of a serious Russian naval presence in the Black Sea, Britain was losing interest in the hoary old issue of control of the Straits. Germany, on the other hand, had begun to take an economic and political interest in Turkey, symbolized by the projected Berlin–Baghdad railway. Perhaps most importantly, the Balkan states which had acquired (or been given) independence from Ottoman rule in the nineteenth century began to pursue policies which were at once more aggressive and more autonomous. In 1886 it had been possible for Russia to kidnap the Bulgarian king when he showed signs of pursuing a policy of his own (even when the policy was not so different from Russia's own of creating a 'big Bulgaria'). The government of Serbia, however, was never so subject to St Petersburg; and its policy was aggressively nationalist and expansionist. What Greece had done in the Peloponnese in the 1820s, what Belgium had done in Flanders in the 1830s, what Piedmont had done in Italy in the 1850s and what Prussia had done in Germany in the 1860s – that was what the Serbs wanted to do in the Balkans in the 1900s: to extend their territory in the name of 'South Slav' nationalism.

The success or failure of small states to achieve independence or enlargement always hinged, however, on the constellation of great power politics. It was the balance, or lack of balance, between Leopold von Ranke's 'pentarchy' of great powers which mattered. Thus the Greeks and Serbs were (partially) successful against the Turks in the 1820s only as far as the powers allowed them to be. Typical of the way new states were created was the 1830 international agreement which turned Greece into a tame monarchy with a German king. The same thing happened in the 1830s when the Belgians broke away from the Dutch: it was only in 1839 that the conflicting interests of the great powers were harmonized in the fateful agreement neutralizing the new state. The creation of Rumania out of the provinces of Moldavia and Wallachia in 1856 – the only lasting consequence of the Crimean imbroglio – was another case.

Piedmont and Prussia, by contrast, were the beneficiaries of international disagreement and disinterest. Cavour got his North Italian confederation with the support of Napoleon III; the subsequent acquisition of the papal states, Naples and Sicily was one of the rare occasions when the few real nationalists – in the form of Garibaldi's Thousand – won the day. Prussia created the German Reich partly by defeating Denmark, Austria and France, mainly because Britain and Russia had no objection. Bulgarian independence was a Russian project scaled down by British threats of intervention: hence the short-lived Ruritanian statelet Eastern Rumelia and the continuation of Ottoman rule in Macedonia. Later, Norway won independence from Sweden without anyone else minding. It was a sign of how far nationalism's revolutionary potential went unfulfilled that all the new states were monarchies, and most of the new thrones were filled by scions of the established royal houses. Only two new republics were established in Europe: the French in 1870 and the Portuguese in 1910 – both long-established nation-states.

Nor were any of the new states the ethnically homogeneous and inclusive nation-states of Mazzinian fantasy. Belgium was a linguistic hodge-podge; there were Rumanians aplenty outside Rumania; hardly any Italians spoke or felt themselves to be Italian (least of all in the south, which became a Piedmontese colony); nearly 10 million Germans did not live within the borders of the Reich (though sundry Poles and Danes did), which in any case was a federation, not a unitary nation-state. Moreover, for every state-building project that succeeded, there was one that failed. The Irish did not even manage to win back their parliament ('Home Rule'), though they were on the verge of doing so when war broke out. The Poles' heroic aspirations continued to be squashed by Russia and Prussia: partitioned four times (in 1772, 1793, 1795 and 1815), Poland made two abortive bids for independence in 1830 and 1863 only to be smashed by the Tsar's army. Self-government was a distant dream for the Croats, Rumanians and Germans who had to endure the uncompromising chauvinism of Magyar rule in Hungary. Other minorities were even more firmly under Russian control: Finns, Estonians, Latvians, Lithuanians, Ukrainians and others. A new state was made only to be unmade on the other side of the Atlantic: the Southern Confederacy failed to win its independence from the United States of America. If Bismarck won the German 'Civil War', then Jefferson Davis lost the South's 'War of Unification'.

There were also ethnic minorities who did not much want national independence before 1914, though some would later embrace it. The Czechs and Slovaks in Austria–Hungary, for example; but also the Jews there, with the exception of the few Zionists; and (in another multinational kingdom) the Scots, the majority of whom derived obvious material benefits from the Union and the Empire and who struck even the Czechs as woefully lacking in nationalist sentiment. At a reception after a football match between Slavie and Aberdeen (memorably described by Jaroslav Hašek), the Czech hosts attempt a cultural exchange, regaling their Scottish guests with 'the awakening of the Czech people', introducing them to such national heroes as Hus, Havlícek and Saint John Nepomuk, and singing the Czech anthem. The Scots, however, play not for love of country but for money (on £2 sterling a day), assume Havlícek is a former Slavie player and belt out 'a salty song about a pretty sutler lass'.[2]

Finally, we should also remember the persistence of anomalous states and statelets which defied the first principles of nationalism: Switzerland, a multilingual confederation, or Luxembourg, a tiny but independent duchy enjoying the same international status as Belgium. There was no irresistible force called nationalism, insisting that Bosnia-Hercegovina could not remain as it was: a religiously heterogeneous province, formerly of the Ottoman Empire, then, after the Congress of Berlin's decision in 1878, occupied and administered by Austria–Hungary, and in 1908 formally incorporated (as a crown land under the control of the 'common' Austro-Hungarian Finance Ministry) into the Habsburg monarchy.

The Austrians piled soldiers and bureaucrats into Bosnia, stamped out banditry, built 200 primary schools, 1,000 kilometres of railways and 2,000 kilometres of roads, and tried vainly to improve agriculture (though when a good quality boar was sent to a village for breeding purposes, it was turned into the Christmas roast). In 1910 they established a Bosnian parliament. They even tried – vainly – to persuade the three different religious communities to think of themselves collectively as *Bošnjaci*. It was no use. The only thing Orthodox, Catholic and Muslim could agree on was that they did not care for Austrian rule; indeed, there were members of each of the religious communities in Mlada Bosna (Young Bosnia), a student terrorist group. The more the Austrians clamped down, the more determined the young terrorists became. When the Archduke Francis Ferdinand and his wife Sophie, Duchess of Hohenberg, decided to visit Sarajevo on 28 June (not only the national festival of Vidovdan, but also the anniversary of the Battle of Kosovo), members of Mlada Bosna resolved to kill them. At the second attempt, and thanks to the most famous wrong-turning in history, one of them, a consumptive Serbian student named Gavrilo Princip, succeeded.[3] The Serbian government did not plan the assassination, though Princip and his associates had undoubtedly received assistance from the pan-Serb society the Black Hand, which had links to the head of Serbian Military Intelligence, Colonel Apis. Apis's superiors knew well that their chances of adding Bosnia-Hercegovina to their kingdom would not be improved by a war with the militarily superior Austria–Hungary. On the other hand, they also knew that a general European war might help them. As a Serb journalist told the British minister in Belgrade as early as 1898 (on the eve of the first Hague Peace Conference):

The idea of disarmament does not please our people in any way. The Servian race is split up under seven or eight different foreign governments, and we cannot be satisfied so long as this state of things lasts. We live in the hope of getting something for ourselves out of the general conflagration, whenever it takes place.[4]

This was Serbian foreign policy: a kind of nationalist version of Lenin's dictum 'the worse, the better'. 'Ah yes,' said the Serbian Foreign Minister, 'if the disintegration of Austria—Hungary could take place at the same time as the liquidation of Turkey, the solution would be greatly simplified.'[5] For this to happen, however, an Austrian action had to precipitate, at the very least, a Russian reaction.

Prior to 1908, however, Balkan instability had not had serious ramifications at the great power level. Since 1897 Austria and Russia had agreed not to disagree about the region. Indeed, the Austrian Foreign Minister Baron Aehrenthal consulted his Russian counterpart Alexander Izvolsky before proceeding to annex Bosnia. To be sure, there was a whiff of smoke in 1908–9 when Izvolsky, discovering belatedly that the concession on the Straits he had expected in return was not in Austria's gift, demanded that the annexation be approved by an international conference. Germany, for so long the onlooker in Balkan quarrels, now strongly supported Vienna (the first time this had happened since the brief experiment of Caprivi's 'new course' in the first years of William II's reign).[6] Moltke assured Conrad: 'The moment Russia mobilises, Germany will also mobilise, and will unquestionably mobilise her whole army.'[7] Yet the immediate effect of German intervention was to reduce rather than increase the risk of war: the Russians were far from ready for another war so soon after their humiliation by Japan, and backed down when it became clear that neither France nor Britain was sympathetic. Something similar happened in the autumn of 1912, following the First Balkan War in which Serbia and Bulgaria, assisted by Montenegro and Greece, drove the Turks out of Kosovo, Macedonia and the Sandžak of Novi Pazar (left in Ottoman hands by the Congress of Berlin). Although Poincaré made it clear that 'if Russia goes to war, France will also' and Kiderlen promised the Austrians 'unconditional . . . support', the truth was that neither St Petersburg nor Vienna wanted war. When Aehrenthal's successor Count Berchtold stated his terms – an independent Albania (a surprise to the Albanians) and a ban on the Serbs establishing a port on the Adriatic – Sazonov assured the Serbs that they would get no Russian support if they insisted on the latter. (It should be noted that the Russians were bound by no treaty to assist Serbia in a war.)[8] True, the Russians had upped the ante in the arms race by retaining the conscripts who would normally have completed their military service at the end of the year, but this was something of a reflex action. Their real worry was that the Bulgarians – over whom they had long since lost control – might gazump them by getting all the way to Constantinople. 'I think', Bethmann told Berchtold in February 1913, 'it would be a mistake of immeasurable consequence if we attempt a solution by force . . . at a moment when there is even the remotest possibility of entering this conflict under conditions more favourable to ourselves.'[9] When Bulgaria tried to wrest Macedonia from Serbia (and Salonika from Greece) by going to war in June 1913 – only to lose badly – the German Chancellor expressed the hope that 'Vienna would not let its peace be disturbed by the *cauchemar* of a Greater Serbia'.[10] The most that Berchtold was prepared to do was to chase the Serbs out of Albanian territory.

What made the difference in 1914? Partly, the direct German interest in Turkey, signalled by the German military mission to Constantinople led by General Liman von Sanders: that scared the Russians, dependent as their finances were on grain exports through the Black Sea Straits, weakened as their own Black Sea fleet was, frail as Turkey looked after the Balkan wars. Indeed, this was one of the arguments for the Franco-Russian railway agreement of January 1914 and the arms programme approved by the Duma six months later. Partly, things were changed by the removal of Francis Ferdinand himself, who had been restraining the recklessly bellicose Conrad. But principally it was the German decision to support, indeed to egg on, an Austrian military strike against Serbia in order to end the threat posed by the 'Piedmont of the South Slavs': in Francis Joseph's words to 'eliminate . . . Serbia as a political factor in the Balkans'. Both the Kaiser and Bethmann gave Count Szögyéni-Marich, the Habsburg ambassador, and Count Hoyos, whom Berchtold sent specially, a clear assurance: 'Even if it should come to a war between Austria and Russia . . . Germany would stand by our side.'[11] The puzzle for the historian has always been to explain why the government in Berlin persisted with this venture in the face of ample evidence that it would indeed lead to a European war.

THE GAMBLERS

It is true that during July the German decision-makers repeatedly expressed the hope that the conflict would be localized: in other words that Austria would be able to vanquish Serbia without Russian intervention.[12] However, it is hard to reconcile such aspirations with the frequent allusions elsewhere to the likelihood of a more general conflagration. In February 1913, for example, Bethmann had rejected the idea of a preventive war against Serbia because 'Russian intervention . . . would result in a war-like conflict of the Triple Alliance . . . against the Triple Entente, and Germany would have to bear the full brunt of the French and British attack'.[13] It is striking that when the Kaiser mentioned a preventive war to Max Warburg, the latter clearly assumed he meant a war against Russia, France and Britain – despite his own involvement in attempts to seek a rapprochement with Britain on colonial issues. The Germans had good reason to fear that an Austrian move against Serbia would, if supported by Germany, lead to a full-scale European war. Sazonov made it clear from the moment the Austrian ultimatum was published that Russia would react; while on 25 and 29 July 1914 Grey had restated the British position of December 1912: should 'the position of France as a power' be threatened, England would not stand aside.[14] Given these indications that the war would not be localized, there were ample opportunities for Berlin to back down.[15] Yet the initial British peace-keeping initiatives were given only the most insincere support by Germany.[16] The Germans pressed on, urging the Austrians to make haste, and after 26 July openly rejecting diplomatic alternatives.[17] Only at the eleventh hour did they begin to lose their nerve: the Kaiser first, on 28 July,[18] and then Bethmann who, after hearing of Grey's warning of the 29th to the German ambassador Prince Lichnowsky, frantically sought to persuade the Austrians to apply the brakes.[19] Berchtold tried to respond; but it was the German military which ultimately secured, by a combination of persuasion and defiance, the mobilization orders, the ultimata and declarations of war which unleashed the conflict.[20]

It has, of course, been argued that the Russian decision to mobilize, partially or fully, played its part in unleashing the conflict.[21] However, the Russian argument that their mobilization was not the same as the German and did not mean war was privately accepted by Moltke and

Bethmann. By 27 July it is clear that the Germans' principal concern was, as Müller put it, 'to put Russia in the wrong and then not to shy away from war' – in other words, to portray the fact of Russian mobilization as evidence of an attack on Germany.[22] German military intelligence pulled off the war's first espionage success in delivering evidence of Russian mobilization. The first indications that the 'period preparatory to war' had been proclaimed on the night of 25 July reached Berlin on the morning of Monday the 27th, though Bethmann had already quoted 'unconfirmed news' of this 'from [a] reliable source' in his dispatch to Lichnowsky the previous afternoon.[23] Early reports that general mobilization had been ordered by the Tsar arrived in Berlin on the evening of 30 July, though it was not until the following morning that Moltke was convinced, and even then he insisted on one of the red Russian mobilization posters being obtained and read aloud over the telephone.[24] An hour later, the Germans proclaimed their 'imminent danger of war'.

Why did the Germans act as they did? The best answer which can be offered by the diplomatic historian relates to the structure of European alliances, which had clearly tilted against Berlin since the turn of the century. Russia, France and England had all been able to find issues on which they could agree, but Germany had repeatedly failed (or chosen not) to secure ententes. Even such allies as they did have the Germans had doubts about: declining Austria, unreliable Italy. It can therefore be argued that the Germans saw a confrontation over the Balkans as a means of preserving their own fragile alliance, possibly also creating an anti-Russian Balkan alliance and perhaps even splitting the Triple Entente.[25] Such calculations were by no means unrealistic. As events proved, there was good reason to doubt the Triple Alliance's dependability; and the Triple Entente was indeed fragile, especially where England was concerned.[26] Even before the July crisis began, Colonel House, Woodrow Wilson's envoy to Europe, discerned that 'what Germany really wants is for England to detach herself from the Triple Entente'.[27] Even French support for Russia, although expressed enthusiastically by the ambassador Maurice Paléologue and by Joffre, seemed to waver on 30 July and 1 August.[28] It is therefore possible that, despite being well aware of the implications of war with respect to Belgium, Bethmann and Jagow discerned just enough evidence of dissension within the Triple Entente for the Germans to continue to hope for British neutrality. They knew the risks with respect to Belgium: on 28 April 1913 Jagow himself had refused to provide the Reichstag Budget

Committee with a guarantee of Belgian neutrality, since it would give the French 'a pointer as to where to expect us' – one of those revealing denials which were his peculiar forte.[29] But he and Bethmann chose to gamble for the prize of a diplomatic victory.[30]

Yet none of this satisfactorily explains why the German generals were so determined to go to war and continue fighting *even if the Triple Entente held*; and this is the critical point since it was they who pressed for mobilization after the diplomatic gamble had failed. At this point the military historian offers an explanation, based on the German General Staff's pessimistic calculations about the relative present and future strengths of the European armies, on which depended their argument for a pre-emptive or preventive war. This was a case which had repeatedly been rejected in the past. But in the summer of 1914, as we have seen, it was once again on the *Tagesordnung* as Moltke waged a campaign to convince the Kaiser, the civilian authorities and the Austrians that, as a result of new armaments programmes in France and, above all, Russia, Germany would be at their mercy within a few years. 'Prospects could never come better for us', argued the Deputy Chief of the General Staff, Georg Count Waldersee on 3 July, referring to Russia's unpreparedness; a view repeated by the Kaiser three days later: 'Russia is at the present moment militarily and financially totally unprepared for war.'[31] On 6–7 July Riezler recorded that military intelligence gave 'a shattering picture': 'After the completion of their [the Russians'] strategic railroads in Poland our position will be untenable . . . The Entente knows that we are completely paralysed.'[32] Szögyéni reported the German argument to Berchtold on 12 July: 'Should the Tsar's Empire resolve for war, it would not be so ready from a military point of view and not by any means so strong as it will be in a few years' time.'[33] Jagow duly relayed the argument to Lichnowsky in London on July 18: 'Russia is not yet ready to strike at present . . . [but] according to all competent observation, [she] will be prepared to fight in a few years. Then she will crush us by the number of soldiers; then she will have built her Baltic Sea Fleet and her strategic railroads.'[34] On July 25 the journalist Theodor Wolff was told by Jagow that although 'neither Russia nor France wanted war . . . The Russians . . . were not ready with their armaments, they would not strike; in two years' time, if we let matters slide, the danger would be much greater than at present.'[35] 'War will come soon anyway,' Jagow assured Wolff, and the situation now was 'very favourable'.[36] When Moltke returned to Berlin the next day, therefore, the ground had already been well prepared for his argument: 'We shall never again strike as well as we do now, with France's and Russia's expansion of their armies incomplete.'[37] Bethmann had been persuaded at last: 'If war must break out, better now than in one or two years' time when the Entente will be stronger.'[38] Whenever he showed signs of wavering in the subsequent days, Moltke stiffened his resolve with a reminder: 'The military situation is becoming from day to day more unfavourable for us and can, if our prospective opponents prepare themselves further unmolested, lead to fateful consequences for us.'[39] Thus what began as an argument in favour of war this year rather than in two years became an argument for mobilization today rather than tomorrow.

That the Germans were thinking along these lines was no secret. Grey himself twice commented in July 1914 on the logic, from a German point of view, of a pre-emptive strike against Russia and France, before the military balance deteriorated any further:

The truth is that whereas formerly the German government had aggressive intentions . . . they are now genuinely alarmed at the military preparations in Russia, the prospective increase in her military forces and particularly at the intended construction, at the insistence of the French government and with French money, of strategic railways to converge on the German frontier . . . Germany was not afraid, because she believed her army to be invulnerable, but she was afraid that in a few years hence she might be afraid . . . Germany was afraid of the future.

His only mistake was to think that this would keep the German government 'in a peaceful mood'.[40] On 30 July the German diplomat Kanitz told the American ambassador that 'G[ermany] should go to war when they are prepared and not wait until Russia has completed her plan to have a peace footing of 2,400,000 men'. Colonel House reported to Woodrow Wilson on 1 August that Germany knew 'that her best chance is to strike quickly and hard'; she might 'precipitate action as a means of safety'.[41]

The Kaiser's verdict on 30 July was, of course, divorced from reality: 'England, Russia and France have agreed among themselves . . . to take the Austro-Serbian conflict for an excuse for waging a war of extermination against us . . . The famous encirclement of Germany has finally become a complete fact . . . We squirm isolated in the net.'[42] But he was not the only person to perceive the German position as vulnerable.

Colonel House's famous remark about 'jingoism run mad' in his letter to President Wilson of 29 May should be seen in context:

The situation is extraordinary. It is jingoism run stark mad. Unless someone acting for you can bring about a different understanding, there is some day to be an awful cataclysm. No one in Europe can do it. There is too much hatred, too many jealousies. Whenever England consents, France and Russia will close in on Germany and Austria.

House was later dismissive of British claims to be 'fighting for Belgium'. Britain had sided with France and Russia 'primarily . . . because Germany insisted upon having a dominant army and a dominant navy, something Great Britain could not tolerate in safety to herself.' And he was no Germanophile: after visiting Berlin he remarked that he had 'never seen the war spirit so nurtured and so glorified as it is there . . . Their one thought is to advance industrially and to glorify war.' House was also an early proponent of the theory that Germany had gone to war partly in order that the 'group of militarists and financiers' who governed her could 'conserve their selfish interests'. But his analysis left room for the possibility that German security had indeed been threatened.[43]

There is thus no need to posit, as Fischer does, pre-existing German war plans to create spheres of influence in Central Europe and Africa, to destroy France as a power and to carve up Russia's Western Empire.[44] The evidence points far more persuasively to a military 'first strike', designed to pre-empt a deterioration in Germany's military position – though this is by no means incompatible with the idea that the outcome of such a strike, if successful, would have been German hegemony in Europe. The only real question is whether or not this strategy deserves the apologetic name of 'preventive war'.[45] It is to condescend to the German decision-makers to caricature them as irrational duellists, going to war 'in a fit of anger', for the sake of an antiquated sense of honour. The Germans did not care about losing 'face'; they cared about losing the arms race.[46]

That said, the extent of German malice aforethought must not be exaggerated. For men who were planning a war, the senior members of the Great General Staff were uncannily relaxed in July 1914. At the time the Kaiser issued his famous 'blank cheque' to the Austrians, Moltke, Waldersee, Groener, chief of the Railway Section, and Major Nicolai, the head of key intelligence agency 'Section IIIb', were all on holiday (in separate resorts, it should be said). Tirpitz and Admiral von Pohl were too. It was only on 16 July that Nicolai's stand-in, Captain Kurt Neuhof, was advised to step up surveillance of Russian military activity. Even this did not strike Waldersee as adequate when he returned from Mecklenburg on 23 July, while Nicolai himself was not back at his desk for another two days. Even then his orders to the so-called 'tension travellers' (*Spannungsreisende*) – i.e. German spies in Russia and France – were merely to find out 'whether war preparations are taking place in France and Russia'.[47]

SMASHING THE TELEPHONE

With hindsight, the biggest question of 1914 – the one which would decide the war – was what Britain would do. At the time, however, it seemed unimportant to many of the key decision-makers on the continent. Though Bethmann sometimes dreamt of British neutrality, the German generals were indifferent: they doubted that Britain's small army could influence the outcome of a war. Nor did the French generals care much. Joffre was bullish enough to believe that he could win the war in the West without assistance.

When, in the wake of the Sarajevo assassinations, it became clear in London that the Austrian government intended demanding 'some compensation in the sense of some humiliation for Serbia', Grey's first reaction was to worry about how Russia might react. Seeing the possibility of a confrontation between Austria and Russia, he sought to exert indirect pressure *via* Berlin to temper any Austrian reprisals, hoping to repeat the success of his Balkan diplomacy of the previous year. The Russian ambassador in Vienna made it clear as early as 8 July that 'Russia would be compelled to take up arms in defence of Serbia' if Austria 'rushed into war'; Grey's belief that a distinction could be drawn between cessions of territory by Serbia and some less serious form of reprisal was never really shared in St Petersburg. (Revealingly, Grey warned Lichnowsky that 'in view of the present unpopularity of England in Russia' he would 'have to be careful of Russian feelings'.)[48] At first Grey urged Austria and Russia to 'discuss things together' in the hope that terms could be devised for the Serbs which both sides would find acceptable, but this was dismissed by Poincaré, who happened to be visiting St Petersburg. Doubting his ability to exercise a moderating influence over Russia, and suspecting that the German government might actually be 'egging on' the Austrians (a suspicion confirmed by the terms of their ultimatum to Serbia), Grey changed tack, warning Lichnowsky that Russia would stand by Serbia and suggesting mediation between Austria and Russia by the four other powers.[49]

From the outset Grey was extremely reluctant to give any indication of how Britain might respond to an escalation of the conflict. He knew that if Austria pressed extreme demands on Belgrade with German backing, and Russia mobilized in defence of Serbia, then France might well become involved – such was the nature of the Franco-Russian entente and German military strategy, so far as it was known in London. Part of Grey's strategy in trying to turn the ententes with France and Russia into quasi-alliances had been to deter Germany from risking war. However, he now feared that too strong a signal of support for France and Russia – such as Crowe and Nicolson predictably urged – might encourage the Russians to do just that. He found himself in a cleft stick: how to deter Austria and Germany without encouraging France and Russia – hence his characteristically convoluted statement to Lichnowsky on 24 July that:

there was no alliance . . . committing us to . . . France and Russia . . . On the other hand . . . the British government belonged to one group of powers, but did not do so in order to make difficulties greater between the two European groups; on the contrary, we wished to prevent any questions that arose from throwing the groups . . . into opposition . . . We should never pursue an aggressive policy, and if there was a European war, and we took part in it, it would not be on the aggressive side, for public opinion was against that.

Lichnowsky interpreted this, as Grey doubtless intended, as a warning that 'in case France should be drawn in, England would [not] dare to remain disinterested', a point he repeated with growing anxiety as the crisis intensified. But Bethmann and Jagow evidently concluded that a show of German support for four-power mediation would suffice to satisfy Grey.[50] The King took a similarly ambiguous line with the German Crown Prince when they met on 26 July:

I don't know what we shall do, we have no quarrel with anyone and I hope we shall remain neutral. But if Germany declared war on Russia and France joins Russia, then I am afraid we shall be dragged into it. But you can be sure that I and my government will do all we can to prevent a European war.

Prince Heinrich concluded that England would remain neutral 'at the beginning', though he doubted 'whether she will be able to do so in the long run . . . on account of her relations with France'.[51] However, neutrality in the short run might be all the German government needed if the army could establish a strong enough military position on the continent. In short, British policy was so garbled that it could be interpreted more or less according to taste. By Sunday 26 July the French thought they could count on Britain, while the Germans felt 'sure' of English neutrality. As Jagow put it to Cambon: 'You have your information. We have ours'; unfortunately, the source was identical in each case. The German government continued undeterred, feigning interest in Grey's proposals for mediation, which it had no intention of pursuing.[52]

To be fair to Grey, his tactic of studied ambiguity very nearly paid off. So exposed did the Serbian government feel itself to be, that – despite Grey's dismay at Vienna's 'formidable' terms – it all but accepted the Austrian ultimatum, seeking only the most limited modifications to it.[53] Moreover, to the dismay of both Bethmann and Moltke, who had been urging the Austrians not to take Grey's mediation proposal seriously, the Kaiser hailed the Serbian reply as a diplomatic triumph. In the belief that *every cause for war* [now] falls to the ground', he urged Vienna simply to 'Halt in Belgrade', in other words to occupy the Serbian capital temporarily, much as Prussia had occupied Northern France in 1870, 'as a guaranty for the enforcement and carrying out of the promises'. This compounded the confusion which Jagow had created by stating that Germany would *not* act if Russia mobilized only in the south (that is, against Austria but not Germany).[54] At the same time Sazonov unexpectedly changed his mind about the possibility of bilateral talks between Austria and Russia, an idea Grey immediately returned to when it became clear that the German government did not really favour his scheme for a four-power conference. As Nicolson commented huffily, 'One does not really know where one is with Mr Sazonov.'[55] (Nor did one know where one was with the Germans: Jagow now argued that a four-power conference would 'amount to a court of arbitration', putting Austria and Serbia on an equal footing, while at the same time Bethmann deliberately omitted to mention Sazonov's proposal for bilateral talks to Lichnowsky on the ground that the ambassador was 'informing Sir Edward [Grey] of everything'.)[56] For a moment, it seemed that the continental war might be averted. To be sure, Sazonov had no intention of accepting the occupation of Belgrade by Austria, which would have represented in his eyes a serious reverse for Russian influence in the Balkans.[57] But he declared himself willing to halt mobilization 'if Austria ... declares itself ready to eliminate from its ultimatum those points which infringe on Serbia's sovereign rights'. An increasingly desperate Bethmann seized on this as a basis for negotiation and the Austrian government actually accepted Sazonov's offer of talks on 30 July.[58]

Unfortunately, however, military logic had now begun to supersede diplomatic calculation. Even before the Austrian bombardment of Belgrade began, Sazonov and his military colleagues issued orders for partial mobilization, which they then desperately tried to turn into full mobilization on being warned that Germany in fact intended to mobilize even in the case of Russian partial mobilization. The Russians in fact began mobilizing in the southern districts of Odessa, Kiev, Moscow and Kazan on 29 July – a decision which the Tsar later said had been taken four days before – assuring the German ambassador that this was 'far from meaning war'. But on being told by Pourtalès that Germany would none the less 'find herself compelled to mobilise, in which case she would immediately proceed to the offensive', the Russians concluded that a partial mobilization would be inadequate, and might even jeopardize full mobilization. There followed a hysterical series of meetings and telephone conversations as Sazonov and his colleagues tried to persuade the vacillating Tsar to agree to full mobilization. He finally did so at 2 p.m. on 30 July and mobilization began the next day. (As in Berlin, the much-vaunted power of the monarch proved to be illusory at the moment of decision.)[59] This was precisely the pretext the Germans wanted to launch their own mobilization against not only Russia but also France.[60] The idea of Austro-Russian talks was forgotten in a bizarre 'reverse race', in which, for the sake of domestic opinion, Germany tried to get Russia to mobilize first. Continental war was now surely unavoidable. Even when Bethmann, grasping at last that Britain might intervene immediately in response to an attack on France, sought to force the Austrians to the negotiating table, they refused to suspend their military operations.[61] Royal appeals to St Petersburg to halt mobilization were equally futile, as the Chief of the Russian General Staff General Nikolai Yanushkevich had resolved (as he told Sazonov) to 'smash my telephone and generally adopt measures which will prevent anyone [i.e. the Tsar] from finding me for the purpose of giving contrary orders which would again stop our mobilization'.[62] And if Russia continued to mobilize, the Germans insisted they had no option but to do the same. That meant the invasion of Belgium and France.[63] In short, 'war by timetable' commenced the moment Russia decided on full mobilization – that is, war by timetable between the four continental powers (as well, of course, as Serbia and Belgium). What still nevertheless remained avoidable was Britain's involvement (and for that matter the involvement of Turkey and Italy).

WHY BRITAIN FOUGHT

Not surprisingly, it was at this point that the French and Russian governments began seriously pressing Grey to make Britain's position clear.[64] The French argued that if Grey were to 'announce that in the event of a conflict between Germany and France . . . England would come to the aid of France, there would be no war'.[65] But Grey, who had been trying for some days to intimate this to Lichnowsky, knew that he alone could not make such a commitment to France. True, he already had the hawks at the Foreign Office behind him arguing that a 'moral bond' had been 'forged' by the Entente (Crowe), and that therefore 'We should at once give orders for the mobilisation of the army' (Nicolson).[66] But, as had repeatedly been made clear since 1911, he could not act without the support of his Cabinet colleagues and his party – to say nothing of that nebulous and frequently invoked entity 'public opinion'. And it was far from clear that he could rely on any of these to back a public military commitment to France. It was therefore decided simply to decide nothing, 'for [as Herbert Samuel put it] if both sides do not know what we shall do, both will be the less willing to run risks'.[67] The most Grey could do was once again to tell Lichnowsky *privately* – 'to spare himself later the reproach of bad faith' – that 'if [Germany] and France should be involved, then . . . the British government would . . . find itself forced to make up its mind quickly. In that event, it would not be practicable to stand aside and wait for any length of time.'[68] That this impressed Bethmann where Grey's previous statements had not can be explained by the fact that, for the first time, Grey implied that any British action in defence of France would be swift.[69] An equally deep impression was made in London by Bethmann's bid for British neutrality – which he made just before he heard Grey's warning to Lichnowsky – principally because it made Germany's intention to attack France so blatantly obvious.[70] But although it was sharply rebuffed, even this did not prompt a commitment to intervene, and Churchill's limited naval preparations of 28–29 July certainly did not have the same significance as the continental armies' mobilization orders.[71] On the contrary: having issued his private warning, Grey took a markedly *softer* official line with Germany, in a last bid to revive the idea of four-power mediation.[72] Indeed, on the morning of 31 July Grey went so far as to say to Lichnowsky:

If Germany could get any reasonable proposal put forward which made it clear that Germany and Austria were still striving to preserve European peace, and that Russia and France would be unreasonable if they rejected it, I would support it . . . and go the length of saying that if Russia and France would not accept it, His Majesty's Government would have nothing more to do with the consequences.

The 'reasonable proposal' Grey had in mind was that 'Germany would agree not to attack France if France remained neutral [or kept her troops on her own territory] in the event of a war between Russia and Germany'.[73] Even the pessimistic Lichnowsky began to think on hearing this that 'in a possible war, England might adopt a waiting attitude'.[74] Reactions in Paris were correspondingly bleak. On the evening of 1 August Grey told Cambon baldly:

If France could not take advantage of this position [i.e. proposal], it was because she was bound by an alliance to which we were not parties, and of which we did not know the terms . . . France must take her own decision at this moment without reckoning on an assistance that we were not now in a position to promise . . . We could not propose to Parliament at this moment to send an expeditionary military force to the Continent . . . unless our interests and obligations were deeply and desperately involved.[75]

A private warning to Lichnowsky was not, as Grey explained to Cambon, 'the same thing as . . . an engagement to France'.[76] Grey was not even prepared to give the Belgian ambassador a guarantee that 'if Germany violates the neutrality of Belgium, we would certainly assist Belgium' – although later the government would make much of its legal obligation to do so.[77]

Grey's conduct in these crucial days was circumscribed by domestic political considerations. As we have seen, there was a substantial body of Liberal politicians and journalists who strongly opposed such a commitment.[78] On 30 July twenty-two Liberal members of the back-bench Foreign Affairs Committee intimated through Arthur Ponsonby that 'any decision in favour of participation in a European war would meet not only with the strongest disapproval but with the actual withdrawal of support from the Government'.[79] Asquith estimated that around three-quarters of his parliamentary party were for 'absolute non-interference at any price'.[80] The Cabinet roughly reflected this, with the proponents of the continental commitment still in a decided minority. The nineteen men who met on 31 July were divided into three unequal groups: those who, in common with the bulk of the party, favoured an immediate declaration of neutrality (including Morley, Simon, John Burns, Earl Beauchamp and C. Hobhouse), those who were in favour of intervention (Grey and Churchill only) and those who had not made up their minds (notably McKenna, Haldane, Samuel, Harcourt, the Quaker Joseph Pease and the Marquess of Crewe, but probably also Lloyd George – as well, of course, as Asquith himself).[81] Morley argued forcefully against intervention on the side of Russia, and it seemed clear that the majority was inclining to his view. However, Grey's threat to resign if 'an out-and-out uncompromising policy of non-intervention' were adopted sufficed to maintain the stalemate.[82] The Cabinet agreed that 'British opinion would not now enable us to support France . . . we could say nothing to commit ourselves'.[83]

Nor was the deadlock really broken when, on the night of 1 August, while Grey played billiards at Brooks's, Churchill was able to persuade Asquith to let him mobilize the navy on the news of the German declaration of war on Russia.[84] This merely prompted Morley and Simon to threaten resignation at the next morning's meeting and the majority once again to close ranks against Grey's repeated pleas for an unambiguous declaration of commitment. The most that could be agreed in the first session of that crucial Sunday was that 'if the German fleet comes into the Channel or through the North Sea to undertake hostile operations against the French coasts or shipping, the British fleet will give all the protection in its power'.[85] Even this – which was far from being a declaration of war, given that such German naval action was highly unlikely – was too much for John Burns, the President of the Board of Trade, who resigned. As Samuel noted, 'Had the matter come to an issue, Asquith would have stood by Grey . . . and three others would have remained. I think the rest of us would have resigned.'[86]

At lunch at Beauchamp's that day, seven ministers, among them Lloyd George, expressed reservations about even the limited naval measures. Morley felt with hindsight that if Lloyd George had given a lead to the waverers, 'the Cabinet would undoubtedly have perished that evening'; but Harcourt's appeal to Lloyd George to 'speak for us' was in vain.[87] Had they realized that Grey had already surreptitiously 'dropped' his proposal to Lichnowsky for French neutrality in a Russo-German war, and that Lichnowsky had been reduced to tears at Asquith's breakfast table that morning, they might have acted on those reservations.[88] As it was, Morley, Simon and Beauchamp now joined Burns in offering their resignations, following the commitment to Belgium which Grey had only been able to secure that evening by himself threatening to resign. A junior minister, Charles Trevelyan, also handed in his notice.[89]

So why did the government not fall? The immediate answer is, as Asquith recorded in his diary, that Lloyd George, Samuel and Pease appealed to the resigners 'not to go, or at least to delay it' whereupon 'they agreed to say nothing today and sit in their accustomed places in the House'.[90] But why did only Morley, Burns and Trevelyan in the end go?[91] The traditional answer can be expressed in a single word: Belgium.

Certainly, it had long been recognized in the Foreign Office that the decision to intervene on behalf of France 'would be more easily arrived at if German aggressiveness . . . entailed a violation of the neutrality of Belgium'.[92] And Lloyd George and others later cited the violation of Belgian neutrality as the single most important reason for swinging them – and 'public opinion' – in favour of war.[93] At first sight, the point seems irrefutable. On 6 August 1914 Britain's 'solemn international obligation' to uphold Belgian neutrality in the name of law and honour, and 'to vindicate the principle . . . that small nations are not to be crushed', provided the two central themes of Asquith's 'What are we fighting for?' speech to the Commons.[94] It was also the keynote of Lloyd George's successful Welsh recruitment drive.[95]

Nevertheless there are reasons for scepticism. As we have seen, the Foreign Office view in 1905 had been that the 1839 treaty did not bind Britain to uphold Belgium's neutrality 'in any circumstances and at whatever risk'. When the issue had come up in 1912, none other than Lloyd George had expressed the concern that, in the event of war, the preservation of Belgian neutrality would undermine the British blockade strategy. Significantly, when the issue was raised in Cabinet on 29 July, it was decided to base any response to a German invasion of Belgium on 'policy' rather than 'legal obligation'.[96] The government's line was therefore to warn the Germans obliquely by stating that a violation of Belgium might cause British public opinion to 'veer round'. Thus Grey was able to respond to German prevarication on the subject with a unanimous Cabinet warning that 'if there were a violation of Belgian neutrality . . . it would be extremely hard to restrain public feeling'.[97] But that did not commit the government itself. This is not so surprising, as a number of ministers were in fact rather keen to welch on the Belgian guarantee.

Lloyd George was one of those who, as Beaverbrook recalled, tried to argue that the Germans would 'pass only through the furthest southern corner' and that this would imply 'a small infraction of neutrality. "You see", he would say [pointing to a map], "it is only a little bit, and the Germans will pay for any damage they do." '[98] It was widely (though wrongly) expected, in any case, that the Belgians would not call for British assistance, but would simply issue a formal protest in the event of a German passage through the Ardennes. The German bid for British neutrality on 29 July had very clearly implied an incursion into Belgium; but even on the morning of 2 August, after Jagow had refused to guarantee Belgian neutrality, Lloyd George, Harcourt, Beauchamp, Simon, Runciman and Pease agreed that they could contemplate war only in the event of 'the invasion *wholesale* of Belgium'. Charles Trevelyan took the same view.[99] Hence the careful wording of the Cabinet's resolution that evening, communicated by Crewe to the King, that 'a *substantial* violation of the neutrality of [Belgium] would place us in the situation contemplated as possible by Mr Gladstone in 1870, when interference was held to compel us to take action'.[100]

The news of the German ultimatum to Belgium therefore came as something of a relief to Asquith when it reached him on the morning of 3 August. Moltke's demand for unimpeded passage through the *whole* of Belgium, the subsequent appeal of King Albert, indicating that Belgium intended to resist any infraction of her neutrality, and the German invasion the next day distinctly 'simplified matters', in Asquith's words, because it allowed both Simon and Beauchamp to withdraw their resignations.[101] The last-minute attempts by Moltke and Lichnowsky to guarantee the post-war integrity of Belgium were therefore as futile as the Germans' cynical lies about a French advance into Belgium.[102] When Bethmann lamented to Goschen that 'England should fall upon them for the sake of the neutrality of Belgium' – for '*un chiffon de papier*' –

he was missing the point. By requiring a German advance through the whole of Belgium, the Schlieffen Plan helped save the Liberal government.[103]

Yet it was not so much the German threat to Belgium which swung the Cabinet behind intervention as the German threat to *Britain* which Grey and the hawks at the Foreign Office had always insisted would arise if France fell. This can be inferred from Asquith's note to his mistress Venetia Stanley of 2 August in which he set down the six principles by which he was guided: only the sixth referred to Britain's 'obligations to Belgium to prevent her being utilized and absorbed by Germany'. The fourth and fifth were more important, stating as they did that, while Britain was under no obligation to assist France, 'It is against British interests that France should be wiped out as a Great Power,' and 'We cannot allow Germany to use the Channel as a hostile base.'[104] Likewise, the main argument of Grey's famous speech to the Commons of 3 August – delivered before the news of the German ultimatum to Belgium – was that 'if France is beaten in a struggle of life and death . . . I do not believe that . . . we should be in a position to use our force decisively to . . . prevent the whole of the West of Europe opposite to us . . . falling under the domination of a single Power.'[105] The strategic risks of non-intervention – isolation, friendlessness – outweighed the risks of intervention. As Grey put it in a private conversation the next day: 'It will not end with Belgium. Next will come Holland, and after Holland, Denmark . . . England['s] . . . position would be gone if Germany were thus permitted to dominate Europe.' German policy, he told the Cabinet, was 'that of the great European aggressor, as bad as Napoleon'.[106] That this argument also won over waverers like Harcourt seems clear. As he explained on 5 August:

I have acted not from any obligation of Treaty or of honour, for neither existed . . . There were three overwhelming British interests which I could not abandon:

1. That the German fleet should not occupy, under our neutrality, the North Sea and English Channel.
2. That they should not seize and occupy the North-Western part of France opposite our shores.
3. That they should not violate the ultimate independence of Belgium and hereafter occupy Antwerp as a standing menace to us.[107]

This had been Pitt's argument for fighting France: an argument rooted in the assumption that sea power was the alpha and omega of British security. (The first Zeppelin raid exposed its obsolescence.) Morley was thus not far wrong when he said that Belgium had furnished a 'plea . . . for intervention on behalf of France'.[108] This was also the view of Frances Stevenson, Lloyd George's mistress, and Ramsay MacDonald, who dined with Lloyd George on the evening of 2 August.[109]

There was, however, another and arguably even more important reason why Britain went to war at 11p.m. on 4 August 1914. Throughout the days of 31 July–3 August one thing above all maintained Cabinet unity: the fear of letting in the Conservative and Unionist opposition.[110] It must be remembered how bitter relations between the two major parties had become by 1914: after the battles over Lloyd George's budgets and the powers of the House of Lords, the Liberals' decision once again to try to enact Home Rule for Ireland had inflamed Unionist sentiment. Attempts to reach a compromise over the temporary exclusion of Northern Ireland had failed at the Buckingham Palace conference. With Ulster Protestants arming themselves to prevent the imposition of 'Rome Rule' – the Ulster Volunteer Force had 100,000 men and at least 37,000 rifles – the possibility of civil war was real and the attitude of leading Tories, to say nothing of senior army officers, was not unsympathetic to the Protestant cause.[111] The sudden onset of the European diplomatic crisis served, as Asquith remarked, to pour oil on the stormy Irish waters (that was 'the one bright spot in this hateful war'); but at the same time it gave the Tories a new stick with which to beat the government. For it had long been obvious that the Conservative leadership viewed the German threat more seriously than most Liberal ministers. In 1912, for example, Balfour had published an article on Anglo-German relations in which he explicitly accused the German government of planning a war of aggression with the purpose of resurrecting the Holy Roman Empire on the continent and extending her overseas empire. Britain, he wrote, had:

too bitter an experience of the ills which flow from the endeavour of any single state to dominate Europe; we are too surely convinced of the perils which such a policy, were it successful, would bring upon ourselves . . . to treat them as negligible.

As we have seen, Grey was regarded by the Tories as a 'sound man', carrying on their own policies as best he could against the opposition of very unsound colleagues. But since 1911 the Foreign Secretary had been on the defensive, if not in retreat. Unionists like Frederick Oliver were appalled at the prospect of a crucial foreign policy decision being taken by 'a government which has so messed and misconceived our domestic situation'.[112] Looking back on the crisis in December 1914, Austen Chamberlain expressed what was probably the dominant Conservative view of the Liberals' handling of the crisis:

There had been nothing beforehand in official speeches or official publications to make known to [our people] the danger that we ran to prepare them for the discharge of our responsibilities and the defence of our interests. Those who knew most were silent; those who undertook to instruct the mass of the public were ignorant, and our democracy with its decisive voice on the conduct of public affairs was left without guidance by those who could have directed it properly, and was misled by those who constituted themselves its guides.[113]

His brother Neville shared his dismay: 'It fairly makes one gasp', he had exclaimed in August, 'to think that we were within a hair's breadth of eternal disgrace.'[114]

The cue for Tory action was provided by the knife-edge Cabinet meetings of 2 August. That morning, at the suggestion of Balfour, Lansdowne and Walter Long, Bonar Law wrote to Asquith making clear the Tory view that 'any hesitation in now supporting France and Russia would be fatal to the honour and future security of the United Kingdom'. The 'united support' offered by Bonar Law 'in all measures required by England's intervention in the war' was nothing less than a veiled threat that Conservatives would be willing to step into Liberal shoes if the government could not agree on such measures.[115] After years of bellicose criticism from the Tory press, this was the one thing calculated to harden Asquith's resolve. Resignation, he told the Cabinet, might seem the ordinary course for a government so divided. But, he went on, 'the National situation is far from ordinary, and I cannot persuade myself that the other party is led by men, or contains men, capable of dealing with it'.[116] Samuel and Pease immediately grasped the point, telling Burns: 'For the majority of the Cabinet now to leave meant a ministry which was a war one and that was the last thing he wanted.' 'The alternative government', as Pease put it, 'must be one much less anxious for peace than ourselves.' He said the same to Trevelyan three days later, by which time Simon and Runciman had taken up the refrain.[117] Margot Asquith later remarked that it was 'lucky for this country that the Liberals were in power in 1914, as men might have been suspicious of acquiescing in such a terrible decision at the dictation of a Jingo Government'.[118]

Probably unbeknown to the rest of the Cabinet, one of their own number was in fact poised to defect if the advocates of neutrality won the day. As early as 31 July Churchill secretly asked Bonar Law *via* F. E. Smith whether, in the event of up to eight resignations, 'the Opposition [would] be prepared to come to the rescue of the Government . . . by forming a Coalition to fill up the vacant offices.'[119] Bonar Law declined Churchill's invitation to dine with him and Grey on 2 August; but his letter to the Cabinet had said enough. This was not the first time the idea of a coalition had been broached by a member of Asquith's government. None other than Lloyd George had flirted with the idea in 1910.[120]

At first sight, the fact that the Conservatives were more eager than the Liberals for war might seem to strengthen the case for an inevitable British intervention: if Asquith had fallen, then Bonar Law would have gone to war just the same. But would it have been just the same? Let us suppose Lloyd George – defeated on his Finance Bill, beset by financial panic, assailed by pacifist editorials in the *Guardian* and the *British Weekly* – had deserted Grey at the critical Cabinet meeting on 2 August and given leadership to the opponents of intervention. Grey would certainly have resigned; Churchill would have rushed off to join Bonar Law. Would Asquith have been able to hang on? Almost certainly not. But how quickly could a Conservative government have been formed? The last change of government had been a protracted affair: Balfour's administration had shown the first signs of disintegrating over tariff reform as early as 1903, had actually been defeated in the Commons on 20 July 1905, had lost the confidence of the Chamberlainites the following November and had finally resigned on 4 December. The general election which confirmed the strength of Liberal support in the country was not over until 7 February 1906. It is conceivable that matters would have moved more swiftly had Asquith been forced to resign in early August 1914. Certainly Churchill's plan for a coalition was designed to minimize delay. But would a declaration of war on Germany have been possible under such circumstances before a general election? Much would have depended on the King, who, like his cousins in Berlin and St Petersburg, had shown little enthusiasm for war once he looked over the edge of the abyss.[121] It seems reasonable to assume that a change of government would have delayed the despatch of the British Expeditionary Force (BEF) by at least a week.

In any case, even with the government unchanged, the despatch of the BEF was not a foregone conclusion and did not go according to the plans which had been worked out in consultation with the French General Staff. This was because, as we have seen, a clear decision in favour of the continental commitment had never actually been made, so that all the old arguments against it immediately resurfaced when war broke out. The navalists insisted, as they had always insisted, that sea power alone could decide the war and until 5 August most ministers seemed to agree.[122] Indeed, Bertie reported from Paris that the expeditionary force would not be needed; he was assured by General de Castelnau, Deputy Chief of the French General Staff, that 'the French, even if they suffer reverses, must win in the end, provided that England will aid by closing the sea approaches to Germany'.[123] They also tended to favour keeping part or all of the army at home: not to fend off an invasion, which was not expected, but to preserve social peace (the economic consequences of the war were indeed already making themselves felt).[124] At the 'rather motley' war council of generals and ministers called by Asquith on 5 August, confusion reigned and no decision was reached pending consultation with a representative of the French General Staff. The next day the Cabinet decided to send just four infantry divisions and the cavalry division to Amiens, whereas Henry Wilson had long before resolved to send all seven divisions to Maubeuge to aid the French. It was only six days later that Earl Kitchener, hastily recalled from Egypt and installed as Secretary of State for War, was persuaded to revert to Maubeuge, and not until 3 September that the Cabinet agreed to send the last remaining division to France.[125]

Did it – as its proponents claimed and subsequent apologists have argued – make a decisive difference to the outcome of the war? Was Major A. H. Ollivant right to argue in his memorandum for Lloyd George of 1 August that 'the presence or absence of the British army will . . . very probably decide the fate of France'?[126] As we have seen, the Schlieffen Plan would probably have failed anyway even without the BEF, such were the flaws Moltke had introduced into the plan. Perhaps the French could therefore have halted the German offensive unassisted, had they themselves not attempted to launch their own almost suicidal offensive rather than concentrating on defence. But they did not; and, even allowing for German errors, it seems likely that, despite the initial, desperate retreat from Mons and the failure of the feint at Ostend, the presence of British troops at Le Cateau on 26 August and at the Marne (6–9 September) *did* significantly reduce the chances of German victory.[127] Unfortunately, what it could not do was to bring about a German defeat. After the fall of Antwerp and the first battle of Ypres (20 October–22 November), a bloody stalemate had been reached which was to endure on the Western Front for three and a half years. If the proponents of a neutral or a naval strategy had prevailed and Britain had not sent the BEF – or even if its departure had been delayed while a new government was formed – the German chances of victory over France would without question have been enhanced.

THE KAISER'S EUROPEAN UNION

That Britain could have limited its involvement in a continental war is a possibility which has been all but ignored by historians.[128] Even those who deplore the *way* the war was fought generally neglect this counter-factual. Yet it should now be clear that the possibility was a very real one. Asquith and Grey themselves later acknowledged this in their memoirs. Both men emphasized that Britain had not been obliged to intervene by any kind of contractual obligation to France. In Asquith's words, 'We kept ourselves free to decide, when the occasion arose, whether we should or should not go to war.'[129] Nor did Grey make any secret of the political opposition within his own party which had prevented him making a commitment to France in July.[130] Despite his talk elsewhere of irresistible historical forces, he admitted that there had been a choice.

Of course, Grey naturally insisted that the Cabinet's choice had been the right one. But what were his arguments *against* neutrality? In his memoirs, he set these out:

If we were to come in at all, let us be thankful that we did it at once – it was better so, better for our good name, better for a favourable result, than if we had tried to keep out and then found ourselves . . . compelled to go in . . . [Had we not come in] we should have been isolated; we should have had no friend in the world; no one would have hoped or feared anything from us, or thought our friendship worth having. We should have been discredited . . . held to have played an inglorious part. We should have been hated.[131]

For Grey, then, the war was at root 'a matter of honour': the legal commitment to Belgium and, even more, the moral commitment to France. Nevertheless, the desire not to be cast as 'perfidious Albion' was only the veneer behind which strategic calculations lay. Grey's fundamental argument was that Britain could not risk a German victory, because such a victory would have made Germany 'supreme over all the Continent of Europe and Asia Minor'.[132]

But was that really the German objective? Was the Kaiser really Napoleon? The answer to that question depends, of course, on what one thinks Germany's 'war aims' actually were in 1914. According to Fritz Fischer and his pupils they were every bit as radical as the British Germanophobes feared. The war was an attempt 'to realize Germany's political ambitions, which may be summed up as German hegemony over Europe' through annexations of French, Belgian and possibly Russian territory, the founding of a Central European customs union and the creation of new Polish and Baltic states directly or indirectly under German control. In addition, Germany was to acquire new territory in Africa, so that her colonial possessions could be consolidated as a continuous Central African area. There was also to be a concerted effort to break up the British and Russian empires through fomenting revolutions.[133]

Yet there is a fundamental flaw in Fischer's reasoning which too many historians have let pass. It is the assumption that Germany's aims as stated after the war had begun were the same as German aims beforehand.[134] Thus Bethmann's 'September Programme' – 'provisional notes for the direction of our policy' for a separate peace with France, drafted on the assumption of a swift German victory in the West – is sometimes portrayed as if it were the first open statement of aims which had existed before the outbreak of war.[135] If this were true, then the argument that war was avoidable would collapse; for it is clear that no British government could have accepted the territorial and political terms which the September Programme proposed for France and Belgium,[136] as these would indeed have realized the 'Napoleonic nightmare' by giving Germany control of the Belgian coast. But the inescapable fact is that no evidence has ever been found by Fischer and his pupils that these objectives existed *before* Britain's entry into the war. It is in theory possible that they were never committed to paper, or that the relevant documents were destroyed or lost, and that those involved subsequently lied rather than concede legitimacy to the 'war guilt' clause of the Versailles treaty. But it seems unlikely. All that Fischer can produce are the pre-war pipedreams of a few Pan-Germans and businessmen, none of which had any official status, as well as the occasional bellicose utterances of the Kaiser, an individual whose influence over policy was neither consistent nor as great as he himself believed.[137] It is of course true that the Kaiser occasionally fantasized about 'a sort of Napoleonic supremacy',[138] and that, when it belatedly dawned on him on 30 July that Britain would intervene, he gave vent to the wildest of global designs:

Our consuls in Turkey and India, agents etc., must fire the whole Mohammedan world to fierce rebellion against this hated, lying, conscienceless nation of shop-keepers; for if we are to be bled to death, England shall at least lose India.[139]

Moltke too envisaged 'attempts . . . to instigate an uprising in India, if England takes a stand as our opponent. The same thing should be attempted in Egypt, also in the Dominion of South Africa.'[140] But such flights of fancy – worthy of John Buchan's wartime thriller *Greenmantle*, and as realistic – should not be seen as serious German war aims. Before the war the Kaiser was just as prone to remind British diplomats: 'We fought side by side a hundred years ago. I want our two nations to stand together again in front of the Belgian monument at Waterloo.'[141] This was hardly Napoleonic talk. It is also of interest that as early as 30 July the Kaiser expected war with Britain to 'bleed Germany dry'. Indeed, even when the Kaiser did compare himself with Napoleon, it was with the Emperor's ultimate fate in mind: 'Either the German flag will fly over the fortifications of the Bosphorus', he declared in 1913, 'or I shall suffer the same sad fate as the great exile on the island of St Helena.'[142]

The critical point is that had Britain not intervened immediately, Germany's war aims would have been significantly different from those in the September Programme. Bethmann's statement to Goschen of 29 July 1914 shows that he was prepared to guarantee the territorial integrity of both France and Belgium (as well as Holland) in return for British neutrality.[143] Moltke's notorious 'Suggestions of a military–political nature' of 2 August said the same: the assurance that Germany 'would act with moderation in case of a victory over France . . . should be given . . . unconditionally and in the most binding form', along with guarantees of the integrity of Belgium.[144] Had Britain in fact stayed out, it would have been foolish to have reneged on such a bargain. So Germany's aims would almost certainly not have included the territorial changes envisaged in the September Programme (except perhaps those relating to Luxembourg, in which Britain had no interest); and they certainly would not have included the proposals for German control of the Belgian coast, which no British government could have tolerated. The most that would have remained, then, would have been the following proposals:

1. *France.* . . A war indemnity to be paid in instalments; it must be high enough to prevent France from spending any considerable sums on armaments in the next 15–20 years. Furthermore: a commercial treaty which makes France economically dependent on Germany [and] secures the French market for our exports . . . This treaty must secure for us financial and industrial freedom of movement in France in such fashion that German enterprises can no longer receive different treatment from French.

2. . . . We must create a *central European economic association* through common customs treaties, to include France, Belgium, Holland, Denmark, Austria–Hungary, Poland, and perhaps Italy, Sweden and Norway. This association will not have any common constitutional supreme authority and all its members will be formally equal, but in practice will be under German leadership and must stabilise Germany's economic dominance over *Mitteleuropa.*

[3.] *The question of colonial acquisitions*, where the first aim is the creation of a continuous Central African colonial empire, will be considered later, as will that of the aims realised *vis-à-vis* Russia . . .

4. *Holland.* It will have to be considered by what means and methods Holland can be brought into closer relationship with the German Empire. In view of the Dutch character, this closer relationship must leave them free of any feeling of compulsion, must alter nothing in the Dutch way of life, and must also subject them to no new military obligations. Holland, then, must be left independent in externals, but be made internally dependent on us. Possibly one might consider an offensive and defensive alliance, to cover the colonies; in any case a close customs association . . .[145]

To these points – in effect, the September Programme without annexations from France and Belgium – should be added the detailed plans subsequently drawn up to 'thrust [Russia] back as far as possible from Germany's eastern frontier and [break] her domination over the non-Russian vassal peoples'. These envisaged the creation of a new

Polish state (joined to Habsburg Galicia) and the cession of the Baltic provinces (which would either be independent, incorporated in the new Poland or annexed by Germany itself).[146] Even this edited version of the September Programme probably exaggerates the pre-war aims of the German leadership. Bülow, of course, was no longer Chancellor; but his comments to the Crown Prince in 1908 were not so different from Bethmann's view that war would strengthen the political left and weaken the Reich internally:

No war in Europe can bring us much. There would be nothing for us to gain in the conquest of fresh Slav or French territory. If we annex small countries to the Empire we shall only strengthen those centrifugal elements which, alas, are never wanting in Germany . . . Every great war is followed by a period of Liberalism, since a people demands compensation for the sacrifices and effort war has entailed.[147]

Would the limited war aims outlined above have posed a direct threat to British interests? Did they imply a Napoleonic strategy? Hardly. All the economic clauses of the September Programme implied was the creation – some eighty years early, it might be said – of a German-dominated European customs union. Indeed, many of the official statements on the subject have a striking contemporary resonance: for example, Hans Delbrück's, 'It is only a Europe which forms a single customs unit that can meet with sufficient power the over-mighty productive resources of the transatlantic world'; or Gustav Müller's enthusiastic call for a 'United States of Europe' (a phrase used before the war by the Kaiser) 'including Switzerland, the Netherlands, the Scandinavian states, Belgium, France, even Spain and Portugal and, *via* Austria–Hungary, also Rumania, Bulgaria and Turkey'; or Baron Ludwig von Falkenhausen's aspiration to:

match the great, closed economic bodies of the United States, the British and the Russian empires with an equally solid economic bloc representing all European states . . . under German leadership, with the twofold purpose:

1. of assuring the members of this whole, particularly Germany, mastery of the European market, and
2. of being able to lead the entire economic strength of allied Europe into the field, as a unified force, in the struggle with those world powers over the conditions of the admission of each to the markets of the other.[148]

Even some of the German 'scaremongers' of the pre-war period had argued in these strangely familiar terms. In *The Collapse of the Old World*, 'Seestern' (Ferdinand Grauthoff) had declared prophetically: 'The *union* of the European peoples alone can win back for them the undisputed political power and the dominion of the seas that they have lost. Today the centre of political gravity is in Washington, St Petersburg, and Tokyo.' Karl Bleibtreu's *Offensive Invasion against England* concludes: 'Only a peacefully united Europe can maintain itself against the growing strength of other races and against the economic domination of America. Unite! Unite! Unite!'[149]

To be sure, Bethmann and his confidant Kurt Riezler had no doubt that this 'Middle European Empire of the German Nation' was merely 'the European disguise of our will to power.' Bethmann's aim, as Riezler put it in March 1917 was:

to lead the German Reich which by the methods of the Prussian territorial state . . . cannot become a world power . . . to an imperialism of the European form, to organize the Continent from the centre outward (Austria, Poland, Belgium) around our tacit leadership.[150]

That is not the way German politicians talk today. But even put like that, Germany's European project was not one with which Britain, with her maritime empire intact, could not have lived.

Of course, it was not to be: the bid for British neutrality was, as we know, rejected. Yet German historians have been too quick to dismiss Bethmann's proposal as wild miscalculation; or even to argue that the Germans themselves did not expect to secure British neutrality. The evidence does not bear this out. On the contrary, it shows that Bethmann's calculations were far from unreasonable. He can be forgiven for not anticipating that, at the very last minute, the arguments of Grey and Churchill would prevail over the numerically stronger non-interventionists; and that the majority of Members of Parliament would accept what would prove to be the Foreign Secretary's most misleading assertion: 'If we are engaged in war, we shall suffer but little more than we shall suffer even if we stand aside.'[151]

7

The August Days: The Myth of War Enthusiasm

TWO VOLUNTEERS

It was once an axiom of historiography that the people of Europe greeted the outbreak of war with fervent patriotic enthusiasm. The following passage may be taken as typical of the kind of evidence usually cited to substantiate this:

The struggle of the year 1914 was not forced on the masses – no, by the living God – it was desired by the whole people.

People wanted at length to put an end to the general uncertainty. Only thus can it be understood that more than two million German men and boys thronged to the colours for this hardest of all struggles, prepared to defend the flag with the last drop of blood.

To me, those hours seemed like a release from the painful feelings of my youth. Even today, I am not ashamed to say that, overpowered by stormy enthusiasm, I fell down on my knees and thanked Heaven from an overflowing heart for granting me the good fortune of being permitted to live at this time.

A fight for freedom had begun, mightier than the earth had ever seen . . . The overwhelming majority of the nation had long been weary of the eternally uncertain state of affairs . . . I too was one of these millions . . . My heart, like that of a million others, overflowed with proud joy . . .

For me . . . there now began the greatest and most unforgettable time of my earthly existence. Compared to the events of this giant struggle, everything past receded to shallow nothingness . . . A single worry tormented me at that time, me, as so many others: would we not reach the Front too late?[1]

Yet it is hard to believe that any sentiment felt by Adolf Hitler was as universal as he himself claimed. What little we know of Hitler's career as a soldier in the Bavarian army confirms that he was no typical volunteer; his comrades in the Bavarian infantry found him something

174

of an oddball – humourless and punctiliously patriotic, he sternly disapproved of the unofficial 'Christmas truces' of 1914–15.[2]

Compare Hitler's retrospective account of volunteering for active service with that of Harry Finch, an English gardener, as he recorded it at the time in his diary:

1915. Jan: 12th Tuesday. I went to Hastings this morning to the recruiting office in Havelock Road, and enlisted in Kitchener's army for war service. I passed the doctor and was put into No: 1 Company, 12th Battalion, The Royal Sussex Regiment (2nd South Downs.) I went back home again with order to report to my Battn: at Bexhill on the 18th inst: The recruiting office was full of men enlisting.

Jan: 18th Monday. Reported myself to-day to Company Sergeant Major Carter of No: 1 Coy: at the Down Schools, Bexhill. Had wire mattress and straw bed issued me with 3 blankets. My first impression was that barrack room language was a trifle warm. My bed seemed rather hard and I did not sleep much. Of course being a rookie I found myself with a broken bed.[3]

This contrast is emphatically not intended to suggest a difference of *national* character. Though there have been many attempts by cultural historians to suggest a difference in the way Germans and Britons responded to the outbreak of war,[4] the evidence presented below is intended to show how diverse responses were in all the combatant states. The difference between Hitler and Finch – who, incidentally, had a more successful wartime career than Hitler, rising to the rank of sergeant – was a difference of personal not national character.

CROWDS AND IMPOTENCE

There was, of course, some enthusiasm. We may view the testimony of Hitler with suspicion, but there are many other more reliable witnesses. Writing in 1945, the great liberal historian Friedrich Meinecke echoed Hitler's recollection: 'To all those who experienced it, the exaltation [*Erhebung*] of the August days of 1914 belongs among the most unforgettable memories of the highest sort . . . All the divisions within German people . . . melted away suddenly in the face of the common danger . . .'[5] At the time, Meinecke even rushed out a book on the subject of 'the German exaltation'.[6]

In practice, exaltation meant crowds.[7] Hitler's account in *Mein Kampf* is memorably corroborated by the photograph of a mass of people in Munich's Odeonsplatz in which his ecstatic face can be picked out. In Vienna Stefan Zweig was thrilled to find himself part of a patriotic crowd; while Josef Redlich was impressed to see workers demonstrating for war against Serbia on 26 July.[8] The night before, there had been the first nationalist demonstrations in Berlin and these were repeated on the 26th.[9] In Hamburg similar crowds gathered from 25 July at the Alster Pavilion on Jungfernstieg.[10] This was a mood which persisted throughout the first months of the war, with trains leaving for the Front decorated with flowers, and crowds gathering outside the stock exchange to celebrate the victory at Tannenberg.[11] In *The Comedy of Charleroi*, Drieu La Rochelle's hero described the pleasurable feeling of being in such a crowd in Paris: 'I was . . . lost in the middle of it all, exulting in my anonymity.'[12] E. C. Powell, a seventeen-year-old bank clerk, recalled arriving back in London on 3 August from a Bank Holiday trip to the Chilterns to find the city 'in a state of hysteria. A vast procession jammed the road from side to side, everyone waving flags and singing patriotic songs. We were swept along . . . bitten by the same mood of hysteria.'[13] It was, recalled Lloyd George, 'a scene of enthusiasm unprecedented in recent times'.[14]

Even those who did not themselves feel enthusiastic commented on the phenomenon (and Lloyd George himself did not much like being cheered by a 'jingo crowd' so reminiscent of those which had celebrated the relief of Mafeking). Karl Kraus's portrayal of the Vienna crowd is profoundly cynical – it takes the imagination of a newspaper reporter to transform the gangs of drunken xenophobes into a patriotic throng – but it does not deny that the crowd was there.[15] Elias Canetti remembered having to be rescued from a crowd in Berlin on 1 August when he and his brothers were heard singing 'God Save the King' (a military band had struck up the original German tune).[16] Even the Social Democrat leader Friedrich Ebert could not deny that the mood of the reservists he saw piling into trains after mobilization was 'confident' and that the crowds waving them off were filled with 'strong enthusiasm'.[17] Bertrand Russell observed the 'cheering crowds . . . in the neighbourhood of Trafalgar Square' and 'discovered to my horror that average men and women were delighted at the prospect of war'.[18] William Beveridge saw them too, 'thick-standing in the roadway, sitting on the railings opposite the Houses of Parliament, and sitting in tiers on the base of Nelson's column'.[19]

During the July crisis politicians – especially in Britain – made frequent reference to 'public opinion'. On 25 July 1914 Sir Edward Grey told his ambassador in Russia that 'public opinion would [not] ... sanction our going to war over a Serbian quarrel', a view echoed by Francis Bertie in Paris.[20] Six days later Pease noted in his diary the Cabinet's conclusion that 'public opinion would not enable us to support France', though 'a violation of Belgium might alter [that] opinion', a statement which Grey solemnly read out to the German ambassador Lichnowsky.[21] 'British public opinion', Jules Cambon reported to Paris, 'plays such an important role in what is happening' that every effort should be made to avoid mobilizing before Germany.[22] Later, in 1915, Grey remarked that 'one of his strongest feelings' about the events of July and August the previous year had been 'that he himself had no power to decide policy, and was only the mouthpiece of England'.[23] If public opinion was as enthusiastic as the numerous descriptions of crowds would seem to suggest, then the various decisions for war begin to look less avoidable than has been suggested in the previous chapter.

Yet there is a growing body of evidence which qualifies, if it does not wholly refute, the thesis of mass bellicosity. Crowds there may have been, but to describe their mood as simply one of 'enthusiasm' or 'euphoria' is misleading. Under the circumstances, feelings of anxiety, panic and even millenarian religiosity were equally common popular responses to the outbreak of war.

It is striking that even the politicians and generals who began the war did not feel much war enthusiasm. We have already seen how pessimistic both Bethmann and Moltke were, to say nothing of the Kaiser. Indeed, Moltke was literally on the brink of nervous collapse even as the German offensive was launched. When the German Foreign Secretary Jagow received the news of the English declaration of war on 4 August, one witness recalled, 'his features showed ... an expression of anguish'.[24] The previous evening, Grey had famously likened the war to 'the lamps going out all over Europe', telling a friend: 'We shall not see them lit again in our lifetime' – the epitaph of an era.[25] Alone together in his office at the Commons earlier that afternoon, Asquith and his wife 'could not speak for tears' after he told her simply: 'It's all up.'[26] Churchill was the exception. He told Violet Asquith on 22 February 1915:

I think a curse should rest on me – because I *love* this war. I know it's smashing & shattering the lives of thousands every moment – & yet – I *can't* help it – I enjoy every second of it.[27]

But Churchill was at heart an incurable optimist who never quite ceased to believe that there was an easy way to win the war. His wife evidently did not share his keenness.[28]

It goes without saying that a great many members of socialist and pacifist organizations regarded the outbreak of war with horror – no small matter given the extent of socialist electoral success before 1914 (see Chapter 1). Of course, the socialist parties and trade unions of Europe conspicuously failed to stop the war: after all the debates and resolutions, the Second International essentially dissolved into its national components when war came. The proponents of a general strike against militarism found themselves out-bid by appeals to support a war which all the combatant governments were somehow able to portray as defensive. The case of the German Social Democrats (SPD) is best known, though the British Labour Party behaved in much the same way.

For most of July the main SPD newspaper *Vorwärts* expressed grave reservations about Austrian policy towards Serbia, urging the government to reach an 'understanding' with France and Britain.[29] So exposed did the party's leaders feel that two of them, Ebert and Otto Braun, left Germany for Switzerland on 30 July as a precaution lest the government decide to act against the party. The day before, however, Ebert and his party colleagues had assured the government that 'no action (general or particular strike, sabotage or the like) was planned or need be feared'. By 4 August a number of SPD deputies – notably the revisionist Eduard David – were even to be seen applauding Bethmann's speech in the Reichstag. In all just fourteen Social Democrat deputies out of 110 opposed the parliamentary party's vote for war credits (among them that most unrelenting opponent of militarism, Karl Liebknecht, who only two weeks before had given a well-received speech – in French – to around 10,000 French socialists at Condé-sur-Escaut).[30] Nine days later Ebert recorded unquestioningly in his diary the government's bogus claim that France and Italy had begun to mobilize against Germany as early as 23 July.[31] He, like most of the leaders of the SPD, accepted the government line that the war was necessary to defend Germany against the aggression of autocratic Russia – *der Krieg gegen Zarismus* – and seized the olive branch of the 'fortress peace' (*Burg-*

frieden) offered by Bethmann in the hope of advancing their unofficial reformist agenda.[32] In just the same way, Arthur Henderson – who had co-authored with Keir Hardie a passionate anti-war *Appeal to the Working Class* in August 1914 – joined the Asquith government as Minister for Education in May 1915, along with two other Labour MPs who accepted junior office.

Nevertheless, those on the Left who continued to oppose the war despite all talk of national unity were more than an irrelevant minority. It is hard to believe that the 'thousands of workers' who had 'overfilled meetings and on the street demonstrated against war and for peace' in Berlin on 29 July disappeared in a puff of gunsmoke a week later; they were among nearly half a million people who participated in anti-war demonstrations in Germany in the last days of July.[33] The same goes for the 10,000 Parisian socialists who heard Liebknecht speak on 13 July.[34] Those German socialists who dissented from the party line in August were not without some popular backing, which proved remarkably resilient in the face of official harassment. When Liebknecht and his associates set up an anti-war newspaper called the *Internationale* in 1915 they were able to sell 5,000 copies before the state intervened to confiscate the remaining 4,000.[35] In Britain too the Independent Labour Party (ILP) had modest but committed support – especially in Scotland, where leaders like James Maxton seem to have relished confrontation with the authorities, even if it led to imprisonment. Maxton's position is perhaps best encapsulated in the anti-war song he wrote:

> Oh, I'm Henry Dubb
> And I won't go to war
> Because I don't know
> What they're all fighting for
>
> To Hell with the Kaiser
> To Hell with the Tsar
> To Hell with Lord Derby
> And also GR [Georgius Rex].[36]

Humour was indeed one of the Left's better cards. As early as 30 July 1914, the socialist newspaper the *Herald* ran a short story by J. C. Squire in which he imagined how a historian writing in 1920 would describe the war which was about to begin:

The British overseas force was wiped out to a man at Bois le Duc . . . a hundred thousand Germans fell into a trap near Cracow and only one-tenth lived to tell the tale . . . The food supplies in every country ran out . . . millions died by hunger, torture and fire . . . riots raged in every capital, and the Black Death . . . once more swept Europe from East to West.

To make the point unambiguously clear, the newspaper ran a leader on the same day entitled 'Hurrah for War! . . . Hurrah for blood and entrails, for lungs shot through, for weeping mothers and fatherless children, for death and disease abroad and destitution at home . . .'[37]

In the Labour Party itself, Ramsay MacDonald was one of those who explicitly opposed the war in the House of Commons after Grey's speech of 3 August. The Foreign Secretary, declared MacDonald, had 'not persuaded me' that 'the country is in danger'. He was dismissive of Grey's appeal to the nation's honour: 'There has been no crime committed by statesmen of this character without those statesmen appealing to their nation's honour. We fought the Crimean War because of honour. We rushed to South Africa because of honour.' Nor was MacDonald impressed by the argument that the war must be fought for the sake of Belgium (though here his argument was conspicuously convoluted):

If the Rt. Hon. Gentleman could come to us and tell us that a small European nationality like Belgium is in danger, and could assure us that he is going to confine the conflict to that question, then we would support him. [But] what is the use of talking about coming to the aid of Belgium, when . . . you are engaging in a whole European war . . .

And MacDonald went on to attack, rather more effectively, Grey's policy of ententes:

The Rt. Hon. Gentleman said nothing about Russia. We want to know about that. We want to try to find out what is going to happen, when it is all over, to the power of Russia in Europe . . . So far as France is concerned, we say solemnly and definitely that no such friendship as the Rt. Hon. Gentleman describes between one nation and another could ever justify one of those nations entering into war on behalf of the other.

On 5 August, after the declaration of war on Germany, MacDonald even managed to get his party's National Executive to pass a resolution condemning Grey's action and declaring the Labour movement's desire

1. John Gilmour Ferguson, private number s/22933, 2nd Battalion, Seaforth Highlanders. The author's grandfather – one of half a million Scots who served in the British army during the First World War.

2. 'H. M. the King and the King of Belgium': from the album of General R. H. Butler. Officially, George V's subjects were fighting to uphold the neutrality of Albert II's kingdom. In fact, Britain would have violated Belgian neutrality herself if Germany had not.

3. The Western Front epitomized: the mythical landscape of no man's land, from an album of photographs by James Francis (Frank) Hurley, an accredited Australian photographer. Hurley was already an established photographer when the war broke out, and worked in both France and Palestine. These soldiers must, in fact, have been quite far from the Front line to expose themselves helmetless and in daylight.

4. The Western Front idealized: officer and man side by side in the mud, from an album of photographs by Frank Hurley. Good relations between officers and men were vital in maintaining morale, but the equal and even friendly relationship implied by this picture was unusual.

5. The Eastern Front epitomized: German soldiers posing with villagers at an unidentified location, from a German soldier's album.

6. The Eastern Front idealized: German horsemen of the apocalypse, from the album of a soldier in the 84th Infantry Division. The homo-erotic connotations should probably be ignored; the real point is that on the Eastern Front a man got to ride and bathe.

7. 'Stacks of food etc.': from the album of Richard Harte Butler, deputy chief of staff to Douglas Haig. Good, plentiful food was crucial for morale. The Entente powers had a massive advantage in this respect, though the tactic of blockading Germany to reduce her food imports was less successful than the pre-war 'navalists' had hoped.

8. The life cycle of a shell, part 1. 'Gauging Dept. No. 2': Women making striking chambers for rifle grenades at Suckling Ltd., part of Kingsway House War Productions. Note the male foreman.

9. The life cycle of a shell, part 2. 'British corporal checking shells arriving on a light railway'. Official photograph issued by the Press Bureau.

10. The life cycle of a shell, part 3. 'This speaks for itself': from the album of Richard Harte Butler. Soldiers on both sides were often motivated by the desire for revenge, and not just for the sake of friends they had lost. In 1915 Captain Charles Fryatt had attempted to ram a German submarine in order to save his ship, the Channel steamer *Brussels*. He was subsequently captured and, after being found guilty of piracy by a court martial, executed – a well publicized example of German 'frightfulness'.

11. The life cycle of a shell, part 4. Spent shells: from the album of Frank Hurley.

12. The life cycle of a shell, part 5. The Germans prepare to fire back. A German boy poses in uniform by shells destined to be fired in Ludendorff's fateful spring 1918 offensive; from a German gunner's album.

13. Images of death, 1. 'Realistic Travels, no. 152 [caption indecipherable]': German corpse on British wire. This photograph was one of the large number by accredited press photographers which were reproduced for use in stereoscopic viewers. The horror of war was concealed from the public less than is sometimes thought.

14. Images of death, 2. 'Realistic Travels, no. 23: The Leicesters brave charge battles the Kaiser's bid to wipe out the old Contemptables [*sic*] at Ypres'; reproduced for use in stereoscopic viewers. Note the number of British casualties (nine out of seventeen), unusually high for an officially approved photograph.

15. Images of death, 3. 'Hun dead rolled into shell crater as an easy means of burial': from the album of Frank Hurley.

16. Images of death, 4. 'Dead Scot at Fosse 8': from the album of a German soldier. Ordinary German soldiers often snapped pictures of enemy corpses – as trophies?

17. (*overleaf*) Images of death, 5. 'Captured English trenches: No loop-holes for shooting, not many duckboards, dirty, disorderly': page from a German soldier's album, Langemark. The Germans' sense of their own superiority as soldiers was reinforced when they saw how much shoddier British and French trenches were than their own.

12

Eroberte englische

9

Kleine Schiesschartm, wenig Unterstände,
schmutzig, unordentlich.

Gräben.

Boches ready
to be buried
Chateau Thierry

Dead German Corporal

Dead Boche Chateau-Thierry

After the Marne fighting (1914-1916)

Deadman's hill - Verdun 1916.

Dead Boche (Amiens)

18. Images of death, 6. Postcards of 'dead Boches': from an American sailor's album. Soldiers were fascinated by death. Photographs of enemy corpses were widely circulated and can be found in many such albums, though it is unusual to find a whole page devoted to them.

'to secure peace at the earliest moment'. Although he failed to carry the parliamentary party with him – it voted for war credits on the same day – his attacks on Grey were applauded by members of the ILP.[38]

Mention should also be made of the non-socialist opponents of the war. In Germany the New Fatherland League (*Bund neues Vaterland*) was set up in the autumn of 1914 to supersede the enfeebled Pacifist Society. German pacifists were also involved in the pan-European Central Organization for a Durable Peace which met in neutral territory.[39] In Britain there were two groups set up in July 1914 to oppose intervention: the British Neutrality League, set up by Norman Angell and others, and the British Neutrality Committee, whose members included J. A. Hobson.[40] The latter published a letter on 3 August which described Germany as 'wedged between hostile states, highly civilized' and 'racially allied' to Britain.[41] Later came the Stop the War Committee and the No-Conscription Fellowship. In his own idiosyncratic way, as we have seen, George Bernard Shaw opposed the war for reasons not so different from those propagated by these (broadly speaking) radical groups.[42]

Different in tenor was the opposition to the war of that clique of somewhat narcissistic intellectuals known as 'Bloomsbury'. Lytton Strachey, Duncan Grant, David Garnett, Gerald Shove, E. M. Forster and Virginia Woolf's brother Adrian Stephen – nearly all the Bloomsbury men were conscientious objectors (though only Shove was a true pacifist). Their snobbishly libertarian views are perhaps best summed up by the letter Grant wrote to his father:

I never considered the possibility of a great European war. It seemed such an absolutely mad thing for a civilised people to do . . . I began to see that one's enemies were not vague masses of foreign people, but the mass of people in one's own country and the mass of people in the enemy country, and that one's friends were people of true ideas that one might and did meet in every country one visited. I still think this and think the war utter madness and folly.[43]

For Clive Bell and Lady Ottoline Morrell, the war was, in Virginia Woolf's words, 'the end of civilization', rendering 'the rest of our lives worthless': Bell's article *Peace at Once* (1915) argued simply (and not inaccurately) that the war would reduce the sum of human happiness: 'Our labour will purchase worse food, shorter holidays, smaller rooms, less fun, less ease, in a word, less well-being than it used to purchase.'[44]

Rather different arguments against the war could be heard in the

European universities. In Vienna – admittedly after a patriotic moment – Sigmund Freud attacked 'the warring state' for 'permit[ting] itself every such misdeed, every such act of violence, as would disgrace the individual man'.[45] In Berlin Albert Einstein and the physician Georg Friedrich Nicolai, author of *The Biology of War*, were among the signatories of a 'Manifesto to the Europeans' which was designed as a riposte to the bombastically pro-war address 'To the World of Culture' signed by ninety-three intellectuals (see Chapter 8). The Marburg law professor Walther Schücking was one of the most prominent German pacifists, arguing throughout the war for a system of international relations based on law and arbitration not military conflict.[46] In Paris the musicologist Romain Rolland denounced the war as 'the collapse of civilization . . . the greatest catastrophe in history . . . the ruin of our holiest hopes for human brotherhood'.[47] The involvement of the Cambridge philosopher Bertrand Russell with the Union of Democratic Control (UDC) and the No-Conscription Fellowship is well documented: according to Russell, Grey was a 'warmonger' and the war was the result of a failure to pursue a rational policy of appeasement towards Germany.[48] True, Russell was an isolated figure in Cambridge; indeed, his involvement with the UDC cost him a fellowship at Trinity. On the other hand, war enthusiasm was far from being the majority sentiment. Professor J. J. Thomson was one of those who opposed British intervention publicly in 1914, as was the historian F. J. Foakes-Jackson, one of the signatories of the 1 August Scholars' Protest. Another historian (though no longer a fellow at Cambridge) who publicly opposed 'the participation of England in the European crime' was G. M. Trevelyan.[49] Few dons were such keen Germanophobes from the outset as Henry Jackson of Trinity. John Maynard Keynes's father, Neville, was probably more typical of the Cambridge mood, miserably playing golf to take his mind off the horror of 'this terrible war'.[50] At the London School of Economics Graham Wallas was a member of the British Neutrality Committee. To be sure, many of the early opponents of intervention – including Wallas and George Trevelyan – changed their minds after 4 August.[51] In a letter of 13 August Trevelyan accepted the view that 'the present awful struggle is to save England, Belgium and France from the Junkers, and to save our island civilization, with its delicate fabric, from collapse'.[52] But this was a long way from war enthusiasm and primarily reflected the appeal of the Belgian issue to a mind steeped in the nineteenth-century liberal tradition.

Less well known are the expressions of anti-war sentiment in more conservative Oxford. Two Oxford dons were among those who signed the 'Scholars' Protest against War with Germany' published as a letter to *The Times* on 1 August, which declared:

We regard Germany as a nation leading the way in the Arts and Sciences, and we have all learnt and are learning from German scholars. War upon her in the interests of Servia and Russia will be a sin against civilization . . . We consider ourselves justified in protesting against being drawn into the struggle with a nation so near akin to our own, and with whom we have so much in common.[53]

This view was endorsed by no less a figure than the vice-chancellor, T. B. Strong of Christ Church, in his speech at the beginning of Michaelmas term 1914, in which he described Germany as 'the one power in Europe with which we have had the closest affinity'. The *Oxford Magazine* paid tribute to German Oxonians who were killed in the war and in January 1915 published a letter from Kurt Hahn – a former Christ Church man – blaming Grey's foreign policy for the war. To be sure, Oxford historians played a leading role in anti-German propaganda (see next chapter) and the student magazine *Varsity* adopted an increasingly Germanophobe tone as the war dragged on. But over a hundred people signed a letter of protest against the magazine's harassment of the German professor H. G. Fiedler (which culminated in a call to boycott German examinations).[54] There was perhaps a note of irony in the vice-chancellor's oration of 1916, when he declared that Oxford would henceforth 'proceed upon our own lines and not attempt to import German methods and German rigidity . . . into our system': it was in fact during the war that the degree of Doctor of Philosophy was introduced, in conscious imitation of the German postgraduate system.[55] Nor did the Rhodes Trustees succumb to pressure to terminate the Rhodes Scholarships for Germans until March 1916.[56] The 'more in sorrow than in anger' mood was well captured by H. Stuart Jones, a Fellow of Trinity, in a letter published in a northern newspaper:

I yield neither to Norman Angell nor to any other man in my detestation of war; but when he tells us that Germany was restrained from provoking hostilities in a previous crisis by fears of trouble in Alsace-Lorraine and predicts if she acquired Rotterdam, Antwerp and Dunkirk she would be held back from aggression by the difficulty of governing her subject populations, one wonders whether to laugh or weep at such abysmal folly.[57]

It should also be emphasized that many left-leaning Liberals who gave their support to the war effort did so with the very reverse of enthusiasm. William Beveridge and John Maynard Keynes toiled in the service of the British war economy for the duration; both privately regarded the war as a mistake. Beveridge told his mother on 3 August that though

it seems necessary and in a sense our duty . . . it's all against the grain with me to go in against Germans with French and Russians. I can only hope that if we do go in we shall understand and that the German will also understand that there is no rancour in it, and that our readiness will always be for an early peace.[58]

A fortnight later he wrote despairingly:

I detest my work . . . All the things I've been working at will be swamped in militarism for the next ten years, and I shall be too busy with them to have any part in any of the new movements for disarmament that may come from this war.[59]

Keynes sought vainly to dissuade his brother Geoffrey and his Hungarian friend Ferenc Békássy from joining up. When his friend Freddie Hardman was killed in late October 1914, he wrote to Duncan Grant: 'It makes one bitterly miserable and long that the war should stop quickly on almost any terms. I can't bear it that he should have died.'[60] The subsequent deaths of Rupert Brooke, another Cambridge friend, and Békássy intensified his anguish.[61] In February 1916, despite being exempt from combatant service because of his 'work of national importance' at the Treasury, Keynes insisted on applying for exemption on the ground of conscientious objection to the war. On 4 January he told Ottoline Morrell that he wished for 'a general strike and a real uprising to teach . . . those bloody men who enrage and humiliate us'. He told Duncan Grant in December 1917: 'I work for a government I despise for ends I think criminal.'[62]

Even those who volunteered to fight were not uncritical of the politics of the war. That legendary war enthusiast, the former apostle, school-teacher and poet Rupert Brooke, lamented on 3 August: 'Everything's just the wrong way round. I want Germany to smash Russia to fragments, and then France to break Germany. Instead of which, I'm afraid Germany will badly smash France and then be wiped out by Russia . . . Prussia is a devil. [But] Russia means the end of Europe and any decency.

I suppose the future is a Slav Empire, world-wide, despotic and insane.'[63] Such ambivalence towards Britain's eastern ally was felt by government ministers too. 'I am dead against carrying on a war of conquest to crush Germany for the benefit of Russia,' Lloyd George wrote to his wife on 11 August. 'Beat the Junker but no war on the German people &c. I am not going to sacrifice my . . . boy for that purpose.'[64]

It might be argued that such views were those of the small, educated élite. Yet such evidence as can be gleaned from British newspapers (and especially their letter columns) in 1914 suggests that less exalted minds thought along similar lines. On 3 August 1914 a Mr A. Simpson wrote to the *Yorkshire Post*:

Now as to England and Germany. There ought not to be any war between us. Our ties of commerce, ideas and religion are too close and too real to allow any such thing . . . The Germans have intellect, moral forces, staying power. No possible European combination can prevent Germany from attaining to greater might and power. Even if she were defeated this year or next year (or any time) by England, Russia, and France, she would retire within herself, dig her foundations, and by the power within her and her intensity of purpose . . . ultimately emerge, and the future of Europe would be with her . . . Russia stands for brute force, any dominance by her in European affairs would be a setback for all the ideals of humanity.[65]

This Russophobia was echoed in a sermon by the Rector of St Mary's, Newmarket, who denounced 'the government of Russia [as] the most horrible, the most barbarous government in the world'.[66] On 5 August – by which time it was too late – the *Barrow Guardian* published a letter from one C. R. Buxton urging 'Liberals [to] stick to their principles and keep their heads. The Tory press is trying to rush us into a war with which we have no concern.'[67]

How seriously should the opponents of the war – who were without question a small minority – be taken? Governments took them seriously enough. Under the authority of the 1851 Prussian Law on the State of Siege (which applied throughout the Reich except in Bavaria and came into force on the outbreak of war), independent socialists and pacifists were systematically persecuted in Germany. The pre-war Peace Society had its journal banned and its leader Ludwig Quidde was forbidden to engage in 'any further proselytizing activity'. The New Fatherland League was subjected to censorship in 1915 and wholly outlawed in 1916. Schücking was effectively gagged: forbidden to express his views orally or on paper. In Britain, those who had been responsible for counter-espionage before the war lost no time in extending their ambit to include domestic opponents of the war. Postal censorship, initially introduced to identify German spies, allowed lists to be compiled of 34,500 British citizens with alleged ties to the enemy, a further 38,000 'under suspicion by reason of any act or hostile association' and 5,246 associated with 'pacifism, anti-militarism, etc.'. In addition to the ILP, the Stop the War Committee and the No-Conscription Fellowship were subjected to official investigation.[68] The Defence of the Realm Act (DORA) was used to imprison not only ILP leaders like Maxton, but also individuals whose scruples against the war were ethical and even religious rather than political. In December 1915, for example, two men received six-month sentences for publishing a leaflet which set out the Christian doctrine on war according to the Sermon on the Mount.[69] Bertrand Russell was prosecuted in June 1916 for an anti-conscription pamphlet, and finally imprisoned in 1918 for 'insulting an ally'. In one of the most shocking episodes of the whole war, thirty-four British conscientious objectors were sent to France, court martialed and sentenced to death, sentences which were later commuted to hard labour following protests by Russell and others.[70] The only reason this had no parallel in Germany or Austria–Hungary was because they had no system of conscientious objection.

PANIC

It was not, however, only the politically articulate who regarded the war with trepidation. In regions where civilians had to reckon with enemy incursions, there was a mood closer to panic. Paris, famously, experienced a mass exodus. This began even before the first bombardment of the city (30 August 1914); memories of the siege of 1870 sufficed. Approximately 700,000 civilians appear to have fled Paris by September, of whom around 220,000 were children under 15; among the adults were the entire government and civil service, who fled to the safety of Bordeaux.[71] There were similar streams of refugees on the Eastern Front. Gregor von Rezzori, an ethnic German born in 1914 in the Bukovina, was told by his parents that 'because someone claimed to have seen their [the Russians'] flat caps – in truth he had mistaken the visorless field-grey caps of our German comrades-in-arms – panic broke out among the population'. His mother joined the mass exodus from the area; ultimately she and her two children ended up in Trieste.[72]

The pioneering work of Jean-Jacques Becker has shown how ambivalent the French mood in 1914 was, even in those areas not directly menaced by war.[73] Fortunately for the historian, the French Minister of Education, Albert Sarraut, circulated primary school teachers in certain departments with a questionnaire which included the following: 'Mobilization. How was it done? Public mood, typical phrases one could hear repeated.' Becker's analysis of the teachers' responses for six departments shows that enthusiasm was *not* the principal reaction of ordinary French people to the war. Before the news of war, one teacher in Mansle noted, 'everybody said that no one would be so insane or criminal as to inflict such a scourge.' The most frequently expressed response to the news of mobilization in over 300 communes surveyed in the department of Charente was 'stupefaction', followed by 'surprise'. Analysing the specific phrases used to describe the popular mood, Becker found that 57 per cent were negative, 20 per cent 'calm and composed' and only 23 per cent indicative of patriotic fervour. Within the negative category, the most frequently mentioned reactions to mobilization were 'weeping' and 'desolation': these appeared no fewer than ninety-two times, compared with just twenty-nine references to 'enthusiasm'.

That said, there was no resistance to mobilization (as there was in Russia); and the mood undoubtedly became more positive by the time troops began to leave – the number of mentions of 'enthusiasm' went up to seventy-one. But even then it was a qualified enthusiasm. 'The songs of those who were blustering and boasting', wrote one teacher in Aubeterre, 'rang false to me and it seemed that they had drunk in order to screw up their courage and hide their fear.' Nor did people allude much to the motivations for war which historians used to cite for France: revenge for 1870–71 and the recovery of Alsace-Lorraine. The principal rationale for war was, as elsewhere, defensive. As one typical report of the mood put it: 'France did not want war; she was attacked; we will do our duty.' Moreover, the evidence from five other departments suggests that enthusiasm was probably above average in the department of Charente. In the Côtes du Nord, around 70 per cent of reactions to mobilization were negative.[74] No equivalent evidence exists to allow a comparable study of the mood in Britain; however, one survey of the press in the north of England identifies anti-war

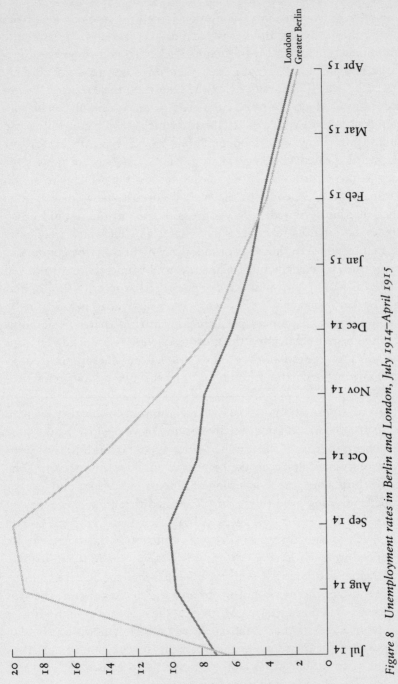

Figure 8   Unemployment rates in Berlin and London, July 1914–April 1915

Source: Lawrence et al., 'Outbreak of War', p. 586.

meetings in Carlisle and Scarborough.[75] There is similar evidence of mixed feelings in Germany.[76]

Most of Becker's evidence relates to rural France, of course, whereas anecdotal evidence tends to suggest that the patriotic crowd in 1914 was an urban phenomenon. Yet even here there are grounds for scepticism. Apart from anything else, it is important to recollect that the most immediate effect of the outbreak of war on urban economies was to plunge them into economic recession. In Berlin unemployment among trade union members jumped from 6 per cent in July 1914 to 19 per cent in August, peaking at just under 29 per cent the following month. In London the unemployment rates for workers covered by national insurance rose from 7 to 10 per cent (see Figure 8). These percentages almost certainly understate total unemployment, since casual (usually non-unionized or uninsured) workers were more likely to be laid off. Worst affected was Paris, not least because so many employers fled the capital. Total employment in the Paris region fell by some 71 per cent in August. Although much of that decline was due to the departure of workers for the army, there were at least 300,000 Parisians registered as unemployed in October: around 14 per cent of the city's total workforce.[77]

Of course, unemployment was mainly a working-class phenomenon; whereas it would seem from photographic and other evidence that the majority of patriotic demonstrators in 1914 were middle-class. There are no proletarian caps to be seen around Hitler in the Odeonsplatz crowd; straw boaters and panamas predominate. In Berlin too, according to the report in *Vorwärts*, the crowd which took to the streets on 26 July and 27 July was mainly composed of 'young men, dressed in the newest, most modish fashion, German nationalist students and clerks'.[78] Newspaper reports suggest that the crowd around Buckingham Palace and Whitehall on 3 August – the size of which the *Daily Mail* estimated at 60,000, though 20,000 seems more likely – was predominantly suburban and middle-class. It was a Bank Holiday Monday, and the city's 'Pooters' were acting rather as they had during the Boer War, though the mood was, according to some reports, rather more sober.[79]

In any case, however much jingoism there was among southern bank clerks in August 1914, war enthusiasm was conspicuously absent from the financial markets which employed them.

Before 1914 it had been argued by authors like Ivan Bloch and

Norman Angell that the financial consequences of a major European war would be so grave as to render such a war practically impossible. Bloch had estimated the cost of a major war at £4 million a day for five warring nations, and calculated that it would cost roughly £1.46 billion just to feed all the soldiers involved for a year:

'But could they not borrow and issue paper money?' [his English editor asked.] 'Very well,' said Mr Bloch, 'they would try to do so, no doubt, but the immediate consequence of war would be to send securities all round down from 25 to 50 per cent, and in such a tumbling market it would be difficult to float loans. Recourse would therefore have to be had to forced loans and unconvertible paper money . . . Prices . . . would go up enormously.'[80]

The problem would be especially acute for countries which had to rely partly on foreigners to finance their pre-war debts. As Angell argued, 'the profound change effected by credit' and 'the delicate interdependence of international finance' meant that war would be more or less impossible: 'No physical force can set at nought the force of credit.' If a battleship belonging to a foreign power sailed up the Thames, it would be the foreign economy which would suffer, not the British, as investors dumped the aggressor's bonds.[81] The French socialist Jean Jaurès was merely parroting Angell when he declared that 'international movement of capital is the biggest single guarantor of world peace'.

The idea of economic constraints on war was widely believed, and not just on the political Left. Schlieffen had devised his plan on precisely the assumption that:

The [economic] machine with its thousands of wheels, from which millions earn their living, cannot stand still for long. One cannot move from position to position in battles of twelve days' length for one or two years, until the belligerents are completely exhausted and worn out, both beg for peace, and both accept the *status quo*.

In an article published in 1910 he repeated the same argument: '[Long] wars are impossible at a time when the existence of a nation is founded upon the uninterrupted progress of commerce and industry . . . A strategy of attrition will not do if the maintenance of millions requires [the expenditure of] billions.'[82] Similar arguments were heard during July. The Russian chargé d'affaires in Berlin warned a German diplomat as early as 22 July that 'German shareholders' would 'pay the price with their own securities for the methods of the Austrian politicians'.[83]

The next day Sir Edward Grey predicted (in conversation with the Austrian ambassador Count Mensdorff) that war 'must involve the expenditure of so vast a sum of money and such an interference with trade, that a war would be accompanied or followed by a complete collapse of European credit and industry'.[84] A continental war, he informed Lichnowsky on the 24th, would have 'absolutely incalculable . . . results': 'total exhaustion and impoverishment; industry and trade would be ruined, and the power of capital destroyed. Revolutionary movements like those of the year 1848 due to the collapse of industrial activities would be the result.'[85] (This was no mere rhetorical device: there were genuine fears in London in early August of 'an incipient food panic', which would result in 'serious trouble' if it 'spread to the mass of the labouring population'.)[86] On 31 July Grey went so far as to use this as an argument in favour of British non-intervention, as Paul Cambon reported to Paris:

It is thought that the coming conflict will plunge the finances of Europe into trouble, that Britain was facing an economic and financial crisis without precedent and that British neutrality might be the only way of averting a complete collapse of European credit.[87]

Although they were to prove wrong in the medium term, these predictions were in fact right in both the short term and the long term. The Vienna stock exchange had begun to slide as early as 13 July. In Hamburg, Max Warburg had begun to 'realize what could be sold, and reduce our engagements' immediately after the Sarajevo assassinations, and by 20 July the main Hamburg banks had to take the first measures to counter a panic on the stock exchange.[88] The earliness of the crisis in Hamburg was probably due to a series of official indications that war was imminent. On 18 July the Kaiser requested that the shipowner Albert Ballin be informed of possible mobilization; three days later the Reich Chancellery wrote to the Senate about the need for regional labour exchanges to allocate labour in the event of a war; and on 23 July the Foreign Office sent an official to Hamburg with a copy of the Austrian ultimatum to Serbia.[89] When news reached Hamburg on the evening of 28 July that the German government had rejected Grey's proposal for a conference of foreign ministers in London, there was such acute panic on the Hamburg bourse that Warburg felt compelled to contact the Wilhelmstrasse. He was authorized to announce that although the German government did not regard the proposed conference as 'feasible', nevertheless 'the [bi-lateral] negotiations from Cabinet to Cabinet, which had already been initiated with the utmost success, would be continued'. Although this disingenuous statement was greeted with applause, the bourse was not re-opened that evening.[90]

The crisis was not really detectable in London until 27 July – the day before the Austrian declaration of war on Serbia – when German banks began to withdraw deposits and wind up positions.[91] That this was only the beginning became apparent the next day when – in a development which took Lord Rothschild wholly by surprise – his Paris cousins sent a coded telegram requesting the sale of 'a vast quantity of Consols here for the French Govt & Savings banks'. He refused, first on the purely technical ground that 'in the actual state of our markets it is quite impossible to do anything at all'; then adding the more political argument that it would produce 'a deplorable effect . . . if we were to send gold to a Continental Power for the purpose of strengthening itself at a moment when "War" is in the mouths of everyone'.[92] Despite his assurances to the French Rothschilds that their telegrams were being kept strictly secret, Rothschild at once warned Asquith of what had happened. With heroic understatement, Asquith described this to Venetia Stanley as 'ominous'.[93] In his diary he was more frank: 'The City . . . is in a terrible state of depression and paralysis . . . The prospect is very black.'[94]

The first real symptom of the crisis was a sharp fall in bond prices – the customary sign of an international crisis. On 29 July consols plunged from above 74 to 69.5 and continued to fall when the market re-opened; and consols were usually the investor's penultimate resort (before gold) in a crisis. The five-point drop on 1 August was, according to the *Economist*, unprecedented, as was the widening of the bid–ask spread (the gap between buyers' offers and sellers' asking prices) to a full point compared with a historic average of one-eighth. The bonds of the other powers slumped even further.[95] In short, Bloch's prediction of 25 to 50 per cent falls in bond prices had begun to come true. The slump affected share prices too, even those of non-European companies. Keynes had made some 'courageous' purchases of Rio Tinto and Canadian Pacific shares on 28 June on the assumption that Russia and Germany would not 'join in' an Austro-Serbian war.[96] He was one of many investors now looking at severe losses.

In addition to giving an idea of the magnitude of the crisis, Figure 9 allows us to assess City expectations. As we have seen, what remained uncertain until 3 August was whether Britain would actually enter the war. The prices to 1 August therefore allow us to infer what the City expected to happen in a purely continental conflict. Between 18 July and 1 August (the last day when quotations were published), the bonds of all the major powers slumped, but some fell further than others. Russian 4 per cents fell by 8.7 per cent, French 3 per cents by 7.8 per cent – but German 3 per cents by just 4 per cent. In the absence of British intervention, the City was putting its money on Moltke, just as it had in 1870. However, the British decision to tip the balance in favour of France by intervening put a new complexion on everything, for it portended a long war, and a global war. Had the European stock markets remained open after 1 August, prices of all securities would have fallen further; indeed, there is every reason to think that the collapse would have overshadowed all the crises of the preceding hundred years, including 1848.

Just as Jaurès and the rest had predicted, bankers therefore strove as far as they were able to avoid war in 1914: they saw even more clearly than the politicians that the outbreak of a major war would bring financial chaos. As Lord Rothschild told his cousins on 27 July, '[N]o one [in the City] thinks and talks about anything else but the European situation and the consequences which might arise if serious steps were not taken to prevent a European conflagration.'[97] '[C]lumsy as Austria may have been', he wrote on 30 July, 'it would be ultra-criminal if *millions of lives* were sacrificed in order to sanctify the theory of murder, a brutal murder which the Servians have committed.'[98] The next day he urged his French cousins to get Poincaré to 'impress upon the Russian Govt':

1) that the result of a war, however powerful a country their ally may be, is doubtful, but whatever the result may be, the sacrifices and misery attendant upon it are stupendous & untold. In this case the calamity would be greater than anything ever seen or known before.

2) France is Russia's greatest creditor, in fact the financial and economic conditions of the two countries are intimately connected & we hope you will do your best to bring any influence you may have, to bear upon your statesmen even at the last moment, to prevent this hideous struggle from taking place, and to point out to Russia that she owes this to France.[99]

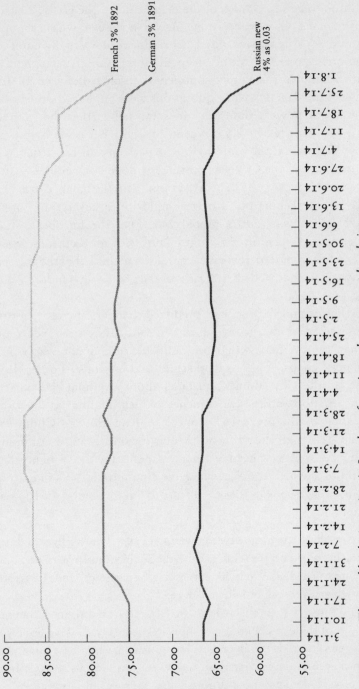

Figure 9   *The weekly closing prices in London of continental government bonds in 1914*

Source: *Economist.*

On 31 July Rothschild implored *The Times* to tone down its leading articles, which were 'hounding the country into war'; but both the foreign editor Henry Wickham Steed and his proprietor Lord Northcliffe regarded this as 'a dirty German-Jewish international financial attempt to bully us into advocating neutrality' and concluded that 'the proper answer would be a still stiffer leading article tomorrow'. 'We dare not stand aside,' Saturday's leader duly thundered. 'Our strongest interest is the law of self-preservation.'[100] Rothschild frantically sought to keep his channels of communication to Berlin via Paul Schwabach open;[101] he even sent a personal appeal for peace directly to the Kaiser.[102] As Asquith told Venetia Stanley, opinion was 'particularly strong in the City . . . to keep out at all costs'.[103] Echoing Wickham Steed, Cambon informed the Quai d'Orsay of the

Extraordinary efforts . . . being made by the business world to prevent the Government from intervening against Germany. The City financiers, governors of the Bank of England, more or less under the domination of bankers of German origin, are carrying on a very dangerous campaign.[104]

Yet it suddenly became apparent that the bankers were impotent after all. For Angell and the rest had got it the wrong way round: the banks could not stop a war – but war could stop the banks. This was because of the paralysing effect of the prospect of a war involving Britain on trade with the continent. Enough was known about British war plans (and enough was recollected of the experience of a century before) for it to be assumed that this trade would now effectively halt: no more shipments of German goods to Britain, no more shipments of British goods to Germany. Yet payment for the ships which would now never sail had invariably been made in advance by the issue of commercial bills. The acceptance houses who financed this trade by discounting such bills were therefore in desperate straits, with around £350 million of acceptances outstanding and an unknowable proportion of them unlikely to be honoured.[105] Table 18 shows the extent of the problem.[106]

As Keynes pointed out, this had major implications for the banking system as a whole: 'The [clearing] banks . . . are depending on the accepting houses and on the discount houses; the discount houses are depending on the accepting houses; and the accepting houses are depending on foreign clients who are unable to remit.' The possibility was now dawning that an acute liquidity crisis emanating from the acceptance houses could threaten the entire British financial system. By

Table 18 The London acceptance market: liabilities on acceptances at year end, 1912–1914 (£ million)

	Barings	Kleinwort Sons	Schröders	Hambros	N. M. Rothschild	Gibbs	Brandts	Total of 'big seven'	All acceptances
1913	6.64	14.21	11.66	4.57	3.19	2.04	3.33	45.64	140
1914	3.72	8.54	5.82	1.34	1.31	1.17	0.72	22.62	69

Source: Chapman, Merchant Banking, p. 209.

the 30th, the Bank of England had advanced £14 million to the discount market and a similar amount to the banks, but was forced to protect its own reserves (which fell from 51 per cent of liabilities to just 14.5 per cent) by pushing up Bank rate from 3 to 4 per cent. Already on 27 July the Russian central bank had been forced to suspend gold convertibility. When the Bank of England sought to avoid the same fate by doubling its base rate to 8 per cent on 31 July, followed by a further 2 per cent hike the following day, the market simply crashed. To avert a complete implosion, the stock exchange had to be closed on the 31st, a step which was also taken in Berlin and Paris. Closure of the bourse had happened in Paris before (in 1848 for example); but not even the worst crisis of the nineteenth century had previously necessitated such a drastic measure in London. The next day (as in 1847, 1857 and 1866), Lloyd George gave the Governor of the Bank a letter permitting him to exceed, if need be, the note-issue limit set by the Bank Charter Act. Fortuitously, 1 August was a Saturday and the following Monday a Bank Holiday; further breathing space was provided by extending the holiday for the rest of the week. The stock exchange remained closed 'until further notice'. There was also, as in Paris, a temporary moratorium on debts (a measure successfully avoided in Berlin).[107]

The gloom of bankers may be imagined. In Hamburg the entry of England into the war plunged Ballin into a despair which startled even Warburg. By September, however, he too had given up hope of a swift victory.[108] 'No Government has ever had a more serious and painful task before it,' Alfred de Rothschild wrote to his Paris cousins on 3 August, when it was clear to him that Britain would intervene. He could not think of the 'military & moral spectacle which we have before us with its painful details looming in the distance ... without shuddering'.[109] There may indeed have been people in 1914 who sincerely believed that the war would be short and sweet. But the bankers were not among them – any more than were the German General Staff, whose pessimism has already been described.

JOINING UP

The best evidence of war enthusiasm is, of course, the willingness of men to fight. Of course, on the continent they had little choice. Those who were performing or had recently performed their military service were immediately mobilized on the outbreak of war. Still, it is note-worthy that there was little resistance to mobilization, even where (as in parts of France) it was greeted with muted enthusiasm. Only in Russia was there violent resistance on the part of peasants who resented the incursion of the military authorities on the eve of the harvest; and even this was sporadic.[110] Moreover, even in those countries which already had compulsory military service, it was still possible for those who had not 'served' in peacetime to volunteer to fight in the war; and many did. Adolf Hitler was one (he had avoided his Austrian military service by moving to Munich, but hastened to volunteer for the Bavarian army in August 1914). Ernst Jünger was another: as he recalled, he was treated with 'a certain puzzlement by old soldiers. The common soldier took it to be a sort of bumptiousness on our part.'[111] In Hamburg, as elsewhere, it was the middle class who rushed to the colours of their own free will: boys like the fifteen-year-old Percy Schramm, from a grand Hanseatic merchant family,[112] or the Frankfurt Jew Herbert Sulzbach, who toyed as early as 14 July 1914 with the idea of 'start[ing] my military service instead of going to Hamburg as a commercial trainee'; after some hesitation, he volunteered on 1 August.[113]

In Britain and the British Empire, by contrast, conscription was not introduced until the beginning of 1916. All those who joined the army before that date therefore did so voluntarily. The figures are impressive. On 25 August 1914 Kitchener stated his aims for voluntary recruitment: thirty divisions, a figure which rose steadily until it had reached seventy a year later. The total number of men he called for in the first month of the war was 200,000.[114] In fact, no fewer than 300,000 men enlisted (see Figure 10). In a single week (30 August–5 September) 174,901 men joined up.[115] The daily total rose from 10,019 on 25 August to a peak of 33,000 on 3 September.[116] Altogether just under 2.5 million men volunteered to fight in the British army, something like 25 per cent of those eligible. Of these, 29 per cent joined in the first eight weeks of the war. Almost as many men joined the army voluntarily as joined after the introduction of conscription; indeed, on an annual basis, the total entry tended to decline regardless of compulsion.[117] In an attempt to slow down the early rush, the War Office raised the minimum height for recruits by three inches to 5'6" on 11 September, though it had to lower it again at the end of October and to restore it to its old level on 14 November.[118] In addition, many men over serving age served as Volunteers or Special Constables.[119] Until the Battle of the Somme the

British mostly fought because they wanted to, not because they had to.

A number of qualifications need to be made, however. Not all Britons were equally keen to fight. It is certainly not true (as was claimed after the war) that 'all classes . . . gave equally'.[120] Nor is it true that the New Army was composed of 'the same class of average recruit as the average run of regular recruit' before the war.[121] As many contemporaries remarked, including the great recruiting-sergeant Lord Derby, there were many middle-class men – potential officer material – who enlisted as privates in their eagerness to see action. 'There were barristers, solicitors, bank clerks, qualified engineers,' recalled one who joined the City of Birmingham regiment, though there were also substantial working-class recruits of the traditional, malnourished type.[122] Within the working class, textile workers were under-represented while (insanely from the point of view of the war economy) miners were over-represented: 115,000 miners volunteered in the first month of the war, nearly 15 per cent of the membership of the Miners' Federation, and by June 1915 the figure had reached 230,000. Some mining towns were virtually emptied of young men.[123] But the most striking imbalance was the high proportion of men employed in the service sector compared with those from industry: 40 per cent of men in finance, commerce and the professions had enlisted by February 1916, compared with a proportion of 28 per cent for industrial employees.[124] This was partly because white-collar employees were taller and fitter; partly because some effort was made to keep vital industrial workers in their jobs; but also because the middle class was keener to fight.

Even more striking, perhaps, are the national variations within Great Britain and the British Empire. The Scots, slightly under-represented in the pre-war army, were the keenest to volunteer for war. By December 1915 just under 27 per cent of Scottish men aged between 15 and 49 had volunteered.[125] Australians were keen too: it was the only part of the Empire which did not need to resort to conscription.[126] The Irish, by contrast, were relatively reluctant: only 11 per cent of those eligible enlisted willingly, though here too there was substantial regional variation, with the South reluctant especially after 1916.[127] Similar political factors affected recruitment in Canada – which sent the largest number of soldiers of all the Dominions (641,000). Only 5 per cent of these were French-speaking Canadians, despite the fact that they accounted for 40 per cent of the population.[128]

Why did men join up? In the majority of cases, it was certainly not

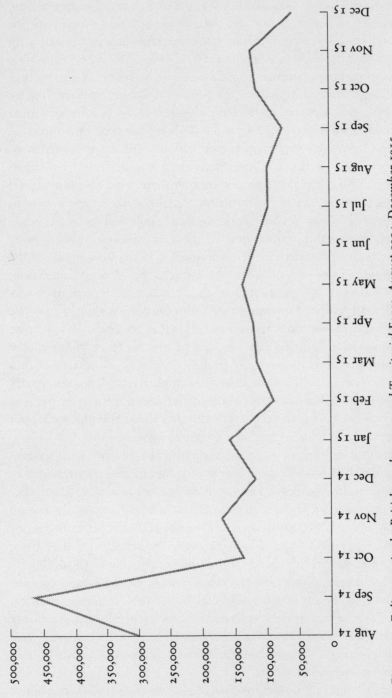

Figure 10 Enlistment in the British regular army and Territorial Force, August 1914–December 1915

Source: Beckett and Simpson, *Nation in Arms*, p. 8.

to enforce the 1839 treaty concerning the neutrality of Belgium (much less to defend Serbia against Habsburg retaliation for the Sarajevo assassination). To be sure, some of the more famous memoirs by combatants do allude to the Belgian issue. Graves recalled being 'outraged . . . [by] the Germans' cynical violation of Belgian neutrality'; Sassoon read in the newspapers 'that German soldiers crucified Belgian babies'.[129] Sir William Lever assured a member of the exiled Belgian government that 'all the men' in the New Army were 'full of keenness to get to the Front, and to avenge the wrongs done to Belgium'.[130] However, it seems doubtful that this sentiment was widely felt, especially among the 'other ranks'. Herbert Read's model 'Other Ranks' Letter Home' ends: 'Well, they say it's all for little Belgium, so cheer up says I: but wait till I gets hold of little Belgium.'[131] There is even a story – though it may be apocryphal (or the soldiers' black humour) – of British troops embarking to cross the Channel singing 'We're going to bash the Belgians.'[132]

A less precise 'love of country' is more usually seen as the typical volunteer's motive.[133] The patriotic 'spirit of 1914', it is argued, was the product of years of indoctrination – in schools, universities, nationalist associations and (on the continent) in the armies themselves. Not without reason is one of the villains in *All Quiet on the Western Front* the schoolmaster. The masses – or at least the middle classes – had been 'nationalized' by relentless exposure to nationalist music, nationalist poetry, nationalist art, nationalist monuments – and, of course, nationalist history. Even some of the cultural trends we think of as 'modernist' contributed to war enthusiasm by depicting war as an agency of spiritual renewal as opposed to annihilation.[134] This argument has a particular appeal when one considers how the products of English public schools conceived of war in the language of the playing fields: Sir Henry Newbolt's 'Vitaï Lampada' ('Torch of Life', 1898) is the text most often cited in this context: on a remote desert battlefield, 'the voice of the schoolboy rallies the ranks: "Play up! Play up! and play the game."'[135] The public schools of England, so it has been argued, inculcated precisely the right qualities for war: 'loyalty, honour, chivalry, Christianity, patriotism, sportsmanship and leadership'. Eton, Winchester, Harrow, Shrewsbury: these were the gateways to the trenches in 1914–15 (just as, until recently, they were reputed to be the ideal preparation for a term of imprisonment). All but eight of the 539 boys who left Winchester between 1909 and 1915 volunteered. The *Eton Chronicle* said explicitly that 'it was there that they learnt the lessons which are to enable them to stand the ordeal which must now be undergone'.[136] Much the same could be said of the German *Gymnasien*, though here sport was rather less of an obsession; while the German universities, with their duelling fraternities instead of rowing eights, certainly outdid Oxford and Cambridge in martial culture. French schools too instilled patriotism as part of the curriculum, before and during the war.[137] Young Frenchmen duelled more than other Europeans, too.

There is no doubting the patriotic fervour of many who volunteered in 1914–15; probably this did have a lot to do with school. Kenneth Kershaw described joining the Gordon Highlanders in June 1915 as 'the happiest day of my life without exception. I am chosen at last to fight for my country, my whole and only ambition in life.'[138] But what is striking is how nebulous this love of country was: what exactly did fighting in Belgium or Northern France have to do with fighting for Britain (much less the Scottish Highlands)? For many public-school volunteers, however, the impact of their education was to diminish interest in the reasons for the war. Sir John French's ideal new officers – 'country men . . . accustomed to hunting, polo and field sports' – tended to regard the war as 'the greatest game': in Sassoon's words, 'a mounted . . . picnic in perfect weather'.[139] To men like Francis Grenfell, German soldiers were a species of fox or boar, to be hunted for sport.

What, in any case, of the 'ordinary men': those who had not enjoyed the benefits of a public-school education? One such who volunteered later recalled his own assumption that the aim of the BEF was to prevent Germany invading Britain:

We weren't fighting for king and country because we'd never met the king. I think it's because there was a war on and everybody felt that was something we could do. There was an army opposed to us and we didn't want them to get into England, and we thought the best way to stop them was to keep them where they were, in France.[140]

This was almost plausible, though wrong: as we have seen, there was no German plan to invade Britain. Still, the defensive motive was probably sincerely felt: it is significant that the peak of recruitment more or less coincided with the nadir of the British Expeditionary Force's fortunes (the retreat from Mons), when the Germans seemed on the point of taking Paris.

But others from this social milieu were less strategically minded.

George Coppard, a sixteen-year-old Croydon boy with only an elementary education, 'knew nothing about' what was going on in France when he volunteered on 27 August.[141] Harry Finch did not even bother to mention a motive for his decision to join up in January 1915; his brother had been in the army before the war, so perhaps he would have joined even if peace had endured.

If British soldiers – among the most literate in the war – were unsure what they were fighting for, the confusion was even greater in the armies on the Eastern Front. At the beginning of Hašek's *The Good Soldier Švejk*, the imbecilic Czech hero first hears of the Archduke Francis Ferdinand's assassination when the charwoman in his local pub tells him: 'They've killed our Ferdinand.' Once she has explained which Ferdinand she means, Švejk offers a wildly off-beam analysis of the implications of the assassination: 'I expect the Turks did it,' he muses. 'You know, we never ought to have taken Bosnia and Hercegovina from them.' This is overheard by a plain-clothes policeman, who informs Švejk that the assassins were in fact 'the Serbs':

'You're wrong there', replied Švejk. 'It was the Turks, because of Bosnia and Hercegovina.' And Švejk expounded his views on Austrian foreign policy in the Balkans. In 1912 the Turks lost the war with Serbia, Bulgaria and Greece. They had wanted Austria to help them, and when this didn't happen, they shot Ferdinand . . . 'Do you really think His Imperial Majesty is going to put up with this sort of thing? If so, you don't know him at all. There'll have to be a war with the Turks. "You killed my uncle, so I'll bash your jaw." War is certain. Serbia and Russia will help us in it. There won't half be a blood bath.'

Švejk looked beautiful in his prophetic moment. His simple face, smiling like a full moon, beamed with enthusiasm. Everything was so clear to him.

'It may be', he said, continuing his account of Austria's future, that if we have a war with the Turks, the Germans'll attack us, because the Germans and Turks stick together. You can't find bigger bastards anywhere. But we can ally ourselves with France which has had a down on Germany ever since 1871. And then the balloon'll go up. There'll be war. I won't say more.[142]

For these insights, the hapless Švejk is arrested and subsequently drafted.

Of course, this is comedy. Nevertheless, it seems doubtful that Švejk was very much worse informed than the majority of the millions of soldiers who found themselves, like him, in uniform and marching into war within five weeks of the Archduke's death. Certainly, few Russian conscripts knew what the war was about, as General Alexei Brusilov recalled:

Time after time I asked my men in the trenches why we were at war; the inevitable senseless answer was that a certain Archduke and his wife had been murdered and that consequently the Austrians had tried to humiliate the Serbians. Practically no one knew who these Serbians were; they were equally doubtful what a Slav was. Why any German should want to make war on us because of these Serbians, no one could say . . . They had never heard of the ambitions of Germany; they did not even know that such a country existed.

A farm agent from Smolensk noted the remarks of peasant soldiers in the first weeks of the conflict: 'If the Germans want payment, it would be better to pay ten roubles a head than to kill people.'[143] Describing the Russian peasantry's response to mobilization in 1914, the British military attaché in St Petersburg wrote: 'The bulk of [the Russian soldiers] went willingly to war in the first instance, chiefly because they had little idea what war meant. They lacked . . . intelligent knowledge of the objects they were fighting for . . .'[144]

The Austrian draft-dodger Adolf Hitler's first reaction to the news of the assassination was to be:

seized with worry that the bullets may have been shot from the pistols of German students, who, out of indignation at the heir apparent's continuous work of Slavisation, wanted to free the German people from this internal enemy . . . But when, soon afterwards, I heard the names of the supposed assassins, and moreover read that they had been identified as Serbs, a light shudder began to run through me at this vengeance of an inscrutable Destiny.

The greatest friend of the Slavs had fallen beneath the bullets of Slav fanatics.[145]

T. E. Lawrence described how Arabs and Turks fighting in the Middle East would preface combat with 'torrents of words . . . After the foulest insults of the languages they knew would come the climax, when the Turks in frenzy called the Arabs "English", and the Arabs screamed back "Germans" at them. There were, of course, no Germans in the Hejaz, and I was the first Englishman.'[146] Clearly, the Arabs were not fighting for Belgium (indeed, Lawrence had considerable difficulty persuading them to fight for their own independence).

Why then did British men volunteer in such numbers? Five motives suggest themselves:

1. *Successful recruitment techniques*. The efforts of the Parliamentary Recruiting Committee (PRC) may well have been successful in increasing recruitment. It certainly built up an impressive organization of 2,000 volunteers who managed to organize 12,000 meetings at which some 20,000 speeches were delivered, to send out 8 million recruiting letters and to distribute no fewer than 54 million posters, leaflets and other publications. On the other hand the PRC was not formed until 27 August, did not have its first meeting until 31 August and was not really in action until after the biggest surge in recruitment.[147] Memoir evidence – from Croydon to Lancashire – suggests that the stirring sound of military bands playing outside recruitment offices in the very early stages of the war was more effective than any number of speeches by local dignitaries.[148] Perhaps newspapers also played a part: there were certainly numerous leaders like that in the *Newcastle Daily Chronicle* on 1 September urging that 'We must have more men from Britain – our allies have already given the full extent of their manhood.'[149]

2. *Female pressure*. There is ample evidence of women handing men not in uniform white feathers symbolizing cowardice. Government propaganda capitalized on this. The PRC poster, with its clever implication that the addressee's husband or son would survive either way, was well-aimed: 'When the war is over and someone asks your husband or your son what he did in the Great War, is he to hang his head because you did not let him go?' Cruder, but perhaps more effective, was the suggestion that the man who would not fight might be capable of other forms of backsliding: 'Is your best boy wearing khaki? . . . if your young man neglects his duty to King and Country, the time may come when he will neglect *you*.'[150] 'Why', asked Mrs F. Boas in a PRC pamphlet, 'won't any chap here in Little Bidworth fight another chap twice his size any day if he sees him doing a bit of bullying on a kid?'[151] Even suffragette leaders like Emmeline and Christabel Pankhurst fell into line, arguing that Germany was 'a male nation' and that a German victory would be 'a disastrous blow to the women's movement', eagerly pressing for conscription and welcoming the influx of women workers into the munitions factories.[152] Small wonder Wilfred Owen reserved a special hatred for Jessie Pope, author of 'The Call': 'Who's for the trench – / Are you, my laddie?'[153]

3. *Peer-group pressure*. There is no doubting the importance of the so-called 'Pals' Battalions' in getting groups of friends, neighbours or colleagues to join up together. The earliest of these – the Stockbrokers'

Battalion of the Royal Fusiliers (founded on 21 August), the 'mercantile and professional men's' battalion of the Gloucester Regiment and the three Liverpool clerks' battalions – testify to the desire to transmit not only local and regional allegiances but also civilian occupational structures (and presumably also class structures) into army life.[154] As if to confirm the British thesis that the war was a game, there was even a footballers' battalion and a boxers' company.[155] To begin with, exclusivity was possible: some battalions even demanded an entry fee of up to five pounds.[156] By the spring of 1915, however, heavy casualties had depleted the ranks of 'pals' and men had to accustom themselves to fighting alongside strangers, often from quite different social and regional backgrounds.[157] Now the 'pals' theme acquired a less spontaneous, more subtly coercive tone in PRC propaganda: 'You're proud of your pals in the Army, of course! But what will your pals think of YOU?'[158] At the beginning, such thoughts did not need to be articulated. In August 1914 even so un-military an individual as William Beveridge felt so 'wildly jealous' of those joining up that he 'made one or two half-hearted efforts' to do so himself.[159]

4. *Economic motives*. Scepticism has been expressed by some historians about the role of economic factors in the decision to enlist. As a Canadian soldiers' newspaper put it in December 1917: 'The party who said he joined up to get a clasp knife and a razor must have been pretty keen.'[160] Dewey found no correlation between low wages and enlistment; rather the reverse.[161] Yet there is no question that the peak of enlistment in Britain coincided with the peak of unemployment caused by the August financial and commercial crisis. Nine out of ten of the working men laid off in Bristol in the first month of the war joined up;[162] enlistment rates were clearly lower in areas where business quickly picked up again. Men were not wholly irrational in 1914. In his pamphlet *How to Help Lord Kitchener*, A. J. Dawson was at pains to show that 'for many working men . . . enlistment would certainly involve no monetary loss', though this manifestly would not be the case if, in his chosen example of a married man with three children, the husband were to be killed or permanently disabled.[163] When the Cardiff Railway Company offered its employees job security, dependants' allowances and pensions if they joined up, the response was so huge that the offer had to be retracted.[164]

Employers were also in a position to exert pressure. On 3 September the West Yorkshire Coal Owners' Association passed a resolution to raise a battalion from among its members' employees; the Newcastle Chamber of Commerce did the same.[165] On the same day the stock-brokers Foster & Braithwaite circulated a notice which stated simply: 'The firm expects that all the unmarried staff under 35 . . . will join Earl Kitchener's army at once, and also urges those who are married and eligible to take the same course.'[166] With similar appeals James Dalrymple, manager of the Glasgow Tramways, was able to raise the 15th Battalion of the Highland Light Infantry in a matter of hours.[167]

5. *Impulse*. Finally, as Avner Offer has pointed out, allowance must be made for the fact that some men volunteered impulsively, with little thought of the consequences for themselves, much less the causes of the war.[168]

REVELATIONS

Yet no general theory of motivation in 1914 will cover all cases. When the philosopher Ludwig Wittgenstein enlisted in the Austrian army on 7 August 1914 he wrote in his diary: 'Now I have the chance to be a decent human being, for I'm standing eye to eye with death . . . Perhaps the nearness to death will bring light into life. God enlighten me.' What he wanted was 'a variety of religious experience . . . to turn [him] into a different person'.[169] Wittgenstein approached the war in a mood not of enthusiasm but of deep pessimism. As early as 25 October he was privately expressing deep gloom at 'our – the German race's – situation. The English – the best race in the world – *cannot* lose. We, however, can lose, and will lose, if not this year then the next. The thought that our race will be defeated depresses me tremendously.' Repelled by his uncouth crew mates on board the ship on the Vistula where he spent the first phase of the war, Wittgenstein contemplated suicide.[170]

The brilliant, tortured, Jewish and Cambridge-educated Wittgenstein might seem the supreme exception. Yet he was not alone in regarding the war in a religious light. The outbreak of war saw an upsurge in religious observance in nearly all the combatant countries. At an interdenominational service in front of the Reichstag in Berlin, a congregation sang Protestant and Catholic hymns together in the week war was declared.[171] Even in Hamburg – perhaps the least religious of German cities in this period – people were seized by religious fervour: Percy Schramm's sister Ruth exulted that 'our people have come to

God'.[172] In France, where anti-clericalism had been in the political ascendant for years (and certainly did not vanish during the war), the Catholic Church hailed 'the great return to God in the masses and among the combatants'. The cult of the Sacré-Coeur flourished – to the point that some militant clergymen urged the superimposition of the image on the tricolour – and there was a marked increase in pilgrimages to Lourdes, Pontmain and La Salette.[173]

As is well known, many ministers and priests encouraged the idea that the war was a holy war, often in a quite grotesque way. In Germany this was true not only of conservative pastors like Reinhold Seeberg; liberal theologians like Otto Baumgarten were just as likely to invoke 'Jesu-Patriotismus', and it was Martin Rade's *Christliche Welt* which published a grotesque pastiche of the Lord's Prayer shortly after the war had begun ('Give us each day the enemy dead . . .').[174] In *The Last Days of Mankind* Karl Kraus satirized the bellicose sermons of Protestant ministers – metaphorically fighting on the 'Sinai Front'. In fact, these scenes are not strictly satirical: as Kraus said of the play as a whole, 'the most grotesque inventions are quotes', and there is every reason to believe that the words 'Killing [in wartime] is a Christian duty, is indeed divine service' really were uttered.[175] French priests too did not hesitate to assure their flocks that France was fighting a just war – though with some justification.[176] The most egregious example of militarist churchmanship in England was the shocking Advent sermon preached in 1915 by the Bishop of London, A. F. Winnington-Ingram (later published in a collection of his sermons in 1917), in which he described the war as:

a great crusade – we cannot deny it – to kill Germans: to kill them, not for the sake of killing, but to save the world; to kill the good as well as the bad, to kill the young men as well as the old, to kill those who have shown kindness to our wounded as well as those fiends who crucified the Canadian sergeant, who superintended the Armenian massacres, who sank the Lusitania, and who turned the machine-guns on the civilians of Aershott and Louvain – and to kill them lest the civilization of the world should itself be killed.[177]

To be sure, Winnington-Ingram was attempting in a rather crass way to make the point that the war was 'an outbreak of viler passions than has been seen in the world for a thousand years'; but he nevertheless insisted that Britain was fighting 'a war for purity, for freedom, for international honour and for the principles of Christianity . . . and everyone who dies in it [is] a martyr'.[178] This was not far removed from Horatio Bottomley's phrase 'everyman a saint'. Indeed, Winnington-Ingram went so far as to inform the *Guardian* that:

The Church can best help the nation first of all by making it realize that it is engaged in a Holy War . . . Christ died on Good Friday for Freedom, Honour and Chivalry and our boys are dying for the same thing[s] . . . You ask for my advice in a sentence as to what the Church is to do. I answer MOBILIZE THE NATION FOR A HOLY WAR.[179]

The poet laureate Robert Bridges agreed that the war was 'primarily a holy war'.[180] Although such extraordinary sentiments were condemned by some in the Church, others – including Michael Furse, Bishop of Pretoria – heartily endorsed them. The Germans, wrote Furse, were 'enemies of God'.[181] In the United States there was even more of this sort of thing. Billy Sunday began his prayer in the House of Representatives: 'Thou knowest, O Lord, that no nation so infamous, vile, greedy, sensuous, bloodthirsty ever disgraced the pages of history', adding gratuitously, 'If you turn hell upside down, you'll find "Made in Germany" stamped on the bottom.'[182]

In their turn, generals and politicians too liked to conceive of the war in religious terms. For Churchill, child as he was of the nineteenth century, the workings of 'Providence' – a very Gladstonian term – must lie behind the 'extraordinarily arbitrary and haphazard way in which death & destruction are meted out': 'It *cannot* matter as much as one thinks whether one is alive or dead. The *absolute* planlessness here makes one suspect a bigger plan elsewhere.'[183] It is impossible to understand Haig's dour character without the knowledge that he belonged to the Church of Scotland: 'I feel that every step in my plan has been taken with the Divine help,' he told his wife on the eve of the Battle of the Somme. Protestantism seems to have reconciled some men to high casualties: Robert Nivelle, responsible for one of the greatest slaughters of French soldiers of the entire war, was one of the 1.5 per cent of the French population who were Protestants.[184] The author of the equally disastrous Schlieffen Plan was, as we have seen, a Pietist (though the man who failed to execute it, Moltke, was a theosophist). For many, the First World War was thus a kind of war of religion, despite an almost complete absence of clear denominational conflicts; a crusade without infidels. Even on the Western Front, where Protestants, Jews and Catholics fought on both sides, men were asked to believe that they had God on their side. And where religious divisions did seem to coincide with political ones, the results were especially gruesome, the most obvious example being the Turkish genocide of the Armenians.

Yet there was an immense difference between the cannon-blessing Christianity of a Winnington-Ingram and the millenarian despair of a Moltke. It is tempting to suggest that the latter was more typical of the religious atmosphere of 1914. Percy Schramm's aunt Emmy's reaction to the outbreak of war was explicit in its allusion to the Last Days: 'It all must come to pass; for it is foretold in the Bible, and we can only thank God if Satan's rule is soon to be destroyed. Then will come at last the true Empire of Peace, with our Lord Jesus Christ as ruler!'[185] As Klaus Vondung has argued, there was an apocalyptic quality to the German 1914. But not only the German. 'Like most people of my generation', H. G. Wells had written in 1906, 'I was launched into life with millennial assumptions . . . There would be trumpets and shoutings and celestial phenomena, a battle of Armageddon and the Last Judgement.'[186] Writing in the *Observer* in August 1914, J. L. Garvin used equally eschatological language: 'We have to do our part in killing a creed of war. Then at last, after a rain of blood, there may be set the greater rainbow in the Heavens before the visions of the souls of men. And after Armageddon war, indeed, may be no more.'[187] On 4 August 1914 the Rector of St Mary's, Newmarket, warned his congregation that:

The horrors of war in ancient times would be nothing compared with the horrors of war today . . . All the resources of science had been called upon to perfect weapons of destruction for mankind. To-day England was no longer isolated as she used to be . . . the air was open as a way of attacks by a fleet of airships. No town in England was now safe. At night it might be turned into a smouldering ruin and its inhabitants into blackened corpses.[188]

Thus did the Book of Revelation meet H. G. Wells in the Fens. Such pessimistic sermons were not unusual. On 3 August a minister in Norwich warned his flock: 'A continental war could be nothing short of disastrous when one thought of the militarism of Europe, of the hell of the battlefield, of the miseries of the wounded, of ruined peasants.'[189] Even feminists caught the apocalyptic mood. Charlotte Perkins Gilman's novel *Herland*, which visualized a female utopia following a cataclysm fatal to all men, was published in 1915.[190] Perhaps this sense that the world had arrived at the Biblical Armageddon was the most powerful of all the 'ideas of 1914'.

And how like Armageddon it proved:

[T]here were voices, and thunders, and lightnings; and there was a great earthquake, such as was not since men were upon the earth, so mighty an earthquake *and* so great.

And the great city was divided into three parts, and the cities of the nations fell: and great Babylon came in remembrance before God, to give unto her the cup of the wine of the fierceness of his wrath. And every island fled away, and the mountains were not found. And there fell upon men a great hail out of heaven . . . and men blasphemed God because of the plague of the hail; for the plague thereof was exceeding great.[191]

8

The Press Gang

THE WAR OF THE WORDS

Shortly after the war Jean Cocteau bought a copy of *Le Figaro* in Paris only to find that he had been charged double the cover price and that the paper was also two years out of date. When he complained, the vendor replied: 'But, *cher monsieur*, that is precisely why it is more expensive – because there is still a war in it.'[1]

The First World War was the first media war. Wars, of course, had been reported in newspapers before. And sometimes – as in the case of the Crimean and Boer wars – press coverage had influenced the conduct of the war: one thinks of *The Times*'s castigation of the generals' conduct of the siege of Sebastopol in December 1854, the criticism of the South African war in the Liberal press or the German Catholic press's attacks on Bülow for his handling of the Herero revolt in South-West Africa. But never before 1914 had the mass media, which were themselves of comparatively recent origin when the war began, been used as a *weapon* of warfare. Indeed, one of the greatest of all myths about the First World War is that it was actually decided by the media, in their capacity as channels for government propaganda.

Not all governments learned at the same pace, it has been argued: hence the claim that superior Entente propaganda played a decisive role in the Central Powers' defeat. 'Today words have become battles', declared Ludendorff: 'The right words, battles won; the wrong words, battles lost.'[2] In their memoirs both he and Hindenburg saw propaganda as the key to the 'demoralization' of their troops in 1918. 'We were hypnotized . . . as a rabbit by a snake,' wrote Ludendorff. 'In the neutral countries we were subject to a sort of moral blockade.'[3] In particular, German post-war analysis focused on the role of Lord Northcliffe: the elder of the two Harmsworth brothers, who by 1914 had built up

Britain's biggest newspaper group.[4] Already loathed by Liberals in Britain before the war, Northcliffe became a hate-figure in Germany on account of the propaganda he directed at German soldiers in the last stages of the war. As one embittered German wrote in an open letter to him in 1921:

German propaganda was in spirit the propaganda of scholars, privy councillors and professors. How could these honest and unworldly men cope with devils of journalism, experts in mass poisoning like yourself? German propaganda, what there was of it, was addressed to the reason, to the intelligence, the conscience . . . How could such dry stuff as facts cope with the gaudy yarns, the hate hypnotism, the crude . . . sensations you dished up . . . The German . . . steadfastly refused to descend to your level.[5]

This was a view echoed by a pacifist on the winning side: Norman Angell called British newspapers in the war 'a more reptile instrument than Bismarck could ever hope to make'.[6] For Hitler, by contrast, Northcliffe's war propaganda had been 'an inspired work of genius': 'I myself learned enormously from this enemy propaganda,' he declared in *Mein Kampf*.[7] In *Propaganda and National Power* (1933) the Nazi propagandist Eugen Hadamovsky stated bluntly: 'The German people were not beaten on the battlefield, but were defeated in the war of words.'[8] A number of studies carried out in the Third Reich developed the argument in more detail, attempting to show how propaganda had been responsible for securing Italy's support for the Entente powers.[9] The obverse of this argument, of course, was that German propaganda had been a failure and that the Jewish and/or socialist press had systematically undermined German morale: an early example of the application of the 'stab-in-the-back' legend to the press was Alfred Rosenberg's attack on the *Berliner Tageblatt*.[10]

Those reponsible for Allied propaganda – not surprisingly – agreed. 'If the people really knew,' Lloyd George told C. P. Scott of the *Manchester Guardian* at a low point in December 1917, 'the war would be stopped tomorrow. But of course they don't – and can't know. The correspondents don't write and the censorship would not pass the truth.'[11] The novelist John Buchan, who played an important role in British propaganda, agreed: 'So far as Britain is concerned,' he commented in 1917, 'the war could not have been fought for one month without its newspapers.'[12] Beaverbrook asserted that the newsreels he had produced as Minister for Information were 'the decisive factor in maintaining the moral [sic] of the people during the black days of the early summer of 1918'.[13] Northcliffe even went so far as to claim that 'good propaganda had probably saved a year of war, and this meant the saving of thousands of millions of money and probably at least a million lives.'[14] The propagandist's calling was not, to be sure, a noble one. In the words of A. R. Buchanan, 'A cynic might be tempted to say that while some patriots went to the battle front and died for their country, others stayed at home and lied for it.'[15] But the sacrifice of integrity made by those who ran the British media during the war continues to be widely accepted as worthwhile (or at least effective).[16]

The offices given to newspaper proprietors during the war seem to speak for themselves. Northcliffe was entrusted with a special mission to the United States by Lloyd George in May 1917, and in February 1918 accepted the role of director of propaganda in enemy countries. His brother was appointed director-general of the Royal Army Clothing Department in 1916 and a year later became Air Minister. The Canadian businessmen and Unionist MP Sir Max Aitken, who had acquired a controlling interest in the *Daily Express* in December 1916, served as Chancellor of the Duchy of Lancaster and, from February 1918, as Minister for Information. The flow of honours told a similar story. Northcliffe (who had received his peerage in 1905) became a viscount in 1917. His brother Harold became a baron in 1914 and Viscount Rothermere in 1919. In December 1916 Aitken became Lord Beaverbrook, having been knighted in 1911 and made a baronet in January 1916. Waldorf Astor, owner of the *Observer*, became a viscount in 1917. Sir George Riddell, owner of the *News of the World*, got a peerage in 1918, as did Henry Dalziel of United Newspapers and W. E. Berry of the *Sunday Times* and *Financial Times* in 1921. In 1916 Robert Donald, editor of the *Daily Chronicle*, was offered a baronetcy, though he turned it down. At least twelve press knighthoods were conferred.[17] This was Lloyd George's way of thanking the 'press lords' for their loyal service.

The idea that the press wielded excessive power without adequate responsibility was not, of course, an invention of the First World War. But in every country the war seemed markedly to increase media power. Indeed, the Viennese satirist Karl Kraus's thesis was that the press was the principal beneficiary – and perhaps even the instigator – of the war. Even President Wilson's famous Fourteen Points are said to have been drafted in response to a request from Edgar Sisson, the American Commissioner of the Committee on Public Information in Petrograd.[18]

DISCORDANT VOICES

Yet the idea that there was a profound difference between the propaganda techniques used by the two sides, convenient as it is for those seeking a non-military explanation of the war's outcome, does not stand up to close scrutiny. As Georges Weill remarked, 'each of the warring nations persuaded itself that its government had neglected propaganda, whereas the enemy . . . had been most effective'.[19] In no country was the press completely restricted, nor was uniformity ever imposed. In every case, institutions for censoring and managing news had to be improvised and did not work efficiently. Most propaganda was initially directed at neutral states, rather than at domestic opinion. When attempts were made to influence the 'Home Front' the main objective was negative: to suppress dissent. The principal positive aims were to boost sales of war bonds or (in Britain and her Empire) recruitment. For most of the war hardly any propaganda was directed at the fighting men themselves; yet it was they, after all, who determined the outcome of the war.

It is worth emphasizing the sheer diversity of European press opinion at the moment the war began. On 30 June 1914 the *Neue Freie Presse*, that bastion of liberal Viennese opinion, pronounced that, despite the Sarajevo murders, 'the fundamental aims of the policy of the monarchy' remained 'peace with honour and without weakness and with the defence of [our] interests', adding on 2 July that 'Wars of revenge are out of the question these days.'[20] Two weeks later it continued to view the international scene with equanimity. 'The man who . . . would give the order . . . to set the world aflame for the sake of Greater Serbia is not to be seen,' it declared, reaffirming on 16 July 'the peaceful attitude of the Monarchy'. Even when it began to adopt a more bellicose tone towards Serbia, it consistently argued that 'local conflicts should not spread into world wars' (18 July).[21] The Hungarian *Pester Lloyd* adopted an equally restrained tone throughout July.[22]

In Germany the liberal *Berliner Tageblatt* was unusual in seeing the 'Greater Serbian question' as 'one of the most threatening and most worrying [questions, one which] concerns us all.' But on 30 July it was still insisting: 'The German people are absolutely peaceful', and would go no further than calling for the 'securing of the border' when it received official notification of Russia's mobilization.[23] Its counterpart in western Germany, the *Frankfurter Zeitung*, was no keener on war.[24] Nor was the Catholic press bellicose: on 30 July *Germania* insisted that the German people wanted 'peace above all', though it is true that the *Kölnische Zeitung* evinced an extreme 'Hurrah-patriotism' after the war had started.[25] The conservative (and traditionally government-inspired) *Norddeutsche Allgemeine Zeitung* argued consistently for the localization of the conflict between Austria and Serbia,[26] and even rebutted the *Berliner Tageblatt*'s pessimistic warning of 1 August that war was inevitable.[27] Of course, this diversity of opinion may be attributed to the Machiavellianism of the German government, seeking to mask its belligerent actions with pacific editorials. However, this seems anachronistic; far more probable is a simple lack of clear guidance from a government entirely preoccupied with diplomatic and military matters.[28]

In Britain, with a sole exception, the press at first viewed the approach of war with disinterest or distaste. The *Manchester Guardian* could confidently state in July 1914 that there was 'no danger of [Britain] being dragged into the conflict [between Austria and Serbia] by treaties of alliance'.[29] On 1 August its editor C. P. Scott argued that intervention would 'violate dozens of promises made to our own people, promises to seek peace, to protect the poor, to husband the resources of the country, to promote peaceful progress'.[30] When war came, the paper angrily protested that 'by some hidden contract England has been technically committed behind her back to the ruinous madness of a share in the violent gamble of a war between two militarist leagues.' Though it eventually concluded that 'Our front is united,' the *Guardian* solemnly warned, 'It will be a war in which we risk everything of which we are proud, and in which we stand to gain nothing . . . Some day we will regret it.'[31]

Even more loath to 'sacrifice . . . British life . . . for the sake of Russian hegemony of the Slav world' was the *Daily News*. On 1 August it published an article by A. G. Gardiner entitled simply: 'Why we must not fight.' 'Where in the world do our interests clash with Germany?' Gardiner asked, and retorted: 'Nowhere.' 'If we crush Germany in the dust and make Russia the dictator of Europe and Asia, it will be the greatest disaster that has ever befallen Western culture and civilization.'[32] On the 3rd the paper averred that there was 'no war party in this country' because 'the horrors of war have already seized on the popular imagination'.[33] Though the *News* finally conceded that Britain had to win the war it had entered, even on the 4th it deplored 'the terrible conflict' and Grey's 'mistaken course of foreign policy'.[34] Sir George Riddell, proprietor of the popular Sunday *News of the World*, spoke for most Liberal journalists when he told Lloyd George of his 'feeling of intense exasperation . . . at the prospect of the government embarking on war'.[35]

Nor was the Liberal press in the provinces enthused. The *Yorkshire Evening News* maintained on 29 July that it was 'certainly in Great Britain's interest that she should keep out of the quarrel.' The *Northern Daily Mail* went further: Britain 'could and ought to remain neutral throughout the whole course of the war,' it argued on 28 July.[36] 'The worst has happened', exclaimed the *Carlisle Journal* on 4 August. There was 'little doubt that the majority of Englishmen regard the prospect of being dragged into this war with feelings of amazement and horror'.[37] It was not until 8 August that papers like the *Lancaster Guardian* and *Barrow News* were convinced that war was necessary to 'save these small but sturdy independent States from the German maw'.[38]

In all Europe only one major newspaper consistently argued for war between the great powers, and that was *The Times*. It anticipated a European war as early as 22 July and five days later called for British involvement, an argument it repeated in leaders on 29 and 31 July.[39] We have already seen how Northcliffe and his foreign editor, Steed, rebuffed appeals from the Rothschilds to soften the paper's line. In this light, there is something to be said for the former Liberal minister Lord Fitzmaurice's claim on 31 July that the Northcliffe press was waging 'a campaign to drive this country into joining the war'.[40] (Revealingly, when the London correspondent of the *Figaro* was despairing of the British government, he exclaimed: 'Cannot Lord Northcliffe and the *Mail* do something?')[41]

Yet even Northcliffe was far from clear about what role he wanted Britain to play in the war. He was slow to appreciate the significance of the Balkan crisis in July.[42] When war came, his newspapers made no attempt to understate the calamitous implications. Even *The Times* on 3 August foresaw 'the most terrible war [in Europe] . . . since the fall of the Roman Empire'. It found 'the losses of human life and in the accumulated wealth of generations which such a contest must involve . . . frightful to think of'.[43] And as late as 5 August Northcliffe astonished his senior executives by coming out strongly against the sending of the BEF. 'What is this I hear about a British Expeditionary Force for France?' he demanded of the *Mail* editor, Thomas Marlowe:

It is nonsense. Not a single soldier shall leave this country. We have a superb Fleet, which shall give all the assistance in its power, but I will not support the sending out of this country of a single British soldier. What about invasion? What about our own country? Put that in the leader. Do you hear? Not a single soldier will go without my consent. Say so in the paper to-morrow.

He even wrote a leader to this effect and only agreed to print Marlowe's alternative version – arguing for sending the BEF – after a heated debate.[44]

Even in late November 1914 *The Times* saw no reason to varnish the truth about what was happening at the Front. 'All the spectacular side of the war has gone, never to reappear,' its correspondent reported grimly:

Trenches and always trenches, and within range of the concealed guns invisibility the supreme law . . . Day after day the butchery of the unknown by the unseen . . . War has become stupid . . . The strain on the infantry is tremendous, and it is endless . . . At the cost of thousands of lives a few hundred yards may be gained, but rarely indeed does [even] the most brilliant attack produce anything . . . Fresh troops brought up under cover of a tremendous artillery fire which opens by surprise may effect a breach . . . But only with heavy loss can such an attack be carried through.[45]

This was hardly calculated to encourage the hope that Tommy would be celebrating Christmas in Berlin.

Nor was this the only jarring note sounded by Conservative newspapers. In late July the *Yorkshire Post* ran an editorial declaring that it was

not convinced that if Russia and France were to crush Germany and Austria the position of this country would be any better than if victory lay on the other side; the disturbance of existing conditions would, one way or the other, we believe, prove highly disadvantageous to us. Therefore, we are by no means of the opinion that the British Government should hasten to join in a European war, on one side or the other.[46]

On 1 August the *Pall Mall Gazette* pronounced it 'a cruel stroke of fate that [Britain and Germany] should be brought face to face at the moment when ill-will appears to have abated', adding:

We believe that the Emperor WILLIAM and his advisers have laboured ardently for peace. If, as seems all too probable, their efforts have been overborne by force beyond the control of man, why should we utter a word of bitterness towards them? We will not. If doomed, with heavy heart . . . to draw the sword, we will fight like gentlemen and respecting a knightly foe.[47]

Horatio Bottomley's editorial in *John Bull* for the week ending 8 August was even more eccentric. 'TO HELL WITH SERVIA', it began, adding: '*Servia must be wiped out*. Let Servia be removed from the map of Europe.' This outdid even the most strident Austrian leader-writers. However, Bottomley went on, the British government should

avail itself of the crisis to get rid once and for all of the German menace . . . [F]ailing a satisfactory assurance of modification in the plans of our Teutonic rival, the only course of far-seeing patriotic statesmen would be to annihilate the German fleet at once . . .

Once more – 'TO HELL WITH SERVIA!'
GOD SAVE THE KING.[48]

As this bizarre line of argument nicely illustrates, there was anything but a uniform press response to the outbreak of war.

Nor did governments ever succeed in establishing uniformity; indeed, it is far from clear that they even attempted to do so. To begin with, not much more was attempted than censorship to prevent publication of military information which might be useful to the enemy. For this there were usually precedents. In Britain, where there was already a tradition of censorship of the arts which vested power in the Lord Chancellor, newspapers had already accepted a system of self-censorship on military matters under the aegis of a Joint Standing Committee set up in 1912.[49] The Defence of the Realm Act (DORA) passed on 8 August 1914 (and subsequently extended six times) drastically increased the state's power in this regard. Regulation 27 explicitly prohibited reports or statements 'by word of mouth or in writing or in any newspaper, periodical . . . or other printed publication' which were 'intended or likely' to undermine loyalty to the King, recruitment or confidence in the currency.[50] The censors also banned publication of news of troop movements, or even speculation about them, on 26 September 1914. The following March the press was warned against exaggerating the extent of British success, though (as one proprietor retorted) such over-optimism was Sir John French's own stock-in-trade.[51] Casualty lists were not published before May 1915. Although moves to impose even tighter censorship were successfully resisted in the autumn of 1915, the press remained tightly controlled throughout the war. The press was also subject to censorship in most parts of the British Empire.[52] Although the system of 'D-Notices' provided the editors of forty publications with confidential information about the war, this was expressly not for publication; the same applied to the copious inside information supplied to *The Times*'s war correspondent Charles à Court Repington (himself a former army colonel). As Lloyd George himself acknowledged, 'The public knows only half the story'; the press knew something more like three-quarters.[53]

What DORA was to British writers, 'Anastasie' was to their French counterparts: the personification of wartime censorship.[54] This was imposed on the basis of the 1849 and 1878 state of siege laws which entitled the military authorities to forbid any publications detrimental to public order. The Ministry of War set up a Press Bureau to enforce this on 3 August. A law passed two days later went further, prohibiting the press from publishing information relating to military operations other than that specified by the government.[55] By September, when the Minister of War Alexandre Millerrand tightened the rules again, a ban had also been imposed on the publication of the names of casualties.[56]

In Germany, as in France, an old state of siege law (that of 1851) came into force when hostilities began, which suspended 'the right to express opinion freely by word, print or picture' and empowered regional military commanders to censor or prohibit publications. To discourage further the publication of 'unreliable information', the Reich Chancellor issued a circular to the press listing twenty-six specific prohibitions. Additional recommendations were issued by the War Ministry in 1915, banning among other things the publication of casualty totals (even rolls of honour were not to use consecutive numbering).[57] Altogether some 2,000 such censorship rules had been issued by the end of 1916. As a result of inconsistencies in their application by military commanders, however, a Central Censor's Office (Oberszensurstelle) was set up in February 1915 which became the War Press Office (Kriegspresseamt) seven months later.[58] In Austria the same function was performed by a War Supervision Office (Kriegsüberwachungsamt).[59] Similar arrangements were introduced in Italy even before her entry into the war.[60]

Censorship was a blunt instrument. In 1915 both *The Times* and the *Labour Leader* were fined for violating censorship rules. On 14 August the *Figaro* fell victim, much to its embarrassment, over a report about

Morocco.[61] Clemenceau's *L'Homme Libre* was suspended for publishing a story about transports of wounded soldiers so filthy that the men contracted tetanus; when it reappeared as *L'Homme Enchaîné* it was banned again.[62] As Alfred Capus put it on 27 September 1914:

Provided one did not mention in one's writings the authorities, the government, politics . . . the banks, the wounded, the German atrocities [or] the postal service, one could express everything freely with the permission of two or three censors.[63]

Among the German newspapers censored or suppressed for revealing military information was the obscure and innocuous *Tägliche Rundschau für Schlesien und Posen*.

Gradually, however, all countries went beyond censorship of military information and used their wartime powers in a more overtly political way. In Britain, newspapers or magazines which were suppressed at one time or another during the war included the *Irish Worker*, the *Irish Volunteer*, *Irish Freedom* and *Sinn Féin*, as well as the *Nation* and the pacifist *Tribunal*. Particular care was taken to prevent the export of anything regarded as potentially harmful to the 'war effort'. Detailed lists were compiled of contraband literature: not only the journals of Irish nationalist, pacifist and socialist groups but also school magazines which had inadvertently published too-detailed reports of Old Boys' movements at the Front, and railway gazettes which revealed supposedly sensitive information about the British transport system. The British Old Heidelbergers' Association Magazine also fell victim.[64] DORA also bid to take over the Lord Chancellor's role as the nation's literary nanny. The book version of Fenner Brockway's play *The Devil's Advocate* was banned in 1914. Four years later Rose Allatini was prosecuted under DORA for her novel (published pseudonymously) *Despised and Rejected*, which revolved around a homosexual conscientious objector: the publisher was fined and copies of the book destroyed.[65] Wartime Britain thus became by stages a kind of police state. In 1916 alone the Press Bureau, assisted by the secret service department MI7(a), scrutinized over 38,000 articles, 25,000 photographs and no fewer than 300,000 private telegrams.[66] Metternich would have been envious. As the *Nation* justly lamented in May 1916, it was 'a domestic tragedy of the war that the country which went out to defend liberty is losing its own liberties one by one, and that the Government that began by relying on public opinion as a great auxiliary has now come to fear and curtail it'.[67]

The same thing happened everywhere. In 1917 a French court judged that the legislation of 1914 banning the publication of unauthorized military information could also be used to prohibit the publication of 'expressions of defeatism'.[68] On this basis, the pacifist *Bonnet Rouge* was censored no fewer than 1,076 times between May 1916 and July 1917.[69]

In Germany *Vorwärts* was banned between 27 and 30 September 1914 and only allowed to resume publication if it eschewed references to 'class hatred and class struggle'; a similar ban was imposed in January 1918 when the paper advocated a general strike.[70] Foreign films were banned early in the war and the existing system of film censorship altered so that only films likely to 'uphold morale and promote patriotism' would be passed.[71] In early 1915 journalists were warned against 'questioning the national sentiment and determination of any German'; interestingly, they were also asked to desist from 'repulsive . . . demands for a barbaric conduct of the war and the annihilation of foreign peoples'. There followed in November 1915 a ban on public discussion of German war aims. Beginning in 1916, interviews with generals, discussions of German–American relations and references to the Kaiser all had to be cleared by the War Press Office before publication. In addition, local military commanders issued their own orders as they saw fit.[72] The *Berliner Tageblatt* fell victim to the political prejudices of the general responsible for censorship in the Marks region when it was temporarily suppressed for *defending* Bethmann against the attacks of annexationists![73]

Yet in no continental country was censorship on a totalitarian scale. The French censors, for example, allowed the newly founded and mischievous *L'Oeuvre* (slogan: 'Imbeciles Don't Read *L'Oeuvre*'), to serialize Barbusse's *Le Feu*.[74] Nor did the censors do much to restrain the satirical magazine *Le Canard Enchaîné* launched in September 1915 by Maurice Maréchal and his friends.[75] In Germany debates in the press about war aims (following the suspension of the ban on discussion in November 1916) ranged more widely than would have been permitted in France. Even more remarkable is the fact that the German censors never banned the publication of Allied military communiqués in German papers.[76]

Moreover, the European – and even the British – experience tends to pale alongside the draconian measures adopted in the United States: a reflection, no doubt, of American uncertainty about the extent of patriotism in a multi-ethnic population. (14.5 million of 100 million Americans in 1914 had been born abroad; around 8 million Americans were first- or second-generation Germans.)[77] After the 1917 Espionage Act was amended by the Sedition Act of May 1918, even criticizing the war in a lodging house became illegal. More than 2,500 Americans were indicted under this legislation, of whom nearly 100 received prison sentences of between ten and twenty years. The director of a supposedly patriotic film called *The Spirit of '76* was sentenced to fifteen years because (as may be inferred from the title) it was anti-British.[78] Not even Britain approached this level of suppression of free speech during the war. It made a mockery of the Allied powers' claim to be fighting for freedom.

Institutions for the active *management* of news (especially the coverage of the war in neutral countries) had to be improvised. The earliest British military communiqués were simply read aloud to members of the Shadow Cabinet by ministers at closed meetings; it was not until September that Major Ernest Swinton was given the task of relaying dispatches to the press, which were duly published under the byline 'Eyewitness' (Max Aitken performed a similar role for the Canadian forces). For more detailed information, Sir George Riddell of the Newspaper Proprietors' Association acted as a press representative in the corridors of power, relaying what he heard from Asquith, Churchill *et al.* to his fellow proprietors and their editors at weekly conferences, an arrangement formalized in March 1915.[79] Only in November 1915 was a system of accredited war correspondents introduced; their reports, however, were tightly controlled.[80]

The first steps to co-ordinate an active British propaganda abroad were taken when Charles Masterman, the Chancellor of the Duchy of Lancaster, invited a select band of eminent writers of fiction and non-fiction to Wellington House at Buckingham Gate (the offices of the National Insurance Commission, which was thought a good 'front').[81] By the end of 1914 it had translated more than twenty publications for distribution in neutral countries; by June 1915 it had commissioned and published some 2.5 million books. It also sent a newsletter to some 360 American newspapers and sponsored a series of films, mostly documentaries. In addition, a hastily constituted Parliamentary War Aims Committee set up a Press Bureau under the direction of the Unionist F. E. Smith in August 1914.[82]

However, in 1916 Lloyd George requested the *Daily Chronicle* editor

Robert Donald to review the performance of Wellington House and, as a result of his criticisms, a new Department of Information was set up. Two months later, in February 1917, the job of running it was given to the popular novelist, lawyer and occasional imperial administrator John Buchan.[83] When the department was made into a full ministry in July 1917, Buchan was notionally subordinated to the Ulster Unionist leader Sir Edward Carson; but the latter's lack of interest drove the press advisory committee to resign in protest, forcing Lloyd George to create a new Ministry of Information under Beaverbrook (February 1918).[84] This prompted a sustained rearguard action by the Foreign Secretary Balfour, aimed at retaining control over the dissemination of British propaganda abroad.[85] A parallel domestic role was played by the cross-party National War Aims Committee set up in June 1917, which between September and March 1918 organized 1,244 public meetings and by the spring of 1919 had distributed 107 million copies of its literature and provided 650 newspapers with standardized pro-government leaders.[86]

Institutional developments were not so different on the continent as has often been claimed. In October 1914 the French army set up an Information Section under its Military Intelligence Division, which at first simply edited and published military communiqués three times a day, but later provided newspapers with more or less anodyne reports of life at the Front. General Nivelle later revitalized this as the Information Service for the Armies and for the first time allowed accredited journalists (rather than army officers) to report from the Front. Meanwhile the Foreign Ministry set up its own office of Press and Information (Bureau de la presse et de l'information). Only in January 1916 was a Press House (Maison de la Presse) created to co-ordinate French propaganda abroad.[87]

In Germany there were daily (11 a.m.) briefings for correspondents by a General Staff officer from 3 August onwards, summaries of which were given to the Wolff Telegraph Bureau; in September 1915 the new War Press Office added a second evening briefing and also produced three military news bulletins. As in Britain, information was sometimes made available on the understanding that it would not be published.[88] At first there was a degree of institutional dualism. The Foreign Office had its own News Department (Nachrichtenabteilung) which was responsible for propaganda in neutral countries. In 1917, however, the Supreme Command established a dedicated press service, the German

War News Service (Deutsche Kriegsnachrichtendienst), part of the general centralization of government favoured by Ludendorff. Though the new Chancellor Georg Michaelis tried to reassert civilian control over propaganda by appointing a Press Chief in late summer 1917, the generals retained control to the last.[89]

Austria too established a War Press Office (Kriegspressequartier), which produced official bulletins for domestic and foreign consumption.[90] When they entered the war, the Americans did more or less exactly the same, creating a Committee on Public Information in April 1917 which by the end of the war had produced and distributed no fewer than 75 million copies of pro-war publications.[91]

Besides trying to sway foreign opinion, a major aim of all this activity was to fortify domestic resolve. Of particular importance was the need to raise money. The British films *You*! and *For the Empire* (commissioned by the Committee on War Loans for the Small Investor) both exhorted audiences to invest in war bonds; the latter went into great detail to show 'the quantity of munitions' the investment of 15s. 6d. would provide.[92] Germany relied even more on the willingness of her own citizens to lend to the government; accordingly, a large number of posters were produced to encourage the public to buy war bonds. Lucian Bernhard's poster of 1917 depicts a naval officer explaining to a soldier as they watch an enemy ship sinking: 'That's how your money helps you to fight. Turned into a U-boat, it keeps enemy shells from you. So subscribe to war loans!'[93] In America too the First Liberty Loan campaign saw the distribution of 2 million posters, and by the third loan this number had increased to 9 million.[94]

By contrast, attempts to indoctrinate soldiers with anything more than the traditional ethos of obedience to orders were extremely limited. And attempts to influence the minds of enemy soldiers came only late in the war. In July 1917 bogus editions of German newspapers like the *Frankfurter Zeitung* were smuggled into Germany by French agents.[95] The British secret service was up to the same trick, though the technique only came to public notice with the appointment of Northcliffe to the Ministry of Information's 'Crewe House' department. In the six months from June 1918 nearly 20 million leaflets were dropped on the retreating German troops with titles like 'Hello Homeland' ('Grüße an die Heimat') and details of German casualties and the collapse of Germany's allies.[96]

The Central Powers attempted nothing on this scale. The Germans preferred to try to infiltrate pacifist newspapers by means of bribery in the form of investments by frontmen in neutral countries. The notorious cases in France concerned *Le Journal*, which received around 10 million francs from German sources, *Le Pays*, the new paper set up in 1917 to promote Joseph Caillaux's idea of a negotiated peace with Germany, and the *Bonnet Rouge*, whose publisher and editor were both arrested and charged with treason in July 1917 (one committed suicide in jail, the other was found guilty and executed).[97]

THE AUTONOMY OF PROPAGANDA

Thus far it has been assumed that by propaganda we mean government propaganda. In fact, much wartime propaganda was not produced by governmental agencies at all, but by autonomous organizations or private individuals, so that much of the time the role of the institutions described above was merely one of co-ordination.[98] This is well illustrated by the case of cinema – the most expensive of media, and therefore the one in which one would expect the government to play the biggest role. Was the Parliamentary Recruiting Committee, for example, a governmental agency? Not really – its work was done on a voluntary basis by MPs and other public figures. It was the PRC, however, and not the War Office, which commissioned the recruiting feature film *You!* in 1915.[99] True, the War Office had begun to use the cinema to attract recruits even before the war, commissioning *The British Army Film* (1914).[100] But it did little more than tolerate the activities of the British Topical Committee for War Films, a cartel of independent production companies which paid the War Office for the privilege of filming at the Front and then sold the resulting footage to the government for propaganda use. The first cinema feature produced in this way – *Britain Prepared* – was screened in December 1915. It was followed by *The Battle of the Somme* (August 1916) and *The German Retreat and the Battle of Arras* (June 1917).[101] Far from influencing the documentary style of these films, the War Office tended to distance itself from them. British film-makers produced around 240 films between 1915 and 1918 in addition to the bi-weekly newsreel introduced in May 1917. The proportion of these directly inspired by government departments was quite small – though then as now British film-makers were always on the lookout for state subsidies.

In Germany too so-called 'field-grey' films, like *How Max Won the Iron Cross, On the Field of Honour, Miss Field-grey* and *It Should be All of Germany*, were produced by the private sector with minimal prompting from the authorities.[102] The ban on foreign films helped, as did the secret commissions (beginning in 1916) from the War Office. But essentially German war cinema was self-propelled. It was the film producer Oskar Messter who opportunistically approached the military authorities with a proposal to manage filming in the various theatres of war. The 'Messter-Woche' newsreel quickly established an almost monopolistic position by virtue of Messter's official control over licences to film at the Front, much to the chagrin of competitors. It was only quite late in the day that the Supreme Command established a bureaucratic control over the cinema, beginning in October 1916 with the creation of the Military Film and Photo Office (Militärische Film- und Photostelle), which became the Photographic and Film Office (Bild- und Filmamt) in January 1917. When Ludendorff sought to step up film propaganda with a programme of 'patriotic instruction' in the second half of 1917, it was entrusted to a new company, the Universum-Film-AG (Ufa), which was financed jointly by the state and private industry. After the war this rapidly emerged as the biggest private film company in Europe.[103]

Least of all interested in government involvement was the American cinema. Largely at its own initiative, Hollywood set up its National Association of the Motion Picture Industry, which was responsible for such bellicose movies as *How the War Came to America, The Kaiserite in America* and *German War Practices*.[104]

Moreover, a good deal of less expensive 'propaganda' was produced without any reference whatever to government by associations like Sir Francis Younghusband's Fight for Right Movement, the Council of Loyal British Subjects, the Victoria League, the British Empire Union and the Central Council for National Patriotic Organisations.[105] The same can be said for Germany, where the Pan-German League and the new Fatherland Party performed a similarly independent role. In America the search for the enemy within was conducted less by the Justice Department than by vigilante groups like the American Patriotic League, the Patriotic Order of Sons of America and the Knights of Liberty. Such organizations were responsible for hundreds of incidents of extra-legal violence during the war years, including lynchings of individuals suspected of harbouring sympathy for the enemy.[106]

It was not only a media war but a media dons' war. On 4 October 1914, at the suggestion of the Naval Office, ninety-three prominent German academics, artists and intellectuals (including the scientists Max Planck and Fritz Haber, the playwright Gerhard Hauptmann and the economists Lujo Brentano and Gustav Schmoller) published a manifesto in the German press entitled 'To the World of Culture!' which justified German actions in Belgium (including the burning of Louvain) and denounced Britain's intervention on the side of 'barbaric' and 'half-Asiatic' Russia. 'It is the fault of England', declared the signatories (not incorrectly), 'that the present war is extended to a world war.'[107] This was followed by a similar statement published by the Cultural League of German Scholars and *Why We Are At War* by the historians Friedrich Meinecke and Hermann Oncken.

British writers were if anything quicker off the mark. As is well known, the counter-manifesto by fifty-two 'well-known men of letters' published in *The Times* on 18 September 1914 was the result of a meeting organized by Masterman on 2 September at Wellington House.[108] But the signatories did not need much encouragement; most of them were already chomping at the bit. Among those who came to Wellington House or signed *The Times* 'Declaration by Authors' were G. K. Chesterton, Arthur Conan Doyle, John Masefield, Rudyard Kipling and the editor of *Punch*, Owen Seaman – a Who's Who of patriotic, not to say Tory, writers. Also present and eager for verbal action were H. G. Wells, the prophet of war now vindicated, and Thomas Hardy. More unexpected were the signatures of the novelists Arnold Bennett, John Galsworthy, the classicist Gilbert Murray and the historian G. M. Trevelyan, none of whom had greeted the outbreak of war with much enthusiasm.[109]

An especially striking example of intellectual self-mobilization is the case of the Oxford History Faculty. Working with a speed unusual, perhaps even unprecedented, in the annals of the university, five Oxford historians led by H. W. C. Davies and Ernest Barker wrote *Why We Are At War: Great Britain's Case* – also sometimes called *The Red Book* – which the University Press managed to publish as early as 14 September (barely two weeks after the manuscript was delivered).[110] Later came a series of Oxford Pamphlets for 'the intelligent working man'. Historians from the 'provincial' universities also waded in, including D. J. Medley from Glasgow and Ramsay Muir from Manchester. There were lectures in major cities to counter the possible belief 'among many of our working men . . . that if Germany wins they will be no worse off than they are now'.[111] Dons from other faculties contributed to the genre. In addition to signing the 'Men of Letters' manifesto, Gilbert Murray wrote *How Can War Ever Be Right?* and *The Foreign Policy of Sir Edward Grey 1906–15*, an apologetic account published in June 1915 and rightly dismissed by Ramsay MacDonald as an 'extraordinary exercise in whitewash and putty'.[112]

It should be noted that few of the established authors mentioned above accepted payment for their wartime writings: Galsworthy and Wells both bashed out their Wellington House articles for nothing, to the alarm of their literary agent.[113] It was not until late in the war that the more assiduous writers like Arnold Bennett became government employees in Beaverbrook's Ministry of Information. Much the same thing happened in France.[114]

Poets mobilized themselves too. *The Times* estimated that it received around a hundred poems a day in August 1914, the vast majority in the patriotic/romantic vein. According to one estimate, no fewer than 50,000 war poems were written in Germany every day in the same month. A bibliography of British war poetry, nearly all of it patriotic, lists over 3,000 volumes; an equivalent estimate for Germany of 350 may be an underestimate – or perhaps the *Denker* came to outnumber the *Dichter* after the August days.[115] To be sure, the poetasters were encouraged by governments: the journalist Ernst Lissauer, for example, was awarded the Iron Cross for his 'Hymn of Hate'. But he wrote it at his own initiative. Likewise, playwrights needed no prompting to scribble patriotic pieces for the theatre.[116]

At every level of society war propaganda did not have to be produced by governments; it produced itself. Academics, journalists, amateur poets and ordinary people churned it out unprompted. Businesses manufactured it too. Nothing perhaps illustrates this better than the production of toys and comics for children, a phenomenon discernible in nearly all the combatant countries.[117] In Britain there were toy tanks (available six months after they were first used in battle); in France, Lusitania jigsaws and a militarized version of Monopoly; in Germany, miniature artillery pieces which fired peas.[118]

Because so much propaganda was not government controlled, it often took on a life of its own. Typical of the way the nationalist ginger-groups undermined Bethmann Hollweg was Wolfgang Kapp's tract *Nationalist Circles and the Reich Chancellor* (1916), part of the relentless campaign waged (admittedly with the connivance of the Naval Office) to remove the restrictions on submarine warfare.[119] An even better example is the quite extraordinary way in which Northcliffe harassed successive British governments. Charles à Court Repington sometimes referred during the war to 'the Government Press', meaning the press loyal to the government; but at times Britain seemed to be heading for a Press Government.[120] Northcliffe used his papers to campaign against Haldane in 1914, Kitchener in 1915, Asquith in 1916 and finally Lloyd George as well as Milner after the war was over. His papers conducted a succession of campaigns aimed at intensifying the British war effort: for the internment of aliens, for a Munitions Ministry, for the introduction of a national register of men capable of bearing arms, for a special War Council, for more machine-guns and, of course, for conscription. So troublesome were these interventions that the Earl of Rosebery, seconded by Churchill, suggested that *The Times* be nationalized; but this was not done.[121] Asquith lived to regret it. Though Northcliffe was not the sole architect of his downfall as prime minister – Beaverbrook also played a part – there is no question that the press lords hastened it.[122]

Typical of Northcliffe's approach was his instruction to the *Daily Mail* editor, Tom Clarke, in December 1916: 'Get a smiling picture of Lloyd George and underneath it put the caption "DO IT NOW", and get the worst possible picture of Asquith and label it "WAIT AND SEE".'[123] By the later stages of the war (especially after his ego-boosting trip to the US)[124] Northcliffe was evincing something like megalomania. 'Tell the Chief', he told one of Haig's staff in the autumn of 1917, 'that if [Lloyd] George ventures to do anything against him, I will put him out of office.'[125] On 3 October 1918 he went so far as to tell Riddell: 'I do not propose to use my newspapers and personal influence to support a new Government . . . unless I know definitely and in writing, and can consciously approve, the personal constitution of the Government.'[126]

Moreover, the relative autonomy of the press frequently put pressure on governments to adopt more ambitious war aims. Although the war aims debate in Germany is notorious thanks to Fischer, there was a very similar debate in Britain and indeed in all combatant states. Among the more extreme options canvassed by British journalists as war aims, for example, was the dissolution of the German Reich. Other demands – the destruction of the Habsburg and Ottoman Empires – only seem less fantastic than their German counterparts because they were actually achieved.[127]

HIGH AND LOW DICTION

The content of propaganda need not long detain us. In all countries there was a torrent of what Paul Fussell has called 'high diction': a friend became a 'comrade', a horse became a 'steed', the enemy became the 'foe'.[128] In *The Barbarism of Berlin* G. K. Chesterton claimed that Britain was 'fighting for the trust and the tryst . . . for the long arm of honour and remembrance'. Poetry was the preferred vehicle for such sentiments. 'Death is no death to him that dares to die', intoned Sir Henry Newbolt, not untypically, in his 'Sacramentum Supremum'.[129] 'Who stands if freedom fall?' asked Kipling in 'For All We Have and Are'; 'Who dies if England live?' No aspect of the war, no matter how unromantic, was safe from this idiom. Newbolt could adopt it even when writing about a war film ('O living pictures of the dead, O songs without a sound . . .').[130] Alfred Noyes, another poet of the old school, described Glaswegian female munitions workers 'lavishing all the passion of motherhood' on their 'gleaming brood of shells . . . brought forth to shield [sic] a dearer brood of flesh and blood'.[131] Gilbert Murray sought to justify such drivel, arguing that

the language of romance and melodrama has now become . . . the language of our normal life . . . The old phrase about . . . 'Death being better than dishonour' – phrases that we thought were fitted for the stage or for children's stories – are now the ordinary truths on which we live.[132]

He protested too much. A more sober critic was closer to the mark when he dismissed wartime high diction as 'word paint'.[133]

For British propaganda the violation of Belgian neutrality was the ace in the pack and it was played *ad nauseam*. Britain, so the 'Men of Letters' put it, was fighting 'to uphold the rule of common justice between civilized peoples [and] to defend the rights of small nations'.[134] The Oxford *Red Book* contrasted Britain, a state guided by the rule of law, with treaty-breaking Germany. The 'solemn treaty more than once renewed' was, Gilbert Murray argued in *How Can War Ever Be Right*, the decisive argument for war.[135] Harold Spencer too assured doubting liberals that Britain had gone to war to enforce the law and 'on that account alone'.[136] The author Hall Caine published *King Albert's Book: A Tribute to the Belgian King and People*, a 'covenant . . . signed on the desecrated altar of a little nation's liberty'.[137] Galsworthy and the historian Arnold Toynbee were among the many who inveighed in print against German 'frightfulness'. Hardy even wrote a poem on the subject entitled 'On the Belgian Expatriation' and the more sanctimonious Anglican clergymen never tired of the theme.[138] Nor did the Parliamentary Recruiting Committee: its poster 'The Scrap of Paper' actually reproduced the seal and signatures on the 1839 treaty. By comparison, very little British propaganda referred to the strategic argument – so important within the Cabinet in 1914 and so dear to the pre-war Germanophobes – that Belgium and France must be defended to prevent Germany building naval bases on the Channel coast.[139]

Notoriously, Entente propaganda exaggerated the 'atrocities' inflicted on the Belgian population by the advancing German armies. After the war, the Liberal pacifist Arthur Ponsonby gave a celebrated (but in fact bogus) illustration of how a report in the *Kölnische Zeitung* – 'When the fall of Antwerp became known, the church bells were rung' – was supposedly transmuted via successive Entente papers into:

The barbaric conquerors of Antwerp punished the unfortunate Belgian priests for their heroic refusal to ring the church bells by hanging them as living clappers to the bells with their heads down.[140]

But pre-war photographs of Russian pogroms genuinely were reprinted to 'illustrate' stories of German behaviour in Belgium. The *Sunday Chronicle* was one of many British papers which alleged that the Germans had cut off the hands of Belgian children, while the former scaremonger William Le Queux related with ill-disguised relish 'the wild orgies of blood and debauchery' in which the Germans allegedly indulged, including 'the ruthless violation and killing of defenceless women, girls and children of tender age'. Other writers had great fun imagining sixteen-year-old girls being 'forced to drink' and then 'violated successively' on the lawn before having their breasts 'pierced . . . with bayonets'. The bayonetted baby was another favoured image. J. H. Morgan even threw in a charge of 'sodomy . . . of little children'. At least eleven pamphlets on this subject were published in Britain between 1914 and 1918, including Lord Bryce's official *Report . . . on Alleged German Atrocities* (1915),[141] and Wellington House under Masterman ensured that a high proportion of them were translated and sent abroad. Atrocities exported well. Several American Liberty Loan posters used images of scantily clad Belgian nymphs at the mercy of simian Huns to entice prurient savers to buy war bonds.[142]

More circumspect British writers sought to distinguish between 'the free and law-abiding ideals of Western Europe' or 'the English-speaking race' and 'the rule of "Blood and Iron"' favoured by Germany's 'military caste'.[143] Anthony Hope, author of *The Prisoner of Zenda*, mocked German militarism in parodies of Bernhardi including *The German (New) Testament*. Hardy too denounced 'the writings of Nietzsche, Treitschke, Bernhardi etc.'[144] This line of argument allowed conscience-stricken Liberals on the *Daily News* to draw a distinction between the German people, with whom they maintained they had no quarrel, and the 'tyranny which has held them in its vice'. Thus the war could be portrayed as 'the last supreme struggle of the old dispensation against the new'.[145]

Another theme of British propaganda, designed specifically for American consumption and seized upon by H. G. Wells, was the idea that Britain was fighting a war against 'Kruppism . . . this huge fighting machine . . . this sordid enormous trade in the instruments of death'.[146] In Wells's early war writings, improbably enough, the war became a war for 'disarmament and peace throughout the earth'.[147] Even more accurately pitched at American sentiment was his seminal pamphlet *The War that Will End War*, dashed off on 14 August, from which sprouted much of Woodrow Wilson's later rhetoric.

Propagandists also enjoyed denigrating one another's national cultures. Partly in response to the German manifesto 'To the World of Culture', British writers let fly at the 'truculence, and stodgy erudition' of the 'Teutonic professorship'.[148] British academics, for decades made to feel inferior by the rigour of the German universities, warmed to this theme. Gilbert Murray was not above a sneer at German scholars who 'spend their lives in narrow and absorbed pursuit of some object which . . . possesses no very great importance and no particular illumination or beauty'. In Cambridge Sir Arthur Quiller-Couch declared war on 'the dry chaff of [German] historical research and criticism'.[149] 'The age of German footnotes', declared one Oxford optimist, 'is on the wane.'[150] Thomas Mann's verbose denunciation of British 'civilization' as inferior to German *Kultur* (especially Wagner) was cut from the same shabby cloth and proved that footnotes were the least of the things wrong with German intellectual life.[151] It is scarcely credible, but true, that intelligent men in Britain thought they were fighting footnotes and intelligent men in Germany thought they were defending E-flat chords.

The counterpart of this was the claim that war would have a purifying effect on one's own national culture, exemplified by the comments in *Poetry Review* in 1914, which looked forward to 'a "Katharsis" of the morbid secretions so much in evidence of late'.[152] Edmund Gosse was a notable British exponent of this view, predicting that war, like 'disinfectant' would clean out 'the stagnant pools and clotted channels of the intellect'; in particular, he hoped it would get rid of Vorticism.[153] The German poet Richard Dehmel hoped likewise that the war would make ordinary Germans think less about 'freedom, equality and the like' and more about 'the trees growing'.

What made the more pompous claims of such writers so ludicrous was precisely the cultural debasement which the war seemed to cause. Far from national uplift, there was a carnival of vulgarity. Crass slogans like *Jeder Tritt ein Britt* ('for every step, a Brit'), *Jeder Stoss ein Franzos* ('for every blow a Frog') and *Jeder Schuss ein Russ* ('for every shot a Russki') had equivalents everywhere: 'Hang the Kaiser', for example. Humorous postcards trivialized the war: one German card attempted to joke about a gas attack, while the Italians tried to see the funny side of Belgian atrocities.[154]

This trivialization was part of a wider effort to glamorize, or at least to sanitize, the fighting itself. In the reports Northcliffe himself wrote from the Front, the war was represented as a kind of jolly summer holiday: 'The open-air life, the regular and plenteous feeding, the exercise and the freedom from care and responsibility, keep the soldiers extraordinarily fit and contented.' A favourite British theme was that the war was a form of sport: 'the greater game' or 'a fast run with the hounds'.[155] Even death was viewed through this Panglossian prism. *The Times* quoted Lloyd George as saying that 'the British soldier is a good sportsman . . . has fought as a good sportsman [and] by the thousands he has died a good sportsman'. The British corpse, according to W. Beach Thomas in the *Daily Mirror*, looked 'more quietly faithful, more simply steadfast, than others . . . as if he had taken care when he died that there should be no . . . heroics in his posture'.[156] This whitewash was dispensed most liberally when casualties were highest – in this case at the time of the Somme. The French press had to use the same tactics in the disastrous opening phase of the war, assuring readers that German shells were ineffective, and again in 1915, when there was an implausible emphasis on the good humour of the *poilus*, 'going into battle as to a fête . . . They looked forward to the offensive as to a holiday. They were so happy! They laughed! They joked!'[157]

Finally, propagandists sought to encourage their fellow-citizens with the prospect that victory would pay domestic political dividends. To begin with, governments trumpeted the national unity called forth by the conflict: France had its *Union sacrée*, Germany its *Burgfrieden* and Britain gladly forgot about Ireland and reverted to 'business as usual' (part of the slogan's significance lay in the fact that business had not been quite usual in 1913–14). Lloyd George was one of the first politicians to give this line of argument a political spin, telling his audience at the Queen's Hall in September 1914 that he saw

amongst all classes, high and low, shedding themselves of selfishness, a new recognition that the honour of the country does not depend merely in the maintenance of its glory on the stricken field, but also in the protection of its homes from distress.[158]

This amounted to a coded pledge to his Liberal supporters that, as with the dreadnoughts, the costs of war would not be incompatible with social policy and progressive taxation. Later in the war, of course, British war propaganda made more explicit promises that the war would materially improve the lot of the British people – hence 'homes fit for heroes'.

THE AUDIENCE

But did propaganda work? The evidence needed to answer such a question is scant; but we have enough to hazard a verdict.

Censorship probably did achieve something; the very fact that journalists complained so much about it speaks in its favour. It certainly kept a good deal secret in a way which would prove impossible in the Second World War, when private radios with international range undermined even Goebbels's grip on the press. The embarrassing loss of the battleship *Audacious* off Ireland in October 1914 was not reported in Britain, nor was the Battle of Jutland until some time after it was over. The Germans had no idea how serious the French mutinies of 1917 were; probably few French civilians did either.

Propaganda proper may also have achieved something. It certainly sold well. The Oxford *Red Book* sold 50,000 copies, of which only 3,300 went to the Foreign Office for use abroad. By September 1915 eighty-seven different Oxford pamphlets had come out, with a total print-run of 500,000. Priced at between 1 and 4 pence, they sold well: just under 300,000 had gone by January 1915.[159] John Masefield's bland account of the Somme, *The Old Front Line*, sold 20,000 copies in Britain and nearly 4,000 in America. Arnold Bennett's *Statement of the British Case* sold 4,600 copies in Britain; Gilbert Murray's *Foreign Policy of Sir Edward Grey* also did well.[160] The film *For the Empire* was a major hit: perhaps as many as 9 million people had seen it by the end of December 1916.[161] In the last year of the war it has been estimated that the National War Aims Committee reached over a million readers with its flood of publications.[162]

On the other hand, it seems unlikely that Alfred Leete's famous Kitchener poster was as effective as its post-war fame would suggest.[163] The film *You!* (which had the same aim) was a commercial failure.[164] Moreover, some works critical of the war were also commercial successes. Shaw's *Common Sense about the War* sold 25,000 copies; Wells's disillusioned *Mr Britling Sees it Through* went through thirteen editions before the end of 1916 and made him £20,000 in royalties in the US alone.[165] Barbusse's *Le Feu* was a bestseller.

Even more ambiguous is the evidence for the reception of films like *The Battle of the Somme*. How far this can really be regarded as propaganda is itself open to question. No less than 13 per cent of its seventy-seven minutes' running time was given over to shots of the dead and wounded; in the case of the last quarter of the film more than 40 per cent. The titles were unflinching: 'British Tommies rescuing a comrade under shell fire. (This man died twenty minutes after reaching a trench.)' Yet the film was a huge success. *Kine Weekly* called it 'the most wonderful battle picture that has ever been written'. By October 1916 it had been booked by over 2,000 cinemas across the country, nearly half the total of 4,500. It made around £30,000.[166]

On the other hand, not everyone enjoyed what they saw. *The Times* and the *Guardian* both received letters lamenting 'an entertainment which wounds the heart and violates the very sanctities of bereavement' (in the words of the Dean of Durham). And many of those who approved of the film did so precisely because it made audiences sob at the horror of the war.[167] Moreover, it may well be doubted how much good was done by such films when they were shown to foreign audiences. Diplomats' reports reveal that (for example) Nicaraguans were bored by long sequences of 'destroyers . . . rushing about in a foggy sea with an occasional picture of a mascot', while Khartoum audiences wanted more 'dead Germans or Turks' and Chinese cinema-goers objected to the lack of actual fighting.[168] When *The Battle of the Somme* was shown in The Hague, the Red Cross saw it as a perfect opportunity to raise money for their anti-war league. In the United States, as Buchan was informed by his man in New York, there were 'so many letters of complaint about the horrors of the Somme films, and the disastrous effects they were having in preventing recruitment and putting people against the war, that . . . we called in the films and subjected them to strong censorship'.[169] This alone must cast doubt on the myth of Britain's brilliant war propaganda.

By contrast, there is good reason to think that German use of cinema was more successful. Oskar Messter claimed that as many as 18 million people had seen his newsreels in Germany and allied countries, and more than 12 million in neutral countries.[170] If true, these were immense figures. A striking difference between German and British war films was the preponderance of dramas over documentaries: while the Germans produced numerous 'field-grey' romances and adventure movies, *Hearts of the World* (1916) was the exception in Britain; conspicuously, it had an American director. There is good reason to question whether British producers like Geoffrey Malins were right to think that showing 'death in all its grim nakedness' would stiffen public resolve.[171]

Perhaps the best measure of the success of Entente propaganda abroad was the number of rebuttals it elicited from the German side. The German Central Bureau for Foreign Service produced an entire 'White Book' devoted to denials of the allegations that atrocities had been committed by German troops. The atrocity reports disturbed many ordinary Germans too. The Hamburg art historian Aby Warburg spent much of the war obsessively collecting evidence from newspapers to disprove the charges.[172] What is less clear is how far propaganda genuinely succeeded in swaying neutral opinion. It is clear, for example, that the American decision to intervene was not due primarily or even secondarily to Entente propaganda.[173] And it is tempting to conclude that both sides wasted a good deal of money in trying to buy journalistic support in countries like Italy and Greece.[174] As for the effect of Allied propaganda on German opinion, evidence is scant: if any inference can be drawn from the behaviour of some German soldiers (and more particularly sailors) in November 1918, it was the Bolsheviks who achieved the most in this regard.[175]

Moreover, even if jingoistic journalism bolstered morale on the home front, it is far from clear that the men doing the fighting were impressed. Soldiers certainly read the Northcliffe press: the *Daily Mail* was sold by French boys at the entrances to communications trenches, and even at the height of the Battle of the Somme the papers arrived from London only a day after publication.[176] As we shall see, atrocity stories did have an influence on soldiers. But the more unrealistic accounts of life and death at the Front were held up to ridicule. 'Eyewitness' was nicknamed 'Eyewash' and Hilaire Belloc's jingoistic style lampooned, as in the *Wipers Times*'s parody of 'Belary Hilloc' in February 1916:

In this article I wish to show plainly that under existing conditions everything points to a speedy disintegration of the enemy. We will take first of all the effect of war on the male population of Germany. Firstly let us take our figures [of] 12,000,000 as the total fighting population of Germany. Of these 8,000,000 are killed or being killed, hence we have 4,000,000 remaining. Of these 1,000,000 are non-combatants, being in the Navy. Of the 3,000,000 remaining, we can write off 2,500,000 as being temperamentally unsuited for fighting, owing to obesity and other ailments engendered by a gross mode of living. This leaves us 500,000 as the full strength. Of these 497,240 are known to be suffering from incurable diseases, of the remaining 600, 584 are Generals and Staff. Thus we find that there are 16 men on the Western Front. This number I maintain is not enough to give them even a fair chance of resisting four more big pushes . . .[177]

Siegfried Sassoon's 'Fight to the Finish' expresses his own loathing of the 'yellow-pressmen', whom he imagines being bayoneted by 'the boys' after their victory parade through London.[178] French soldiers felt much the same about their more gung-ho papers.[179] Saxon soldiers at Ypres in July 1915 even threw a stone into the English line with a message attached: 'Send us an English newspaper so that we may hear the verity.'[180]

British soldiers preferred to produce and read their own trench newspapers (around half of which were edited by other ranks).[181] So did the French, who produced a host of 'trench newspapers' – as many as 400[182] – with titles like *Le Rire aux Eclats* and, inevitably, *Le Poilu*. One of the most enduring French satirical magazines, *Le Crapouillot*, began life in the trenches in August 1915.[183] German soldiers were equally sceptical of their own government's propaganda. To be sure, many educated soldiers (like the artist Otto Dix) carried Nietzsche's works in their packs and sincerely believed they were 'defending the German feeling against Asiatic barbarism and Latin indifference'.[184] But that was at the beginning. When a newsreel entitled *From the*

Front was shown to troops in 1916 it was greeted with derision.[185]

Perhaps the grim truth about war propaganda was that it had the greatest influence on the social group which mattered least to the war effort: children. In *The Last Days of Mankind* Karl Kraus depicts Viennese children merrily exchanging war slogans. Hänschen greets Trudchen with '*Gott strafe England*', while two toddlers discuss their 'duty' to subscribe to war loans:

KLAUS: The way we were encircled, every child knows that.
DOLLY: British envy, French vengefulness, Russian rapacity . . . Germany wanted a place in the sun.
KLAUS: Europe was a powder keg.
DOLLY: The Belgian treaty was a scrap of paper.[186]

There is evidence that this was only mild exaggeration. When children in two London schools were asked which kind of films they liked best, war films came second; asked to list their five favourite films, a majority put either *The Battle of the Somme* or *The Battle of the Ancre* first. One schoolboy's breathless description of the latter shows how even the most realistic battle scenes could be recast by an impressionable mind exposed at an early age to the works of Buchan and his ilk:

Now the whistle shrills, and they leap over the parapet, rat, tap, tap, go the German machine guns, but nothing daunts our soldiers. Crack! and their gallant captain falls. This enrages the men to fury. At last they reach the German lines. Most of the Germans flee for their lives shouting 'Kamerad! Kamerad!' etc. Now the British and German wounded are brought in . . . Soon after follow the German prisoners, some vicious-looking scoundrels I should not like to meet on a dark night . . .[187]

AT THE CASH REGISTER OF HISTORY

One of the most compelling of all arguments about the role of the press during the war was advanced by the Viennese satirist Karl Kraus in his one-man magazine *Die Fackel* and his epic play about the war, *The Last Days of Mankind*.

Kraus was at once fascinated and appalled by the way newspapers treated the war, with a mixture of conscious cynicism and unconscious irony, as the ultimate 'good story'. At the beginning of *The Last Days*, it is reporters who turn xenophobic drunks into patriotic crowds and an editor who supplies the 'mood' conspicuously absent from Francis Ferdinand's funeral. Cameramen exchange stories of photogenic deaths – 'completely natural' – and executions – 'too bad you weren't there'. When seventeen Austrian soldiers are hit by shrapnel while reporters are on the scene it is 'the greatest compliment the press has so far received in the war'. When a wounded soldier begs for money from a journalist, the latter retorts crossly: 'Excuse me, what do you want from me, *I* had eighty lines censored from last Monday's paper.' In cinemas a newsreel of the sinking of the Lusitania is preceded by the announcement: 'Smoking permitted at this point in the programme.' A film about the Somme is itself 'the greatest event of the war'.

The greatest of the many reptilian journalists of *The Last Days* is Alice Schalek, the female war correspondent for whom the suffering of soldiers is merely wonderful 'colour' for her copy. To Schalek the war is no different from the plays she reviewed in peacetime: 'performances' at the Front are 'first class' and officers are treated to interviews as if they were stars of the stage ('How did you feel?' is her favourite question). Anticipating Hemingway, Schalek herself takes a turn with a gun and finds it 'interesting' when (as she has been warned) the enemy returns fire with interest. Throughout the play Kraus shows how journalistic language distorts the war: 'the public masses' in 'thousands upon thousands' (louts threaten foreigners); 'with true manliness Vienna accepts the fateful decision . . . far removed from over-confidence or weakness' (more louts threaten foreigners); 'the leader of our glorious army makes an important announcement' (a senile general drools incomprehensibly); 'soldiers are freed' (men are obliged to fight by their employers). Moreover, this language infects everyone: the military authorities begin to use it and so, as we have seen, do children. A little girl refuses to play with her friends because sport is an English frivolity, while Germans only work. Delighted, her mother suggests sending her 'golden words' to the *Berliner Abendzeitung*.

This was no mere consequence of the war. On the contrary: according to Kraus, it was the war which was a consequence of the impoverishment of the imagination brought about by the mass press. 'Through decades of practice', he argued,

the newspaper reporter has brought to us that degree of impoverishment of the imagination which makes it possible for us to fight a war of annihilation against ourselves. Since the boundless efficiency of his apparatus has deprived us of all capacity for experience and for the mental development of that experience, he can now implant in us the courage in the face of death which we need in order to rush off into battle . . . His abuse of language embellishes the abuse of life.[188]

The key to the war, then, was 'the mental self-mutilation of mankind through its press'. His central argument in the essay 'In These Great Times' was that 'acts not only produce reports, reports are also responsible for actions', so that 'if the newspaper publishes lies about atrocities, atrocities will be the result'. Kraus made the same point in *The Last Days*: 'Paper burns and has set the world alight. Newspaper pages have acted as the kindling for the world conflagration . . . Would the war have been possible at all without the press – possible to begin or possible to continue?'

Yet the press was only acting in its own interest: as one of Kraus's journalists says, 'the public must have its appetite whetted for the war and for the paper, one is inseparable from the other'. Crowds cheer 'for Austria, Germany and the *Neue Freie Presse*'. 'Are those our men?' one reporter near the front line asks another. 'You mean from the press corps?' replies the other. The only 'international' which has benefited from the war, argues Kraus's alter ego 'the Grumbler', is 'the black and white international'.[189]

This argument is bound to strike a chord with a modern reader, anticipating as it does later commentators such as Walter Benjamin, Marshall McLuhan and Jean Baudrillard. At the very least, it provides a salutary reminder that the power of the mass media is no recent development, nor the enthusiasm of newspapers for wars. But was Kraus right? The implication of his argument was that the war boosted newspaper circulation and hence also the profits of newspapers: indeed, he memorably denounced Moritz Benedikt, the proprietor of the *Neue Freie Presse*, as 'the man who sits at the cash register of world history'.[190] Although a good deal has been written about war propaganda, hitherto there has been no attempt to assess the impact of the war on the European press in terms of circulation and profitability.

At first sight, Kraus had a point: there is striking evidence that the war did boost newspaper sales. The circulation of the *Daily Mail* soared from 946,000 before the war to just under 1.5 million during the first weeks of August 1914 and remained at 1.4 million until June 1916.

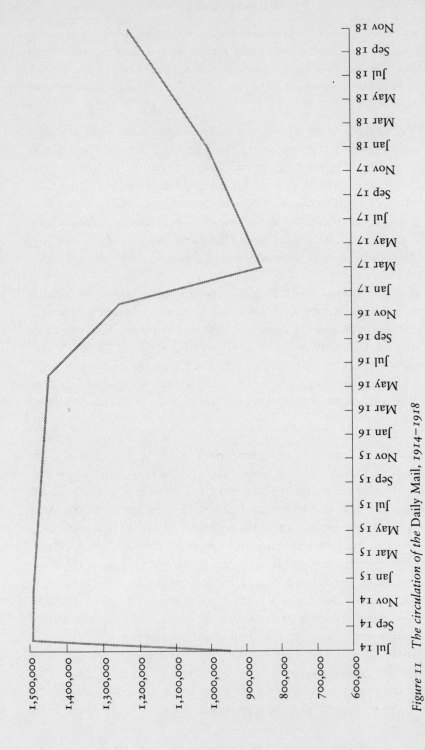

Figure 11 The circulation of the Daily Mail, *1914–1918*

Source: Grünbeck, *Presse*, vol. I, p. 150.

Table 19   The circulation of selected British newspapers, 1914–1918 (thousands)

	1914	1915	1916	1917	1918
The Times	183		184	137	131
Daily Mail	946	1,105	1,172	938	973
Daily Express	295	373	434	450	579
Daily News	550	800			
Daily Chronicle	400		758		
Daily Mirror	1,000		1,307		
Daily Sketch	800	1,500		820	
Sunday Times	35				50
Observer	133	194	224	188	195
News of the World		2,000		2,750	

Source: McEwen, 'National Press', pp. 468–83.

Even at the end of the war it remained above its pre-war level (Figure 11).

One evening newspaper experienced an increase in circulation of 144 per cent on August 3 1914; but this was beaten on 16 December, when news broke of the first German naval raid on the East coast. *The Times* saw sales rise to 278,000 on 4 August 1914 and 318,000 the following month. The *Evening News* also gained nearly 900,000 readers in the second half of 1914. The *Daily Express* very nearly doubled its circulation during the war; while Horatio Bottomley's *John Bull* was selling as many as 2 million copies by late 1918, a figure beaten only by the new *Sunday Pictorial* and the *News of the World*.

In France *Le Matin* experienced a similar boom. In Germany the circulation of the *Berliner Tageblatt* rose from 220,000 in 1913 to 300,000 in 1918.[191] Between 1913 and 1918 the total circulation of German newspapers increased by nearly 70 per cent.[192] A selection of seven titles for which figures are available suggests a substantial wartime growth in readership across the board (see Table 20).

Even the neutral countries' press benefited: the circulation of the *Neue Zürcher Zeitung* doubled during the war, while that of the *New York Times* rose 48 per cent before US entry.[193] There is no question, then, that war sold papers just as Northcliffe had foretold. The same argument holds good for cinema. Before the war there had been just

Table 20   The circulation of selected German newspapers, 1913–1918 (thousands)

	1913	1914	1915	1916	1917	1918	1913–18 (% increase)
Berliner Tageblatt	228	230	238	245		300	31.6
Neue Augsburger Zeitung	38	40	38			58	52.6
Berliner Morgenpost	360	400	430			457	26.9
Cottbuser Anzeiger	16	17	17			28	71.9
Darmstädter Tageblatt	15	15				22	51.7
Jenauische Zeitung	6	7	7	8	8	8	30.6
Leipziger Neueste Nachrichten	142	182	205	196	207	215	51.5
All German newspapers	16,320					27,720	69.9

Source: Heenemann, 'Auflagenhöhe', pp. 70–86.

one German newsreel series; by September 1914 the number had risen to seven. By the end of the war the number of cinemas in Germany had increased by 27 per cent and the number of film companies from 25 to 130.[194]

Yet Kraus's argument needs to be qualified. As the figures for the British press show, not all the gains in circulation proved permanent. Overall, *The Times* lost readers during the war. Other papers rose only to fall; some stagnated (the *Telegraph* for instance). Some of those papers which put on circulation had already been doing so before the war. Other papers did not increase sales during the war, while a substantial number (especially socialist papers) lost readers.[195] Moreover, there were several economic disadvantages which prevented higher circulation from being translated into higher profits. Advertising revenue fell everywhere and, like other service sector industries without a direct role in arms production, the press lost skilled labour. Especially damaging were the paper shortages and the general price inflation caused by the war. In Britain paper rationing was introduced in 1918, reducing allocations by 50 per cent, though papers had been forced to reduce their pagination long before because of the drop in advertising revenue.[196] In France daily papers were reduced to two pages from August 1914 onwards and although this maximum was later raised for certain days in the week to six, physical shortages cut paper sizes back to four pages five days a week in 1917.[197] In Germany newsprint began to be rationed as early as April 1916. The number of pages in editions therefore had to be reduced: the main Berlin titles were around half their pre-war size by 1916.[198] Everywhere newsprint grew more expensive: in France by a factor of more than five and even in the United States by 75 per cent.[199] The price of ink and other materials also rose sharply: in Germany it very nearly quadrupled during the war.[200] Yet with papers shrinking in size it was difficult to put the cover price up by as much as the costs of newsprint and ink without losing readers. The price of *The Times* went up from 1d. in March 1914 to 1½d. in November 1916 and 2d. in March 1917, finally reaching 3d. in March 1918. Northcliffe was also forced to double the price of the *Mail*. Circulation duly fell. This was the norm throughout Europe. Most British papers doubled their cover price during the war.[201] All French papers were ordered to do so in September 1917,[202] and in Germany 88 per cent of German newspapers had doubled their price by 1918.[203] The same was true in neutral Switzerland.[204] Thus, even well established papers which attracted new readers suffered financially. Profits at *Le Matin* declined sharply in 1914–15 and only returned to pre-war levels in 1918; and when adjustment is made for inflation, this recovery turns out to be illusory.[205]

These economic problems help explain why the war saw a significant reduction in the number of newspaper titles in a number of combatant countries. Some papers simply folded. In France, for example, *Gil Blas, l'Aurore, l'Autorité* and the *Paris-Journal* were among the more famous names to vanish in 1914.[206] In Germany around 300 papers ceased publication in the first year of war and more than ten times that number had suffered at least some interruption in production by 1918. Although some papers managed a comeback, the final net reduction in titles was just over 500.[207] The total number of newspapers in Germany decreased permanently from 4,221 in 1914 to 3,719 during the war, a decrease of around 12 per cent.

As might be expected, it was mostly the smaller papers which suffered. Moreover, many of those which survived as titles lost their commercial independence as the larger newspaper publishers used their wartime profits to expand their empires – the most obvious example being the empire built up by the Krupp director Alfred Hugenberg, who took over August Scherl's group (including the *Berliner Lokal-Anzeiger* and

Der Tag) in 1916. According to one estimate, the so-called *Maternpresse* accounted for some 905 newspapers.[208] There was, however, an unexpected political dimension to the contraction. While the proportion of German newspapers supporting the liberal parties, the SPD or the Centre rose between 1914 and 1917 (from 28.2 per cent to 32.4), the percentage of conservative papers fell from 22.6 to 16.8.[209] And Hugenberg's was only one of three media empires, the other two of which remained politically liberal: the two groups associated with the names Rudolf Mosse (*Berliner Tageblatt, Berliner Morgenzeitung*) and Leopold Ullstein (*Berliner Zeitung, Berliner Abendpost, Berliner Morgenpost* and the *Vossische Zeitung*). It was these big concerns, rather than the press as a whole, which truly did benefit from the war.

TRUE STORIES

There is a final point to be made. As the French satirist Alain said, there were two wars: the one fought and the one talked. But the former was the one which counted. *Pace* Kraus, there would have been no war propaganda without the war, no atrocity stories without atrocities. Although the Entente press wildly exaggerated what went on in Belgium, there is no question that the German army *did* commit 'atrocities' there in 1914. According to evidence from the diaries of German soldiers and other reliable sources, all the advancing German armies executed civilians, including women and priests. Altogether about 5,500 Belgian civilians were deliberately killed by the German army, most of them in the eleven-day period from 18 to 28 August 1914; and at least another 500 in France.[210] The Germans also used civilians as human shields and razed numerous villages to the ground. In one case an eighteen-year-old girl was bayoneted to death. There were also numerous rapes in occupied France.[211] Le Queux was not fantasizing after all.

To be sure, the questions of international law raised by these incidents were more complicated than Entente propaganda implied. The Hague Convention of 1899 was in fact not very precise about how civilians should be treated in invaded territory; it certainly did not rule out the death penalty for those who continued to resist after a country had been defeated and occupied.[212] The Germans recalled the casualties inflicted on their predecessors in 1870 by *francs-tireurs*, French guerrillas who continued sniping at them after their army had been defeated. In the pandemonium unleashed by the German invasion in 1914, tired and trigger-happy conscripts were inclined to see any hostility by Belgian civilians as threatening, especially as the reserves of the Belgian Civil Guard wore only the most rudimentary of uniforms (a Brabant chemise and an arm-band). Indeed even accidental shots by the Germans themselves were blamed on phantom *francs-tireurs* and on occasion led to reprisals against entirely blameless Belgians.[213]

Still, the fact remains that the Germans behaved a great deal worse in Belgium than the Russians did at the beginning of the war in East Prussia or Galicia, as the Germans themselves had to admit. It is worth noting that as many as a thousand Serb civilians were killed by the Austrians, compared with just twenty-two Habsburg subjects killed by the Russians in Galicia up until February 1915.[214] By the same token, there is no denying that 1,198 passengers (including 80 children and 128 Americans) did drown when the *Lusitania* was sunk in May 1915. The Germans argued, rightly, that the ship had been carrying ammunition for the Entente powers and that Britain was also guilty of violating the freedom of the seas in enforcing its blockade of Germany; but no ships were sunk without warning and no citizens of neutral countries were deliberately killed by the Royal Navy.

Hitler thought that the lesson to be learned from Entente propaganda in the First World War was to lie repetitively and on a grand scale. In this he was wrong. The real lesson was that the most effective propaganda was that which was based on the truth. Unfortunately for the Entente powers, their moral superiority over the Central Powers with respect to neutrals and non-combatants was one of the few respects in which they truly were superior. Another was that they were much richer. But when it came to waging war, as we shall see, they were greatly inferior – a harsh reality for which no amount of propaganda could compensate.

9

Economic Capability: The Advantage Squandered

THE GREAT IMBALANCE

To the economic historian, the outcome of the First World War looks to have been inevitable from the moment the majority of Asquith's Cabinet swallowed their Liberal scruples and opted for intervention. A war which was longer than most people had expected and more expensive than anyone had predicted was, it might be thought, bound to be won by whichever coalition had Britain on its side. Without Britain, France and Russia had a combined national income approximately 15 per cent smaller than that of Germany and Austria–Hungary. With Britain, the tables were more than turned: the Triple Entente had a combined national income 60 per cent greater than that of the Central Powers. The Central Powers accounted for 19 per cent of the world's manufacturing output in 1913; the Triple Entente for 28 per cent. In terms of Kennedy's measure of 'industrial potential', the ratio of advantage to the Entente was not far off 1.5 to 1.[1] In manpower terms the advantage looked even greater. The combined population of the Central Powers (including Turkey and Bulgaria) when the war began was roughly 144 million; that of the British Empire, France, Russia, Belgium and Serbia around 656 million – a ratio of advantage of 4.5 to one. Around 25 million men fought for the Central Powers in all between 1914 and 1918; the other side put more than 32 million in the field. True, the Central Powers managed to knock out populous Russia in 1917. But new allies more than compensated for this loss (see Table 21).

In financial terms too Britain made the difference thanks to her huge stock of accumulated overseas capital – roughly three times more than Germany's (see Table 4, Chapter 2) – and her superior fiscal system. In 1913 the combined military budgets of Russia and France were not

Table 21   The demographic imbalance

	Total Central Powers*	Total Entente in 1914†	Total Allies in 1918‡
Population, c. 1910–14	144,282	655,749	690,245
Total mobilized, 1914–18	25,100	32,080	30,580

Notes: *Germany, Austria–Hungary, Turkey, Bulgaria; †Great Britain, British Empire, France, Russia, Belgium, Serbia; ‡Great Britain, British Empire, France, Serbia, Italy, Rumania, Greece, Portugal, USA, Japan. Source: Parker, *The Times Atlas of World History*, pp. 248f.

much more than those of Germany and Austria–Hungary. The addition of Britain increased the differential to nearly £100 million.[2]

Nothing happened during the war to close this gap. On the contrary: the Central Powers suffered from economic contraction, while the main Entente economies achieved growth. Table 22 gives inflation-adjusted estimates for net or gross national product for four major combatants. The available index suggests that Germany's net national product contracted by around a quarter.[3] Austria–Hungary probably fared

Table 22   Estimates for real net/gross national product for four combatants, 1913–1918 (1913 = 100)

	Germany	Britain	Russia	Italy
1913	100	100	100	100
1914	88	101	101	97
1915	79	109	114	104
1916	78	109	122	111
1917	76	109	77	113
1918	73	107	n/a	107

Notes: Germany: net national product; Britain and Italy: gross national product; Russia: national income.
Sources: Mitchell, *European Historical Statistics*, pp. 409–16; Stone, *Eastern Front*, p. 209; Witt, 'Finanzpolitik', p. 424. Lyashchenko, *National Economy*, p. 697, gives lower figures for Russia.

worse. Britain and Italy, by contrast, achieved real growth of the order of 10 per cent between 1914 and 1917. Until the revolutionary collapse, Russia did even better: by 1916 total output was more than a fifth higher than in 1913.

Inevitably, the disruption of trade and the diversion of factors of production into the work of destruction created problems for industry on both sides. However, the problem of falling industrial output was particularly severe in Germany (Table 23). The index for Britain shows a fall of the order of 10 per cent between 1914 and 1917; for Germany the figure is 25 per cent.[4] Russia by contrast (and contrary to the view that Tsarism was economically doomed) managed to increase industrial output by 17 per cent between 1914 and 1916.

Apart from non-ferrous metals (which Germany had traditionally imported) the output of all Germany's major industries fell between 1913 and 1918 – coal by 17 per cent and steel output by 14 per cent. In Britain, by comparison, steel production rose by a quarter, though coal production fell by just over 20 per cent. Moreover, Russia had managed a 16 per cent increase in coal production by 1916 as well as a 7 per cent increase in petroleum output (a substance the Central Powers were chronically short of) and a fractional increase in steel output. German electricity output increased by as much as 62 per cent between 1913 and 1918; but Britain and Italy both managed to double their output and even France managed a 50 per cent increase.[5]

None of the economic blows the Central Powers struck against their enemies proved fatal. True, France lost more than half her coal capacity

Table 23 *Indices of industrial production in four combatant countries (1914 = 100)*

	Germany	Britain	Russia	Italy
1914	100	100	100	100
1915	81	102	115	131
1916	77	97	117	131
1917	75	90	83	117
1918	69	87	n/a	113

Sources: Mitchell, *European Historical Statistics*, pp. 181ff; Wagenführ, 'Industriewirtschaft' p. 23; Stone, *Eastern Front*, p. 210 (again Lyaschenko, *National Economy*, p. 761, gives lower figures for Russia).

and two-thirds of her steel capacity, which happened to be in the disastrously ill-defended north of the country.[6] Yet by 1917 coal production was back to 71 per cent of pre-war levels and steel production to 42 per cent. Nor was occupied Belgium as rich a source of coal as might have been hoped: total Belgian coal output fell by 40 per cent during the war and steel production more or less ceased. Rumania also disappointed: it only supplied around 1.8 million tons of food and fodder between the time of its invasion in 1916 and July 1918 (6 per cent of the annual German harvest) for the simple reason that wheat production under the occupation slumped to a quarter of its pre-war level.[7] To be sure, the collapse of Russia into revolution in 1917 more than reversed the great advances in production achieved since 1914, but the entry of the United States more than made up for this loss. In terms of 'industrial potential' the ratio of advantage to the American-backed Allies was now 2.6 to 1.[8] Steel production in the US rose by an astounding 235 per cent between 1913 and 1917.[9] The Germans had brought the United States into the war by gambling on unrestricted warfare. But they could not build submarines as fast as the Allies could replace sunk merchant ships. By 1917 the output of Germany's shipyards had fallen to around a fifth of its pre-war level, compared with a figure for the British Empire of 70 per cent. In America, shipbuilding output rose by a factor of four between 1914 and 1917; by the last year of war it was a staggering fourteen times higher.[10]

German agriculture had some success, paradoxically, in boosting its production of certain staples of consumption. Tobacco production rose and that of wine went up by no less than 170 per cent, while the output of sugar fell less than the output of pig iron.[11] Unfortunately, the Germans were much less successful at producing the staff of life: bread. Total grain production slumped by nearly half between 1914 and 1917 (the figures for wheat in Table 24 somewhat understate the crisis: the production of oats fell by 62 per cent).[12] The decline in the yields per hectare of all major crops was primarily due to the choking off of imported fertilizers by the British blockade, the significance of which the Reich Interior Ministry had wholly underestimated before the war. The increased use of potash and nitrates produced by the Haber-Bosch process could not compensate.[13] Beer production was reduced in all the European combatants, but the reduction was more severe among the Central Powers: a fall of two-thirds for Germany, compared with just over half for Britain.[14] There were also drastic declines in the numbers

Table 24   Wheat production, 1914–1917 (thousand metric tons)

	Austria	Hungary	Germany	Bulgaria	Britain	France	Russia	Italy
1914	1,376	2,864	4,343	632	1,772	7,690	68,864	4,493
1917	163	3,354	2,484	791	1,784	3,660	60,800	3,709
Percentage change	−88.2	17.1	−42.8	25.2	0.7	−52.4	−11.7	−17.4

Source: Mitchell, *European Historical Statistics*, pp. 108–25; Stone, *Eastern Front*, p. 295.

of German pigs and poultry, a smaller but still significant decline in cattle numbers, as well as reductions in average weights at slaughter and milk yields.[15] Admittedly, these were bad years in most countries for climatic reasons. Austria and France both fared worse, and even the US saw a 28 per cent decline in its wheat crop. On the other hand, Hungary and Britain managed to increase wheat production and Russia and Italy experienced only modest declines.

Trade further lengthened the odds against the Central Powers: they were unable to import as much from neutral countries as their opponents. The disruption caused by British naval action to German sea-borne trade was undoubtedly severe. The German shipping journal *Hansa* foresaw on 1 August that if Britain entered the war 'economic life [would] suffer a collapse unprecedented in history'.[16] This proved only too true. The inability of the German navy's surface vessels to contest control of the North Sea meant that German merchant shipping in home ports at the outbreak of war was effectively confined to the Baltic, with occasional forays into the North Sea, for the duration.[17] The result was that by 1915 German imports had fallen to around 55 per cent of their pre-war level. Small wonder erstwhile Anglophiles like the shipowner Albert Ballin railed against the 'sickening' and 'wretched shopkeepers' methods' adopted by the British 'with the sole purpose of excluding us from the world market'.[18]

That said, the naval blockade proved a much less lethal weapon than British navalists had assumed. No attempt was made at first to halt the flow of goods to neutrals which might then find their way to Germany. Indeed, in the first nine months of war, British exports and re-exports to northern neutrals soared from 10 per cent of total exports to 24 per cent.[19] Much of this went on to Germany. It took time for the Entente powers to work out a system of preclusive purchase of supplies from neutral countries which might otherwise go to the enemy.[20] Moreover, it was not until the US entered the war that there was a significant decline in American exports to the Central Powers' neutral neighbours (from $267 million in 1915/16 to just $62 million in 1917/18).[21] It should also be remembered how much damage the harassment of neutral shipping did to Anglo-American relations, especially in July 1916, when the British government published its blacklist of American firms suspected of trading with the Central Powers (to make matters worse, the naval disruption of American commerce coincided with the suppression of the Easter Rising in Dublin).[22] By comparison, the German submariners did succeed in reducing British imports of foodstuffs to 75 per cent of their 1913 level in 1917 and 65 per cent in 1918.[23] But this was not enough: the introduction of the convoy system sharply reduced the U-boats' success rate; American shipyards proved able to replace ships faster than the Germans could sink them; while increased domestic production and the introduction of rationing did much to mitigate the problem of food shortage in Britain. *Pace* Liddell Hart, naval power did not decide the war.[24]

Thus, although nearly half (48 per cent) of her pre-war imports had come from countries she went to war against, Germany was able to find alternative sources of imports, running a total trade deficit with her Scandinavian and continental neighbours of as much as 15 billion marks, equivalent to around 46 per cent of her total wartime imports.[25] Nevertheless, the figures for Russia, France and Italy are all significantly larger (see Table 25). Even more revealing, the average German trade deficit during the war was equivalent to around 5.6 per cent of net national product; the equivalent British figure was double that (11.3 per cent). The German inferiority was partly due to the British naval blockade, of course, but it was also – and perhaps even more – because Germany lacked the invisible earnings, the reserves of overseas assets and the credit abroad to finance a large trade deficit. During the war, Britain earned £2.4 billion from 'invisibles' (mainly shipping), sold altogether £236 million of foreign investments and borrowed £1,285 million from foreign countries. Germany could not match this, not least because of enemy measures which were in many ways more successful than the blockade itself. In 1914 Germans had held overseas investments worth between £980 and £1,370 million, much of them in what became enemy economies. As a result of British, French, Russian and later

Table 25 *Average annual wartime trade deficits as a percentage of imports*

Britain	41.5
France	63.0
Italy (from 1915)	66.6
Russia (to 1917)	58.3
Germany	45.8
Austria–Hungary (to 1916)	55.7

Source: Eichengreen, *Golden Fetters*, pp. 82f.

American legislation, beginning with the first Alien Enemies (Winding Up) Ordinances in October 1914, at least 60 per cent of this was confiscated.[26] German merchant houses with branches in British territory found themselves summarily expropriated. Particularly hard hit were the shipping lines. As a result of sinking or confiscation, the German shippers lost up to 639 ships with a total tonnage of 2.3 million gross tons – a staggering 44 per cent of the total pre-war merchant fleet.[27] Germany thus had no invisible earnings to speak of and did well to raise as much as £147 million by selling foreign securities. Nor did the government borrow much from abroad, at first because it felt it did not need to, later because it could not. To finance its balance of payments deficit Germany therefore had to rely on selling bullion amounting to £48 million (double the British figure) and short-term private credits from foreign suppliers.[28]

TORTOISES AND HARES

In the light of the massive advantage which the Entente powers enjoyed throughout the war it is rather mysterious that historians have for so long concerned themselves with the defective organization of the German war economy. Although the discrepancy in economic resources might seem a sufficient explanation for the Central Powers' failure to win the war, historians have (like Hitler) felt it necessary to blame the German government for misallocating them as well.

The consensus is that Germans made a bigger hash of economic mobilization than their opponents. This is odd, since German businessmen and politicians were more ideologically predisposed to accept large-scale state intervention in economic life than their British counterparts. Indeed, contemporaries and some later historians sought to portray the German war economy as a new kind of economy: the 'planned economy', 'state socialism', the 'common economy', 'state-monopoly-capitalism', 'organized capitalism' – all these concepts owe a debt to Germany in the First World War.[29] Yet the reality fell far short of this billing. In fact the German war economy was undermined by bureaucratic bungling and the military leadership's lack of realism, typified by the crude and unsuccessful *dirigisme* of the Hindenburg Plan.[30]

British historians have tended to propagate a complementary view. True, the British began the war with cheerful naivety, typified by the phrase 'business as usual' (coined by H. E. Morgan of W. H. Smith and turned into an advertising slogan by Harrods) – an attitude which owed less to *laissez-faire* dogma than to the assumption that Britain would be fighting an old-style naval war. Prices would not be controlled, nor exports, nor shipping.[31] But the shocks of 1915 woke the British up. Led by the heroic figure of Lloyd George and organized by his creation, the Ministry of Munitions, the British magnificently adapted to the exigencies of total war – their only real sin being the haste with which they forgot the lessons they had learned as soon as the war ended.[32] Thus the pleasingly paradoxical conclusion: amateur Britain groped, fumbled and stumbled to an improvised victory over professional Germany.[33] This, in fact, was the way the *Glasgow Herald* rather smugly saw it in June 1916:

We are incapable of existing under a cast-iron system of rules and regulations such as that which prevails in Germany, and which is so apt to break down when it is over-strained . . . It is true that we too frequently 'muddle through', but is there any other nation capable of doing so successfully as we and coming out on top in the end?[34]

Even French economic policy can be portrayed in this way, with Etienne Clémentel as the Lloyd George figure, belatedly imposing organizational efficiency from the Ministry of Commerce.[35] According to Jay Winter, Britain and France undertook 'a unique and unplanned experiment in state capitalism' which was 'relatively successful':

In Britain the wartime state was never a 'business' state. That is to say, output of war material was assured within a framework which placed national interests above employers' interests . . . [F]or the bulk of the British population . . . the wartime state succeeded where it mattered most, namely, in delivering the goods, both to the men in uniform and to the civilian population.

Germany, by contrast, adopted a 'corporatist' system which

left the management of the economy to a tangled bureaucracy working through the large firms and the army. The result was chaos. Labour shortages remained chronic [while] the big firms benefited . . . profits soared . . . thus ensuring the progressive acceleration of the wartime inflationary spiral, steeply declining real wages, and a subsistence crisis which undermined the regime itself. The German war economy . . . was one of the earliest and least successful examples of a 'military-industrial complex' in action. The 'corporatist' solution to Germany's economic difficulties was no solution at all . . . Germany's leaders never established effective political control over the war economy . . . They could, therefore, not hope to balance the claims of competing sectors for scarce resources. The outcome . . . was a vast free-for-all. In effect the German state dissolved under the pressure of industrial war . . . The situation on the other side of the line was different. This . . . is the appropriate context in which to place . . . the history of the outcome of the war . . .[36]

Elsewhere Winter has gone so far as to suggest that 'if German workers in 1917–18 had commanded the real incomes of their British counterparts, and if their families had been able to maintain the nutritional levels [of British families], the outcome of the war may well have been reversed'.[37] In Germany, he has argued (on the basis of a detailed study of Berlin), there was a deficiency of 'citizenship'. Whereas

in Paris and London the entitlements of citizenship helped preserve communities at war by enforcing a balance of distribution of necessary goods and services as between civilian and military demands . . . in Berlin . . . the military came first, and the economy created to serve it completely distorted the delicate economic balance at home.

In a nutshell, the Allied system was 'more equitable and efficient'.[38]

Like the story of the tortoise and the hare, which it so closely resembles, this is – a story. For if the Entente powers had really been more efficient than the Central Powers *as well as* vastly better endowed with resources, there would be no *1914–18* war to write about: the war would have been over by the winter of 1916–17, when hardship within Germany was at its worst. The literature on war economies perfectly illustrates the dangers of writing national history without adequate comparative perspective. Once this is introduced it becomes clear that the 'defective organization' hypothesis is no more than a respectable version of the *Dolchstosslegende* (stab-in-the-back theory) propagated by the far Right and the German military leadership during and after Germany's defeat. Merely transferring the blame from the 'November criminals' (socialists and Jews) to Germany's wartime leaders does not make it true that the war was lost on the Home Front. On the contrary, there is good reason to think that, considering the limited resources with which they had to work, the Germans were significantly better at mobilizing their economy for war than the Western powers.

In part, the negative view of German mobilization was born of disappointed expectations at the time. The pre-war assumption had been that the German military authorities were the epitome of efficiency. In August 1914 Albert Ballin was able to 'derive some pleasure from the magnificent discipline and accomplishment of the General Staff'.[39] Experience of other government departments almost immediately shattered his illusions. On 6 August Ballin and Max Warburg were driven to Berlin to discuss the question of food imports with officials of the Ministry of the Interior, the Treasury Office, the Foreign Office and the Reichsbank. The chaos of the journey (during which they were repeatedly stopped by armed civilians searching for spies) was matched by the confusion of the meeting, which foundered on the erroneous assumption of the Foreign Office representative that Germany would somehow be able to make use of the American merchant marine.[40] As the war went on, Ballin grew ever more despondent as he struggled to secure some economic compensation for the immense losses of shipping his company had suffered at Allied hands. He was intensely frustrated when the government prohibited him from selling ships which had been marooned in neutral harbours. Addressing the National Liberal Party's Reichstag deputies in February 1918, Ballin denounced 'the dangerous notion of running the national economy and international trade from the parade ground', and demanded 'freedom from the Berlin planned economy'.[41]

Ballin, of course, was a Hamburg free trader. Walther Rathenau of the electrical engineering giant AEG was, by contrast, an early convert to the belief that the war would require a transformation of the German economy from a free market system into a quasi-socialist system based on corporatist structures and planning. As early as 14 August 1914, in his memorandum proposing the creation of a War Raw Materials Department, he renounced individualism and the other economic 'gods to whom, before August 1914, the world prayed'.[42] Later, in his book *Things to Come* (1917), he outlined his utopian vision of a German 'common economy' (*Gemeinwirtschaft*). Yet when he met Hindenburg at Kovno in 1915 Rathenau was sorely disappointed:

Hindenburg is big, and has rather run to fat, his hands are unusually plump and soft and the lower half of his head resembles the portraits . . . [but] the nose itself is very weak and undefined, his eyes swollen and dull . . . Conversation was conducted in a cordial and friendly way yet remained unproductive. His remarks had little colour and towards the end when I told him of the great unanimity of popular feeling, such as had not been seen in Germany since the time of Luther and of Blücher, he remarked, in his unpretentious and friendly way, that he did not deserve such enthusiasm, but probably ought to fear that it might arouse envy and ill will in the country. I was rather astonished at this apprehension and tried to divert his attention; [but] he came back to it again.[43]

Like many other businessmen, Rathenau transferred his hero-worship to Hindenburg's second-in-command, Ludendorff, but he too turned out to be thick-headed. In July 1917 Rathenau tried to persuade Ludendorff that from a strictly economic viewpoint Germany needed domestic political reform and a negotiated peace soon. The country's 'power arrangements', Rathenau complained, were 'unbelievably confused':

The Under-Secretaries of State cannot do anything because the Chancellor is there. The Chancellor cannot do anything if he does not have the confirmation of the [military] headquarters. In the headquarters Ludendorff is hindered by Hindenburg. The latter in his turn gives way just as soon as the Kaiser pats him on the shoulder. The Kaiser himself feels he should rule constitutionally, and thus the circle is closed.

Annexations to protect German industry in the Rhineland–Ruhr area were not worth holding out for: 'If the war goes on for two more years, then we will not have to concern ourselves about our Aachen industry because by then we would not know whether there will still be any industry there.' But Ludendorff just did not get it.[44]

Ballin and Rathenau were not alone. German businessmen – especially those not based in Berlin – complained endlessly about the way the war was being run. The President of the Hamburg Chamber of Commerce likewise lambasted 'the concentration of all business transactions . . .

in the hands of the war companies . . . the almost exclusive distribution of army contracts to Berlin industry . . . [and] the countless, commerce-inhibiting Bundestag decrees.'[45] Even in the heavy industrial camp there were critical voices by the last year of the war, notably that of Hugo Stinnes.[46] German farmers never ceased griping about the way government managed the distribution of food.[47]

However, historians have taken these complaints too literally (rather as they have taken the attacks on pre-war German militarism too literally). If one considers the experience of the other war economies, it becomes apparent that all experienced very similar problems and that, given the far narrower resource base with which the Germans had to work, the remarkable thing is not their inefficiency but the very reverse. In fact, it was the Entente powers which were inefficient, not to say wasteful, in the way they mobilized their economies. Of course there was bureaucratic confusion in Germany; but the point is that there was more in Britain, France and Russia. The fact that Germany ultimately lost the war has concealed this. But a proper comparison demolishes the argument that it lost because of relative organizational inefficiency.

PROCUREMENT AND RAW MATERIALS

In every country it took time before anyone questioned the fundamental assumption that the vastly increased needs of the armed forces should be met by placing contracts with private companies, working with a view to profit. It was typical of the problems which beset German wartime procurement that, in order to balance the competing interests of the separate states, the War Ministry resorted to allocating contracts on a matricular basis (i.e. in proportion to state populations) – a patently absurd system.[48] But the British and French systems were worse. The businessman George Booth could not believe the shambolic way the War Office organized procurement in the first phase of the war, and the suspicion with which he and other businessmen who offered to help were viewed by Asquith. First not enough equipment was ordered; then too much at exorbitant prices.[49] In the end the army was probably over-supplied with clothing.[50] As for munitions, the difficulties which beset Entente procurement in 1914–15 – the British 'shells crisis' which led to the creation of the Ministry of Munitions in June 1915, its Russian equivalent and the contemporaneous battles between Albert Thomas and the French arms companies – are well known.[51] But the subsequent improvements are only impressive by comparison with what had gone before. The contribution of the British National Factories could have been greater, as could the pressure on the private companies' profit margins.[52] French shell production exceeded British by a considerable margin, suggesting that Britain was still not punching its industrial weight; but the French effort to expand state production by building a huge arsenal at Roanne in late 1916 was one of the great economic fiascos of the war, costing 103 million francs to build but contributing only 15 million francs worth of useful products.[53]

Nothing the Germans did wrong can compare with this. The Germans never suffered from serious shortages of shells (see Table 26);[54] though it is true that by 1918 the Allies had a 30 per cent superiority in guns of all calibres and a 20 per cent superiority in planes, these differentials were not the reason Ludendorff's spring offensive failed. The most serious German weakness was their lack of tanks and armoured vehicles, of which they had just 10 to the Allies' 800; and of lorries (23,000 to 100,000). It is not wholly clear whether this was a result of shortages of fuel (and rubber) or of technological Luddism in the High Command: after all, tanks were just the sort of thing the German industry ought to have been good at making.

Did businessmen have excessive power in the German war economy? One of the main innovations of the war years on the supply side was

Table 26 *British and German armaments production: selected statistics*

		1914	1915	1916	1917	1918
Machine-guns	Britain	300	6,100	33,500	79,700	120,900
	Germany	2,400	6,100	27,600	115,200	
Rifles	Britain	100,000	600,000	1,000,000	1,200,000	1,100,000
	Germany	43,200		3,000,000		
Explosives (tons)	Britain	5,000	24,000	76,000	186,000	118,000
	Germany	14,400	72,000	120,000	144,000	

Sources: Hardach, *First World War*, p. 87; Herwig, *First World War*, pp. 254ff. (using monthly figures multiplied by 12).

the delegation of monopolistic controls over the distribution of raw materials to trusts made up of the industrial consumers – the so-called 'war corporations' – over which a new official body, the War Raw Materials Office (KRA), exercised supervision. By the end of the war there were twenty-five war corporations controlling the distribution of everything from metal to tobacco. Athough it was the brainchild of a businessman, there is not much that can be said against this way of proceeding. Indeed, it is significant that the most vehement criticism of the KRA came from Hanseatic businessmen who disliked its centralizing tendencies – which should probably be interpreted as proof that the system was doing its job.[55] More open to attack was the German practice of delegating the setting of certain industrial production targets to industrial cartels like the Rhineland-Westphalian Coal Syndicate.[56] This allowed the big industrial concerns and their umbrella organizations not only to regulate the production of essential materials but also to control their prices. There is no question that this made it hard for government to control prices of goods in short supply and no doubt helped boost big business profits. Finally, it can be argued that too much heed was paid to business associations like the Central Association of German Industry and the League of Industrialists, which formed a joint War Committee of German Industry during the war.

Yet what was the alternative to relying on big business? In all countries it quickly became apparent that the people best able to grapple with the organizational problems of the war economy were businessmen with experience of large corporations: most civil servants were out of their depth by comparison. Bureaucrats like William Beveridge might sneer at the dominance of 'amateurs' in the British war effort,[57] but it is not without significance that attempts at direct state control of production were generally ill-starred wherever they were made. The question is which country best struck a balance between the private interests of business and the needs of the war economy as a whole. Whatever one calls the German system – and 'corporatist' is not necessarily a term of abuse in wartime – it at least had the merit of institutionalizing relationships between business and the state, even if neither side was much enchanted by the experience.

In France, by contrast, businessmen continued to regard the state more as a customer than a partner until relatively late in the war.[58] The campaign to oust Thomas over the Roanne affair, which led to the appointment of the businessman Louis Loucheur as Minister of

Armaments in September 1917, was partly a reflection of the hostility felt by some business interests towards the idea of a state arsenal.[59] It was not until late 1917 that proper institutions were set up in France to co-ordinate the allocation of raw materials, and this was only really done to appease France's allies. Despite Clémentel's denials in June 1918, the French consortiums set up to allocate raw materials were little different from the German corporations; just much later in coming.[60] In this light, the comparative speed with which a 'corporatist' system was developed in Germany was a sign of strength not weakness.

In Britain too there was an *ad hoc* quality to the way businessmen were drawn into the war effort. Rather than creating institutional mechanisms for collaboration, Lloyd George preferred to take businessmen away from their businesses and give them government departments to run. Something of a legend surrounds this recruitment of 'men of push and go' into the public sector. No doubt individuals like George Booth or Alfred Mond were good at what they did, though civil servants like Christopher Addison were maddened by their unsystematic approach to paperwork. No doubt too they were scrupulous about distinguishing their private interest from the public interest when they accepted civil service jobs. But it is a mistake to regard these men as in any way typical of wartime relations between the British state and business. The big British companies which dominated the arms market were not manifestly more restrained in their pricing policies than their German counterparts.[61] While D. A. Thomas (later Lord Rhondda) argued for public control of the coal industry from the start, not all the pit proprietors shared his view, and some continued to oppose control until as late as 1917.[62] True, coal was effectively brought under direct state control when the Coal Controller was created in 1917, but there is little evidence that this contributed to improved productivity. Indeed, the Coal Control system has been described as no more than a system for guaranteeing the pit-owners' profits.[63] The engineering employers (especially those in Clydeside) were also conspicuously slow to abandon the confrontational style of industrial relations of the pre-war period. Time and again civil servants trying to resolve disputes in Glasgow found the employers as recalcitrant as their employees.[64]

In 1917–18, the same problems arose in the United States, which experienced surprisingly serious economic dislocation following its entry into the war. The War Industries Board, set up under the banker Bernard M. Baruch in July 1917, proved wholly unequal to the task of mobilizing the economy for direct participation in the war. 'Today', complained one of its members in January 1918, 'there is no body . . . in our Government whose function it is to decide what is to be done.'[65]

It is interesting to contrast the Western powers' experience with that of Russia which, in terms of sheer increased output, had the most successful war economy. Here big business won its battle with the War Minister, Vladimir Sukhomlinov, who had resisted pressure to boost private sector arms production: he was not only dismissed but arrested in May 1915, and a new 'Special Council for Examination and Harmonization of Measures required for the Defence of the Country' was set up with Petrograd industry well represented. Just as in Germany, other business groups lamented the dominance of the big concerns. Just as in Germany, there was a plethora of War-Industries Committees and local government offices all meddling in the allocation of raw materials and contracts. Just as in Germany, pre-war cartels like the metal-producers' *Prodameta* wielded great power over prices. And just as in Germany (only more so), there was waste, inflated profits and malpractice, as in the cases of Solodovnikov, owner of the Revdinskoye factory in the Urals, and Putilov in Petrograd, both of whom defrauded the state of millions.[66] Yet the system delivered the goods, as the impressive figures for arms production testify: Russian artillery production came close to out-stripping British and French in 1916–17 and by November 1918 a huge reserve of 18 million shells had accumulated.[67]

The one obvious point of international comparison – the level of profits achieved by business – certainly does not convict the Germans of aberrant practice. There are, of course, notorious examples. Profits at Krupp AG rose from 31.6 million marks to 79.7 million in 1916–17.[68] Hugo Stinnes expanded his already immense coal, iron and steel empire, buying stakes in shipping lines and other travel companies as part of a strategy of 'vertical integration'. Among Rathenau's pet projects for the AEG during the war was to invest in air transport and shipbuilding: the seeds of the future Lufthansa were planted during the war. The steel giant Gutehoffnungshütte also made sufficient profits to invest in an entirely new shipbuilding company, Deutsche Werft. Indeed shipbuilding provides a good illustration of German industry's wartime performance. Net profits at the shipbuilders Blohm & Voss (which received orders for ninety-seven submarines during the war) rose steadily from 1.4 million marks in 1914–15 to 2.7 million marks (13.5 per cent) in 1917–18. The firm was able to expand its annual output to around

600,000 gross tons, acquiring a new dock and machine factory from a smaller yard, to increase its share capital from 12 million marks to 20 million and to enlarge its workforce from 10,250 to 12,555. This was by no means exceptional: between 1914 and 1920 the 13 main German shipyards increased their capital by 120 per cent. While employment in engineering overall only rose by 6.6 per cent during the war, in the shipyards it rose 52 per cent. The government was in no doubt that 'the ship-building industry has . . . done much better during the war than in the preceding peacetime years'; and indeed accused the shipyards of concealing the true extent of their profits 'whether through depreciation allowances or transfers of all kinds'.[69]

Yet this may have exaggerated the benefits of war-time contracts: the principal reason for expanding the workforce was the much lower quality of the workers available as a consequence of indiscriminate conscription. Blohm & Voss's profits, if deflated to allow for inflation, can be shown to have risen only slightly from the trough of 1914 – as a percentage of capital, profits only went up from 11.4 per cent to 13.5 per cent – and the yard's expansion was in many ways a gamble on the anticipated post-war boom in demand for shipping. Moreover, these profits were above average: for German industry in general, profits as a percentage of capital and reserves went up from 8 per cent in 1913–14 to just 10.8 per cent in 1917–18. Taken as a whole, the German iron and steel industry suffered badly,[70] and the Hanseatic cities – with the exception of the shipyards – fared worse.[71] A good indication of how business fared was the contraction of aggregate joint stock capital in real terms. The Reich's total share capital fell by 14 per cent in real terms during the war; Hamburg's fell by over a third.[72] Especially hard hit were the big shipping lines and the small merchant houses which suffered more severe capital losses during the war than any other sector: the Hapag's post-war accounts recorded a 25 per cent fall in the real value of its total assets, rising to 53 per cent if only its physical assets are considered. Earnings were also dramatically reduced: calculations based on the Hapag's post-war accounts suggest that, adjusting for inflation, it was able to earn only 43.9 million marks during the war years: an 84 per cent fall in annual earnings.

The situation was little different in other economies. Arms firms in France, Britain and especially Russia recorded substantial increases in nominal profits, and these were probably understated in published accounts.[73] In Britain profits at Nobels' Explosives rose threefold, though the chemicals firm Brunner, Mond could only manage a 50 per cent rise and shipping profits were only a third up after tax. Mining as a whole saw profits treble during the war; in the case of a firm like Cardiff Collieries Ltd, 1916 was the peak year, though the imposition of controls probably lowered profits below their pre-war level in real terms. Courtaulds and Lever Brothers registered huge increases in capitalization.[74] Profits in Russia may have been even higher. Gross profits in the Russian metallurgical industry rose from 26 per cent of capital in 1913 to 50 per cent in 1916; equivalent figures for metal-processing firms are 13.5 and 81 per cent.[75] Even British farmers made higher wartime profits than German industry: as a percentage of capital, farm profits rose from 6.1 per cent (1909–13) to a peak of 14.3 per cent in 1917.[76] And as in Germany, small businesses in Britain, France and Russia all lost out in relative terms.[77]

In many respects, then, all war economies faced similar problems. This can clearly be seen in the case of rail transport. In Germany most of the railways had been in state control since they had been built, so that placing them under direct Reich control was simply a matter of administrative centralization; whereas the French and British governments had to impose controls on companies which remained formally in the private sector. But the effect of control during the war was essentially the same. In each case, the volume of freight traffic was sharply reduced – in the German case to around 59 per cent of pre-war levels by 1917, in the French to around 66 per cent. Yet state control ensured that the lines were kept in a reasonable condition for military use: German investment in locomotives exceeded pre-war levels by 23 per cent.[78] The Russian railway network was also well maintained – 2.5 billion roubles were spent on it between August 1914 and September 1917 – though it had to cope with significantly higher levels of passenger and freight traffic due to the extraordinary economic upsurge called forth by the war in Russia.[79]

The case of shipping was, however, rather different. In Germany there was not much the government could do but pay the shipping lines cash compensation for the tonnage they lost to enemy action. In Britain the government began by subsidizing insurance but soon had to create a Requisitioning Committee to ensure that food supplies were given priority and this was followed in January 1916 by the creation of a Shipping Control Committee. Finally in December 1916 a Ministry of Shipping was set up.[80] France was essentially dependent on Britain for shipping.[81] Trade control was obviously simpler for the Central Powers as they had less trade to control and the Austrians (though not the Hungarians) were relatively easy to bully. At the outset of the war an Imperial (later Central) Purchasing Corporation (*Einkaufsgesellschaft*) was set up in Hamburg to co-ordinate imports.[82] There seemed no need to restrict exports until January 1917, when an export licensing system was introduced to prevent iron and steel producers seeking higher prices for essential products in the foreign markets still accessible to them.[83]

Nevertheless, the difficulties of the Entente powers in managing their combined trade – the key to their economic survival – perfectly illustrate the organizational weakness from which they suffered. In Britain trade control had begun with the restriction on coal imports imposed in the summer of 1915. This was followed at the end of 1916 with the introduction of a system of import licensing controlled by a new Import Restriction Department at the Board of Trade. Up until that point there had been something approaching a free-for-all in purchasing from the United States, with the Admiralty and the War Office both resisting Treasury efforts to subordinate them to the New York bankers J. P. Morgan. Quite why the Treasury wanted to do this is hard to say: buying arms for export to Britain was not at all the kind of thing the Morgan group did (it specialized in bond issues), and the monopoly the firm was being granted over British import finance promised immense profits – between 1 and 2 per cent of $18 billion dollars, as it turned out. Nor did the decision to give Morgan the job solve the trans-Atlantic procurement problem: there continued to be considerable friction between the different British business and government interests represented on the British Munitions Board set up in September 1915.[84]

Inevitably, because of Britain's merchant fleet and greater financial resources, she became the quartermaster of the Entente powers, with J. P. Morgan as her banker.[85] But the British thought the French were cheating them, or at least wasting resources.[86] As a result, they sought to impose controls on them by withdrawing half the shipping they had leased to France and threatening to take the rest if the French did not adopt the British system. When Clemenceau charged Clémentel with this task there were loud protests from French business and the press. It was not until November 1917 that an integrated Anglo-French shipping pool was introduced; and not until the last year of the war, under American pressure, that an Interallied Council for War Purchases and Finance was set up to co-ordinate all imports. Trying to harmonize trade policy with the Russians proved even harder, especially when Russian inspectors fussily rejected as sub-standard American mass-produced goods which Britain and France had paid for.[87] The Italians too disliked being treated as mercenaries by the British; though, as Keynes pointed out, that was in financial terms what they and Britain's other allies became.

MANPOWER: THE BRITISH PROBLEM

The allocation of manpower was perhaps the most difficult economic problem which the combatant states faced. Everywhere it proved extremely difficult to find the correct balance between the needs of the armed forces and the needs of domestic production of food and material. Many skilled workers who would have been better employed in their peacetime jobs volunteered to fight or were conscripted. If they were then killed, the economy was permanently worse off; but even if they survived they were not making their optimal contribution to the war effort.

In the German case, the number of men under arms rose from 2.9 million in the first month of war to 4.4 million by the beginning of 1915, and over 7 million at its peak in early 1918. Altogether 13 million men served.[88] Many of those who fought were industrial workers. By January 1915 firms like Blohm and Voss which had substantial war contracts were requesting the return of skilled workers called up.[89] Bosch in Stuttgart lost 52 per cent of its workforce in the first months of the war; the chemicals firm Bayer lost slightly under half its workers. By December the Hibernia mining company had lost nearly 30 per cent of its 20,000 pre-war workforce.[90] However, the Germans moved quite quickly to keep essential workers in their jobs. By early 1916 a total of 1.2 million workers were classed as exempt from military service, of whom 740,000 had been passed as fit for active service. Two years later 2.2 million workers were exempt, of whom 1.3 million were *kriegsverwendungsfähig*.[91] To make up the shortfall in male labour, the employment of women was increased (an additional 5.2 million entered the labour market), some 900,000 prisoners-of-war were put to work and up to 430,000 foreign workers were imported, including many reluctant Belgians.[92] As a result, the civilian labour force in July 1918 was only around 7 per cent smaller than it had been in 1914.[93]

This was not ideal (though quite what would have been is hard to say: no formula exists for optimal labour allocation in wartime). But were the Entente powers any better at allocating labour? The answer is probably no. Total civilian employment in Britain fell by about as much as in Germany (6.5 per cent), but fewer men had to fight: 4.9 million in all joined the army, less than half the German figure. The soldiers' places were taken by 1.7 million new male employees entering the labour force and an increase in the female labour force of 1.6 million.[94] It will at once be noticed that the Germans made much more use of female labour during the war. In both Britain and France women accounted for around 36–7 per cent of the industrial workforce by the end of the war, compared with 26–30 per cent before August 1914. In Germany the proportion rose from 35 per cent to 55 per cent.[95] It should also be remembered that the British enlistment system attracted not only dispensable clerks and Oxford graduates but also essential skilled workers. By the end of 1914, 16 per cent of all employees in small-arms factories had joined up and nearly 25 per cent of the chemical and explosives industry's workforce, not least because many of them were laid off in the first chaotic month of war. Twenty-one per cent of those employed in mining and 19 per cent of those employed in metal industry had enlisted by July 1915.[96] Getting the War Office to relinquish skilled workers proved exceedingly difficult and devices such as 'badging' (introduced in 1915), the Munitions Volunteers and 'bulk release' were only half-measures.[97] As Lloyd George told the Commons, 'get[ting] men from the Colours ... [was] like getting through barbed wire entanglements with heavy guns'.[98] When a Cabinet committee sought to 'co-ordinate ... the military and financial effort' in January 1916, its report acknowledged the problem of conflicting departmental priorities:

The method of investigation adopted by the Committee at the outset of their enquiry was to obtain from the War Office, the Treasury, and the Board of Trade a statement of their respective desiderata in regard to the size of the army, the expenditure that can be devoted thereto, and the numbers that can be spared for military service without disastrous results on the trade and industry of the country. The proposals originally put forward by the Departments were not reconcilable; those of the Treasury would not have found the money, and those of the Board of Trade would not have furnished the men needed to maintain an army of the size proposed by the War Office.[99]

In order to allay the Board of Trade's fears of a 'disaster to trade' if conscription were too indiscriminate, a system of reserved occupations was introduced; but this was relatively limited in its scope.[100] Moreover, the 'trade card' scheme introduced for skilled workers in late 1916 was more a response to trade union pressure than the result of government planning.[101] Skilled agricultural workers were not given exemption until July 1917, miners were still being recruited in January 1918 and in April whole classes of protected occupation were cancelled in the panic induced by the German spring offensive.[102] Nor can it be claimed that the new Ministry of Labour did much to improve matters, as its competence was soon challenged by the Ministry for National Service.[103] When the minister of that department (Auckland Geddes) drew up a 'manpower budget' in October 1917, it made sobering reading: the projected surplus of available men over men required for 1918 was just 136,000 men.[104] As late as April that year Geddes complained to Lloyd George: 'The Admiralty, War Office, Board of Agriculture, Ministry of Labour, National Service are all fishing in the same pool, and the employers and men are playing us off one against the other.'[105] This was a shocking indictment after three and a half years of war.

What made this so serious both in the short and in the long term was the exceptional dependence of the British economy on skilled labour. At the outbreak of war, for example, 60 per cent of British engineering workers were classified as skilled. Economic historians have argued that this was one reason British employers did not hasten to introduce new machinery or mass production techniques: for one thing, British skilled workers were affordable and, for another, they would make employers' lives hell if attempts were made to impose standardized piece rates on them.[106] This may also be the reason why the First World War stands out as the watershed in modern British industrial history.[107] The death of a very high proportion of Britain's skilled workers left a hole which was not easily filled. 'Dilution' was precisely what befell the British labour force; blood was the dilutant.

Gregory's suggestion that the British volunteer system ensured a more equitable distribution of casualties than the conscription system is therefore open to question; to argue that this 'helped to safeguard political stability' seems a step too far.[108] The most important consequence of the British system was that it killed off skilled workers who would have been better employed in their usual jobs. This 'lost generation' was the one that mattered; the more familiar one, composed of peers, public school boys and Oxbridge men,[109] was much more easily replaced and was probably more use employed as officers than in any other capacity. Angell had warned that war promoted 'the survival of the unfit'; in Britain, however, it was the unskilled and uneducated who survived.[110]

In France, where the labour supply was tighter than in any other combatant economy, labour was misallocated for different reasons: the strong political pressure for an 'equality of sacrifice'. The popular view was that (as in the 1790s) the blood tax – *l'impôt du sang* – should be borne by all, including skilled workers. Those who were brought back from the Front to relieve the shell shortage of 1915 – who accounted for nearly half the total munitions workforce by the end of the year – were derided as shirkers (*embusqués*).[111] Men recalled from the colours (apart from war wounded) accounted for only 30 per cent of the increase in the French armaments workforce during the war.[112]

In all the combatant economies, labour shortages inevitably created problems: workers were in a position to bid up wages and/or to lower their productivity by 'going slow' or, if managements sought to resist wage demands, by striking. The experience of a single not untypical firm may illustrate how these problems manifested themselves in Germany. At first the management at the Hamburg shipyard Blohm & Voss sought to compensate for labour shortages by lengthening working hours and increasing work intensity, taking advantage of trade union weakness to do so. Junior managers and foremen sometimes took these tactics to extremes: in March 1916 instructions had to be issued discouraging 'forms of words towards insubordinate workers such as: "You're headed for the trenches"' (illustrating neatly Karl Kraus's point that a 'hero's death' was simultaneously at once an honour and a punishment in wartime rhetoric). A year later, shifts lasting over twenty-four hours were ruled excessive.[113] Workers responded in a variety of ways, more often resorting to individual and spontaneous acts than to collective strike action.[114] There was a recurrent problem of indiscipline: lunch-breaks were extended, work was half-hearted, absenteeism was rife and materials were constantly being stolen (usually to be used as firewood). Above all, workers took advantage of the high demand for their services to change jobs regularly: traditionally high labour mobility reached unprecedented levels, so that 10,000 workers had to be replaced in the year after October 1916 – a problem which the Auxiliary Service Law of December 1916 exacerbated by recognizing the worker's right to change jobs for a higher wage.[115] As a result, the no-strike agreement concluded in August 1914 gradually crumbled. In October 1916 the rejection by Blohm & Voss of a wage claim led to the first major strike of the war. There were major strikes at the Vulkan yard four months later and again in May 1917 (a month after the great Berlin strike sparked by a reduction in the flour ration); and in January 1918 the yards were swept by a nationwide wave of industrial action which had begun in Berlin. These strikes are traditionally seen as the harbingers of the November 1918 revolution – a symptom if not a cause of Germany's inevitable defeat.[116]

But again we must ask whether things were really any better in the Entente economies. One important though crude test of war efficiency is the extent to which wages rose during the war.[117] For social historians it is almost axiomatic that an increase in real wages is a good thing. A great deal of work has gone into showing that in this sense Britain did 'better' than Germany. However, this is economic nonsense: it would have been disastrous for the German war economy if money wages had risen as fast as in Britain. In any comparison, the only criterion which should be applied is whether or not real wages increased in step with productivity. The more wages rose in real terms ahead of output, the less efficient the economy was, in that higher living standards for manual workers (though doubtless pleasant for those workers themselves) were not the first priority for the economy as a whole. The figures in Table 27 show that by this standard it was Britain not Germany which was the less efficient war economy. These admittedly somewhat crude figures would seem to suggest that British workers made wage gains ahead of productivity – i.e. undeserved gains – whereas German wages fell in real terms almost in perfect step with falling industrial output.

Of course, such average indices tell us nothing about wage differentials, which clearly changed a good deal during the war. Again, social historians often point to widening differentials as evidence of increased inequality which they generally regard as a bad thing per se. But this is economically wrongheaded too. Again the question is whether wage differentials accurately reflected the great shift in the structure of labour demand occasioned by the war. The more they did so, the better, as a relative increase in the wages of unskilled workers in munitions factories would have the effect of attracting individuals into that vital sector.

In all countries labour shortages in strategically vital sectors gave

Table 27 *Industrial production and real wages in Germany and Britain,*
1914–1918

	Germany		Britain	
	Industrial production	Real wages	Industrial production	Real wages
1914	100	100	100	100
1915	81	88	102	87
1916	77	79	97	81
1917	75	65	90	81
1918	69	66	87	94

Sources: Mitchell, *European Historical Statistics*, pp. 33ff., 181ff.;
Wagenführ, 'Industriewirtschaft', p. 23; Horne, *Labour at War*, p. 395;
E. Morgan, *Studies*, p. 285; Bry, *Wages*, pp. 53, 331.

bargaining power to groups who were traditionally at the lower end of
the income scale. Four key gaps tended to narrow: between workers in
different sectors; between unskilled and skilled workers; between female
and male workers; and between younger and older workers. In Germany,
for example, between July 1914 and October 1918 the hourly wage of
an average male worker at Blohm & Voss rose by 113 per cent in
nominal terms, while a youth employed at the same yard earned 85 per
cent more than in peacetime and a textile worker earned 74 per cent
more. By comparison, a junior clerical worker earned only 62 per cent
more, a book-keeper only 37 per cent more and a chief cashier a
meagre 30 per cent more. Manual workers thus clearly did better than
white-collar employees.[118] The narrowing of differentials meant that,
after inflation is taken into account, a shipyard worker lost far less in
real terms (9 per cent) than a senior civil servant (52 per cent). Put
another way, in 1914 the civil servant's monthly income had been
roughly five times that of the worker; by 1918 it was less than three times
as great.[119] Nor do such figures take account of the wage supplements and
child benefits paid to certain categories of workers, which by the end
of the war could account for up to a third of an unskilled worker's
income.[120]

It is very hard to say whether things were significantly different in
other countries, because of the extreme difficulty of making comparisons
between the available wage statistics. It has been tentatively suggested

Table 28   The ratio of skilled to unskilled wages in the building trade in three capital cities, 1914–1918

	1914	1918	Percentage change
German construction (hourly rates)	1.47	1.07	−27.3
French construction (daily salaries)	1.90	1.47	−22.6
British construction (hourly wages)	1.53	1.31	−14.2

Source: Manning, 'Wages', pp. 262f.

that London wage differentials were narrowed more during the war than Berlin wages; but the figures presented in Table 28 would seem to prove just the opposite, though they tell us only about the building trade in the three capital cities.[121]

Changes in wage levels and differentials – for better or for worse – were not exogenously determined: they had a good deal to do with the relative power of organized labour. In which country did workers have most leverage? Mindful of the events of November 1918, German historians have sometimes tended to assume that their labour movement was exceptionally militant. However, this accolade seems in reality to have belonged to the British workforce which put up stiff resistance to attempts by all employers or government to hold down nominal wages or to 'dilute' the skilled labour force.[122] Ultimately, even Lloyd George was unable to restrict the mobility of workers, the crucial lever in the wage spiral: the system of leaving certificates envisaged by Clause 7 of the 1915 Munitions of War Act was a failure in practice and was finally killed off in August 1917.[123] After 1916 it is only a slight exaggeration to say that British employers steadily lost control over wage awards which were determined by a combination of labour pressure and state fiat.[124]

One possible explanation for this is that the German trade unions were hit harder by the war than their west European counterparts. Another way of comparing the different war economies is to consider the figures for union membership (see Table 29). Not too much should be read into these statistics. In Britain, France and Germany alike, trade union leaders lent support to the war effort in the hope of entrenching their position on an equal footing with employers; and everywhere ordinary union members jibbed at the concessions made by their leaders. Nevertheless it cannot be without significance that trade union member-

Table 29   Trade union membership in Britain, France and Germany,
1913–1918

	Britain (TUC)	France (departmental and federations)	Germany (Free, 'yellow', clerical)
1913	2,232,446	593,943	3,024,000
1914	n/a	493,906	2,437,000
1915	2,682,357	81,617	1,396,000
1916	2,850,547	183,507	1,199,000
1917	3,082,352	559,540	1,430,000
1918	4,532,085	1,175,356	2,184,000

Sources: Petzina *et al.*, *Sozialgeschichtliches Arbeitsbuch*, vol. III,
pp. 110–18; Horne, *Labour at War*, p. 398.

ship roughly doubled in Britain and France during the war, while in
Germany it fell by more than a quarter. It went up by around 85 per
cent in the US too.[125]

Finally, figures for strikes show that once again Germany was not
especially susceptible. There was significantly more strike activity in
Britain, where attempts to replace strikes with compulsory arbitration
(as the 1915 Munitions of War Act envisaged for 'controlled establishments' in the arms industry) proved unenforceable. By striking and
demanding that dismissed men be given leaving certificates, the Clyde
coppersmiths made a mockery of the Munitions Tribunal which sought
to enforce 'dilution' measures in Glasgow.[126] Likewise, Lloyd George's
attempts to flatter the miners into accepting a strike ban fell flat when
the Welsh miners walked out in July 1915.[127] As he himself admitted,
it was 'impossible to summon and try 200,000 men'; and as for nationaliz-
ing the pits, that was precisely what the radicals in the workforce
wanted.[128] No German politician had to endure the type of humiliation
inflicted on Lloyd George by the Glaswegian shop stewards. Confronting
them in 1916 (when the papers *Forward* and the *Worker* were banned
and radical leaders arrested and deported from the area) did nothing
much to improve productivity; it was a symbolic showdown.[129] No
German union regarded 'the privileges of skilled labour as almost
Gospel' in the way the Amalgamated Society of Engineers (ASE) did.[130]
The big engineers' strike in May 1917 ended in a decisive victory for

Table 30   Strikes in Britain and Germany, 1914–1918

	Britain		Germany	
	no. of strikers	days lost	no. of strikers	days lost
1914	326,000	10,000,000	61,000	1,715,000
1915	401,000	3,000,000	14,000	42,000
1916	235,000	2,500,000	129,000	245,000
1917	575,000	5,500,000	667,000	1,862,000
1918	923,000	6,000,000	391,000	1,452,000

Sources: Wilson, *Myriad Faces*, p. 221; Horne, *Labour at War*, p. 396; Petzina *et al.*, *Sozialgeschichtliches Arbeitsbuch*, vol. III, pp. 110–18.

the ASE: as Beveridge recalled, the union 'won the most important concession they had asked for . . . without giving anything for which the government had asked'.[131] Unbelievably, 22,000 engineering workers went on strike in April 1918, with the Germans less than fifty miles from Paris. The War Cabinet's instruction to its negotiators was succinct: 'If an imminent strike appeared to be inevitable, all the concessions asked for should be granted.'[132] The contrast with the way the German government broke the January 1918 Berlin strike after a week could not be starker.[133] Also worth noting is the fact that six out of seven of the Berlin strikers' demands were political: they wanted the war to stop, not more pay.

In short, it was fortunate for Britain that Lloyd George was wrong when he described the war in a speech to the TUC as 'a conflict between the mechanics of Germany and Austria on the one hand and the mechanics of Great Britain and France on the other'.[134] With the exception of Russia, British labour relations were quite simply the worst of the war: neither Germany nor Italy nor France suffered as many strikes.[135] Moreover, many of the strikes which swept France in the summer of 1917 affected the non-essential clothing industry and many of the strikers were non-unionized women who went back to work when they were given pay rises.[136] A flurry of more politicized strike action in May 1918 seems to have fizzled out in the face of public criticism, not least from men in uniform.[137]

HUNGER, HEALTH AND INEQUALITY

Was Germany starved into defeat? The idea is one of the most tenacious in modern European historiography.[138] Yet it is almost certainly wrong. In aggregate terms, of course, the average German suffered more than the average Briton, for the simple reason that real per capita income fell in Germany – by around 24 per cent – during the war, while in Britain it actually rose.[139] As we have seen, the blockade certainly reduced the German food supply not only by reducing imports of food but, more seriously, by cutting off supplies of fertilizer. And there is no question that grave administrative errors were made, not least the piecemeal way price maxima were imposed by the Federal Council (*Bundesrat*), which led to price ceilings being lowest for the goods most in demand, and the wholly counterproductive slaughter of 9 million pigs (the notorious *Schweinmord*) in the spring of 1915, which was supposed to release grain and potatoes for human consumption.[140]

Yet the case can be overstated. As Table 31 shows, German food consumption was reduced, but so was British – and the British suffered far less of an aggregate shortage thanks to the expansion of domestic production. Indeed, according to other figures, German per capita consumption of potatoes and fish was actually higher in 1918 than in 1912–13.[141] Much criticism has been heaped on the German wartime system of food rationing; but it is at least arguable that Britain's *laissez-faire* approach was more wasteful and inefficient. The Germans introduced bread rationing in January 1915 and established a War Food Office in May 1916. The Ministry of Food, by contrast, was not set up until December 1916 and was notably ineffective (despite the pleas of William Beveridge) until June 1917, when Lord Davenport was replaced as minister by Lord Rhondda. Alarmed by the appearance of food queues in many cities, the government now introduced rationing of sugar, and began to build up a system of regional and local food distribution; but it was not until April 1918 that a nationwide system of meat rationing was in place, and only three months later that all the basic staples were being rationed.[142] Beginning in mid-1915, France moved much more quickly to requisition grain and control food distribution, but it was only under Anglo-American pressure that steps towards fully fledged rationing were taken, and as late as October

Table 31   British and German food consumption as a percentage of
peacetime consumption, 1917–1918

	Britain	Germany
Meat	25.3	19.8
Butter	37.4	21.3
Potatoes	100.0	94.2

Notes: Britain: working class families' average weekly consumption, Oct.
1917–May 1918; Germany: official rations in Bonn, July 1917–June 1918.
Sources: Winter, Great War, p. 219; Burchardt, 'War Economy', p. 43.

1918 there was a major scandal about profiteering by the consortium
responsible for vegetable oil supplies.[143] Historians who extrapolate
German ineptitude from grumbles about food shortages and prices
should read the identical grumbles which were heard in France in
1917.[144] Yet the Germans had to cope with far more of a food deficit.

Germans certainly went hungry. Instead of the sausages and beer,
they had to make do with nasty ersatz products and East European wine.
They got thinner: the nutritionist R. O. Neumann lost 19 kilogrammes in
seven months by living exclusively on the official ration.[145] But the
evidence that anyone starved – much less the fantastic figure of 750,000
still cited by some otherwise sensible historians[146] – is not to be found.
True, the female mortality rate rose from 14.3 per 1,000 in 1913 to 21.6
per 1,000, a significantly bigger rise than in England (12.2 to 14.6 per
1,000).[147] According to one estimate, around a third of the entire pre-war
population of German psychiatric asylums died of hunger, disease or
neglect.[148] There was also an increase in the number of people killed by
lung disease (1.19 per 1,000 to 2.46) and a sharp increase in deaths of
women in childbirth.[149] But the infant mortality rate clearly fell (apart
from in Bavaria, where it rose in 1918, and the exceptional case of
illegitimate children born in Berlin).[150] In this respect things were much
worse in France, where the rate of infant mortality in 1918 was 21 per
cent above its 1910–13 level.[151] Moreover, it is arguable that Winter
has somewhat overstated the improvement in civilian health experienced
in Britain during the war. There was a 25 per cent increase in deaths
from tuberculosis in England and Wales, too, and that seems likely to
have been due in part to poor nutrition.[152] Populations have continued

to fight wars despite suffering far greater hunger than that experienced by Germans in 1918: the Soviet Union in the Second World War is the most obvious case.

The real test of war economics was how well scarce resources were distributed. Here, once again, it has been argued that Germany failed. In the classic study by Kocka, the war economy is portrayed as having heightened class conflict and other kinds of social division, paving the way for revolution in November 1918.[153] The German state in the First World War appeared to increase inequality by its interventions, favouring some social groups and penalizing others. Relations between classes became less important during the war compared with relations between special interest groups and the state.

Yet evidence that Germany became a less equal society between 1914 and 1918 is mixed. Calculations of the 'Pareto coefficient' for Prussia suggest that in 1918 Prussian income distribution was more unequal than at any time since 1850.[154] But these figures may be distorted by the high incomes enjoyed by a relatively few entrepreneurs. Other evidence strongly suggests that the biggest relative declines in standards of living were suffered not by workers but by other groups within that broad sociological band we call the middle class. The narrowing of differentials in nominal pay described above speak for themselves: civil servants were especially badly affected by this, and the higher up the hierarchy, the more they lost out. Moreover, wartime controls tended to favour working-class households at the expense of various propertied strata of society. Laws against excessive prices were hurriedly enacted in the first months of the war and the first price ceilings set in early 1915. However, it was not until the September 1915 Bundesrat decree for the creation of Price Supervisory Boards (*Preisprüfungstellen*) that a coherent policy of price control emerged.[155] Although a host of offences were created (e.g. 'chain selling', which a Tudor Englishman would have recognized as 'regrating'), in essence the Price Supervisory Boards existed to prosecute shopkeepers who breached price maxima; the same system was adopted in Austria.[156] The one set up in October 1916 in Hamburg provides a good illustration of how they worked. In 1917 alone there were 1,538 successful prosecutions, leading to the closure of 5,551 firms, custodial sentences totalling 12,208 days and fines totalling 92,300 marks.[157] Shopkeepers thus found themselves unable to pass on rising wholesale prices to their customers. Something similar happened in the countryside, where controls were steadily tightened in 1916–17 (the so-called 'Turnip Winter'): here farmers found themselves subjected to house searches and confiscations.[158]

As is well known, price control was not strict enough to prevent the development of a large black market to which city dwellers with spare cash and contacts in the countryside readily turned.[159] But which city dwellers could afford black market prices (which were sometimes as much as fourteen times above official prices)? Clearly those workers in the booming arms industry were now in a better position than low-grade civil servants. This was certainly how it appeared to the military authorities in Hamburg:

Fruit and fresh vegetables . . . are purchased by the upper ten thousand and the now universally well-paid workers, who have no need to shirk the high prices. But the situation is becoming increasingly difficult for the *Mittelstand* or the civil service [*Beamtentum*], upon whom the burdens of the war weigh most heavily.[160]

Similar sacrifices were exacted from what had been, before the war, one of the most powerful political forces in Germany: urban landlords. Despite the exodus of men to the Front, there remained some pressure on the housing stock because of the almost complete suspension of house-building caused by the war: between 1915 and 1918 just 1,923 new homes were added to the Hamburg housing stock, compared with 17,780 in the two pre-war years.[161] The more people moved into the big cities to work in war industries, the more demand for housing rose. But a succession of regulations controlling rents prevented landlords from benefiting. On the contrary, rents were frozen so that in real terms they actually fell. The Hamburg Property Owners' Association estimated the cost of the war to its members at 80 million marks, largely as a result of compulsory rent reductions which were imposed on over half the existing tenancies in Hamburg during the war. By the end of 1918 monthly rents had been reduced to almost half their July 1914 level.[162] Similar controls were, of course, adopted in Britain, where rents began to rise in 1914–15 and a housing shortage later developed.[163] But landlords in Germany were almost certainly harder hit, as were the other professional classes who after the war loudly lamented their 'proletarianization'.[164]

All this makes it tempting to conclude that the war had shifted the balance of socio-economic power away from the middle class, and especially the *Mittelstand*, towards the working class and big business.[165]

Price and rent controls were used to subsidize working-class living standards at the expense of retailers and landlords; civil servants' salaries were held down, while the nominal wages of workers in strategic sectors were allowed to rise. The experience of the Schramm family – a Senatorial family at the pinnacle of the Hamburg *Grossbürgertum* – illustrates the trauma of bourgeois deprivation. For Ruth Schramm, the war meant more than just physical deprivation; it was a time of moral and cultural humiliation. The 'lugubrious and unfriendly public'; the war profiteers; the corruption and violence of 1917 – all this represented a grotesque mockery of the ideals of the *Burgfrieden* three years before. To have to eat meat-paste made from the Alster swans was symbolic of Hamburg's degradation; to have to buy food on the black market represented a stark break with 'the principles which held firm for me before 1914'.[166] When her brother returned to the family home from the Front in December 1918, he found that his parents had taken in a lodger on the second floor and closed up the ground floor to save on heating. Although they still ate with silver spoons, he at once recognized 'the end of the grand-bourgeois lifestyle'.[167]

Such genteel impoverishment, however, does not necessarily lead to internal collapse, much less to revolution. On the contrary: it was precisely the social groups who were hardest hit in relative terms by the war who were the most avid supporters of official war aims. An explanation of the German defeat which emphasizes the collapse of the Home Front thus simply will not work. At no time, including the period of strikes in April 1917 and January 1918, did domestic morale in Germany come as close to collapsing as it did in Russia and nearly did in France.[168] In purely chronological terms, it was the Western Front not the Home Front which collapsed first; and when revolution did sweep from the northern ports southwards to Berlin and Munich in November 1918, it was a revolution made not by the war's economic losers but by its relative winners: the soldiers and sailors, who had been better fed than civilians, and the industrial workers, whose real wages had fallen least.

The only plausible argument which can be made about the German and Russian war economies is that they were *too* successful: the stimulus of arms production *à tout prix* eventually put too much strain on urban consumers, leading ultimately to a collapse in morale. As we shall see, there are problems with this thesis, however; and even if it were true it would be no great vindication of British, French and American achievements. If the Western powers did strike a better balance between civilian and military needs, it was by accident not design. Moreover, they paid a high military price for it – so high, indeed, that they came close to losing the war.

IO

Strategy, Tactics and the Net Body Count

STRATEGIES

Given the enormous economic disadvantage under which they laboured, but given also the relative inefficiency of their enemies, could the Germans have won the war? Few historians think so. Carl von Clausewitz's *On War* (published shortly after his death in 1831) had famously defined war as 'the continuation of political intercourse [*des politischen Verkehrs*] with the intermixing of other means [*mit Einmischung anderer Mittel*].' The great mistake of Germany's war leaders, it has often been argued, was that they forgot this precept. As Germany became more and more a military dictatorship, politics became merely one of the other means, intermixed with the paramount activity of warfare. Strategic errors were consequently made which ultimately guaranteed their country's defeat.

German strategy from the outset was characterized by an exceptionally high willingness to gamble. It might be argued that this had to be the case, precisely because of the odds against Germany: convinced of their own relative inferiority over the long run, the Germans were irresistibly attracted by risky strategies designed to bring victory in the short run. Still, there is no denying that at least some of Germany's strategic gambles were reckless; that is to say based on estimates of probable costs and benefits which were obviously – and not just with the benefit of hindsight – unrealistic.

The German gamble which has been subjected to most criticism was the gamble that unrestricted submarine warfare, which involved the sinking without warning of ships believed to be carrying war supplies to Britain, would defeat Britain before the United States could make an effective military contribution to the war. This strategy was tried three times: between March and August 1915, when the *Lusitania* and

Arabic were sunk; between February and March 1916; and finally from 1 February 1917, when the Admiralty Staff promised that Britain would have to sue for peace 'within five months'. In fairness to the German naval planners, the U-Boats initially exceeded the original target of sinking 600,000 tons a month; indeed, they bagged 841,118 in April. But their calculations were in every other possible respect wrong. They had underestimated:

1. Britain's ability to expand her own wheat production;
2. the normal size of the American wheat crop (1916 and 1917 were exceptionally bad years);
3. Britain's ability to switch scarce wood from house construction into mine-pit props;
4. the tonnage available to Britain;
5. the British state's ability to ration food in short supply;
6. the effectiveness of convoys; and
7. the ability of the Royal Navy to develop anti-submarine technology.

Incredibly, they had also over-estimated the number of submarines they themselves possessed or could possess: between January 1917 and January 1918 some 87 new U-Boats were built, but 78 were lost. The total force at the outset of the final campaign was around a hundred, of which no more than a third were able to patrol British waters at any one time.[1] By 1918 the loss rate among convoys was down to below 1 per cent; for U-Boats the figure was over 7 per cent.[2]

Nor was this the only respect in which the Germans bungled the war at sea. It is sometimes said that the naval war was inconclusive because the British and German surface fleets never fought a decisive encounter, Dogger Bank and Jutland being draws. But this is nonsense. The Royal Navy succeeded in doing the job of confining the German battle fleet to the North Sea, give or take a few militarily insignificant raids on the English east coast: it was Tirpitz who stood to gain from a full-scale sea battle, not Jellicoe. Indeed, Tirpitz's entire pre-war strategy depended on the British fleet's attacking Germany; it never dawned on him that, as they already dominated the High Seas, the British could simply sit tight at Scapa Flow.[3] Moreover, having lost at Coronel, the Royal Navy won the battle of the Falkland Islands. It was also very successful in incapacitating German merchant shipping in the first phase of the war, a heavy blow to the German balance of payments. True, the German submariners sunk a great deal of British and American shipping before

Lloyd George managed to bully the Admiralty into adopting the convoy system; but the proportion sunk was smaller than the proportion of German merchant shipping seized or sunk by the British (44 per cent).

It is striking how few voices were raised in Germany against the gamble on unrestricted submarine warfare. Max Warburg was one of the few influential German businessmen who opposed the lifting of restrictions on submarine warfare, on the grounds that, however great the impact on British food supplies, the risk of alienating the United States was too grave. 'If America is cut off from Germany', he argued in February 1916, 'that means a 50 per cent reduction in Germany's financial strength for the war, and an increase of 100 per cent for England's and France's . . . Everything should . . . be done to avoid a breach with America.'[4] 'The war is lost if it [unrestricted submarine warfare] goes ahead: financially, because our loans will no longer be bought; economically, because the masses of raw materials which we continue to get from abroad and which we cannot do without will be cut off.'[5] On 26 January 1917 he expressed forebodings which seem prescient: 'If we end up at war with America, we will face an enemy with such moral, financial and economic strength that we will have nothing more to hope for from the future; that is my firm conviction.'[6] Warburg went unheard (not least because, with two brothers living in the United States, he was regarded as biased): the restrictions on submarine warfare were lifted, and in just over two months the United States declared war on Germany. Here, it has been argued, was a classic example of a decision based on 'bounded rationality': the Germans made their calculations of the likely impact of unrestricted U-Boat war without taking into account awkward facts and possibilities.[7] For this blunder they were ultimately punished with defeat; for once the United States entered the war they could not hope to win – so the conventional argument runs.

The Germans can also be accused of having gambled in the war they waged on land. In August 1914 they gambled on victory in a two-front war in the belief that to wait any longer would allow Russia and France to establish an unassailable superiority. At the same time, they gambled that Austria–Hungary would make an effective contribution to the war in the East. Virtually no attempt had been made to check that this could be relied upon; or indeed what form the Habsburg contribution would take.[8] Neither gamble came off. If one believes that the Schlieffen Plan was expected to deliver a swift military victory in the West then it was a complete failure; and one that was preordained by logistical deficiencies in the plan.[9] The gamble on alliance with Austria also went wrong. Time and again the Germans had to divert men to the Eastern theatre to bail out the Austro-Hungarian army: in 1915, when Russia's Galician offensive forced Falkenhayn to counter-attack at Gorlice, and again in the wake of the Brusilov offensive in 1916.[10] Another frequently criticized gamble was Falkenhayn's decision to attempt to 'bleed the enemy white' at a 'decisive point': the 'meatgrinder' fortress of Verdun. That ended up costing the Germans almost as many men as the French (337,000 casualties to 377,000), thanks to General Philippe Pétain's successful use of artillery and rapid rotation of divisions; and the original goal was lost sight of as the Germans came to believe that they really needed to capture the fortress.[11]

Finally, Ludendorff has been accused of committing strategic suicide with Operation Michael in the spring of 1918. Tactically brilliant, driving the Allies back as far as 40 miles and capturing 1,200 square miles of territory, the Germans' offensive was nevertheless foredoomed to fail because they lacked the reserves and the supply structures to consolidate their gains. By extending the front line, the Germans stretched their own forces to breaking point, so that the Allied counter-offensive was almost certain to succeed. Moreover, the subsequent offensives against the Chemin des Dames and Reims at the end of May eroded German reserves to little effect.[12]

Indeed, it is plausible to argue that the Germans lost the war precisely because they so nearly won it. It was the huge extent of the victory over Russia which left around a million troops milling around in the chaos of post-Brest-Litovsk Eastern Europe at a time when they were needed in the West. It was the unprecedented distance covered by the Germans in the spring of 1918 which laid them open to the heaviest casualties since 1914: more than a fifth of the original 1.4 million-strong force was lost between 21 March and 10 April.[13] Moreover, the offensive in the West left Germany's allies in the South-East and South fatally exposed;[14] it was here that the defeat of the Central Powers began, with the Bulgarian request for a separate armistice on 28 September. Thus Ludendorff's confession to Hindenburg that evening that an armistice was urgently needed because 'the position could only grow worse' was the admission of a defeat which was at least partly self-inflicted.[15]

Related to these strategic arguments is a critique of German diplomacy. States in stronger positions than that of Germany in 1917 have sought to negotiate peace rather than risk ultimate defeat. However, the longer the conflict went on and the greater the sacrifices it entailed, the greater became the expectations of its ultimate rewards. The formulation of war aims, which began as a preliminary to possible negotiations, rapidly escalated into a public debate involving economic interests and domestic politics as much as – indeed, more than – grand strategy. The longer this debate went on, the more divorced from reality it tended to become. At the same time, the German generals repeatedly interfered in diplomacy – for example, replacing Jagow as Foreign Secretary in 1916 with Arthur Zimmermann, whose name will always be associated with one of the great diplomatic blunders of modern times (the telegram offering to help Mexico recover New Mexico, Texas and Arizona from the US). Germany's defeat can therefore be portrayed as the consequence of political rather than material factors. It was due to a failure of policy not production.

Of course, the Germans had their undeniable victories on the Eastern Front. They attempted as early as 1915 to woo the Tsar with a separate peace;[16] had this been successful, the Germans might well have won the war (and Russia would almost certainly have been spared Bolshevism). When the Russians spurned these advances, the Germans went on to inflict total defeat on them. The magnitude of this achievement should not be understated. The war had been launched by the General Staff to pre-empt a deterioration in Germany's strategic position relative to Russia. By 1917 this had in fact been achieved. Nor was it entirely fanciful to envisage breaking up Tsarist dominion in Eastern Europe. As Norman Stone has said, Brest-Litovsk was a 'might have been' more than a fantasy, and Britain might have been willing to accept German hegemony in Eastern Europe as a bulwark against Bolshevism if that had been Germany's only objective. On 5 November 1916 – nearly two and a half months before Woodrow Wilson made his famous call for a 'peace without victory' on the basis of self-determination – the Germans had seized the initiative by proclaiming the independence of Poland. Under Brest-Litovsk, Finland and Lithuania also won their independence, even if Latvia, Courland, the Ukraine and Georgia were to be the victims of (in Warburg's words) 'thinly veiled annexation, with an all too transparent façade provided by the right of national self-determination'.[17] This was one of the moments when the Germans would have been better advised to seek a negotiated peace in the West before American forces became numerous enough to tip the military balance irreversibly.

Yet almost from the moment Bethmann Hollweg's September programme raised the possibility of annexations of territory from France and Belgium, that option was ruled out. Some German aims for Western Europe were, as we have seen, not wholly unacceptable to Britain: the idea of a Central European trading bloc, for example, was one she could have lived with. But the desire for territory in the West as well as the East proved the fatal stumbling block to a negotiated peace. Tirpitz, his deputy Rear-Admiral Paul Behncke and others at the Naval Office argued for annexation of Belgian territory as early as September 1914, a demand repeated on numerous occasions after Henning von Holtzendorff replaced Tirpitz in 1916.[18] Beginning with the memorandum by Hermann Schumacher in the autumn of 1914, heavy industrialists argued that Germany must retain a substantial part of Belgium and the ore-rich Briey-Longwy region of France. In May 1915 these demands were included in the list of war aims submitted by the six big economic associations, which also envisaged the annexation of the Pas-de-Calais region, the fortresses of Verdun and Belfort and a strip of the northern French coast to the mouth of the Somme.[19] Few shared Albert Ballin's view that there should be 'no annexation' since 'English policy cannot sacrifice Belgium to us'; and even he envisaged 'economic and military dependence . . . especially for the ports'.[20]

Time and again the Belgian issue prevented negotiations from getting off the ground: as early as November 1914, when Falkenhayn realistically warned Bethmann that Germany could not hope to achieve a peace with major annexations; in January 1916, when Colonel House proposed peace on the basis of the *status quo ante*; in December 1916, when Bethmann thought of concessions but Hindenburg bullied him out of it; and again in July 1917, when Pope Benedict XV sought to mediate.[21] As Foreign Secretary, Richard von Kühlmann argued for relinquishing Belgium in September 1917; but the generals and the admirals would not let go. When Max Warburg (acting on Chancellor Hertling's instructions) went to Belgium for unofficial talks with the American ambassador in Holland in March 1918, the German government was still insisting on 'minor cessions' of Belgian territory 'in order to have assurances . . . that Belgium would not be used as a *pied à terre* by the English and the French'.[22] Hugo Stinnes was adamant until the very last weeks of the war that Germany must endeavour to annex territory in the West to provide a 'buffer' for the protection of her – or rather his – western iron and steel plants. He also had no qualms about proposing the thoroughgoing expropriation of the industrial plants and the elimination of the Belgian management' in any annexed territory, to say nothing of ruling that territory 'in a dictatorial manner for a number of decades'.[23] That he continued to take this position even after the failure of Ludendorff's Western offensive perfectly illustrates the way the German war aims debate became divorced from diplomatic and strategic realities. Stinnes was by no means unique; the senior naval commander Captain von Levetzow proposed as late as 21 September 1918 that Germany should acquire Constantinople, Valona, Alexandretta and Benghazi after the war.[24]

The proponents of annexation fatally underestimated the advantages Germany would have been able to retain if, in agreeing to restore Belgium, she had been able to secure a negotiated end to the war before her own collapse. German plans for colonial acquisitions from Britain and France – typified by the numerous wish-lists of Hamburg business associations – were less important, but also testified to the lack of realism which pervaded the war-aims debate, given Germany's clear maritime inferiority.[25] The same can be said of the German admirals' daydreams about bases at Valona (Albania), Dakar, the Cape Verde Islands, the Azores, Tahiti and Madagascar; to say nothing of their imagined African *imperium*.[26]

Defects in German strategy had their origins in defects in the political structure of the Reich, which even before the war had been short of institutions capable of co-ordinating policy between the various Reich departments of state. Notoriously, the authority of both the Chancellor and the Kaiser declined during the war; the military came to dominate, with the Supreme Command of Hindenburg and Ludendorff constituting after 1916 a 'silent' (i.e. unstated) military dictatorship.[27] In practice, Ludendorff came to be the sole master of German strategy, and much else besides. Partly for this reason, it was inevitable that the war aims debate would become inextricably bound up with the debate on Germany's constitutional arrangements. Those who felt that diplomatic opportunities were being squandered questioned not only the calibre of the *Auswärtiges Amt* but also the extent of the Reich Chancellor's subordination to the military. Those for whom Bethmann was a 'traitor' and a 'criminal against the Fatherland' wished conversely to see the power of the generals increased. War aims – whether annexations,

Mitteleuropa, the *status quo ante* or a revolutionary peace based on self-determination and working-class solidarity – came to be identified with domestic aims – dictatorship, some degree of parliamentarization or socialist revolution. Events between February and September 1917 made the alternatives clear. In the wake of the February Revolution in Russia, the founding of the Independent Socialist Party at Gotha gave organizational substance to the idea of 'peace through democratization' and pushed the Majority Social Democrats in the same direction. In the Reichstag, the latter allied with the Centre Party and the Progressives to pass a resolution calling for 'peace without forced cessions'. But Bethmann, having persuaded the Kaiser to accept democratization of the Prussian franchise, was ousted by Hindenburg and Ludendorff and replaced by the nonentity Michaelis; a move endorsed by Tirpitz and Wolfgang Kapp's new Fatherland Party, which by July 1918 had 2,536 branches and 1.25 million members.[28]

By now the military dictators and their supporters had moved well beyond traditional monarchical conservatism. One Pan-German leader, Konstantin von Gebsattel, warned that if no annexations were achieved at the end of the war there would be popular 'disappointment and embitterment': 'The people, disillusioned after all their achievements, will rise. The monarchy will be endangered, even overthrown.' German politics polarized. Those who favoured a negotiated peace had little choice under these circumstances but to embrace the idea of some degree of domestic reform, if only to increase the power of the Reich Chancellor over the military and to reduce the power of the heavy industrial lobby. The problem was that these elements only gained control in Germany in October 1918 after Ludendorff had frittered away the last remnants of German military bargaining power. As the Bavarian Colonel Mertz von Quirnheim had lamented in July 1917:

What a tremendous impression it would make if General Ludendorff (through the voice of Hindenburg) were to declare: 'Yes, OHL is also in favour of universal suffrage for Prussia, because our Prussian soldiers have fully deserved it.' I believe Ludendorff would be carried aloft in triumph, all danger of strikes etc. would be removed . . . But General Ludendorff lacks all understanding for such an exploitation of political ideas for the purpose of the war.[29]

Thus the circle from domestic politics to defective strategy and back to domestic politics seems complete; and it only remains to draw the reassuring conclusion that democracies wage war better than dictatorships.

A third and perhaps more surprising area of German failure was the relative slowness of the Reich to exploit new military technologies. To be sure, the Germans were the pioneers of high quality trench fortifications, of steel-cored bullets capable of piercing enemy parapets and of incendiary bullets to get rid of observation balloons. They were also, notoriously, the first army to use chlorine gas on the battlefield (at Ypres on 22 April 1915) – though the French had been using grenades filled with ethyl bromo-acetate (essentially tear gas) from the outset and the Germans had already tried 'T-shells' containing xylyl bromide in Poland.[30] Flame-throwers too were a German innovation (first used at Hooge in July 1915); as were trench mortars (the feared *Minenwerfer*) and steel helmets.[31] But in three crucial areas they lagged behind. As Herwig has argued, the Germans fell short in terms of air power, though simply counting the number of planes available in the spring of 1918 (3,670 to 4,500) may understate the achievements of the Zeppelin fleet and Gotha bombers in killing, injuring and terrifying British civilians, as well as in damaging property.[32] The same was true of motorized transport. In 1918 they had around 30,000 vehicles, mostly with steel or wooden tyres; as against 100,000 on the Allied side, mostly with rubber tyres. Finally, the Germans did not manufacture enough tanks. They produced only 20 in 1918, and many of them broke down; the Allies by then had 800.[33] Hence the paradox that the country with the most renowned technical expertise and manufacturing industry before the war failed to win the *Materialschlacht*. Another technological lapse was the German failure to match British espionage: in particular, the Germans were unaware that most of their signals to the fleet were intercepted by the Admiralty and deciphered in Room 40.[34]

ENTENTE AND ALLIED STRATEGY

There are, however, a number of difficulties with this critique of German strategy and diplomacy. For one thing, it could be argued that the strategy of the Entente powers was not a great deal better than that of the Central Powers.[35] Liddell Hart, for example, contended that Germany could have been defeated without embroiling Britain in a prolonged and bloody continental stalemate if more troops had been made available for indirect approaches such as the Dardanelles invasion.[36] In *The Donkeys*, Alan Clark suggested that Britain could have avoided using ground forces altogether, relying instead on her naval power to starve Germany into submission.[37]

No historian since the official historian Edmonds has done more to rebut these notions than John Terraine, who has consistently argued for nearly forty years that Britain fought the war as well as could have been expected under the circumstances. According to Terraine, there was no alternative to sending the British Expeditionary Force; no alternative to launching the offensives at the Somme and Passchendaele; and it is therefore 'unprofitable to look for the causes of the [high British] loss[es] very far beyond the quality of the enemy . . . and the technical character of the war itself.[38] Correlli Barnett has been among the supporters of this view, though he also argues that victory did nothing to halt Britain's long-term economic and strategic decline, which was (by a curious irony) partly due to her failure to become more *like* Germany.[39]

It is certainly hard to see a plausible alternative to winning the war on the Western Front. In the first place, nothing could have been *more* likely to ensure a German victory in France than the commitment of larger numbers of British troops to a protracted campaign against Turkey. Nor would much have been achieved by a British triumph at Gallipoli. The principal strategic beneficiary would have been Russia, which would have come a step closer to realizing her long-cherished aim of controlling Constantinople. Britain would simply have won the right to supply Russia with more arms through the Straits at her own expense; it is far from certain that this would have been the optimal use of British resources. Meanwhile the French would have been crumbling without enough British soldiers to bail them out.[40] Indeed, it might even be argued that every major deployment of British troops elsewhere was strategically perilous: not just Gallipoli, but also Mesopotamia, Salonica and Palestine. The gains made in non-European theatres doubtless proved useful when it came to enlarging the Empire in the peace negotiations; but if the Germans had won the war in Flanders and France, then all bets in the Middle East would have been off.

As for the pure navalist strategy, that would not have delivered victory over Germany either. Despite the fact that Germany lost the war at sea, Britain's naval strategy indubitably failed to starve German civilians into submission as it was supposed to: as we have seen, the principal German victims of the blockade were among social groups which were not crucial to the war effort. If Britain had fought the war only at sea, she would have found herself in command of only the waves around Europe; without the armies raised by Kitchener, Germany would have won the land war.

The war had to be won on the Western Front, then. But that does not mean that the principal strategy adopted there – to fight a war of attrition – should be accepted as correct without qualification.

The origins of attrition can be traced back as far as October 1914 when Kitchener told Esher that 'before Germany relinquishes the struggle, she will have exhausted every possible supply of men . . .' At first Kitchener hoped to play a long game, building up the New Army with a view to intervening decisively (à la Wellington) once the French had done the dirtier work of wearing the Germans down. Sir Charles Callwell, the Director of Military Operations, cheered everyone greatly in January 1915 by writing a report which proved that the Germans would run out of men 'in a few months hence'. Five months later Brigadier Frederick Maurice, Callwell's successor as DMO, was still confidently predicting that if the army could 'keep hammering away . . . we shall wear Germany out and the war will be over in six months'. Kitchener's view was that 'attrition' would not exhaust German reserves of manpower until 'about the beginning of 1917'; nonetheless he favoured allowing the Germans 'to burn themselves up by costly attacks to shatter our lines' – hence Balfour and Churchill's talk in July 1915 of an 'active defence, inflicting as much loss on the enemy as possible, and nibbling and gnawing along the whole front'. The enemy was to be 'reduced . . . to the point at which further resistance will have become impossible' (Selborne); he was to be 'exhausted' and 'worn down' (Robertson and Murray); his reserves were to be 'used up' (Robertson). The generals even began to set targets: 200,000 German casualties a month was one (in December 1915).[41] The French reasoned in much the same way. In May 1915 their General Staff concluded that 'the break-through followed by exploitation' would not be possible 'until the enemy has been . . . so worn down that he has no reserves available to close the gap'.[42]

'Active defence' soon shaded into attack. Sir Henry Rawlinson's draft plan for the Somme attack was 'to kill as many Germans as possible with the least loss to ourselves' by seizing points of tactical importance and waiting for the Germans to counter-attack.[43] 'We are fighting primarily to wear down the German armies and the German nation,' wrote Brigadier-General Sir John Charteris in his diary on 30 June. To be sure, Haig continued to cling to the notion that a breakthrough could be achieved, fearing that in a 'wearing-out' battle 'our troops will be used up no less, possibly more than those of the enemy'.[44] This was true, but Haig's preferred option of a massive assault on the German line was even more costly: on the first day of the Somme the British army sustained 60,000 casualties, as is well known; the full significance of this figure becomes clear when it is realized that the German defenders suffered only 8,000. When the breakthrough failed to materialize, all reverted to the arguments of attrition, fantasizing that 'the Germans are now getting to their last legs, with few reserves and doubting – even the officer prisoners – whether they can escape defeat'.[45] The reality was that at best, if one accepts the British official figure for German casualties of 680,000, the Somme was a draw (the British lost 419,654 casualties, the French 204,253). If, as is more likely, the German figure for casualties was correct (450,000), then the strategy of attrition was self-defeating. Even Haig began to divine that by remaining on the defensive, it was the Germans who were 'wear[ing] out our troops';[46] nothing showed this more clearly than the suicidal Nivelle offensive of April 1917, which should never have been launched after the German withdrawal to the Hindenburg Line. By May 15 the French had suffered 187,000 losses, the Germans 163,000.

Yet when the French mutinied, Haig prescribed more attrition: whatever gains were made by the British offensive at Arras (April–May 1917), they did not match the losses of 159,000 in just 39 days. In May Robertson and Haig were still arguing in unison for 'wearing down and exhausting the enemy's resistance'; but the attack at Messines the following month still cost 25,000 British casualties to 23,000 German. Attrition was invoked to justify Third Ypres too.[47] Haig still dreamt of a breakthrough, but now even Robertson admitted that he 'stuck to' this strategy 'because I see nothing better, and because my instinct prompts me to stick to it' rather than because he had 'any convincing argument by which I can support it'.[48] In the event, both sides suffered around 250,000 casualties. It is hard not to agree with Lloyd George's verdict: 'Haig does not care how many men he loses. He just squanders the lives of these boys.'[49] The Prime Minister's bitter joke – 'When I look at the appalling casualty lists I sometimes wish it had not been necessary to win so many [great victories]' – hit the nail on the head.[50] The heaviest casualties suffered by the German Army were in the spring of 1918, when Ludendorff launched *his* offensive. Total German casualties by the end of Operation Michael were 250,000 to 178,000 British and 77,000 French; by the end of April the figures were 348,000 to 240,000 and 92,000. In terms of total casualties, it was yet another 'draw', but the Entente could better withstand the losses, as they now had American reinforcements. Only in June 1918 did British commanders recognize that 'engag[ing] and wear[ing] down' the enemy was only worth while if there was 'sufficient deliberation and artillery preparation to secure economy of men'.[51]

By their own criteria, then, the British generals failed. As Table 32 shows, the greatest of all the paradoxes of the First World War is that, despite being disastrously disadvantaged in economic terms, the Central Powers were far more successful in inflicting death on their enemies. According to the best available totals for wartime military deaths, some 5.4 million men fighting for the Entente powers and their allies lost their lives, the overwhelming majority of them killed by the enemy. The equivalent total for the Central Powers is just over 4 million. The Central Powers' superiority in killing was thus of the order of 35 per cent. The official British statistics published shortly after the war give an even higher margin of 50 per cent, as do the figures in a number of modern textbooks.[52] In other words, the Central Powers were at least a third better at mass slaughter. Elias Canetti said of the strategy of attrition: 'Each side wants to constitute the larger crowd of living fighters and it wants the opposing side to constitute the largest heap of the dead.'[53] Judged by that measure, the Central Powers 'won' the war.

An even bigger discrepancy existed with respect to the other most effective means of incapacitating the enemy: prisoner taking. Between 3.1 and (at most) 3.7 million soldiers fighting for the Central Powers were taken prisoner during the war, compared with between 3.8 and (at most) 5.1 million Entente and Allied soldiers (see Chapter 13 for a discussion of the figures). The 'net body count' here too is strongly in favour of the Central Powers, who succeeded in capturing between 25 and 38 per cent more men than they lost as prisoners to the enemy. Only in one respect does the balance of advantage seem to have lain with the Entente and Allied powers: the available statistics suggest that 1.3 million more soldiers of the Central Powers were wounded as a result of enemy action. However, these are of all the figures the least reliable (for example, the Germans did not record minor wounds in their official statistics, whereas the British did). In any case, wounding the enemy was the least effective way of inflicting damage because a

Table 32   *Total casualties in the First World War*

	Official British deaths figures	Revised deaths figures	Men held as prisoners at end of war	Wounded	Total casualties
France	1,345,300	1,398,000	446,300	2,000,000	3,844,300
Belgium	13,716	38,000	10,203	44,686	92,889
Italy	460,000	578,000	530,000	947,000	2,055,000
Portugal	7,222	7,000	12,318	13,751	33,069
Britain	702,410	723,000	170,389	1,662,625	2,556,014
British Empire	205,961	198,000	21,263	427,587	646,850
Rumania	335,706	250,000	80,000	120,000	450,000
Serbia	45,000	278,000	70,423	133,148	481,571
Greece	5,000	26,000	1,000	21,000	48,000
Russia	1,700,000	1,811,000	3,500,000	1,450,000	6,761,000
USA	115,660	114,000	4,480	205,690	324,170
Total Allies	4,935,975	5,421,000	4,846,376	7,025,487	17,292,863
Bulgaria	87,500	88,000	10,623	152,390	251,013
Germany	1,676,696	2,037,000	617,922	4,207,028	6,861,950
Austria–Hungary	1,200,000	1,100,000	2,200,000	3,620,000	6,920,000
Turkey	325,000	804,000	250,000	400,000	1,454,000
Total Central Powers	3,289,196	4,029,000	3,078,545	8,379,418	15,486,963
Grand total	8,225,171	9,450,000	7,924,921	15,404,905	32,779,826
'Net body count'	1,646,779	1,392,000	1,767,831	−1,353,931	1,805,900
Percentage difference	50	35	57	−16	12

Notes: The figures for dead include deaths from disease as well as action, which inflates the totals, especially in peripheral theatres of the conflict.

Figures for Portugal: no figures for wounded from Mozambique or Angola.

Greek prisoners figure includes missing and so is probably too high.

Sources: War Office, *Statistics of the Military Effort*, pp. 237, 352–7; Terraine, *Smoke and the Fire*, p. 44; J. Winter, *Great War*, p. 75.

Table 33 Estimates for total casualties (killed, taken prisoner and wounded)

	Maxima	Minima	Best estimates
France	6,100,000	3,791,600	3,844,300
Belgium	92,889	68,605	92,889
Italy	2,190,000	1,937,000	2,055,000
Portugal	33,291	33,069	33,291
Britain and Empire	3,305,000	3,190,235	3,202,864
Rumania	535,706	450,000	450,000
Serbia	481,571	248,571	481,571
Greece	48,000	27,000	48,000
Russia	9,100,000	6,650,000	6,761,000
USA	325,830	324,170	324,170
Total Allies	22,212,287	16,720,250	17,293,085
Bulgaria	250,513	250,513	251,013
Germany	7,437,000	6,501,646	6,861,950
Austria–Hungary	7,000,000	6,920,000	6,920,000
Turkey	2,290,000	970,000	1,454,000
Total Central Powers	16,977,513	14,642,159	15,486,963
Grand total	39,189,800	31,362,409	32,780,048
'Net body count'	5,234,774	2,078,091	1,806,122
Percentage difference	30.8	14.2	11.7

Sources: as Table 32.

substantial proportion of wounded soldiers – 55.5 per cent in the British case[54] – were able to return to active service if they did not die of their injuries. Partly for this reason, attempts to arrive at figures for total casualties are fraught with difficulty. To be accurate, they should be weighted to take account of the fact that killing the enemy was best, taking him prisoner almost as good and perhaps even better (a prisoner had to be fed and sheltered, which ate into resources, but could be made to work), while wounding him was the least damaging of the three. Table 33 summarizes the available minima and maxima and provides what seem like the best estimates for casualties. It will be seen that overall the Central Powers had a margin of advantage of more than 10 per cent. If one ignores the figures for wounded, that margin rises to an astonishing 44 per cent. The Central Powers, in other words,

Table 34   *Manpower available in Germany, 1914–1918*

	Males attaining the age of 18 (approx.)	War deaths	Surplus
1914	670,000	241,000	429,000
1915	674,000	434,000	240,000
1916	688,000	340,000	348,000
1917	693,000	282,000	411,000
1918	699,000	380,000	319,000
1919	711,000		

Source: Maier, 'Wargames', p. 266.

permanently incapacitated 10.3 million enemy soldiers, while losing only 7.1 million in the same way. These are remarkable statistics.

Admittedly, simply calculating the 'net body count' is a somewhat crude measure of military effectiveness; Michael Howard has even said that 'to reduce the criteria of military success to this kind of body-count is a *reductio ad absurdum*'.[55] Yet it is not easy to see how else to assess the performance of armies in the First World War. If one tries to assess the success of offensives in terms of territory won, one merely proves what every schoolboy knows: that for most of the period from 1915 until 1917 war on the Western Front was a zero-sum game.

Furthermore, as Charles Maier points out, throughout the war Britain and her allies never succeeded in killing more Germans than attained the age of 18 (Table 34). If attrition really had been the way to win the war, it would still have been going strong in 1919, with the German cohort of new recruits at its highest level of any year since 1914. In Stone's words, 'manpower was, to all intents and purposes, inexhaustible'.[56]

Of course, it could be argued that in relative terms the strategy of attrition was successful because of the much greater quantity of manpower at the Entente generals' disposal. To put it crudely, they could afford to sustain higher losses than the Central Powers: what counted was not the absolute number of enemy soldiers killed or captured but the proportion of available manpower. Table 35 relates death figures to the available manpower of the combatants. It will be seen at once that in relative terms the Central Powers were indeed harder hit by the war, losing 11.5 per cent of their adult men to a figure of just 2.7 per cent on the other side. Some would say that this by itself is a sufficient explanation of the Allied victory. Yet the Allied figures are heavily distorted by the very large numbers of men on the Entente and Allied side who did not serve. In all only 5 per cent of the total population were actually mobilized on the Entente and Allied side, compared with 17 per cent for the Central Powers. It may well be asked how willing these unused men would have been to fight had they been required to. This applies especially to large parts of the British Empire, but one could also ask how many more men the Americans would have been able to mobilize if the war had dragged on; as it was, draft evasion in the US amounted to 11 per cent (337,649 cases in all).[57] If one considers the differential as set out in the first column (killed as a percentage of men actually mobilized), the gap shrinks to 15.7 per cent for the Central Powers as against 12 per cent for the other side.

Furthermore, if one considers what was strategically the most important country in the war – France – it becomes clear that the Germans succeeded in inflicting heavier relative losses in every respect. The French and Germans mobilized more or less the same proportion of their populations; but the Germans killed more Frenchmen than the French were able to kill Germans. Worse still, the French had fewer young men available each year to fight than the more fertile Germans. Yet the French army did not collapse (though it suffered a debilitating crisis of morale in 1917). It was the Russian army – whose casualties were comparatively low as a proportion of men mobilized and very low as a proportion of all adult males – which collapsed first. As we have already seen, the Scots were (after the Serbs and Turks) the soldiers who suffered the highest death rate of the war; yet the Scots regiments fought on to the end. A mechanistic explanation of the Central Powers' defeat of the sort advanced by proponents of attrition will therefore not do. Indeed, the differentials presented here as the net body count make it quite hard to understand how Germany and her allies lost the First World War.

The most sophisticated study of casualty figures for both World Wars by Trevor Dupuy concludes that on average the Germans were 20 per cent more effective than British or American troops. Dupuy studies fifteen First World War battles and awards 'scores' for 'casualties per day as a percentage of the force inflicting the casualties', then adjusts these to take account of 'the known operational advantage which is conferred by the defensive posture' (1.3 for Hasty Defence, 1.5 for

Table 35   Military deaths as percentages of manpower

Country	Total killed as a percentage of total mobilized	Total killed as a percentage of males 15–49	Total killed as a percentage of population
Scotland	26.4	10.9	3.1
Britain & Ireland	11.8	6.3	1.6
Canada	9.7	2.6	0.8
Australia	14.5	4.4	1.2
New Zealand	12.4	5.0	1.5
South Africa	5.1	0.4	0.1
India	5.7	0.1	0.0
British Empire (excluding GB)	8.8	0.2	0.1
France	16.8	13.3	3.4
French colonies	15.8	0.5	0.1
Belgium	10.4	2.0	0.5
Italy	10.3	7.4	1.6
Portugal	7.0	0.5	0.1
Greece	7.4	2.1	0.5
Serbia	37.1	22.7	5.7
Rumania	25.0	13.2	3.3
Russia	11.5	4.5	1.1
United States	2.7	0.4	0.1
Allied Total	12.0	2.7	0.7
Germany	15.4	12.5	3.0
Austria–Hungary	12.2	9.0	1.9
Turkey	26.8	14.8	3.7
Bulgaria	22.0	8.0	1.9
Central Powers' Total	15.7	11.5	2.6
Grand Total	13.4	4.0	1.0

Source: J. Winter, *Great War*, p. 75.

Prepared Defence and 1.6 for Fortified Defence). The average 'score effectiveness' for German forces is 5.51, or 2.61 if Russian prisoners are omitted (though there is no real reason to do so); the figure for the Russians is 1.5, for the Western Allies an even lower 1.1.[58]

The argument can be pursued in more detail for the crucial Western Front. Official monthly casualty figures may not be the most reliable of historical sources, but they are not so useless that they deserve to be ignored (as they generally have been by historians). They show clearly that, for all but eight out of sixty-four months between February 1915 and October 1918, the Germans succeeded in inflicting heavier casualties on Britain in the British sector of the line – and three of those eight months were at the very end of the war (August–October 1918) (see Figure 12). It should also be noted that for most of the war officer casualties were much higher on the British side than on the German: in every year of the war the Germans killed or captured more officers in the British sector than they lost.[59] Figure 13 combines the available French, British and German figures to show that from August 1914 until June 1918 there was *not a single month* in which the Germans failed to kill or capture more Entente soldiers than they lost themselves. True, throughout this period the British army on the Western Front was growing, so that the proportional rate of loss of both officers and men was certainly falling. When the British figures are combined with the French figures and compared with total German casualties on the Western Front, it seems that the Entente armies did improve. However, it was only in the summer of 1918 that the net body count turned in their favour; and that primarily reflected the sharp increase in the number of Germans surrendering rather than a major improvement in net killing by the Allies (see Chapter 13). Indeed, if one considers the figures for deaths in the British sector (which are admittedly incomplete because many of those listed as missing subsequently turned out to have been killed), it looks as if the war ended with the net body count turning back in Germany's favour after the horrendous losses of the spring offensive. These figures suggest that in August, September and October 1918 the Germans were achieving a killing surplus over the British rivalled only by the period of the Battle of the Somme.

J. E. B. Seely, who commanded the Canadian Cavalry brigade, summed up the absurdity of attrition when he remarked in 1930: 'Some foolish people on the allied side thought that the war would be ended on the Western Front by killing off the Germans. Of course this method could only succeed if we killed a great many more of them than we lost ourselves.'[60] That only proved impossible when, as a result of Ludendorff's offensive, the British were forced to defend. Their own offensive operations, with remarkably few exceptions, tended to inflict

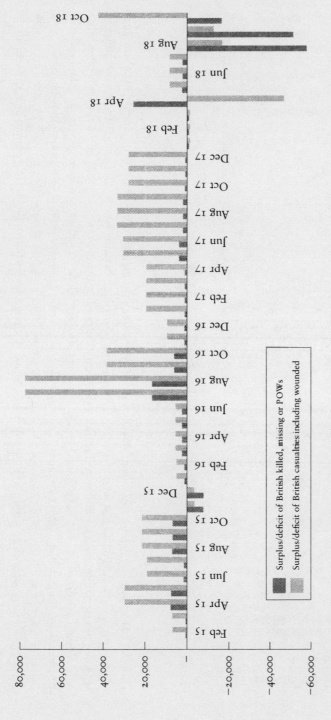

Figure 12 The 'net body count': British casualties minus German casualties in the British sector of the Western Front, 1915–1918

Note: The figures are not always for individual months, so in a number of cases average monthly figures are given. This may understate the impact of certain military events in particular months.

Source: War Office, *Statistics of the British Military Effort*, pp. 358–62.

Legend within figure:
- Surplus/deficit of British killed, missing or POWs
- Surplus/deficit of British casualties including wounded

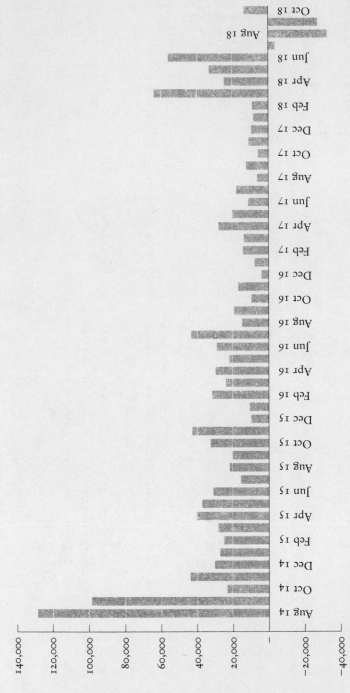

Figure 13   The 'net body count': British and French soldiers permanently incapacitated minus German, August 1914–July 1918 (Western Front)   Note: For August–October 1918 German permanently incapacitated figures are for the British sector only, so the extent of German losses is understated. Typically, the German official statistics from the 1930s omit the months after July. Deist, 'Military Collapse', p. 203, gives a total for dead and wounded from mid-July to 11 November of 420,000 plus 340,000 prisoners and missing, which implies average casualties of around 245,000 per month (August to October) plus 15,000 in November. However, the figures above also omit American permanent losses, which amounted to a total of 110,000 killed and 11,480 prisoners, most of them sustained in precisely this period. If these were included, the net body count against Germany in late 1918 would be reduced.

Sources: War Office, *Statistics of the British Military Effort*, pp. 253–65; Reichswehrministerium, *Sanitätsbericht*, vol. I, pp. 140–1; Guinard *et al., Inventaire*, vol. I, p. 213.

as many permanent losses on their own forces as on the enemy's, if not more. In short, the Germans achieved and maintained a higher level of military effectiveness in the crucial theatre for most of the war. This makes the possibility that they might have won the war, despite the economic odds against them, seem a good deal less fantastic.

EXCUSES

How can we account for the immense discrepancy in both effectiveness and efficiency between the Entente and Central Powers in the decisive war on land?

The most popular explanation still remains that the Entente generals were 'donkeys', characterized in the British case by 'a captious and jealous rigidity of outlook, a purblind psychology . . . as a consequence of their narrow education'.[61] As T. E. Lawrence memorably put it, 'the men were often gallant fighters, but their generals as often gave away in stupidity what they had gained in ignorance'.[62] Lloyd George was another who sneered at the generals' 'brains . . . cluttered with useless lumber, packed in every niche and corner. Some of it was never cleared out to the end of the war . . . they knew nothing except by hearsay about the actual fighting of a battle under modern conditions.'[63] Such views continue to inform modern writers such as Laffin, for whom the British generals were Blimpish 'butchers and bunglers'.[64] More academic writers have recently sought to refine the critique. The generals, it is argued, were slow to understand the nature of trench warfare; ordered attacks that were insufficiently prepared or supported by artillery and lacked clear objectives; continued them long after the chance of success had gone; sought to break through the German lines rather than inflict maximum casualties; and sought to gain ground, regardless of its tactical value, while at the same time failing to appreciate the value of ground suitable for artillery observation. According to Bidwell and Graham, the pre-war army lacked any real doctrine of warfare and failed to adapt tactics to the new technology of war;[65] a view which has been echoed by Travers.[66]

In defence of the much maligned 'brass hats', a number of explanations have been offered for the relatively high British casualties:

1. The British army had to attack while the Germans (and in Gallipoli the Turks) were able to defend. Modern firepower had driven soldiers

off the battlefield into entrenchments and dug-outs. With enough artillery and shells these defences could be breached, but such breaches could not be exploited. The very artillery that created the opportunity also took it away as the shells churned up the ground and therefore made it extremely difficult for the guns to be brought forward and the advance resumed under their protective fire. While attacks tended to get bogged down, enemy reserves could be quickly brought forward by rail. Terraine has likened the attacking army to a prizefighter with one leg in plaster: strong but sluggish.[67] It was the same nearly everywhere: in Fuller's words, 'it was the bullet, spade and wire which were the enemy on every front'.[68]

The other technical problem was poor command, control and communications.[69] In 1914 the BEF had yet to develop adequate means for air observation, aerial photography and signals communication. Maps were inaccurate. Communication networks stopped at the front line, so that as soon as troops left that point their position was unknown. During battle, despite elaborate precautions such as burying cables in triplicate along different routes, communications were more than likely to be cut by enemy shellfire. Generals therefore had to rely on fragmentary reports from runners.[70] It was not until 1918 that armies developed sophisticated signals services and had access to wireless sets. This flaw in communications technology cannot be overestimated as an explanation for high casualties on the attacking side.[71] As Holmes has put it, 'it was not primarily the growth of killing power that gave the Western Front its distinctive character: it was the fact that communications consistently lagged behind weaponry. It was always easier for a defender, driven back on his own communications, to reinforce his failure than it was for an attacker, his communications stretched across the abrasive edge of the battlefield, to reinforce his success.'[72]

2. The British were also repeatedly forced into premature offensives because of the exigencies of coalition warfare. The British Expeditionary Force would not have launched the premature offensives of 1915 had it not seemed (in Kitchener's words) 'doubtful how much longer [the Russian army] could withstand the German blows'.[73] He also warned the Cabinet that they 'could not without serious and perhaps fatal injury to the Alliance refuse the cooperation which Joffre expected'.[74] According to Esher in January 1915, 'the French are splendid but they cannot bear more than a certain amount of strain'.[75] It was not untypical that when the French cancelled an attack on Vimy Ridge which was

supposed to coincide with the British attack on Neuve Chapelle in March 1915, Sir John French went ahead anyway to prove his willingness to 'cooperate loyally and in the most cordial manner'.[76] Likewise, the date, time and place of the Somme offensive were decided by the French, not by Haig, who would rather have attacked in Flanders.

This continued into 1917. Third Ypres was justified by Charteris because of a fear that France might 'give way' if British troops were diverted to another sideshow (this time the Adriatic to support faltering Italy) as Lloyd George wished.[77] It was not until Messines (June 1917) that the British Army was able to take the strategic initiative, that is, to decide when and where to attack. But independence of action was not really the way to win the war. What was needed was effective co-ordination of Allied efforts. Only in the face of the German offensives of 1918 did the British army accept the consequences of a continental commitment: unity of command under the French.[78] Even then problems persisted; the Americans under Pershing, for example, strongly resisted amalgamation under Pétain, spurning the chance to be guided by more experienced commanders.[79]

3. Unlike the German army, the British army was not designed for a continental war. In June 1919 Haig recalled that 'we went into this war lacking preparation for it . . . Throughout the whole process of the war we were making desperate efforts to catch up.'[80] For example: only one divisional staff had been maintained during peacetime, partly because of financial restrictions, but mostly because there was no intention to have any tiers of command between GHQ and the BEF.[81] Allenby, who was in command of the Cavalry Division, found that he only had two staff officers. He was given others but they were inexperienced.[82] British generals were therefore forced to improvise from the beginning.

The trouble was – and here the excuses must stop – that the entire culture of the British regular army militated against effective improvisation. The command structure was based on obedience to superiors and suspicion of subordinates; men could still advance according to their connections; and commanders could still be 'unstuck' by personal quarrels.[83] This could have serious repercussions: when Haig questioned Rawlinson's original Somme plan, the latter felt unable to stand his ground, with the result that Haig was able to insist on the suicidal breakthrough objective. As Rawlinson said, 'It is a gamble to go for an unlimited offensive but D. H. wants it and I am prepared to undertake anything within reason [*sic*].'[84] An Army Commander did not presume to correct the Commander-in-Chief, even when tens of thousands of men's lives were at stake.[85] Similar inhibitions existed at every level. Orders were issued at the top and fed down the line; there was little traffic in the other direction. As a result, officers, NCOs and men grew accustomed to 'waiting for orders'. In battle, as J. M. Bourne has remarked, 'when German shelling interrupted communications paralysis set in'. To adapt the not inappropriate language of industrial organization, this was 'line management', and it provided no mechanism by which the views of 'junior line managers' could be relayed back to head office.[86] Partly for this reason, the proponents of a more technocratic approach made slow headway against the traditional believers in war as a moral rather than material contest.[87] Too much emphasis was placed on morale, courage and discipline; not enough on fire-power and tactics.[88]

Nor did these problems abate as the old army was diluted by new men; rather the reverse. Bigger meant more bureaucratic. As Charteris put it, the army became responsible for:

Food supply, road and rail transport, law and order, engineering, medical work, the Church, education, postal service, even agriculture, and for a population bigger than any single unit of control (except London) in England . . . Add to that, the purely military side of the concern . . . The amazing thing is that with the exception of the transportation and the postal services, every particular part of the organization is controlled by regular soldiers . . . Each department is under its own head, and all the heads take their orders from one man only – the Chief. He does not see any of the heads of these great departments more than once a day, and then very rarely for more than half an hour at a time . . .[89]

Command itself, as Martin van Creveld has argued, became bureaucratic: 'the conduct of war had reached back from the battlefield into the factory and into the office' and imperceptibly 'the methods of the office and of the factory' filtered back 'to dominate the battlefield'.[90] According to Dominic Graham, it was precisely this organizational tendency which made the BEF's learning curve so lamentably flat between Neuve Chapelle and Cambrai.[91] Thus, while the BEF learned how to fight defensively, it was slow to discern how best to attack, failing to co-ordinate the different arms at its disposal, failing to master the interplay of fire and movement.[92] No one troubled to spell out in the manuals the plain principle that 'fire tactics were concerned with the progressive occupation of advantageous fire-positions and their effective use by all arms to inflict casualties on the enemy', without of course incurring comparable casualties of one's own.[93]

Furthermore, weapons such as artillery and tanks tended to be seen as mere accessories to the infantry rather than component parts of a combined system. A classic illustration often cited is the fact that it took thirteen months for a prototype tank to be accepted by the War Office, another seven months for tanks to be deployed in combat (at Flers–Courcelette in September 1916) and fourteen more months for an attack to be made with significant numbers. This despite the fact that the component parts of the tank – armour plating, the internal combustion engine and caterpillar track system – were all available from around 1900, as was the concept of armoured fighting vehicles. And even once tanks were made available, army commanders tended to ignore expert advice as to how they should be employed.[94] Even after Amiens, Haig rejected the idea of mechanical warfare, continuing to believe that manpower was the key to victory.[95] Conservatism at the top was compounded by the phenomenon of 'cap badge loyalty', which encouraged officers and men to identify with their battalion, rather than the brigade or the division.[96]

British use of artillery provides other, more telling evidence of deficiency; for artillery was in many ways the key to a war of great sieges.[97] From 1914 until the Somme the British were simply out-gunned, lacking powerful enough guns and adequate stocks of shells (High Explosive was in especially short supply).[98] Artillery was primarily 'observed', which meant that gunners could only hit targets they could see (this precluded both indirect and counter-battery fire); there was little use of maps; and batteries were dispersed, making concentration of fire difficult. The Battle of Loos in September 1915 saw around 60,000 British casualties when infantry were ordered to attack without enough artillery support. Only gradually did it dawn that artillery and infantry had to co-ordinate their efforts.

By the end of 1915 British gunners had learned about indirect fire and the first use was being made of aerial reconnaissance. More and more heavy guns (especially howitzers and larger-calibre guns) appeared, as did vast quantities of ammunition to cope with rising rates of fire. Artillery was centrally controlled for the initial bombardment. The first experiments were made with lifting barrages. However, these few advances pale into insignificance alongside the inefficiencies which characterized the Somme offensive. Entente commanders now believed that since the artillery's aim was to destroy the enemy's defences, bombardments should be protracted. In Sir John French's words, 'If sufficient ammunition is forthcoming, a way can be blasted through the [enemy] line.'[99] Or, as Pétain put it, 'Artillery now conquers a position and the infantry occupies it.' Weight of shell was now supposed to make up for any lack in accuracy. Yet Haig's decision to bombard the second German line as well as the first effectively halved the weight of the bombardment. More seriously, ammunition was found to be defective (up to 30 per cent did not explode) and a quarter of guns were simply worn out through overuse. There were still too few High Explosive shells, as well as numerous technical shortcomings: calibration was a matter of guesswork, map-surveying was inaccurate, poor communications hindered observed fire and counter-battery work was ineffective. In addition, the British fire plan was too rigid.[100] Worst of all, the bombardments of 1916 not only failed in their primary task of destruction (Haig underestimated the strength of the German defences), but hindered the subsequent infantry advance. It was the same story at Arras in April 1917, where the destruction was much more efficient and the initial success much greater, but where the ground was so broken up that the guns could not be brought up quickly enough and the breach was stemmed. The need for shorter bombardments to ensure surprise was still not yet realized, while adhesion to a rigid fireplan prevented the exploitation of early success.[101] Messines saw further technical improvements, not least the devastating explosion of nineteen mines under the German positions and the successful creeping barrage; but (as noted above) British casualties were still 2,000 more than German. The short, concentrated bombardment before the tank attack at Cambrai was another step in the right direction; but as so often there were too few reserves to resist the German counter-attack.

By comparison, the German army was a model of operational and tactical proficiency. Michael Geyer has argued that Ludendorff's reorganization of the German army in 1916 was the watershed in the military response to the First World War, displacing 'the well-tried hierarchical control of men over men in favour of a functional organization of violence'.[102] Where the British merely grafted the new weapons on to their existing unchanging concepts and remained preoccupied with manpower, the Germans shaped tactics around new technology.[103]

The classic German advances were the development of 'defence in depth' (in fact pirated from a captured French document);[104] Colonel Georg Bruchmüller's development of the 'creeping barrage' and the 'hurricane' bombardment;[105] and the development of the stormtroops (*Stosstruppen*), specially trained, highly mobile and powerfully armed units whose job it was to infiltrate and disrupt enemy lines. Seen at their most effective in the spring of 1918, these were already in existence as early as August 1915.[106]

It was the defence in depth which most impressed post-war British analysts like G. C. Wynne. In essence, the Germans replaced the system of a large line firing frontally with small groups firing at the attacker's flanks.[107] The front line (which was the prime target for enemy artillery fire) was weakly held, but behind that there was a zone of continuous defence, so that the 'line' included scattered outposts and machine-gun nests and strength was reserved for the counter-attack. When used to repel Allied offensives in 1917, the effect was impressive.[108] It was not until early 1918 that the Allies began to imitate the defence in depth, and it is arguable that they never really mastered it. A similar principle, applied to the attack, underlay stormtroop tactics: once again, the emphasis was on small groups acting with mobility and flexibility.

These German tactical strengths were rooted in a distinctive military culture. According to Dupuy, the German military establishment had 'discovered the secret of *institutionalizing* military excellence'.[109] Martin Samuels likewise points to a distinctively German philosophy of combat, which acknowledged its fundamentally chaotic character.[110] This in turn influenced the way command structures evolved. The Germans favoured 'directive command' (task-oriented and decentralized decision making, flexible at all levels) whereas the British preferred 'restrictive control', which deliberately discouraged initiative.[111] Differences in training also followed logically from this. German 'chaos theory' demanded a high level of training to promote adaptability; the British approach required only obedience. Moreover, the German officer did not stop learning on obtaining his commission; the officer corps was meritocratic, and dud officers were ruthlessly weeded out.[112] This line of argument has been further developed by the work of Gudmundsson on stormtroop tactics, which (he argues) depended for their success on the existence of a 'self-educating officer corps'.[113]

Before the war, critics of Prussian militarism used to sneer that it inculcated in soldiers *Kadavergehorsamkeit*, zombie-like obedience.

Lord Northcliffe once fatuously boasted that the British soldier had a greater sense of initiative than the German, thanks to the British traditions of individualism and team sports. Nothing could be further from the truth. In reality, it was the largely amateur British army which was characterized by excessive rigidity in its command structure and a culture of unthinking obedience below the NCO level – and when officers and NCOs were incapacitated, of unthinking inertia ('If you knows of a better 'ole . . .'). By contrast, the Germans throughout the war encouraged their men to take the initiative on the battlefield, recognizing (as Clausewitz had taught) that 'friction' and breakdowns in communications would quickly make detailed operational plans obsolete.

UNDEFEATED IN THE FIELD?

Apologists for Britain's war effort invariably remind us that 'Britain *did* win the war' (or was on the winning side). By the same token, few historians of Germany have patience with the claim, famously expressed by Friedrich Ebert, soon to be the first President of the Weimar Republic, that their army had been undefeated in the field.[114] Yet the evidence above makes it easy to see why so many Germans believed this.

How then are we to explain the German defeat in 1918? According to Paddy Griffith, there is a pleasing answer to this question, namely that the BEF won the war because – eventually – it got better at fighting it. By 1918 the British had at last worked out how to use tanks, aircraft, armoured cars, cavalry, and above all to co-ordinate their infantry and artillery. At the same time, the infantry had learned new tactics, such as advancing in small groups in diamond formations or behind tanks, and had incorporated new forms of mobile firepower (hand grenades, Stokes trench mortars, rifle grenades and Lewis guns).[115]

The artillery too got better. Eventually it was appreciated that attacks had to be supported by a creeping barrage if they were to succeed, and that more use had to be made of aerial reconnaissance, field survey and intelligence. Mortars were used to cut wire and machine-gun barrages were introduced. Elaborate fireplans made the best use of all available guns. Guns were better concentrated.[116] The importance of counter-battery fire was also acknowledged, as well as the use of smoke shells to protect the infantry. Accurate calibration, better positioning of guns, survey, flash and sound spotting enabled accurate predicted fire without preliminary registering, which had previously acted as a mere trailer for intended attacks. Above all, the prolonged inaccurate bombardment was replaced by the hurricane bombardment over the entire depth of the defensive zone. At last it was understood that the artillery's prime task was not to obliterate but to neutralize enemy defences and guns long enough for the infantry to advance. This not only minimized physical disruption to the terrain, but also restored the element of surprise, which had hitherto been wholly lacking in most British offensives.

The culmination of these advances, so it is argued, was the triumph of the 'Hundred Days' in 1918. Attacks like Beaumont-Hamel and above all Amiens saw the British successfully combining infantry, artillery, tanks and planes in ways which military historians regard as prefiguring the Second World War. Bailey has gone so far as to speak of 'the birth of . . . the Modern Style of Warfare', a change so revolutionary 'that the burgeoning of armour, airpower and the arrival of the Information Age since then amount to no more than complements to it'.[117] Griffith has called it 'a veritable revolution in technique'.[118] Thus Terraine seems vindicated: 'The enemy was fundamentally outmatched by the British weapons system.'[119]

The possible flaw in this argument is that the German retreat in the summer of 1918 never became a rout. On the contrary: the Germans continued to be highly effective at killing the enemy. To be sure, the months August–October 1918 saw the net body count turn against the Germans for the first time in the war: altogether around 123,300 more Germans than British were recorded as killed, missing or taken prisoner in the British sector of the Western Front in those months. However, a very high proportion of German casualties were men who surrendered. The official British statistics, though imperfect, show that the net kill count was still in the Germans' favour, to the tune of around 35,300 men. By that measure, the nadir of the German army's fortunes was not August but April 1918, when the British estimated a surplus of German over British killed of around 28,500.

We must, of course, treat these figures with caution, as many of those recorded as missing in the decisive months of 1918 had in fact been killed. But the evidence seems to suggest strongly that the key to the Allies' victory was not an improvement in their ability to kill the enemy, but rather a sudden increase in the willingness of German soldiers to surrender. As will be argued in the next two chapters, it cannot safely be assumed that this decline in German morale was necessarily due to the improvements in British tactics described above; there is at least a possibility that the decline in morale was an endogenous phenomenon. A similar point can be made about the Austro-Hungarian collapse on the Grappa and the Piave. Between 26 October and 3 November the Italians took 500,000 prisoners, but they inflicted only 30,000 battle casualties.[120] Was this because Marshal Diaz had revolutionized Italian tactics? It seems more likely that it was because Austro-Hungarian morale imploded as non-German soldiers ceased to be willing to fight for the moribund Habsburg Empire.

More detailed studies show the limits of Allied military success against the Germans. Rawling's study of the Canadian Corps reveals, not surprisingly, that it suffered its highest proportionate casualties at Ypres in 1915 and the Somme in 1916 – in other words, at the bottom of its tactical learning curve. However, there was no sustained improvement thereafter. The casualty rate at Vimy Ridge in 1917 was 16 per cent; at Passchendaele 20 per cent; at Amiens 13 per cent; at Arras 15 per cent; and at Canal du Nord 20 per cent – exactly what it had been at Passchendaele.[121]

The evidence of heavy losses in 1918 is even more obvious in the case of the American Expeditionary Force, an important part of the combined Allied force, but one which was too inexperienced to share in the supposed tactical revolution. It was commonly claimed at the time (and some people still believe it) that the Americans 'won the war'. In reality, the AEF suffered disproportionately large casualties, mainly because Pershing still believed in frontal assaults, dismissed British and French training as over-cautious, and insisted on maintaining outsized and unwieldy divisions. The American First Army's operations against the Hindenburg Line (the Kriemhilde Stellung) in September–October 1918 were old-fashioned and wasteful. It was not until the last week of October that the German defences were finally penetrated after a succession of frontal assaults which cost around 100,000 casualties (many of them caused by gas, which other armies had more or less learned how to deal with). Trask has concluded that 'the most important service of the AEF' was simply 'to appear in France'; they were more useful in relieving British and French troops in quiet sectors of the Front and in implying to the Germans the inexhaustible manpower available to the Allies.[122] If this was what made German soldiers decide to surrender, it was hardly a triumph of revolutionary tactics.

The Allied advance was in fact slowing down by the end of October 1918; as they neared their own *Heimat*, the resolve of German troops returned. Austen Chamberlain asked his wife: 'A year hence we shall have lost how many more men?'[123] Haig too seized the chance of an armistice with relief. As late as 19 October he told Henry Wilson: 'Our attack on the 17th inst. met considerable resistance, and . . . the enemy was not ready for unconditional surrender. In that case, there would be no armistice, and the war would continue for another year.'[124] As Lloyd George recalled, 'The military advice we obtained did not encourage us to expect an immediate termination of the war. All our plans and preparations . . . were therefore made on the assumption . . . that the War would certainly not conclude before 1919.'[125]

It was not Allied tactical superiority which ended the war, then: it was a crisis of German morale, and this can only partly be attributed to the exogenous force of Allied infantry and artillery. The key point to note is that those Germans who kept fighting still proved better at killing the enemy. It was those Germans who elected to surrender – or to desert, shirk or strike – who ended the war. No doubt they were influenced in their decision to do so by the improved fighting capability of the enemy; the events of 8 August outside Amiens truly were 'the greatest defeat the German Army had suffered since the beginning of the war'.[126] But what made the day truly black was the German High Command's *admission* of defeat. On 10 August Ludendorff offered the Kaiser his resignation, admitting that 'the martial spirit of some divisions leaves much to be desired'. Though he did not accept Ludendorff's offer, William II responded with uncharacteristic realism: 'I see that we must draw up a balance sheet, we are on the brink of solvency. The war must be ended.'[127] Three days later Ludendorff

reviewed the military situation, the condition of the Army and the position of our Allies, and explained that it was no longer possible to force the enemy to sue for peace by an offensive. The defensive alone could hardly achieve that object, and so the termination of the war would have to be brought about by diplomacy . . . the logical conclusion [was] that peace negotiations were essential.[128]

If that was how it seemed to both Germany's *de facto* ruler and her *de jure* ruler, it is little wonder their soldiers now began to surrender or otherwise give up the fight. It was not until 2 October that the Reichstag and the German public were formally made aware that the High Command wanted an armistice. It is nevertheless obvious that many ordinary soldiers sensed more than a month earlier that their leaders regarded the war as lost.

Yet it is now clear that the exhausted and ill Ludendorff was over-reacting. Just as Germany's war had begun with a nervous breakdown (Molke's) at the top, so it ended with one: Ludendorff's. A tired and sick man after the failure of his offensives, Ludendorff jumped to the conclusion that the army would collapse if he did not secure an armistice; it seems more likely that his desire for an armistice was what made it collapse. Haig believed that the German army was 'capable of retiring to its own frontiers and holding that line'.[129] That was also the view of Julian Bickersteth, an experienced front-line army chaplain, who wrote on 7 November (the day the armistice was signed):

The enemy ... is ... fighting a clever rear-guard action and I do not see how we can hope to get him moving any faster. The difficulties about our communications as we advance are appalling – with bridges blown up and roads ruined, our progress is of necessity very slow, and the enemy has plenty of time to get back and form new machine-gun posts, which cause us heavy casualties as we advance ... We all, except perhaps the Staff Officers who don't see anything of the fighting or the morale of the Germans, anticipate another six months of fighting at least.[130]

It was Ludendorff who delivered the fateful stab, and it was in the German front, not the back. To adapt Ernst Jünger's phrase (though he was referring to Langemark, and meant something rather different): 'The German met with a superior force: he encountered himself.'[131]

If November 1918 had witnessed a true Allied victory, British, French and American soldiers would have marched in triumph down Unter den Linden. That, after all, was what Pershing, Poincaré and many others wanted to see. The main reason it did not happen was that Haig, Foch and Pétain doubted their armies had the strength to do it. The Allies had beaten the Bulgarians, the Austro-Hungarians and the Turks, no doubt; but they had not completely defeated the Germans. Instead it was German troops who marched to Berlin, in good if sombre order.

THE LOST VICTORY?

On 31 May 1918 Sir John du Cane, head of the British Mission at Foch's headquarters, had voiced to Sir Maurice Hankey his

considerable misgivings about the future . . . [He] was particularly anxious at the idea of our having two and a half million hostages on the Continent in the event of a French defeat. He envisages the possibility of the French Army being smashed and cut off from us, the enemy demanding as a condition of peace the handing over of all the ports from Rouen and Havre to Dunkirk, and, in the event of a refusal, the remorseless hammering of our Army by the whole German Army. He does not think we can get our Army away and considers that, if we wanted to go on with the war, we should have to face the prospect of over a million prisoners in France.[132]

These were not the views of one isolated Cassandra. Five days later, Sir Maurice Hankey, Sir Henry Wilson and Lord Milner met at 10 Downing Street to discuss 'the proposed evacuation of Ypres and Dunkirk' and 'the possibility of withdrawing the whole army from France if the French crack'. Milner's view as late as 31 July was that 'we shall never thrash the Boches'.[133]

Events proved these views too pessimistic; but they attest to the fact that a German victory in the First World War seemed a not unrealistic possibility. The Central Powers had defeated Serbia (in 1915), Rumania (in 1916) and Russia (in 1917). They had very nearly defeated Italy too. The defeat of France and Britain in 1918 thus looked far from inconceivable; after all the Germans came within forty miles of Paris that May. And all this despite an immense inferiority in economic resources. This achievement was primarily due to the tactical excellence of the German army.

In the light of the well-worn criticisms of German strategy, it is therefore tempting to pose another counter-factual question. Were there alternative strategies Germany could have pursued after war had broken out which might have delivered victory? A number suggest themselves.

Some historians have implied that the old *Ostaufmarsch* plan for an initial concentration on defeating Russia in 1914 would have been preferable to the Schlieffen Plan. However, it can be argued that the Schlieffen Plan was not designed to win a *Blitzkrieg*, but merely to give Germany the strongest defensible position for a protracted war;[134] in those terms, it was relatively successful. It should also be remembered that the Germans were hugely successful in killing Frenchmen in the opening months of the war: few armies in history have sustained so many casualties in so few weeks and survived.

More credible is the argument that Falkenhayn erred in attacking at Verdun: it would have been better to have maintained a defensive posture in the West and concentrated on Russia. However, once the British and French stepped up their production of guns and shells, defence turned out to be not a great deal less costly than attack. It is far from clear that the Germans would have been better off sitting tight and waiting for the British and French to commit suicide by attacking. Historians who ridicule the pre-war 'cult' of the offensive have tended to overlook the point that defending as the Germans had to at the Somme genuinely was more demoralizing than attacking, and not much less costly in terms of life and limb.[135] In any case, victory over Russia in 1917–18 created almost as many problems as it solved. To have ensured the maximum concentration of force in the West, the Germans would have needed to resist the temptation to which they succumbed in 1918, to attempt large-scale expansion in Eastern Europe.

Similarly, the arguments against the use of unrestricted submarine warfare overlook the fact that without it Britain would have been able to import even *more* goods and munitions from across the Atlantic. And it was only a mistake if it can be shown that Germany could not have won the war before the Americans reached France in sufficient numbers to guarantee Allied victory.

The crucial question may therefore be: Should Ludendorff have resisted the temptation to attack in the spring of 1918? With the wisdom of hindsight, this is an easy argument to make. Yet there was nothing wrong with his diagnosis on 11 November 1917 that 'our general situation requires that we should strike at the earliest moment, if possible at the end of February or the beginning of March, before the Americans can throw strong forces into the scale. We must beat the British.'[136] There were only 287,000 Americans in France in March 1918, of which only three divisions were in the line. By November 1918 there were 1,944,000. On the other hand, the French army had shrunk from 2,234,000 in July 1916 to 1,668,000 in October 1918, though the Germans were also well below their peak strength. No doubt Ludendorff erred in diverting his attack southwards to separate the British and the French; perhaps two converging attacks on Flanders and Péronne would have been better. However, the real mistakes came after Ludendorff had realized that he could not shatter enemy resistance completely (5 April). That was the moment to relinquish Belgium for the sake of a negotiated peace; not to launch yet more probing offensives.[137] And when these failed (as they were bound to), Ludendorff should not have sought an armistice so hurriedly; instead of attacking at Reims on 15 July, the Germans should have been withdrawing to the Hindenburg Line.[138]

Finally, it was a miscalculation to endorse Woodrow Wilson's Fourteen Points, as the Germans effectively did when appealing to him for an end to the hostilities. Morale both at home and at the Front would almost certainly have been fortified by the knowledge that France's military leaders, industrialists and radical nationalists had repeatedly called for the separation of the left bank of the Rhine from Germany, if not the complete dismemberment of the Reich, to be a French war aim. This was no secret; such proposals had appeared in the pages of right-wing papers like the *Echo de Paris* and *Action Française*: for example, Charles Maurras called for the complete dissolution of the Reich in a series of articles in the latter in late 1916. His proposals bore a close resemblance to the plan drawn up for Joffre in the same year by Colonel Dupont of his Headquarters Staff, which envisaged not only the return of Alsace-Lorraine to France but also the annexation of the Saar coal basin and two chunks of Baden (at Kehl and Germersheim); the detachment of the Rhineland and its conversion into a French satellite or group of satellites; the enlargement of Belgium, which would exchange her neutral status for dependence on France; the dismemberment of Prussia; and the dissolution of the Reich into nine small states. Austria–Hungary was also to be broken up. Even the minimal programme adopted by Aristide Briand's government in October 1916 envisaged the detachment and neutralization of the Rhineland.[139] To stop this there seems little doubt that many German soldiers would have fought on; what they refused to do was to fight on while their masters haggled for an armistice.

II

'Maximum Slaughter at Minimum Expense': War Finance

FINANCE AND WAR

Bertrand Russell once defined the objective of war economics as 'maximum slaughter at minimum expense'. By this yardstick too it is tempting to say that the Central Powers 'won' the First World War.

In order to grasp the sheer scale of the Central Powers' superiority in waging war it is necessary to consider not only military effectiveness but also economic efficiency. Chapter 9 followed previous economic historians by considering the war economies of the combatants in more or less complete isolation from the actual business of destruction. This, of course, rather misses the point. As Russell said, the ultimate objective of all wartime economic activity was slaughter of the enemy. Any assessment of efficiency in wartime must therefore take that slaughter into account, just as any assessment of military effectiveness must take account of the expenses incurred. In order to do this in a meaningful way we must now turn to war finance.

As we have seen, despite their piecemeal efforts to allocate physical resources by fiat, most states even by the end of the war were still running their economies principally through the market mechanism and relying on regulation of prices to check its more egregious distortions. Nowhere did the state act as if it owned materials, companies or men (as the Soviet Union could in the Second World War): everything had to be paid for. That meant that traditional war finance was as crucial to economic mobilization as any of the more or less bureaucratic devices for the allocation of resources discussed in Chapter 9.

It had often been asserted before 1914 that a war between the great European powers would be unaffordable; any attempt to wage one would simply end in financial collapse. When war did break out, the immediate economic impact seemed to confirm these predictions (see Chapter 7). On 10 August 1914 Keynes excitedly explained to Beatrice Webb that

he was quite certain that the war could not last more than a year ... The world, he explained, was enormously rich, but its wealth was, fortunately, of a kind which could not be rapidly realised for war purposes: it was in the form of capital equipment for making things which were useless for making war. When all the available wealth was used up – which he thought would take about a year – the Powers would have to make peace.[1]

Such sloppy thinking was commonplace in London in 1914. Asquith assured George Booth that the war would be over 'in a few months'.[2] Sir Archibald Murray, chief of the General Staff of the British Expeditionary Force, assured Esher that the war would last 'three months if everything goes well, and perhaps eight months if things do not go satisfactorily. Beyond that he thinks it impossible to feed the armies in the field and the populations concerned, and the financial strain would be more than Europe could bear.'[3] It was as if they had all read their Bloch and Angell.

Needless to say, however, the financial crisis of August 1914 did not render the First World War impossible. An intelligent American diplomat named Lewis Einstein had foreseen this as early as January 1913. In his article 'The Anglo-German Rivalry and the United States', published in the *National Review*, he astutely argued against the view that financial collapse would soon stop a war:

A more likely possibility would be that of a contest long drawn out ... wherein neither [side] could obtain decisive advantage. In spite of the paper proof that a lengthy war presents today an economic impossibility, there is no practical evidence to substantiate this theory, and there are distinguished economists who believe that the modern system of credit is peculiarly adapted to facilitate the prolongation of war.[4]

This was spot on. Kitchener made the same point in August 1914, much to the alarm of his more Panglossian colleagues. The war, he warned Esher, could last for 'two or three years at least' because 'no financial pressure has ever yet stopped a war in progress'.[5] Unprecedented though the costs of the war were in nominal terms, European taxpayers and, more importantly, the international capital and money markets were well able to sustain some three years of slaughter before the sort of collapse which Bloch had predicted finally came.

But did it come, as has often been claimed, to Germany? Certainly, economic historians have long portrayed German war finance between 1914 and 1918 in a far from flattering light, blaming it for 'sky-high' inflation.[6] The principal criticism has been that the government did not raise direct taxes sufficiently and relied too heavily on inflationary forms of borrowing.[7] Even Theo Balderston, in an illuminating comparison of British and German finance, still starts from the assumption that it is German failure to control inflation which needs to be explained. Balderston convincingly argues that, in fact, Germany did not finance a substantially smaller share of wartime public spending by taxation than did Britain. But his conclusion is nevertheless concerned with a more subtle German deficiency: it was (among other things) the relative incapacity of the German financial markets to absorb short-term government debt which led to the growth of a much bigger monetary overhang in Germany than in Britain.[8] It seems not implausible to link this monetary overhang to the alleged problem of German administrative inefficiency discussed in the previous chapter. Suppressed inflation – held in check only by a complex system of price controls – led to the development of a black market. This, so it is argued, worsened an already existing problem of resource misallocation, contributing to that decline in efficiency alleged for the German economy as a whole.

The story of German war finance can therefore be told along the following doleful lines. The war cost most than even the pessimists had expected. Including the communes and social insurance system, total public spending rose from around 18 per cent of net national product before the war to 76 per cent at its peak in 1917.[9] Only a limited proportion of this expenditure was met out of taxation.[10] The failure of the government to impose higher direct taxation attested to the powerful political position of business; for it was business, and especially industry, which made the biggest gains in income and wealth during the war. Typical was the resistance to the turnover tax (*Umsatzsteuer*), a flat-rate levy on all business activity introduced in June 1916. Instead, the bulk of spending was financed by borrowing; and, as Germany was only able to borrow a limited amount abroad, the greater part of the burden of borrowing fell on the German capital market. However, as the public sector deficit spiralled, the level of borrowing exceeded the public's willingness to lend long to the government. By November 1918 the Reich's floating debt had reached 51.2 billion marks, 34 per cent of the total Reich debt.[11] High levels of public borrowing in turn led to rapid monetary expansion following the (illegal) suspension of cash payments by the Reichsbank on 31 July 1914. Legislation on 4 August created the potential for unlimited monetary growth through a number of modifications to the Reichsbank's reserve rule.[12] Thereafter cash in circulation grew at an annual average rate of 38 per cent.[13] Monetary expansion led in turn to inflation, though this was less than might have been expected thanks to controls on prices.[14] However, price controls distorted the market when they created artificial differentials,[15] leading to the development of black markets for goods in demand and exacerbating shortages on the official market.[16] This growing overhang of frustrated purchasing power in turn reduced economic efficiency, so driving Germany into a downward spiral towards internal collapse and defeat.

The obverse of this argument is the contention that Britain's financial superiority assured her of victory. That was certainly Lloyd George's view. As Chancellor of the Exchequer he had begun the war with a nasty fright when, as we have seen, the acceptance houses had come close to collapse and the clearing banks had attempted to bounce the Bank of England into a full suspension of gold convertibility. (This would have allowed them to supply their clients with liquidity at a rate lower than Bank rate.) The decision to impose a moratorium and an extended Bank Holiday saved the acceptance houses, but despite the pleas of the clearing banks the Treasury and Bank of England preferred to follow post-1844 convention and to avoid suspension by any means. The compromise reached was that convertibility should be maintained but Bank rate lowered by a further 1 per cent. A week later the acceptance market was relieved by the decision that the Bank would discount all bills accepted before 4 August at the new lower rate. This was a success and Lloyd George's self-confidence as Chancellor received an enormous boost as a result.

As in 1909, when the City had predicted ruin if the People's Budget were passed, Lloyd George had got the better of the bankers. A sense of the hubris this inspired can be gathered from a passage in his famous speech in the Queen's Hall a few weeks later: 'Have you any £5 notes about you? (Laughter and Applause) . . . If you have burn them; they are only scraps of paper . . . What are they made of? Rags . . . What are they worth? The whole credit of the British Empire. (Loud Applause)'[17] It was generally assumed that the whole credit of the Empire guaranteed victory. 'I think,' he told another audience that September, that cash is going to count much more than we can possibly imagine at the moment.'[18] Even Keynes, who later became the arch-pessimist on this subject, began the war with the same optimism. In January 1915 he assured his friends Leonard and Virginia Woolf: 'We are bound to win – and in great style too, having at the last minute applied all our brains' – he meant his own – 'and our wealth to the problem.'[19]

THE COST OF KILLING

Yet the now familiar problem here presents itself. Why, if German war finance was so defective, did the Entente powers, backed by the superior British financial system, take so long to win the war?

The most striking point of all about the financing of the First World War is that it cost much more – roughly twice as much – to win it than to lose it. Various attempts have been made to compute the cost of the war to all combatants in dollar terms. According to one set of calculations, the total of 'war expenditure' (i.e. the increase in public spending over and above the pre-war 'norm') amounted to $147 billion for the Allied powers (France, Britain, the British Empire, Italy, Russia, the United States, Belgium, Greece, Japan, Portugal, Rumania and Serbia), compared with a figure of $61·5 billion for the Central Powers (Germany, Austria–Hungary, Turkey and Bulgaria).[20] Another estimate arrives at figures of $140 billion and $83 billion.[21] My own rough calculations – summarised in Table 36 – confirm these orders of magnitude: Britain ($45 billion) spent nearly half as much again as Germany ($32 billion).[22]

In relying principally on borrowing to raise these huge sums, Germany was acting no differently from the other combatants. As Balderston has shown, when the states' budgets are added to the Reich's – as they should be when making comparisons with non-federal states like Britain, France and Russia – the large differences identified by Knauss and others are much reduced.[23] While Germany financed between 16 and 18 per cent of public spending by taxation during the war, that was not significantly less than Britain (23–6 per cent). Nor was British tax policy

Table 36   Total expenditures, 1914–1918 (millions of dollars)

	Germany (Reich and states)	Britain	France	Russia	Italy	USA
1914/15	2,920	2,493	1,994	1,239	979	761
1915/16	5,836	7,195	3,827	3,180	1,632	742
1916/17	5,609	10,303	6,277	4,585	2,524	2,086
1917/18	8,578	12,704	7,794	2,774	3,012	13,791
1918/19	9,445	12,611	10,116		4,744	18,351
Total	32,388	45,307	30,009	11,778	12,892	35,731

Notes: Russian figure for 1914 for last five months only; for 1917 for 8 months only. Italian and American figures for year ending 30 June; others for year ending 31 March. Dollar figures arrived at using appropriate average dollar exchange rates.

Sources: Balderston, 'War Finance', p. 225; Bankers Trust Company, *French Public Finance*, pp. 119–23; Apostol, Bernatzky and Michelson, *Russian Public Finance*, p. 217.

significantly more progressive than German: the effective income tax rate rose about equally for top and middle earners during the war and excess profits taxes were only levied on businesses in Britain (whereas in Germany individuals had to pay as well).[24] On average, 13.9 per cent of German wartime expenditures were met out of direct taxation; the British figure was 18.2 per cent – hardly an earth-shattering difference.[25] Indeed, German tax policy compares quite favourably with French, Italian and Russian. Prussia actually had, like most of the larger German states, an effective income tax before the war began, whereas the income tax finally passed in France on the eve of the war did not come into effect until 1916 and yielded relatively little.[26] The French war profits tax was already relatively light and easy to avoid.[27] On average, the French met only 3.7 per cent of total wartime expenditure out of direct taxation, a figure even worse than that for Italy (5.7 per cent).[28] Similarly, the illusory quality of revenue from the 1917 German coal tax (much of which was in fact paid from the extraordinary Reich budget) was a minor problem compared with the muddles of Russian wartime taxation. As we have seen, one of the Tsarist regime's principal sources of revenue was the vodka monopoly; but the government abolished the trade in spirits for the duration of the war, so the money (unlike the populace) dried up. The income tax and excess profits duty which were introduced in 1916 yielded together 186 million roubles: 'less than enough to pay for a week-end of war'.[29] In short, all the warring states ran very large deficits, adding substantially to their respective national debts (see Table 37).

Once again, the striking thing is not so much that German deficits were slightly larger in relation to expenditure than those of the Entente powers, but how much more the Entente powers had to borrow in absolute terms. Table 38 shows that in nominal terms the French national debt rose by a factor of five, the German national debt (again, for the Reich and the states combined) by a factor of eight and the British by a factor of eleven between 1914 and 1919. The equivalent figures for Italy are five and for the United States nineteen. Between August 1914 and October 1917 Russia's debt increased by a factor of four.[30] Such figures, however, are slightly misleading, partly because some states (like the US) began the war with relatively small debts, and partly because some debts were denominated in weaker currencies. For this reason, I have computed at the bottom of the table the value of the total net addition to the national debt in dollar terms by the end of the war. This shows that the real increase in Germany's national debt was less than half the increase in Britain's.

All countries therefore relied heavily on the willingness of their citizens to lend money to the war effort by buying war bonds. As we have seen, maintaining that willingness became one of the principal themes of war propaganda. The German poster discussed in Chapter

Table 37 *Government deficits as a percentage of total expenditures, 1914–1918*

	Hungary	Germany	Bulgaria	Britain	France	Russia	Italy	Rumania	Greece	USA
1914	−38.4	−73.5	−23.0	−61.3	−54.8	−57.0	−6.1	1.0	−55.0	−0.1
1915	−72.4	−94.4	−37.9	−79.8	−79.4	−63.0	−45.3	n/a	−41.0	−8.4
1916	−81.4	−92.7	−59.4	−75.0	−86.6	−67.0	−64.9	−63.0	5.0	6.7
1917	−74.6	−90.8	−65.3	−76.1	−86.1	−55.0	−69.6	−76.0	−26.0	−43.7
1918	−59.1	−93.8	−56.2	−69.2	−80.0	n/a	−70.2	−75.0	n/a	−71.2

Sources: Eichengreen, *Golden Fetters*, p. 75; Mitchell, *European Historical Statistics*, pp. 376–80, E. Morgan, *Studies in British Financial Policies*, p. 41; Apostol, Bernatzky and Michelson, *Russian Public Finance*, p. 220.

Table 38   National debts in millions of national currencies, 1914–1919

	Germany (Reich and states, marks)	Britain (£)	France (francs)	Italy (lire)	USA ($)
1914	22,043	650	32,800	15,719	1,338
1915	34,323	1,098	40,008	18,707	1,344
1916	57,477	2,124	58,465	26,146	1,225
1917	87,119	4,025	82,504	38,449	2,976
1918	125,523	5,802	114,200	59,518	12,244
1919	179,050	7,280	171,353	79,348	25,482
Difference (1919–1914)	157,007	6,630	138,553	63,629	24,144
Difference in dollars	*15,135*	*30,432*	*25,423*	*7,364*	*24,144*

Note: French figures for 1 January of each year, German and British for 31 March, Italian and American for 30 June. Dollar values arrived at using appropriate monthly rates.
Source: Balderston, 'War Finance', p. 227; Schremmer, 'Taxation and Public Finance', p. 470; Bankers Trust Company, *French Public Finance*, p. 139.

8 had its counterparts in all the combatant states. The following titles from the British war film *For the Empire* speak for themselves.

One Dreadnought costs £2,000,000, but we must win the war. Never mind the cost.

Three things are essential – money, men, munitions.

There are only two alternatives: either give your money or give your blood.

Damn the cost, we must win this war.[31]

The American Treasury Secretary William Gibbs McAdoo memorably declared in 1917: 'A man who can't lend his government $1.25 at the rate of 4 per cent interest is not entitled to be an American citizen.'[32] There was not a great deal to choose between the practicalities of war bond issues either. In Britain there were three War Loans, in 1914, 1915 and 1917, followed by a 'Victory Loan' in 1919.[33] In France there were four National Defence loans.[34] In Russia there were six war loans under the Tsar and a seventh 'Liberty Loan' under the Provisional Government;[35] the US also favoured the label 'Liberty Loans' as they encouraged citizens to lock up their money. The Germans' nine loans were more numerous than those of the Entente, but there is no reason to think they performed significantly worse.[36] In every country investors had to be tempted by slightly higher yields as the war went on, especially when the war was going badly: the decline of French subscriptions in late 1917 is a case in point.[37] The German system whereby war bonds could be used as collateral for loans from the State Loan Banks (*Darlehnskassen*), so that war bonds did not in practice soak up liquidity, had an exact parallel in Russia.[38] Much the same happened in France.[39]

Again, there was nothing unusual in the fact that Germany could only finance a limited proportion of this borrowing by selling long-term bonds. The fact that on average 32 per cent of the German debt was floating (short-term) between March 1915 and March 1918 whereas for Britain the figure was just 18 per cent reflects,[40] as Balderston has argued, structural differences in the nature of the Berlin and London financial markets; but it also reflects the fact that the British Treasury made large issues of medium-term paper. Around 31 per cent of the British national debt in December 1919 was made up of bonds due for redemption in between one and nine years.[41] By comparison with France, indeed, the German authorities were successful in selling their long-term bonds: only 19 per cent of the amount raised by borrowing during the war came from sales of long-term *rentes*, probably because France's long-term debt was already relatively large before the war began.[42] On average, 37 per cent of the French debt during the war was short-term (compared with 32 per cent for Germany); by March 1919 the French short-term debt was bigger in relative terms than the German (44 per cent of the total, as opposed to 42). Russia too was more reliant than Germany on short-term borrowing: by 23 October 1917 some 48 per cent of its total debt was in the form of short-term Treasury Bills.[43] Only the United States was able to fund its war deficits more or less exclusively by sales of long-dated bonds.[44]

THE DOLLAR SCARE

It is often assumed that foreign lending made a decisive difference to the outcome of the First World War. This is partly because of the histrionics which surrounded British financial negotiations with the United States, especially in the period between November 1916 and

April 1917, which may have led some writers to exaggerate the economic importance of American money to the Allied war effort.[45] The process of exaggeration can be traced back to John Maynard Keynes, who became one of the British Treasury's most influential advisers during the war. Keynes, as noted already, had started out an optimist about Britain's prospects. But his mood quickly changed, not least because of the pressure he came under from his Bloomsbury friends, who disapproved of the war more viscerally than he did. Though his work in the Treasury gratified his sense of self-importance, the war itself made Keynes deeply unhappy. Even his sex life went into a decline, perhaps because the boys he liked to pick up in London all joined up.[46] In September 1915, just eight months after predicting that German finance was 'crumbling', Keynes was warning that unless peace was achieved by the following April, there would be a 'catastrophe', as 'the expenditure of the succeeding months would rapidly render our difficulties insupportable'. When no catastrophe came – despite alarming threats of a prohibition on loans by Wilson following the introduction of blacklists of American firms selling to the Central Powers[47] – Keynes rescheduled his prophecy. In late 1916 he drafted a memorandum for the Chancellor, Reginald McKenna, which warned that 'by next June or earlier the President of the American Republic will be in a position if he wishes to dictate his own terms to us'.[48]

It is true that there were grounds for concern in late 1916, not least because of the mounting opposition of Germanophiles within the Federal Reserve Board to the way Britain was financing its burgeoning American overdraft; this culminated in a 'warning' to US investors not to invest in British Treasury bills.[49] However, as a *soi-disant* conscientious objector, Keynes had an interest in supporting the efforts of Woodrow Wilson to bring the war to a negotiated conclusion; and (as Sir Edward Grey pointed out on 28 November) financial pressure was clearly one way to do this.[50] In February 1917, after Britain had weathered a severe run on the Bank of England's gold reserve, Keynes tried again, claiming that Britain only had sufficient resources to carry on fighting for four weeks. Even after American entry into the war, he did not give up. On 20 July he drafted a memorandum for Bonar Law, threatening that 'the whole financial fabric of the alliance' would 'collapse in a matter not of months but of days'.[51] Wilson himself concluded the next day that England and France would soon be 'financially in our hands'.[52]

There is no doubt that it assisted Britain to be able to purchase essential war supplies in the United States at an over-valued exchange rate, shored up by loans raised on Wall Street. It would have been not only embarrassing but inflationary if the pound had slipped much below $4.70.[53] But it is too much to claim that a weakening of the pound, which was pegged at around $4.76 (2 per cent below par) for most of the war, would have been as fatal to the British war effort as Keynes claimed. It must be remembered that, although Britain borrowed more than $5 billion in the USA during the war, it did not end the war a net debtor, but remained a net creditor. In March 1919 Britain's external debts, primarily to the USA, totalled £1,365 million; but she was owed £1,841 million by her Allies and the Dominions and Colonies, leaving a net balance of nearly half a billion.[54] All that had happened was that Britain had used her own good credit rating (based initially on the large dollar holdings of British subjects) to borrow money in New York which she then lent on to her much less creditworthy allies. France too had borrowed from Britain and the US, while lending to Russia and others.[55] Nor should it be assumed that the Central Powers were somehow 'cut off' from the international capital market by the might of J. P. Morgan.[56] According to one estimate, around $35 million of the $2,160 million lent by the US to the combatant states before April 1917 went to the Central Powers.[57] From the point of view of prosecuting the war, it mattered less how many war bonds could be sold on Wall Street than how large a trade deficit could be financed by any means, and in that respect the Germans did surprisingly well despite the constraints of the blockade. A higher level of external finance certainly helped Britain and France to spend more on waging war than Germany and Austria–Hungary. The fact that some 18 per cent of Britain's war debt was held by foreigners at the end of the war speaks for itself. But external finance was no guarantee of victory: witness the defeat and default of Russia, despite the accumulation of debts to her allies totalling 7,788 million roubles (£824 million): no less than 30 per cent of the country's total wartime borrowings.[58]

What is really remarkable is that the Entente war effort should have come – in Keynes's eyes at least – to *depend* on American loans, when, as we have seen, the Entente had begun the war with such a massive financial advantage in its own right. The war had exposed the limits of British imperial power: those great accumulations of overseas assets with which Britain entered the war proved a much less firm financial cushion than had been expected, not least because (as George Booth noted): 'When one is forced to sell, one is a weak seller and the seller's position tempts the buyer to make the most of the situation. Many sales [of overseas assets] were made that were shown afterwards to have been at pathetically low valuations.'[59] On the other hand, by 1916 the British had the distinctive position of strength in relation to Wall Street which the big debtor always enjoys. By the beginning of 1917, J. P. Morgan was so committed to Britain and to sterling that a real crisis was well-nigh unthinkable; the 'state of elation' in Morgan's office when it was announced that the US was severing diplomatic relations with Germany may well be imagined:[60] it was Morgan as much as Britain which was bailed out in 1917. Thereafter the threat of a sterling crisis was no more or less than a stick with which the Americans sought to beat the British into accepting American diplomatic objectives.[61] As Wilson put it, the beauty of having financial leverage over Britain and France was that 'when the war is over we can force them to our way of thinking'.[62]

PAPER AND PRICES

Was Germany unique in allowing its money supply to grow rapidly during the war? Certainly not. All the combatant states altered the pre-war monetary rules, whether by informally suspending gold convertibility (Russia and Germany), restricting exports of gold (Russia, Germany, Britain and France), imposing temporary moratoriums on and then monetizing certain forms of debt (Britain), or creating new forms of paper legal tender (Britain and Germany).[63] The initial objective of these changes was to avoid a catastrophic monetary contraction. But once confidence had returned, the effect – in conjunction with high levels of short-term government borrowing and limited new taxation – was to inject liquidity on a large scale. The money supply ceased to be meaningfully related to central bank reserves of bullion. The resulting increase in note circulation (more sophisticated monetary indicators are unavailable for some combatant states) was certainly greater for Germany than for Britain, France and Italy. In Germany broad money grew by 285 per cent between 1913 and 1918, compared with 110 per cent in Britain. Taking annual averages for central bank note circulation in the same years, the increase for Germany was of the order of 600 per cent, compared with around 370 per cent for Italy and 390 per cent for France. However, the increases in note circulation were substantially larger for Austria–Hungary and Russia (see Table 39).

Inevitably, given the shortages of certain goods which coincided with this monetary expansion, inflation was a universal problem. Once again, Germany's wartime experience was far from exceptional. Wholesale prices actually rose less in Germany between 1914 and 1918 (105 per cent) than in Britain (127 per cent), France (233 per cent) or Italy (326 per cent), though the available cost-of-living indices suggest that consumer prices rose by about twice as much in Germany (204 per cent) as in Britain (110) or France (113). This still compares very favourably with Austria (1,062 per cent) (see Table 40).

But was it such a bad thing to allow prices to rise during the war? Not necessarily. As has often been pointed out, inflation (particularly

Table 39   Money supply figures (broad money and currency in circulation, millions of national currency)

	Broad Money (31 Dec.)		Currency in circulation (annual av.)					
	Germany (marks)	Britain (£)	Germany (marks)	Austria (crowns)	Britain (£)	France (francs)	Italy (lira)	Russia (roubles)
1913	17,233	1,154	1,958	2,405	29	5,665	1,647	
1914	19,514	1,329	2,018	2,405	36	7,325	1,828	2,321
1915	23,175	1,434	5,409	6,249	34	12,280	2,624	2,946
1916	29,202	1,655	6,871	8,352	35	15,552	3,294	5,617
1917	43,801	1,939	9,010	12,883	40	19,845	4,660	9,097
1918	66,359	2,429	13,681	24,566	55	27,531	7,751	27,900
Percentage increase 1913–1918	285	110	599	921	91	386	371	1,102

Notes: Broad money: For Germany I have used Holtfrerich's definition of M3 in his *German Inflation*; for Britain, Capie and Webber, *Survey of Estimates*.
Currency: Figure for Austria monthly average for July; for Russia, figures for 1 August 1914, and 1 January 1915–1918.
Sources: Balderston, 'War Finance', p. 237; Kindleberger, *Financial History*, p. 295; Bordes, *Austrian Crown*, pp. 46f.; Carr, *Bolshevik Revolution*, vol. II, pp. 144f.; Bresciani, *Economics of Inflation*, p. 164; Apostol, Bernatzky and Michelson, *Russian Public Finance*, p. 372.

Table 40   Cost-of-living indices (1914 = 100)

	Austria–Hungary	Germany	Britain	France	Russia	Belgium	USA
1914	100	100	100	100	100	100	100
1915	158	125	125	120	146	156	98
1916	336	165	161	135	199	328	109
1917	671	246	204	163	473	746	143
1918	1,162	304	210	213		1,434	164

Sources: Maddison, *Capitalist Development*, pp. 300f.; E. Morgan, *Studies in British Financial Policy*, p. 284; Fontaine, *French Industry*, p. 417; Stone, *Eastern Front*, p. 287.

at this level and over this period of time) acts as a form of tax, easily collected and not generally recognizable as such. One effect of currency depreciation was to reduce the real burden of the national debt and therefore the costs to taxpayers of interest payments. This is, of course, an important explanation of the lower cost of the war in dollar terms to Germany and Austria, whose currencies depreciated significantly against the dollar, particularly in the second half of 1918 when the defeat of the Central Powers seemed imminent. Nevertheless, it is important not to exaggerate the extent of this depreciation: the Russian and Italian currencies both fared worse (Figure 14).

All things considered, then, German war finance was hardly as 'disastrous' or 'pathetic' as has often been claimed. On the contrary, it can be regarded as something of a marvel that Germany was able to sustain its war effort for as long as it did when its financial resources were so much more limited than those of its enemies.

THE PRICE PER DEATH

When asked in 1917 when he thought the war would end, *The Times*'s war correspondent Charles à Court Repington replied:

Since nations counted money no more than pebbles on a beach, and all would probably repudiate in one form or another at the end of the war, there seemed no reason for stopping, especially as so many people were growing rich by the war; the ladies liked being without their husbands, and all dreaded the settlement afterwards, industrial, political, financial and domestic.[64]

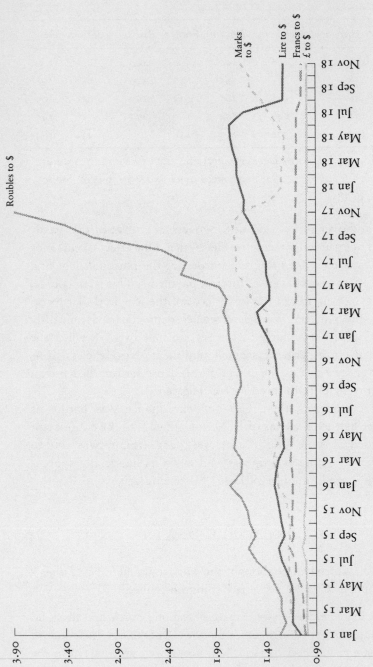

Figure 14 Exchange rates of the dollar, 1915–1918 (1913=1).

Notes: London prices except for the mark (New York).

Sources: E. Morgan, *Studies in British Financial Policy*, pp. 345–9; Statistisches Reichsamt, *Zahlen zur Geldentwertung*, p. 6; Bordes, *Austrian Crown*, p. 114.

For Repington, the only way to end the war was to inflict a decisive military defeat on the Central Powers. This was quite right. Only victory in the field would do. Given the Entente Powers' immense economic superiority, however, it was far from easy to explain why in 1917 that had still not been achieved. Indeed, many American observers began to think in the course of that year that it would never be achieved. Historians, like Keynes, have tended to be fixated on the exchange rate when considering transatlantic financial relations. Yet if one considers bond yields – an indicator, as we have seen, of considerably more importance in the pre-war world – a different picture emerges. Once Britain and France began to issue bonds in New York, they were exposed to precisely that scrutiny by investors to which other states had been exposed before the war when they borrowed in Paris and London. Figures for yields of one of the most important war-time issues, the 1915 Anglo-French loan (a $500 million loan to Britain and France),[65] reveal the extent of the crisis of confidence in the Allied war effort (Figure 15). It is fascinating to note that the nadir of American confidence in the Allied war effort came in December 1917 – not when one might have expected, in the spring of 1918.

Even more surprising, this was a crisis of confidence in France and Britain, not in the US war effort. Figure 16 shows that the end of 1917 saw a sharp widening of the gap between Anglo-French and American bond yields: on 14 December it reached a maximum of 3·8 per cent. This was no quirk of the New York market: the yield of consols in London reached a wartime peak of 4.92 in November 1917.[66]

Investors had good reason to be worried about the West European powers. Serbia and Rumania had been defeated; Italy was reeling after Caporetto (October 1917). In Russia the Bolshevik revolution in November heralded the complete victory of Germany on the Eastern Front. In France morale was at its nadir in the second half of 1917: less than 30 per cent of letters scrutinized by censors in Bordeaux that September expressed support for peace on the basis of outright victory; more than 17 per cent explicitly favoured a negotiated peace.[67] To be sure, the British army had finally made effective use of tanks at Cambrai; but the success proved ephemeral and certainly did not compensate for the losses which had been sustained at Passchendaele. The Americans had confidence in themselves; but their army was as yet embryonic and by the end of 1917 they were close to losing confidence in their own allies' ability to fight on. Perhaps it was Lord Lansdowne's letter

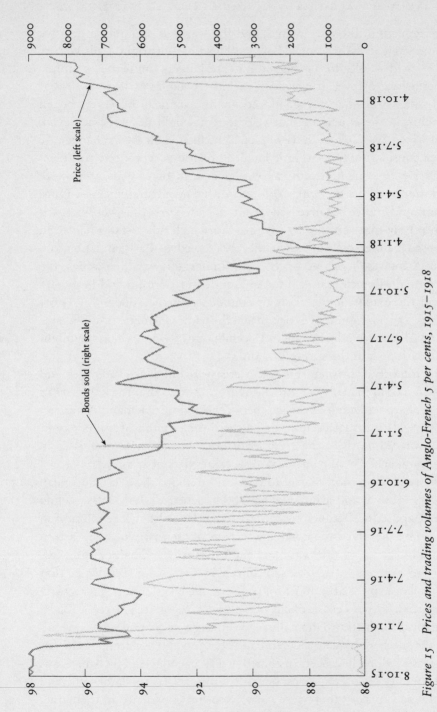

Figure 15   *Prices and trading volumes of Anglo-French 5 per cents, 1915–1918*

Source: *Commercial and Financial Chronicle, 1915–18.*

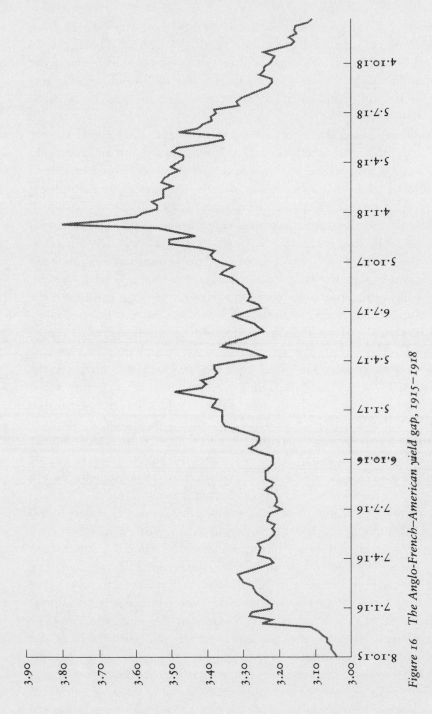

Figure 16 *The Anglo-French–American yield gap, 1915–1918*

Source: *Commercial and Financial Chronicle*, 1915–18.

arguing for a negotiated peace (published by the *Daily Telegraph* on 29 November) which prompted the jitters on Wall Street. The surprising thing is that the New York market remained so bullish about the Anglo-French bonds the following spring, when many influential figures in Britain and France sincerely feared that Germany was on the brink of victory.

Nothing can detract from the central fact that the Central Powers were significantly more successful at killing, wounding and capturing the enemy than the Entente Powers. But what is even more astonishing is that they did so at a much lower cost. One (admittedly rather callous) way of expressing the difference between the two sides in a way which takes not only military effectiveness but also economic resources into account – in other words, a way which measures integrated war *efficiency* – is to say that Germany succeeded far better than the Entente in inflicting 'maximum slaughter at minimum expense'. As we have seen, the Allies spent approximately $140 billion between 1914 and 1918, the Central Powers around $80 billion. Yet the Central Powers killed many more members of the Allies' armed forces than were killed of their own men. On this basis, a simple calculation can be made: whereas it cost the Entente powers $36,485.48 to kill a serviceman fighting for the Central Powers, it cost the Central Powers just $11,344.77 to kill a serviceman fighting for the Entente (Table 41). To complete the macabre balance sheet, these figures could, of course, be related to Bogart's estimates of the notional economic *value* of each individual soldier killed to his country of origin. According to Bogart, an American or British soldier was worth 20 per cent more than a German ($1,414 compared with $1,354), but nearly double the cash value of a Russian or a Turk ($700). But no soldier was worth as much as it cost to kill him.[68] Ultimately, the financial historian can therefore do no more than pose a question to military historians: why on earth did Germany and her allies – who were more than three times more efficient at killing the enemy than Britain and her allies – end up losing the war? One possible answer is simply that because Britain felt sure of her economic advantage, she could afford to be somewhat wasteful in the way she waged war. However, that is not easy to reconcile with the fears of a dollar crisis which surfaced in 1916 and 1917 and ought to have encouraged parsimony. Perhaps, as Keynes suggested to Beatrice Webb in March 1918, it was Britain rather than Germany whose government 'habitually put finance last of all relevant considerations and believed

Table 41   The cost of killing: war expenditure and deaths

	'War expenditure' ($ billion current)	*Deaths*
Great Britain	43.8	723,000
British Empire (excl. Britain)	5.8	198,000
France	28.2	1,398,000
Russia	16.3	1,811,000
Italy	14.7	578,000
USA	36.2	114,000
Other	2.0	599,000
Entente and Allied Powers	147.0	5,421,000
Germany	47.0	2,037,000
Austria–Hungary	13.4	1,100,000
Bulgaria and Turkey	1.1	892,000
Central Powers	61.5	4,029,000
Grand total	208.5	9,450,000

Sources: Hardach, *First World War*, p. 153; J. Winter, *Great War*, p. 75.

that action however wasteful is preferable to caution and criticism, however justified'.[69]

One way of answering this question is to try to see if Britain became more efficient in the course of the war. This is not easy, but in order to arrive at a very rough and tentative hypothesis I have calculated ratios of British to German 'slaughter' and expenditure; the former using the numbers of soldiers permanently incapacitated in the British sector of the Western Front; the latter using total annual expenditures converted into dollars. The figures suggest that when Britain was most markedly outspending Germany (by a ratio of 1.8 to 1), Germany was achieving her most favourable net body count in the British sector (1.4 to 1). This was in 1916, the year of expensive but self-destructive British offensives. However, the continued if somewhat reduced British superiority in financial terms (1.3 to 1) may help explain the subsequent deterioration in the German net body count to just 0.7 to 1 in 1918, the year of Ludendorff's offensive and the subsequent mass German surrenders. This would seem to suggest a relative improvement in military efficiency on the British side: in 1917 and 1918 the Germans were closing the financial gap, but the net body count ultimately turned against them.[70] It remains to be explained, however, exactly how, if at all, the superior spending power of the Allies was linked to the collapse of German morale which ended the war.

12

The Death Instinct: Why Men Fought

LIFE IN HELL

Contrary to the theory of attrition, victory is won not just by killing the enemy: as important is getting him to desert, mutiny or surrender. Thus the key to the German victory over the Russians in 1917 lies here rather than in the statistics of dead Russians. The same goes for the Austro-Hungarian and German defeats in 1918.

There is, of course, a natural temptation to conclude that there is a direct causal relationship between the two: the higher the number of deaths inflicted, the more likely men were to give up fighting. But this was not the case; indeed it has even been suggested by one writer that 'high casualty rates may have helped to prolong the war' because high troop turnover prevented fatigue and despair from becoming too widespread.[1] If killing had been the key, the Germans would have won the war for the reasons discussed in the previous chapter. In fact, high casualty rates do not correlate consistently with collapses in morale. Some of the most reliable regiments on both sides were the ones which suffered the highest casualties. The British 29th Division suffered casualties equivalent to seven times its original strength during the war but was still regarded as the élite force of the BEF.[2] The resilience of the Scottish regiments is another good example. This leads us to a conclusion which at first sight seems odd: that those much-derided pre-war generals who believed that the war would be decided not by *matériel* but by morale – 'the human factor', or 'grit' as Sir John Robertson called it – were right.[3]

This takes us to the heart of the matter. What made men keep fighting? And what, besides being killed or wounded, made them stop? How, when the chances of a swift victory were greatly outweighed by the chances of being killed, can we explain the willingness of millions of men to carry on fighting?

339

To the mind of the modern reader, fighting in the First World War is all horror and misery: 'a million men, moving one against the other', as Ford Madox Ford described it in 1916, 'impelled by an invisible moral force into a hell of fear that surely cannot have had a parallel in this world'.[4] It was certainly no picnic. The slaughter of the French soldiers in the opening phase of the war was unmatched in the rest of the conflict: 329,000 killed in the space of two months and half a million by the end of the year. The highest number of men the Germans lost in a single two-month period was 68,397 in March–April 1918. The worst two months for the BEF in France were July–August 1914, when 'only' 45,063 men and officers were killed. As one French officer described the experience of combat in 1914, men were sent to their deaths senselessly: 'All day long they lie there, being decimated, getting themselves killed next to the bodies of those killed earlier.'[5] Machine-guns – and rifles capable of firing eighteen rounds a minute – simply scythed the *poilus* down as they endeavoured to implement the insane Plan XVII. Nearly two years later the British still had not learned the simple lesson that to advance in a line was a form of mass suicide. Once the trenches were dug, men were still vulnerable (even when they were not going 'over the top') to machine-gunners and snipers, who by 1916 were positioned approximately every 21 yards along the British line.[6] When Edwin Campion Vaughan led his 'D' Company into action at Passchendaele he lost seventy-five out of ninety men:

Poor old Pepper had gone – hit in the back by a chunk of shell; twice buried as he lay dying in a hole, his dead body blown up and lost after Willis had carried it back to Vanheule Farm. Ewing hit by machine gun bullets . . . Chalk . . . had been seen to fall riddled with bullets; then he too had been hit by a shell.[7]

Men were not just killed in such big offensives, the battles so beloved by traditional military history. Routine patrols in no man's land, and the practice of 'raiding' the enemy line for intelligence, training or wrecking, pushed up casualties on both sides even in 'quiet' periods. Between December 1915 and June 1916 some 5,845 British soldiers died in such 'minor trench operations'.[8]

Worst of all was the shelling. Although experienced soldiers learned to distinguish the directions and types of enemy shell, in heavy bombardments at the Front there was next to nothing in the way of evasive action which could be taken and only a few shelters deep and strong enough to be genuinely proof against a direct hit. The feeling of helpless vulnerability this induced was almost certainly the most excruciating mental strain the war inflicted. As one French trench journal (*Le Saucisse*) put it:

There's nothing more horrible in war than being shelled. It's a form of torture that the soldier can't see the end of. Suddenly he's afraid of being buried alive ... He conjures up the atrocious agony ... The man stays put in his hole, helplessly waiting for, hoping for, a miracle.[9]

Ernst Jünger knew this feeling well:

It is as if one were tied to a post and threatened by a fellow swinging a sledgehammer. Now the hammer is swung back for the blow, now it whirls forward, till, just missing your skull, it sends the splinters flying from the post once more ... The brain links every separate sound of whirring metal with the idea of death and so the nerves are exposed without protection and without pause to the sense of absolute menace ... Hours such as these were without doubt the most awful of the whole war.[10]

Anyone inclined to think that the defenders had an easy time of it at the Somme should pause over Jünger's diary description of the German front line at Guillemont in August 1916: 'Among the living lay the dead. As we dug ourselves in we found them in layers stacked up on top of one another. One company after another had been shoved into the drum-fire and steadily annihilated.' It was this experience, he wrote, which 'first made me aware of the overwhelming effects of the war of material (*Materialschlacht*)'. Had the shell which fell at his feet not been a dud, he would not have written another word; as it was he only missed the annihilation of his company because of a leg wound.[11] In March 1918 another company led by Jünger suffered a direct hit from a shell as they advanced towards Cagnicourt on the eve of the great offensive: 63 out of 150 men were killed. Jünger, an almost psychopathically brave officer, ran from the spot in terror, then broke down and wept in front of the survivors.[12] Small wonder so many men on both sides suffered from 'shell shock', a term used to describe a variety of mental disorders resulting from combat stress. After the war, around 65,000 British ex-soldiers were drawing disability pensions because of 'neurasthenia' – 6 per cent of the total – of whom 9,000 were still in hospital.[13] One study of 758 cases estimated that no more than 39 per cent returned to 'normal' after the war, and this did not mean complete, symptomless recovery.[14] German soldiers evinced similar symptoms and, as in Britain, there was a tendency to punish as much as treat the victims with electric shocks and other equally painful 'remedies'. If there was a German equivalent of Charles Rivers Wilson, who at least had a humane way of getting men back to their work of killing, his deeds have gone unsung.[15] And if a man like Jünger could experience a complete (if brief) loss of nerve, it seems fair to assume that few, if any, soldiers did not experience extreme fear under a bombardment. Siegfried Sassoon had courage in common with Jünger: his poem 'Repression of War Experience' gives a harrowing insight into the psychological impact of shelling:

> Hark! Thud, thud, thud, – quite soft . . . they never cease –
> Those whispering guns – O Christ, I want to go out
> And screech at them to stop – I'm going crazy;
> I'm going stark, staring mad because of the guns.[16]

That was written while he was convalescing in Kent.

While in action, men also suffered from intense fatigue. Private John Lucy's description of the retreat from Mons gives a good insight into this – 'Our minds and bodies shrieked for sleep . . . Every cell . . . craved rest and that one thought was the most persistent in the minds of the marching men' – but countless other examples could be cited from the works of Aldington, Barbusse, Jünger and others.[17] Indeed, Jünger believed that it was not 'danger, however extreme . . . that depresses the spirit of men, so much as over-fatigue and wretched conditions'. In his first tour of duty near Orainville, he got just two hours' sleep a night.[18]

Conditions were certainly often wretched. Even if (as Barnett long ago remarked) men from the slums of Glasgow were used to rain, cold, lice, rats and violence,[19] it would be absurd to pretend that the trenches were not worse: the slums were bad, but they were not made of mud and nor did Catholic tenants shell Protestants. 'Hell is not fire,' declared the French soldiers' paper La Mitraille. 'The real hell is the mud.' Le Crapouillot begged to differ: it was the cold which was the worst.[20] Jünger sometimes thought 'wet and cold' did more damage to the resistance of troops than artillery.[21]

Even when they were not cold, dirty and wet, men in the trenches suffered. They grieved for friends who had been killed (especially if they were relatively 'green').[22] And contrary to Northcliffe's tales of a healthy outdoor life, they were often ill (though less often fatally than in past wars). The German statistics show that for the war as a whole an average of 8.6 per cent of the total fighting strength of the army was sick, with the percentage leaping upwards in the summer of 1918; it was no fault of Ludendorff's that his army was smitten by the world-wide influenza epidemic in the summer of 1918.[23]

Psychologically too it was hard to feel cheerful when surrounded by 'rusty barbed wire', 'upturned earth' and 'ghostlike trees . . . splintered with shell scars' – though once again, aversion to the scenery was mainly confined to rookies.[24]

And for all this the soldier was paid a comparative pittance (a much more serious grievance for most men than the ugliness of their surroundings). British soldiers on a shilling a day in 1917 reacted with indignation when they came into contact behind the lines with colonial troops on five or six times as much (hence 'fuckin' five bobbers' as a derogatory term for Dominion soldiers); even more galling was the sight of officers drinking themselves under the table when their men could not afford a glass of wine (a subaltern got 7s. 6d. a day, a 2s. lodging allowance and a field allowance of 2s. 6d.).[25] George Coppard's memoirs are full of references to the British Tommy's feeling of poverty;[26] and yet he was better off than most French conscripts, who had to get by on a miserable 25 centimes a day. All the armies which had begun the war were mortified by the wealth of the Americans when they arrived on the scene: there were pitched battles at Brest between *poilus* and the newcomers precipitated by the latter's unfair advantage in bedding women.[27]

Given the awfulness of the conditions soldiers had to endure, the most surprising thing of all about the war, perhaps, is that military discipline did not break down much more often, or earlier, than it did. Disproportionate attention has been paid to the famous Christmas truces of 1914, when British and German soldiers 'fraternized' with one another in no man's land;[28] and even more to the so-called 'live and let live' system which developed in certain sectors of the Western Front in 1914 and 1915. Essentially, there were tacitly agreed ceasefires at mealtimes, or when wounded were being rescued; a 'tit for tat' system evolved whereby for every unprovoked shot two would be returned in retaliation.[29] Rival night patrols would carefully avoid one another in no man's land. Snipers stopped shooting to kill if they shot at all. Later, when staff orders came to resume fighting, violence was merely 'ritualized'.[30] These phenomena have been cited by social scientists and even by Darwinian biologists as evidence of, respectively, the readiness of human beings to co-operate[31] and the determination of individuals' selfish genes to avoid being annihilated.[32]

Unfortunately for such elegant theories, such behaviour did not catch on. If the First World War really did resemble the famous iterated Prisoner's Dilemma game,[33] then for most of it both sides persistently defected.[34] One Gordon Highlander spoke for many soldiers when he returned from one Christmas truce fingering his dagger and musing: 'I don't trust these bastards.'[35] Hitler was not alone, then, in his distaste for the truces.[36] Jünger describes exactly how they tended to break down:

The occupants of the trenches on both sides had been driven to take to the top [by appalling rain] and now there was a lively traffic and exchange going on in schnapps, cigarettes, uniform buttons etc. in front of the wire . . . Suddenly there was a thud that dropped one of our fellows dead in the mud.

On Christmas Day 1915 another of his men was killed by a flanking shot. 'Immediately after the English attempted a friendly overture and put up a Christmas tree on their parapet. But our fellows were so embittered that they fired and knocked it over. And this in turn was answered with rifle grenades.'[37] Instead of increasing, trust diminished. It is not convincing simply to blame the end of 'live and let live' on pushy staff officers who wanted an 'active front' for the sake of their own promotion prospects.[38] Orders not to fraternize (like those given to the 16th Division in February 1917) were quite willingly obeyed. George Coppard relished machine-gunning the German line at Christmas: 'The age-old sentiment of "goodwill to all men" meant nothing to us.'[39]

If co-operation did not become the norm, what of another kind of defection – desertion from one's own side? Despite myths of an army of deserters who roamed in no man's land, there was in fact relatively little desertion on either side of the Western Front. Early in the war peasant recruits and conscripts on both sides would often try to get home at harvest time; and late in the war German morale crumbled. By November 1917 as many as 10 per cent of troops were using transport trains to desert, something which became easier after the Russian collapse; by the summer of 1918 as many as 20 per cent of replacement troops were melting away en route to Army Group Prince Rupprecht.[40]

But for most of the war desertion was at such a low level that it did not undermine military effectiveness: in the British army the number of men shot for deserting was just 266.[41] Between 1914 and 1917 an annual average of 15,745 French soldiers were recorded as absent without leave; much of this was more like lateness in returning from leave than desertion.[42] Nor was there as much desertion by Austro-Hungarian troops as might have been expected, considering the high proportion of ethnic Slavs in the ranks; the ethnically homogeneous Italians were only slightly less prone to steal away, especially if they came from the *Mezzogiorno* and regarded their northern officers as not much less foreign than the enemy. Until the last stages of the war it was the Russians who deserted in large numbers, especially if they got wind of impending offensives. However, it was not until quite late in 1917 that Russian desertions reached the level of hundreds of thousands – even millions.[43]

Mutinies too were few and far between. The forty-nine French divisions which mutinied in the summer of 1917[44] and the Saxon and Württemberg units who did so on a smaller scale that summer are conspicuous as the exception which proves the rule of a remarkable lack of disorder on the Western Front.[45] Of course, not even the French mutinies were as revolutionary in intent as the French High Command feared: mainly they reflected the *poilus'* loss of confidence in Nivelle's generalship. They certainly did not signify an intention to let the Germans win the war. Still, defiance of orders by 30,000 to 40,000 men at such a critical stage in the war was serious. Nothing of this sort happened in the British army. The only significant breakdown in discipline (at the detested Étaples base in September 1917), involving men of the 51st Highland Division, the Northumberland Fusiliers and Australians, was principally directed against the Military Police after they shot dead a long-serving regular army corporal for trying to cross a bridge into the nearby town.[46] At most, British working-class soldiers behind the lines would revert to peacetime techniques of protest when dissatisfied at their treatment. Some 25th Division units held mass meetings to protest against poor billets in 1916;[47] while the Workers' and Soldiers' Council set up at Tunbridge Wells in June 1917 formulated its grievances like a strike committee: allowances should be raised to keep pace with food prices and soldiers should not be used as 'blacklegs' to do civilian work.[48] Typical of British discipline was that the orders most commonly disobeyed towards the end of the war were to disband into new units.[49]

Yet when called on to fight against appalling odds at Third Ypres, the morale of British soldiers remained 'amazingly high' in the view of Sir Hubert Gough, who commanded the Fifth Army: 'Our private soldiers . . . only knew that they were asked to fight under impossible conditions, with death above, around, below . . . It was little short of marvellous that men could stand such an intense strain.'[50] Considering that they came from the country with the least experience of mass conscription, he was right.

STICKS

So why did men keep fighting? There is, of course, the possibility that they were forced to do so. Certainly, the war saw a great increase in the extent of the state's power to coerce its citizens. A substantial part of the increased public expenditure between 1914 and 1918 went on burgeoning administrative structures employing hundreds of thousands of people whose job was to force their fellow citizens to fight. This expansion of bureaucracy had predated the war and had occurred not only in the public sector but also in the sphere of voluntary associations and business: never had men been so well organized as in 1914. Giant industrial concerns employed tens of thousands of men and were run by their own managerial bureaucracies. Trade unions had vast member-ships. When such structures were harnessed to the task of mass slaughter they were remarkably effective.

Moreover, it is at least arguable that the British army was more ruthless in its use of coercion to maintain military discipline than those armies which ultimately suffered collapse. Members of the No Conscription Fellowship who refused to do war work only narrowly avoided execution by the military authorities, and of the 1,540 pacifists who were condemned to two years' forced labour seventy-one died as a result of their ill treatment.[51] Notoriously, 3,080 British soldiers were sentenced to death for desertion, cowardice, mutiny or other offences – of whom 346 unfortunates had their sentences carried out (more than the French and around seven times the equivalent German figure, though less than half the number the Italians shot of their own men).[52] Lists of those executed were then read out at parades *pour encourager les autres*: George Coppard was shocked but impressed by this. Max Plowman was almost as amazed to see a man tied spread-eagled to a wheel: a field punishment dating back to Wellington's day which was not abolished until 1923.[53] There was 1 military policeman for every 291 British servicemen by 1918, compared with a ratio of 1 to 3,306 at the start of the war.[54] The British army also had a far higher ratio of officers to men than the German: 25 per battalion, compared with a German figure of 8 or 9.[55] Considering the lack of military experience of the overwhelming majority of British soldiers before the war, the army ended up being a remarkably disciplined organization. Indeed, as we have seen, it instilled a much higher level of blind obedience than the German.[56] John Lucy recalled a man wounded in the head asking permission before he fell out of line.[57] More commonly observed in the British 'other ranks' was an ethos of passivity and even apathy: men would not lift a finger until ordered to do so.[58] Indeed, this hierarchical, deferential structure – this dependence on the orders of a superior officer – has been identified as a source of weakness in the British army in comparison with the German culture which encouraged men to show initiative in the absence of clear commands from above.[59]

Yet the extent to which men were forced to fight should not be exaggerated. The number of soldiers shot for cowardice was a minute percentage of the total number (5.7 million) who served in the British army during the war. What is more, many of these (including a substantial proportion of those actually shot) were suffering from shell shock – like the unfortunate Private Harry Farr of the West Yorkshire Regiment, who faced a firing squad in October 1916.[60] He had not consciously refused to fight; he simply could not go on, and it must be doubted whether Haig was right to think that the war would be lost if these few wretched individuals were pardoned. In reality, wartime military discipline was a good deal more subtle than it would later become in Trotsky's Red Army (if you advance you have a chance of surviving, if you retreat, you will definitely be shot). During the war, discipline had much more to do with the extent of respect felt by men for their NCOs and officers. This varied greatly, with the Russians supremely bad (treating their men like serfs, absenting themselves during fighting)[61] and the Italians not far behind. The French officer was somewhere in the middle.[62] It may be that by 1918 the famed German officer had begun to forfeit the respect of his men too, though this became such a politically sensitive issue during the revolution that it is hard to distinguish myth from reality.[63]

How good relations actually were between officers and men in the British army remains debatable. There was, of course, an immense change in the social composition of the officer corps during the war: 43 per cent of permanent commissions were granted to NCOs compared with just 2 per cent before the war, and around 40 per cent of temporary officers were from working-class or lower-middle-class backgrounds.[64] For officers of the old regular army this was hard to take: one was aghast to hear officers in the Manchesters telling their men to 'shoot oop' and 'bugger off'.[65] On the other hand, this social 'dilution' greatly reduced the social gap which there had once been between officers and men (in contrast with the German army, which did not promote NCOs above the rank of *Feldwebelleutnant*).[66] For their part, many of the new officers tended to portray their relations with their men in a rosy light when they came to write their memoirs. Some recalled 'comradeship . . . that was the despair of the more crusted Regular martinet'.[67] Others went still further: one thinks of Herbert Read's passionate ode to 'my company' ('O beautiful men, O men I loved . . .'), Guy Chapman's similarly fervent declaration to the 'firm ranks' of the soldiers under his command, or Robert Graves's supremely camp suggestion that a platoon of men would 'get a crush on . . . a good-looking gallant young officer . . . [I]t's a very, very strong romantic link.'[68] On 4 June 1918 Siegfried Sassoon wrote in his diary: 'After all, I am nothing but what the Brigadier calls a "potential killer of Germans (Huns)." O God, why must I do it? *I'm not.* I am only here *to look after* some men.' Five months later Wilfred Owen assured his mother that 'I came out in order to help these boys – directly by leading them as well as an officer can; indirectly, by watching their sufferings that I may speak of them as well as a pleader can.'[69] Undoubtedly there was sometimes an erotic dimension to the relationships forged between homosexual officers like these and their men. T. E. Lawrence admitted as much in his *The Seven Pillars of Wisdom*:

The public women of the rare settlements we encountered in our months of wandering would have been nothing to our numbers, even had their raddled meat been palatable to a man of healthy parts. In horror of such sordid commerce our youths began indifferently to slake one another's few needs in their own clean bodies – a cold convenience that, by comparison, seemed sexless and even pure. Later, some began to justify this sterile process, and swore that friends quivering together in the yielding sand with intimate hot limbs in supreme embrace, found there hidden in the darkness a sensual co-efficient of the mental passion which was welding our souls and spirits in one flaming effort.[70]

This, however, was very likely fantasy: it seems unlikely that many of these public-school/Oxbridge 'crushes' were ever consummated. In the period 1914–19 twenty-two officers and 270 other ranks were court-martialled for 'indecency' with another man. Generally homosexual officers slept with officers and men with men: as Lawrence observed coyly, 'Hut 12' had shown him 'the truth behind Freud'.[71]

To George Coppard, the officers were remote beings who communicated indirectly via NCOs: the gulf might narrow while units were in the trenches, but it was still a gulf both materially and socially.[72] In so far as it is possible to generalize, what the men liked in an officer was not his good looks but his willingness to 'muck in'. Positive comments about officers were often prompted by their 'digging and filling sand bag[s] . . . like the rest', 'having guts . . . in a trench' or 'handl[ing] a spade'.[73] As the poet and private Ivor Gurney noted, a measure of leniency was also welcome. 'Do you think you might crawl through there, Gurney: there's a hole', one of his officers once said to him. 'I'm afraid not, sir,' Gurney felt able to reply.[74] On the other hand, other officers (including Guy Chapman on a separate occasion) admitted that they barely even knew the names of the men they commanded, turnover was so high,[75] and sometimes that was exactly how the men felt about the officers, who got killed at an even higher rate (not least by trying to win the respect of their men).[76]

In any case, it seems clear that morale was only partly dependent on discipline – and could indeed be undermined if discipline took the form of gruelling drill (as at Étaples) and pointless button-polishing when men had seen real action. As Westbrook has argued, military morale is as dependent on the carrots of remuneration and reward as on the sticks of discipline; and more dependent than either on the moral and social ties which bind an army together.[77]

CARROTS

The best accounts of army life during the First World War emphasize the importance of quite humdrum things in keeping men going. Immediate short-term comfort was at a premium. Here is a simple list of the comforts and discomforts that mattered most:

1. Warm and comfortable clothing. In September 1915, French school-teachers in Doubs sent 4,403 hand-knitted balaclavas as part of their contribution to the war effort; by the winter these must have been very welcome.[78] Though British officers had their clothes tailor-made, the men were issued with coarse uniforms which rarely fitted – and they were the best dressed of all the armies. German uniforms were much more cheaply made, and good boots an object of desire (see *All Quiet on the Western Front*), while the Russian army was so short of footwear in 1914 that many men went into battle barefoot. The Highland regiments took great pride in the wearing of the kilt (under a khaki apron), but it was in many ways a handicap in trench warfare and finally had to be abandoned when it was realized that mustard gas burnt the sweatier parts of the body, with disastrous consequences.[79]

2. Decent accommodation. The German trenches were generally far better constructed than the British; it was rare that a British soldier could write home praising the dugout he was in, while the Germans (see plate 17) were amazed at the shoddiness of the enemy's line when they captured sections of it. Conversely, British soldiers were 'stagger[ed] to see the high standard of the [German] trenches' compared with their own 'lousy, scratchy holes'.[80] Mention should also be made here of latrines: the German soldier was inordinately, scatologically fond of his 'thunder box', while the more prudish British soldier often had to make do with ditches.[81]

3. Food. Nearly all war memoirs make it clear that morale was heavily dependent on good rations. It is, in many ways, the central leitmotif of *All Quiet*. The smell of bacon in the morning cheered men (including Jünger and Liddell Hart) on both sides; conversely, as George Coppard recalled, 'a slight deficiency in the rations would arouse mutinous mutterings'.[82] If Jünger's experience was typical, the German army's rations began to deteriorate markedly in the second half of 1917 ('thin mid-day soup . . . the third of a loaf . . . half-mouldy jam'), with important consequences: when the Germans broke through the Allied line in the spring of the following year they wasted precious time in plundering. Colonel-General von Einem lamented that his 3rd Army had degenerated into a 'bunch of thieves'.[83] But not too much should be read into this: lust for plunder is not a bad source of motivation. In any case, French soldiers' letters are full of gripes about bad or insufficient food: 'We have had nine meals in a row of bully beef and Saigon rice,' complained one in June 1916. 'They must take us for chickens.'[84]

4. *Drugs*. Without alcohol, and perhaps also without tobacco, the First World War could not have been fought. When Sergeant Harry Finch of the Royal Sussex Regiment advanced into no man's land on the eve of the Passchendaele offensive (31 July 1917), he was struck by the fact that most of the men in his section 'fell fast asleep' as they lay waiting to attack. That was the effect of the rum issue as much as tiredness.[85] 'Had it not been for the rum ration,' one medical officer later declared, 'I do not think we should have won the war.'[86] This was only an understatement in the sense that it did not mention the huge quantities of drink men consumed when they were not in the front line. Ordinary soldiers would get drunk at every opportunity; they had, as one officer in the Highland Light Infantry put it, a 'marvellous talent' for it.[87] The apex of misery for George Coppard was having to 'mouch [*sic*] around in a lonely village without the price of a drink' while 'the officers [drank] their duty-free whisky'. Likewise, when wine was unavailable, unaffordable or undrinkable, morale in French units tended to plummet.[88] A soldier-poet wrote in the *Aussie* trench paper in June 1918:

> You say we're mad when we strike the beer,
> But if you'd stood in shivering fear
> With the boys who bring the wounded back
> Cross no-man's land where there ain't no track
> You'd read no psalms to the men that fight
> You'd take the drink to forget the sight
> Of torn out limbs and sightless eyes
> Or the passing of a pal that dies.[89]

The Germans were no different: Jünger repeatedly refers to orgies of drunkenness: 'Though ten out of twelve had fallen, still the last two, as sure as death, were to be found on the first evening of rest over the bottle drinking a silent health to their dead "companions"':

351

We . . . drank heavily until . . . we treated the whole world as no more than a laughable phantom that circled round our table . . . All the devastation of every kind that surrounded one was seen in the light of humour and in a state of bliss, however fleeting it might be, and was finally lost altogether in . . . light-hearted independence of time . . . One broke through time . . . and rejoiced for an hour or two in a boundless world.[90]

5. *Rest*. Three-fifths of an infantryman's time was in fact spent in the rear, not the front lines: the 7th Battalion, Royal Sussex Regiment, was typical in spending 42 per cent of their time in the front line or in close support between 1915 and 1918.[91] An individual soldier like Harry Finch would often serve less if he were taken ill or received a 'Blighty' wound (as Finch did, luckily for him, on the first day of the Somme): reading his diary gives a good insight into the infrequency of the really horrendous periods of fighting.[92] Guy Carrington spent only around a third of 1916 under fire, of which just sixty-five days were in the front line.[93] And of course some sectors of the line were quiet: to be near Festubert after 1915 was infinitely safer than to be near Ypres, for example.[94] Some soldiers had 'cushy' jobs: a third of a million men were occupied exclusively with supplying the BEF.[95] 'Rest areas' usually meant anything but rest (there was endless digging, repairing, loading and unloading to be done), but the private soldier was an accomplished 'skiver', always contriving to do the barest acceptable minimum of work.[96] More serious was shirking, when men sought to avoid actual fighting: one estimate of the number of German shirkers (*Drückeberger*) in the summer of 1918 puts it as high as 750,000; this amounted to a 'covert military strike', with retreating men even shouting 'strike-breakers' at those going to the Front.[97]

6. *Leisure*. Men joked: as one British trench newspaper put it, 'were it not for the spirit of bonhomie and cheerfulness, we should find it hard to keep going'.[98] A good insight into the sometimes black hue of trench humour is given by the comic names British soldiers bestowed on the things around them: a cemetery became a 'rest camp', while going over the top became 'jumping the bags' and Foncquevillers became 'Funky Villas'.[99] Men read and wrote letters, even if only by filling in Form A 2042, the Field Service Post Card (also known as the 'Quick Firer'), which was usually sent with everything save 'I am quite well' struck out. The English idiom of understatement was, as Fussell has said, well suited to the trenches.[100] Men collected souvenirs, including

enemy badges, buttons, bayonets and helmets.[101] They were entertained by professional and amateur concerts.[102] They saw films at field cinemas.[103] They played football, in the British case obsessively and with official encouragement: significantly, officers and men played together on an equal footing just as 'gentlemen' and 'players' did in peacetime, though familiarity ceased with the final whistle. There was also baseball for the Canadians and even horse-racing for the Australians.[104] And, of course, there was sex, quite a lot of it with prostitutes, to judge by memoirs[105] and the figures for venereal disease, which indicate that there were as many as 48,000 cases among British troops in 1917 and 60,000 cases including Dominion troops in 1918. After the war, there were alarmist claims that one soldier in five had syphilis; in fact the annual rate for the British army was 4·83 per cent, a slight improvement on the pre-war figure, though rates for Dominion troops were much higher: in the case of Canadian soldiers in 1915, no less than 28·7 per cent.[106] Otherwise there was always pornography, masturbation and, for a few, buggery.

7. *Leave*. Soldiers naturally looked forward to their home leave; the *poilu* in particular (it has been argued) sustained himself with visions of his home and family.[107] He did not see them often: although French soldiers were supposed to get seven days' leave for every three months' service, few did.[108] British soldiers were allowed home even less often. For much of the war the average Tommy got only ten days' leave for every fifteen months' service; by the summer of 1917 100,000 had not had any for eighteen months and four times that number had served without leave for a year.[109] For Australians, of course, home leave was more or less out of the question.[110] Yet it is clear that for many soldiers the pleasure of homecoming was tainted by feelings of hostility towards civilians whose experiences seemed so tame by comparison with their own and whose knowledge of front-line conditions was based on sanitized press reports. In their memoirs and elsewhere, Robert Graves and Siegfried Sassoon repeatedly allude to this. As Graves later related, 'The funny thing was you went home on leave for six weeks or six days but the idea of being and staying at home was awful because you were with people who didn't understand what this was all about.'[111] R. H. Tawney, later an eminent economic historian, fulminated as he recovered from being wounded at the Somme at 'your papers and . . . your conversation . . . You have chosen to make to yourselves an image of war, not as it is, but of a kind which [is] picturesque . . . because you . . . cannot bear . . .

the truth.'[112] In reality, civilians were probably less starry-eyed than the soldiers imagined: Red Cross reports on the wounded and missing were only slightly toned down before being relayed to relatives.[113] Many a *Frontschwein* felt just as alienated. German soldiers, like Hitler, were shocked by the mood of defeatism they encountered when they returned from the Front in 1918; others, however, picked up the mood and brought it back with them.[114]

The corollary of this sense of alienation was a strong sense of comradeship between soldiers. This was the key to what men looked back on with nostalgia as the 'front experience': 'love passing the love of women of one pal for his half section', intense friendships between men who fought alongside one another.[115] As one British private later wrote, it was the desire not to 'let down the others' more than any 'fear of Redcaps' which kept him from turning tail.[116] The French historian Marc Bloch agreed.[117] An entire theory of 'primary group' cohesion has developed which argues that this is the key to military effectiveness.[118] Yet there is a need not to overstate the importance of 'pals'. Many of the literary officers whose experience so interests Fussell clearly derived as much pleasure from the isolated enjoyment of reading as from comradely friendships. Moreover, the fact that units often went into action shortly after being formed, or that friendships were so often terminated by death, meant that such individualist, inward ways of coping in the end probably counted for as much, if not more. At the same time, soldiers often identified with the larger organizational units to which they belonged. Carefully cultivated traditions of regimental identity were designed to forge ties of loyalty at a less intimate level, ties which could survive even decimation. Although the growth of the army did much to weaken these regimental ties, the great reshuffle of battalions in 1918 was very unpopular with men, some of whom refused to obey orders to move to new 'homes'.[119]

It can also be argued that a fundamental loyalty to their own country motivated soldiers (even if they were often in the dark about their government's precise strategic objectives). Clausewitz had argued that military strength depended on morale: 'An army that maintains its cohesion under the most murderous fire', he wrote, '. . . that is mindful of all [its] duties and qualities by virtue of the single powerful idea of the honour of its arms – such an army is imbued with the true military spirit.' For Clausewitz, the mobilization of national feeling had been one of the keys to the French army's morale under Napoleon; many modern analysts would agree that this is the key to the resilience of an army.[120] In the First World War too men fought for *la patrie*, as well as for the Empire and *das Vaterland*. In the French case this was perhaps most obvious: the fact that the enemy was on French soil combined with folk memories of the 1790s to create a potent sense of patriotic resolve.[121] A more understated sense of British superiority probably acted as cement too.[122] But here too there is a need for qualification. Though predominantly English, the British Expeditionary Force was a multinational force. The Scots in particular had a strong sense of their own distinct identity, keen to show as they marched behind the bagpipes that 'we – WE – were winning the war'.[123] The Irish too, though much less keen on the war than the Scots, produced regiments with a distinctive culture, even when Englishmen had to be drafted in to keep up the numbers: so distinctive in fact that senior English officers tended to underestimate their fighting quality out of sheer prejudice.[124] Although a high proportion of Canadian and Australian soldiers who fought were British-born, they too had very clear-cut identities; the Australian 'diggers' in particular worried British generals by their lack of deference, a trait which seems to modern eyes attractive but was not invariably an asset.[125] On the German side too there was a perceptible difference between Prussian and South German troops: the Saxons in particular were regarded as 'safer' opponents than the Prussians. And, of course, national identity clearly counted for little in the Austro-Hungarian army – or for that matter in the Russian, where many peasant conscripts thought of themselves as being 'from Tambov' rather than Russia, which to them was equivalent to 'the world'. Yet both armies fought for nearly as long without internal crisis as the more homogeneous armies of France (who in any case had their own problems of regional division: the Breton soldiers one officer had to lead spoke four different dialects and few understood French).[126]

We have already seen that soldiers were unimpressed by the jingoistic propaganda carried in newspapers. However, an alternative 'official' source of motivation which offered rather more subtle ways of coping with the slaughter was religion. For the men on the Western Front, who were overwhelmingly Christians, their own sufferings could be easily interpreted in a rhetoric of sacrifice derived from Christ's Passion. (Fussell cites numerous examples of this kind of identification in the literature and letters written by officers at the front: Sassoon's 'The Redeemer', Owen's Christ being taught 'to lift his cross by numbers' and the numerous analogies with Christian in Bunyan's *Pilgrim's Progress*.) There was even a widely repeated story about a wounded Canadian soldier whom the Germans crucified in full view of his comrades. The war was also a time of apparitions. Soldiers imagined they saw angels hovering above Mons; just as three illiterate Portuguese children saw the Blessed Virgin bemoaning the Russian Revolution outside the village of Fatima in May 1917, so soldiers in Belgium and Northern France believed they heard words of prophecy from the Madonnas in roadside shrines. Spiritualism thrived in the trenches, where many exhausted men believed they saw or heard ghosts. French soldiers reared on the *images d'Epinal* came to believe the Germans had been repulsed by phantom *poilus* at Bois-Brûlé in 1916.[127] The most striking vision of the Virgin was in fact real: the gilded Virgin on top of the basilica of Notre Dame des Brebières in Albert, which leant forward precariously as a result of shelling: it was said that the war would end when the statue finally fell (it didn't).[128] The Saarburger Cross – a statue of the crucified Christ which a stray shell had freed from the cross – was another ambivalent image of war: part holy, part unholy.

Yet there are limits to how far the idea of the First World War as a religious war can be taken. Robert Graves, for one, was struck by the lack of religious feeling among British soldiers. Apart from anything else, it was obvious to even the least sophisticated soldier that there was a difference between the teaching of the Sermon on the Mount and that of the drill instructor on the use of the bayonet. The 8,000 Catholic priests who took part in the war on both sides had to contend with the embarrassment of Benedict XV's opposition to the war, most apparent when he appealed for an end to the suicidal hostilities on 1 August 1917: this failed to impress the more Gallican believers in France and Belgium. Feelings about the 3,480 British army chaplains were also mixed. 'Woodbine Willie' – the Revd G. A. Studdert Kennedy – typified a kind of muscular, not to say bloodthirsty, Christianity which not everyone found attractive: he delivered sermons after the congregation had been treated to exhibitions of boxing, wrestling and bayoneting.[129] As the trench paper the *Mudhook* put it, a chaplain like that of the 63rd Division had a strangely schizoid role to play:

> I do not wish to hurt you
> But (Bang!) I feel I must.
> It is a Christian virtue

> To lay you in the dust.
> You – (Zip! That bullet got you)
> You're really better dead.
> I'm sorry that I shot you –
> Here, let me hold your head.[130]

On the other hand, other chaplains had the reputation for avoiding danger.[131] Haig famously declared that 'a good chaplain was as valuable as a good general'. As a verdict, that can be read in a different sense from the one he intended.

THE JOY OF WAR?

There is another possibility which has received too little attention in the historiography of the First World War, for the simple reason that it is not very palatable. That is the thesis that men kept fighting because they wanted to.

In his wartime essay 'Thoughts for the Times on War and Death', Sigmund Freud argued that the war signified the reassertion of primitive instincts which society had previously repressed. 'When the frenzied conflict of this war shall have been decided', he wrote,

every one of the victorious warriors will joyfully return to his home, his wife and his children, undelayed and undisturbed by any thought of the enemy he has slain . . . If we are to be judged by the wishes in our unconscious, we are, like primitive man, simply a gang of murderers . . . Our unconscious is just as . . . murderously minded towards the stranger, as divided or ambivalent towards the loved, as was man in earliest antiquity . . . War . . . strips us of the later accretions of civilization and lays bare the primal man in each of us.

At the same time, however, Freud also detected a 'disturbance that has taken place in our attitude towards death'. Before the war, he argued, there had been 'an unmistakable tendency to "shelve" death, to eliminate it from life. We tried to hush it up . . . The psychoanalytic school could venture the assertion that at bottom no one believes in his own death . . . [I]n the unconscious everyone is convinced of his own immortality.' Freud disapproved of this, arguing that disbelief in death had the effect of 'impoverishing life'. The war, he suggested, had made life 'interesting again' because it had swept away 'this conventional treatment of death'.[132]

Freud further developed this line of argument after the war in his *Beyond the Pleasure Principle* (1920), in which he suggested that 'beside the instinct preserving the organic substance and binding it into ever larger units, there must exist another in antithesis to this, which would seek to dissolve those units and reinstate their antecedent inorganic state; that is to say, the death instinct as well as Eros'. It was the interaction of the death instinct and the erotic instinct which he now saw as the key to the human psyche:

The tendency to aggression is an innate, independent, instinctual disposition in man, and . . . constitutes the most powerful obstacle to culture . . . Eros . . . aims at binding together single human individuals, then families, then tribes, races, nations into one great unity, that of humanity. Why this has to be done we do not know; it is simply the work of Eros. These masses of men must be bound to one another libidinally; necessity alone, the advantages of common work, would not hold them together.

The natural instinct of aggressiveness in man, the hostility of each against us all and of all against each one, opposes this programme of civilization. The instinct of aggression is the derivative and main representative of the death instinct we have found alongside Eros, sharing his rule over the earth. And now, it seems to me, the meaning of the evolution of culture is no longer a riddle to us. It must present to us the struggle between Eros and Death, between the instincts of life and the instincts of destruction.[133]

Though it is now fashionable to sneer at Freud, there is something to be said for this interpretation – at least with respect to the behaviour of men at war. Today's neo-Darwinian genetic determinism may be more scientifically respectable than Freud's mixture of psychoanalysis and amateur anthropology, but the latter seems better able to explain the readiness of millions of men to spend four and a quarter years killing and being killed. (It is certainly hard to see how the deaths of so many men who had not yet married and fathered children could possibly have served the purposes of Dawkins's 'selfish genes'.) In particular, there is a need to take seriously Freud's elision of the desire to kill – 'the destructive instinct' – and the lack of desire not to be killed – the striving of 'every living being . . . to work its ruin and reduce life to its primal state of inert matter'.

There is some evidence to support Freud's thesis. In June 1914 – before the war in which he would fight had even begun – the 'Vorticist' artist Wyndham Lewis wrote:

Killing somebody must be the greatest pleasure in existence: either like killing yourself without being interfered with by the instinct of self-preservation – or exterminating the instinct of self-preservation itself.[134]

In August 1914 Arthur Annesley, a middle-aged Londoner, was driven to commit suicide by 'the feeling that he was not going to be accepted for service': he chose death because he could not kill.[135] Robert Graves too had an authentically Freudian quirk: he superstitiously preserved his own chastity throughout the conflict, making precisely the kind of link made by Freud between Eros and Thanatos.[136] By suppressing the sexual impulse, Graves sought to ward off the suicidal one. In his 'Two Fusiliers', the eponymous soldiers are said to have 'found Beauty in Death'.[137] For many, the proximity of death was exciting: 'If I'd never had a shell rush at me', one of Ernest Raymond's characters exclaims in *Tell England*, 'I'd never have known the swift thrill of approaching death – which is a wonderful sensation not to be missed.'[138] At the other extreme, one French trench newspaper alluded to the way depression made soldiers 'tired of living'.[139] Intimations of mortality were a frequent preoccupation of soldiers in the trenches: Jünger was worried on the eve of a battle by a 'confused dream in which a death's head played a part'.[140] Yet at the same time he admitted to being fascinated by the first corpses he encountered in a captured French trench:

A young fellow lay on his back, his glazed eyes and his fingers fixed in their last aim. It was a weird sensation to look into those dead and questioning eyes . . . The horrible was undoubtedly a part of that irresistible attraction that drew us into the war . . . Among [the] questions that occupied us [before the war] was this: What does it look like when there are dead [people] lying about? . . . And now at our first glance of horror . . . [we could] make nothing of it. So it was that we had to stare again and again at these things that we had never seen before, without being able to give them meaning . . . We looked at all these dead with dislocated limbs, distorted faces, and the hideous colours of decay, as though we walked in a dream through a garden full of strange plants.[141]

Not everyone was repelled by the corpses, as Wilfred Owen was. A. P. Herbert confessed to the same 'hideous fascination' as Jünger felt.[142] Another poet, W. S. Littlejohn, wrote lines which seem perfectly to illustrate Freud's thesis, except that Littlejohn's death instinct seems to have become a conscious death wish:

So there is just a laughing death-song in my heart as up I plod
To the trenches, where my need will be six-foot stretch of sod
With a plain wood cross above it – leave the rest of me to God.[143]

Finally, there was the post-war sense of guilt felt by the survivors, like the character in Joseph Roth's *The Emperor's Tomb* who was 'found unfit for death'.[144] Good Wagnerian that he was, Thomas Mann's post-war verdict on Wilhelmine Germany was that its culture had been too bound up with death: *Todesverbundenkeit* was its fateful vice, the war its climactic *Liebestod*.[145]

Alternatively, and perhaps worse, men may have fought simply because fighting was fun. Martin van Creveld (no Freudian) has written perceptively on this same subject:

War . . . far from being merely a means, has very often been considered an end – a highly attractive activity for which no other can provide an adequate substitute . . . War alone presents man with the opportunity of employing all his faculties, putting everything at risk, and testing his ultimate worth against an opponent as strong as himself . . . However unpalatable the fact, the real reason why we have wars is that men like fighting.[146]

In the final analysis, this may be the best explanation of all for the continuation of the conflict: Oh! What a Lovely War, literally. Julian Grenfell, the archetypal upper-class cavalry chap, is often regarded as exceptional for thinking the war a great lark:

Four of us were talking and laughing in the road when about a dozen bullets came with a whistle. We all dived for the nearest door, which happened to be a lav, and fell over each other, *yelling* with laughter . . . I *adore* war. It is like a big picnic without the objectlessness of a picnic. I've never been so well or so happy.[147]

But such feelings were widespread. On the eve of his death at Loos Alexander Gillespie told his father: 'It will be a great fight, and even when I think of you, I would not wish to be out of this.'[148] When Captain W. P. Nevill of the 8th East Surreys led his company over the top at the start of the Somme offensive, he just had time to kick a football towards the German lines before he was shot dead: sport and war had fused fatally in his mind.[149] Others saw the war as an extension of hunting (as indeed cavalry officers were supposed to): Sassoon most obviously, but the analogy crops up everywhere. Francis Grenfell's last recorded words to his commanding officer at Second Ypres were: 'Hounds are fairly running!'[150] A Scottish sniper considered 'seven sure hits' and another four possible hits in a single day 'good hunting'.[151] The Germans got their own back: Jünger describes fleeing Highlanders whom his men massacred in March 1918 as 'hunted game'.[152] The sheer compulsiveness of war as sport is nicely captured in some lines in Robert Nichols' poem 'The Assault':

> 'Look, sir! Look out!'
> Ha! Ha! Bunched figures waiting.
> Revolver levelled quick!
> Flick! Flick!
> Red as blood.
> Germans. Germans.
> Good! O good!
> Cool madness.[153]

War, one Canadian private recalled, was 'the *greatest adventure of my life*, the memories of which will remain with me for the remainder of my days, and I would not have missed it for anything'; for another English stretcher-bearer, 'everything that happened after [the war] was an anti-climax'.[154] War was 'a mistress' to Guy Chapman: 'Once you have lain in her arms you can admit no other.' He later confessed to missing 'the sense, fleeting, beyond price, of living in every nerve and cell of one's body and with every ghostly impulse of one's mind'.[155] The French priest Pierre Teilhard de Chardin echoed this when he described the exaltation he had felt as a stretcher-bearer: 'You . . . see emerging from *within yourself* an underlying stream of clarity, energy and freedom that is to be found hardly anywhere else in ordinary life.'[156]

No man can have enjoyed the war more than Ernst Jünger. To him, battle was an 'opiate whose immediate effect is to stimulate the nerves though the subsequent effect is to deaden them'. A nearly disastrous raid was a 'brief and sporting interlude' and 'a good tonic for the nerves'; the war, he later reflected, had been 'an incomparable schooling of the heart'. But Jünger was not alone; he detected the same attitude among his men:

Often . . . it is quite jolly. Many of us take quite a sporting interest in the job. [The] hotheads are forever puzzling out the best possible ways of slinging over bombs with home-made catapults . . . Another time they creep out over the top and tie a bell on to the wire and to this a long string which can be pulled in order to excite the English posts. Even the war is a joke to them.[157]

Those women who got close to the action enjoyed it too. 'I wouldn't have missed this run for the world', was May Sinclair's comment in her journal, referring to her time in a Belgian ambulance unit; she recalled 'exquisite moments of extreme danger'. Vera Brittain and Violetta Thurstan, who also became nurses, relished 'the thrill' and 'great fun' of life near the Front. In the lesbian Radclyffe Hall's post-war story 'Miss Ogilvy Finds Herself', the heroine's time in an all-female unit is described as having been 'glorious'.[158]

What made war fun for some was precisely that it was dangerous. Van Creveld echoes Freud unconsciously when he writes: 'The true essence of war consists not just of one group killing another but of its members' readiness to be killed in return if necessary.' Killing and death co-existed in the soldier's mind.

So why, if not because of some subconscious desire for death, did men want to kill the enemy at the risk of their own lives? One strong motivation was revenge. That was what motivated John Lucy at the Aisne in September 1914 and at Neuve Chapelle – a chance to give the Germans some 'gyp' back after the hellish retreat from Mons and his brother's death:

We let them have it. We blasted and blew them to death. They fell in scores, in hundreds, the marching column wilting under our rapid fire. The groups melted away and no man was able to stand in our sight within five minutes. The few survivors panicked, and tried to keep their feet in retreat. We shot them down through the back. A red five minutes . . . We had cancelled out our shell-tortured day with a vengeance.[159]

At the Somme, the 9th Welch were motivated by the same desire to even the score for their losses at Loos.[160] A French agricultural worker from Puy-de-Dôme told his parents how he felt 'a terrible rage against these barbaric people. I'd be pleased to see a whole lot of them come along. I guarantee there wouldn't be any left alive for very long. I'm proud when I see them fall on the field of battle.'[161] Jünger noticed the same mood among his men. When a member of an entrenching party was killed in the Altenburg Redoubt, 'his comrades lay in wait a long while behind the parapet to take vengeance. They sobbed with rage. It is remarkable how little they grasp the war as an objective thing. They seem to regard the Englishman who fired the fatal shot as a personal enemy. I can understand it.' When he led his men into action on 21 March 1918 they switched from telling 'coarse jokes' to saying:

> 'Now we'll show what the 7th Company can do.'
> 'I don't care for anything now.'
> 'Vengeance for the 7th Company.'
> 'Vengeance for Captain von Brixen.'[162]

Note the words: 'I don't care for anything now': the desire for vengeance was often laced with a disregard for one's own life. It is impossible to read Sassoon's account of his experiences in the winter of 1915–16 without detecting the satisfaction he derived from killing Germans, but also his own preparedness to die. From the moment his close friend Dick was killed, he embarked on a succession of reckless raids on German trenches, simultaneously pursuing vengeance and death:

I went up to the trenches with the intention of trying to kill someone . . . it was this feeling which took me out patrolling the mine craters whenever an opportunity presented itself . . . I had more or less made up my mind to die because in the circumstances there didn't seem to be anything else to be done.

However, many men simply took pleasure in killing. Julian Grenfell recorded in his diary an 'exciting' episode in October 1914 when he crawled into no man's land and caught sight of a German 'laughing and talking. I saw his teeth glisten against my foresight, and I pulled the trigger very steady. He just gave a grunt and crumpled up.'[163] Australians at Gallipoli took pride in their skill as snipers and with the bayonet, partly to 'get even' but partly just to do the job 'beautifully'.[164] This kind of professional detachment contrasts with the violent hatred for 'the Boche' expressed by other soldiers. In the eyes of two officers in the Royal Berkshire Regiment, the Germans were 'unutterable vermin'; 'They have no sort of pity or compunction for them', one of their fellow-officers noted; 'the more they kill the better.'[165] Hate flourished in the other ranks too. When asked by a prisoner his view of the Germans, one British other ranker simply replied: 'We just looks on you as vomit.'[166] Few felt remorse of the sort felt by the character Jaretzki in Hermann Broch's *The Sleepwalkers*, who reasons that the loss of his left arm is a punishment for his having 'flung a hand-grenade between a Frenchman's legs'. But even he reasons that:

when one has deliberately done in a few ... well it seems to me one hasn't any need to look into a book for all the rest of one's life ... it's a sort of feeling I've got ... one has achieved everything ... and that's the reason too why the war will never end.[167]

In killing, all these men were simultaneously risking being killed. This willingness to risk death may not have been the result of a subconscious death wish, of course; it may simply have been because men could not (or chose not to) calculate the odds on their own survival. The average British soldier who served in France had rather more than a one in two chance of being a casualty of some sort; men who were actually in the front line, especially during offensives, had a far higher probability of being killed let alone wounded or taken prisoner. The odds were even worse for French *poilus*. 'Death lies ceaselessly in wait, especially before an attack', wrote a soldier in the journal *L'Argonaute* in 1917.[168] Though men had no way of knowing their precise chances of survival (casualty totals were kept strictly secret), it was not difficult to hazard a guess from experience. Some men clearly did have a keen awareness of their own chances of being killed. Norman Gladden remembered the 'torturing ... last hours before a battle': 'I could see no valid reason why I should again escape mutilation or death.'[169]

Yet such thoughts seem to have done little to discourage men from fighting for most of the war. This was because men persuaded themselves that the odds did not apply to them personally. The longer a man survived unscathed, the more other men he saw die, the more pronounced this sense became that an exception had been made to the laws of probability. Jünger noticed the way men used the open road from the Altenburg Redoubt despite the risk from snipers: this was 'the old indifference of the old soldier to the risk of a bullet. As a rule it was all right, but one or two victims were claimed daily.' Men were also reckless with unexploded shells and grenades. When Jünger watched his own brother being stretchered away under heavy fire he was more worried about him than he was about himself. 'This may be explained partly by the confidence in his own luck everyone has. The belief that nothing can happen to himself makes each man underestimate the danger.' At the same time, knowing that their lives could be lost or saved by the unpredictable trajectory of a shell, men became fatalistic. 'Thank God we can only die once,' exclaimed Jünger's men as they advanced into the storm of steel in the spring of 1918.[170] 'There on the open field of death', wrote Patrick McGill of the London Irish, 'my life was out of my keeping.'[171] As Cruttwell observed, 'Nearly every soldier becomes a fatalist on active service; it quietens his nerves to believe that his chance will be favourable or the reverse. But his fatalism depends on the belief that he has a chance.'[172] This fatalism sometimes manifested itself in a seeming callousness about the deaths of other men. Numerous eye-witnesses commented on the way experienced soldiers would barely react when one of their comrades was suddenly killed or wounded: a dead man suddenly became 'not a matter of horror but replacement': 'One got to regarding men as mere matter.'[173] In short, each man (as Freud himself noted) believed that he as an individual would not be killed:

No instinct we possess is ready for a belief in [our own] death. This is perhaps the secret of heroism. The rational explanation for heroism is that it consists in the decision that the personal life cannot be so precious as certain abstract general ideals. But more frequent, in my view, is that instinctive and impulsive heroism which . . . flouts danger in the spirit of . . . 'Nothing can happen to *me.*'[174]

Or, as the British soldiers sang on their way to the Front: 'The Bells of hell go ting-a-ling-a-ling / For you but not for me.' They sang it with irony, but fought believing it.

Crucial to such skewed calculations was the distortion of the soldier's time-horizon. Many soldiers came to half-believe that the war would never end. Becker has shown how French soldiers' expectations about the war's duration gradually grew more pessimistic until by 1917 the end had ceased to be foreseeable. Even in August 1918 André Kahn was one of many soldiers who expected it to last another year.[175] As early as 1916 Siegfried Sassoon's fellow officers joked about commuting by train from England to the Front, as if to a civilian office job. A year later an officer calculated that it would take 180 years to reach the Rhine if the pace of advance achieved at the Somme, Vimy and Messines were maintained. There were jokes about how the Front would look in 1950. Even in the 1930s Sassoon still dreamt of having to return to it. Ivor Gurney died in a mental hospital in 1937 still convinced the war was not over.[176]

Yet in the heat of battle, time telescoped inwards: men who had spent the night before dreading death ceased to think about anything but the immediate future once an attack began. (As Graves put it, 'I didn't want to die – not before I'd finished *The Return of the Native* anyhow.') And that made action a relief: as one French soldier observed, 'the attack freed you from the terrible anguish of waiting, which disappear[ed] as soon as the action start[ed]'.[177] Countless soldiers' memoirs testify to this, and to the anaesthetic quality of combat. As a private in the Royal Welch Fusiliers recalled of his part in the attack on Mametz Wood:

It was life rather than death that faded away into the distance, as I grew into a state of not-thinking, not-feeling, not-seeing. I moved past trees, past other things; men passed me by, carrying other men, some crying, some cursing, some silent. They were all shadows, and I was no greater than they. Living or dead, all were unreal . . . Past and future were equidistant and unattainable, throwing no bridge of desire across the gap that separated me from my remembered self and from all that I hoped to grasp.[178]

Such feelings, at once exalted and morbid, help explain why soldiers in the most exposed positions were rarely those whose morale cracked. For morale to crack, men needed time to weigh their chances of survival. In combat there was no opportunity to do so. Instead of a rational assessment of survival chances, men acted on impulse: usually they fought, trusting that they as individuals would be lucky.

13

The Captor's Dilemma

THE RATIONALE OF SURRENDER

There was, however, another reason that men kept fighting; and that was that they could see no more attractive course of action. As Norman Gladden said about the eve of Third Ypres: 'If only some alternative were open. But I knew I had no choice.' But was that true? This brings us to the crucial point. There was, of course, a choice. The previous chapter considered only the more difficult options: desertion back into one's own lines, which in the West was hard to get away with (especially for monoglot Tommies like Eric Partridge, who 'had not even the courage to desert');[1] or mutiny, the most difficult form of resistance to military authority. One might also add the techniques of shooting oneself in the foot and, indeed, suicide; both extremely difficult to do since immediate, certain, self-inflicted pain rarely seems preferable to future and possibly avoidable pain inflicted by others. For that reason the numbers of SIWs (self-inflicted wounds) and suicides was never very high.

But there was another option: to surrender.

Surrender was the key to the outcome of the First World War. Despite the huge death rolls, it proved impossible to achieve the ideal objective of pre-war German doctrine, 'the annihilation of the enemy': demography meant that there were more or less enough new conscripts each year to plug the gaps created by attrition. For that reason the 'net body count' in the Central Powers' favour was not enough to bring them victory. However, it did prove possible to get the enemy to surrender in such large numbers that his ability to fight was fatally weakened.

People at the time knew that large captures of enemy troops were a good sign. Around 10 per cent of the British film *The Battle of the*

Somme is devoted to pictures of German POWs. Interestingly, there is a sequence at the end of Part III in which a British soldier threatens a German POW, though elsewhere 'wounded and nerve-shattered German prisoners' are seen being given drink and cigarettes.[2] Official photographers were encouraged to snap such scenes. The Germans too produced postcards and newsreels showing foreign prisoners of war being marched through German cities.[3] The significance of surrendering was never more obvious than on the Eastern Front in 1917; for the key to Russia's military defeat was the huge number of surrenders in that year. Overall, more than half of total Russian casualties were accounted for by men who were taken prisoner. Austria and Italy also lost a large proportion of men in this way: 32 and 26 per cent of all casualties. Yet for most of the war surrender rates for the British, French and German armies were much lower. Just 12 per cent of French casualties were taken prisoner, 9 per cent of German and 7 per cent of British.

It was only at the very end of the war, as Figure 17 shows, that German soldiers began to give themselves up in large numbers, beginning in August 1918. According to one estimate, 340,000 Germans surrendered between 18 July and the armistice.[4] Between 30 July and 21 October – less than three months – the British alone took 157,047 German prisoners. In the whole of the rest of the war they had captured only slightly more than that (190,797). In the last week alone 10,310 gave themselves up.[5] This was the real sign that the war was ending. The figures for men *killed* in fact tell a completely different story. In the last three months of fighting, 4,225 British officers were killed and 59,311 men, compared with equivalent figures for Germans (in the British sector) of 1,540 and 26,688.[6] In terms of killing, in other words, the losers in the war were still more than twice as effective as the winners. But in terms of prisoner-taking there was no doubt that the Germans were losing. To explain this, it is not enough simply to say that the Germans were 'war-weary', 'demoralized' or, for that matter, cold and hungry. It is also necessary to examine their attitude towards the enemy to whom they were surrendering; and the way that enemy reacted to surrender.

There was a good reason for this general reluctance of soldiers in the West to surrender – and it was not just superior discipline and morale. Surrender on the Western Front was dangerous; indeed, for much of the war most soldiers felt that the risks a man ran by surrendering were greater than the risks he ran by fighting on.

Table 42   Prisoners of war, 1914–1918

Country of origin of POWs	Minima	Maxima	Prisoners as a proportion of total casualties
France	446,300	500,000	11.6
Belgium	10,203	30,000	11.0
Italy	530,000	600,000	25.8
Portugal	12,318	12,318	37.2
Britain	170,389	170,389	6.7
British Empire	21,263	21,263	3.3
Rumania	80,000	80,000	17.8
Serbia	70,423	150,000	14.6
Greece	1,000	1,000	2.1
Russia	2,500,000	3,500,000	51.8
USA	4,480	4,480	1.4
Total Allies	3,846,376	5,069,450	28.0
Bulgaria	10,623	10,623	4.2
Germany	617,922	1,200,000	9.0
Austria–Hungary	2,200,000	2,200,000	31.8
Turkey	250,000	250,000	17.2
Total Central Powers	3,078,545	3,660,623	19.9
Total prisoners	**6,924,921**	**8,730,073**	24.2
Net prisoner count	767,831	1,408,827	
Percentage difference	25	38	

Notes: The Greek prisoners figure includes missing so probably overstates number of POWs. Rumanian figures are very approximate.
Sources: War Office, *Statistics of the Military Effort*, pp. 237, 352–7; Terraine, *Smoke and the Fire*, p. 44.

Why was surrendering dangerous? The answer is that on numerous occasions on both sides men were killed not only as they tried to surrender but after they had surrendered. These are, it might be said, the forgotten 'atrocities' of the First World War; but they were arguably the most important. For so long as such things happened – and they happened often enough for men on both sides to be aware of them – there was a substantial disincentive to surrender. That was one of the most important reasons why men kept fighting even when they found

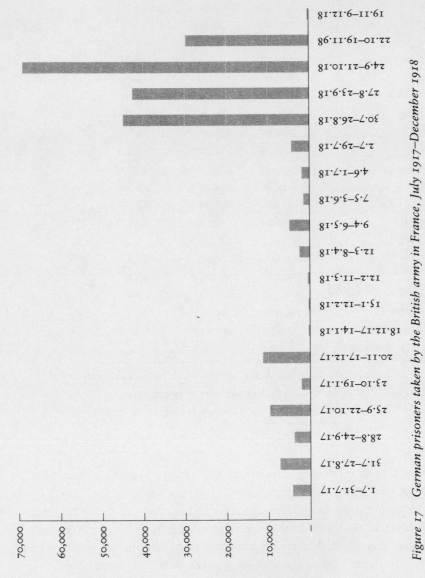

Figure 17 German prisoners taken by the British army in France, July 1917–December 1918

Source: War Office, *Statistics of the Military Effort*, p. 632.

themselves in dangerous, if not hopeless, positions. Had it been safer to surrender in 1917–18, it seems plausible that many more men would have done so in order to escape from the terrible battles of those years; the fact that it was not safe to surrender thus prolonged the war. Once the Germans lost their fear of surrendering to the Allied armies, the war was over. If the French or British had surrendered in comparable numbers in the spring of 1918 Ludendorff would have been forgiven all his sins of strategic omission.

To make the problem of surrender clearer – and it is a perennial problem in warfare – it is helpful to imagine a theoretical game: instead of the prisoner's dilemma, the captor's dilemma. The captor's dilemma is simple: accept the enemy's surrender, or kill him. The captor has been fighting an opponent who has been trying to kill him, when suddenly the opponent makes as if to surrender. If he is sincere, then the right thing to do is to accept his surrender and send him back down through the line towards a prisoner-of-war camp. That is the rational course of action for four reasons. A prisoner may be used as:

a. a source of intelligence;
b. a source of labour;
c. a hostage; and
d. an example to his comrades (if by treating him well you can induce them to give themselves up too).

Of these points, the first and second were regarded as especially important during the First World War. Captured Germans were interrogated for intelligence purposes and Haig relied heavily on the results of such interrogations.[7] Moreover, captured POWs provided a useful source of cheap labour at a time when that was in short supply. Though Haig was initially opposed to keeping captured Germans in France for this purpose, he was effectively overruled by the Cabinet. By November 1918 German POWs accounted for 44 per cent of the BEF's Labour units. Technically, under the Hague Convention, they were not to be given tasks connected with military operations, but that was a distinction which was more or less impossible to maintain and the term 'preparation work' came to be very flexibly interpreted (the French even used POWs to dig trenches).[8] Indeed, the deployment of POWs in areas closer than 30 kilometres to the front line prompted a protest by the German government in January 1917, accompanied by reprisals whereby British prisoners were moved into the vicinity of the German lines in France and in Poland.[9] Prisoners were also used as hostages: the Germans put prisoners in camps at Karlsruhe, Freiburg and Stuttgart to act as 'lightning conductors', in the hope of deterring Allied bombing raids.[10] Less attention was, however, paid to the fourth argument in favour of taking prisoners, in the sense that little was done to broadcast the fact that prisoners were being reasonably well treated.

What are the arguments on the other side of the captor's dilemma: against taking prisoners? One is that the supposed surrenderer may be bluffing. Time and again during the Great War, men were warned by their commanders of such ruses: a man would appear to surrender, the attackers would relax their efforts and vigilance, whereupon concealed enemy forces would open fire. Typical was the experience of the British troops at the Aisne in September 1914 who were killed when they accepted a bogus gesture of surrender.[11] In the same way, Lieutenant Louis Dornan of the Dublin Fusiliers was killed at the Somme when some Germans who had apparently surrendered 'shot him through the heart'.[12] On other occasions no duplicity was intended: while some members of a group of soldiers would surrender, others would fight on. At Bullecourt in 1917 an Australian officer named Bowman ordered his men to surrender and proceeded to do so himself. 'Two German soldiers were escorting the officer away when our fellows shot both of them. They also threatened to shoot Lieutenant Bowman.'[13] It could equally well be the other way round, as in the case of Lieutenant-Colonel Graham Seton Hutchison, who reputedly shot 38 of his own men for attempting to surrender, before resuming the war against the Germans.[14]

In other words, accepting surrender is therefore itself risky.[15] It may also be quite difficult to transport a prisoner back to the lines – in the First World War the army specified a ratio of between one and two escorts to every ten prisoners[16] – and anyone given this job has to be subtracted from the attacker's force. The problem is increased if the man surrendering is wounded and incapable of walking unassisted. The simple solution is to shoot the prisoner and forget about him; had he kept fighting that would have been his fate anyway and while he was fighting he probably inflicted casualties on the attacker. But though prisoner shootings solved an immediate problem, they were illegal under military and international law: to be precise, under the Hague Convention, Regulation 23(c), which stated that it was forbidden to kill or wound a prisoner who had surrendered by laying down his arms, and Regulation 23(d), which prohibited the order that no quarter be given.[17] Moreover, killing prisoners had negative consequences in practice because it encouraged resistance by other enemy troops who might otherwise have surrendered. Thus the captor's dilemma: to accept a surrender, with all the personal risks entailed; or to shoot the surrenderer, with the likelihood that resistance would be stiffened, thus increasing the risks to one's own side as a whole.

CHARGE AND COUNTER-CHARGE

It was in fact the Germans who started the illegal and ultimately irrational practice of taking no prisoners. Thus Soldier Fahlenstein of the 34th Fusiliers recorded in his diary that orders were carried out on 28 August 1914 to kill wounded French prisoners. At around the same time NCO Göttsche of the 85th Infantry Regiment was told by his captain near the fort of Kessel, near Antwerp, that no English prisoners were to be taken. According to the diary of a German doctor, French wounded were bayoneted to death by a company of German sappers on 31 August. A Silesian newspaper even reported (under the heading 'A Day of Honour for our Regiment') that French prisoners were finished off in late September.[18] The soldiers concerned were almost certainly following verbal orders such as those given to the 112th (Baden) and 142nd regiments. According to one German soldier's diary for 27 August, 'French prisoners and wounded are all shot because they mutilate and maltreat our wounded'; this at any rate was what he had been told by his superiors. Another conscript, named Dominik Richert, confirmed that his regiment (the 112th Infantry) had been ordered to kill prisoners; interestingly, he noted that most but not all of the soldiers disliked the order.[19]

Such behaviour continued throughout the war. In March 1918 Ernst Jünger described how an orderly in another officer's company shot 'a good dozen or more' English prisoners who were 'hasten[ing] with upstretched arms through the first wave of storm troops to the rear'. Jünger's feelings were ambivalent: 'To kill a defenceless man', he wrote, 'is a baseness. Nothing in the war was more repulsive to me than those heroes of the mess tables who used to repeat with a fat laugh the familiar tale [sic] of the prisoners marched in: "Did you hear about the massacre? Priceless!"' Yet he felt he could 'not blame the men for their bloodthirsty conduct'.[20]

It is tempting merely to add these episodes to the charge sheet of German *Schrecklichkeit*. But this will not quite do. For it seems clear that the Entente powers did not take long to reply in kind. Karl Kraus made this point in *The Last Days of Mankind*. In Act V, scene 14, German officers are seen ordering their men to kill French prisoners at Saarburg. In the next scene, however, French officers discuss the bayoneting of 180 German prisoners near Verdun.[21] As so often, the more grotesque a scene in Kraus's drama, the closer to the truth it turns out to be.

In 1922 August Gallinger, a former army doctor and, from 1920, Professor of Philosophy at Munich University, published a book entitled *Countercharge*, in which he listed a series of allegations to the effect that Allied soldiers had committed atrocities against German prisoners.[22] Most historians would be inclined to dismiss such a work as mere special pleading, a feeble attempt by a German to prove that 'two blacks do make a white' in response to the wartime allegations of German atrocities. However, Gallinger's charges merit more serious consideration.

Gallinger himself served with the Bavarian army and was one of the many Germans captured late in the war (by the French in September 1918). He did not much care for his treatment, though he was honest enough to admit that he personally did not witness any incidents of prisoner killing. As we shall see, however, there probably were fewer such incidents at that stage in the war (which was perhaps why so many Germans were willing to surrender).

After the war Gallinger began to assemble statements from other former POWs. They make hair-raising reading. To be sure, some describe incidents of the sort which happen in most conflicts in the heat of battle. But others describe acts which can only be described as cold-blooded murder. Often these prisoners were wounded men whom the French simply finished off. Karl Alfred of Mehlhorn described how, after his company's trench had been stormed, 'French soldiers appeared from either hand and ruthlessly killed off the wounded, either with the butt end of their rifles or with bayonets. Those lying near me were killed one after the other by bayonet thrusts through the head. I pretended to be dead and so escaped.'[23] 'Johann Sch.' of Dortmund described seeing 'French reserves marching to the front plac[ing] five or six badly wounded Germans in a row, and took delight in shooting these helpless wretches. The company officer, among others, was killed by two blows on the head.'[24] According to Gallinger, this kind of behaviour was not necessarily spontaneous: the French 151st Division specifically charged *nettoyeurs* with the task of killing enemy wounded on the grounds that 'German soldiers after holding up their hands in sign of surrender, have frequently shot their captors in the backs'.[25] But it was not only the wounded who were killed. John Böhm from Fürth related how 'A French sergeant came and asked us to what nation we belonged. The first man questioned, replied "Bavarian", whereupon he was shot through the head at close range and at once fell dead. The sergeant did the same with the others.'[26] In October 1914, according to the affidavit of Sergeant Feilgenhauer, '150 men of the 140th infantry were butchered behind the trench, only 36 men escaping, all in the presence of a [French] officer'.[27] Another witness described being shot at by a French officer as he and other prisoners were marched through the French lines.[28] Max Emil Richter of Chemnitz recalled how he and his comrades were ordered by their French captors to 'unbuckle our arms and climb down into a small trench, but while doing so, our opponents shot at us, so that we fell on top of one another. Whoever gave a sign of life was felled by gun butt blows or bayoneted ... I myself was shot through the lung and scalp . . .'[29] Adolf K. of Düsseldorf related how in September 1915 he and thirty-nine other men were ordered by their commanding officer to surrender after the French had captured their trench: 'At the command of some superior . . . the French opened fire upon us. We all scattered and I fell into a shell hole, shot through the knee. From there I could see the Frenchmen kill the rest as they lay on the ground, using their feet and rifle butts.' He was the only survivor.[30] In May 1916, Julius Quade, who served in the 2nd Company, 52nd Infantry, was captured at Douamont:

Fifty or sixty metres behind the enemy trench stood a French officer and shot six or seven of my comrades who were disarmed, and some of them even wounded. I myself was shot in the thigh. At his command we had to file past him, and he shot each man at close range.[31]

Though many of Gallinger's stories relate to the French army, his book covers most theatres and armies. There are horror stories about Africans, Moroccans and 'Hindoos' cutting off heads and the like, as well as accounts of Rumanian murders of prisoners.[32] There are also several allegations against British troops. They too, Gallinger claimed, 'shot without ado' prisoners who were too badly wounded to be moved to the rear.[33] And they too murdered healthy POWs in cold blood. One Magdeburg man signed an affidavit which described how, at Pozières in July 1916, 'Four prisoners belonging to the 27th Infantry are shot down by Englishmen and afterwards bayoneted.'[34] In May 1917, according to Sergeant Drewenick of Posen's testimony, 'About 30 men of the 98th Reserve Infantry, who were cut off in a trench and had surrendered to an English sergeant, were killed while being led away.'[35] Four months later, infantryman Oberbeck of Hanover alleged, forty or fifty men of the 77th Reserve Infantry captured at St Julien were 'sent into a concrete house near the English second line. Most of them are killed by handgrenades and revolver shots.'[36] That same month infantryman Stöcken, also of Hanover, witnessed 'systematic killing of the wounded by groups of three of four men after the end of the fight' at Ypres.[37] English soldiers could also be violent in demanding booty from prisoners. According to Hugo Zimmermann, 'One man unable in his excitement to get his belt off quickly enough, was bayoneted through the body' in November 1918.[38] Friedrich Weisbuch of Ettenheimmünster described being as far as '500 metres behind the enemy line when one man was killed and two wounded by three English soldiers, even though they raised their hands in sign of surrender'.[39] Again Gallinger suggests that in some cases men were acting under orders. He cites a statement from one Jack Bryan of 'the 2nd Scottish Regiment' to the effect that 'The order "make [sic] no prisoners" [had been] passed along the company from man to man.'[40] He also cites incidents involving Dominion troops. According to medical sergeant Eller of the 17th Bavarian Reserve Infantry, the Canadians at Messines had been given 'orders . . . to take no prisoners, but to kill all Germans. There had been so many taken however that it could not be done.'[41] Sergeant Walter of Stuttgart testified that 'a Canadian officer [at Miramont] without cause kill[ed] the captured infantryman Mahl and Lieutenant Kübler, both of the 120th Reserve Infantry'.[42]

Were these mere fictions? Certainly, it is possible to find explicit denials from the Allied side that such things happened. Lieutenant-General Sir John Monash claimed in his account of the Australian army's campaign in France in 1918 that 'no case ever came to my notice of brutality or inhumanity to prisoners'.[43]

Yet in support of his argument Gallinger was able to quote from English sources too. In his war memoir *A Private in the Guards*, Stephen Graham described being told by an instructor: 'The second bayonet man kills the wounded . . . You cannot afford to be encumbered by wounded enemies lying about your feet. Don't be squeamish. The Army provides you with a good pair of boots; you know how to use them.' Later Graham described how

the idea of taking prisoners had become very unpopular. A good soldier was one who would not take a prisoner. If called on to escort prisoners to the cage, it could always be justifiable to kill them on the way and say they tried to escape . . . Captain C., who at Festubert shot two German officer-prisoners with whom he had an altercation, was always a hero, and when one man told the story, 'That's the stuff to gi' 'em' said the delighted listeners.

Graham also referred to British soldiers 'vowing never to take any prisoners', adding: 'The opinion cultivated in the army regarding the Germans was that they were a sort of vermin like plague-rats that had to be exterminated.' Graham also related a story he had been told by others:

An old time sergeant goes up to his officer, who by the bye was a poet, and wrote some very charming lyrics and had a taste for art, and salutes: 'Leave to shoot the prisoners, sir?' 'What do you want to shoot them for?' says the poet. 'To avenge my brother's death,' says the sergeant. I suppose the poet tells him to carry on. He pinks the Germans one after one, and some of the fellows say 'Bravo!' and in others the blood runs cold.[44]

Gallinger was also able to quote a similar story from Philip Gibbs's *Now It Can Be Told*, as originally related by Colonel Ronald Campbell, the famously bloodthirsty lecturer on bayonet-drill:

A crowd of Germans were captured in a dugout. The sergeant had been told to blood his men, and during the killing he turned round and asked, 'Where's 'Arry? . . .'Arry 'asn't 'ad a go yet.'

'Arry was a timid boy, who shrank from butcher's work, but he was called up and given his man to kill. And after that 'Arry was like a man-eating tiger in his desire for German blood.

Another Campbell story quoted by Gibbs was as follows: 'You may meet a German who says "Mercy! I have ten children!" Kill him! He might have ten more.'[45] Gallinger was able to quote a French author named Vaillant-Courturier who recalled 'officers who boasted of shooting down German prisoners in order to test their revolvers . . . [and] officers who shot down companies of captured and disarmed prisoners and who were promoted for these atrocities'.[46]

None of this can be treated as impeccable evidence, of course; indeed, the English quotes need to be read with a sense of humour which Gallinger evidently lacked. Had they been written sooner, he might also have quoted Norman Gladden's reminiscences:

Most of our northern compatriots [i.e. Scots] were against [taking prisoners] much to our dismay. Fritz, they insisted, did not take any, so why should we? I did not really believe them though of course in such anarchy anything was possible. Lurid yarns were told of German prisoners who failed to reach the cages for some reason or other. The favoured tale was of a party of warlike Gurkhas who were extremely annoyed at having been detailed for such a time-wasting job as conducting a batch of prisoners to the rear. They discovered a short cut of their own and the authorities had turned a blind eye. Whether true or not the tale was received with satisfaction as an instance of rough justice.[47]

Lieutenant A. G. May related a similar story after the battle of Messines, having seen two Tommies pass with a group of prisoners and then report back without them:

After being much questioned it was learned that the two men had killed the prisoners. 'All right,' said the Staff Captain, 'you'll be court-martialed for this.' 'We don't care, we expected it.' 'Well why did you kill them?' 'They killed my mother in an air-raid,' said one. 'When they bombarded Scarborough they killed my sweetheart,' said the other one.[48]

On 16 June 1915 Charles Tames, a private in the Honourable Artillery Company, described an incident following an attack at Bellewaarde near Ypres:

We were under shell fire for eight hours, it was more like a dream to me, we must have been absolutely mad at the time, some of the chaps looked quite insane after the charge was over, as we entered the German trenches hundreds of Germans were found cut up by our artillery fire, a great number came out and asked for mercy, needless to say they were shot right off which was the best mercy we could give them. The Royal Scots took about 300 prisoners, their officers told them to share their rations with the prisoners and to consider the officers were not with them, the Scots immediately shot the whole lot, and shouted 'Death and Hell to everyone of ye s—' and in five minutes the ground was ankle deep with German blood . . .[49]

Gallinger might also have appreciated Somerset Maugham's stories of French violence towards prisoners which he heard and in one case witnessed in 1914. A Cossack cavalry officer serving with the French described how,

having taken a German officer prisoner, he took him to his quarters. There he said to him: 'Now I will show you how we treat prisoners and gentlemen,' and gave him a cup of chocolate; when he had drunk it, he said: 'Now I will show you how you treat them.' And he smacked his face. 'What did he say?' I asked. 'Nothing, he knew that if he had opened his mouth I would have killed him.' He talked to me about the Senegalese. They insist on cutting off the Germans' heads: 'Then you're sure they're dead – *et ça fait une bonne soupe*.'[50]

In *Goodbye to All That* Robert Graves supplies more anecdotes: 'Some divisions, like the Canadians and a division of Lowland Territorials . . . would . . . go out of their way to finish [enemy wounded] off.'[51] He had no doubt that 'true atrocities, meaning personal . . . violations of the code of war' occurred frequently 'in the interval between the surrender of prisoners and their arrival (or non-arrival) at headquarters':

Advantage was only too often taken of this opportunity. Nearly every instructor in the mess could quote specific instances of prisoners having been murdered on the way back . . . In any of these cases the conductors would report on arrival at headquarters that a German shell had killed the prisoners; and no questions would be asked. We had every reason to believe that the same thing happened on the German side, where prisoners [were regarded] as useless mouths to feed in a country already short of rations.[52]

Such stories, most of them more or less embroidered if not wholly made up, do not constitute adequate corroboration of Gallinger's German testimony, though they testify to the widespread *belief* in prisoner killings. Major F. S. Garwood claimed to be amazed when a German officer taken prisoner at First Ypres 'pretended that he had been told that we shot all our prisoners'; this, declared Garwood, 'shows what lies the Germans spread among their troops'.[53] Herbert Sulzbach had exactly the same reaction when French prisoners told him 'stories about our killing prisoners'; they expressed 'agreeable surprise that it isn't happening'.[54] However, it is clear that on both sides such 'stories' were based on fact.

It is important in this context to try to distinguish between killing which happened in the heat of battle and more cold-blooded killing away from the battlefield. Harry Finch's diary for the first day of

Third Ypres provides a good example of the difficulty of making that distinction: 'We sent back crowds of prisoners,' he wrote. 'They were absolutely frightened to death. Some of the poor devils got shot down in cold blood, through our men being so excited.'[55] In this case, the blood of the soldiers responsible (men of the Royal Sussex Regiment) was not 'cold' at all: this was typical of the kind of battlefield confusion which John Keegan has described so well, in which attacking men find it impossible to suspend their desire to kill the enemy in the face of a gesture of surrender. On 20 September 1917, to give another example, Australian troops had surrounded a two-storey German pillbox and persuaded the men in the lower storey to surrender:

The circle of Australians at once assumed easy attitudes, and the prisoners were coming out when shots were fired, killing an Australian. The shot came from the upper storey, whose inmates knew nothing of the surrender of the men below; but the surrounding troops were much too heated to realise this. To them the deed was treachery, and they forthwith bayoneted the prisoners. One, about to bayonet a German, found that his own bayonet was not on his rifle. While the wretched man implored him for mercy, he grimly fixed it and then bayoneted the man.[56]

Was this done in cold or hot blood? The same question can be asked of the other Great War example cited by Keegan, the story related by Chapman of a sergeant at the Somme shooting a German officer who had explicitly said 'I surrender' – even handing over his field glasses as he did so. Chapman's view was that the man was probably 'half mad with excitement when he got into the trench. I don't suppose he even thought what he was doing. If you start a man killing, you can't turn him off again like an engine.'[57] One veteran of the Somme recalled killing surrendering Germans almost as a reflex action: 'Some of the Germans were getting out of their trenches, their hands up in surrender; others were running back to their reserve trenches. To us they had to be killed.'[58] In the same spirit, the New Zealand Otago Battalion took no prisoners when it stormed Crest Trench.[59] When this sort of thing did *not* happen, it was cause for comment. An Irish lieutenant in the 16th Division at Ginchy in September 1916 was impressed that 'not one' of 200 'Huns' who had been 'engaged in slaughtering our men up to the very last moment was killed' after surrendering. 'I did not see a single instance of a prisoner being shot or bayoneted,' he added. 'When you remember that our men were worked up to a frenzy of excitement, this crowning act of mercy to their foes is surely to their eternal credit.'[60] The fact that he was so struck by this suggests that it was the exception rather than the rule.

It would be easy to list many similar cases of formally 'improper' violence which was nevertheless bound to happen sometimes in close-quarters fighting; probably a number of Gallinger's cases were more like these than his accounts imply. In *All Quiet on the Western Front*, Remarque gives a vivid account of the split-second decisions which determined the fates of surrendering men:

We have lost all feelings for others, we barely recognize each other when somebody else comes into our line of vision, agitated as we are. We are dead men with no feelings, who are able by some trick, some dangerous magic, to keep on running and keep on killing.

A young Frenchman falls behind, we catch up with him, he raises his hands and he still has a revolver in one of them – we don't know if he wants to shoot or to surrender. A blow with an entrenching tool splits his face in two. A second Frenchman sees this and tries to get away, and a bayonet hisses into his back. He leaps in the air and then stumbles away, his arms outstretched and his mouth wide open in a scream, the bayonet swaying in his back. A third throws down his rifle and cowers with his hands over his eyes. He stays behind with a few other prisoners-of-war, to help carry off the wounded.[61]

Ernst Jünger himself admitted that:

The defending force after driving his bullets into the attacking force at five paces' distance, must take the consequences. A man cannot change his feelings again during the last rush with a veil of blood before his eyes. He does not want to take prisoners but to kill. He has no scruple left; only the spell of primeval instinct remains.[62]

However, Jünger also cited an incident of German prisoners shooting their captor and of a British officer himself being captured when attempting to take some Germans prisoner![63] This was precisely the kind of thing which made men like the Norfolks in Ivor Maxse's 18th Division at the Somme take no prisoners. As one subaltern recalled:

I saw parties of Germans during the attack fire on our fellows until they were within a few yards of them; then, as soon as they found out that there was no hope for them they threw down their arms and rushed forward to shake our men by the hands. Most of them got their desserts [sic] and were not taken prisoner. Some of the wounded Germans were shooting our men in the back after they had been dressed by them. They are swine – take it from me – I saw these things happen with my own eyes.[64]

It was particularly gratifying to kill a man who appeared to be surrendering and then find that he had intended foul play. 'Lying on his stomach, he turned his head and asked for mercy,' one soldier wrote,

but his eyes said murder. I plunged the bayonet into the back of his heart and he slumped with a grunt. I turned him over. There was a revolver in his right hand under his left armpit. He had been trying to get a shot at me under his body. As I withdrew the bayonet, I pressed the trigger and shot him to make sure.[65]

Mistrust was not the only reason men gave for killing prisoners, however. Graves cited as 'the commonest motives . . . revenge for the death of friends or relatives, jealousy of the prisoner's trip to a comfortable prison camp in England, military enthusiasm, fear of being suddenly overpowered by prisoners, or, more simply, impatience with the escorting job'.[66] Sometimes the threat of a counter-offensive was enough: in October 1917 the 2nd Anzac Corps was said to have killed a large number of prisoners on hearing 'the Boche was massing to counter'.[67] More frequently, men were motivated by the desire for revenge that we have already encountered as a motive for fighting: witness the men described by May who were repaying the Germans for the deaths of their mother and sweetheart in air raids. Probably more usual was the desire to avenge a dead comrade: Lieutenant John Stamforth described how three 'lads' in the 7th Leinsters killed six prisoners after their attack at Vermelles in June 1916, when 'they stumbled upon the body of one of our officers' while leading the prisoners back through the lines.[68] Occasionally a man sought to avenge himself: having himself been shot in the foot by a German raid on a sap near Loos in December 1916, Private O'Neill of the 2nd Leinsters had to be restrained when he attempted to kill a German prisoner subsequently brought in.[69] The classic illustration of the way the cycle of violence rolled forward is given by George Coppard who recalled 'a villainous trick by the Prussians' in the Hohenzollern Redoubt:

Three hundred of them came across No Man's Land feigning surrender, with no rifles or equipment, their hands held high, but with pockets full of egg bombs. Just before reaching our wire they flung themselves to the ground and hurled a rain of bombs into 'B' Company's trench, causing many casualties. The blow was so severe that the remnants of the company were unable to put up any strong retaliation. The rest of the battalion was sullen and furious about the trick and called the Prussians bloody bastards. Many vowed some dark revenge when any prisoners were taken. Most Vickers gunners swore a private vendetta. From then on, the advance of a crowd of Jerries with their hands up would be the signal to fire.[70]

In fact, when Coppard had the chance to pursue his vendetta at Arras by giving some surrendering Germans on the other side of Scarpe canal 'the extreme treatment', 'Lieutenant W. D. Garbutt *decided* they should be taken prisoner'. Understandably the Germans were reluctant to comply when ordered to cross the canal, fearing they would be mown down as they crossed.[71]

However, vengeance was also sometimes wreaked for more remote German acts, including atrocities which soldiers had not themselves witnessed. 'Some [surrendering Germans] would crawl on their knees', recalled another British soldier,

holding a picture of a woman or a child in their hands above their heads but everyone was killed. The excitement was gone. We killed in cold blood because it was our duty to kill as much as we could. I thought many a time of the *Lusitania*. I had actually prayed for that day [of revenge], and when I got it, I killed just as much as I had hoped fate would allow me to kill.[72]

Another man recalled how a friend had to be restrained from killing a captured German pilot:

He tried to find out whether he had been over [London] dropping bombs. He said, 'If he's been over *there*, I'll shoot him! He'll never get away.' He would have done it too. Life meant nothing to you. Life was in jeopardy and when you'd got a load of Jerries stinking to high heaven, you hadn't much sympathy with their *Kamerad* and all this cringing business.[73]

An Australian soldier described in August 1917 how an officer shot two Germans, one wounded, in a shellhole:

The German asked him to give his comrade a drink. 'Yes', our officer said, 'I'll give the — a drink, take this,' and he emptied his revolver on the two of them. This is the only way to treat a Hun. What we enlisted for was to kill Huns, those baby-killing—.'[74]

Note here the influence of fictional atrocities (the killing of Belgian babies) in generating real atrocities: Kraus vindicated. Clearly some soldiers did believe what they read in the Northcliffe press.

ORDERS

More controversial is the question of whether men were obeying orders in shooting prisoners. There are, of course, many examples of senior officers exhorting their men 'to kill Huns'. The commander of the 24th Division urged his men in December 1915 to 'kill every armed German on every possible occasion'; but he specified *armed*.[75] Major John Stewart of the Black Watch told his wife that his battalion 'TOOK VERY FEW PRISONERS' at Loos in 1915, adding that 'the main thing is to kill plenty of HUNS with as little loss to oneself as possible.' But this was a private letter and does not prove he ordered his men not to take prisoners.[76]

The evidence of 'take no prisoners' orders is, however, unambiguous for the Somme, traditionally portrayed as the mass martyrdom of the British army. A brigadier, probably Gore, was heard by a soldier in the Suffolks to say on the eve of the battle: 'You may take prisoners, but I don't want to see them.' A soldier in the 17th Highland Light Infantry recalled the order 'that no quarter was to be shown to the enemy and no prisoners taken'.[77] In his notes 'from recent fighting' by II Corps dated 17 August, General Sir Claud Jacob urged that no prisoners should be taken, as they hindered mopping up.[78] Colonel Frank Maxwell, VC, ordered his men (the 18th battalion of the 12th Middlesex) not to take any prisoners in their attack on Thiepval on 26 September, on the ground that 'all Germans should be exterminated'.[79] On 21 October Maxwell left his battalion a farewell message which was circulated along with battalion orders by his successor. In it he praised his men for having

begun to learn that the only way to treat the German is to kill him . . . I hardly know what a prisoner looks like and one of the reasons for this is that this Battalion knows how to look after its thirsty souls . . . Remember that the 12th 'Die-Hards' DO KILL [and] DON'T TAKE PRISONERS UNLESS WOUNDED.[80]

Captain Christopher Stone took the view that 'a live Boche is of no use to us or to the world in general'.[81]

Similar evidence can be found for 1917 too. Before Passchendaele, Hugh Quigley's commanding officer told his men:

Do not shoot prisoners when such – that is, murder on his own lines [sic]; do not kill wounded if they are in desperate condition and helpless. If prisoners are in your way, you are allowed to dispose of them as you please. Not otherwise![82]

Those were, to say the least, flexible guidelines. Typical of the attitude of many front-line officers is the following exchange between three officers in the mess of the Royal Berkshire Regiment:

L: There was a rather rotten story about that raid last night.
R&F: What was that?
L: Why, they captured a German officer and were taking him back to our lines, and he had his hands tied behind his back, and a chance bullet hit one of the men forming his escort, and so they turned on him and killed him.
R: I don't see anything wrong about that . . . More Bosch you kill the better.
L: But . . . he was a *prisoner*; and it was only a stray bullet that hit his escort, and his hands were tied behind his back; and he could not defend himself; and they simply killed him just as he was.
R: And a damned good job too.[83]

As this exchange suggests, officers differed on the issue. Anthony Brennan of the Royal Irish Regiment described the case of 'one of our Lance-Corporals who had . . . deliberately fired at and killed a German who was coming in with his hands up'. Brennan and his fellow officers 'took a very poor view of this and all kind of maledictions were directed against the murderer'.[84] On the other hand, Jimmy O'Brien of the 10th Dublin Fusiliers recalled being told by his chaplain (an English clergyman named Thornton): 'Well now boys, we're going into action tomorrow morning and if you take any prisoners your rations will be cut by half. So don't take prisoners. Kill them! If you take prisoners they've got to be fed by your rations. So you'll get half rations. The answer is – don't take prisoners.'[85]

However, it is not true to claim that Haig's Chief of Staff Lieutenant-General Sir Lancelot Kiggell encouraged this sort of thing.[86] His order of 28 June 1916 simply reminded officers of German ruses (the use of British words of command, the disguising of machine-guns) and stated:

It is the duty of all ranks to continue to use their weapons against the enemy's fighting troops, unless and until it is beyond all doubt that those have not only ceased all resistance, but that, whether through having voluntarily thrown away their weapons or otherwise, they have definitely and finally abandoned all hope or intention of resisting further. In the case of apparent surrender, it lies with the enemy to prove his intention beyond the possibility of misunderstanding, before the surrender can be accepted as genuine.[87]

This was no more than doing things by the book.

The facts of the matter therefore seem clear: on occasions, and with encouragement from some commanders, men went into battle intending to give no quarter. Even when they did not, they found it difficult to take prisoners – and risk falling for a ruse – when they had the chance to kill them. Of course, there were relatively few such incidents in comparison with the thousands of captures which proceeded smoothly from battlefield, to Straggler Post, to Divisional Cage, to Corps HQ for interrogation, to camp – and finally back home when the war was over (usually a good many months after). Behind the lines, the German prisoner ceased to be an object of hatred and became rather an object of curiosity (like zoo animals or 'music 'all 'uns') and even sympathy;[88] just as the half-starved Russian prisoners arouse the hero's pity in *All Quiet on the Western Front*[89] – though even when they were in camps prisoners were not always safe. Somerset Maugham himself saw a group of French *gendarmes* gratuitously gun down a group of German prisoners. This occurred 25 kilometres from the Front.[90]

Yet the number of incidents is not as important as the impression they made on the culture of the trenches. Men magnified these episodes: they passed into trench mythology. And the more such myths were repeated, the more reluctant men were to surrender. Keegan therefore errs when he dismisses such incidents as 'absolutely meaningless . . . in "win/lose terms"', for *future* decisions about surrender could not but be affected by the perception that the other side were taking no prisoners; or at least finding it difficult to do so.

Only in the last three months of the war did German soldiers begin to surrender in such large numbers that the war could no longer be continued. That was the key to the Allied victory. Yet it is far from easy to say why suddenly the Germans were willing to surrender. The most commonly offered explanation is that the failure of Ludendorff's spring offensive, after its initial success, finally convinced a large number of soldiers that the war could not be won.[91] Another possibility is that the arrival of American troops on the Western Front encouraged Germans to surrender because the Americans had a reputation for treating prisoners well. There is a little evidence to support this. When Elton Mackin of the 21st Battalion, 5th Marine Regiment, encountered dead German machine-gunners as he advanced towards the Meuse on 7 November 1918, he was puzzled:

The enemy had broken away before us, leaving scattered Maxims here and there to slow our advance. Their bravely desperate crews had done the best they could and died.

We never really understood such men. The crews were small, seldom more than two or three, and always young. The young ones stayed and died because their orders told them to. Older fellows would have used their heads – cried 'Kamerad' before the guns grew really hot and men grew coldly bitter.[92]

However, the figures clearly show that only a minority of Germans – around 43,000 – surrendered to the Americans in the last phase of the war, compared with 330,000 captured by the British and French.[93] More probably it was the *idea* of ever-increasing American reinforcements rather than their actual presence which contributed to the collapse of German morale. In any case, it is clear that the US Marines were just as ready to take no prisoners as more seasoned British and French troops. Mackin himself recalled being told by Major-General Charles P. Summerall, commander of the American Expeditionary Force's V Corps: 'Way up there to the north is a railhead . . . Go cut it for me. And when you cut it, you will go hungry if you try to feed the prisoners you will take . . . [N]ow I say, and you remember this, on those three ridges, take no prisoners.'[94] Mackin describes at least one occasion when no prisoners were taken and another when only one wounded German was spared 'for some reason that we younger fellows didn't understand . . . He was the only prisoner taken there – or should we say "accepted".'[95]

A general explanation for the mass German surrenders of late 1918 remains elusive. To say the Germans 'knew' they had lost the war probably implies a bigger grasp of the strategic 'big picture' than many soldiers in the front line had. Decisions about fighting or surrendering had more to do with immediate personal calculation than grand strategy. Why, for example, did Ernst Jünger refuse to surrender when his position was plainly a hopeless one in the weeks before the Armistice?

In refusing to surrender along with his men, he very nearly got himself killed. His motivation seems to have been individual honour; like the mortally wounded German who refused British medical assistance because he wanted 'to die uncaptured'.[96] Why did the young machine-gunners seen by Mackin fight on pointlessly in November 1918?

On 8 July 1920 Winston Churchill declared in the House of Commons:

Over and over again we have seen British officers and soldiers storm entrenchments under the heaviest fire, with half their number shot down before they entered the position of the enemy, the certainty of a long, bloody day before them, a tremendous bombardment crashing all around – we have seen them in these circumstances . . . show, not merely mercy, but kindness, to prisoners, observing restraint in the treatment of them, punishing those who deserved to be punished by the hard laws of war, and sparing those who might claim to be admitted to the clemency of the conqueror. We have seen them exerting themselves to show pity and to help, even at their own peril, the wounded. They have done it thousands of times.[97]

Thousands of times, perhaps; but not always. If either side had been able to do more to encourage the enemy to surrender – rather than allowing the culture of 'take no prisoners' to infect certain units, generating exaggerated impressions on both sides of the risks of surrender – then the war might conceivably have ended sooner; and not necessarily with a German defeat. Conversely, if more men had taken no prisoners the war might have carried on indefinitely. And, then again, perhaps it did.

WAR WITHOUT END

It is usually asserted that men surrendered because they were 'war-weary'. A Bavarian named August Beerman who surrendered at Arras told his captors: 'We were sick of gas, sick of shells, sick of the cold and sick of having no food. We no longer had the will to fight. Our spirit had been broken.'[98] No doubt he spoke for many. Yet there is another paradox: though weary of the war, men do not seem to have been weary of violence. Karl Kraus warned in *The Last Days of Mankind* that the returning warriors will break into the hinterland and there really begin the war. They will grab for themselves the successes which eluded them [at the Front] and the essence of the war – the murder, plunder and rape – will be child's play compared with the peace which will now break out. May the god of battles protect us from the offensives that will then lie ahead! A fearful activity, freed from the trenches, no longer under any command, will reach for arms and for gratification in every situation, and more death and illness will be brought into the world than even the war itself has required of it.[99]

D. H. Lawrence agreed. 'The war isn't over,' he told David Garnett on Armistice night:

The hate and evil is greater now than ever. Very soon war will break out again and overwhelm you . . . Even if the fighting should stop, the evil will be worse because the hate will be dammed up in men's hearts and will show itself in all sorts of ways which will be worse than war. Whatever happens there can be no Peace on Earth.[100]

This proved all too true. Hermann Hesse was quite right when he wrote shortly after the war: 'Revolution is nothing more than war, [just] as war is a continuation of politics by other means.'[101]

War raged far and wide in the 'post-war' world. German *Freikorps*, composed of veterans and students who had been too young to fight, scrapped with Poles and others along Germany's new and contested borders.[102] Herbert Sulzbach was impressed when some of his comrades joined the 'Eastern Border Guard' (*Grenzschutz Ost*): '[J]ust imagine this, soldiers who have been engaged in heavy fighting for years are volunteering straight away, thousands and thousands of them . . . Could there be more splendid proof of spirit and conviction than this?' Other irregular units fought Spartacist and Communist 'hundreds' in the big German cities: there were *putsch* attempts from the Right or the Left in every year between 1919 and 1923. The Majority Socialists used *Freikorps* units against the extreme Left in 1919; a year later they had to mobilize a workers' 'Red Army' in the Ruhr to stop a coup by military conservatives led by the former Fatherland Party leader Wolfgang Kapp. In 1921 the Communists staged a 'March Action' in Hamburg; in 1922 there was a spate of assassinations by right-wing extremists (among the victims was Walther Rathenau); and in 1923 both Left (the Hamburg *Aufstand*) and Right (the Bürgerbräukeller *putsch*) attempted coups. The extent of violence in urban Germany is hard to quantify: suffice to say that in 1920 it was estimated that 1.9 million rifles were being held illegally, along with 8,452 machine-guns; demobilization had not included disarmament.[103]

The egomaniacal Italian poet Gabriele D'Annunzio seized Fiume (now Rijeka) in September 1919 to prevent its being ceded to Yugoslavia; this ephemeral escapade attracted support from demobilized and disgruntled *arditi* (shock troops), whose black shirts shortly became the emblem of the new violence-loving political movement known as Fascism. Desultory fighting also continued in Albania; and the Italians landed other troops at Adalia (now Antalya) in southern Anatolia. Though the Italian government gave up Fiume and Albania in 1920, this merely imported the violence. In the Romagna and in Tuscany the phenomenon of *squadrismo* burgeoned as landowners and socialists took up arms against one another: the archetypal ex-soldier proto-Fascist was Italo Balbo of Ferrara. The Fascist 'March on Rome' (26–30 October) was a sham, no doubt: the 25,000 ill-armed Fascists who gathered around Rome could easily have been dispersed if the Italian king had not panicked and summoned Mussolini to power; but with their uniforms and salutes the Fascists were reading from a script based loosely on the war.[104]

In the Balkans too 'peace' meant war in the countryside, at its worst in northern Croatia; there was also the first sign that the Serbs would use force to impose their dominance on the ethnic minorities in the new 'Kingdom of the Serbs, Croats and Slovenes': according to one report, as many as a thousand Muslim men were killed and 270 villages pillaged in Bosnia in 1919.[105] Turkey had seemed prostrate in 1918, at last ready to be carved up by France, Britain and Italy. All three at once fell to quarreling over the spoils. Egged on by Lloyd George, the Greeks landed a rival force at Smyrna.[106] They underestimated the Turks who, under the leadership of Mustapha Kemal, drove them out in 1921.

Violence was endemic within the British Empire too. In Ireland 'Black and Tans' and 'Auxies' – veterans of the British army – were deployed against Republicans; once the British had given up, the nationalists killed one another in a civil war which claimed at least 1,600 lives.[107] In the Middle East Britain's newly established rule was beset by riots in Egypt in 1919; and revolts in Palestine and Iraq in 1920.[108] British troops displayed extreme violence in suppressing these disturbances: some 1,500 Egyptians were killed in the space of eight weeks, while in Iraq General Sir Aylmer Haldane even contemplated using poison gas.[109]

On 11 April 1919, in one of the seminal atrocities of British imperial history, soldiers killed 379 people at a political meeting in Amritsar. Brigadier-General Reginald Dyer, who gave the order to shoot, would have killed more if he had been able to deploy two armoured cars with machine-guns.[110] Thus did men export the techniques of mass murder which had been patented on the Western Front.

The world was not weary of war, in other words; just weary of the First World War. For many men who had fought, violence had become addictive; and once the violence stopped on the Western Front, they sought it elsewhere. This included men who had been taken prisoner during the war: the Czech Legion in Russia is the classic example. And the veterans found ready accomplices in men like the Bolsheviks, German students and Irish Republicans who had not fought, but thirsted to taste blood.

The extreme case was indeed Russia. It was the Russian army which collapsed first, the Russian soldier who had been most ready to surrender rather than fight on. Yet nowhere was violence more prolonged after the supposed end of the war than in Russia. More Russians lost their lives during the Russian Civil War than during the First World War. Between October 1917 and October 1922, somewhere in the region of 875,818 men who served in the Soviet armed forces were killed or died of wounds and disease (roughly 13 per cent of all those called up); the best available mortality estimate for the White armies is 325,000. This total (1.2 million) should be compared with the total number of Russian soldiers killed during the war (1.8 million).

Table 43   Casualties in the Russian Civil War, 1918–1922

Total numbers called up, 1918–20	6,707,588
Maximum strength of all armed forces, Nov. 1920	5,427,273
Average strength of all armed forces, 1918–20	2,373,137
Irrecoverable losses (killed, missing, prisoners, died) 1918–20	701,647
Sick and wounded, 1918–20	4,322,241
Average strength of all armed forces, 1921–2	1,681,919
Irrecoverable losses (killed, missing, prisoners, died) 1921–2	237,908
Sick and wounded, 1921–2	2,469,542
Total irrecoverable losses (killed, missing, prisoners, died)	939,755
Total sick and wounded	6,791,783

Source: Krivosheev, *Soviet Casualties*, pp. 7–39.

However, these figures for the Civil War omit large numbers of people who died in the hundreds of peasant rebellions or anti-Soviet risings which also occurred in this period, but which were not really part of the White war effort: for example, around 250,000 people were probably killed in the various 'Bread Wars' as peasants sought to resist grain requisitioning. One estimate of the number of victims of the 'Red Terror' directed by the secret police (the Cheka) against political opponents of the regime puts it as high as 500,000, among them 200,000 people officially executed; the figure may indeed be even higher.[111] Perhaps as many as 34,000 people also died inside or on their way to the concentration and labour camps set up after July 1918.[112] Nor should the numerous pogroms perpetrated by both Whites and Reds against Jews be forgotten: a 1920 report mentions a total of 'more than 150,000 reported deaths'.[113] Finally, around 5 million people died as a result of famine and a further 2 million from disease. From all these causes, almost as many people died during the Civil War period as people of all nations during the First World War: one estimate for total demographic losses in the Civil War period is as high as 8 million; around 40 per cent of these deaths can be attributed to the Bolshevik policies.[114]

In one respect, Kraus's thesis that it would be the returning soldiers who would unleash civil war was quite wrong. The White armies, led by seasoned Tsarist generals, were certainly responsible for a large number of atrocities against civilians;[115] as were Red Army units led by equally experienced former imperial officers (by the end, three-quarters of the senior commanders of the Red Army were former Tsarist officers; among the bigger 'catches' was Brusilov). However, the peculiarly extreme violence of the Civil War owed much to the bloodthirstiness of men who had not fired a shot during the war against Germany. In particular, there is something uncanny about the way Lenin and Trotsky gloried in setting new standards in military ruthlessness: two wordy intellectuals who had watched the war from what Volkogonov has called 'the Russian émigré's grand circle';[116] who had come to power in 1917 by denouncing the Provisional Government for prolonging the war; who had promised to bring peace to Russia; who had been willing to hand over most of Russia's European possessions to end the war with Germany. Yet Lenin meant only to turn the imperialist war into a civil war against the bourgeoisie of his own country. In their pursuit of that goal, and in their resistance to the efforts of the White armies and other opponents of the revolution, he and Trotsky sought to resolve the problem of surrender and desertion which had dogged the Tsarist army by means of terror. Though they had been far from the battlefields during the imperialist war, their imaginations – stimulated by extensive knowledge of the history of Jacobin France – were more than equal to the task of devising new rules of warfare which far exceeded in their brutality even those which had come to prevail on the Western Front by 1917.

After reintroducing conscription in May 1918, the Bolsheviks had to deal with levels of desertion greater even than those which had wrecked the Tsarist war effort. In 1920 20,018 men deserted from the front-line troops, including fifty-nine commanding officers; but the rate of desertion by men shortly after call-up was as high as 20 per cent. Altogether some 4 million men deserted from the Red Army in 1921; many peasant deserters formed their own 'Green' forces to resist conscription.[117] The Bolsheviks responded by introducing draconian discipline: a Temporary Central Commission for Combating Desertion was set up in December 1918. In seven months alone in 1919, 95,000 men were found guilty of desertion in aggravated circumstances, of whom 4,000 were sentenced to death and 600 actually shot.[118] In 1921 some 4,337 men were executed in Russia and the Ukraine by military tribunals.[119] It was Trotsky who set the pace here. 'Repression' was his watchword: in November 1918 he demanded 'merciless punishment for the deserters and shirkers who are paralysing the will of the 10th Army ... No mercy for deserters and shirkers.' 'It is', he declared in 1919, 'impossible to maintain discipline without a revolver.'[120] The families of officers were to be arrested in cases of desertion. Above all, it was Trotsky who in December 1918 ordered the formation of 'blocking units' equipped with machine-guns, whose role was simply to shoot front-line soldiers who attempted to retreat. Thus was born the elementary rule that if Red Army soldiers advanced they might be shot, but if they fled, they would definitely be shot.[121]

Lenin was, if anything, even more intoxicated by the possibilities of terror. In August 1918 he cabled to Trotsky: 'Shouldn't we tell the [Red Army commanders] that from now on we're applying the model of the French Revolution and putting on trial and even executing the senior commanders if they hold back and fail in their actions.' At the same time he urged the Party boss in Saratov to 'shoot conspirators and waverers without asking anyone or any idiotic red tape'.[122] His letter to the Bolsheviks of Penza in the same month gives a good insight into the new ethos of violence against civilians which characterized the Civil War period:

Comrade! The kulak [rich peasant] uprising in [your] five districts must be crushed without pity. The interests of the whole revolution demand it, for the 'final and decisive battle' with the kulaks everywhere is now engaged. An example must be made. 1) Hang (and I mean hang so that the *people can see*) *not less than 100* known kulaks, rich men, bloodsuckers. 2) Publish their names. 3) Take *all* their grain away from them. 4) Identify hostages ... Do this so that for hundreds of miles around the people can see, tremble, know and cry: they are killing and will go on killing the bloodsucking kulaks ...

Yours Lenin.
P.S. Find tougher people.[123]

Surprisingly, the Bolshevik leaders drew the line at prisoner killing: Trotsky explicitly forbade it in an order of 1919.[124] But the fact that the order had to be issued suggests that the practice of shooting captured Whites was widespread. In August of that year the Red Army Commander-in-Chief S. S. Kamenev ordered that 'no prisoners be taken' in repulsing an attack by Don Cossacks:

Wounded or captured [White] officers were not only to be finished off and shot, but tortured in every possible way. Officers had nails driven into their shoulders according to the number of stars on their epaulets; medals were carved on their chests and stripes on their legs. Genitals were cut off and stuffed in their mouths.[125]

Figes reproduces a picture of a Polish officer, captured by the Red Army in 1920, being hanged naked upside down and beaten to death.[126] This kind of barbaric behaviour may have proved effective against the ill-disciplined, dispersed and outnumbered White armies; against the Poles, however, it merely stiffened resistance. The Civil War thus represented a major advance on the terror tactics of the earlier world war. The next major war on the Eastern Front would be fought under these new 'rules': death for deserters; exemplary violence against civilians; and no quarter for prisoners. This truly was 'total' war: and to Hitler and Stalin, both of whom issued orders to these effects, it seemed the logical conclusion to be drawn from German and Russian defeat in the First World War. Of course, nothing could have been better calculated to make that war one of unprecedented violence, in which men on both sides fought to the end because they no longer had any alternative.

14

How (not) to Pay for the War

ECONOMIC CONSEQUENCES

Imagine a country which, as a result of the First World War, effectively lost 22 per cent of its national territory; incurred debts equivalent to 136 per cent of gross national product, a fifth of it owed to foreign powers; saw inflation and then unemployment rise to levels not seen for more than a century; and experienced an equally unprecedented wave of labour unrest. Imagine a country whose newly democratic political system produced a system of coalition government in which party deals behind closed doors, rather than elections, determined who governed the country. Imagine a country in which the poverty of returning soldiers and their families contrasted grotesquely with the conspicuous consumption of a hedonistic and decadent élite; a country which one disgusted conservative could dismiss as:

a nation without standards, kept in health rather by memories which are fading than by examples which are compelling. We still march to the dying music of great traditions, but there is no captain of civilization at the head of our ranks. We have indeed almost ceased to be an army marching with confidence towards the enemy, and have become a mob breaking impatiently loose from the discipline and ideals of our past ... We are ... [a] nation of half-educated people, and it is the mark of the half-educated to be sceptical, apathetic, unimaginative, and capricious.[1]

The effects of inflation were most severely felt by the middle classes, as another post-war writer vividly lamented:

[A] whole body of decent citizens [is] slipping down by inexorable God-made or man-made or devil-made laws into the Abyss: as if a table was suddenly tilted slanting and all the little dolls and marionettes were sent sliding on to the floor . . . [T]he whole mass, despite resistance, is falling through the bottom of the world.

Here . . . is a complete and startling transformation of values; not slowly changing from one to another, but suddenly and almost brutally forced upon the life of millions by causes altogether outside their control . . .[2]

Middle-class spokesmen lamented the new 'corporatist' alliance of capital and labour which the war had forged – an analysis of the war's consequences since endorsed by historians.[3]

This was not Germany – as the reader may forgivably have assumed – but Britain, the supposed victor of the First World War, in the years immediately after 1918. The territory lost consisted of the twenty-six counties of Southern Ireland, where the spark of revolt ignited in Dublin at Easter 1916 had become a blaze of civil war in the 1920s, and where the *de facto* partition of 1922 had, by 1938, become *de jure* secession under the constitution of the Republic of Ireland.[4] The external debts were owed principally to erstwhile Allies, with the US accounting for the lion's share (slightly more than £1 billion in March 1919). The cost of living reached nearly treble its pre-war level in November 1920, and annual inflation touched 22 per cent; the unemployment rate reached 11.3 per cent the following year, higher than in 1930, and the worst figure since records had begun. Some 2.4 million British workers were involved in strikes in 1919, 300,000 more than in revolutionary Germany. In 1921 86 million days were lost in industrial disputes; the German figure was 22.6 million.[5] The electorate was increased from 7.7 million to 21.4 million by the 1918 Representation of the People Act, more or less giving Britain the franchise Germans had enjoyed since 1871 (universal male suffrage).[6] Lloyd George, who had come to power in 1916 as a result of a backroom coalition deal, called a snap election three days after the Armistice was signed. His coalition won; but he himself was turned out of office in October 1922 when Conservative MPs, meeting at the Carlton Club, killed the coalition. To writers like Harold Begbie and Charles Masterman – the authors of the passages quoted above – Britain seemed sick despite her victory.

Yet the great paradox was – and remains – the belief that Germany, the loser, was worse off. No doubt she should have been, having lost the war. Even then, British sympathy for the vanquished foe would be hard to explain. But in many ways Germany came out of the war no worse off than Britain, and in some respects better off. The one respect in which post-war Germany did fare worse was that inflation ran completely out of control, so that the Reichsmark was worth virtually nothing by the end of 1923 (see Figure 18). At the nadir in December 1923 the cost of living index reached 1.25 trillion times its pre-war level (1,247,000,000,000). A loaf of bread cost 428 billion marks; a dollar 11.7 trillion. Though most combatant countries experienced some measure of inflation and few were able to return to their pre-war gold standard parity, this was the worst case. Poland did better despite having to fight a war: its price level rose by a factor of 1.8 million; even Russian prices went no higher than 50 billion times the pre-war level before the currency was reformed.[7] As we shall see, the Germans blamed their monetary troubles on the harsh peace terms which had been imposed on them; oddly, most educated British contemporaries seem to have believed them. In March 1920 the Oxford Union debated the motion 'That the Peace Treaty is an economic disaster for Europe': it was carried by a majority of 20 per cent. Three months later it voted by 80 to 70 votes for 'the immediate re-establishment of cordial relations' with Germany. The Union motions on foreign affairs in this period read like a chronicle of the genesis of appeasement. In February 1923 the Union voted by 192 to 72 votes to 'deplore the present policy of France' in occupying the Ruhr after the Germans had defaulted on reparations. In March a motion was carried which declared 'the overwhelming defeat of Germany a misfortune for Europe and this country'. Two months later a majority of 25 per cent of those in the chamber agreed 'That the selfishness of French policy since 1918 has condemned humanity to another war.'[8]

In reality, the peace terms were not unprecedented in their harshness and the German hyperinflation was mainly due to the irresponsible fiscal and monetary policies adopted by the Germans themselves. They thought they could win the peace by economic means. In British minds they did. The Germans were also more successful than any other country in defaulting on their debts, including the reparations demanded from them by the Allies. However, this victory was pyrrhic: it was won by democratic politicians at the expense of democracy and their own power.

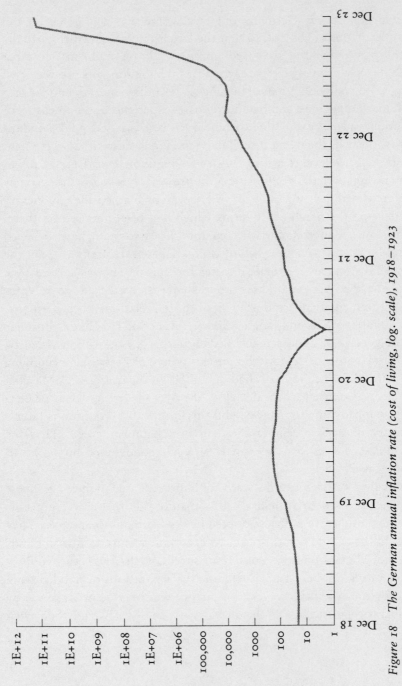

Figure 18 The German annual inflation rate (*cost of living, log. scale*), 1918–1923

Source: Statistisches Reichsamt, *Zahlen zur Geldentwertung.*

CAN'T PAY

The idea that the Versailles treaty imposed on Germany in 1919 was excessively harsh was a truth universally acknowledged in Germany itself; however, it would never have gained much credence outside Germany, and especially in Britain, had it not been for John Maynard Keynes, whose pamphlet *The Economic Consequences of the Peace* was (along with Lytton Strachey's *Eminent Victorians*) one of the bestsellers of 1919.

As we have seen, Keynes had become an influential voice at the Treasury thanks to his Cassandra-like utterances about British war finance. It was therefore logical for him to become involved in preparations for the peace once it became clear that the Germans wanted an armistice. The question of reparations had been a subject of debate even before the war's end.[9] Keynes soon emerged as the leading advocate of a relatively low indemnity, arguing as early as October 1918 that 20 billion goldmarks was a realistic total figure for reparations.[10] Although he doubled this figure in the memorandum he drafted in December 1918 'on the Indemnity payable by the Enemy Powers for Reparation and other Claims', he was careful to stress the problems that would arise from imposing such a burden. The Treasury memorandum acknowledged from the outset that even 'if every house and factory and cultivated field, every road and railway and canal, every mine and forest in the German Empire could be carried away and expropriated and sold at a good price to a ready buyer, it would not pay for half the cost of the war and of reparation added together'.[11] More importantly, Keynes's memorandum anticipated an argument which was to become central to the subsequent debate by distinguishing between 'two eventualities' which might arise from the transfer of reparations:

The first, in which the usual course of trade is not gravely disturbed by the payment, the amount of it being approximately equal to the sum which would accrue to the paying country abroad in any case, and would have been invested abroad if it were not for the indemnity; the second, in which the amount involved is so large that it cannot be paid without . . . a far-reaching stimulation of the exports of the paying country . . . [which] must necessarily interfere with the export trade of other countries . . . In so far as this country receives the indemnity, there is a heavy off-set to this injury. But, in so far as the indemnity goes into other hands, there is no such off-set.

For this reason, Keynes advocated a policy of 'obtain[ing] all the property which can be transferred immediately or over a period of three years, levying this contribution as ruthlessly and completely, so as to ruin entirely for years to come Germany's overseas development and her international credit; but, having done this . . . to ask only small tribute over a term of years'.[12] However, he also warned that a German fiscal crisis might lead to open debt repudiation or a break-up of the Reich.[13] In short, Keynes's intellectual reservations about excessive reparations were to a large extent established before he arrived in France for the armistice and peace negotiations.

There is, however, no question that a series of meetings with one of the German representatives at Versailles added an emotional dimension to Keynes's position. Carl Melchior was Max Warburg's right-hand man at the Hamburg bank of M. M. Warburg & Co.: a Jewish lawyer with a distinguished war record both on the battlefield and in economic policy-making. It may be that Keynes's subsequent declaration that he 'got to love' Melchior during the armistice negotiations at Trier and Spa obliquely alluded to a sexual attraction. As we have seen, Keynes was an active homosexual at this time. However, it seems more probable that Keynes was simply captivated by the sound of his own pessimism – the product of long-standing doubts about the morality of the war – being articulated by another.[14] Melchior (as Keynes later recalled) painted a bleak picture of a Germany on the brink of a Russian-style revolution:

German honour and organization and morality were crumbling; he saw no light anywhere; he expected Germany to collapse and civilization to grow dim; we must do what we could; but dark forces were upon us . . . The war for him had been a war against Russia; and it was the thought of the dark forces which might issue from the Eastwards which most obsessed him.[15]

The implication was clear: the Allies risked unleashing Bolshevism in Central Europe if they treated their vanquished foe too harshly. These arguments struck a resounding chord with Keynes. As the German Foreign Office official Kurt von Lersner observed after Lloyd George seemed to change his mind on the question of financing food imports to Germany: 'Thanks to Dr Melchior's clear explanation, Herr Keynes has realised that there is a danger for the Allies in delaying [matters] and is trying to find common ground with us.'[16] Significantly, in the immediate aftermath of the conference, Keynes warned that 'an immediate rapprochement between Germany and Russia' might be 'the only chance . . . [of] central Europe being able to feed itself'.[17]

The most detailed – and, for Keynes, influential – statement of the German view came in the counter-proposals drawn up in May at Warburg's instigation in response to the Allied terms.[18] The central theme (developed in a 'Supplement on Financial Questions') was that the Allied terms meant 'the utter destruction of German economic life', condemning Germany politically to 'the fate of Russia'.[19] Given the economic constraints being imposed by the peace – in particular, the loss of industrial capacity, colonies, overseas assets and the merchant navy – Germany could not pay war damages as defined by the Allies; attempting to force her to do so would have dire consequences. On the one hand, to pay reparations from current government revenue would require that 'expenditures for the payment of interest on the war loans, for the allotments of the disabled German soldiers and for the pensions of the dependents of the fallen soldiers, must cease or be cut down, as well as the expenditures for cultural purposes, schools, higher education etc.'. This would simply 'destroy' German democracy: 'Any ability and inclination to pay taxes would disappear and Germany would be for decades to come the scene of uninterrupted social class struggles of the bitterest kind.' Financing reparations by borrowing, on the other hand, posed equally grave problems:

In the immediate future it will be impossible to place German state loans in large amounts either at home or abroad, so that compensation [to the owners of assets expropriated for reparations] could be made only by means of large issues of notes. The inflation, already excessive, *would increase constantly if the peace treaty as proposed should be carried out. Moreover, great deliveries of natural products can only take place if the state reimburses the producers for their value; this means further issues of notes.* As long as these deliveries last, there could be no question of the stabilizing of the German currency even upon the present level. *The depreciation of the mark would continue. The instability of the currency would affect not only Germany, however, but all the countries engaged in export, for Germany, with her currency constantly depreciating, would be a disturbing element and would be forced to flood the world market with goods at ridiculously low prices.*[20]

Only if the Allies were to leave Germany with her territory, colonies and merchant fleet intact could reparations be paid.[21] Under these conditions, the Germans offered to pay interest plus amortization on bonds worth 20 billion goldmarks between 1919 and 1926; and amortization only on bonds up to a maximum of 80 billion goldmarks – the annuities 'not [to] exceed a fixed percentage of the German imperial and state revenues'.[22]

Whatever its significance for the history of German foreign policy,[23] the striking thing about this document is the way it foreshadows Keynes's subsequent critique of the treaty. This is perhaps not surprising. We know that Keynes was impressed by the refusal of the German delegation to sign the unamended peace treaty.[24] Indeed, he all but repeated the Germans' prophecies of doom:

Germany's . . . industry will be condemned to stagnation . . . Germany will collapse economically . . . and millions of Germans will die in civil conflicts or will be forced to emigrate . . . The result will be an 'economic Balkans' in the heart of Europe which will create endless unrest and constant danger of its spreading to the rest of the world.[25]

That was the German version. This was Keynes's:

The Peace is outrageous and impossible and can bring nothing but misfortune . . . They can't possibly keep the terms, and general disorder and unrest will result everywhere . . . Anarchy and revolution is the best thing that can happen . . . The settlement . . . for Europe disrupts it economically and must depopulate it by millions of people.[26]

Nor was Keynes out of touch with the Germans during the period when he was preparing his own prophecies for publication. In October 1919 he attended a small conference of bankers and economists in Amsterdam at the invitation of Warburg's American brother Paul.[27] Then he and Warburg jointly composed an appeal to the League of Nations which effectively called for a reduction in reparations, the cancellation of war debts and a loan to Germany.[28] However, by the time the final version of the memorandum was published in January 1920, it had ceased to matter. It had been overshadowed completely by the appearance of *The Economic Consequences*, a draft of which Keynes had read to Melchior and Warburg at Amsterdam.[29]

To say that Keynes's argument in this book was the same as that put forward by the German financial experts at the conference would be to exaggerate. But the resemblances are very close; nor did Keynes deny their influence on him.[30] Like them, he blamed the French for the 'Carthaginian' economic provisions of the Treaty and denounced the

Reparations Commission as 'an instrument of oppression and rapine'.[31] Like them, he insisted that Germany 'had not surrendered unconditionally, but on agreed terms as to the general character of the peace' (the Fourteen Points and subsequent American notes).[32] And like them, he stressed that the loss of Germany's merchant marine, her overseas assets, her coal-rich territories and her sovereignty in matters of trade policy severely limited her capacity to pay reparations. The Allies claimed compensation for damage and pensions amounting to some 160 billion goldmarks, which an asset-stripped Germany could only hope to pay out of her export earnings. Yet to turn the traditional German trade deficit into a surplus would put pressure on Allied business, while necessitating intolerable reductions in German consumption. Even leaving Germany with her essential assets (including the Silesian coal-fields), 41 billion goldmarks was the most she could be expected to pay, three-quarters in the form of interest-free annuities spread over thirty years.[33] Nor did Keynes omit the apocalyptic warnings he had heard from Melchior at Versailles, predicting a Malthusian crisis in Germany and the destruction of capitalism in Central Europe:

The policy of reducing Germany to servitude for a generation, of degrading the lives of millions of human beings, and of depriving a whole nation of happiness [will] . . . sow the decay of the whole civilised life of Europe . . . 'Those who sign this treaty will sign the death sentence of many millions of German men, women and children.' I know of no adequate answer to these words . . . If we aim deliberately at the impoverishment of Central Europe, vengeance, I dare predict, will not limp. Nothing can then delay for very long the final civil war between the forces of Reaction and the despairing convulsions of Revolution, before which the horrors of the late German war will fade into nothing, and which will destroy, whoever is victor, the civilization and the progress of our generation.[34]

Nothing short of 'a general bonfire' of international debts and a German-led programme of economic reconstruction in Eastern Europe, he argued, would avert this catastrophe.[35]

The setting of the final reparations bill – postponed at Versailles because of Allied dissension – prompted a new broadside from Keynes. In April 1921, after much haggling and prevarication, a definitive total bill was set at 132 billion goldmarks, backed by the threat that the Ruhr would be occupied if the Germans did not submit. This 'London Ultimatum' demanded that, beginning at the end of May 1921, Germany pay interest and amortization on so-called 'A' and 'B' bonds totalling 50 billion goldmarks in the form of a 2 billion goldmarks annuity. It also specified that, beginning in November 1921, a payment equal to 26 per cent of the value of German exports should be made; this implied a total annual payment of around 3 billion goldmarks. When German exports had reached a level sufficient to pay off the 'A' and 'B' bonds, non-interest bearing 'C' bonds with a face value of 82 billion goldmarks would be issued.[36]

Keynes's response to the London schedule involved some back-of-envelope sums. He estimated the burden of reparations at between a quarter and a half of national income, which, in purely fiscal terms, he considered impossibly heavy. 'Would the whips and scorpions of any government recorded in history have been potent enough to extract nearly half their income from a people so situated?' he asked readers of the *Sunday Times*.[37] In December 1921 he suggested that 21 billion goldmarks was the most which could be paid.[38] However, he remained sceptical about the possibility of any payment in hard currency as long as Germany was unable to run a balance of payments surplus: this was what would later be called 'the transfer problem'. Keynes doubted that Germany would obtain a loan from abroad to facilitate matters: by the time of the Genoa conference in April 1922 (which he 'covered' for the *Manchester Guardian*), he dismissed the German proposal for an international loan as 'an illusion [as big] as reparations on a grand scale'.[39] Nor did he believe that payments in the form of raw materials (as envisaged by Walther Rathenau) could ease the situation.[40] He also saw no possibility of a German export surplus in view of the country's large post-war appetite for imports. In any case, as he had already argued in 1919,

[even] if Germany could compass the vast export trade which the Paris proposals contemplate, it could only be by ousting some of the staple trades of Great Britain from the markets of the world ... I do not expect to see Mr Lloyd George fighting a general election on the issue of maintaining an Army to compel Germany at the point of the bayonet to undercut our manufacturers.[41]

In other words, the schedule of payments was unworkable. In the short term, Germany would only be able to raise the monthly payments by selling paper marks on the foreign currency markets; but this would inexorably drive down the exchange rate until the process became unsustainable.

19. Images of death, 7. 'WAR!!!!!': from an American soldier's album. To American soldiers arriving in Europe in 1917–18, the battlefields were gruesomely fascinating.

20. Comradeship, 1. 'East Yorks marching to the trenches before the attack': from the album of Richard Harte Butler. False jollity before the slaughter – or did some soldiers genuinely look forward to battle?

21. Comradeship, 2. 'Realistic Travels, no. 4: A Bosche sniper worries the Seaforths, who are snatching an hour's respite with their mascot'; reproduced for use in stereoscopic viewers. The Highland regiments – 'devils in skirts' – were especially disliked by the Germans, not least because of their reluctance to take prisoners.

22. Comradeship, 3. 'Bringing in the wounded. This man is actually under fire. He brought in 20 wounded in this manner': from the album of Richard Harte Butler. Men risked their lives for their friends more than for their country.

23. Rest . . . 'Asleep within 100 yards of Thiepval': from the album of Richard Harte Butler. This is no romantic image. Exhausted soldiers in the front line grew used to snatching sleep when they could, though to fall asleep while on sentry duty was a capital offence.

N⁰ 1840 Strassenbild aus d. wiedereroberten Görz 1.

24. . . . and Relaxation. 'Street scene in recaptured Görz [Gorizia], 1 November 1917': from the album of a soldier in the German 16 Korpscommando. Most soldiers drank as much alcohol as they could get their hands on.

25. Prisoners, 1. 'British Tommies with wounded Germans': from the album of Richard Harte Butler. Prisoner-taking was crucial to the outcome of the war. When soldiers felt confident of good treatment they were more likely to surrender. Unfortunately, such confidence was sometimes misplaced; in the heat of battle, men who surrendered were often shot. This encouraged their comrades to fight on – hence the captor's dilemma.

26. Prisoners, 2. 'This man knew London. He was a waiter and is anxious to return there.' Official photograph issued by the Press Bureau.

27. Prisoners, 3. 'Battle of Menin Road – Three Dejected-Looking Boches – They Came Out of the Fight for Vampire Farm Terribly Shaken by the Tremendous British Artillery Barrage.' The British lived in hope of bombarding the Germans into submission. Official photograph issued by the Press Bureau.

28. Prisoners, 4. 'One of our soldiers being carried in. He has his hand up shouting "I am not a German"': from the album of Richard Harte Butler. Note the German prisoners-of-war acting as stretcher-bearers.

29. (*overleaf*) The war in the air, 1. 'Bombs falling. East of Courtrai, 31 January 1918 9am': from a British pilot's album. As an American pilot said, 'From the air, it is often very difficult to distinguish where the lines are or to tell just what is going on.' (Hynes, *Soldier's Tale*, p.13) To drop bombs from this height was surely a pointless exercise. Aerial reconnaissance was important, however.

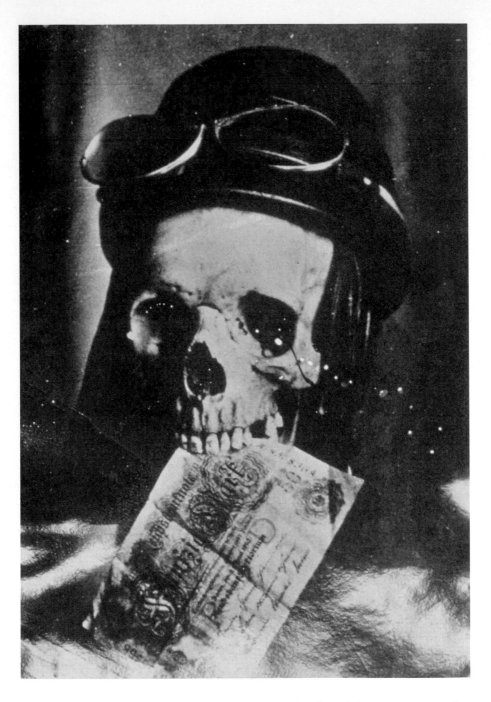

30. The war in the air, 2. A pilot's protest: a skull with a flying helmet and a 50-mark note, from the album of a German aviator. This image became a kind of photographic shorthand for the idea that a pilot's life was cheap.

31. The war in the air, 3. A German airman's cartoon of his squadron as donkeys, Armee Flugpark 'C', Easter 1917. The contrast between the way the pilots saw themselves and the way they were seen by the soldiers in the trenches – as 'knights of the sky' – is striking. Note the implication that the bombs they were carrying were no better than rotten eggs.

32. Oh! What a lovely War, 1: from an album of photographs by Frank Hurley. Not the 1960s musical, but a wartime concert party, revealing that soldiers at the time were well able to satirize themselves.

33. Oh! What a lovely War, 2. 'Poets and actors in the officers' mess': from a German officer's album (Western Front). The Germans had a sense of humour too.

34. Europe post-war. 'The Great British Advance in the West: The Germans destroyed the beautiful château of Calincourt and blew it into the Somme, and our men made a passage for the water': from the album of Richard Harte Butler. The German scorched-earth policy in 1918 did little to halt the victorious Allies, but added a few more million francs to the reparations bill worked out after the Versailles Treaty.

It was in August 1922 that Keynes's influence on the reparations issue reached its zenith, when he was invited to address a gathering of politicians and businessmen at the Hamburg 'Overseas Week' – in effect, an unofficial conference on German foreign policy – shortly after the French President Raymond Poincaré's speech calling for 'productive pledges' at Bar-le-Duc on 21 August.[42] The response this elicited from Keynes five days later was extraordinary. Introduced as 'the man most responsible for the changed attitude of the English-speaking world towards Germany', he was cheered to the echo; and it is tempting to wonder how far the applause influenced the content of his speech. In it Keynes made a fateful prediction:

I do not believe . . . France may actually carry into effect her threat of renewing war . . . One or two years ago France might have acted thus with the necessary inner conviction. But not now. The confidence of the Frenchmen in the official reparations policy is utterly undermined . . . They know in their hearts that it has no reality in it. For many reasons they are reluctant to admit the facts. *But they are bluffing.* They know perfectly well that illegal acts of violence on their part will isolate them morally and sentimentally, ruin their finances and bring them no advantage whatever. M. Poincaré . . . may make harsh speeches and inflict futile minor outrages . . . but he will not act on a big scale. Indeed, his speeches are an alternative not a prelude to action. The bigger he talks the less he will do . . .

To cap this, he dismissed the idea that inflation was causing 'the disintegration of German life':

One must not lose sight of the other side of the balance sheet . . . The burden of internal debt is wiped off. The whole of Germany's payments to the Allies so far . . . have been entirely discharged by the losses of foreign speculators. I do not believe that Germany has paid a penny for these items out of her own resources. The foreign speculators have paid the whole of these liabilities and more too.[43]

His conclusion amounted to a repetition of the now-familiar German demands for a moratorium, a loan and a reduced reparations burden.[44]

In private, it is true, Keynes was rather less rash. But it was the public remarks which had the greatest impact; not least because he was telling the Germans what they wanted to hear. Poincaré's 'bluff' should be called: this was the message relayed to the government in Berlin.[45] Nor was this the speech's only significance. Keynes's prediction in the same speech that 'the day of scientific, administrative and executive skill was at hand . . . not this year, indeed, but next year' echoed earlier calls by Warburg and his associates that precedence be given to 'the men of business over the diplomats and politicians in all questions of world economics'.[46] These calls were answered in early November with the appointment as Chancellor of Wilhelm Cuno, Albert Ballin's successor as head of the Hamburg–Amerika shipping line.[47] Keynes in England was enthusiastic. Eagerly, he urged the new Chancellor to 'call . . . out in a clear voice', and confessed to 'envy[ing] Cuno his job'.[48]

It would, of course, be absurd to lay the blame for the French occupation of the Ruhr and the final, irretrievable collapse of the German currency solely on Keynes. But there is no question that he played a role in encouraging both. Nor was he dismayed by the revelation that Poincaré had not, after all, been bluffing. Throughout the early weeks of the French occupation of the Ruhr, he encouraged the Germans to 'hold out to the limit of [their] endurance' and the government to 'keep its nerve'.[49] Only in May 1923, with the French grip on the Ruhr showing no sign of weakening and the German economy plunging ever deeper into the hyperinflationary abyss, did Keynes admit that the strategy had failed.[50]

This is not the place to describe the events which led to Cuno's fall, nor the protracted process by which passive resistance was wound up.[51] Suffice to say that Keynes's own account in his *Tract on Monetary Reform* (published in December 1923) was a trifle harsh, given his intimate involvement with the decisions to confront Poincaré and wage passive resistance:

It is necessary to admit that Cuno's failure to control incompetence at the Treasury and at the Reichsbank was bound to bring [his fall] about. During this catastrophic period, those responsible for the financial policy of Germany did not do a single wise thing, or show the least appreciation of what was happening.[52]

It is difficult to escape the conclusion that here Keynes was being wise after the event – having been rather unwise during it. For the counter-inflationary remedies he now urged – monetary restriction and a capital levy – had been conspicuously absent from his advice to the Germans prior to December 1923. Indeed, on a number of occasions, Keynes had congratulated the Germans on the large-scale expropriation of foreign wealth which had been brought about by the inflation. And ultimately, it seems, he could not resist judging the inflation a success in terms of economic diplomacy:

The remarkable experience of Germany during this period [he wrote in June 1929] may have been necessary to convince the Allies as to the futility of their previous methods for extracting reparations and was perhaps an inevitable prelude to the Dawes Scheme.[53]

As he put it in a speech in Hamburg in 1932 (exactly ten years after the Overseas Week appearance): 'I have often been doubtful during the past years about the wisdom of what you call the Policy of Fulfilment. If I had been a German statesman or economist, I think that I should probably have opposed it.'[54]

WON'T PAY

The man Keynes 'got to love' at Versailles called *The Economic Consequences of the Peace* 'magnetizing' and 'a landmark for a new development in . . . post-war history.'[55] In this Melchior was certainly right. Keynes's attack on the Versailles treaty without question contributed a good deal to that guilty feeling of having wronged Germany which so inhibited British diplomacy between the wars. Even today the idea that reparations were to blame for Germany's descent into hyperinflation continues to enjoy widespread scholarly support. The German budget was already badly out of kilter, Haller has argued, but the Allies' demand for cash reparations made matters much worse.[56] Because of a structural balance of payments deficit, Germany had no option but to buy hard currency by selling papermarks, thus driving down the exchange rate, pushing up import prices and hence the domestic price level.[57] Barry Eichengreen has put it bluntly: reparations were 'ultimately responsible for the inflation' because without reparations there would have been no budget deficit.[58] A conclusion frequently drawn is that German governments – expected by the Allies to raise taxes to pay for reparations which were almost universally unpopular – had no alternative but to seek to avoid paying. The most obvious way to do this was to allow inflation to continue, for, in Graham's words, the view was 'by no means without justification that improvement in the public finances would lead to still more severe exactions'.[59] It also supposedly made political sense to allow currency depreciation to continue unchecked, since that had the effect of boosting German exports.[60] This should have put pressure on the Allied economies, forcing them to accept that reparations could only be paid at the expense of Allied industry. Depreciation was therefore, according to Holtfrerich, 'in the national interest' – the most effective way of 'persuading the rest of the world of the need for a reduction of the reparations burden'.[61] Indeed, the strategy had a double advantage: because so much of the money lent to Germany in the period was never repaid, one historian has gone so far as to speak of 'American "Reparations" to Germany'.[62] In his definitive study of the German inflation, Feldman is unequivocal: the Allied peace terms 'made impossible demands and promoted intoler-able choices'; reparations were 'a disincentive to stabilise'.[63] These are Keynes's arguments, alive and well eighty years on. Yet historians have failed to recognize the extent to which Keynes was manipulated by his German friends; and the extent to which he erred in his analysis of the consequences of the peace.

Those involved in the German government's peace delegation in 1919 were well aware that they faced a tough peace. After all, they would have imposed a tough peace on the other side if they had won the war. The American diplomat who wrote the following during the war was not far wrong:

The Germans want somebody to rob – to pay their great military bills. They've robbed Belgium and are still robbing it of every penny they can lay their hands on. They robbed Poland and Servia . . . They set out to rob France and . . . if they got to Paris there wouldn't be 30 cents worth of movable property there in a week, and they'd levy fines of a million francs a day.[64]

Contemplating his country's burgeoning war debt in August 1915, the German Finance Minister Karl Helfferich had declared: 'The instigators of this war have earned this dead weight of billions . . . How this debt is cast off will be the biggest problem since the beginning of the world.'[65] Even the comparatively liberal Warburg had accepted this argument: in November 1914 he proposed 50 billion marks as an appropriate level of reparations for Germany to impose, assuming a war lasting just four months; as late as May 1918 he was still envisaging an Allied indemnity as high as 100 billion marks.[66] A supplementary financial agreement signed on 27 August 1918 had imposed on Russia an indemnity of 6 billion marks, despite the declaration in the original Treaty of Brest-Litovsk of March 1918 that there would be no reparations.[67] This was in addition to huge cessions of territory: Finland and the Ukraine became independent, while Poland and the Baltic states of Lithuania, Estonia, Courland and Livonia became German satellites. (In the surreal atmosphere of 1918, German princes bickered over who should rule them: the Duke of Urach wanted to be king of Lithuania; the Austrian Archduke Eugen demanded the Ukraine; the Kaiser's brother-in-law Friedrich Karl of Hesse had his eye on Finland; while the Kaiser himself coveted Courland.)[68] The territory in question represented around 90 per cent of the Russian Empire's coal capacity and 50 per cent of its industry.[69] By comparison with this, the territorial terms of the Versailles treaty were relatively lenient. Besides her colonies, Germany lost around nine peripheral chunks of territory from the Reich itself;[70] but these amounted to just 13 per cent of its pre-war area, and 46 per cent of the population of these areas was non-German. The Germans lamented the loss of 80 per cent of their iron ore, 44 per cent of their pig iron capacity, 38 per cent of their steel capacity and 30 per cent of their coal capacity; but the Russians had lost more in 1918, while the Austrians, Hungarians and Turks all fared worse in terms of territory (the Hungarians lost 70 per cent of their pre-war area) and perhaps also economic resources under their respective peace treaties. The loss of Germany's colonies was a blow to prestige: but although extensive (just under 3 million square kilometres) and populous (12.3 million people), they were of little economic worth.

Despite their anguished protests when the Allies presented their terms, the Germans had known what to expect. 'The Entente conditions', Warburg commented when invited to join the German delegation, 'would doubtless be extremely hard.'[71] Eugen Schiffer, the new Finance Minister, and Carl Bergmann, the Foreign Office's reparations expert, talked of figures of 20 billion marks and 30 billion marks; but Warburg warned them to brace themselves for an 'absurdly high' figure. As he put it to the Foreign Minister Count Ulrich von Brockdorff-Rantzau in early April: 'We must be prepared for damned hard conditions.'[72] Indeed, Warburg assumed that Germany would be burdened with reparations for between twenty-five and forty years.[73] The only way such a burden could be shouldered, he argued, was by means of an international loan to Germany, which would allow her to pay a fixed capital sum in annuities spread over a period of twenty-five to forty years.[74] By April he was envisaging a loan of 100 billion goldmarks.[75]

The best argument to justify such relatively generous treatment, the

Germans believed, was that without it Germany would descend into Bolshevism, fulfilling the next stage of Trotsky's plan for world revolution. As Warburg's friend Franz Witthoefft noted, shortly after agreeing to join the German delegation to Versailles:

Bread and peace are the preconditions for order and work; otherwise we are headed for Bolshevism, and that will be the end of Germany. Yet I detect in this very danger of Bolshevism a certain safety valve with regard to the efforts of the Entente to checkmate us absolutely. If this malaise spreads from Hungary over Germany, neither France nor England will be immune; and that means the end for all Europe.

During a meeting with ministers in Berlin in late April, Melchior argued that 'leanings towards Russia' must be contemplated as a future diplomatic strategy for Germany; a view which was endorsed by the Reich President Friedrich Ebert.[76] This was a very different tone from the apocalyptic one he adopted with Keynes. No doubt Melchior genuinely was worried about the political situation in Germany when he first met Keynes: after all, his home town was under the control of a Workers' and Soldiers' Council, and it was far from clear that the revolution of November 1918 was going to end in a compromise between Moderate Social Democrats, the more liberal 'bourgeois' parties and the old political, military and economic élites. Nevertheless, it seems clear that he did his best to exaggerate the Bolshevik threat for Keynes's benefit. The Red Army's successes in late 1919 and early 1920, and continuing social unrest in Germany, prompted renewed prophecies from Melchior of 'a kind of League of the Vanquished . . . between Russia and Germany'.[77] Melchior did not mean a word of this; he and Warburg were in fact appalled when Rathenau did a deal with the Russians over reparations during the 1922 Genoa Conference (the Treaty of Rapallo).[78]

At the same time, the Germans made no serious effort to balance their budget, the only way reparations could be paid in the absence of an international loan. To be sure, as Finance Minister Mathias Erzberger made substantial changes to the German tax system, enhancing the fiscal power of the central government. He also attempted a drastic increase in direct taxation before his departure from office in March 1920: the 'Reich Emergency Levy' (*Reichsnotopfer*) taxed property at rates rising to 65 per cent, while the Reich income tax had a top rate of 60 per cent. Yet this did not suffice to reduce the deficit (which averaged around 15 per cent of net national product between 1919 and 1923). Firstly, there was considerable evasion, much of it within the law. For example, the 'Emergency Levy' was payable in instalments over periods as long as 47 years, with interest charged at only 5 per cent after December 1920.[79] So long as inflation remained above 5 per cent, delayed payment was clearly advantageous. Likewise, those whose incomes were not paid as wages (from which tax was deducted at source) could easily defer payment of the new Reich income tax.[80]

This was not accidental: tax reform was deliberately botched out of the desire to avoid reparations. As Chancellor Joseph Wirth himself put it in arguing against a property levy (or 'seizure of real values', in the contemporary catch-phrase): 'The goal of our entire policy must be the dismantling of the London Ultimatum. It would therefore be a mistake if, by initiating a seizure of real values at this moment, we were [in effect] to declare the Ultimatum to be 80 per cent possible.'[81] The domestic debate on financial reform between May 1921 and November 1922 was therefore a phoney debate, as the Chancellor himself was not in earnest. Schemes like the property levy had to be discussed in order to appease the Reparations Commission, but they were never intended to 'close the hole in the budget'.[82] Similarly, the idea for a 1 billion goldmark forced loan was devised primarily in response to the Allies' demand for a financial reform plan at Cannes; the Finance Ministry fixed the multiplier for converting paper marks into gold at such a low level that the tax yielded just 5 per cent of the target figure.[83] State Secretary David Fischer captured the prevailing mood when he described the Reparations Commission's 'wish for a further increase in taxes' as implying a 'wish for the economic destruction of Germany'.[84] Real income from taxation actually fell in the second half of 1921, and rose only slightly in the first half of 1922.[85]

Keynes was too trusting. In November 1921, responding to the claim that the Germans were deliberately exacerbating inflation to avoid paying reparations, he wrote: 'I do not believe a word of the silly stories that the German government could be so bold or so mad as to engineer on purpose what will in the end be a great catastrophe for their own people.'[86] Unfortunately, those 'silly stories' were correct. The Germans believed that through continued deficits and continued currency depreciation they would be able to increase their exports; and these would, in the words of Melchior, 'ruin trade with England and America, so that the creditors themselves will come to us to require modification'.[87]

When the mark slumped against the dollar from 14 marks to 99 marks between June 1919 and February 1920, following the lifting of German exchange controls,[88] the Economics Minister Robert Schmidt was explicit about what he hoped this would achieve: 'The tossing out of German goods abroad at slaughter prices . . . will compel the Entente to allow us to bring our exchange into order.'[89] As Felix Deutsch of the electrical engineering giant AEG put it: 'Our good fortune in the midst of misfortune is our poor currency, which enables us to export on a large scale.'[90] In order to preserve this good fortune, the Economics Ministry took the step of intervening *against* the mark between March and June 1920, buying substantial amounts of foreign currency to limit the appreciation of the mark.[91] Warburg made the rationale of the strategy quite explicit in a speech he drafted in October 1920: 'Even at the risk of sometimes selling our own products too cheaply abroad . . . the world must be made to understand that it is impossible to burden a country with debts and at the same time deprive it of the means of paying them . . . The most complete collapse of the currency . . . cannot be avoided if the peace treaty is maintained in its present form.'[92]

COULD HAVE PAID?

The reality was that the economic consequences of the Versailles Treaty were far less severe for Germany than the Germans and Keynes claimed. Apart from the US, all the combatant countries had emerged from the war with heavy losses on their capital accounts. The sums owed by the prospective recipients of reparations to the US were already equivalent to around 40 billion goldmarks.[93] Similarly, it was not just Germany which had lost shipping: the total losses to world shipping during the war (the better part of them inflicted by Germany) had totalled more than 15 million tons. In any case, the significance of these lost assets should not be exaggerated: shipping in particular was swiftly replaced. In the short run the world economy boomed as businessmen rushed to replace inventories and plant run down during the war, and as trade links which had been disrupted by front lines, warships and submarines were restored. By 1920 international trade had recovered to 80 per cent of its pre-war level. The monetary expansion generated by war finance fuelled this upswing. Germany's net national product grew by an estimated 10 per cent in 1920 and 7 per cent in 1921.[94] Although her agriculture continued to languish, indicators of industrial output show a sharp upward trend: up 46 per cent in 1920 and 20 per cent in 1921, with certain industries (notably shipbuilding and coal) experiencing especially rapid growth.[95]

From a foreign point of view, this combination of rapid growth and a weak exchange rate appeared contradictory, and invited speculation. As a result, the German trade deficit in 1919–20 was financed not by large-scale foreign loans but by numerous, small-scale purchases of paper marks by foreigners. Foreign deposits at the seven Berlin great banks rose from 13.7 billion marks in 1919 to 41.6 billion marks in 1921, and accounted for almost a third of total deposits.[96] Purchases of marks in New York totalled 60 million goldmarks between July 1919 and December 1921.[97] Keynes was dimly aware of this. 'The speculation', he noted in early 1920, was 'on a tremendous scale and was, in fact, the greatest ever known'.[98] But he wholly overlooked the likely impact this would have on the exchange rate. In March 1920 the mark suddenly ceased falling against the dollar and rallied, rising from a rate of 99 marks to a peak of 30 marks in June. In the following months all the trends of the previous eight months were reversed. Domestic prices in Germany fell by around 20 per cent from a peak in March 1920 to a trough in July, and then fluctuated at roughly thirteen times their pre-war level until the summer of 1921. In May 1921 the annual inflation rate sank to a post-war low of 2 per cent. At the same time the gap between German prices and world market prices abruptly closed.[99] This not only stopped the German export drive in its tracks.[100] It also cost Keynes over £20,000 (most, but not all, his own) which he had invested on the assumption that the economic consequences of the peace would be as he had forecast.[101] It was not until some time later that he fully grasped what had happened:

[From] itinerant Jews in the streets of the capitals . . . [to] barber's assistants in the remotest townships of Spain and South America . . . the argument has been the same . . . Germany is a great and strong country; some day she will recover; when that happens the mark will recover also, which will bring a very large profit. So little do bankers and servant girls understand of history and economics.[102]

In fact, the slowing of inflation reflected more than just ill-informed speculation. This was a time of international deflation as the British and American monetary and fiscal authorities took the first steps to settle the bills run up during the war and to end inflation by raising taxes and restricting credit. Sharp price falls occurred in 1921 in both countries, and this deflation tended to spread to their trading partners.[103]

Nor can it credibly be maintained that the reparations total set in 1921 constituted an intolerable burden. Eighty-two of the 132 billion gold marks were to some extent 'notional', in that the 'C' bonds to that value would only be issued at some unspecified future date when German economic recovery was sufficiently advanced.[104] This cast a shadow over the future and certainly limited the Reich's ability to borrow on the international market, but it meant that Germany's immediate obligations in 1921 were less than 50 billion goldmarks – as little, in fact, as 41 billion (taking account of what had been paid after 1919). That had been the sum regarded by Keynes himself as payable in *The Economic Consequences of the Peace*. Moreover, inflation had already substantially reduced the real value of the Reich's internal debt by mid-1921 to around 24 billion goldmarks, so, as a proportion of national income, the Reich's total liabilities including the 'A' and 'B' bonds amounted to around 160 per cent. This was certainly a higher debt burden than France had faced after the Franco-Prussian War: if one adds together the indemnity demanded by Bismarck (5,000 million francs) and the existing French national debt (11,179 million francs), the total liability is equivalent to around 84 per cent of 1871 net national product. However, the German debt burden in 1921 was actually slightly *less* than the ratio of the total British national debt (internal and external) to gross national product in the same year (165 per cent). The ratio of debt to national income had been even higher for Britain in 1815: close to 200 per cent. Yet Britain had become the nineteenth century's most successful economy – and its most stable polity – despite that burden.

Nor was the annual payment being demanded from Germany excessive. As we have seen, annual reparations as scheduled by the London Ultimatum implied a total annuity of around 3 billion goldmarks. At least 8 billion goldmarks and perhaps as much as 13 billion goldmarks were actually handed over in the period 1920–23: between 4 and 7 per cent of total national income. In the hardest year, 1921, the figure was just 8.3 per cent (see Figure 19). This was far less than Keynes's guess of between 25 and 50 per cent of national income.[105] To be sure, this was a much bigger proportion of national income than that subsequently paid under the Dawes plan (at peak, around 3 per cent); and far outstrips the burdens imposed on developing countries by international debt in the 1980s, let alone the sums currently paid by Western countries in the form of aid to the Third World.[106] But between June 1871 and September 1873, France paid Germany 4,993 million francs: around 9 per cent of net national product in the first year, and 16 per cent in the second.

Finally, it was not wholly fantastic to expect Germany to pay a lower annual burden over a longer period than had been the case in the 1870s. The Young Committee's report of 1929 is often ridiculed for proposing that Germany continue to pay reparations until 1988. But since 1958 Germany has paid more than 163 billion marks to the rest of Europe in the form of net contributions to the European Economic Community/ European Union budget. Of course, the annual sums involved have represented a very small proportion of national income; but the final total is rather more in nominal terms than was asked for in post-Versailles reparations; this was precisely the long, scarcely perceptible transfer the Young Plan aimed at.

Keynes was right on one point: reparations implied an acute international conflict of interests.[107] If Germany were to run a trade surplus of 3 billion goldmarks, there would have to be a drastic contraction of German imports and an expansion of German exports. But which of Germany's trading partners would pay the price for this? British and French business representatives repeatedly argued that measures should be taken after the war 'to prevent Germany, who will still be a most dangerous economic enemy, from flooding our markets'.[108] A Board of Trade report on post-war commerce discerned in January 1916

a general fear that, immediately after the war, this country will be flooded with German and Austro-Hungarian goods, sold at almost any price, and that the competition in price which was going on before the war will be accentuated, with resultant serious difficulty to all manufacturers of goods of kinds exposed to this competition, and positive disaster to those manufacturers who have been encouraged to extend their operations, or engage in new branches of industry, with a view to capturing trade hitherto carried on by enemy countries.[109]

The issue of post-war discrimination against German trade was discussed and limited resolutions adopted at the Anglo-French conference in Paris the following June.[110] A committee of inquiry into post-war economic policy concluded in December 1917 that 'present enemy countries should not, for a time at least, be allowed to carry on trade

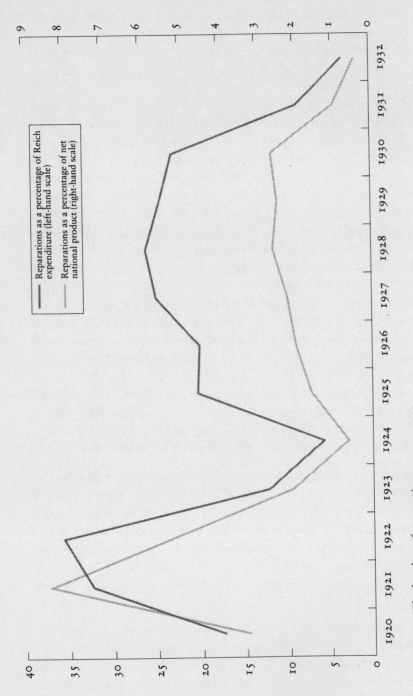

Figure 19 The burden of reparations, 1920–1932

Source: Ferguson, *Paper and Iron*, p. 477.

with the British Empire in the same unrestricted manner as before the war, or on terms equal to those accorded to Allies or Neutrals'.[111] Such resolutions manifested themselves after the war as special duties on German imports: the Germans called them 'hate discounts'.[112]

If, on the other hand, reparations were to be financed by loans to Germany, whose claims would take precedence – the reparations recipients, or the new lenders? As Schuker has argued, the Germans received at least as much in the form of loans from abroad which were never repaid as they themselves paid in reparations.[113] Between 1919 and 1932 Germany paid altogether 19.1 billion goldmarks in reparations; in the same period she received 27 billion goldmarks in net capital inflows, mainly from private investors, which were never repaid as a result of her defaults in 1923 and 1932.

Yet it does not necessarily follow from this that the German government was therefore right not to *attempt* to pay reparations. The question is not whether the transfer was sustainable; but whether the strategy adopted by the Germans and endorsed by Keynes was the best way of convincing the Allies that it was not. 'Economic revisionism' was supposed to pressurize the Allied economies by promoting a flood of German exports. This undoubtedly happened in 1919; but it did not last long. Even the very sharp depreciation of the mark against the dollar between May and November 1921 did not bring about a repeat of the immediate post-war 'fire sale' (*Ausverkauf*). True, the available export statistics point to a 35 per cent increase in the goldmark value of monthly exports in the year after May 1921, while annual figures suggest a two-thirds increase of exports in volume terms.[114] Graham's calculations for 43 categories of commodity also point to increases in exports.[115] But at the same time imports grew even faster. This was of critical importance, since only a trade *surplus* would have had the intended effect of exerting economic pressure on the Allies. Estimated annual figures point to a trade deficit of around 690 million goldmarks in 1921 and over 2,200 million goldmarks in 1922, compared with a tiny surplus in 1920.[116] Monthly figures provide a more precise record: the trade gap widened between May and September 1921, narrowed to record a small surplus in December 1921, and then widened again to reach a peak in July 1922. The data for trade volumes tell the same story, but suggest an even more dramatic widening of the deficit after February 1922, despite the fact that by this stage the proportion of semi-finished and finished goods had risen to a third of all imports.[117]

And these figures may actually understate the extent of the trade gap. While Economics Ministry officials continued to claim that exports were being underestimated and that the deficit in 1922 was negligible (claims which have misled later historians), there was 'complete consensus' in the Reich Statistical Office 'that the balance of trade deficit was being significantly underestimated'.[118]

In other words, contrary to the predictions of the proponents of economic revisionism, the trade deficit widened at the times of most rapid nominal exchange rate depreciation and narrowed when the mark stabilized.[119] Precisely when Germany was supposed to be putting the reparations collectors under pressure by flooding their markets with cheap exports, she was in fact relieving the pressure on them by providing a bouyant market for *their* exports.[120] This may well have been good for the world economy, helping to lift it out of a slump which might otherwise have become a depression;[121] but it was wholly counter-productive from the point of view of German diplomacy.

The reasons for the unexpectedly large German trade deficit are clear. Hostility to German exports abroad may have been a factor, but the real problem was that, although in nominal terms the mark clearly depreciated against the other major currencies, in real terms – allowing for changes in relative prices – there was no significant improvement in German competitiveness.[122] This reflected the low level of British and American prices, continuing foreign speculation in the mark and more rapidly adjusting German domestic prices and wages.

The idea that continuing depreciation would help Germany avoid paying reparations was thus fundamentally misconceived. If anything, it had the reverse effect. Inevitably, this begs the question: would not a policy of stabilization have been more effective in exerting pressure on the Allies by dampening German demand for imports? The experience of the period after 1930, when severely deflationary policies drastically reduced German imports, suggests that it might have been. After all, reparations survived the crisis of 1923 to be restored – rescheduled but not reduced – in 1924; but they were as good as dead and buried after the Hoover Moratorium in 1931. This was the pyrrhic victory of Weimar foreign policy: the moment at which Germany's external war debt – notionally worth around $77 billion in 1931 – was effectively cancelled at the expense of her former enemies (see Table 44). Considering that the total value of reparations actually paid by Germany cannot have exceeded $4·5 billion dollars, the conclusion seems clear. What hyper-

Table 44   *Outstanding war debts and reparations liabilities in 1931*
(£ thousands)

	suspended receipts	suspended payments	net loss (−) or gain
USA	53,600		−53,600
Great Britain	42,500	32,800	−9,700
Canada	900		−900
Australia	800	3,900	3,100
New Zealand	330	1,750	1,420
South Africa	110		−110
France	39,700	23,600	−16,100
Italy	9,200	7,400	−1,800
Belgium	5,100	2,700	−2,400
Germany		77,000	77,000
Hungary		350	350
Austria		300	300
Bulgaria	150	400	250

Source: Eichengreen, *Golden Fetters*, p. 278.

inflation did for the internal war debt, the depression did for the external burden imposed in the form of reparations. Having already fought the First World War on the cheap, the German Reich ultimately succeeded in avoiding paying all but a fraction of the war's financial cost.

CAN'T COLLECT

The real problem with the peace was not that it was too harsh, but that the Allies failed to enforce it: not so much 'won't pay' as 'can't collect'. In 1870–73 the Germans had occupied large tracts of northern France and linked the payment of the indemnity to their withdrawal: the faster the French paid, the sooner the Germans left. In 1919, by contrast, the Allies imposed the reparations total in 1921 after they had lifted the naval blockade, and with only a minimal force on the ground in the Rhineland. Rather than using occupation as an incentive to encourage reparation-payment, the Allies – or rather the French – sought to use the threat of a larger occupation as a sanction to discourage default. This was psychologically misconceived, as it encouraged the Germans to gamble that (as Keynes rashly suggested in 1922) the French were bluffing. The alternative course of action was – in effect – voluntarily to pay reparations; not surprisingly, democratically elected politicians were extremely reluctant to approve taxes for this purpose. The difficulty facing Weimar politicians – even those few who sincerely believed that Germany must fulfil the peace terms – was simple: they had to reconcile competing claims on the Reich budget from, on the one hand, their own electors, and on the other, Germany's former enemies. To put it simply: the Allies might want reparations for the damage done to them by the war; but German voters also felt entitled to 'reparations' for the hardship they had endured since 1914.

According to German budgetary figures, total real expenditure under the terms of the Versailles treaty in the years 1920 to 1923 amounted to between 6.54 and 7.63 billion goldmarks. This accounted for around 20 per cent of total Reich spending and 10 per cent of total public spending. Put another way, reparations accounted for a fifth of the Reich deficit in 1920, and more than two-thirds in 1921.[123] But even if one subtracts reparations payments, total public spending was still running at around 33 per cent of net national product, compared with around 18 per cent before the war.[124] And although without reparations inflation might have been lower and revenues therefore higher, it is still conceivable that there would have been deficits. It cannot be assumed that domestic spending would not have risen had reparations magically been abolished.

In addition to the dwindling real costs of servicing the funded debt, German reparations to Germans – which is how these domestic expenditures may be regarded – included higher spending on public sector pay, doles for the unemployed, of which the Reich paid half, subsidies for housing construction and subsidies to keep down the costs of food.[125] There was also the cost of paying pensions to over 800,000 war wounded, 533,000 war widows and 1.2 million war orphans.[126] The most notorious 'hole' in the budget, however, was the deficit run by the rail and postal systems: the deficit on the Reichsbahn accounted for around a quarter of the total Reich deficit between 1920 and 1923. In part, this was a consequence of purchases of new rolling stock and a failure to maintain the real value of fares and freight rates.[127] But it was also partly due to the government's concern to maintain employment levels, which led to chronic over-manning.[128] The situation was similar in the postal, telegraph and telephone system.[129] In addition, the cost of reconstructing the German merchant marine (aimed at maintaining employment in the shipbuilding industry) accounted for as much as 6 per cent of total Reich expenditures in 1919 and 1920.[130] Such 'domestic reparations' were more important than actual reparations in generating the German fiscal deficit.

All the former combatants faced the same problem, of course: a debt burden so high that paying the interest on it precluded generous expenditures on welfare of the sort which had been dangled, carrot-like, before voters during the war. The 'shopping list' drawn up by the British Minister of Reconstruction Christopher Addison in February 1918 was typical:

an adequate housing programme . . . involving purchases of materials and acquisition of land on a large scale . . . a considerable transfer of agricultural lands to public authorities for the purpose of small holdings, soldiers' settlements, afforestation and reclamation . . . the reconstruction of roads and the repair of railways and their equipment . . . the financing for a time in whole or in part by the State of certain essential industries . . . an extension of unemployment insurance to meet the dislocation of industry that is to be expected during the transition period . . . a strengthened health service both at the centre and locally.[131]

Addison opposed 'the view that everything should be subordinated to the paying off of debt', arguing instead that Britain should be 'prepared to incur expenditure essential for establishing at the earliest possible moment, the fullest measure of national productivity'. This was not so different from the arguments heard in post-war Germany. The difference was that in Britain the proponents of debt-service and amortization won; whereas in Germany the proponents of welfare spending did. That was why inflation gave way to deflation in Britain in 1921, while in Germany the printing presses kept rolling until the currency's final collapse.

As early as 1922 the German national debt had been reduced by inflation so much that in dollar terms it was almost exactly what it had been in 1914 ($1.3 billion compared with $1.2 billion on the eve of the war). By contrast, Britain's was almost ten times its pre-war level and America's more than a hundred times larger (see Table 45). Six years later, after the German hyperinflation and the British return to pre-war parity, the difference was even more pronounced. The combined debts

of the Reich and states had been equivalent to around 40 per cent of
GNP in 1913. In 1928 the figure was a mere 8.4 per cent. By contrast,
Britain's national debt had increased from 30.5 per cent of GNP in
1913 to a crushing 178 per cent in 1928.[132] Despite the protests of
advocates of full 'revaluation' in Germany, the Finance Minister Hans
Luther had succeeded in effectively cancelling Germany's war debt. In
drawing up the third Emergency Tax Decree of February 1924, which
promised modest (10–15 per cent) revaluation of private mortgages
and debentures, he explicitly ruled out similar treatment for the 60
million marks worth of war bonds still in circulation (until reparations
had been paid). Georg Reimann's wartime prediction that Solon's
seisachtheia would be re-enacted in Germany had been fulfilled.[133]

The choice between inflation and deflation had important macroeconomic, and hence social, implications. In his *Tract on Monetary
Reform* Keynes presented these as more or less straightforward: a
government which balanced its budget and restored its currency to
pre-war parity ran the risk of reducing aggregate economic output
and employment; a government which continued deficit finance and
therefore inflation, on the other hand, would boost output and employment levels, albeit at the expense of bondholders and other savers with
paper assets. Thus in Britain the war was paid for – and more, in that
the real value of the war debt actually rose – by imposing deflation and
hence unemployment on the working class; while in Germany (and of
course in Russia) it was the bondholders who paid.

But which was preferable? In his *Tract* Keynes suggested that though
inflation was 'worse' than deflation 'in altering the *distribution* of

Table 45   *National debts in dollar terms, 1914 and 1922*

	1914	1922	1922 *as a percentage of 1914*
USA	1,338	23,407	1,749
Britain	3,440	34,251	996
France	6,492	27,758	428
Italy	3,034	8,689	286
Germany (Reich)	1,228	1,303	106

Source: Bankers Trust Company, *French Public Finance*, p. 137.

wealth', deflation was 'more injurious' in 'retarding the *production* of wealth.' Though he expressed sympathy for the middle class, 'out of which most good things have sprung', he therefore favoured the former, 'because it is worse in an impoverished world to provoke unemployment than to disappoint the rentier'.[134] In fact, Keynes explicitly identified as an exception to this rule 'exaggerated inflations such as that of Germany'; however, this important qualification has since tended to be forgotten. In the words of Frank Graham, for example, 'the balance of material gains and losses' of the German inflation was 'on the side of gains'.[135] This line of argument was developed in the 1960s by Laursen and Pedersen, among others. Not only did output increase in 1920, 1921 and 1922, they argued, but so did investment, creating a potential for sustained growth which only the depressed conditions of the post-1924 period prevented from being put to use.[136] A vital piece of evidence in this case is the fact that German employment levels were unusually high by international standards in the years 1920–22[137] – this was what Graham principally had in mind when he wrote that 'Germany accomplished the actual process of transition from the war to a stable post-war monetary structure at a lower real cost' than Britain and the US.[138] Most recent economic history textbooks have been at pains to stress these relative advantages of inflation, at least for the pre-hyperinflation period.[139] By implication, an alternative policy would have led to lower growth, lower investment and higher unemployment.

To explain the different policy choices in each country, historians have invoked a mixture of sociology and political culture. Thus it has been suggested that in Britain some social groups whose material interests were actually harmed by deflation nevertheless supported the 'conventional wisdom' of sound money for economically irrational reasons, equating Gladstonian orthodoxy with moral rectitude.[140] In France a middle course was adopted, which moderately devalued the national debt – a recognition of the relative but not absolute power of the *rentier* in French society. In Italy the distributional conflict proved impossible to resolve within a parliamentary system, so that the stabiliz-ation of the currency had to be undertaken by Mussolini's dictatorship. In Germany, by contrast, a crucial section of the bourgeoisie – entrepreneurs and the managerial business élite – defected to the side of the working class, supporting inflationary policies in the pursuit of a rapid physical expansion of German industry, but at the expense of share-holders, bondholders and banks. Whereas earlier accounts portrayed big business as the sole beneficiaries of the inflation, reaping the benefits of low real interest rates, low taxation and a weak exchange rate, it is now argued that workers also did relatively well.[141] The inflation was thus the unplanned outcome of a tacit 'inflationary consensus' between industry, organized labour and other social groups averse to deflation.[142] The loser was the rentier; but the overall effect was to make society as a whole better off and more equal than it would have been if deflation had been attempted.[143] This line of argument has political implications. In an influential article Hans Haller estimated that tax levels would have needed to exceed 35 per cent of national income to balance the budget without further government borrowing; a level of taxation we would now consider modest but which, according to Haller, would have been politically intolerable in the early 1920s. Inflation is thus said to have 'secured the parliamentary form of government for the period of the Weimar Republic', since any attempt to have stabilized fiscal and monetary policy would have led to a political crisis.[144]

In fact, all of these justifications for the inflation have their origins in the contemporary policy debate. At a meeting with the American ambassador in Berlin in June 1922, Rathenau (now German Foreign Minister) and the industrialist Hugo Stinnes offered two differing, but complementary justifications for German policy:

[Rathenau] held . . . that inflation was no worse economically than controlling rents and maintained it only took from those who had and gave to those who had not, which in a country as poor as Germany was entirely proper. Stinnes . . . declared the choice had been between inflation and revolution and as between the two he favoured inflation.[145]

To Stinnes, inflation was 'the only way of giving the population a regular employment, which was necessary to secure the life of the nation'.[146] 'It was', he later told Houghton, 'politically necessary to put at work three million men coming back from the war. It was . . . a question of your money or your life.'[147] Melchior made a similar point:

It was politically and socially necessary at the time and . . . could it have been controlled, no permanent harm would have occurred. It was not planned . . . It became involved in the creation of new capital to enable industry to hire the returning soldiers.[148]

Elsewhere he argued that the huge deficit on the publicly owned railways was necessary 'to avoid putting . . . 100,000 disposable employees . . .

onto unemployment benefit and thus handing them over to political radicalism'.[149] Writing in November 1923, Max Warburg underlined the point: 'It was always a question of whether one wished to stop the inflation and trigger the revolution.'[150] Nor were such views peculiar to businessmen. The trade unionist Paul Umbreit was essentially making the same point when he argued against cuts in social expenditures. 'If economic and social effects are set in opposition to one another, then the social interests have to be given precedence.'[151]

There are, however, good reasons to doubt the wisdom of these arguments. The inflation had far higher costs than Graham or Laursen and Pedersen appreciated. The Italian economist Costantino Bresciani-Turroni, who wrote one of the first serious studies of the subject in 1931, listed them as follows: falling productivity; a misallocation of resources; 'profound disequilibrium in the economic organism'; 'the vastest expropriation of some classes of society that has ever been effected in time of peace'; and declines in public health and morality:

It annihilated thrift [he went on] . . . It destroyed . . . moral and intellectual values . . . It poisoned the German people by spreading among all classes the spirit of speculation and by diverting them from proper and regular work, and it was the cause of incessant political and moral disturbance . . . [Moreover,] by reinforcing the economic position of those classes who formed the backbone of the 'Right' parties, i.e. the great industrialists and financiers, [it] encouraged the political reaction against democracy.[152]

Although he had come down on the side of inflation, Keynes himself elsewhere expressed similar views. In his *Economic Consequences* he famously endorsed the view (which he attributed to Lenin) that 'the best way to destroy the Capitalist System was to debauch the currency':

By a continuing process of inflation, governments can confiscate, secretly and unobserved, an important part of the wealth of their citizens. By this method, they not only confiscate, but they confiscate *arbitrarily*; and, while the process impoverishes many, it actually enriches some. The sight of this arbitrary rearrangement of riches strikes not only at security, but at confidence in the equity of the existing distribution of wealth. Those to whom the system brings windfalls . . . become 'profiteers', who are the object of the hatred of the bourgeoisie, whom the inflationism has impoverished not less than of the proletariat. As the inflation proceeds . . . all permanent relations between debtors and creditors, which form the ultimate foundation of capitalism, become so utterly disordered as to be almost meaningless ... There is no subtler, no surer means of overturning the existing basis of society ... In Russia and Austria–Hungary this process has reached a point where for the purposes of foreign trade the currency is practically valueless ... There the miseries of life and the disintegration of society are too notorious to require analysis; and these countries are already experiencing the actuality of what for the rest of Europe is still in the realm of prediction.[153]

The most modern research has provided ample support for these arguments. In particular, the claim that the inflation stimulated invest-ment has been called into question by the work of Lindenlaub, whose detailed study of engineering firms suggests that rising prices (or to be precise, uncertainty about future prices) actually discouraged invest-ment. The year of stable prices – 1920 – was when firms undertook new capital projects, and many of these had to be abandoned when inflation resumed in 1921.[154] More generally, it seems hard to deny that whatever benefits the inflation conferred in 1921 and 1922 were compensated for by the sharp falls in production and employment after hyperinflation set in. It has also been persuasively argued by Balderston that, because of its damaging effects on the banking system and the capital market, the inflation was indirectly responsible for the onset and peculiar severity of the 1929–32 Slump in Germany.[155] Economi-cally, then, the costs of inflation seem to have outweighed the benefits.

The sociological explanations of the divergent national outcomes are too simplistic. They tend to overlook the fact that, in fiscal terms, the conflict which really mattered was between holders of government debt and tax-payers; and that these were far from being distinct groups. Everywhere the number of bondholders had been greatly increased by the war. If one adds together the total number of subscriptions to the nine German war loans, just under half were for amounts of just 200 marks or less; for the last four war loans the proportion of such small subscriptions averaged 59 per cent.[156] In 1924 around 12 per cent of the internal British national debt was held by small savers.[157] It is also sometimes forgotten that many of the biggest holders of war bonds were institutional rather than individual investors – insurance companies, savings banks and so on – whose large wartime purchases were effec-tively made on behalf of small savers. For example, 5.5 per cent of the British debt in 1924 was held by insurance companies and 8.9 per cent by the clearing banks.

At the same time there was an increase in the number of people paying direct tax. In Britain the number of income taxpayers more than trebled from 1,130,000 in 1913/14 to 3,547,000 in 1918/19, while the proportion of wage-earners rose from 0 to 58 per cent. To be sure, wage-earners only accounted for around 2.5 per cent of the net revenue from the income tax; but they could hardly be indifferent to the £3.72 each of them on average paid in 1918/19.[158] In Germany tax deducted from wages at source accounted for a steadily rising share of total direct tax revenue as middle-class taxpayers delayed payment of their tax bills, leaving inflation to reduce them in real terms. German working-class taxpayers were therefore even more concerned about direct tax. It is also vital to remember the post-war changes to electoral franchises, which had previously been restricted by wealth or income qualifications in most countries: democratization might have been expected to increase the political representation of voters who were neither bondholders nor direct taxpayers. In Britain, however, the ratio of voters to income taxpayers actually fell from 6.8 to 1 before the war to 6 to 1 in 1918 – the number of taxpayers had increased by more than the number of voters (by 214 per cent compared with 177 per cent).

Class analysis of the sort favoured by sociology therefore simply will not work because the crucial groups – bondholders, taxpayers and voters – had been too much altered by the war and overlapped in ways which defy the old class-based models. Winners in one respect could simultaneously be losers in another: in this German peasants were no exception.[159] Thus the sacrifices made by the rich élite in Britain before 1914 (in the form of super tax and death duties) and during the war were to some extent compensated for after the war in the form of a real increase in the value of their financial assets and the income they yielded. By contrast, the rich in Germany, who were so successful in opposing or evading higher direct taxation before, during and after the war, were penalized after the war by paying a massive inflation tax on their mark-denominated securities. In a sense, the 'choice' for Europe's middle class was whether to receive income in the form of interest on war bonds, but lose it in higher taxation, or avoid the taxation but lose the war bonds to inflation.

There is no question which was politically the more hazardous course. In Britain middle-class voters might whinge about the 'servant problem' and other signs of their relative impoverishment since 1914, but they remained solidly loyal to parliamentary Conservatism. In Germany, on the other hand, middle-class respect for parliamentary politics was dealt a fatal blow by the experience of inflationary expropriation: as the Prussian Minister of Justice Hugo am Zenhoff rightly foresaw in November 1923, 'such a failure of the legal order must lead to a serious shattering of the legal sensibility and confidence in the state'.[160] The disintegration of the 'bourgeois parties' in Germany can be dated from the elections of 1924; six years later many of the voters who had defected from them to form transient splinter groups like the Economy Party turned to National Socialism.[161]

Hitler's line on inflation was always tough. As early as 1922 he denounced 'this weak republic [which] throws its pieces of paper about wildly in order to enable its party functionaries . . . to feed at the trough'. The Nazi party's manifesto in 1930 – the year of the party's biggest electoral advance – stated: 'The other parties may have come to terms with the thievery of the inflation, may recognise the fraudulent republic [but] National Socialism will bring the thieves and traitors to justice.' 'I'll see to it that prices remain stable,' Hitler promised voters. 'That's what my stormtroopers are for.'[162] Though Nazi propaganda made much of the 'Unknown Soldier' Hitler's (and the fighter ace Goering's) own war service – even using parades by disabled veterans in election campaigns[163] – the movement was in fact only indirectly a product of the 'Front experience'. After all, around 38 per cent of those who voted Nazi in 1933 had been sixteen or younger when the war ended, while the biggest post-war veterans' association had been founded by the SPD.[164] It was the post-war economic crisis, not the war, which spawned Nazism; and with it the next war.

ALTERNATIVES TO HYPERINFLATION

The question remains whether the calamity of hyperinflation could have been avoided.

Clearly, any attempt to restore the mark to pre-war parity on the British pattern was out of the question; a drop in output of nearly 5 per cent and an unemployment rate of over 10 per cent (the effect of British deflationary policies in 1920–21) would, it seems fair to say, have been politically unsustainable. But could not the mark have been stabilized at, say, 50 marks to the dollar or 8 per cent of its pre-war value? Such a stabilization (not dissimilar from that which occurred in Yugoslavia, Finland, Czechoslovakia and France) would not have entailed a British-style slump.[165]

The first step towards an enduring German stabilization in 1920 would have been a bigger (though not, it should be stressed, a total) reduction in the budget deficit.[166] As a proportion of estimated net national product, the deficit fell from around 18 per cent in 1919 to 16 per cent in 1920 and 12 per cent in 1921. More could have been done. Better-designed taxes could have raised more revenue: Webb has calculated that, if the revenues from income tax had not been eroded by renewed inflation after mid-1921, the real deficit (net of debt service) for the period July 1920 to June 1921 would have been just 4 per cent of NNP).[167] More practically, if Erzberger had also increased taxes on consumption, his whole tax package might have seemed less like 'fiscal socialization' to the middle classes. Under Erzberger's reforms, the share of Reich tax revenue coming from direct taxation rose to around 60 per cent in 1920/21 and 75 per cent in 1921/2, compared with just 14.5 per cent (including stamp taxes) before the war.[168] This was too high. What is more, higher taxes on consumption – though seen on the left as politically retrograde – would have been easier to collect. Some corresponding cuts in public expenditure could also have been made. To have halved the 1920 deficit would have required tax increases of around 1.5 billion goldmarks and spending cuts of the same order.

Fiscal policy alone cannot explain the failure of stabilization to endure, of course. Although monetary policy was largely influenced by the monetization of government debt, it was far from being a wholly dependent variable. The problem can be stated simply. In terms of currency in circulation, the rate of monetary growth was actually higher in 1920 than it was in either 1919 or 1921.[169] This expansion was only partly due to the continuation of government deficits, since a rising share of treasury bills was held outside the Reichsbank in the same period.[170] It reflected above all the high liquidity of the money markets and the static discount rate policy of the Reichsbank, which kept market interest rates at around 3.5 per cent and the discount rate at 5 per cent until 1922.[171] Although the Reichsbank actually threatened to stop discounting treasury bills in 1919,[172] it made no attempt whatever to tighten credit conditions for the private sector. Indeed, at the first sign of such a tightening, it stepped in to maintain business liquidity by discounting commercial bills.[173]

Yet there was an alternative monetary policy. The Reichsbank's traditional reserve requirements remained formally in force until May 1921. Admittedly, these rules had been substantially diluted by the decision to treat *Darlehnskassenscheine* (supplementary wartime notes) as equivalent to gold in the reserve. But by late 1920 the total volume of such notes had fallen by 12.5 per cent compared with the previous year; while the Reichsbank's gold reserve was almost exactly at its 1913 level at 1,092 million goldmarks – 19 per cent of the real value of currency in circulation, compared with 18 per cent in 1913.[174] A *de facto* stabilization of monetary policy could thus have been undertaken in 1920 without necessarily causing a significant real monetary contraction. To avoid the legal quagmire of an internal currency reform (with all the protests from creditors that would have elicited even in 1920), the easiest way of doing this would have been to peg the paper mark's exchange rate against the dollar at around 5 or 10 gold pfennigs.

Why was this not done? Some historians have tended to stress the low quality of German economic theory in this period; and certainly there were many economists who explicitly opposed policies of stabilization on thoroughly spurious grounds.[175] Yet politicians were not unaware of the risks they were running by letting inflation run out of control. On 28 June 1920 Chancellor Konstantin Fehrenbach urged Reichstag deputies 'to promote the reform of the Reich's finances with the utmost urgency':

The relentless increase of our floating debt depresses the purchasing power of our money, restricts our credit and pushes prices to fraudulent heights. The volume of paper money is no sign of prosperity, (*Quite right!*) but a measure of increasing impoverishment. (*Renewed agreement.*) And the more the value of money collapses, the more violent become the struggles over wages and salaries, which despite everything are rarely able to keep pace with the rise in prices. An endless ratchet! It poses the gravest possible threat to trade and transport, to every branch of industry and labour. This danger must be countered with every available means, if we are to protect our people from the fearful misery of a collapse not only of the state finances but also of the nation's economy. God forbid that our people should only come to understand the full extent of our present plight as a consequence of [such] a collapse![176]

The expressions of agreement which greeted his remarks show clearly that German politicians understood the risks of deficit finance and knew what they had to do to stabilize the currency.

What were the arguments at the time against such a stabilization? There were some advanced specifically against devaluation. For example, it was argued, firms and individuals with wartime foreign currency debts would be deprived of the theoretical possibility of some longer-term recovery of the mark. More important, however, was the fear of a domestic liquidity crisis or 'credit shortage'. Even without a policy of stabilization, there were around two and a half times as many bankruptcies in the first half of 1921 as in the first half of 1920.[177] It was not, of course, bankruptcies *per se* which were feared, but the increased unemployment which would arise as a consequence. Yet the assumption that policies of retrenchment would have triggered a 'second revolution' merits reassessment.

There is no doubt that stabilization would have increased unemployment in the short term. In ending foreign speculation in the mark and deterring future investment in German-mark denominated assets, devaluation would also have ruled out that expansion in the German trade deficit which occurred in 1921 and 1922, thus placing a ceiling on domestic consumption. On the other hand, there is good reason to think that price stability and a devalued currency would have encouraged businesses to continue with the programmes of investment which they were beginning in 1920, but subsequently cancelled. Nor is there any reason to think that foreign lending would have ceased permanently. After all, it resumed very quickly in 1924, despite far heavier losses than a 1920 devaluation would have entailed. It seems reasonable to assume that any stabilization crisis in 1920/21 would have been less severe than the contraction experienced in 1923/24, when, in circumstances of complete monetary collapse, NNP fell by around 10 per cent and unemployment rose to a peak of 25 per cent of trade union members, not including more than 40 per cent who were on short-time work. Such levels of unemployment were not seen again in Germany until 1931. By contrast, unemployment in 1920 only exceeded 5 per cent in two months (July and August); for the year as a whole it averaged just 4.1 per cent. The experience of France, where a strategy of the sort suggested here was actually adopted, suggests that at most unemployment would have doubled in the event of stabilization. A rate of unemployment of around 10 per cent of trade union members would have represented a significantly 'softer landing' than that of 1923/24.

Weimar politicians' fears of the social consequences of such unemployment were exaggerated. To be sure, there were numerous small-scale demonstrations by the unemployed at the time of the mark's relative stabilization in 1920. Coming in the wake of the anti-Kapp general strike and coinciding as they did with sporadic consumers' protests against high prices, it is not surprising that these caused anxiety. Yet there was a certain illogic in lumping together these various manifestations of popular discontent as a single potentially revolutionary threat. For a policy of stabilization would have tended to reduce the radicalism of organized labour and the dissatisfaction of consumers precisely by stabilizing prices, reducing the incentive to strike for higher wages and adding a disincentive by pushing up unemployment. By contrast, the government's policy of subsidies to workers in sensitive sectors such as transport bought only the most illusory kind of social peace; for expanding the numbers and wage-packets of such workers only served to bolster the position of the more radical elements in the unions and the works' councils, to antagonize employers and hence to exacerbate industrial friction.

In practice, of course, too many economic interests were too well represented in the host of competing institutions which made Weimar policy for an even slightly deflationary policy to have stood a chance of success. Even in 1923–4, when Fehrenbach's worst fears had been realized for all to see, it was only possible to reform the currency by using the President's emergency power to rule by decree. This, of course, was precisely the instrument used after 1930 to emasculate the Weimar system. But perhaps it would have been better if Germany had had a more authoritarian government ten years earlier. If the mark had been successfully stabilized in 1920, rather than allowed to fall into the abyss of hyperinflation, German history might have taken a less disastrous course in the 1930s. As it was, Keynes all too soon had to start working out how to pay for the next war.[178]

Conclusion:
Alternatives to Armageddon

At the end of *Crime and Punishment*, the nihilist murderer Raskolnikov has a feverish and clearly allegorical dream in which 'the whole world . . . suffered a terrible, unprecedented and unparalleled plague':

Those infected were seized immediately and went mad. Yet people never considered themselves so clever and unhesitatingly right as these infected ones considered themselves. Never had they considered their decrees, their scientific deductions, their moral convictions and their beliefs more firmly based. Whole settlements, whole cities and nations, were infected and went mad. Everybody was in a state of alarm, and nobody understood anybody; each thought the truth was in him alone; suffered agonies when he looked at the others; beat his breast; wept and wrung his hands. They did not know whom to bring to trial or how to try him; they could not agree on what to consider evil, what good. They did not know whom to condemn or whom to acquit. People killed each other with senseless rage. Whole armies were mustered against each other, but as soon as the armies were on the march they began suddenly to tear themselves apart. The ranks dispersed; the soldiers flung themselves upon each other, slashed and stabbed, ate and devoured each other. In the cities, the alarm bells rang for a whole day. Everybody was called, but nobody knew by whom or for what, and everybody was on edge. The most ordinary trades were abandoned, because everyone proposed his own ideas, his own criticisms, and they could not agree. Agriculture came to a halt. In some places, knots of people would gather together, reach some agreement, and swear not to separate; no sooner was this accomplished, however, than something quite different from what they had proposed took place. They started accusing each other, fighting each other, and stabbing away. Fires blazed up; hunger set in. Everything and everybody went to wrack and ruin.[1]

That vision was more or less realized in Europe between 1914 and 1918.

What, if anything, was achieved by this Armageddon? Belgium and northern France were cleared of German troops; so were Rumania, Poland, the Ukraine and the Baltic states. The German, Russian and Turkish empires were diminished; the Austrian altogether destroyed. Hungary shrank; so too did Bulgaria – and Great Britain, which by stages lost most of Ireland. New states were formed: Austria and Hungary went their separate ways; the Serbs achieved their goal of a South Slav state – called after 1929 'Yugoslavia' – along with the Croats and Slovenes (as well as the Bosnian Muslims); Czechoslovakia, Poland, Lithuania, Latvia, Estonia and Finland became independent. Italy grew, though less than her leaders had hoped, acquiring the South Tyrol, Istria, part of Dalmatia and the Dodecanese islands (in 1923). France reclaimed Alsace and Lorraine, lost in 1871. She and Britain also enlarged their colonial empires in the form of 'mandates' of former enemy possessions: Syria and Lebanon for France, Iraq and Palestine for Britain, who had committed herself to the creation of a Jewish National Home in the latter. Cameroon and Togoland were also shared between the two victors. In addition, German South-West Africa went to South Africa, German Samoa to New Zealand and German New Guinea to Australia. Britain also snapped up German East Africa, to Belgian and Portuguese chagrin (they were fobbed off with less desirable African territory). Sassoon had been right after all in July 1917: it had become 'a war of . . . conquest'; the map, as Balfour said, had yet 'more red on it'.[2] In the British War Cabinet's concluding meeting before the Versailles Conference, Edwin Montagu had commented drily that he would like to hear some arguments *against* Britain's annexing the whole world.[3] America, however, rivalled Britain as the world's banker; it stood on the brink of global economic supremacy. And President Wilson's vision of a 'new world order' based on a League of Nations and international law was realized, if not quite in the utopian form of his dreams. Little heed was paid to the pretensions of Japan, which laid claim to Shantung, another German relic, as its share of the spoils. Nor were serious objections raised when, in breach of the Treaty of Sèvres, Turkey and Russia partitioned briefly independent Armenia.[4]

Perhaps most remarkably, the Romanovs, Habsburgs and Hohen-zollerns were toppled (the Ottoman Sultan did not last much longer); republics took their place. In that respect, the First World War turned out to be a turning point in the long-running conflict between monarchism and republicanism; a conflict which had its roots in eighteenth-century America and France, and indeed further back, in seventeenth-century England. Though two monarchies had in fact fallen in 1911 – the Chinese and the Portuguese – republicanism had been relatively feeble in 1914; some conservatives thought the war might help to kill it off altogether. In practice the war dealt a fatal blow to three of the major European monarchies and severely undermined the position of a number of others. On the eve of the war descendants and other relatives of Queen Victoria had sat on the thrones not only of Great Britain and Ireland, but also of Austria–Hungary, Russia, Germany, Belgium, Rumania, Greece and Bulgaria. In Europe only Switzerland, France and Portugal had been republics. Despite the imperial rivalries of pre-war diplomacy, the personal relations between the monarchs themselves had remained cordial, even friendly: the letters exchanged between 'George', 'Willy' and 'Nicky' testify to the continuing existence of a cosmopolitan, multi-lingual royal élite with at least some sense of collective interest. And despite the incessant abuse heaped on the Kaiser's head by British war propagandists (and since echoed by many historians), William II had not been personally responsible for the outbreak of war in 1914; indeed, he had vainly sought to limit Austria to the occupation of Belgrade when it had transpired that Britain would support France and Russia in a general war. The Tsar too had seemed too pacifically inclined to his own Chief of General Staff: hence the talk of smashing telephones. Though the monarchs' power relative to the professional politicians and soldiers had varied, they had all ultimately hesitated to enter a full-scale war with one another, sensing that, just as Bethmann had predicted in May 1914, 'war would topple many a throne'. Ultimately, the position of the monarchs was bound to be threatened by a war which mobilized millions of men: at root, the First World War was democratic.

Thus, when the strain of the war began to tell, it was the monarchy which was among the first established institutions to lose legitimacy; so that the war led to a triumph of republicanism undreamt of even in the 1790s. In July 1918 Nicholas II and his family were murdered at Ekaterinburg, their bodies thrown down a mineshaft (where they remained for eighty years); the Kaiser stole away to exile in Holland, whose government resisted calls for his extradition as a war criminal; the last Habsburg Emperor, Karl I, went to Switzerland then Madeira; the last Ottoman Sultan was hustled out of Constantinople to a waiting British ship. True, the institution of monarchy survived in Britain, Belgium, Rumania, Bulgaria, Italy, Yugoslavia, Greece and Albania, as well as in Holland and Scandinavia, which had stayed out of the war; and new monarchies were also established in the ruins of the Ottoman Empire. However, the post-war map of Europe saw the emergence of republics in Russia, Germany, Austria, Hungary, Czechoslovakia, Poland and the three Baltic States, as well as Belorussia, West Ukraine, Georgia, Armenia and Azerbaijan (which were forcibly absorbed into the Union of Soviet Socialist Republics in 1919–21), and eventually in Southern Ireland. This must rank as one of the least intended consequences of the war. In Russia, moreover, the new republic was a tyranny far more bloodthirsty and illiberal than that of the tsars. Russia's descent into civil war might have seemed like the achievement of Germany's original war aim: to knock out the military threat in the East. But all the other combatants (the Germans included) came to regret the triumph of Lenin. Though there were revolutionary manifestations from Glasgow to Beijing, from Córdoba to Seattle, fears that Bolshevism would sweep across the world like the Spanish influenza proved exaggerated.[5] But gradually it dawned that Soviet Russia had the potential to be an even greater military power than Imperial Russia, even if it was not until the 1940s that the extent of the new regime's resilience became manifest to a new generation of German soldiers.

The victors of the First World War had paid a price far in excess of the value of all their gains; a price so high, indeed, that they would very shortly find themselves quite unable to hold on to most of them. All told, the war claimed more than 9 million lives on both sides, more than one in every eight of the 65.8 million men who fought in it. In four and a quarter years of mechanized butchery, an average of around 6,046 men were killed every day. The total number of fatalities for the British Empire as a whole was around 921,000: the originator of the Imperial War Graves Commission, Sir Fabian Ware, calculated that if the dead were to march abreast down Whitehall the parade past the Cenotaph would last three and a half days.[6] In 1919 Ernest Bogart attempted to work out the capital value of the dead; he estimated the total cost to Germany at $7 billion, to France at $4 billion and to Britain at $3 billion.[7] The demographic reality was that the dead (though not always their skills) were quite quickly replaced. Fewer British men were killed during the war than had emigrated in the decade before it.[8] Although the German birth-rate had fallen sharply since 1902 (from above 35 per cent to a nadir of 14 per cent in 1917), there was no shortage of young men in the immediate post-war period; rather the reverse. As a percentage of the population as a whole, men aged between fifteen and forty-five rose from 22.8 in 1910 to 23.5 per cent in 1925.[9] In England and Wales the number of men aged between 15 and 24 was also higher in 1921 than it had been in 1911; as a proportion of the total population it fell only slightly (from 18.2 to 17.6 per cent).[10]

More of a problem were those among the 15 million men wounded during the war who were permanently crippled. Of the 13 million German men who at one time or another 'served', as many as 2.7 million were permanently disabled by their wounds, of whom 800,000 received invalidity pensions.[11] These were the pathetic cripples depicted by Otto Dix: the erstwhile Front heroes reduced to begging in the gutter.[12] There were at least 1.1 million war wounded in France, of whom 100,000 were totally incapacitated.[13] Over 41,000 British servicemen had limbs amputated as a result of the war; two-thirds of them lost a leg and 28 per cent an arm; a further 272,000 suffered injuries which did not require amputation. In the late 1930s 220,000 officers and 419,000 servicemen were still receiving disability pensions.[14] In addition, there were those whom the war unhinged: 65,000 British ex-soldiers received disability pensions because of 'neurasthenia'; many, like the poet Ivor Gurney, were hospitalized for the rest of their lives.

Then there was the grief. Historians have recently turned their attention to the multitude of ways in which the survivors – parents, spouses, siblings and friends – sought to cope with the loss of those who died. No doubt, as Jay Winter has argued, many derived some solace from the symbolic aids to grieving provided by war memorials. No doubt religion – including the fashionable if unorthodox practice of communicating with the 'spirits' of the dead – helped too. The European peoples had lost more people to the war than were subsequently murdered in the Holocaust; the British social élite had indeed lost a generation; yet the manner of their dying, and the existence of a traditional language of Christian sacrifice meant that the survivors were less traumatized than the Jews who lived past 1945.[15] Yet no symbol – not the Trench of Bayonets at Verdun, nor Käthe Kollwitz's agonizing statues of bereft parents, nor the 73,367 names of the dead at Thiepval, nor even the simple pathos of the Cenotaph at Whitehall – could do more than provide a focus for personal anguish. If anything, the real purpose of such memorials was to transmit the pain to those who had been lucky enough to suffer no immediate loss: that was the whole point of the South African Sir Percy Fitzpatrick's suggestion that all Britain observe two minutes' silence on the eleventh hour of the eleventh day each November. The testimony of those who lost sons – Asquith, Bonar Law, Rosebery, Kipling, Sir Harry Lauder – confirms the universal truth that no pain equals the pain of losing a child.[16] Kipling had the supreme outlet of writing: his history of his son John's regiment is one of the war's most admirable memorials, marvellous for its understatement,[17] while his poems on the subject ('When you come to London stone / (Grieving – grieving!)') have a melancholy beauty. Yet pain was not diminished by remembrance. Private David Sutherland was killed during a raid on 16 May 1916. His platoon commander, Lieutenant Ewart Mackintosh, who had vainly carried him back across no man's land, wrote a poem which it is impossible to read unmoved:

> So you were David's father,
> And he was your only son,
> And the new-cut peats are rotting
> And the work is left undone,
> Because of an old man weeping,
> Just an old man in pain,
> For David, his son David,
> That will not come again.[18]

Quite apart from the killing, maiming and mourning, the war literally and metaphorically blew up the achievements of a century of economic advance. As we have seen, one estimate of the cost of the war puts it as high as $208 billion; that grossly understates the economic damage done. The economic misery of the post-war decades – a time of inflation, deflation and unemployment due to monetary crises, shrinking trade and debt defaults – could not have contrasted more bleakly with the unprecedented prosperity which had characterized the years 1896–1914, a time of rapid growth and full employment based on price stability, growing trade and free capital flows. The First World War undid the first, golden age of economic 'globalization'. Men marvelled that, after so much slaughter, there could be unemployment; after so much destruction, so little work – if only repair-work – to do. Aside from swift demographic recovery, the problem was in restoring fiscal and monetary stability. With hindsight Keynesians may criticize governments for endeavouring to balance budgets instead of borrowing to finance job-creation; but the combatant powers had already borrowed up to the hilt and it is very doubtful that the benefits of running new deficits would have outweighed the costs. Eichengreen has argued that the problems of the inter-war world economy were largely due to the quixotic attempt to restore the now inappropriate gold standard.[19] Democratic parliaments resisted the implementation of the old gold standard rules. Rigidities in the labour market – the refusal of unionized labour to accept nominal wage cuts – condemned millions to the dole. Yet what was the alternative? Those countries which sought to evade their war debts by letting their currencies depreciate ended up faring worse economically than those which painfully returned to gold. It is doubtful that a system of floating exchange rates would have worked any better.

At the time, critics of the Paris peace bemoaned its financial terms, insisting that the burden of reparations on Germany doomed Europe to a new war. This was incorrect, as we have seen. The Weimar economy was not wrecked by reparations; it wrecked itself. Nor should too much significance be attached to the failure of French schemes for Franco-German economic co-operation in the Rhineland–Ruhr region; though interesting to historians as harbingers of post-1945 European integration, these were irrelevances between the wars. The real defects of the peace lay elsewhere: in the naive belief that disarmament could suffice to eradicate militarism (with the army restricted to 100,000 men the Reichswehr was merely streamlined by Versailles); and, even graver, in the invocation of the principle of 'self-determination'.

As early as December 1914 Woodrow Wilson had argued that any peace settlement 'should be for the advantage of the European nations regarded as Peoples and not for any nation imposing its governmental will upon alien people'.[20] On 27 May 1915 he went further in a speech to the League to Enforce Peace, stating unequivocally that 'every people has a right to choose the sovereignty under which they shall live'.[21] On 22 January 1917 he repeated this principle: 'Every people should be left free to determine its own polity';[22] he elaborated on its implications in points five to thirteen of his Fourteen Points (8 January 1918), by which time it had been adopted – with varying degrees of disingenuousness – by the Bolsheviks, the Germans and Lloyd George.[23] As devised by Wilson, the League of Nations was not simply to guarantee territorial integrity of its member states but could accommodate future territorial adjustments 'pursuant to the principle of self-determination'.[24]

Quite apart from the American Senate's repudiation of the Treaty of Versailles, there was one fatal problem with this; and that was the

Table 46   The German populations of European states, c. 1919 (000s)

	Germans	Total population	Percentage
Reich	61,211	62,410	98.1
Austria	6,242	6,500	96.0
Denmark	40	3,260	1.2
Czechoslovakia	551	4,725	11.7
Italy	199	38,700	0.5
Yugoslavia	505	11,900	4.2
Rumania	713	18,000	4.0
Poland	1,059	27,100	3.9
Estonia	18	1,100	1.6
Latvia	70	1,900	3.7
Lithuania	29	2,028	1.4
Total	70,637	177,623	39.8

ethnic heterogeneity of Central and Eastern Europe – and in particular the existence of a large German diaspora outside the borders of the Reich. Table 46 gives an approximate breakdown of the distribution of the German-speaking population of Central and Eastern Europe *circa* 1919. The key point is that there were at least 9.5 million Germans outside the borders of the post First World War Reich – around 13 per cent of the total German-speaking population. These figures would be increased by the inclusion of Germans in Alsace–Lorraine and the Soviet Union (the so-called 'Volga Germans'); and do not include self-consciously German communities outside continental Europe. (Indeed, the Association for Germandom Abroad put the total figure of Germans outside the Reich at closer to 17 million after 1918; Nazi propaganda later inflated this to 27 million.)

The adoption of 'self-determination' as a guiding principle of the peace was fatal because it could not be applied to Germany without aggrandizing her far beyond the territory of the pre-1919 Reich. The choice was between an organized hypocrisy, which denied Germans the right of self-determination granted to others; or an irresistible revisionism, which would end by granting the Germans a substantial part of the annexationist aims of 1914–18. From the outset there was inconsistency: no *Anschluss* of the rump Austria to the Reich; but plebiscites to determine the fates of Schleswig, southern East Prussia and Upper Silesia. Philip Gibbs said that it was the peace treaties' 'disregard of racial boundaries [and] their creation of hatreds and vendettas, which would lead, as sure as the sun should rise, to new warfare'.[25] He was half-right; rather it was the fact that peacemakers invoked self-determination, a principle which could not be applied in Central and Eastern Europe without renewed violence. The way ahead was shown in the Balkans and Anatolia, where 1.2 million Greeks and half a million Turks were 'repatriated' – meaning expelled from their homes. The population of Greece rose by a quarter, wholly altering the ethnic balance of Greek Macedonia.[26] Similar transfers of population happened with varying degrees of compulsion in Europe: 770,000 German-speakers had quit the 'lost territories' for the Reich by 1925, more than a fifth of those who had lived there in 1910.[27] The criteria in the Greek case were in fact religious; future mass expulsions would be based on the looser categories of race. Especially vulnerable would be the approximately two million refugees who were technically 'stateless', most of them refugees from the Russian Civil War, many of them Jews fleeing White and Red pogroms.[28] What the Germans might have done had they won the war is not difficult to imagine. Even Max Warburg argued in the course of 1916 for the creation of German 'colonies' in the Baltic territories of Latvia and Courland:

The Latvians would be easily evacuated. In Russia, resettlement is not regarded as cruel in itself. The people are used to it . . . Those alien [i.e. non-Russian] peoples who are of German descent and are currently so ill-treated can be allowed to move into this area and found colonies. [These] do not need to be integrated into Germany, but must merely be affiliated, albeit with cement, so that their slipping back to the Russian side is ruled out.[29]

For the Jews of Eastern Europe, however, conquest by comparatively philo-Semitic Imperial Germany would have been preferable to conquest by Bolshevik Russia; conquest by the Third Reich proved fatal.

SOME CONCLUSIONS

This book set out to answer ten questions about the Great War:

1. Was the war inevitable, whether because of militarism, imperialism, secret diplomacy or the arms race?
2. Why did Germany's leaders gamble on war in 1914?
3. Why did Britain's leaders decide to intervene when war broke out on the Continent?
4. Was the war, as is often asserted, really greeted with popular enthusiasm?
5. Did propaganda, and especially the press, keep the war going, as Karl Kraus believed?
6. Why did the huge economic superiority of the British Empire not suffice to inflict defeat on the Central Powers more quickly and without American intervention?
7. Why did the military superiority of the German army fail to deliver victory over the British and French armies on the Western Front, as it delivered victory over Serbia, Rumania and Russia?
8. Why did men keep fighting when, as the war poets tell us, conditions on the battlefield were so wretched?
9. Why did men stop fighting?
10. Who won the peace?

The answer to the last question has already been given above. The answers I have attempted to give to the other nine may be summarized as follows:

1. Neither militarism, imperialism nor secret diplomacy made war inevitable. Everywhere in Europe in 1914 anti-militarism was in the political ascendant. Businessmen – even the 'merchants of death' like Krupp – had no interest in a major European war. Diplomacy, secret or otherwise, was successful in resolving imperial conflicts between the powers: both on colonial and even naval questions, Britain and Germany were able to settle their differences. The main reason relations between Britain and Germany did not produce a formal Entente was that Germany, unlike France, Russia, Japan or the US, did not seem to pose a serious threat to the Empire.

2. The German decision to risk a European war in 1914 was not based

on hubris: there was no bid for world power. Rather, Germany's leaders acted out of a sense of weakness. In the first instance, this was based on their inability to win either the naval or the land arms race. The ratio of British to German warship tonnage on the eve of the war was 2.1:1; the ratio of manpower in a war which pitted Russia, France, Serbia and Belgium against Germany and Austria–Hungary was 2.5:1. This differential was emphatically not due to a lack of economic resources. It was due to political and especially fiscal constraints: the combination of a relatively decentralized federal system with a democratic national parliament made it more or less impossible for the Reich government to match the defence expenditure of its more centralized neighbours. Moreover, by 1913–14 it was becoming increasingly difficult to increase Reich borrowing, after a decade and a half in which the national debt had increased by 150 per cent. Thus Germany spent only 3.5 per cent of gross national product on defence in 1913–14, compared with figures of 3.9 per cent for France and 4.6 per cent for Russia. Paradoxically, if Germany had been as militarist in practice as France and Russia, she would have had less reason to feel insecure and to gamble on a pre-emptive strike 'while [she] could more or less still pass the test', in Moltke's telling phrase.

3. Britain's decision to intervene was the result of secret planning by her generals and diplomats, which dated back to late 1905. Formally, Britain had no 'continental commitment' to France; this was repeatedly stated by Grey and other ministers in parliament and the press between 1907 and 1914. Nor did the Liberal government feel bound by the 1839 treaty to uphold Belgian neutrality; if Germany had not violated it in 1914, then Britain would have. The key was the conviction of a minority of generals, diplomats and politicians that, in the event of a continental war, Britain must send an army to support France. This was based on a misreading of German intentions, which the proponents of intervention imagined to be Napoleonic in scale. Those responsible were culpable in other ways: they misled the House of Commons, but at the same time they did virtually nothing to prepare Britain's army for the envisaged strategy. When the moment of decision came on 2 August 1914, it was by no means a foregone conclusion that Britain would intervene against Germany; the majority of ministers were hesitant, and in the end agreed to support Grey partly for fear of being turned out of office and letting in the Tories. It was a historic disaster – though not for his own career

– that Lloyd George did not support the opponents of intervention at this crucial juncture; for 'standing aside' would have been preferable to an intervention which could not be conclusive in the absence of a much bigger British army. German objectives, had Britain remained out, would not in fact have posed a direct threat to the Empire; the reduction of Russian power in Eastern Europe, the creation of a Central European Customs Union and acquisition of French colonies – these were all goals which were complementary to British interests.

4. Nor was Britain swept into the war on a wave of popular enthusiasm for 'little Belgium'; one reason so many men volunteered in the first weeks of the war was that unemployment soared because of the economic crisis the war had unleashed. The financial crisis of 1914 is indeed the best evidence of war pessimism. For many people in Europe, the war was not a cause for jubilation but trepidation: apocalyptic imagery was as frequently employed as patriotic rhetoric. People recognized Armageddon.

5. The war was certainly a media war: propaganda was less the result of government control than of spontaneous self-mobilization by the press, as well as academics, professional writers and film-makers. At first, newspapers thrived on the war which brought enormous increases in circulation for many titles. However, the economic problems of wartime meant that the period was on balance financially damaging for most newspapers. Moreover, much of the vilification of the enemy and mythologizing of the *casus belli* in which newspapers and other propagandists indulged was not taken seriously by those who fought; the efficacy of propaganda was in inverse relation to proximity to the Front. Only when based on truth, as in the case of the Belgian atrocities or the *Lusitania* sinking, was propaganda effective in bolstering the will to fight.

6. The Entente Powers enjoyed an immense economic superiority over the Central Powers: a combined national income 60 per cent greater, 4.5 times as many people and 28 per cent more men mobilized. In addition, the British economy grew during the war while the German contracted. Economic warfare could not compensate for these great economic differentials. Yet it is a myth that the Germans mismanaged their war economy. Taking the difference in resources into account, it was the other side – and especially Britain and the United States – which

waged war inefficiently. In particular, Britain made a mess of manpower allocation, with the result that a high proportion of the skilled workers on which her manufacturing industry relied were enlisted, and many of them killed or wounded. At the same time, those who stayed in or entered the factories were paid higher wages in real terms than were justified in terms of productivity. This reflected the greater power of the trade unions, which in Britain and in France roughly doubled their membership during the war; in Germany membership fell by more than 25 per cent. There were around 27 million working days lost due to strike action in Britain between 1914 and 1918; the figure for Germany was 5.3 million. Finally, it is implausible to argue that maldistribution of income and scarce food undermined the German war effort, as the groups worst affected were relatively unimportant: landlords, senior civil servants, women, the insane and illegitimate babies. They did not lose the war, nor make a revolution.

7. The Central Powers were far more successful in killing the enemy than the Entente and Allied armies; they killed at least 35 per cent more men than they lost. They also succeeded in taking prisoner 25–38 per cent more men than were captured by the other side. The Central Powers permanently incapacitated 10.3 million enemy soldiers; they lost only 7.1 million. To be sure, the Central Powers had smaller armies; but their mortality total was only 15.7 per cent of men mobilized, only slightly more than the equivalent figure for the other side (12 per cent). In any case, high mortality rates do not explain the outcome of the war: otherwise France, not Russia, would have collapsed and the Scots regiments would have mutinied. This means that the Entente powers lost the war of attrition: their principal strategy, in a word, was a failure – almost as big a failure as their second most important strategy, that of starving the Germans into submission through the naval blockade. Between August 1914 and June 1918 the Germans consistently killed or captured more British and French soldiers than they lost themselves. Even when the tide turned in the summer of 1918 it had more to do with errors of German strategy than with improvements on the Allied side. The extent of German success and Allied failure is even more evident when military and financial figures are combined: it cost the Central Powers just $11,345 to kill an enemy soldier; the equivalent figure for the Entente and Allied powers is $36,485, more than three times as much.

8. Why, then, did men keep fighting? Conditions at the Front were undoubtedly wretched. Death and injury were meted out daily by machine-guns, snipers, shells, bayonets and the rest of the instruments of carnage. In addition to the pain of being 'hit', men felt fear, horror, grief, fatigue and discomfort: the trenches were damper, dirtier and more vermin-infested than the worst slum. Yet there was relatively little fraternizing with the enemy; desertion was comparatively rare for most of the war, especially on the Western Front; mutinies were few.

It would be reassuring, in many ways, if we could prove that men fought because they were coerced into doing so by the huge state bureaucracies generated before and during the conflict. Some men undoubtedly were; but the evidence clearly shows that those who had to be coerced into fighting were a tiny minority. Military discipline was not about compelling men to fight, but encouraging them – hence the importance of relations between officers and men.

It would be less reassuring, but still bearable, if we could show, as Kraus suggested, that men fought because of the jingoistic propaganda of a censored or cynical press. Yet even this hypothesis, for all its contemporary resonance, seems unpersuasive. Some men no doubt believed in the causes their governments told them they were fighting for. However, many either did not understand the political arguments for war or disbelieved them. Their reasons for carrying on with the fighting were different.

Morale was dependent on ordinary comforts and discomforts: warm clothing, habitable billets, food, alcohol, tobacco, rest, leisure, sex and leave. Comradeship at the level of the unit was also an important cement. It is unlikely that the war was kept going by its homoerotic undertones, though some public-school-educated officers were not oblivious to these. The nature of the male bonds of the trenches is better conveyed by words which still retain a flavour of that period: men stuck by their pals or mates. Such comradeship, however, was to be found on all sides. Larger collective identities (regimental, regional and national) were more important because they were more pronounced in some armies than in others – French soldiers felt more French than Russians felt Russian. Some evidence also exists that religion helped motivate the opposing armies. The motifs of holy war and Christian self-sacrifice employed by clergymen on both sides enabled soldiers to rationalize the slaughter they found themselves perpetrating and suffering, despite the fact that the sides on the Western Front were little different in their religious character.

But the crucial point is that men fought because they did not mind fighting. Here I take issue with the idea that the war was entirely 'piteous' in Wilfred Owen's sense, and the men who fought it pitiable. For most soldiers, to kill and risk being killed was much less intolerable than we today generally assume. This is in many ways the most shocking argument which it is possible to advance about the war, given the influence of Owen's poetry. Yet even the most famous war writers provide evidence that murder and death were not the things soldiers disliked about the war. Killing aroused little revulsion and fear of death was suppressed, while non-fatal 'Blighty' wounds were even coveted. Freud was close to the mark when he suggested that a kind of 'death instinct' was at work in the war. For some, revenge was a motivation. Others undoubtedly relished killing for its own sake: to those intoxicated by violence, it really could seem 'a lovely war'. At the same time, men underrated their own chances of being killed. Though the chances of a British soldier in France being a casualty were around 50:50, most men assumed the bells of hell would not ring for them as individuals and became to some extent inured to the sight of others suddenly dead (it was watching a man die slowly which was distressing). Time horizons were warped: in combat men lived from second to second, relieved to be out of the preceding night's long wait. And as the war itself began to seem as if it would never end, fatalism set in.

9. This brings us to the final and most difficult question: Why, if the war was bearable, did men stop fighting? The best answer to that question lies in the complex calculus of surrender; for it was the mass surrendering, not the mass killing, of the enemy which signalled victory on all the Fronts. The German collapse began in August 1918 with a huge increase in the number of Germans taken prisoner. This dramatic change is not easily explained; but the key may lie in the fact that to surrender (and indeed to take prisoners) was dangerous. There were many incidents on both sides of prisoner-killing, including an unknown number in which prisoners were murdered in cold blood, away from the immediate fighting area. This was despite the value of prisoners as sources of intelligence and cheap labour. In part, prisoner killing was a by-product of the bloodthirsty Front culture described above: some men killed prisoners for revenge. But there is also evidence that some

officers encouraged a policy of 'take no prisoners' to heighten the aggression of their men. Possibly such incidents grew less frequent in 1918, but it seems unlikely. It is more probable that a general decline in morale due to the manifest failure of the spring offensive, Ludendorff's request for an armistice and the increasing problem of illness encouraged German soldiers to attach a higher cost to fighting on than they had in 1917. However, it would be wrong to regard this willingness to surrender as a general weariness with violence. Although the fighting ceased along the Western Front in November 1918, war continued unabated in Eastern Europe and elsewhere; and it was waged by the Whites and Reds in the Russian Civil War with even greater ferocity.

OTHER MEMORIES

In the light of all this, it is worth re-examining critically the assumption discussed in the introduction to this book that the memory of war in literature and art was one of unmitigated horror. Even some of the most famous war poets were less 'anti-war' than is commonly realized. Of 103 complete poems in the standard edition of Owen's complete works only thirty-one (by my count) can really be classified as anti-war.[30] As for Sassoon's 'The Kiss' – addressed to 'Brother Lead and Sister Steel' – it is at best ambivalent about the hand-to-hand fighting at which the poet (known at the Front as 'Mad Jack') was so good:

> Sweet Sister, grant your soldier this:
> That in good fury he may feel
> The body where he sets his heel
> Quail from your downward darting kiss.[31]

Sassoon's most famous denunciation of the war as one 'of aggression and conquest' delighted a small clique of pacifists; but his friends and superiors saw it as a symptom of 'neurasthenia'. Instead of court-martialling him, they indulgently sent him to 'Dottyville', the psychiatric hospital at Craiglockhart.[32] After treatment by Rivers, both he and Owen returned from there to active service of their own volition. Other 'war poets' were at most ambivalent rather than hostile to the war: a good example is Charles Hamilton Sorley, whose 'When You See Millions of the Mouthless Dead' (1915) is solemn but not 'anti-war'. Appollinaire too was no anti-war poet: he never doubted that 'material, artistic and moral progress . . . [had] to be victoriously defended' against Germany.[33] Nor was Ungaretti: though cryptically modern in style, poems like 'Rivers' and 'Italy' are movingly patriotic.[34]

It is also worth recalling how many famous poems in this canon were in fact written by non-combatants: Thomas Hardy was seventy-eight when he wrote 'And There Was a Great Calm', with its final, despairing 'Why?' Ezra Pound's 'Hugh Selwyn Mauberley (Life and Contacts)' (1920) is not a war poem at all but a parody of one by a writer who never went near a trench:

> Died some, pro patria,
>
> > non 'dulce' non 'et decor' . . .
>
> walked eye-deep in hell
> believing in old men's lies, then unbelieving . . .

Among the most haunting condemnations of the war in German poetry are Rilke's *Duino Elegies*; but although he was called up and briefly served in the 1st Reserve Rifle Regiment, he did not fight.[35] In its revised second edition, *The Penguin Book of First World War Poetry* includes works by Hardy, Rudyard Kipling, D. H. Lawrence, Ford Madox Ford and, in deference to feminist sensibility, nine female poets. None fought. There are also several poems which are more or less enthusiastic about the war, notably works by Brooke – by far the most popular of all the war poets[36] – Julian Grenfell, John McCrae and Edward Thomas, often considered an archetypal martyr of a senseless war, whose 'This is No Case of Petty Right or Wrong' is in fact a defence of it. In any case, it cannot be overemphasized that such selections are anything but representative. The overwhelming majority of the vast number of poems written during the war by combatants and non-combatants alike were patriotic ditties.[37]

There are difficulties too with the notion of anti-war prose. As Hugh Cecil has observed, although *All Quiet on the Western Front* was and is probably the most widely read of all First World War-inspired books, it was quite untypical of the 400 or so works of war fiction published in Britain between 1918 and 1939.[38] During the war the patriotic tone predominated. Ian Hay's *The First Hundred Thousand* (1915) is full of early war enthusiasm. Jingoistic wartime fiction included William J. Locke's *The Red Planet* (1916) and *The Rough Road* (1918), and Joseph Hocking's *The Curtain of Fire* (1916). After the war too, the mood was not all disenchanted. *Disenchantment* itself did not sell spectacularly well: by 1927 it had sold just over 9,000 copies in Britain.[39] *Medal Without Bar*, though admired by the ex-soldiers who read it for its accuracy, sold 10,000.[40] These were respectable sales figures, no doubt; but far more successful was the former army chaplain Ernest Raymond's saccharine *Tell England*, a book which has only one thing in common with *All Quiet on the Western Front*, namely that all the young friends who join up in 1914 get killed. This 'Great Romance of Glorious Youth' was reprinted fourteen times in 1922.[41] Although the central character in Wilfred Ewart's *Way of Revelation* (1921) – another bestseller – has to contend with a girlfriend who succumbs to decadence on the home front, his criticisms of the war itself were muted.[42]

Nor were all war memoirs wholly disenchanted in tone. There is in fact much less anti-war sentiment in the works of Sassoon, Blunden and Graves than is sometimes asserted; indeed Graves was surprised when his own *Goodbye to All That* was reviewed as if it were 'a violent treatise against war'.[43] Graves in fact brilliantly explains how men 'calculated' their own survival chances:

To take a life we would run, say, a one-in-five risk, particularly if there was some wider object than merely reducing the enemy's manpower; for instance, picking off a well-known sniper . . . I only once refrained from shooting a German I saw . . . Perhaps a one-in-twenty risk to get a wounded German to safety would be considered justifiable [in the Royal Welch] . . . When exhausted and wanting to get quickly from one point in the trenches to another without collapse, we would sometimes take a short cut over the top . . . In a hurry, we would take a one-in-two-hundred risk; when dead tired, a one-in-fifty risk.[44]

Graves also describes how 'the regimental spirit persistently survived all catastrophes'; whereas 'the battalion cared as little about the success or reverses of our Allies as about the origins of the war.'[45] He cites as evidence of the violent culture of the 'other ranks' the two men of the Royal Welch who were court-martialled and shot for having murdered one of their own sergeants; and remarks that 'it was surprising there were so few clashes between the British and the local French – who returned our loathing'.[46] Nor does he omit the fact that 'base venereal hospitals were always crowded'. None of this is intended to convey outrage; Graves simply, and with a certain black humour, explains. Blunden's *Undertones of War* has its share of horrors, but it also conveys the ordinary soldier's fascination with death (witness the 'squints' men took at exposed graves in a shelled churchyard), and their mastery of understatement: ' "Never did see such shelling," he said. It was exactly as if he had been talking of a break by Willie Smith, or art for art's sake.'[47] As for Sassoon's thinly fictionalized memoirs, they unblinkingly recall going 'up to the trenches with the intention of killing someone' to avenge a dead friend;[48] and later, feeling 'elated at the prospect of battle . . . as though going over the top were a species of religious experience'. As Sassoon puts it, he was 'no believer in wild denunciations of the War . . . in 1917 I was only beginning to learn that life for the majority of the population is an unlovely struggle against unfair odds, culminating in a cheap funeral'.[49] He also acknowledges the death instinct: 'the semi-suicidal instinct which haunted me whenever I thought about going back to the line . . . an insidious craving to be killed'.[50]

Even Remarque (like Barbusse) acknowledges the redeeming role of the comradeship of the Front: the communal crapping, the coarse banter, the obsession with food which results in the hilarious theft of a goose, the ability to forget a dead comrade and inherit his boots.[51] Gilbert Frankau's *Peter Jackson, Cigar Merchant* (1920) expresses criticism of army mismanagement and even corruption, but only because they inhibit the effective prosecution of the war.[52] Less well-known memoirists like Ronald Gurner, William Barnet Logan and Edward Thompson all repudiated the notion of disenchantment.[53] Moreover, even some of those who did feel in some way disenchanted – men like Montague and Edmonds – were more so with the peace than with the war itself.[54] The military historian Douglas Jerrold was not an isolated voice when he published his pamphlet *The Lie about the War: A Note on Some Contemporary War Books* in 1930, accusing sixteen authors (including Remarque and Barbusse) of 'deny[ing] the dignity of tragic drama to the war in the interests of propaganda'. His colleague Cyril Falls agreed in his *The War Book: A Critical Guide* (1930): it was quite wrong, he argued, to imply that 'the men who died in [the war] were driven like beasts to the slaughter, and died like beasts . . .' Predictably, the few senior officers who stooped to reading Remarque were dismissive.[55] Many ordinary soldiers also shared Sidney Rogerson's dislike of books which 'pil[ed] corpse on corpse, heap[ed] terror on futility'.[56] As has often been remarked, the memoirs of the 1920s and 1930s were disproportionately the work of public school and university-educated men with little pre-war experience of hardship, much less war. Their disillusionment was predicated on the illusions of privileged youth;[57] whereas little of the discomfort they complained about was new to the 'other ranks'.[58] A fine example of the cheerful Tommy's view is Coppard's memoir, which perfectly illustrates how men were sustained by a combination of fatalism – 'If it's got your bloody number on it, there's nothing you can do about it' – nicotine addiction – 'as important as ammunition' – and hatred: 'The enemy were bloody bastards always.' Coppard even admits that he would not have refused to shoot a court-martialled man if he had been ordered to do so.[59]

It is also a great mistake to imagine that there was a uniform tone to post-war writing about the war. One of the best books directly inspired by the Central Powers' war effort was Jaroslav Hašek's *The Good Soldier Švejk* (1921–3).[60] It is one of the funniest books ever written. At the other extreme there are Ernst Jünger's war novels. To Jünger, as we have seen, the war was an exhilarating test of the individual's ability to master fear for the sake of honour; despite acknowledging the discomforts and terrors of the trenches, he constantly reiterates the satisfaction he derived from his time as a stormtroop officer.[61] 'Combat is one of the truly great experiences', he wrote in *Combat as Inner Experience* (1922), 'and I have still to find someone to whom the moment of victory was not one of shattering exaltation.' In war, 'the true human being makes up in a drunken orgy for everything that he has been neglecting. Then his passions, too long dammed up by society and its laws, become once more uniquely dominant and holy and the ultimate reason.' When he called war 'a great school' and 'the anvil on which the world will be hammered into new boundaries and new communities', Jünger was echoing what pre-war Social Darwinists had written: far from invalidating militarism, the war had enhanced its appeal to many Germans. There were numerous war memoirs published in the Weimar years which expressed similar sentiments in less exalted prose: for example Rudolf Binding's memoir, *Vom Kriege* (1924), Georg von der Vring's *Soldat Suhren* (1927), Werner Beumelburg's *Trommelfeuer um Deutschland* (1929) and *Gruppe Bösemüller* (1930).[62] The memoirs of those soldiers who continued to fight after the Armistice in irregular *Freikorps* express, besides their now notorious misogyny, a quite unrepentant bloodthirstiness.[63] In Italy too the advent of the Fascist regime in 1922 ensured that, despite the country's wretched wartime experience, the war would be glorified in literature. Indeed, this process began even before 1922, thanks to D'Annunzio.[64] In the Soviet Union, of course, the Bolshevik regime encouraged writers to shrink the events before October 1917 into a mere prelude to the revolution. It is significant that in Stalin's favourite book, Mikhail Bulgakov's *The White Guard*, the story begins with the flight of the German armies from Ukraine, and ends with the Bolsheviks arriving to halt the anarchy of the Civil War. Still, there was no attempt in the 1920s to deprecate violence as such; on the contrary, it was praised as a necessary tool in the class struggle.

Nor can it really be said that the drama inspired by the war was uniformly anti-war. Though it is set in a dugout near St Quentin on the eve of Ludendorff's great spring offensive, R. C. Sherriff's *Journey's End* (1928) is not a pacifist play. The senior officer drinks, another has lost his nerve and their two colleagues die in a doomed raid; but the ethos of the play is public school stiff-upper-lip.[65] The British playwright who was most critical of the war was George Bernard Shaw; but his anti-war journalism and pamphleteering won virtually no popular support and the oblique digs at the war in *Heartbreak House* and the preface to *Back to Methuselah* are ineffectual compared with Kraus's *magnum opus*.[66] Such music as was composed about the war also defies simple categorisation. Havergal Brian's *The Tigers* (begun in 1916) may fit the bill as a 'satirical anti-war opera'; but what of John Foulds's overblown *World Requiem* (1918–21), performed for four successive years on Armistice Day at a commemoration service sponsored by the British Legion? As 'a message of consolation to the bereaved of all countries', this was scarcely anti-war.[67] Nor can Stravinsky's *L'Histoire du Soldat* really be characterized in that way, nor even Ernst Krenek's jazz-tinged opera *Jonny spielt auf* (premiered in 1927); Krenek's use of an air-raid siren to drown out the final chorus is, if anything, a comic touch.

The most famous films inspired by the war were, of course, *All Quiet on the Western Front* and its German counterpart *Westfront 1918*. Of the five war films released in 1930, *All Quiet* is the one which is still regularly shown in Britain; and no one who has seen it will forget the scene (which does not appear in the less sentimental book) in which the young hero is shot as he stretches out, near the war's end, to touch a butterfly on a parapet. More harrowing still, perhaps, is the image of the dead rising from their graves in Abel Gance's *J'Accuse*, the greatest of the French anti-war films along with Jean Renoir's *La Grande Illusion*. But we should not forget that released in the same year as *All Quiet* were a screen version of *Journey's End* and two more straightforward adventures set in the most romantic of all the war's theatres – the air.

The 1920s had also seen the release of six British-made war films: *The Battle of Jutland, Armageddon* (about the war in Palestine), *Zeebrugge, Ypres, Mons* and *Battles of the Coronel and the Falkland Islands*. One irritated critic described them as 'full of the kind of sentimentality that makes one shudder', presenting the war '*entirely* from a romantic boy-adventure book angle'.[68] But was that not what cinema audiences between the wars liked best?

And which art was the true 'war art'? In the more 'Whiggish' art history textbooks it used to be said that the horrors of the war had in some way accelerated the evolution of modernism by discrediting romantic conventions of representation; this is debatable. Romantic imagery came through the war more or less intact: witness John Hassall's *Vision of St George over the Battlefield* (1915), Lucy Kemp's *Forward the Guns!* (1917) or George Bellows' *Edith Cavell* (1918) and his extraordinary sequence of canvases depicting Belgian atrocities, which echo Titian's *Flaying of Marsyas*.[69] The most radical development in modernism between 1914 and 1918 – Dadaism – was largely the work of artists like Hugo Ball and Richard Huelsenbeck who had decamped to neutral Switzerland.[70] For those who fought, the war provided geometric subject matter for painters (like Wyndham Lewis, Fernand Léger or Oscar Schlemmer) who had already been exponents of Vorticism or Cubism; explosive subject matter for those (like Otto Dix) already attracted to expressionism; and grotesque subject matter for those (like George Grosz) already filled with misanthropy. To be sure, none of these artists appear to the modern eye to have glorified war. Yet the number who, like Paul Nash, saw their work serving a didactic, anti-war function was relatively small. Remarkably few of the thirty or so war-time drawings Grosz published during and after the war in collections like the two *Mappen* (1917), *Im Schatten* (1921), *Die Räuber* (1923), *Ecce Homo* (1923) and *The Marked Men* (1930) explicitly allude to the war. Though disabled veterans are depicted in the frantic, shabby Berlin streets, nearly all the caricatures are of civilians. Only the two 1915 cartoons, 'Battlefield with Dead Soldiers' and 'Captured', and the nine cartoons in *Gott mit uns* (1920) give any suggestion that Grosz himself had personal experience of the army. Much the same can be said of Grosz's paintings: even *Explosion* (1917), which might be construed as an imagined air raid on Berlin, was directly inspired by Ludwig Meidner's pre-war *Burning City* (1913). It was not until 1928 (with *Hintergrund*) that Grosz produced a series of explicitly anti-war cartoons.[71]

Moreover, a number of modern artists relished the aesthetics of total war. Having eulogized war before 1914, the Italian Futurist Filippo Marinetti could hardly do otherwise after it. But it was not only Futurists who viewed the war in a positive light. Lewis, Léger and Dix were at the very least ambivalent about the horrors they witnessed. Lewis, who had urged fellow Vorticists not to 'miss a war, if one is going', later wrote with undisguised relish of:

those grinning skeletons in field-grey, the skull still protected by the metal helmet: those festoons of mud-caked wire, those miniature mountain-ranges of saffron earth, and trees like gibbets – these were the properties only of those titanic casts of dying and shell-shocked actors, who charged this stage with *a romantic electricity*.[72]

Léger was 'stunned by the sight of the open breech of a .75 cannon in full sunlight, confronted with the play of light on white metal'.[73] The war, he wrote, gave him a sudden revelation of 'the *depth* of the present day':

The sight of swarming squadrons. The resourceful private soldier. Then again and again fresh armies of workmen. Mountains of pure raw materials, of manufactured objects . . . American motors, Malaysian daggers, English jam, troops from all countries, German chemicals . . . everything bearing the stamp of tremendous unity.[74]

His *The Card Game* (1917) was, as one critic commented, 'at once a cry of rage against the war's imposing on men the terrible mechanical uniformity of robots, and, at the same time, a hymn of strength of man who has created these machines, the very rhythm of which exalts man's controlling power'.[75] If, as Willett has suggested, Franz Jung was the author of the Dadaist Berlin Manifesto of April 1918, it seems reasonable to link its bellicose language to his experience as a conscript at the battle of Tannenberg:

The highest art will be that . . . which one can see allowing itself to be bowled over by last week's explosions, which is repeatedly gathering its limbs together after the previous day's shock. The best . . . artists will be those who are [for]ever collecting the shreds of their bodies from the confusion of life's cataracts, as they cling to the intellect of the age with bleeding heart and hands.[76]

Russian artists too produced more pro- than anti-war art. Y. Pimenov's *Disabled Veterans* (1926) is conspicuous for its debt to German artists like Grosz and Dix; but K. Petrov-Vodkin's *Death of Commissar*, completed in the same year, illustrates once again the Bolshevik need to distinguish between the wicked imperialist war and the heroic Civil War.[77]

Perhaps the most striking of all counter-examples is that of Otto Dix. Dix, who fought throughout the war on both Western and Eastern Fronts, regarded war as 'a natural occurrence' and horrified his friend Conrad Felixmüller by describing the pleasure of 'sticking a bayonet in someone's guts and twisting it around'. Often misinterpreted as denunciations of war – perhaps because Dix's agent sought to catch the pacifist wave of 1920s Germany – grotesque paintings like *The Trench* (1923, since lost) or the *War* triptych (1929–32) and the fifty war etchings (1924) in fact owed as much to the artist's desire as a young volunteer to 'experience all the ghastly, bottomless depths of life for myself'. As he later explained, 'I had to experience how someone beside me suddenly falls over and is dead and the bullet has hit him squarely. I had to experience that quite directly. I wanted it.' 'The war was a horrible thing,' he recalled, 'but there was something tremendous about it too.'[78] A keen reader of Nietzsche before and during the war, Dix more than any other artist was inspired by the aesthetics of mass death and destruction. As he wrote in one of the postcard sketches he sent to his friend Helen Jakob: 'In the ruins of Aubérive – the shell holes in the villages are full of elemental energy . . . It's a singular and rare beauty that speaks to us.'[79] A much less sophisticated German soldier-artist also painted and sketched shelled villages: the mood of these little-known works by Adolf Hitler, a corporal in the 16th Bavarian Reserve Infantry Regiment, can only be described as serene.[80]

Some later British art inspired by the war shares this ambivalence: Stanley Spencer said of his own *Resurrection of the Soldiers* at Burghclere – in some ways stylistically similar to Dix's post-war work – that he wished to communicate 'a feeling of joy and hopeful expectancy'.[81] Even when, during the war, he had been required to paint the signs differentiating the sergeant's toilets from other ranks', he had sought to uplift, by decorating the S for Sergeant with a halo of roses.[82] The Burghclere *Resurrection* is hardly a joyful work; but its reconfiguration of the war in Christian iconography is intended to console, not to anger; in this Spencer resembled Georges Rouault, whose cycle of fifty-eight etchings, *Miserere*, is perhaps the supreme attempt to render the war intelligible in religious terms.[83]

WHAT IF?

In 1932, with reparations and war debts frozen and the world in the depths of the Depression, the writer J. C. Squire published an entertaining (though now largely forgotten) collection of what he called 'lapses into imaginary history'. Three of his eleven contributors chose to rewrite history in such a way as to 'avoid' the First World War. André Maurois did it by imagining away the French Revolution. As his omniscient 'Archangel' explains, the imaginary world after a century and a half more of Bourbon rule in France 'is divided somewhat differently. The United States did not break away from England, but so vast have they grown that they now dominate the British Empire . . . The Imperial Parliament sits in Kansas City . . . the capital of . . . the United States of Europe . . . in Vienna.' There has been no 'war of 1914–1918'.[84] Winston Churchill entertained a similar fantasy by assuming a Confederate victory at Gettysburg and the subsequent emergence in 1905 of an 'English Speaking Association' of Britain, the Confederacy and the Northern United States:

Once the perils of 1914 had been successfully averted and the disarmament of Europe had been brought into harmony with that already effected by the E.S.A., the idea of 'An United States of Europe' was bound to occur continually. The glittering spectacle of the great English-speaking combination, its assured safety, its boundless power, the rapidity with which wealth was created and widely distributed within its bounds, the sense of buoyancy and hope which seemed to pervade the entire populations; all this pointed to European eyes a moral which none but the dullest could ignore. Whether the Emperor Wilhelm II will be successful in carrying the project of European unity forward by another important stage at the forthcoming Pan-European Conference at Berlin in 1932, is still a matter for prophecy . . . If this prize should fall to his Imperial Majesty, he may perhaps reflect how easily his career might have been wrecked in 1914 by the outbreak of a war which might have cost him his throne, and have laid his country in the dust.[85]

In a slightly more realistic vein, Emil Ludwig suggested that, if the German Emperor Frederick III had not died of cancer in 1888 (after just ninety-nine days on the throne), German political development might have taken a more liberal course: in this alternative world, a longer-lived Frederick parliamentarizes the constitution and concludes an Anglo-German alliance, dying contentedly at the age of eighty-three on 1 August 1914.[86] Only Hilaire Belloc imagined a counter-factual outcome worse than historical reality. Like Maurois, Belloc undid the French Revolution; but this time France's decline as a power is accelerated, allowing the Holy Roman Empire to wax into a federation of Europe 'stretching from the Baltic to Sicily and from Königsberg to Ostend'. Thus, when war breaks out with this Greater Germany in 1914, it is Britain which loses, ending up as a 'Province of the European Commonwealth'.[87]

Apart from the common preoccupation with that idea of European unification which, as we have seen, had indeed been a German objective in 1914, the striking thing about all of these essays is how far back the authors felt they had to go in order to find a turning point at which European history could credibly have turned another way. Yet eighty years after the Armistice of 1918 less remote counter-factuals seem more plausible. What if Germany had pursued a less risky defence strategy, spending more on her peacetime defences rather than staking everything on the Schlieffen Plan? What if Britain had stayed out of the war in 1914?

If the First World War had never been fought, the worst consequence would have been something like a First Cold War, in which the five great powers continued to maintain large military establishments, but without impeding their own sustained economic growth. Alternatively, if a war had been fought, but without Britain and America, the victorious Germans might have created a version of the European Union, eight decades ahead of schedule.

If the British Expeditionary Force had never been sent, there is no question that the Germans would have won the war. Even if they had been checked at the Marne, they would almost certainly have succeeded in overwhelming the French army in the absence of substantial British reinforcements. And even if the BEF *had* arrived, but a week later or in a different location as a result of a political crisis in London, Moltke might still have repeated the triumph of his forebear. At the very least, he would have been less inclined to retreat to the Aisne. Then what? Doubtless the arguments for British intervention to check German ambitions would have continued – especially with Bonar Law as Prime

Minister. But only intervention of a very different kind would have been conceivable. The expeditionary force would have been rendered obsolete by French defeat; had it been sent, a Dunkirk-like evacuation would probably have been the *dénouement*. The navalists' old schemes for landings on the German coast would also have been consigned to the rubbish-bin, as they were anyway. It is possible that some version of the Dardanelles invasion would still have emerged as the most credible use for the army (especially if Churchill had remained at the Admiralty, as he almost certainly would have). Besides that hazardous enterprise – which might, of course, have fared better if the full BEF had been available – the most Britain could have done would have been to use its naval power to wage the kind of maritime war against Germany which Fisher had always advocated: rounding up German merchant vessels, harassing neutrals trading with the enemy and confiscating German overseas assets.

Such a dual strategy would certainly have been an irritant to Berlin. But it would not have won the war. For the evidence is strong that the blockade did not starve Germany into submission, as its advocates had hoped it would. Nor would a victory over Turkey have significantly weakened the position of a Germany which had won in the West, though it would certainly have benefited the Russians by realizing their historic designs on Constantinople. Without the war of attrition on the Western Front, Britain's manpower, its economy and its vastly superior financial resources could not have been brought to bear on Germany sufficiently to ensure victory. A far more likely outcome would have been a diplomatic compromise (of the sort which Lord Lansdowne actually advocated), whereby Britain ended hostilities in return for German guarantees of Belgian integrity and neutrality. That, after all, had been Bethmann's objective all along. With France beaten and the German offer to restore Belgium to the *status quo ante* still on the table, it is hard to see how any British government could have justified continuing a naval and perhaps Middle Eastern war of unforeseeable duration. For what? It is possible to imagine embittered Liberals still calling, as they did, for a war against Germany's 'military caste', though the argument cut little ice with Haig and would have been hard to sustain if, as seems probable, Bethmann had continued that policy of collaboration with the Social Democrats which had begun with the 1913 tax bill and borne fruit with the vote for war credits.[88] But a war to preserve Russian control over Poland? To hand Constantinople to the Tsar? Although Grey at times seemed ready to fight such a war, he would surely have been overruled by those like Sir William Robertson, who could still argue in August 1916 for the preservation of 'a strong ... Teutonic ... Central European power' as a check against Russia.[89] Germany's proposed Central European Customs Union would have been difficult to reject.

Had Britain stood aside – even for a matter of weeks – continental Europe could therefore have been transformed into something not wholly unlike the European Union we know today – but without the massive contraction in British overseas power entailed by the fighting of two world wars. Perhaps too the complete collapse of Russia into the horrors of civil war and Bolshevism might have been averted. Though there would still have been formidable problems of rural and urban unrest, a properly constitutional monarchy (following Nicholas II's probably inevitable abdication) or a parliamentary republic would have stood more chance of success after a shorter war. And there plainly would not have been that great incursion of American financial and military power into European affairs which effectively marked the end of British financial predominance in the world. Granted, there might still have been Fascism in Europe in the 1920s; but it would have been in France rather than Germany that radical nationalists would have sounded most persuasive. This would have come as no surprise: the French Right had been far more noisily anti-Semitic than the German before 1914 – witness the Dreyfus Affair. And perhaps, in the absence of a world war's economic strains, the inflations and deflations of the early 1920s and early 1930s would not have been so severe.

With the Kaiser triumphant, Adolf Hitler could have eked out his life as a mediocre postcard painter and a fulfilled old soldier in a German-dominated Central Europe about which he could have found little to complain. And Lenin could have carried on his splenetic scribbling in Zurich, forever waiting for capitalism to collapse – and forever disappointed. It was, after all, the German army which gave Hitler not only his beloved 'Front experience' but also his introduction to politics and public speaking immediately after the war. It was also the German army which sent Lenin back to Petrograd to undermine the Russian war effort in 1917. It was ultimately because of the war that both men were able to rise to establish barbaric despotisms which perpetrated still more mass murder. Both saw it as conclusive proof of their conflicting but complementary theories: that the Jews were intent on destroying the Aryan race; that capitalism was bound to self-destruct.

In the final analysis, then, the historian is bound to ask if acceptance of a German victory on the continent would have been as damaging to British interests as Grey and the other Germanophobes claimed at the time, and as the majority of historians have subsequently accepted. The answer suggested here is that it would not have been. Eyre Crowe's question had always been: 'Should the war come, and England stand aside . . . [and] Germany and Austria win, crush France and humiliate Russia, what will then be the position of a friendless England?'[90] The historian's answer is: better than that of an exhausted England in 1919.

Immanuel Geiss has recently argued:

There was nothing wrong with the conclusion . . . that Germany and continental Europe west of Russia would only be able to hold their own . . . if Europe pulled together. And a united Europe would fall almost automatically under the leadership of the strongest power – Germany . . . [But] German leadership over a united Europe in order to brave the coming giant economic and political power blocs would have to overcome the imagined reluctance [sic] of Europeans to domination by any one of their peers. Germany would have to persuade Europe to accept German leadership . . . to make crystal clear that the overall interest of Europe would coincide with the enlightened self-interest of Germany . . . in order to achieve in the years after 1900 something like the position of the Federal Republic today.[91]

Though his assumptions perhaps unconsciously reflect the hubris of the post-reunification era, in one sense he is absolutely right: it would have been infinitely preferable if Germany could have achieved its hegemonic position on the continent without two world wars. It was not only Germany's fault that this did not happen. It was Germany which forced the continental war of 1914 upon an unwilling France (and a not so unwilling Russia). But it was the British government which ultimately decided to turn the continental war into a world war, a conflict which lasted twice as long and cost many more lives than Germany's first 'bid for European Union' would have, if it had only gone according to plan. By fighting Germany in 1914, Asquith, Grey and their colleagues helped ensure that, when Germany did finally achieve predominance on the continent, Britain was no longer strong enough to provide a check to it.

The title of this book, then, is at once a sincere allusion to Wilfred Owen's twice-used phrase and an echo of the understated idiom of the ordinary private soldier in the trenches. The First World War was at once piteous, in the poet's sense, and 'a pity'. It was something worse than a tragedy, which is something we are taught by the theatre to regard as ultimately unavoidable. It was nothing less than the greatest *error* of modern history.

Notes

Introduction

1. It was not known as such then: the 'World War' and 'European War' were the usual designations; the 'Great War' came later; and the name '*First* World War' is usually attributed to *The Times*'s military correspondent Charles à Court Repington who discerned, as early as September 1918, that it would not live up to H. G. Wells's optimistic billing as 'The War That Will End War'.

2. Spiers, 'Scottish Soldier', p. 314. For a lower estimate, see Harvie, *No Gods*, p. 24. Note that the Serbs and Turks probably lost more men to disease.

3. PRO WO 95/1483, History of the 2nd Battalion, Seaforth Highlanders, 1916–1918, War Diary.

4. *Sic:* most soldiers were not demobilized until that year.

5. It is, of course, just another way of saying 'Their name liveth for evermore', the biblical phrase suggested by Rudyard Kipling for the Great War Stones erected by the Imperial War Graves Commission.

6. I am grateful to Dennis Goodwin and Cathy Stevenson for this information.

7. Around 723,000 British servicemen died in the First World War; in the Second the figure was 264,443. More civilians died in the Second, however, around 92,573; German air and naval raids on Britain in the First World War claimed around 1,570 lives: Davies, *Europe*, p. 1328; Banks, *Military Atlas*, p. 296.

8. Fitzgerald, *Tender Is the Night*, pp. 67f, 70.

9. Fitzgerald, *The Great Gatsby*, p. 72.

10. Reynolds, *Young Hemingway*, pp. 18ff., 55f.

11. Though it should be remembered that twice as many Civil War fatalities were due to disease than to battle.

12. Born, *International Banking*, p. 204; Eichengreen, *Golden Fetters*, p. 85.

13. A useful chronicle is provided by Gilbert, *First World War*. Other excellent textbooks are Ferro, *Great War*, an inspired mixture of strategy and social history; Robbins, *First World War*; and Warner, *World War One*. Taylor's *First World War* is still the most readable, if idiosyncratic, short account.

14. For an admirably broad portrayal of Britain's war, see Wilson, *Myriad Faces*. See also Bourne, *Britain and the Great War*; DeGroot, *Blighty*. Not to be missed are the relevant sections of Taylor, *English History*, pp. 1–119. Woodward, *Great Britain*, has worn less well.

15. See the otherwise excellent Hardach, *First World War*, which says virtually nothing about military effectiveness, and Kocka, *Facing Total War*. Cf. Chickering's excellent new synthesis, *Imperial Germany*, and Herwig, *First World War*, which gives military matters due primacy and skillfully weaves together German and Austro-Hungarian experiences. More eccentric, though rich in detail, is Moyer, *Victory Must Be Ours*.

16. Fussell, *Great War*; Hynes, *War Imagined*.

17. Among the many recent volumes of essays which I have found useful are Liddle (ed.), *Home Fires*; Mommsen (ed.), *Kultur und Krieg*; Michalka (ed.), *Erste Weltkrieg*; Cecil and Liddle (eds.), *Facing Armageddon*. Mention should also be made of Becker and Audoin-Rouzeau (eds.), *Sociétés Européennes et la Guerre*; idem *et al.* (eds.), *Guerre et Cultures*; and Hirschfeld *et al.* (eds.), *Keiner fühlt sich mehr als Mensch*.

18. See the insightful discussion in Winter, *Great War*, pp. 289–300.

19. Sassoon, *War Poems*, p. 22.

20. Hynes, *War Imagined*, p. 239.

21. Only four of Owen's poems had been published when he was killed a week before the Armistice, and although seven appeared in Edith Sitwell's magazine *Wheels* in 1919 it was not until late the following year that twenty-three of his *Poems* were edited and published by Sassoon. Cf. Owen, *Poems*.

22. Blunden, *Undertones*, pp. 256–60.

23. Others who wrote unambiguously anti-war poems in English included Herbert Read, David Jones and Isaac Rosenberg. See the examples of their work in Silkin (ed.), *Penguin Book*.

24. Willett, *New Sobriety*, p. 22.

25. See in general Marsland, *Nation's Cause*.

26. Silkin (ed.), *Penguin Book*.

27. E.g. Balcon (ed.), *Pity of War*; Hibberd and Onions (eds.), *Poetry of the Great War*.

28. Holroyd, *Shaw*, vol. II, pp. 348ff.

29. Hynes, *War Imagined*, pp. 83ff.

30. Ibid., p. 106. He changed his name from Ford Madox Hueffer in 1919; among the victims of the war were a large number of German surnames.

31. Ibid., pp. 131, 169.

32. Agnes Hamilton, *Dead Yesterday* (1916); Rose Allatini, *Despised and Rejected* (1918); the latter, which linked pacifism and homosexuality, was banned.

33. Hynes, *War Imagined*, pp. 137, 326. See also pp. 347f.

34. Ibid., pp. 286f.

35. Ibid., pp. 318ff.

36. Ibid., pp. 432f.

37. Ibid., p. 351.

38. Ibid., pp. 344ff.

39. Buchan, *Prince of the Captivity*.

40. Gibbon, *Scots Quair*, esp. pp. 147–82.

41. Forester, *The General*, esp. chapters 16 and 17.

42. Herbert, *Secret Battle*. In fact, Dyett's case had already been taken up by that least anti-war of journalists, Horatio Bottomley.

43. Grieves, 'Montague', pp. 49, 54.

44. Ibid., pp. 424f.; Cecil, 'British War Novelists', p. 809. Cf. Barnett, 'Military Historian's View', pp. 1–18.

45. Céline, *Voyage au bout de la nuit*. Cf. Field, 'French War Novel', pp. 831–40.

46. Weber, *Hollow Years*, p. 19.

47. Kraus, *Letzten Tage*. There is no full English translation, though some extracts appear in idem, *In These Great Times*, pp. 157–258. Cf. Timms, *Kraus*, pp. 371ff.

48. Hynes, *Soldier's Tale*, pp. 102f.

49. Marwick, *Deluge*, p. 221.

50. Kahn, 'Art from the Front', pp. 192–208.

51. Cork, *Bitter Truth*, p. 171.

52. Ibid., p. 175.

53. Danchev, 'Bunking and Debunking', pp. 281–7.

54. Ibid., pp. 263, 269, 279–81.

55. J. Winter and Baggett, *1914–1918*, pp. 10ff.

56. Mosse, *Fallen Soldiers*, pp. 112f., 154; Cannadine, 'Death and Grief', p. 231.

57. See, e.g., Holt, *Battlefields of the First World War*; R. Holmes, *War Walks*; O'Shea, *Back to the Front*.

58. Danchev, 'Bunking and Debunking', pp. 263f.

59. A. J. P. Taylor, *First World War*, pp. 11, 62.

60. L. Wolff, *In Flanders Fields*; Tuchman, *August 1914*; Clark, *Donkeys*; A. Horne, *Price of Glory*. On the backstage influence of Liddell Hart on these books, see Bond, 'Editor's Introduction', p. 6; Danchev, 'Bunking and Debunking', p. 278.

61. Danchev, 'Bunking and Debunking', p. 268.

62. Macdonald, *Passchendaele; Roses of No Man's Land; Somme; 1914; Voices and Images; 1915*.

63. Laffin, *British Butchers and Bunglers*.

64. Ministère des Affaires Étrangères [Belgium], *Corréspondance Diplomatique*; Ministerium des k. und k. Hauses und des Äussern, *Diplomatische Aktenstücke*; Marchand (ed.), *Un Livre noir*; Auswärtiges Amt, *German White Book*.

65. Hynes, *War Imagined*, pp. 47, 278.

66. Edmonds (ed.), *France and Belgium*. There are substantial official histories of all the theatres of war in which British soldiers fought—including East Africa, Egypt and Palestine, Italy, Macedonia, Mesopotamia,

Togoland and the Cameroons—of which the most important remains Aspinall-Oglander's two volumes on *Gallipoli*. The Admiralty produced Corbett and Newbolt's five-volume *Naval Operations* (1920–31); the role of the Royal Flying Corps is detailed in Raleigh and Jones's six-part *War in the Air* (1922–27). There are also official histories of transport on the Western Front, the Merchant Navy, Seaborne Trade, the Blockade, as well as twelve volumes on the Ministry of Munitions. In addition, the Carnegie Endowment published a number of semi-official volumes of great value to the economic historian: Beveridge's *British Food Control* and Stamp's *Taxation during the War* are especially useful.

67. Reichsarchiv, *Weltkrieg*. The Austrian equivalent is Österreichisches Bundesministerium für Heereswesen und Kriegsarchiv (ed.), *Österreich-Ungarns letzter Krieg*.

68. Anon (ed.), *Documents diplomatiques secrets russes*; Hoetzsch (ed.), *Internationalen Beziehungen im Zeitalter des Imperialismus*.

69. Montgelas and Schücking (eds.), *Outbreak of the World War*. But see the documents produced by Germany's former military leaders: Ludendorff, *General Staff*; Tirpitz, *Deutsche Ohnmachtspolitik*.

70. E. Fischer, Bloch and Philipp (eds.), *Ursachen des Deutschen Zusammenbruches*.

71. Lepsius, Mendelssohn-Bartholdy and Thimme (eds.), *Grosse Politik*. See also from the Austrian side, Bittner and Übersberger, *Österreich-Ungarns Aussenpolitik*.

72. Gooch and Temperley (eds.), *British Documents*.

73. Commission de publication, *Documents diplomatiques français*.

74. In addition, Haig published his *Despatches* in 1919; Jellicoe's *The Grand Fleet, 1914–16* came out the same year, followed by his *The Crisis of the Naval War* (1920).

75. Ludendorff, *Kriegserinnerungen*; Tirpitz, *Erinnerungen*; Falkenhayn, *Oberste Heeresleitung*.

76. Pershing, *Experiences*.

77. Bethmann, *Betrachtungen*.

78. Wilhelm II, *Ereignisse und Gestalten*. Monarchs who were not deposed generally kept mum: a partial exception is Galet, *Albert King of the Belgians*.

79. It was followed much later by *Men and Power*.

80. These books generally sold well: Grey's *Twenty-Five Years* sold nearly 12,000 in its first year, while almost as many copies of volume one of W. S. Churchill's *World Crisis* were printed within a month of publication. By 1937, nearly 55,000 copies of all six volumes of Lloyd George's memoirs had been sold: Bond, 'Editor's Introduction', p. 7.

81. Lloyd George, *War Memoirs*, vol. I, pp. 32, 34f., 47f.

82. W. S. Churchill, *World Crisis*, vol. I, pp. 45, 55, 188.

83. Hitler, *Mein Kampf*, p. 145.

84. Grey, *Twenty-Five Years*, vol. I, pp. 143, 277; vol. II, pp. 20, 30.

85. Hazlehurst, *Politicians at War*, p. 52.

86. Trevelyan, *Grey of Falloden*, p. 250.

87. Jarausch, *Enigmatic Chancellor*, p. 149.

88. Hobsbawm, *Age of Empire*, pp. 321f.; Barnett, *Collapse of British Power*, p. 55; Davies, *Europe*, p. 900.

89. Joll, *Origins*, p. 186.

90. See for example Oncken, *Das Deutsche Reich*; and more recently, Calleo, *German Problem*.

91. Fay, *Origins of the World War*. More inclined to criticize Russia and France was Barnes, *Genesis of the World War*.

92. Lenin, *Imperialism*. Cf. J. A. Hobson, *Imperialism*. For a good discussion of the Left's intellectual adaptation to the war, see Cain and Hopkins, *British Imperialism*, vol. I, pp. 454f.

93. See for a recent example, Hobsbawm, *Age of Empire*, pp. 312–14, 323–27.

94. A. J. P. Taylor, *First World War*; idem, *War by Timetable*.

95. Mayer, *Persistence of the Old Regime*. See also idem, 'Domestic Causes of the First World War', pp. 286–300; Gordon, 'Domestic Conflict and the Origins of the First World War', pp. 191–226. For a critical view see Loewenberg, 'Arno Mayer's "Internal causes"', pp. 628–36.

96. McNeill, *Pursuit of Power*, pp. 310–14.

97. For some recent examples see Eksteins, *Rites of Spring*; Wohl, *Generation of 1914*.

98. Kaiser, 'Germany and the Origins of the First World War', pp. 442–74.

99. Jarausch, *Enigmatic Chancellor*, p. 149.

100. Asquith, *Genesis*, p. 216.

101. Lloyd George, *War Memoirs*, vol. I, pp. 43f.

102. See, e.g., A. J. P. Taylor, *Struggle for Mastery*, p. 527; Joll, *Europe since 1870*, pp. 184ff. See also M. Brock, 'Britain Enters the War', pp. 145–78.

103. W. S. Churchill, *World Crisis*, vol. I, pp. 202f.

104. Ibid., vol. I, pp. 228f.

105. Grey, *Twenty-Five Years,* vol. II, p. 46. See also pp. 9f.

106. Ibid., vol. I, pp. 77, 312.

107. Ibid., vol. II, p. 28.

108. Ibid., vol. I, pp. 335ff.

109. K. Wilson, *Entente,* esp. pp. 96f., 115. See also T. Wilson, 'Britain's 'Moral Commitment''', pp. 382–90.

110. French, *British Economic and Strategic Planning,* p. 87.

111. See, e.g., Howard, 'Europe on the Eve', p. 119; Martel, *Origins,* p. 69; J. Thompson, *Europe since Napoleon,* p. 552.

112. Kennedy, *Rise of the Anglo-German Antagonism,* esp. p. 458.

113. T. Wilson, *Myriad Faces,* pp. 12–16.

114. F. Fischer, 'Kontinuität des Irrtums', pp. 83–101; idem, *Griff nach der Weltmacht.*

115. On the historiography of the 'Fischer controversy', see Moses, *Politics of Illusion;* Droz, *Causes de la première guerre mondiale.* See also Jäger, *Historische Forschung,* pp. 135ff.

116. Kehr, *Primat der Innenpolitik.*

117. F. Fischer, *War of Illusions.* See also Schulte, *Europäische Krise.*

118. See Erdmann, 'Zur Beurteilung Bethmann Hollwegs', pp. 525–40; Zechlin, 'Deutschland zwischen Kabinettskrieg and Wirtschaftskrieg', pp. 347–458; Jarausch, 'Illusion of Limited War', pp. 48–76. See also Zechlin, *Krieg und Kriegsrisiko;* idem, 'July 1914', pp. 371–85; Erdmann, 'War Guilt 1914 Reconsidered', pp. 334–70.

119. Kaiser, 'Germany and the Origins of the First World War'.

120. Berghahn, *Germany and the Approach of War;* Steiner, *Britain and the Origins of the First World War;* Keiger, *France and the Origins of the First World War;* Bosworth, *Italy and the Approach of the First World War;* Lieven, *Russia and the Origins of the First World War;* S. Williamson, *Austria-Hungary and the Coming of the First World War.*

121. Turner, *Origins of the First World War;* Remak, '1914—The Third Balkan War'; D. Lee, *Europe's Crucial Years;* Langhorne, *Collapse of the Concert of Europe;* Barraclough, *From Agadir to Armageddon.* Still valuable is Albertini, *Origins.*

122. See, e.g., Hildebrand, 'Julikrise 1914'; idem, *Vergangene Reich,* pp. 302–15.

123. Geiss, *July 1914,* p. 365. See also idem, *Das Deutsche Reich und der Erste Weltkrieg.*

124. Geiss, *Der Lange Weg,* esp. pp. 23f., 54, 123.

125. Ibid., pp. 123, 128.

126. Ibid., pp. 128, 187.

127. Ibid., p. 214.

128. Schöllgen, 'Introduction', pp. 1–17; idem, 'Germany's Foreign Policy in the Age of Imperialism', pp. 121–33.

129. P. Parker, *Old Lie,* p. 203.

130. *The Lion: Hampton School Magazine* (1914), p. 23. I am grateful to Glen O'Hara for this reference.

131. For a good account of one British memorial, see Inglis, 'Homecoming', p. 583.

132. Prost, 'Monuments aux Morts', p. 202.

133. See in general, J. Winter, *Sites of Memory.*

134. Ferguson (ed.), *Virtunal History,* esp. pp. 1–90.

1. The Myths of Militarism

1. This section is drawn largely from I. Clarke, *Great War.* See also his *Tale of the Next Great War* and his *Voices Prophesying War.*

2. I. Clarke, *Great War,* pp. 129–39.

3. Childers, *Riddle of the Sands,* p. 248.

4. I. Clarke, *Great War,* pp. 326ff.

5. Ibid., pp. 139–52. According to one source, the book sold as many as a million copies.

6. Ibid., pp. 153–66. But see also p. 225 of the edited German edition, which omitted this ending.

7. Ibid., pp. 168–78.

8. Ibid., pp. 339–54.

9. Andrew, *Secret Service,* p. 77.

10. Le Queux, *Spies of the Kaiser.*

11. I. Clarke, *Great War*, pp. 356–63.

12. Ibid., pp. 377–81.

13. Du Maurier was an officer in the Royal Fusiliers: Andrew, *Secret Service*, p. 93.

14. Hynes, *War Imagined*, p. 46.

15. I. Clarke, *Great War*, pp. 179f.

16. Saki, *When William Came*, pp. 691–814.

17. Ibid., esp. pp. 706–11. The idea that Jews were pro-German, somewhat surprising to modern eyes, was a nostrum of the pre-1914 Right in England. Needless to say, the Boy Scout movement defies the defeatist mood.

18. I. Clarke, *Great War*, pp. 364–9.

19. Ibid., pp. 87–98.

20. Ibid., pp. 183–201, 390–98.

21. Ibid., pp. 399–408.

22. Ibid., pp. 385–90.

23. Ibid., pp. 408ff.

24. Ibid., pp. 29–71.

25. Ibid., pp. 72–87.

26. Andrew, *Secret Service*, p. 74. Le Queux's conversion to Germanophobia only came when (like Sir Robert Baden-Powell, the 'hero' of Mafeking and founder of the Boy Scouts) he acquired bogus plans for a German invasion from a gang of forgers based in Belgium: ibid., pp. 83f.

27. Andrew, *Secret Service*, p. 68.

28. I. Clarke, *Voices Prophesying War*, pp. 136–8.

29. Ibid., pp. 102–8.

30. Andrew, *Secret Service*, p. 69.

31. Ibid., pp. 233–47.

32. Ibid., pp. 259–75.

33. Ibid., pp. 276f. On Lockwood, see Andrew, *Secret Service*, p. 84.

34. Hiley, 'Introduction', pp. ix–x.

35. I. Clarke, *Great War*, pp. 313–23. However, the book did not sell well. Andrew, *Secret Service*, p. 78.

36. I. Clarke, *Great War*, pp. 282–92.

37. Ibid., p. 214.

38. Ibid., pp. 296–313.

39. Ibid., p. 233.

40. Ibid., pp. 202–25.

41. Steinberg, 'Copenhagen Complex'. By launching a surprise attack, Lord Nelson had destroyed the Danish navy in Copenhagen harbour in 1801.

42. I. Clarke, *Great War*, pp. 226–32.

43. Förster, 'Dreams and Nightmares', p. 4.

44. Ibid.

45. Bloch, *Is War Now Impossible*.

46. Ibid., p. xxxvii.

47. Ibid., p. lx.

48. Ibid., p. lii.

49. Ibid., pp. lvi–lix.

50. Ibid., pp. x–xi.

51. Ibid., p. xxxi.

52. G. Gooch and Temperley, *British Documents*, vol. I, p. 222. According to Bloch, the 'book was referred by the Emperor of Russia at my request to the Minister of War, with the request that it should be subjected to examination by a council of experts'. Their view was that 'no book could contribute so much to the success of the Conference': Bloch, *Is War Now Impossible*, p. xiii.

53. On the role of the press, see Morris, *Scaremongers*.

54. Lasswell, *Propaganda Technique*, p. 192.

55. Innis, *Press*, p. 31.

56. Andrew, *Secret Service*, p. 73.

57. Morris, *Scaremongers*, pp. 132–9; Mackay, *Fisher of Kilverstone*, pp. 369, 385. Cf. Andrew, *Secret Service*, p. 81; Beresford was one of those to whom Le Queux showed a bogus 'speech' in which the Kaiser supposedly declared his intention to invade England.

58. Andrew, *Secret Service*, p. 77.

59. D. French, 'Spy Fever', pp. 355–65; Hiley, 'Failure of British Counter-Espionage', pp. 867–89; Hiley, 'Counter-Espionage', pp. 635–70; Hiley, 'Introduction', pp. vii–xxxvi; Andrew, *Secret Service*, pp. 90ff. The opening of the pre-1919 MI5 (originally MO5) files in 1997 has revealed further details of the truly farcical early days of British counter-espionage.

60. Public Record Office (PRO) KV 1/7, List of Persons Arrested, 4 Aug. 1914. See also PRO KV 1/9, Report, 31 July 1912; Kell report, 16 Aug. 1912; Report, 29 Oct. 1913; PRO KV 1/46, M.I.5 Historical reports, G Branch report, 'The investigation of espionage', vol. VIII (1921), Appendix C; Major R. J. Dake memorandum, 4 Jan. 1917. See also Andrew, *Secret Service*, pp. 105–16 for a wry survey of the various cases.

61. Andrew, *Secret Service*, pp. 115ff. Once again, the threat these men posed to national security was virtually nil.

62. Ibid., p. 120.

63. Hiley, 'Counter-Espionage', Appendices C and D.

64. Trumpener, 'War Premeditated', pp. 58–85.

65. Hiley, 'Introduction', pp. xix–xxi.

66. Andrew, *Secret Service*, pp. 89f.

67. PRO KV 1/9, Kell report, 7 Nov. 1910. Cf. Andrew, *Secret Service*, pp. 121ff.

68. Andrew, *Secret Service*, pp. 127–33. See also D. French, 'Spy Fever', p. 363; Andrew, 'Secret Intelligence', pp. 12ff.

69. Andrew, *Secret Service*, pp. 133ff.

70. PRO CAB 38/4/9, W. R. Robertson, 'The Military Resources of Germany, and Probable Method of their Employment in a War Between Germany and England', 7 Feb. 1903.

71. Andrew, *Secret Service*, p. 88.

72. Morris, *Scaremongers*, p. 158.

73. PRO FO 800/61, Grey to Lascelles, 22 Feb. 1908. Cf. D. French, 'Spy Fever', p. 363.

74. Andrew, 'Secret Intelligence', p. 13. Perhaps he also wished to ward off allegations of Germanophilia in the right-wing press: Andrew, *Secret Service*, pp. 92f., 98f.

75. Details of the campaign for such a bureau in PRO KV 1/1, Organisation of Secret Service: note prepared for DMO, 4 Oct. 1908; PRO KV 1/2, Edmond to DMO, 2 Dec. 1908; War Office note for Chief of the General Staff, 31 Dec. 1909; Edmonds paper for General Staff, 'Espionage in Time of Peace', 1909. Cf. Public Record Office, *M.I.5*.

76. PRO CAB 3/2/1/47A, Report of CID sub-committee: 'The Question of Foreign Espionage in the United Kingdom', 24 July 1909. See also PRO KV 1/3, Memorandum on meeting for setting up secret service bureau, 26 Aug. 1909.

77. Hiley, 'Introduction', p. xxi. Cf. Andrew, 'Secret Intelligence', p. 14.

78. PRO KV 1/9, Kell report, 25 March 1910; PRO KV 1/10, Kell diary, June–July 1911; PRO KV 1/9, Kell report, 22 Nov. 1911; Kell report, 9 April 1913; PRO KV 1/8, William Melville memoir, 1917 (an unintentionally very funny document). Melville, the former Superintendent of the Special Branch, had begun investigating suspect foreigners for the Foreign Office as early as 1903.

79. PRO KV 1/9, Kell report, 30 April 1914. Cf. D. French, 'Spy Fever', p. 365; Hiley, 'Counter-Espionage', p. 637.

80. Hiley, 'Introduction', p. xxvii.

81. Bernhardi, *Germany*.

82. Searle, *Quest;* Searle, 'Critics of Edwardian Society', pp. 79–96.

83. Summers, 'Militarism in Britain', pp. 106, 113.

84. Bond, *War and Society*, p. 75.

85. Summers, 'Militarism in Britain', p. 120. See also Hendley, '"Help Us to Secure"', pp. 262–88.

86. Price, *Imperial War.* Cf. Cunningham, 'Language of Patriotism', pp. 23–8.

87. E. Weber, *Nationalist Revival in France*.

88. Sumler, 'Domestic Influences', pp. 517–37.

89. Eley, *Reshaping the German Right;* Eley, 'Wilhelmine Right', pp. 112–35. See also Chickering, *We Men*.

90. Eley, 'Conservatives and Radical Nationalists', pp. 50–70.

91. Coetzee, *German Army League*, p. 4.

92. The Army League in south-west Germany had links with the Volunteer Youth Army, the German League against the Abuse of Intoxicating Drinks, the German League for the Combating of Women's Emancipation, the League against Social Democracy and the General German Language Association—as well as, improbably but revealingly, the Württemberg Association for Breeding Pedigree Hunting Dogs: Coetzee, *German Army League*, pp. 55–8, 65.

93. It cost one mark to join the Army League, in return for which a member enjoyed a newspaper, *Die Wehr,* regular slide shows and excursions, and an annual three-day jamboree.

94. Coetzee, *German Army League*, pp. 76–104. Coetzee's attempt to derive a more exact sociological profile of the League from the rolls it kept of members killed in the war gives a similar picture: 29.4 per cent were career soldiers; 16.2 per cent civil servants; 11.4 per cent academics or teachers; 7.7 per cent businessmen; 8.9 per cent other professions; and only 6.5 per cent were clerical employees (pp. 90f.). Unfortunately, there are methodological difficulties with these figures, since they naturally over-represent the young; whereas another sample of 195 pre-war members reveals that 90 per cent were over forty!

95. Chickering, *We Men*.

96. Düding, 'Die Kriegsvereine im wilhelminischen Reich', p. 108. See also Showalter, 'Army, State and Society', pp. 1–18.

97. Greschat, 'Krieg und Kriegsbereitschaft', pp. 33–55.

98. Leugers, 'Einstellungen zu Krieg und Frieden', p. 62. It is significant that crowds in Berlin on 1 and 2 August 1914 sang not only the Protestant *Ein' feste Burg ist unser Gott,* but also the Catholic *Grosser Gott wir loben Dich;* Eksteins, *Rites of Spring*, p. 61.

99. Chickering, 'Die Alldeutschen', p. 25.

100. Bucholz, *Moltke, Schlieffen*, pp. 109–14, 217–20, 273.

101. Bruch, 'Krieg und Frieden', pp. 74–98. It was Dietrich Schäfer whom Max Weber had in mind when he urged academics to leave their politics at the lecture-room door.

102. Berghahn, *Germany and the Approach of War*, pp. 203f.

103. Geiss, *July 1914*, pp. 22, 43.

104. Bruch, 'Krieg und Frieden', pp. 85f.

105. Coetzee, *German Army League*, pp. 85f.

106. Ibid., p. 52; F. Fischer, *War of Illusions*, p. 194.

107. Coetzee, *German Army League*, p. 116.

108. Mann, *Betrachtungen eines Unpolitischen*.

109. Cf. Hildebrand, 'Opportunities and Limits', p. 91; Hillgruber, 'Historical Significance', p. 163.

110. Mommsen, *Max Weber*, pp. 35–40.

111. See F. Fischer, *War of Illusions*, pp. 4–7, 30ff., 259–71, 355–62; cf. Meyer, *Mitteleuropa.*

112. Kroboth, *Finanzpolitik*, p. 278; Eksteins, *Rites of Spring*, p. 91.

113. Förster, *Der doppelte Militarismus*, p. 279.

114. Coetzee, *German Army League*, pp. 45–50; Chickering, 'Die Alldeutschen', p. 30.

115. Coetzee, *German Army League*, pp. 119f.

116. Geiss, *July 1914*, pp. 21f.; Berghahn, *Germany and the Approach of War*, p. 144.

117. Eksteins, *Rites of Spring*, p. iv; Geiss, *July 1914*, p. 48.

118. See in general Nicholls and Kennedy, *Nationalist and Racialist Movements.*

119. See especially Chickering, *Imperial Germany.*

120. Bentley, *Liberal Mind*, pp. 11–15; Barnett, *Collapse of British Power*, pp. 24ff.

121. Weinroth, 'British Radicals', pp. 659–64.

122. Angell, *Great Illusion.* It had originally been called, over-cleverly, *Europe's Optical Illusion.*

123. Ibid., p. 295.

124. Ibid., pp. 137, 140.

125. Ibid., pp. xi–xiii.

126. Ibid., p. 229.

127. Ibid., pp. 268ff.

128. Ibid., p. 361. Emphasis added.

129. Offer, *First World War*, p. 261.

130. Ibid., p. 250.

131. Morris, *Scaremongers*, p. 266.

132. Hynes, *War Imagined*, p. 80.

133. Marquand, *Ramsay MacDonald*, pp. 164ff.

134. Mackenzie and Mackenzie, *Diary of Beatrice Webb*, vol. III, pp. 203f.

135. Holroyd, *Bernard Shaw*, vol. II, pp. 341ff.

136. Hynes, *War Imagined*, pp. 74f.

137. Graves, *Goodbye*, pp. 11f., 25–31.

138. T. Weber, 'Stormy Romance'.

139. Winter, 'Oxford and the First World War', p. 3.

140. Pogge von Strandmann, 'Germany and the Coming of War', pp. 87f.

141. Ferguson, *World's Banker*, Chapter 30.

142. Groh, *Negative Integration.*

143. Winzen, 'Der Krieg', p. 180.

144. Geiss, *Der lange Weg*, p. 269.
145. Cf. the evidence in Eksteins, *Rites of Spring*, pp. 55–63, 193–7, with that in Ullrich, *Kriegsalltag*, pp. 10–21.
146. Dukes and Remak, *Another Germany*, esp. pp. 207–19. In attempting to portray the Reich as *'ein Land wie andere auch'*, Remak goes much further than other critics of the idea of a German *Sonderweg*: cf. Blackbourn and Eley, *Peculiarities of German History*.
147. Liebknecht, *Militarism and Anti-Militarism*, pp. 9–42.
148. In addition to Ritter, *Sword and the Sceptre*, esp. vol. II: *The European Powers and the Wilhelminian Empire, 1890–1914*, see Vagts, *History of Militarism*; Berghahn, *Militarism*. See most recently Stargardt, *German Idea of Militarism*.
149. Zilch, *Die Reichsbank*, p. 40.
150. F. Fischer, *War of Illusions*, pp. 13–25; F. Fischer, *Bündnis der Eliten*.
151. Wehler, *German Empire*, pp. 155–62; Berghahn, *Germany and the Approach of War*, pp. 4, 41, 213.
152. See Mayer, 'Domestic Causes of the First World War', pp. 286–300; Groh; '"Je eher, desto besser!"', pp. 501–21; Gordon, 'Domestic Conflict and the Origins of the First World War', pp. 191–226; Witt, 'Innenpolitik und Imperialismus', pp. 24ff. See also F. Fischer, *War of Illusions*, esp. pp. 61, 83, 94, 258; Wehler, *German Empire*, pp. 192–201. Cf. the critique in Mommsen, 'Domestic Factors in German Foreign Policy', pp. 3–43.
153. Eley, 'Army, State and Civil Society', pp. 85–109.
154. On the growing gulf between the government and the radical right see Eley, *Reshaping the German Right*, pp. 316–34; Mommsen, 'Public Opinion and Foreign Policy'.
155. Bülow, *Memoirs*, p. 400.
156. Geiss, *July 1914*, p. 47.
157. Davies, *Europe*, p. 895.
158. Ferro, *Great War*, p. 179.

2. Empires, Ententes and Edwardian Appeasement

1. *Joll, Second International*, pp. 196f.
2. Buse, 'Ebert', p. 436.
3. Lenin, *Imperialism, passim*.
4. Gutsche, 'Foreign Policy', pp. 41–62.
5. Zilch, *Die Reichsbank*, p. 79.
6. Ferguson, *World's Banker*, Chapter 29.
7. Ferguson, *Paper and Iron*, p. 84.
8. Steed, *Through Thirty Years*, vol. II, pp. 8f.
9. Jahresbericht 1914, pp. 1f., Hamburg, Brinckmann, Wirtz & Co.–M. M. Warburg (MMW), Max Warburg Papers, 'Jahresbericht 1914'. Cf. Warburg, *Aus meinen Aufzeichnungen*, p. 29.
10. J. Williamson, *Karl Helfferich*, pp. 105f., 111ff. See also Feldman, 'Deutsche Bank', pp. 129ff. And see in general on German banks and diplomacy Barth, *Die deutsche Hochfinanz*.
11. Pogge von Strandmann, *Walther Rathenau*, p. 183. See also Rathenau, *Briefe*, vol. I, pp. 156ff.
12. Cf. Zilch, *Die Reichsbank*.
13. Feldman, 'War Aims', pp. 2f.
14. Kennedy, *Rise and Fall of the Great Powers*, esp. pp. 269–77; Kennedy, 'First World War', pp. 7–40.
15. See typically Henig, *Origins*, pp. 8ff.
16. Geiss, *Der lange Weg*, pp. 54, 116, 123.
17. Geiss, 'German Version of Imperialism', p. 114.
18. See e.g. Wilson, *Policy of the Entente*, pp. 96f.; T. Wilson, 'Britain's "Moral Commitment"', pp. 381ff.
19. Calculated from statistics in: Mitchell, *European Historical Statistics*; *Economist, Economic Statistics*; Bairoch, 'Europe's Gross National Product', pp. 281, 303.
20. E. Morgan and Thomas, *Stock Exchange*, pp. 88f.
21. *Financial Times*, 6 May 1997, p. 18: gross direct plus portfolio investment in the period 1990–95 was just under 12 per cent of GDP.
22. Pollard, 'Capital Exports', pp. 491f.
23. Gutsche, 'Foreign Policy', p. 50.
24. See Buchheim, 'Aspects of Nineteenth-Century Anglo-German Trade Policy', pp. 275–89. See also Kennedy, *Rise of the Anglo-German Antagonism*, pp. 46ff., 262ff.; Cain and Hopkins, *British Imperialism*, vol. I, pp. 461f.; Steiner, *Britain and the Origins of the First World War*, pp. 60–63.

25. For a good discussion of the issue see Pollard, *Britain's Prime;* Floud, 'Britain 1860–1914', pp. 1–26.
26. Cain, *Economic Foundations,* pp. 43ff.
27. Edelstein, *Overseas Investment,* pp. 24ff., 48, 313ff.
28. Davis and Huttenback, *Mammon,* pp. 81–117; Pollard, 'Capital Exports', p. 507.
29. Davis and Huttenback, *Mammon,* p. 107.
30. Offer, *First World War,* p. 121.
31. Eichengreen, *Golden Fetters,* pp. 29–66; Eichengreen and Flandreau, 'Geography of the Gold Standard'.
32. Reader, *At Duty's Call,* p. 71.
33. See especially Hentschel, *Wirtschaft und Wirtschaftspolitik,* p. 134. Cf. Sommariva and Tullio, *German Macroeconomic History,* pp. 41–50.
34. Offer, *First World War,* pp. 121–35.
35. Geiss, *Der lange Weg,* pp. 188f.
36. Förster, *Der doppelte Militarismus,* p. 64.
37. Kaiser, 'Germany and the Origins of the First World War', pp. 454f.
38. E. Dugdale, *German Diplomatic Documents,* vol. I, p. 284.
39. A. J. P. Taylor, *Struggle for Mastery,* p. 342.
40. Kennan, *Fateful Alliance.*
41. Stern, *Gold and Iron,* p. 442.
42. Girault, *Emprunts russes,* pp. 159–62; Kennan, *Franco-Russian Relations,* pp. 382f.; Stern, *Gold and Iron,* pp. 446f. Cf. Kynaston, *City,* vol. I, p. 312.
43. Kennan, *Decline of Bismarck's European Order,* pp. 387–90; Poidevin, *Relations économiques,* pp. 46–50. Cf. Davis, *English Rothschilds,* pp. 230–32.
44. Poidevin, *Relations économiques,* pp. 46–50.
45. Girault, *Emprunts russes,* pp. 314–20.
46. Ibid., pp. 73f.
47. Poidevin, *Relations économiques,* pp. 46–50; Girault, *Emprunts russes,* p. 73.
48. Lyashchenko, *History of the National Economy,* p. 714.
49. Figures from Mitchell, *European Historical Statistics,* pp. 218, 253–5, 318.
50. Reader, *At Duty's Call,* p. 61. See also p. 67 for H. M. Stanley's allusion to 'this nightmare of war' with Russia and France.
51. Monger, *End of Isolation,* p. 10.
52. Kennedy, *Rise of the German Antagonism,* pp. 47f.
53. Koch, 'Anglo-German Alliance Negotiations', p. 392; Kennedy, 'German World Policy', p. 625. See also Grey, *Twenty-Five Years,* vol. I, p. 245.
54. See esp. Eckardstein, *Lebenserinnerungen;* Meinecke, *Die Geschichte.*
55. Kynaston, *City,* vol. I, p. 351.
56. Barth, *Die deutsche Hochfinanz,* pp. 39f.
57. Ibid., pp. 142ff.; Kynaston, *City,* vol. II, pp. 125ff.
58. Poidevin, *Relations économiques,* pp. 77–9.
59. Garvin, *Life of Joseph Chamberlain,* vol. III, pp. 248f.; Barth, *Die deutsche Hochfinanz,* pp. 160f.
60. Garvin, *Life of Joseph Chamberlain,* vol. III, pp. 250ff.
61. Barth, *Die deutsche Hochfinanz,* p. 163.
62. Ibid., pp. 166f.
63. Amery, *Life of Joseph Chamberlain,* vol. IV, pp. 139f., 150; Monger, *End of Isolation,* pp. 15, 19f. Cf. Rich and Fisher, *Holstein Papers,* vol. IV, p. 197.
64. Barth, *Die deutsche Hochfinanz,* pp. 280f. See also G. Gooch and Temperley, *British Documents,* vol. II, p. 72.
65. B. Dugdale, *Arthur James Balfour,* vol. I, pp. 258f. For Chamberlain's own notes of the conversations, see Garvin, *Life of Joseph Chamberlain,* vol. III, pp. 259–64.
66. Garvin, *Life of Joseph Chamberlain,* vol. III, p. 270–80.
67. Amery, *Life of Joseph Chamberlain,* vol. IV, pp. 144ff., 153ff.; Monger, *End of Isolation,* pp. 30, 35–8.
68. Rich and Fisher, *Holstein Papers,* vol. IV, p. 275.
69. Garvin, *Life of Joseph Chamberlain,* vol. III, pp. 503ff.; Amery, *Life of Joseph Chamberlain,* vol. IV, pp. 147ff.
70. Garvin, *Life of Joseph Chamberlain,* vol. III, pp. 281, 340f., 505; Amery, *Life of Joseph Chamberlain,* vol. IV, p. 138; E. Dugdale, *German Diplomatic Documents,* vol. III, p. 50; Monger, *End of Isolation,* p. 37.
71. Jay, *Chamberlain,* p. 219.
72. Garvin, *Life of Joseph Chamberlain,* vol. III, pp. 498, 507f., 510–15.
73. Amery, *Life of Joseph Chamberlain,* vol. IV, p. 157. See also pp. 169–80, 191f., 199.

74. Steinberg, 'Copenhagen Complex', p. 27.
75. Langhorne, 'Anglo-German Negotiations', pp. 364ff.; G. Gooch and Temperley, *British Documents*, vol. I, pp. 44–8; Egremont, *Balfour*, p. 139; Steiner, *Foreign Office*, pp. 38f.
76. Rich and Fisher, *Holstein Papers*, vol. IV, p. 71.
77. Garvin, *Life of Joseph Chamberlain*, vol. III, pp. 331–9.
78. Amery, *Life of Joseph Chamberlain*, vol. IV, p. 201; Monger, *End of Isolation*, pp. 105ff.; Kennedy, *Rise of the Anglo-German Antagonism*, p. 259.
79. Barth, *Die deutsche Hochfinanz*, p. 134; Gall, 'Deutsche Bank', pp. 67–77.
80. Monger, *End of Isolation*, pp. 119–23. Cf. Steiner, *Foreign Office*, pp. 186f. To those whose memories extended back to the 1870s, this was a bizarre decision: on that basis, Disraeli's purchase of the Khedive's Suez Canal shares would have been disavowed because French shareholders were in a majority.
81. Monger, *End of Isolation*, p. 13. Cf. Trebilcock, 'War and the Failure of Industrial Mobilisation', pp. 141ff.; Cain and Hopkins, *British Imperialism*, vol. I, p. 452; Barnett, *Collapse of British Power*, pp. 75–83.
82. J. Gooch, *Plans of War*, pp. 42–90; d'Ombrain, *War Machinery*, pp. 5f., 9f., 14, 76.
83. Amery, *Life of Joseph Chamberlain*, vol. IV, p. 144.
84. Rich and Fisher, *Holstein Papers*, vol. IV, pp. 257, 260; Monger, *End of Isolation*, pp. 39–42; Amery, *Life of Joseph Chamberlain*, vol. IV, pp. 163, 182n.
85. Kennedy, 'German World Policy', p. 613.
86. K. Wilson, *Policy of the Entente*, p. 5.
87. Amery, *Life of Joseph Chamberlain*, vol. IV, p. 151; Monger, *End of Isolation*, pp. 23–34.
88. Monger, *End of Isolation*, pp. 17, 39f., 113, 129, 132ff., 144f.; Andrew, 'Entente Cordiale', pp. 11, 19ff.
89. Garvin, *Life of Joseph Chamberlain*, vol. III, p. 275; Amery, *Life of Joseph Chamberlain*, vol. IV, pp. 180, 184ff., 202–6.
90. Monger, *End of Isolation*, pp. 186–98, 223.
91. K. Wilson, *Policy of the Entente*, pp. 71, 74; Andrew, 'Entente Cordiale', pp. 20ff.; Monger, *End of Isolation*, pp. 129–33, 192.
92. B. Williams, 'Strategic Background', pp. 360–66; Monger, *End of Isolation*, pp. 2, 5ff., 33f., 108ff., 115ff., 123f., 132, 140ff., 185, 216–20; J. Gooch, *Plans of War*, pp. 171, 175.
93. Monger, *End of Isolation*, pp. 200–202, 214–21.
94. R. Williams, *Defending the Empire*, pp. 70f.
95. M. Jones, *Limits of Liberty*, pp. 396–411.

3. Britain's War of Illusions

1. K. Wilson, 'Grey', p. 173. Lloyd George recalled Rosebery's prescient warning: 'You are all wrong. It means war with Germany in the end': Lloyd George, *War Memoirs*, vol. I, p. 1. Salisbury and Lansdowne also had doubts: Monger, *End of Isolation*, pp. 135, 212, 226; as did the banker Lord Avebury: Reader, *At Duty's Call*, p. 69. For the doubts of the radical Speaker, see Weinroth, 'British Radicals', pp. 659f.
2. Howard, 'Edwardian Arms Race', pp. 82f.
3. K. Wilson, *Policy of the Entente*, pp. 18–22; Monger, *End of Isolation*, p. 259. On the steady increase in the Liberal Leaguers' influence, especially after Asquith became premier, see Steiner, *Britain and the Origins of the First World War*, p. 140.
4. Rowland, *Last Liberal Governments*, vol. II, p. 361.
5. Lloyd George, *War Memoirs*, vol. I, pp. 56–60.
6. Albertini, *Origins*, vol. III, p. 368; Barnett, *Collapse of British Power*, p. 54; Steiner, *Britain and the Origins of the First World War*, p. 255.
7. K. Wilson, *Policy of the Entente*, pp. 10ff.
8. Semmel, *Imperialism*, p. 75; Russell, *Portraits from Memory*, p. 77. See also O'Hara, 'Britain's War of Illusions'.
9. Bernstein, *Liberalism and Liberal Politics*, p. 182.
10. K. Wilson, *Policy of the Entente*, p. 35.
11. Monger, *End of Isolation*, p. 260.
12. Lloyd George, *War Memoirs*, vol. I, pp. 28f., 60; W. S. Churchill, *World Crisis*, p. 203.
13. Bentley, *Liberal Mind*, p. 12; Hazlehurst, *Politicians at War*, pp. 26f.
14. Monger, *End of Isolation*, pp. 257, 287; K. Wilson, *Policy of the Entente*, pp. 34ff.; Steiner, *Britain and the Origins of the First World War*, pp. 56, 128f., 143, 186.
15. K. Wilson, *Policy of the Entente*, pp. 17, 30ff. Cf. Searle, *Quest*, p. 232.

16. Searle, 'Critics of Edwardian Society', pp. 79–96; Morris, *Scaremongers*, p. 294.

17. Morris, *Scaremongers*, pp. 301–4.

18. On Grey's youth, see Trevelyan, *Grey of Falloden*, pp. 7–20; Robbins, *Sir Edward Grey*, esp. pp. 1, 7. 12.

19. Though it may be evidence of a certain timidity. Grey's two brothers were both keen hunters of big game. One was killed by a lion, the other by a buffalo: Davies, *Europe*, p. 882.

20. Grey, *Fly Fishing*. I am grateful to Mr Sandy Sempliner for this reference.

21. Grey, *Twenty-Five Years*, vol. I, pp. 152–9. Cf. Asquith, *Genesis*, p. 53.

22. PRO CAB 2/2, CID meeting, 9 March 1906; PRO CAB 38/11/9, Military Requirements of the Empire: note by Lord Esher, 26 Feb. 1907; PRO CAB 2/2, Sub-committee on the military requirements of the Empire, 30 May 1907; PRO FO 800/100, Grey to Campbell-Bannerman, 31 Aug. 1907. Cf. B. Williams, 'Strategic Background', pp. 365–73; K. Wilson, *Policy of the Entente*, pp. 6f., 25, 76ff.; Monger, *End of Isolation*, pp. 285–91.

23. PRO FO 800/102, Robertson memorandum on entente with Russia, 29 March, 1906.

24. Sweet and Langhorne, 'Great Britain and Russia', pp. 236, 253f.; K. Wilson, *Policy of the Entente*, p. 83. See also PRO FO 800/90, Ellbank to Grey, 21 Jan. 1909.

25. Grey, *Twenty-Five Years*, vol. I, pp. 163f.

26. A. J. P. Taylor, *Struggle for Mastery*, p. 443.

27. PRO FO 800/92, Grey memorandum of conversation with Clemenceau, 28 April 1908.

28. Sweet and Langhorne, 'Great Britain and Russia', pp. 243ff.; Grey, *Twenty-Five Years*, vol. I, pp. 176–9, 182–9.

29. PRO FO 800/61, Grey to Goschen, 5 Nov. 1908. See also for Hardinge's fear of a 'general European conflagration' beginning in the Balkans, K. Wilson, 'Foreign Office', p. 404. See also Butterfield, 'Sir Edward Grey', pp. 4f., 20f.

30. A. J. P. Taylor, *Struggle for Mastery*, p. 463.

31. Ibid., p. 464.

32. Ibid., p. 475.

33. Renzi, 'Great Britain, Russia', pp. 2f.; Stone, *Europe Transformed*, p. 327.

34. Cf. the reaction of *The Times* with those of the *Nation*, *Daily News* and *Guardian*: Morris, *Scaremongers*, pp. 86, 256f.; Weinroth, 'British Radicals', p. 665. See also Bernstein, *Liberalism and Liberal Politics*, p. 186. For American attacks on Russia in 1911 see G. Owen, 'Dollar Diplomacy in Default', pp. 255.

35. Monger, *End of Isolation*, p. 278.

36. Offer, *First World War*, pp. 223f., 226, 230, 291; Monger, *End of Isolation*, pp. 188f., 206ff.; d'Ombrain, *War Machinery*, pp. 78ff.; D. French, *British Economic and Strategic Planning*, pp. 22f.

37. PRO CAB 38/10/73, General Staff paper on Belgian neutrality during a Franco-German war, 29 Sept. 1905.

38. Monger, *End of Isolation*, p. 238. The meetings took place on 16 or 18 and 21 Dec.; Campbell-Bannerman had agreed to form a government on the 5th, and Grey became Foreign Secretary on the 10th.

39. PRO CAB 38/11/4, Military conference on actions during war with Germany, 19 Dec. 1905; 1 June 1906. Cf. d'Ombrain, *War Machinery*, pp. 83f.; Monger, *End of Isolation*, pp. 240f.

40. Monger, *End of Isolation*, pp. 209f., 229. My emphasis.

41. PRO CAB 38/11/4, Military conference on actions during war with Germany, 19 Dec. 1905. Cf. Mackay, *Fisher of Kilverstone*, pp. 353ff., with McDermott, 'Revolution in British Military Thinking', pp. 174f; and see also d'Ombrain, *War Machinery*, pp. 84f.; Howard, *Continental Commitment*, pp. 32, 43.

42. PRO FO 800/100, Grey to Campbell-Bannerman, 9 Jan. 1906; PRO FO 800/49, Grey to Bertie, 15 Jan. 1906. See also Grey, *Twenty-Five Years*, vol. I, pp. 78–83.

43. Monger, *End of Isolation*, pp. 248–51. Cf. PRO FO 800/49, Grey to Cambon, 21 June 1906. Even a year later only two or three members of the Cabinet knew about them: d'Ombrain, *War Machinery*, p. 90.

44. K. Wilson, *Policy of the Entente*, pp. 88f.; Monger, *End of Isolation*, p. 271. He meant that such a promise would never have to be honoured because of its deterrent effect.

45. PRO FO 800/87, Grey to Tweedmouth, 16 Jan. 1906; K. Wilson, *Policy of the Entente*, p. 65.

46. Monger, *End of Isolation*, p. 282; d'Ombrain, *War Machinery*, p. 89.

47. PRO FO 800/92, Grey memorandum, 20 Feb. 1906. Cf. Grey, *Twenty-Five Years*, vol. I, p. 114.

48. PRO CAB 38/11/4, Military conference: actions during war with Germany, 1 June 1906.

49. Hamilton, 'Great Britain and France', p. 331. Cf. K. Wilson, *Policy of the Entente*, pp. 88f.; Monger, *End of Isolation*, p. 271.

50. Details in d'Ombrain, *War Machinery*, pp. 75–96, 103–9; Monger, *End of Isolation*, pp. 238–52; K. Wilson, *Policy of the Entente*, pp. 63–7.

51. PRO FO 800/100, Grey to Asquith, 16 April 1911. 'What they [the military experts] settled I never knew—the position was that the Government was quite free, but that the military would know what to do if the word was given'.

52. PRO CAB 16/5 XL/A/035374, CID paper E-3, 27 Nov. 1908; CID Sub-committee on the military needs of the Empire, 3 Dec. 1908; 2nd meeting, 17 Dec. 1908; CID paper E-8 (II), Admiralty memorandum, 4 Feb. 1909; CID paper E-11 (B), Note by the General Staff, 5 March 1909; 3rd meeting, 23 March 1909. Cf. Howard, *Continental Commitment*, p. 46; d'Ombrain, *War Machinery*, pp. 93ff., 103; Mackay, *Fisher of Kilverstone*, pp. 405ff.

53. PRO CAB 38/19/50, Churchill memorandum on 'the military aspect of the continental problem', 1 Aug. 1911. In his memoirs Churchill claimed that it was the 'military men' not he who had 'overrated the relative power of the French army': W. S. Churchill, *World Crisis*, vol. I, p. 59.

54. PRO CAB 38/19/47, General Staff memorandum on 'the military aspect of the continental problem', 15 Aug. 1911.

55. PRO CAB 2/2, CID, minutes of the 114th meeting, 23 Aug. 1911. Cf. Collier, *Brasshat*, pp. 117–21.

56. PRO CAB 38/19/48, Admiralty comments on 'military aspect of the continental problem', 21 Aug. 1911; and PRO CAB 2/2, CID, minutes of the 114th meeting, 23 Aug. 1911.

57. Ibid. Cf. Hankey, *Supreme Command*, vol. I, p. 81; Nicolson, 'Edwardian England', p. 149; d'Ombrain, *War Machinery*, p. 102; D. French, *British Economic and Strategic Planning*, pp. 32ff.; K. Wilson, *Policy of the Entente*, p. 64.

58. Mackintosh, 'Committee of Imperial Defence', p. 499.

59. Hankey, *Supreme Command*, vol. I, p. 82; d'Ombrain, *War Machinery*, p. 108; Offer, *First World War*, p. 295.

60. K. Wilson, *Policy of the Entente*, p. 123.

61. Ibid., pp. 65–8; Hankey, *Supreme Command*, vol. I, p. 77; Offer, *First World War*, p. 296.

62. PRO CAB 2/3, CID meeting, 6 Dec. 1912. Cf. Lloyd George, *War Memoirs*, vol. I, pp. 30f.

63. Kossmann, *Low Countries*, p. 435. Cf. Cammaerts, *Keystone of Europe*; Johannson, *Small State*; Thomas, *Guarantee of Belgian Independence*.

64. My emphasis. See on this point PRO FO 800/93, Mallet memorandum, 11 April 1909; PRO FO 800/94, Nicolson to Grey, 4 and 6 May 1912; PRO CAB 2/2, CID meeting, 4 July 1912; PRO FO 800/94, Nicolson to Asquith, Churchill and Grey, 24 July 1912; PRO FO 900/87, Churchill to Grey, 2 Aug. 1912; PRO CAB 41/33/71, Asquith to George V, 21 Nov. 1912; PRO FO 800/62, Grey to Goschen, 28 Oct. 1913. Cf. W. S. Churchill, *World Crisis*, vol. I, pp. 112f.; K. Wilson, 'Foreign Office', p. 411; Rowland, *Last Liberal Governments*, vol. II, pp. 246–50; Hamilton, 'Great Britain and France', pp. 331f.; Steiner, *Britain and the Origins of the First World War*, p. 104.

65. PRO CAB 41/35/13, Asquith to George V, 14 May 1914; PRO FO 800/55, Bertie to Grey, 28 June 1914; Grey to Bertie, 30 June 1914. Cf. Grey, *Twenty-Five Years*, vol. I, pp. 284, 291f.

66. Geiss, *Der lange Weg*, p. 249.

67. F. Fischer, *War of Illusions*, pp. 160–65; Berghahn, *Germany and the Approach of War in 1914*, p. 170; Schulte, *Europäische Krise*, pp. 17ff., 23–31.

68. W. S. Churchill, *World Crisis*, vol. I, p. 94.

69. Langhorne, 'Colonies', pp. 366f.

70. Wilson, *Entente*, p. 10; Langhorne, 'Anglo-German Negotiations', p. 369. See Vincent-Smith, 'Anglo-German Negotiations', pp. 621f.

71. PRO CAB 41/33/71, Asquith to George V, 21 Nov. 1912; PRO FO 800/55, Bertie to Grey, 12 Feb. 1914; Grey to Bertie, 13 Feb. 1914; same to same, 4 March 1914. Cf. Langhorne, 'Anglo-German Negotiations', pp. 370–85; Vincent-Smith, 'Anglo-German Negotiations', pp. 623–9. Cf. Warburg, *Aus meinen Aufzeichnungen*, pp. 27f.; Steiner, *Britain and the Origins of the First World War*, p. 105.

72. Grey, *Twenty-Five Years*, vol. I, pp. 117f.; Monger, *End of Isolation*, pp. 266f., 275–8. This was despite Tweedmouth's warning that 'the acquisition and fortification of ports in Morocco by Germany would constitute a great danger to our naval supremacy': PRO FO 800/87.

73. Lloyd George, *War Memoirs*, vol. I, pp. 25ff. Cf. W. S. Churchill, *World Crisis*, vol. I, pp. 46–50; Grey, *Twenty-Five Years*, vol. I, pp. 219, 222–40; Asquith, *Genesis*, pp. 91–5.

74. PRO FO 800/52, Grey to Bertie, 12 July 1911; PRO FO 800/100, Grey to Asquith, 13 July 1911; PRO FO 800/52, Bertie to Grey, 17 July 1911; PRO FO 800/100, Grey to Asquith, 19 July 1911; PRO FO 800/52, Grey to Bertie, 20 July 1911; PRO FO 800/93, Nicolson to Grey, 21 July 1911; PRO FO 800/52, Bertie to Grey, 21 July 1911; PRO FO 800/62, Grey to Goschen, 24 and 25 July 1911; PRO FO 800/52, Grey to Bertie, 28 July 1911; PRO FO 800/62, Grey to Goschen, 8 and 26 Aug. 1911; PRO FO 800/52, Grey to Bertie, 4 Sept. 1911; Bertie to Grey, 6 Sept. 1911; Grey to Bertie, 8 Sept. 1911. See also Grey's statement to the Commons, *Hansard*, V, 32, pp. 49–59, 27 Nov. Cf. Steiner, *Britain and the Origins of the First World War*, pp. 72–5.

75. F. Fischer, *Germany's Aims*, pp. 45f.; Grey, *Twenty-Five Years*, vol. I, pp. 272–5; Butterfield, 'Sir Edward Grey', p. 4.

76. A. J. P. Taylor, *Struggle for Mastery*, p. 506.

77. *Frankfurter Zeitung*, 20 Oct. 1913.

78. Rothschild Archive, London (RAL), XI/130A/8, Natty, London, to his cousins, Paris, 16 March 1914.

79. Rosenbaum and Sherman, *M. M. Warburg & Co.*, p. 111.

80. Esposito, 'Public Opinion', p. 11.

81. Steiner, *Britain and the Origins of the First World War*, p. 123; J. Gooch, 'Soldiers, Strategy and War Aims', p. 23.

82. Pohl, *Hamburger Bankengeschichte*, p. 110.

83. Ibid., p. 513.

84. Grey, *Twenty-Five Years*, vol. I, p. 149.

85. Berghahn, *Germany and the Approach of War*, p. 67; Morris, *Scaremongers*, pp. 142f.

86. PRO FO 800/92, Grey memorandum, 23 July 1908. Cf. Lloyd George, *War Memoirs*, vol. I, p. 7; A. J. P. Taylor, *Struggle for Mastery*, p. 448; Berghahn, *Germany and the Approach of War*, p. 68.

87. PRO FO 800/61, Goschen to Grey, 21 Aug. 1909; Grey to Goschen, 23 Aug. 1909; PRO FO 800/100, Asquith to Grey, 25 Aug. 1909; PRO FO 800/93, Hardinge to Grey, 25 Aug. 1909; Mallet to Grey, 26 Aug. 1909; Tyrrell to Grey, 27 Aug. 1909; Drummond to Grey, 29 Dec. 1909; Grey note, 29 Dec. 1909; PRO FO 800/61, Grey to Goschen, 31 Dec. 1909; PRO FO 800/87, Grey to McKenna, 27 Jan. 1910; PRO FO 800/52, Grey to Bertie, 13 April 1910; PRO FO 800/62, Goschen to Grey, 6 Aug. 1910; Grey to Goschen, 11 and 16 Aug. 1910; Goschen to Grey, 19 Aug. 1910; PRO FO 800/100, Grey to Asquith, 21 Oct. 1910; Asquith to Grey, 27 Oct. 1910; PRO FO 800/62, Grey to Goschen, 26 Oct. 1910. Cf. Sweet, 'Great Britain and Germany', pp. 229ff.

88. G. Gooch and Temperley, *British Documents*, vol. VI, nos. 442, 446.

89. PRO CAB 41/33/34, Asquith to George V, 3 Feb. 1912. Cf. W. S. Churchill, *World Crisis*, pp. 96ff.; Langhorne, 'Great Britain and Germany', pp. 290–93. For the German side of the story, Steinberg, 'Diplomatie als Wille und Vorstellung'. See also L. Cecil, *Albert Ballin*, pp. 163ff., 180–200.

90. PRO FO 800/62, Goschen to Grey, 3 July 1913; PRO FO 800/87, Churchill to Grey and Asquith, 8 July 1913; Churchill to Grey, 17 July and 24 Oct. 1913; PRO FO 800/62, Grey to Goschen, 28 Oct. 1913; Goschen to Grey, 8 Nov. 1913; Grey to Goschen, 5 Feb. 1914; PRO FO 800/87, Grey to Churchill, 5 Feb. 1914.

91. PRO FO 800/87, Churchill to Grey, 20 May 1914. Cf. R. Churchill, *Winston S. Churchill*, vol. II, part III, pp. 1978–81.

92. Langhorne, 'Great Britain and Germany', pp. 293f. My emphasis. Cf. Asquith's misleading account in *Genesis*, pp. 55f., 100.

93. PRO CAB 41/33/41, Asquith to George V, 16 and 30 March 1912; PRO FO 800/94, Tyrrell memorandum, 3 April 1912; PRO FO 800/100, Asquith to Grey, 10 April 1912; PRO FO 800/87, Grey to Churchill, 12 April 1912; PRO FO 800/62, Grey to Goschen, 27 June and 4 July 1912. Cf. Langhorne, 'Great Britain and Germany', pp. 299, 303f.; Kennedy, *Rise of the Anglo-German Antagonism*, p. 451; Steiner, *Britain and the Origins of the First World War*, p. 96.

94. Berghahn, *Germany and the Approach of War*, pp. 120ff.; Geiss, 'German Version of Imperialism', p. 118.

95. PRO CAB 41/33/36, Asquith to George V, 15 and 21 Feb. 1912. Cf. W. S. Churchill, *World Crisis*, vol. I, pp. 103, 109; Grey, *Twenty-Five Years*, vol. I, pp. 249–52; Asquith, *Genesis*, pp. 77f., 97, 100; Rowland, *Last Liberal Governments*, vol. II, p. 241.

96. K. Wilson, *Policy of the Entente*, p. 8.

97. PRO FO 800/92, Tyrrell to Grey, 27 Aug. 1909; G. Gooch and Temperley, *British Documents*, vol. VI, no. 456, p. 611. Cf. Cain and Hopkins, *British Imperialism*, vol. I, p. 458.

98. Monger, *End of Isolation*, pp. 260, 267ff.

99. G. Gooch and Temperley, *British Documents*, vol. VI, no. 344, p. 461. Cf. Grey, *Twenty-Five Years*, vol. I, pp. 254f.

100. Sweet, 'Great Britain and Germany', pp. 229f.

101. PRO FO 800/62, Grey to Goschen, 27 June 1912.

102. PRO FO 800/92, Mallet to Grey, 26 June 1906.

103. K. Wilson, *Policy of the Entente*, p. 93. See also PRO FO 800/93, Nicolson to Grey, 21 July 1911. Cf. Langhorne, 'Great Britain and Germany', pp. 290f.; Grey, *Twenty-Five Years*, vol. I, p. 251; Steiner, *Britain and the Origins of the First World War*, p. 97.

104. Trevelyan, *Grey of Falloden*, pp. 114f.; Sweet and Langhorne, 'Great Britain and Russia', pp. 243f.

105. K. Wilson, *Policy of the Entente*, pp. 101, 108.

106. Nicolson's phrase, quoted in ibid., p. 38. Grey may initially have been influenced by the fear that Russia and Germany might conclude an alliance which the Kaiser and Tsar sought unsuccessfully to do in 1905. Cf. Butterfield, 'Sir Edward Grey', p. 2; K. Wilson, 'Grey', p. 193; Monger, *End of Isolation*, p. 293.

107. Monger, *End of Isolation*, p. 270.

108. PRO FO 800/92, Hardinge notes, 20 Feb. 1906.

109. K. Wilson, *Policy of the Entente*, pp. 35, 38f.

110. Ibid., pp. 39, 42f., 94, 111, 114f.; Andrew, 'Entente Cordiale', p. 25; *Hansard*, V, 32, p. 60, 27 Nov. 1911; Howard, *Continental Commitment*, p. 57; Grey, *Twenty-Five Years*, vol. I, p. 252. See also Butterfield, 'Sir Edward Grey', p. 2.

111. Trevelyan, *Grey of Falloden*, pp. 114f.

112. Schmidt, 'Contradictory Postures', p. 139.

113. Geiss, *July 1914*, pp. 29ff.

114. PRO FO 800/62, Goschen to Grey, 22 Oct. 1910; K. Wilson, *Policy of the Entente*, p. 100.

115. PRO CAB 2/2, CID meeting, 26 May 1911; Langhorne, 'Great Britain and Germany', p. 298; Steiner, *Britain and the Origins of the First World War*, p. 42.

116. K. Wilson, *Policy of the Entente*, pp. 66f.

117. PRO CAB 38/19/47, General Staff memorandum on the military aspect of the continental problem, 15 Aug. 1911.

118. Cain and Hopkins, *British Imperialism*, vol. I, pp. 450, 456ff.

119. W. S. Churchill, *World Crisis*, vol. I, p. 120; Lloyd George, *War Memoirs*, vol. I, p. 6.

120. J. Gooch, *Plans of War*, p. 25.

121. Monger, *End of Isolation*, pp. 248–55, 273, 279.

122. PRO CAB 16/5 XL/A/035374, CID paper E-2, 11 Nov. 1908. My emphasis.

123. PRO CAB 16/5 XL/A/035374, Proceedings, 23 March 1909. My emphasis. Cf. d'Ombrain, *War Machinery*, pp. 95–8.

124. PRO CAB 2/2, CID meeting, 30 May 1911.

125. PRO FO 800/52, Grey to Bertie, 16 April 1911.

126. Weinroth, 'British Radicals', pp. 674ff.

127. Steiner, *Britain and the Origins of the First World War*, p. 141.

128. PRO FO 800/90, Tyrrell to Grey, 25 Jan. 1912.

129. Grey to Asquith, 16 April 1911, quoted in Grey, *Twenty-Five Years*, vol. I, p. 94. He repeated this view to the CID the following month. K. Wilson, *Policy of the Entente*, p. 85.

130. K. Wilson, *Policy of the Entente*, pp. 57, 69.

131. Steiner, *Britain and the Origins of the First World War*, p. 76; D. French, *British Economic and Strategic Planning*, p. 33; D. French, 'Edwardian Crisis', p. 9.

132. PRO FO 800/100, Asquith to Grey, 5 Sept. 1911. Cf. d'Ombrain, *War Machinery*, p. 106.

133. PRO FO 800/100, Grey to Asquith, 8 Sept. 1911. Cf. Grey, *Twenty-Five Years*, vol. I, p. 95; K. Wilson, 'British Cabinet's Decision for War', pp. 149, 156n.; K. Wilson, *Policy of the Entente*, pp. 28f., 124.

134. PRO CAB 41/33/28, Asquith to George V, 2 Nov. 1911. Cf. Morley, *Memorandum*, p. 17; K. Wilson, *Policy of the Entente*, p. 28.

135. d'Ombrain, *War Machinery*, pp. 106f.; K. Wilson, *Policy of the Entente*, p. 28. Though no longer at the Admiralty, McKenna had seized the opportunity to resume the navalist attack.

136. *Hansard*, V, 32, p. 58, 27 Nov. 1911. Cf. Trevelyan, *Grey of Falloden*, p. 113.

137. Morris, *Scaremongers*, p. 303.

138. PRO FO 800/87, Churchill to Grey, 17 July 1912.

139. Hamilton, 'Great Britain and France', p. 332; W. S. Churchill, *World Crisis*, pp. 112f. My emphasis.

140. K. Wilson, *Policy of the Entente*, p. 29. Harcourt expressly repudiated the term 'Triple Entente' on the grounds that 'no such thing has ever been considered or approved by the Cabinet'; ibid., p. 26. For precisely this reason Grey tried to avoid the term too: A. J. P. Taylor, *Struggle for Mastery*, p. 449.

141. Rowland, *Last Liberal Governments*, vol. II, p. 263.

142. Grey, *Twenty-Five Years*, vol. I, pp. 297ff.

143. Ibid., vol. I, pp. 97f. Cf. Monger, *End of Isolation*, p. 197.

144. Renzi, 'Great Britain, Russia', p. 3. For Nicolson's concern at this time about public lack of 'knowledge' as to 'the very great importance that Russia's friendship is [sic] to us', see K. Wilson, 'Foreign Office', p. 404.

145. *Hansard*, V, 63, p. 458, 11 June 1914. Cf. Grey, *Twenty-Five Years*, vol. I, pp. 289ff.

146. PRO FO 800/92, Grey memorandum, 29 Feb. 1906. Cf. Monger, *End of Isolation*, pp. 281f.; Schmidt, 'Contradictory Postures', pp. 141f. For Crowe's version of the same deterrent theory, see Monger, *End of Isolation*, p. 271. For Nicolson's, see K. Wilson, *Policy of the Entente*, p. 40.

147. Langhorne, 'Great Britain and France', pp. 298, 306; K. Wilson, *Policy of the Entente*, pp. 92, 98; F. Fischer, *Germany's Aims*, p. 32.

148. K. Wilson, *Policy of the Entente*, pp. 29, 39f., 42f., 52f.; Rowland, *Last Liberal Governments*, vol. II, p. 250. Cf. W. S. Churchill, *World Crisis*, vol. I, pp. 65, 203; Grey, *Twenty-Five Years*, vol. I, pp. 73–81, 95, 281.

149. Hamilton, 'Great Britain and France', p. 324; K. Wilson, *Policy of the Entente*, p. 37.

150. PRO FO 800/55, Bertie to Grey, 8 March 1914. Cf. K. Wilson, *Policy of the Entente*, p. 92.

151. Andrew, 'Entente Cordiale', p. 27.

152. Grey, *Twenty-Five Years*, vol. I, pp. 324f.; K. Wilson, *Policy of the Entente*, p. 36. As early as December 1911 C. P. Scott identified Lloyd George, Churchill and Haldane as the ministers who would go with Grey if he resigned.

153. A. J. P. Taylor, *Struggle for Mastery*, p. 479.

154. Grey, *Twenty-Five Years*, vol. I, p. 81; vol. II, p. 44; Asquith, *Genesis*, pp. 57f., 63f., 83.

155. Steiner, *Britain and the Origins of the First World War*, pp. 124, 148, 245, 253. See also Nicolson, 'Edwardian England', pp. 145–8. This possibility was discussed but dismissed by Bertie: K. Wilson, *Policy of the Entente*, pp. 46ff.; Monger, *End of Isolation*, p. 279.

4. Arms and Men

1. *Grey, Twenty-Five Years*, vol. 1, p. 90.

2. Stevenson, *Armaments*, pp. 412, 415, 421.

3. Herrmann, *Arming of Europe*, pp. 228ff.

4. Steinberg, 'Copenhagen Complex', pp. 27ff.; Kennedy, 'German World Policy', pp. 610f., 619f.

5. Monger, *End of Isolation*, p. 12.

6. Amery, *Life of Joseph Chamberlain*, vol. IV, p. 197.

7. F. Fischer, 'Foreign Policy of Imperial Germany', p. 21.

8. Offer, *First World War*, p. 291. See also Steinberg, 'Copenhagen Complex', pp. 32–8.

9. Berghahn, *Germany and the Approach of War*, pp. 40f., 53.

10. Kennedy, 'German World Policy', pp. 618, 621, 625.

11. Marder, *British Naval Policy*, p. 503.

12. Steinberg, 'Copenhagen Complex', pp. 31–8; Monger, *End of Isolation*, p. 189.

13. The *Dreadnought*, launched in 1906, was the first turbine-driven, all-big-gun battleship. On the 1908–9 panic, see Stevenson, *Armaments*, p. 166f.

14. Howard, 'Edwardian Arms Race', pp. 91f.; Berghahn, *Germany and the Approach of War*, pp. 59f.; Mackay, *Fisher of Kilverstone*, pp. 398f.

15. Bond, *War and Society*, p. 193. However, Russia's were not true dreadnoughts.

16. I. Clarke, *Great War*, p. 295.

17. Berghahn, *Germany and the Approach of War*, p. 254.

18. Offer, *First World War*, p. 252. See also Mackay, *Fisher of Kilverstone*, p. 370.

19. Offer, *First World War*, pp. 237f.; D. French, *British Economic and Strategic Planning*, p. 28.

20. PRO FO 800/87, Tweedmouth to Grey, 17 Aug. and 24 Aug. 1907; 1 Jan. 1909; Beresford to Grey, 26 June 1911; Grey to Churchill, 23 Dec. 1911. Cf. Hankey, *Supreme Command*, vol. I, pp. 88, 91, 97–100; Offer, *First World War*, pp. 252, 274–80, and the report of the British delegation in G. Gooch and Temperley, *British Documents*, vol. VIII, pp. 295f. Fisher contemptuously predicted that the resolutions would 'tumble down as soon as the guns went off'.

21. Offer, *First World War*, p. 232.

22. Ibid., pp. 298f.

23. Förster, 'Dreams and Nightmares', p. 19.

24. Langhorne, 'Great Britain and Germany', p. 293.

25. W. S. Churchill, *World Crisis*, vol. I, p. 100.

26. Churchill meant the Triple Alliance, not the rest of the world. See the sceptical comments of McKenna in 1912, PRO CAB 2/2, CID meeting, 4 July 1912: 'This estimate was based upon the assumption that it was necessary to have a sixty per cent superiority over Germany and practical equality with Austria and Italy in the Mediterranean, in other words a three-power standard plus sixty per cent margin.' The German return to the 'two tempo' from 1912 promised a growing British advantage.

27. PRO FO 800/87, Churchill to Grey, 24 Oct. 1913.

28. W. S. Churchill, *World Crisis*, vol. I, p. 168; R. Churchill, *Winston S. Churchill*, vol. II, part III, pp. 1820, 1825–37, 1856f. Cf. K. Morgan, *Lloyd George Family Letters*, pp. 165f.; Lloyd George, *War Memoirs*, vol. I, p. 5.

29. W. S. Churchill, *World Crisis*, vol. I, pp. 178f.

30. Asquith, *Genesis*, pp. 143f.

31. Rowland, *Last Liberal Governments*, vol. II, pp. 278f. This was not as ingenuous as it sounds: Lloyd George was deliberately trying to undercut Churchill's naval estimates (see Chapter 5). Cf. PRO FO 800/87, Churchill to Grey, 8 Jan. 1914; PRO FO 800/55, Bertie to Grey, 8 Jan. 1914.

32. PRO CAB 38/11/15, General Staff paper, 'Possibility of a Raid by a Hostile Force on the British Coast', 26 March 1906. Cf. d'Ombrain, *Military Machinery*, pp. 86f.

33. PRO CAB 38/13/27, CID Sub-committee secretary's notes, 'Invasion', 20 July 1907; PRO CAB 3/14/7, Balfour statement, 29 May 1908; PRO CAB 3/1/1/44A, CID Sub-committee report, 22 Oct. 1908.

34. PRO CAB 38/26/13, CID Sub-committee report, 'Attack on the British Isles from Overseas', 15 April 1914; PRO CAB 38/28/40, CID secretary's note, 'Attack on the British Isles from Overseas', 14 Sept. 1914.

35. Andrew, *Secret Service*, p. 71.

36. Förster, 'Dreams and Nightmares', p. 8.

37. Ibid., p. 9.

38. Ibid., p. 11.

39. Though the possibility of an *Ostaufmarsch* against Russia alone was not wholly abandoned until 1913.

40. Ritter, *Der Schlieffenplan;* Turner, 'Significance of the Schlieffen Plan', pp. 199–221; Rothenberg, 'Moltke, Schlieffen', pp. 296–325.

41. Kehr, 'Klassenkämpfe und Rüstungspolitik', esp. pp. 98f., 110.

42. Förster, *Der doppelte Militarismus*, pp. 1–10, 297–300; Förster, 'Alter und neuer Militarismus', pp. 122–45.

43. Förster, *Der doppelte Militarismus*, p. 92.

44. Ibid., pp. 26f., 91f., 133, 147.

45. Bucholz, *Moltke, Schlieffen*, p. 133.

46. See Craig, *Politics of the Prussian Army*, pp. 232–8; Trumpener, 'Junkers and Others', pp. 29–47. Cf. Demeter, *Das deutsche Offizierkorps*; Kitchen, *German Officer Corps*.

47. Berghahn, *Germany and the Approach of War*, p. 113.

48. Förster, *Der doppelte Militarismus*, p. 251.

49. Ritter, *Sword and the Sceptre*, vol. II, pp. 223ff.; F. Fischer, *War of Illusions*, pp. 180ff.

50. Jaurausch, *Enigmatic Chancellor*, p. 96.

51. Förster, *Der doppelte Militarismus*, pp. 268f.

52. Kroboth, *Finanzpolitik*, p. 211.

53. Dukes, 'Militarism and Arms Policy', pp. 19–35.

54. Figures from Reichsarchiv, *Weltkrieg*, erster Reihe, vol. I, pp. 38f.; *Statistisches Jahrbuch*, p. 343. See also Förster, *Der doppelte Militarismus*, pp. 28, 37, 96f., 129, 190, 248; Bucholz, *Moltke, Schlieffen*, pp. 62, 67, 159; Berghahn, *Germany and the Approach of War*, p. xii; Joll, *Origins*, p. 72; Snyder, *Ideology of the Offensive*, pp. 42, 107.

55. Reichsarchiv, *Weltkrieg*, erster Reihe, vol. I, p. 22.

56. Förster, *Der doppelte Militarismus*, p. 205.

57. Stone, *Eastern Front*, p. 39; Kennedy, *Rise and Fall of the Great Powers*, esp. pp. 261, 307. Cf. Rothenberg, *Army of Francis Joseph*; Rutherford, *Russian Army*.

58. Förster, *Der doppelte Militarismus*, p. 164.

59. Bernhardi, *Germany and the Next War*, pp. 124f.

60. Ritter, *Sword and the Sceptre*, vol. III, p. 246.

61. Stone, *Europe Transformed*, pp. 327f.

62. See E. Weber, *Nationalist Revival in France*.

63. Angell, *Great Illusion*, p. 153. See also pp. 190f. on 'the tide of German Socialism'.

64. Bucholz, *Moltke, Schlieffen*, pp. 106, 128, n. 40.

65. Ibid., p. 316.

66. See Jagow's comments in *July 1914*, quoted in Geiss, *July 1914*, doc. 30.

67. Bucholz, *Moltke, Schlieffen*, pp. 306f.; Stone, *Eastern Front*, pp. 17–42.

68. Stone, *Europe Transformed*, p. 334.

69. Porch, 'French Army', vol. I, pp. 117–43.

70. Herrmann, *Arming of Europe*, p. 25. Joffre was an unfortunate choice of *generalissimo:* his predecessor General Michel had worked out an altogether more realistic strategy for countering the Schlieffen Plan. It is nevertheless true that only a handful of French officers had a realistic view of the war to come: Henri Mordacq was one of the rare pessimists who thought the war would last more than a few weeks: Bond, *War and*

Society, p. 83. The best way to understand the various plans is to study the maps in Banks, Arthur, *Military Atlas*, pp. 16–32.

71. See in general Challener, *French Theory*.

72. Creveld, *Supplying War*, pp. 119–24, 138–41.

73. Förster, 'Dreams and Nightmares', pp. 17f., 24. My emphasis.

74. Ibid., p. 23. See also Förster, 'Der deutsche Generalstab', pp. 61–95.

75. M. Gilbert, *First World War*, p. 7; Geiss, *July 1914*, pp. 36f.

76. Steinberg, 'Copenhagen Complex', p. 41.

77. Förster, 'Dreams and Nightmares', p. 20.

78. Moltke, *Generaloberst Helmuth von Moltke*, pp. 13f.

79. Joll, *Origins*, p. 186.

80. See Bernhardi, *Germany and the Next War*.

81. Stern, 'Bethmann Hollweg', p. 97. Cf. Afflerbach, *Falkenbayn*, pp. 147–71.

82. Jarausch, *Enigmatic Chancellor*, p. 96.

83. Ibid., p. 99.

84. Mommsen, 'Topos of Inevitable War', pp. 23–44.

85. Erdmann, 'Zur Beurteilung Bethmann Hollwegs', pp. 536f.; Stern, 'Bethmann Hollweg', p. 91. Doubt has been cast on the reliability of the Riezler diary for this period.

86. Berghahn, *Germany and the Approach of War*, p. 203.

87. F. Fischer, *War of Illusions*, p. 172.

88. Schulte, *Europäische Krise*, pp. 22f., 48.

89. Stone, *Eastern Front*, pp. 73–82; Stone, 'Moltke and Conrad', pp. 222–51; Herwig, *First World War*, pp. 87ff.

90. Bond, *War and Society*, pp. 86, 94.

91. K. Wilson, *Policy of the Entente*, p. 112.

92. F. Fischer, *War of Illusions*, p. 170.

93. Förster, 'Facing "People's War"', pp. 209–30.

94. Förster, 'Dreams and Nightmares', p. 16n.

95. F. Fischer, *War of Illusions*, p. 172; Bond, *War and Society*, p. 86.

96. Seligmann, 'Germany and the Origins', p. 317.

97. F. Fischer, *War of Illusions*, pp. 164–7, Geiss, *July 1914*, docs. 3, 4. My emphasis.

98. MMW, Max Warburg papers, 'Jahresbericht 1914', pp. 1f.; Warburg, *Aus meinen Aufzeichnungen*, p. 29.

99. Weinroth, 'British Radicals', p. 680.

100. Ibid., p. 512.

101. T. Wilson, 'Lord Bryce's Investigation', pp. 370f.

102. Trumpener, 'War Premeditated', p. 84.

103. L. Farrar, *Short-War Illusion*.

104. Kossmann, *Low Countries*, pp. 518f.; Stevenson, *Armaments*, p. 301.

105. Summers, 'Militarism in Britain', p. 111.

106. Offer, 'Going to War', p. 231.

107. Beckett, 'Nation in Arms', pp. 5ff.; Reader, *At Duty's Call*, p. 107.

108. Collier, *Brasshat*, p. 117.

109. K. Wilson, *Policy of the Entente*, p. 69.

110. Metternich's phrase, quoted in Amery, *Life of Joseph Chamberlain*, vol. IV, p. 151.

111. Dallas and Gill, *Unknown Army*, pp. 17, 24; Bourne, 'British Working Man in Arms', p. 338; Beckett, 'Nation in Arms', p. 7; Fuller, *Troop Morale*; p. 47; Sheffield, 'Officer-Man Relations', p. 413. Cf. Morris, *Scaremongers*, pp. 225–32.

112. J. Gooch, *Plans of War*, pp. 47, 71–89.

113. Travers, 'Offensive', pp. 531–53; Travers, 'Technology', pp. 264–86.

114. Trebilcock, 'War and the Failure of Industrial Mobilisation', pp. 150–61. On the lack of artillery preparations, see Adams, *Arms and the Wizard*; p. 170.

115. K. Wilson, *Policy of the Entente*, pp. 63f. Cf. J. Gooch, *Plans of War*, p. 289; d'Ombrain, *War Machinery*, p. 102.

116. PRO CAB 4/3, CID paper 121-B, 4 Nov. 1910; PRO CAB 2/2, CID meeting, 25 April 1912; PRO CAB 2/3, CID meeting, 5 Aug. 1913. Cf. J. Gooch, *Plans of War*, pp. 97ff., 265, 289, 294f.; d'Ombrain, *War Machinery*, pp. 17, 109ff., 265, 271ff.; D. French, *British Economic and Strategic Planning*, pp. 18, 74–84. Cf. Hankey, *Supreme Command*, vol. I, pp. 122, 178.

117. Albertini, *Origins*, vol. III, pp. 331, 368, 644; Lloyd George, *War Memoirs*, vol. I, pp. 57f.; Hazlehurst, *Politicians at War*, p. 41. For similar views, see Gordon, 'Domestic Conflicts and the Origins of the First World War', pp. 195f.

118. Grey, *Twenty-Five Years*, vol. II, p. 42; Asquith, *Genesis*, p. 202; Trevelyan, *Grey of Falloden*, p. 257. See Nicolson, 'Edwardian England', pp. 145–8.

119. J. M. Hobson, 'Military-Extraction Gap', pp. 461–506. The argument is also made in Friedberg, *Weary Titan*, pp. 301f.

120. McKeown, 'Foreign Policy', pp. 259–72.

121. D. French, *British Economic and Strategic Planning*, p. 10.

122. Hazlehurst, *Politicians at War*, p. 301.

123. K. Wilson, 'Grey', p. 177.

5. Public Finance and National Security

1. Salisbury to Sir C. Scott, 24 Oct. 1898, in G. Gooch and Temperley, *British Documents*, vol. I, p. 221.

2. Howard, 'Edwardian Arms Race', p. 95.

3. See the various figures in *Statistiches Jahrbuch*, pp. 348–55; Andic and Veverka, 'Growth of Government Expenditure', pp. 189, 205, 263; Roesler, *Finanzpolitik* p. 195; Witt, *Finanzpolitik*, pp. 380f.; Hentschel, *Wirtschaft und Wirtschaftspolitik*, p. 149; Schremmer, 'Taxation and Public Finance', p. 474.

4. See J. M. Hobson, 'Military-Extraction Gap', *passim*; Stevenson, *Armaments*, pp. 1–14. My own calculations can be found in Ferguson, 'Public Finance and National Security', pp. 141–68. The data assembled by N. Choucri, R. C. North, J. D. Singer and M. Small at Michigan University are summarized in Offer, 'The British Empire', pp. 215–38. Though there are minor differences between all the various series which have been produced, there is agreement on the 'big picture'.

5. Ferguson, 'Public Finance and National Security'.

6. For some earlier attempts to calculate this, see Q. Wright, *Study of War*, pp. 670f.; A. J. P. Taylor, *Struggle for Mastery*, p. xxviii; and Richardson, *Arms and Insecurity*, p. 87.

7. 1995 figures as given in the *Economist, Britain in Figures 1997*.

8. Figures from Stockholm International Peace Research Institute, *Yearbook 1992*, pp. 264–8; International Institute of Strategic Studies, *Military Balance*, pp. 218–21.

9. Andic and Veverka, 'Growth of Government Expenditure', pp. 262f.; Berghahn, *Modern Germany*, p. 296.

10. Davis and Huttenback, *Mammon*, pp. 160f.; O'Brien, 'Costs and Benefits', pp. 163–200; Kennedy and O'Brien, 'Debate', pp. 186–99. Davis and Huttenback calculated rightly that the per capita cost of defence was much higher for Britain itself than for the empire, but the argument (also advanced by O'Brien) that the British per capita military burden was more than double that of the other European states is misleading. If one calculates the cost of empire in terms of expenditure per square mile of territory, the British empire was much the cheapest to run.

11. Offer, *First World War*, p. 218.

12. Ferguson, 'Public Finance and National Security'. Modifying Hobson's figures slightly, Stevenson arrives at slightly different figures again (for percentages of NNP): Germany—4.9 per cent; Britain—3.4; Austria—3.5; France—4.3; Russia—5.1: *Armaments*, p. 6.

13. O'Brien, 'Power with Profit'.

14. Wagner, *Grundlegung*, p. 895; Timm, 'Das Gesetz', pp. 201–47.

15. F. Fischer, 'Foreign Policy of Imperial Germany', p. 21.

16. Peacock and Wiseman, *Growth of Public Expenditure*, pp. 151–201. Cf. Kennedy, 'Strategy Versus Finance', pp. 45–52.

17. As Chancellor in 1909, Lloyd George naturally had an incentive to remind his colleagues of those pledges: K. Wilson, *Policy of the Entente*, p. 7; Howard, 'Edwardian Arms Race', p. 81. Asquith had managed to reduce the naval estimates in 1906: Bernstein, *Liberalism and Liberal Politics*, pp. 174f.

18. PRO FO 800/87, Churchill to Grey and Asquith, 8 July 1913; Grey to Churchill, 31 Oct. 1913. Cf. R. Churchill, *Winston S. Churchill*, vol. II, part 3, p. 1820; Steiner, *Britain and the Origins of the First World War*, p. 164; Rowland, *Last Liberal Governments*, vol. II, pp. 271–80.

19. PRO FO 800/87, Churchill to Grey, 25 Dec. 1913 and 15 Jan. 1914. Cf. R. Churchill, *Winston S. Churchill*, vol. II, part 3, pp. 1835ff.

20. PRO CAB 41/34/38, Asquith to George V, 11 Dec. 1913; PRO CAB, 41/34/39, Asquith to George V, 20 Dec. 1913. Cf. W. S. Churchill, *World Crisis*, vol. I, p. 172; Bernstein, *Liberalism and Liberal Politics*, p. 179;

Rowland, *Last Liberal Governments*, vol. II, p. 287. In addition to Lloyd George, his opponents included McKenna, Runciman, the Postmaster-General, Herbert Samuel, and Sir John Simon, the Attorney-General.
21. Angell, *Great Illusion*, pp. 140f.
22. PRO CAB 41/35/3, Asquith to George V, 11 Feb. 1914. Cf. W. S. Churchill, *World Crisis*, vol. I, pp. 174–7; Lloyd George, *War Memoirs*, vol. I, p. 5; R. Churchill, *Winston S. Churchill*, vol. II, part 3, pp. 1856f., 1861, 1873; Rowland, *Last Liberal Governments*, vol. II, pp. 280–86; K. Morgan, *Lloyd George Family Letters*, pp. 165f. Both men felt they were re-enacting nineteenth-century battles: Churchill, his father's; Lloyd George, Gladstone's.
23. Rowland, *Last Liberal Governments*, vol. II, p. 283.
24. Delarme and André, *L'Etat*, pp. 50, 721–7, 733.
25. Bankers Trust Company, *French Public Finance* (New York, 1920), pp. 4, 182; Schremmer, 'Taxation and Public Finance', Table 55.
26. Bankers Trust Company, *French Public Finance*, p. 210; Schremmer, 'Taxation and Public Finance', Table 58.
27. P. Gregory, *Russian National Income*, pp. 58f., 252, 261ff.; Gatrell, *Tsarist Economy*, pp. 214–22.
28. Gatrell, *Government, Industry*, pp. 139f.
29. PRO CAB 38/16/6, Edgar Crammond, Paper on the finance of war presented to Institute of Bankers, 20 April 1910.
30. Gall, *Bismarck*, vol. II, p. 317.
31. A maximum estimate for the public sector's share of NNP—including revenues from public sector enterprises, public borrowing and the social insurance system—shows it rising from 13.8 per cent in 1890 to 18.8 per cent in 1913: Hentschel, *Wirtschaft und Wirtschaftspolitik*, p. 148. Cf. Witt, 'Finanzpolitik und sozialer Wandel', pp. 565–74.
32. Schremmer, 'Taxation and Public Finance', pp. 468–94.
33. Witt, *Finanzpolitik*, pp. 1–31; Witt, 'Reichsfinanzen', pp. 146–77.
34. Wehler, *German Empire*, pp. 52–65, 72–83; Berghahn, 'Politik und Gesellschaft', pp. 168–73; Witt, 'Innenpolitik und Imperialismus'; and the contrary view in Rauh, *Föderalismus*; Rauh, *Die Parlamentarisierung*.
35. Crothers, *German Elections*.
36. On the Centre's increasingly *mittelständisch* political tone, see Blackbourn, *Class, Religion*.
37. Hentschel estimates that the indirect tax burden fell from 5 per cent on incomes of less than 800 marks to just 1 per cent on those over 10,000 marks. Tariffs alone cost the average family up to 1.5 per cent of annual income: *Wirtschaft und Wirtschaftspolitik*, Table 37.
38. For the debate on the effectiveness of *Sammlungspolitik*, see esp. Stegmann, *Erben Bismarcks*; Stegmann, 'Wirtschaft und Politik', pp. 161–84; and the critique by Eley, 'Sammlungspolitik', pp. 29–63.
39. Wysocki, 'Die österreichische Finanzpolitik', pp. 68–104.
40. Morton, *Thunder at Twilight*, p. 211.
41. Murray, *People's Budget*.
42. Rowland, *Last Liberal Governments*, vol. II, p. 325ff.
43. J. M. Hobson, 'Military-Extraction Gap', pp. 495f., 499f. For similar suggestions, see Friedberg, *Weary Titan*, pp. 301f. But see McKeown, 'Foreign Policy', pp. 259–78.
44. Butler and Butler, *British Political Facts*.
45. B. Gilbert, *David Lloyd George*, pp. 81ff. The revolt was also a hangover from the row about Churchill's naval estimates: Bernstein, *Liberalism and Liberal Politics*, p. 181.
46. See originally and obliquely Dangerfield, *Strange Death*, later developed by Mayer, 'Domestic Causes of the First World War', pp. 288–92. For critical views see Lammers, 'Arno Mayer', esp. pp. 144, 153; Gordon, 'Domestic Conflict and the Origins of the First World War', pp. 197f., 200, 203–13, 224f. But see also the comments by Nicolson, 'Edwardian England', p. 161, and K. Wilson, 'British Cabinet's Decision for War', p. 148.
47. Schremmer, 'Taxation and Public Finance', Tables 51, 52, 54 and 55; Bankers Trust Company, *French Public Finance*, pp. 184–9. The stamp taxes acted as quasi-direct taxes in that it was mostly the better-off who had to pay them.
48. Sumler, 'Domestic Influences'.
49. Gatrell, *Government, Industry*, p. 150.
50. Kruedener, 'Franckenstein Paradox', pp. 111–23; Witt, *Finanzpolitik*, pp. 15ff.; Hentschel, *Wirtschaft und Wirtschaftspolitik*, pp. 174ff. Cf. Terhalle, 'Geschichte', pp. 274–89.
51. Saxony in 1874, Baden in 1884, Prussia in 1892, Württemberg in 1903 and Bavaria in 1912: Schremmer, 'Taxation and Public Finance', pp. 488ff. By 1913 the states depended on income tax for between 40 and 75 per cent of their revenues. The communes, which accounted for around 40 per cent of total public expendi-

ture by 1913, also relied increasingly on income tax: by 1910 52 per cent of Prussian local government revenue came from surcharges on the state income tax: Hentschel, 'German Economic and Social Policy', pp. 163f.

52. Kroboth, *Finanzpolitik*, p. 29.

53. It suited the Social Democrats, as it has suited many historians, to talk only about Reich finances when stressing the regressive and militaristic character of the German financial system. They said less about the increasingly progressive tax system of the states and communes, around half of the revenues of which were by 1910–13 devoted to 'social' policies (such as health and education provision). Between 1907 and 1913 the percentage of total public revenues coming from direct tax rose from 49 per cent to 57 per cent; the percentage of total public expenditure devoted to 'social' and educational purposes rose from 13.3 per cent (1891) to 28 per cent: see Kroboth, *Finanzpolitik*, pp. 301–5; Hentschel, *Wirtschaft und Wirtschaftspolitik*, p. 150; Schremmer, 'Taxation and Public Finance', Table 95.

54. Berghahn, 'Das Kaiserreich'; Mommsen, 'Die latente Krise'. See also Schmidt, 'Innenpolitische Blockbildungen', pp. 3–32.

55. Kroboth, *Finanzpolitik*, p. 115.

56. The government succeeded in quashing the second and third resolutions: ibid., pp. 170–81.

57. Ibid., pp. 181–273.

58. Groh, '"Je eher, desto besser!"'; Wehler, *German Empire*, pp. 192–201.

59. It was typical that, although the Reichstag raised the yield of the capital gains tax by 18 million marks by making the tax more progressive, it actually increased the total level of expenditure by 22 million marks: Kroboth, *Finanzpolitik*, pp. 220–70.

60. Westarp and Heydebrand had been divided about Conservative tactics; Erzberger's enthusiasm was not shared by all Centre deputies, a number of whom voted against the capital gains tax; there were many in the SPD who objected to voting for any legislation linked to arms spending; while a significant number of National Liberals were unhappy with the introduction of a progressive scale for the Defence Contribution: Kroboth, *Finanzpolitik*, pp. 272ff.

61. Stegmann, *Erben Bismarcks*, p. 356; Eley, *Reshaping the German Right*, pp. 30–34.

62. Kehr, 'Klassenkämpfe und Rüstungspolitik', esp. pp. 98f., 110.

63. Calculated from figures in Mitchell and Deane, *British Historical Statistics*, pp. 6–9, 402f.

64. British Library (BL), MSS Asquith 19, ff. 180–82, Hamilton to Asquith, 22 Jan. 1907.

65. Delarme and André, *L'Etat*, pp. 50, 721–7, 733; Lévy-Leboyer and Bourgignon, *L'Économie française*, pp. 320ff.; Straus, 'Le Financement', pp. 50, 97.

66. Kahan, 'Government Policies', pp. 460–77.

67. P. Gregory, *Russian National Income*, pp. 58f., 252, 261ff.; Gatrell, *Tsarist Economy*, pp. 214–22.

68. Gatrell, *Government, Industry*, pp. 140, 150; Apostol, Bernatzky and Michelson, *Russian Public Finances*, pp. 234, 239.

69. Kroboth, *Finanzpolitik*, p. 122, n. 65.

70. Kroboth estimates the proportion of total Reich debt incurred by the army, the navy and colonies as 65.3 per cent in 1913/14: ibid., p. 33n.

71. Calculated from figures in Witt, *Finanzpolitik*, p. 378.

72. Kroboth, *Finanzpolitik*, p. 33.

73. Hentschel, *Wirtschaft und Wirtschaftspolitik*, p. 144; Kroboth, *Finanzpolitik*, p. 489.

74. Figures from Kroboth, *Finanzpolitik*, pp. 489ff. Cf. Stuebel, *Das Verhältnis*.

75. Rich and Fisher, *Holstein Papers*, vol. III, pp. 302f.

76. Paulinyi, 'Die sogenannte gemeinsame Wirtschaftspolitik', pp. 567–604; März, *Austrian Banking*, pp. 26–30, 99; Bordes, *Austrian Crown*, pp. 232f.; Komlos, *Habsburg Monarchy*, pp. 153, 176.

77. Kroboth, *Finanzpolitik*, p. 235.

78. Ibid., p. 98.

79. Ferguson, *Paper and Iron*, pp. 91ff.

80. Warburg, *Aus meinen Aufzeichnungen*, pp. 29f.

81. M M W, Max M. Warburg papers, 'Geeignete und ungeeignete Mittel zur Hebung des Kurses der Staatspapiere'. Warburg saw Germany's exposure on the international market as part of the problem, and argued for keeping the public debt internal.

82. F. Fischer, *War of Illusions*, pp. 355–62.

83. Angell, *Great Illusion*, pp. xi–xii.

84. Kennedy, *Rise of the Anglo-German Antagonism*, p. 304.

85. Kroboth, *Finanzpolitik*, p. 188.

86. Berghahn, *Germany and the Approach of War*, p. 83.

87. Coetzee, *German Army League*, p. 50.

88. Bernhardi, *Germany and the Next War*, pp. 128f. As Bernhardi remarked (p. 254): '[The Japanese] spent their last farthing in the creation of a powerful army and a strong fleet. This was the spirit that led [them] to victory [over Russia]'.

89. Zilch, *Die Reichsbank*.

90. Coetzee, *German Army League*, p. 28.

91. Ibid., p. 35.

92. Ibid., p. 41.

93. Sterling Library, Yale University, Paul M. Warburg papers, series II, box 8, folder 118, Max M. Warburg, 'Die geplante Reichsfinanzreform: Wie vermeiden wir, dass aus der Beseitigung der Reichsfinanznot eine Bundesstaatsfinanznot entsteht[?]', Nov. 1908.

94. L. Cecil, *Albert Ballin*, pp. 159f.

95. Förster, *Der doppelte Militarismus*, pp. 228f., n. 11, 12.

96. Quoted in Ropponen, *Die russische Gefahr*, p. 98.

97. Berghahn, *Germany and the Approach of War*, pp. 77f.

98. Ibid., pp. 82f.

99. Förster, *Der doppelte Militarismus*, p. 253; cf. Ritter, *Sword and the Sceptre*, vol. II, p. 220.

100. Kroboth, *Finanzpolitik*, pp. 210f.

101. Bodleian Library, Oxford, Harcourt MSS, 577, Churchill memorandum, 3 Nov. 1909. I am grateful to Edward Lipman of Peterhouse for this reference.

102. See O'Hara, 'Britain's War of Illusions'.

103. G. Gooch and Temperley, *British Documents*, vol. VI, nos. 430, 437.

104. PRO FO 371/10281, Goschen to Grey, 3 March 1913.

105. O'Hara, 'Britain's War of Illusions'.

106. RAL, XI/130A/0, Lord Rothschild, London, to his cousins, Paris, 5 April 1906.

107. RAL, XI/130A/1, Lord Rothschild, London, to his cousins, Paris, 3 Jan. 1907.

108. RAL, XI/130A/1, Lord Rothschild, London, to his cousins, Paris, 17 April 1907.

109. RAL, XI/130A/2, Lord Rothschild, London, to his cousins, Paris, 2 April 1908; RAL, XI/130A/3, Lord Rothschild, London, to his cousins, 7 Jan. 1909.

110. See, e.g., E. Dugdale, *German Diplomatic Documents*, vol. III, p. 407.

111. Poidevin, *Relations économiques*, pp. 635, 655–9.

112. Seligmann, 'Germany and the Origins', pp. 315f.

113. Ibid., pp. 318, 320.

114. RAL, XI/130A/1, Lord Rothschild, London, to his cousins, Paris, 28 Jan. 1907.

115. See Mommsen, 'Topos of Inevitable War', pp. 23–44.

116. Ferro, *Great War*, p. 32.

117. See, for example, Hildebrand, *Deutsche Aussenpolitik*, p. 1.

118. Zilch, *Die Reichsbank*, pp. 69–133; Hentschel, *Wirtschaft und Wirtschaftspolitik*, pp. 136–43.

119. Roesler, *Finanzpolitik, passim*.

6. The Last Days of Mankind

1. See esp. Schulte, *Vor dem Kriegsausbruch 1914;* Schöllgen, *Imperialismus und Gleichgewicht.*

2. Hašek, 'Sporting Story' (1911), pp. 67ff.

3. Malcolm, *Bosnia*, pp. 133–55. As A. J. P. Taylor memorably put it: 'If a British royalty had visited Dublin on St Patrick's Day at the height of the Troubles, he too might have expected to be shot at': *Struggle for Mastery*, p. 520. The Serbian government in fact warned the Austrians against the visit, hardly the action of the assassination's mastermind. See also the account in Davies, *Europe*, pp. 877f.

4. G. Gooch and Temperley, *British Documents*, vol. I, p. 220.

5. A. J. P. Taylor, *Struggle for Mastery*, p. 485.

6. On the Austro-Hungarian background, see in addition to S. Williamson, *Austria—Hungary and the Coming of the First World War;* Leslie, 'Antecedents of Austria—Hungary's War Aims', pp. 307–94.

7. A. J. P. Taylor, *Struggle for Mastery*, p. 453.

8. Davies, *Europe*, p. 881.

9. A. J. P. Taylor, *Struggle for Mastery*, p. 495.

10. Ibid., p. 497.

11. Ibid., p. 521. Cf. S. Williamson, *Austria—Hungary and the Coming of the First World War*, pp. 195f.

12. Among many examples, see Biedemann's report to Dresden on 17 July in Geiss, *July 1914*, doc. 28.
13. Ibid., p. 44. Cf. the very pessimistic assessments described by Schoen on 18 July 1914: ibid., doc. 33.
14. Ibid., docs. 97, 98, 99, 122, 130.
15. Ibid., docs. 100, 108, 128, 129, 130, 135, 163, 173, 174.
16. Ibid., doc. 95.
17. Ibid., docs. 96, 101, 110, 165.
18. Ibid., docs. 112, 131; Schmidt, 'Contradictory Postures', p. 149.
19. Geiss, *July 1914*, docs. 130, 133, 134, 143.
20. Ibid., docs. 125, 168, 171, pp. 266, 270, 364; Ritter, *Sword and the Sceptre*, vol. II, pp. 247–75; Berghahn, *Germany and the Approach of War*, p. 207.
21. Turner, 'Russian Mobilisation', pp. 252–68.
22. Ibid., pp. 205f.; Geiss, *Der lange Weg*, p. 320; Pogge von Strandmann, 'Germany and the Coming of War', p. 120.
23. Albertini, *Origins*, vol. II, p. 343.
24. Trumpener, 'War Premeditated', pp. 69f., 80ff. General Hermann von François, one of the three corps commanders stationed in East and West Prussia, warned his wife in a coded telegram on the morning of the 30th that the 'music' was about to begin. The agent who succeeded in smuggling a Russian mobilization poster across the border was a Polish merchant named Pinkus Urwicz. Alas for romance, this more or less coincided with a telegram confirming the news from the German embassy in St Petersburg.
25. Schmidt, 'Contradictory Postures', pp. 143ff. Cf. Berghahn, *Germany and the Approach of War*, pp. 139f., 191f., 200; Geiss, *July 1914*, doc. 30.
26. Geiss, *July 1914*, docs. 162, 170, 175.
27. Seligmann, 'Germany and the Origins', p. 315.
28. Geiss, *July 1914*, docs. 148, 176.
29. Kroboth, *Finanzpolitik*, p. 279.
30. Erdmann, 'Zur Beurteilung Bethmann Hollwegs'; Erdmann, 'War Guilt 1914 Reconsidered', pp. 334–70; Zechlin, 'Deutschland zwischen Kabinettskrieg und Wirtschaftskrieg', pp. 347–458; Jarausch, 'Illusion of Limited War'; Hildebrand, 'Julikrise 1914'. See also Erdmann, 'Hat Deutschland auch den Ersten Weltkrieg entfesselt', and Zechlin, 'Julikrise und Kriegsausbruch 1914'.
31. Berghahn, *Germany and the Approach of War*, p. 180.
32. Ibid., p. 203; Schmidt, 'Contradictory Postures', p. 144.
33. Geiss, *July 1914*, doc. 18.
34. Ibid., p. 123.
35. T. Wolff, *Eve of 1914*, p. 448.
36. Sösemann, *Theodor Wolff: Tagebücher*, vol. I, p. 64.
37. Berghahn, *Germany and the Approach of War*, p. 203.
38. A. J. P. Taylor, *Struggle for Mastery*, p. 522.
39. Geiss, *July 1914*, doc. 125.
40. Schmidt, 'Contradictory Postures', p. 144; Trevelyan, *Grey of Falloden*, p. 244.
41. Seligmann, 'Germany and the Origins', p. 320.
42. Geiss, *July 1914*, doc. 135.
43. Seligmann, 'Germany and the Origins', pp. 322, 330f.
44. F. Fischer, 'Foreign Policy of Imperial Germany', p. 37.
45. F. Fischer, *War of Illusions*, pp. 461–5; Pogge von Strandmann, 'Germany and the Coming of War', pp. 118f.
46. Offer, 'Going to War', pp. 213–41. Moltke was no Instetten.
47. Trumpener, 'War Premeditated', pp. 62–6.
48. Albertini, *Origins*, vol. II, pp. 203–8. Cf. Butterfield, 'Sir Edward Grey', pp. 9f; Geiss, *July 1914*, pp. 95, 138.
49. Albertini, *Origins*, vol. II, pp. 209–14, 329–38; Geiss, *July 1914*, docs. 44, 46, 57, 80, 93.
50. Geiss, *July 1914*, docs. 68, 73, 81, 82, 83, 85, 94, 97, 98, 99; Grey, *Twenty-Five Years*, vol. II, pp. 304f., 317. See also Albertini, *Origins*, vol. II, pp. 336–9, 514; Asquith, *Genesis*, pp. 201f. Nicolson detected the sham: PRO FO 800/94, Nicolson to Grey, 26 July 1914.
51. Albertini, *Origins*, vol. II, pp. 429, 497, 687.
52. Geiss, *July 1914*, p. 221, docs. 95, 96; Grey, *Twenty-Five Years*, vol. I, pp. 319f.
53. Albertini, *Origins*, vol. II, pp. 329–34, 340; Geiss, *July 1914*, docs. 50, 79; W. S. Churchill, *World Crisis*, vol. I, pp. 193f.
54. Geiss, *July 1914*, docs. 103, 110, 112, 114.

55. Ibid., docs. 108, 119, 120; Albertini, *Origins*, vol. II, p. 509; Grey, *Twenty-Five Years*, vol. I, p. 319; Asquith, *Genesis*, pp. 190ff.

56. Geiss, *July 1914*, docs. 90, 100.

57. Ibid., docs. 121, 122, 123, 128; Albertini, *Origins*, vol. II, pp. 510ff.

58. Geiss, *July 1914*, docs. 101, 140, 141a, 153.

59. Ibid., pp. 271, 291; docs. 118, 123, 124a, 137, 138, 147.

60. Ibid., docs. 91, 111, 114, 115, 125.

61. Ibid., docs. 133, 134, 143, 145, 154; Albertini, *Origins*, vol. II, pp. 523–6.

62. Geiss, *July 1914*, doc. 147; Albertini, *Origins*, vol. II, pp. 635–8, 645; vol. III, pp. 378f., 390f.

63. Geiss, *July 1914*, doc. 158; Albertini, *Origins*, vol. II, pp. 634f.; vol. III, pp. 373, 378, 386.

64. Geiss, *July 1914*, docs. 107, 148, 149.

65. Ibid., doc. 152.

66. Ibid., doc. 164; PRO FO 800/94, Nicolson to Grey, 31 July 1914. Cf. Hazlehurst, *Politicians at War*, p. 52; Andrew, 'Entente Cordiale', p. 33; K. Wilson, *Policy of the Entente*, p. 95; Albertini, *Origins*, vol. III, p. 374.

67. Hazlehurst, *Politicians at War*, pp. 78f. See also Grey's repetition of the same formula to Ponsonby: ibid., p. 37. Cf. K. Wilson, 'British Cabinet's Decision for War', pp. 149f.

68. Geiss, *July 1914*, docs. 130, 133.

69. Albertini, *Origins*, vol. II, pp. 501, 514, 523–5.

70. The German offer to guarantee French territorial integrity (but not French colonial possessions) had in fact been trailed by the German ship-owner Albert Ballin in a conversation with Churchill at dinner on 24 July: W. S. Churchill, *World Crisis*, p. 196; L. Cecil, *Albert Ballin*, p. 207. For Bethmann's offer see Geiss, *July 1914*, docs. 139, 167; Albertini, *Origins*, vol. II, p. 506; Grey, *Twenty-Five Years*, vol. I, pp. 325f.

71. Geiss, *July 1914*, doc. 151; Albertini, *Origins*, vol. II, pp. 507, 519, 633; Grey, *Twenty-Five Years*, vol. I, pp. 327f.; R. Churchill, *Winston S. Churchill*, vol. II, part 3, pp. 1989, 1993; K. Wilson, 'British Cabinet's Decision for War', p. 153; W. S. Churchill, *World Crisis*, vol. I, pp. 213ff.; Offer, *First World War*, p. 308; Hazlehurst, *Politicians at War*, p. 23.

72. Albertini, *Origins*, vol. II, pp. 511ff., 521ff.; Asquith, *Genesis*, p. 198.

73. Geiss, *July 1914*, docs. 170, 173, 177. Cf. Albertini, *Origins*, vol. III, pp. 380–85. To Moltke's despair, the Kaiser thought this meant the attack in the West could be called off; he even ordered champagne to celebrate, declaring: 'So now we need only wage war against Russia, we simply advance with the whole army in the east': M. Gilbert, *First World War*, p. 30.

74. Albertini, *Origins*, vol. II, p. 639.

75. Geiss, *July 1914*, docs. 162, 177.

76. Albertini, *Origins*, vol. II, pp. 638f., 646–9; vol. III, pp. 373, 380, 384f., 392ff.

77. Trevelyan, *Grey of Falloden*, p. 260.

78. Kennedy, *Rise of the Anglo-German Antagonism*, pp. 458f.

79. Hazlehurst, *Politicians at War*, pp. 36–9; R. Churchill, *Winston S. Churchill*, vol. II, part 3, pp. 1990f.

80. Hazlehurst, *Politicians at War*, p. 33; Bentley, *Liberal Mind*, p. 17.

81. Beaverbrook, *Politicians and the War*, pp. 19ff. Cf. Trevelyan, *Grey of Falloden*, p. 254; Hazlehurst, *Politicians at War*, pp. 49, 73, 84–91; K. Wilson, 'British Cabinet's Decision for War', pp. 150ff.; K. Wilson, *Policy of the Entente*, pp. 136–9. It is an error to regard Lloyd George as in some way committed to intervention on the basis of his Mansion House speech of 1911. Lloyd George was never committed to anything except Lloyd George.

82. Albertini, *Origins*, vol. III, pp. 369f. See also Morley, *Memorandum*, p. 7; Nicolson, 'Edwardian England', p. 157; Hazlehurst, *Politicians at War*, pp. 49, 86.

83. K. Wilson, 'British Cabinet's Decision for War', p. 150.

84. Beaverbrook, *Politicians and the War*, pp. 28f.; W. S. Churchill, *World Crisis*, vol. I, pp. 216f.; R. Churchill, *Winston S. Churchill*, vol. II, part 3, p. 1997.

85. K. Wilson, *Policy of the Entente*, pp. 138ff.; Hazlehurst, *Politicians at War*, p. 94; Geiss, *July 1914*, doc. 183; Albertini, *Origins*, vol. III, pp. 406f. Cf. Grey, *Twenty-Five Years*, vol. II, p. 2; Offer, *First World War*, p. 317.

86. K. Wilson, 'British Cabinet's Decision for War', pp. 153ff.; Albertini, *Origins*, vol. III, pp. 403f.

87. Albertini, *Origins*, vol. III, pp. 403ff.; B. Gilbert, *Lloyd George*, p. 109; K. Wilson, *Policy of the Entente*, p. 141; Hazlehurst, *Politicians at War*, pp. 66f.

88. Albertini, *Origins*, vol. III, pp. 381f., 386, 399. Grey subsequently denied in the House of Commons that he had made the offer, claiming that Lichnowsky had misunderstood him. This is contradicted by his letter to Bertie of August 1: see Geiss, *July 1914*, doc. 177—unless Grey had been deliberately misleading Cambon in describing his proposal to Lichnowsky.

89. Asquith, *Genesis*, p. 221; Beaverbrook, *Politicians and the War*, p. 21; K. Wilson, *Policy of the Entente*, pp. 138f.; Hazlehurst, *Politicians at War*, pp. 93f.

90. Albertini, *Origins*, vol. III, p. 483; Hazlehurst, *Politicians at War*, pp. 116f.; K. Wilson, 'British Cabinet's Decision for War', pp. 157f.; Asquith, *Genesis*, pp. 220f.

91. On Morley's resignation see Morley, *Memorandum, passim;* Pottle, *Champion Redoubtable*, pp. 39f.

92. PRO CAB 16/5 XC/A/035374, Foreign Office memorandum (CID paper E-2), 11 Nov. 1908. Cf. K. Wilson, 'Foreign Office', p. 409.

93. Lloyd George, *War Memoirs*, vol. I, pp. 30f., 40; W. S. Churchill, *World Crisis*, vol. I, pp. 65, 199, 219.

94. Albertini, *Origins*, vol. III, p. 513; Asquith, *Genesis*, p. 211.

95. Hazlehurst, *Politicians at War*, pp. 177, 303.

96. Ibid., p. 73; K. Wilson, *Policy of the Entente*, p. 136; K. Wilson, 'British Cabinet's Decision for War', p. 149.

97. R. Churchill, *Winston S. Churchill*, vol. II, part 3, pp. 1991, 1996; Geiss, *July 1914*, docs. 166, 174; Albertini, *Origins*, vol. III, pp. 388f., 399f. Cf. Grey, *Twenty-Five Years*, vol. I, pp. 329f.; vol. II, p. 10; Asquith, *Genesis*, p. 209.

98. Beaverbrook, *Politicians and the War*, pp. 22f.; M. Brock, 'Britain Enters the War', pp. 149f.

99. K. Wilson, 'British Cabinet's Decision for War', p. 153; Brock, 'Britain Enters the War', p. 151; B. Gilbert, *Lloyd George*, p. 110; Hazlehurst, *Politicians at War*, pp. 70f.

100. PRO CAB 41/35/23, Crewe to George V, 2 Aug. 1914. Cf. Albertini, *Origins*, pp. 409f. (my emphasis). For vivid proof of Lloyd George's agonizing on the subject, see K. Morgan, *Lloyd George Family Letters*, p. 167. See also Lloyd George's remarks to C. P. Scott in B. Gilbert, *Lloyd George*, p. 112.

101. Albertini, *Origins*, vol. III, p. 494; Brock, 'Britain Enters the War', p. 160. Cf. Grey, *Twenty-Five Years*, vol. II, pp. 9f.

102. Geiss, *July 1914*, docs. 179, 184, 188; Albertini, *Origins*, vol. III, pp. 479, 489, 492, 497.

103. To say that 'if Germany had not invaded [Belgium] there might have been a few more resignations' is to understate the fragility of the government as a whole: Martel, *Origins*, p. 69.

104. Brock, 'Britain Enters the War', p. 145.

105. Albertini, *Origins*, vol. III, pp. 486f.; Grey, *Twenty-Five Years*, vol. II, pp. 14f.; K. Wilson, *Policy of the Entente*, p. 144.

106. W. S. Churchill, *World Crisis*, vol. I, pp. 202f.; Asquith, *Genesis*, pp. 212f.; K. Wilson, *Policy of the Entente*, p. 120; Brock, 'Britain Enters the War', p. 161. Cf. Howard, 'Europe on the Eve', p. 119.

107. Hazlehurst, *Politicians at War*, p. 114.

108. Morley, *Memorandum*, p. 10; K. Wilson, *Policy of the Entente*, p. 146.

109. B. Gilbert, *Lloyd George*, pp. 108, 111.

110. K. Wilson, 'British Cabinet's Decision for War', p. 154.

111. PRO FO 800/100, Grey to Asquith, 23 March and 20 May 1914. Cf. Hazlehurst, *Politicians at War*, pp. 26–32; Lammers, 'Arno Mayer', pp. 147f.

112. Woodward, *Great Britain*, p. 46.

113. K. Wilson, 'In Pursuit of the Editorship', p. 83.

114. Andrew, 'Entente Cordiale', p. 34.

115. Beaverbrook, *Politicians and the War*, p. 31; Albertini, *Origins*, vol. III, pp. 99–404; K. Wilson, *Policy of the Entente*, p. 141.

116. Lammers, 'Arno Mayer', p. 159; K. Wilson, 'British Cabinet's Decision for War', p. 155. Cf. Woodward, *Great Britain*, p. 46, for the reciprocation of this sentiment from the Tory side.

117. K. Wilson, 'British Cabinet's Decision for War', pp. 154f.; K. Wilson, *Policy of the Entente*, pp. 141f. Cf. Shannon, *Crisis of Imperialism*, p. 466. Pease may also have been persuaded to 'stick to the ship' for financial reasons: as his wife pointed out, he would have 'no business prospects to look forward to' if he resigned.

118. Hurwitz, *State Intervention*, p. 53.

119. Beaverbrook, *Politicians and the War*, pp. 13–19. Cf. Hazlehurst, *Politicians at War*, p. 41.

120. Searle, *Quest for National Efficiency*, pp. 175–201.

121. See for example his less than hawkish comments to the German Crown Prince on 26 July.

122. Albertini, *Origins*, vol. III, pp. 407, 503; Hankey, *Supreme Command*, p. 165; A. J. P. Taylor, *Struggle for Mastery*, p. 526; Offer, *First World War*, pp. 5, 308f.

123. PRO FO 800/55, Bertie to Grey, 3 Aug. 1914; Bertie to Tyrrell, 4 Aug. 1914. Cf. Bertie to Grey [cypher telegram], 4 Aug. 1914.

124. D. French, *British Economic and Strategic Planning*, pp. 87f.; Offer, *First World War*, p. 312.

125. Beaverbrook, *Politicians and the War*, p. 36; Hankey, *Supreme Command*, pp. 169ff., 187, 192; Albertini, *Origins*, vol. III, pp. 510f.; K. Wilson, *Policy of the Entente*, p. 125; J. Gooch, *Plans of War*, pp. 301ff.; Collier, *Brasshat*, pp. 162f.; K. Morgan, *Lloyd George Family Letters*, p. 169; d'Ombrain, *War Machinery*, pp. 113f.

126. Hazlehurst, *Politicians at War*, pp. 63f.

127. Woodward, *Great Britain*, pp. 32–5; Hankey, *Supreme Command*, pp. 187–97; Collier, *Brasshat*, pp. 166f., 172–90. See also Guinn, *British Strategy*, pp. 37ff.

128. A rare exception is Johnson, *Offshore Islanders*, pp. 365f. For a detailed discussion see Ferguson, 'Kaiser's European Union'.

129. Asquith, *Genesis*, pp. 57f., 60, 63f., 83.

130. Grey, *Twenty-Five Years*, vol. I, pp. 75, 81, 85, 313, 334f. Cf. Trevelyan, *Grey of Falloden*, pp. 254, 260.

131. Grey, *Twenty-Five Years*, vol. II, pp. 35ff. See also ibid., vol. I, p. 77.

132. Ibid., vol. II, p. 28.

133. See e.g. F. Fischer, *War of Illusions*, p. 470.

134. Butterfield, 'Sir Edward Grey', pp. 1f.; Hatton, 'Britain and Germany', p. 143.

135. F. Fischer, *Germany's Aims*, pp. 103–6.

136. Point one raised the possibility of the cession from France of 'Belfort and western slopes of the Vosges, razing of fortresses and cession of coastal strip from Dunkirk to Boulogne'. The ore field of Briey was to be 'ceded in any case'. Point two stipulated that Liège and Verviers were to be ceded by Belgium to Prussia, and a 'frontier strip' by Belgium to Luxembourg. It left open the 'question whether Antwerp, with a corridor to Liège, should also be annexed'. 'Militarily important ports' were to be occupied by Germany; indeed, the whole Belgian coast was to be 'at our disposal in military respects'. French Flanders with Dunkirk, Calais and Boulogne might then be taken from France and given to Belgium. Point three stated that Luxembourg would become a German federal state and might acquire Longwy from France. Point seven raised the possibility that Antwerp might be ceded to Holland 'in return for the right to keep a German garrison in the fortress of Antwerp and at the mouth of the Scheldt': F. Fischer, *Germany's Aims*, p. 105.

137. F. Fischer, *Germany's Aims*, pp. 10, 28, 32ff., 101f.; Geiss, *July 1914*, pp. 21f.; Berghahn, *Germany and the Approach of War*, pp. 138ff.

138. For example, in 1892: Geiss, *July 1914*, pp. 21f.

139. Ibid., doc. 135.

140. Ibid., doc. 179.

141. G. Gooch and Temperley, *British Documents*, vol. VI, no. 442.

142. Berghahn, *Germany and the Approach of War*, pp. 138ff.

143. See Grey, *Twenty-Five Years*, vol. I, p. 325; Albertini, *Origins*, vol. II, p. 506. It should, however, be noted that Belgian integrity was only guaranteed 'assuming that Belgium does not take sides against us'; and that no assurance was to be given with respect to French colonies. It is possible to deduce from this that Bethmann already contemplated some changes to the extent and status of Belgium, as by this stage the chances of Belgian acquiescence were small. On the other hand, Moltke's draft decree 87 justifying the invasion of Belgium offered not only to guarantee Belgium's sovereign rights and independence in return for its neutrality, but also to evacuate the country immediately after the war was over and to pay compensation for any war damage: Geiss, *July 1914*, doc. 91. The future of Belgium was to be a bone of contention in Berlin throughout the war, and it proved impossible to make the kind of unequivocal commitment to the restoration of Belgian integrity which might have satisfied British opinion; though it should be noted that the issue might have disappeared if, as nearly happened, the Germans had been able to persuade King Albert to drop his country's commitment to neutrality: F. Fischer, *Germany's Aims*, pp. 215–25; 420–28.

144. Geiss, *July 1914*, doc. 179.

145. F. Fischer, *Germany's Aims*, pp. 104f.

146. Ibid., pp. 115ff.

147. Bülow, *Memoirs*, p. 400. Cf. Winzen, 'Der Krieg'.

148. For further details of the German conception of *Mitteleuropa* as it developed during the war, see F. Fischer, *Germany's Aims*, pp. 201–8, 247–56, 523–33. Cf. Berghahn, *Germany and the Approach of War*, pp. 130–38.

149. I. Clarke, *Great War*, pp. 203, 232.

150. Stern, 'Bethmann Hollweg', pp. 99f.

151. Offer, 'Going to War', p. 228.

7. The August Days

1. *Hitler, Mein Kampf*, pp. 148ff.

2. Kershaw, *Hitler*, pp. 92f.

3. Finch, 'Diary', 12 Jan. 1915; 18 Jan. 1915.

4. See esp. Eksteins, *Rites of Spring*, esp. pp. 55–93, 193–7. Also, Wohl, *Generation of 1914*.

5. Meinecke, *Die deutsche Katastrophe*, p. 43.

6. Meinecke, *Die deutsche Erhebung*.

7. See in general Joll, *Origins*, pp. 171–200.

8. Coker, *War and the Twentieth Century*, p. 91; Sösemann, 'Medien', p. 212. It may be that the photograph is a fake.

9. Sösemann, 'Medien', pp. 220f.

10. Ullrich, *Kriegsalltag*, pp. 10–14. See also Schramm, *Neun Generationen*, vol. II, pp. 480f.

11. Schramm, *Neun Generationen*, vol. II, p. 480.

12. Coker, *War and the Twentieth Century*, p. 91.

13. Reader, *At Duty's Call*, p. 103.

14. Lloyd George, *War Memoirs*, vol. I, p. 41.

15. Kraus, *Die letzten Tage*, pp. 69–83.

16. See Canetti, *Tongue Set Free*, p. 90.

17. Buse, 'Ebert', pp. 443f.

18. Joll, *Origins*, p. 184.

19. J. Harris, *William Beveridge*, pp. 199f.

20. Grey, *Twenty-Five Years*, pp. 316f.; Butterfield, 'Sir Edward Grey', p. 14.

21. Hazlehurst, *Politicians at War*, p. 84; Geiss, *Twenty-Five Years*, doc. 174; Albertini, *Origins*, vol. III, pp. 388f. See also Asquith, *Genesis*, p. 209; R. Churchill, *Winston S. Churchill*, vol. II, part 3, p. 1996.

22. Geiss, *July 1914*, doc. 149.

23. Hazlehurst, *Politicians at War*, p. 52.

24. Albertini, *Origins*, vol. III, p. 524.

25. Grey, *Twenty-Five Years*, vol. II, p. 20.

26. Davies, *Europe*, p. 885.

27. Pottle, *Champion Redoubtable*, p. 25.

28. Davies, *Europe*, p. 885.

29. Koszyk, *Zwischen Kaiserreich und Diktatur*, p. 31; Sösemann, 'Medien', p. 200.

30. Sösemann, 'Medien', p. 207.

31. Buse, 'Ebert', pp. 433, 435.

32. See in general Miller, *Burgfrieden und Klassenkampf*.

33. Ibid., p. 40; Buse, 'Ebert', p. 440n.

34. Sösemann, 'Medien', p. 207.

35. Carsten, *War against War*, pp. 48f.

36. G. Brown, *Maxton*, pp. 58ff.

37. A. Gregory, 'British Public Opinion', p. 12.

38. Marquand, *Ramsay MacDonald*, pp. 167ff.

39. Shand, 'Doves', pp. 97ff. Note however that these restrictions were somewhat relaxed in 1917.

40. Marwick, *Deluge*, pp. 71f.

41. See in general Wallace, *War and the Image*, p. 25.

42. Holroyd, *Bernard Shaw*, pp. 348ff. See the discussion in the Introduction.

43. Ibid., p. 326.

44. Hynes, *War Imagined*, pp. 4, 85.

45. Freud, 'Thoughts', pp. 1ff.

46. Shand, 'Doves', p. 103.

47. Davies, *Europe*, p. 895.

48. Ryan, *Bertrand Russell*, pp. 55–80.

49. Butterfield, 'Sir Edward Grey', p. 1.

50. Skidelsky, *John Maynard Keynes*, vol. I, p. 297.

51. Pogge von Strandmann, 'Historians', pp. 9, 14.

52. Cannadine, *G. M. Trevelyan*, p. 78.

53. Hynes, *War Imagined*, p. 68.

54. Winter, 'Oxford', p. 16.

55. T. Weber, 'Stormy Romance', pp. 14–22.

56. Winter, 'Oxford', p. 5.

57. Esposito, 'Public Opinion', p. 37.

58. J. Harris, *William Beveridge*, p. 200.

59. Ibid., p. 202.

60. Skidelsky, *John Maynard Keynes*, vol. I, pp. 295ff.
61. Ibid., pp. 302f.
62. Ibid., pp. 317–21.
63. Davies, *Europe*, p. 892.
64. K. Morgan, *Lloyd George Family Letters*, p. 169.
65. A. Gregory, 'British Public Opinion', p. 9. See also Esposito, 'Public Opinion', p. 28.
66. A. Gregory, 'British Public Opinion', p. 9.
67. Esposito, 'Public Opinion', p. 26.
68. Hiley, 'Counter-Espionage', pp. 637–50.
69. Hynes, *War Imagined*, p. 81.
70. Ryan, *Bertrand Russell*, p. 56.
71. J. Lawrence, Dean and Robert, 'Outbreak of War', pp. 582f.
72. Rezzori, *Snows of Yesteryear*, pp. 7f.
73. Becker, 1914.
74. Becker, 'That's the death knell . . . ', pp. 18ff.
75. Esposito, 'Public Opinion', p. 25. The size of these meetings is, unfortunately, not recorded.
76. Krumeich, 'L'Entrée', pp. 65–74.
77. J. Lawrence, Dean and Robert, 'Outbreak of War', pp. 571ff., 581–7.
78. Sösemann, 'Medien', p. 220.
79. A. Gregory, 'British Public Opinion', pp. 13f.
80. Bloch, *Is War Now Impossible*, p. xlv.
81. Angell, *Great Illusion*, p. 209.
82. Förster, 'Dreams and Nightmares', p. 14.
83. Geiss, *July 1914*, doc. 43.
84. Albertini, *Origins*, vol. II, p. 214; K. Wilson, *Policy of the Entente*, p. 13. For a similar comparison with 1848 by Morley, see D. French, *British Economic and Strategic Planning*, p. 87.
85. Geiss, *July 1914*, doc. 57.
86. Offer, *First World War*, p. 312.
87. Geiss, *July 1914*, doc. 162.
88. M M W, Max M. Warburg papers, 'Jahresbericht 1914', pp. 2f.
89. Geiss, *July 1914*, p. 134; Staatsarchiv Hamburg, Deputation für Handel, Schifffahrt und Gewerbe II Spez. XXXIV 23a, Reich Chancellor to Senate, 21 July 1914; M M W, Max M. Warburg papers, 'Jahresbericht 1914', p. 3.
90. *Hamburger Börsenhalle*, 28 July 1914.
91. R A L, XI/130A/8, Lord Rothschild, London, to his cousins, Paris, 27 July 1914.
92. R A L, XI/130A/8, Lord Rothschild, London, to his cousins, Paris, 28 July (two letters) and 29 July 1914.
93. M. Brock and E. Brock, *H. H. Asquith*, p. 131.
94. Albertini, *Origins*, vol. III, p. 378.
95. Lipman, 'City', pp. 68ff. I am grateful to the author for his help on this point.
96. Skidelsky, *John Maynard Keynes*, vol. I, p. 285.
97. R A L, XI/130A/8, Lord Rothschild, London, to his cousins, Paris, 27 July 1914.
98. R A L, XI/130A/8, Lord Rothschild, London, to his cousins, Paris, 30 July 1914. My emphasis.
99. R A L, XI/130A/8, Lord Rothschild, London, to his cousins, Paris, 31 July 1914.
100. Steed, *Through Thirty Years*, vol. II, pp. 8f.; *The Times, History*, p. 208.
101. Barth, *Die deutsche Hochfinanz*, p. 448.
102. Joll, *Origins*, p. 30. This too was in vain: before a reply could be sent, communications with Berlin were interrupted.
103. Hazlehurst, *Politicians at War*, p. 85.
104. Albertini, *Origins*, vol. III, p. 376.
105. R A L, XI/130A/8, Lord Rothschild, London, to his cousins, Paris, 31 July 1914.
106. See also the description in Wake, *Kleinwort Benson*, pp. 138–42, 207f.
107. R A L, XI/130A/8, Lord Rothschild, London, to his cousins, Paris, 4 Aug. 1914. See also J. Lawrence, Dean and Robert, 'Outbreak of War', pp. 564ff.; Hardach, *First World War*, p. 140.
108. L. Cecil, *Albert Ballin*, pp. 210–14; Warburg, *Aus meinen Aufzeichnungen*, p. 34.
109. Archives Nationales, Paris, 132 A Q 5594/1M192, Alfred de Rothschild, London, to his cousins, Paris, 3 Aug. 1914.
110. Dahlmann, 'Russia at the Outbreak', pp. 53ff.
111. Jünger, *Storm of Steel*, p. 8.

112. Schramm, *Neun Generationen*, vol. II, pp. 467–9.

113. Sulzbach, *With the German Guns*, pp. 21ff.

114. Beckett, 'Nation in Arms', p. 12; Reader, *At Duty's Call*, p. 107.

115. J. Winter, *Great War*, p. 30.

116. Simkins, *Kitchener's Army*, pp. 59, 65f.

117. J. Winter, *Great War*, p. 27; D. Winter, *Death's Men*, p. 29.

118. Reader, *At Duty's Call*, p. 107. The point is misunderstood by Fussell, *Great War*, p. 9.

119. Beckett, 'Nation in Arms', pp. 15ff.

120. H. Wolfe, quoted in Dewey, 'Military Recruitment', p. 200.

121. Quoted in Hughes, 'New Armies', p. 104.

122. J. Winter, *Great War*, pp. 30f. Cf. Dallas and Gill, *Unknown Army*, p. 33; Beckett, 'Nation in Arms', p. 10.

123. See Dewey, 'Military Recruitment', pp. 200–219; J. Winter, *Great War*, pp. 33ff.

124. J. Winter, *Great War*, pp. 36ff. See also A. Gregory, 'Lost Generations', pp. 79f.

125. Spiers, 'Scottish Soldier', p. 315.

126. Offer, 'Going to War', p. 234.

127. J. Winter, *Great War*, p. 27.

128. Armstrong, *Crisis of Quebec*, p. 250.

129. Graves, *Goodbye*, pp. 60f.; Sassoon, *Memoirs of a Fox-Hunting Man*, p. 244.

130. Reader, *At Duty's Call*, p. 110.

131. Fussell, *Great War*, p. 182.

132. A. Gregory, 'British Public Opinion', p. 11.

133. Churchill's phrase, quoted in Englander and Osborne, 'Jack, Tommy and Henry Dubb', p. 593.

134. Wohl, *Generation of 1914*, *passim*; Eksteins, *Rites of Spring*, *passim*; Mosse, *Fallen Soldiers*, pp. 54–66; Hynes, *War Imagined*, pp. 7f., 59.

135. See, e.g., T. Wilson, *Myriad Faces*, p. 11; Fussell, *Great War*, pp. 25f.; Mosse, *Fallen Soldiers*, pp. 60f.

136. P. Parker, *Old Lie*, pp. 17, 130, 204–17; Barnett, *Collapse of British Power*, p. 28; Nicolson, 'Edwardian England', p. 165.

137. Becker, *Great War*, pp. 156–8.

138. Spiers, 'Scottish Soldier', p. 315.

139. Dallas and Gill, *Unknown Army*, p. 28; Sassoon, *Memoirs of a Fox-Hunting Man*, p. 244.

140. Hodgson, *People's Century*, pp. 29f.

141. Coppard, *With a Machine Gun*, p. 1.

142. Hašek, *Good Soldier Švejk*, pp. 9–13.

143. Figes, *People's Tragedy*, p. 258.

144. Pipes, *Russian Revolution*, p. 204.

145. Hitler, *Mein Kampf*, pp. 145f. Everyone thought Francis Ferdinand had it coming; even his own uncle commented: 'God permits no challenge. A higher power has re-established the order which I had no longer been able to maintain'—an allusion to Francis Ferdinand's marriage to Sophie Chotek, which the Emperor had vainly tried to prohibit.

146. T. E. Lawrence, *Seven Pillars*, p. 97.

147. Reader, *At Duty's Call*, pp. 111–18.

148. Coppard, *With a Machine Gun*, p. 1; Offer, 'Going to War', p. 232.

149. Esposito, 'Public Opinion', p. 54.

150. Reader, *At Duty's Call*, p. 115; Offer, 'Going to War', p. 232. See also Hynes, *War Imagined*, p. 92.

151. Reader, *At Duty's Call*, p. 115.

152. Hynes, *War Imagined*, pp. 88f.

153. S. Gilbert, 'Soldier's Heart', p. 209. Owen's poem 'Dulce et Decorum Est' was originally entitled 'To Jessie Pope'.

154. J. Winter, *Great War*, p. 32; Beckett, 'Nation in Arms', p. 7; Reader, *At Duty's Call*, pp. 109f., 132f.

155. Reader, *At Duty's Call*, p. 110.

156. Offer, 'Going to War', p. 233.

157. Hughes, 'New Armies', p. 103ff. Spiers, 'Scottish Soldier', describes how Englishmen began to be sent to the Highland regiments, which tended to suffer exceptionally high casualties.

158. Reader, *At Duty's Call*, p. 114.

159. J. Harris, *William Beveridge*, p. 201.

160. Fuller, *Troop Morale*, p. 36.

161. Dewey, 'Military Recruitment', pp. 206f., 211, 218. Dewey's rather mechanistic analysis finds that age was more important, but that the key factor for the war as a whole was the working of the exemption system—hardly surprising.

162. Beckett, 'Nation in Arms', p. 10.

163. Reader, *At Duty's Call*, p. 119.

164. Hughes, 'New Armies', p. 102; Reader, *At Duty's Call*, p. 121.

165. Esposito, 'Public Opinion', p. 54.

166. Reader, *At Duty's Call*, pp. 120f.

167. Spiers, 'Scottish Soldier', p. 315.

168. Offer, 'Going to War', p. 232.

169. Monk, *Wittgenstein*, p. 112.

170. Ibid., p. 114.

171. Eksteins, *Rites of Spring*, p. 61.

172. Schramm, *Neun Generationen*, vol. II, p. 486.

173. Mayeur, 'Le Catholicisme français', pp. 379ff.

174. See also Greschat, 'Krieg und Kriegsbereitschaft', pp. 33–55.

175. Kraus, *Die letzten Tage*, pp. 355ff.

176. Mayeur, 'Le Catholicisme français', p. 383.

177. Mews, 'Spiritual Mobilisation', p. 258. See also the not wholly convincing apologetic by Diane Y. Thompson, pp. 264f.

178. Mews, 'Spiritual Mobilisation', p. 259.

179. Ibid., p. 260.

180. Bogacz, 'Tyranny of Words', pp. 650n.; see also p. 659.

181. See in general Hoover, *God, Germany*.

182. Nägler, 'Pandora's Box', pp. 11f.

183. Pottle, *Champion Redoubtable*, pp. 25f.

184. Robert, 'Les Protestants français', p. 421.

185. Schramm, *Neun Generationen*, vol. II, pp. 486ff. Cf. Vondung, 'Deutsche Apokalypse'; Greschat, 'Krieg und Kriegsbereitschaft', pp. 33–55.

186. Coker, *War and the Twentieth Century*, p. 101.

187. Marwick, *Deluge*, p. 88.

188. A. Gregory, 'British Public Opinion', pp. 9, 11.

189. Ibid., p. 12.

190. S. Gilbert, 'Soldier's Heart', p. 204.

191. Revelation, 16: 18–21.

8. The Press Gang

1. *Coker, War and the Twentieth Century*, p. 1.

2. Bruntz, *Allied Propaganda*, p. 3.

3. Marquis, 'Words as Weapons', p. 493.

4. Northcliffe owned *inter alia* the London *Evening News* (since 1894), the *Daily Mail* (founded in 1896) and *The Times* (acquired in 1908). In addition his brother Harold, later Lord Rothermere, owned the *Daily Mirror* (acquired from his brother in 1914), the *Sunday Pictorial*, the *Leeds Mercury* and two Glasgow papers, the *Daily Record* and the *Evening News*. Details of the Harmsworth empire, which controlled around forty titles ranging from mass circulation newspapers to children's comics, in Gebele, *Die Probleme*, pp. 420ff. See in general S. Taylor, *Great Outsiders*.

5. Hansen, *Unrepentant Northcliffe*, p. 12. See also Grünbeck, *Die Presse Grossbritanniens*.

6. Gebele, *Die Probleme*, p. 27.

7. Hitler, *Mein Kampf*, p. 161.

8. Marquis, 'Words as Weapons', pp. 493f.

9. See Dresler, *Geschichte*.

10. Sösemann, *Theodor Wolff: Tagebücher*, vol. I, p. 41.

11. Knightley, *First Casualty*, p. 109.

12. Gebele, *Die Probleme*, p. 45.

13. A. J. P. Taylor, *Beaverbrook*, p. 144.

14. Marquis, 'Words as Weapons', p. 493.

15. Gebele, *Die Probleme*, p. 45.
16. Marquis, 'Words as Weapons'; A. Jackson, 'Germany, the Home Front', p. 568; Gebele, *Die Probleme*, p. 43.
17. Marquis, 'Words as Weapons', p. 479; Gebele, *Die Probleme*, p. 43.
18. Marquis, 'Words as Weapons', p. 488.
19. Becker, *Great War*, p. 59.
20. Sösemann, 'Medien', pp. 196f.
21. Ibid., pp. 203, 205, 209, 212.
22. Ibid., pp. 204, 216.
23. Ibid., pp. 223, 229.
24. Ibid., pp. 198, 211.
25. Ibid., pp. 213f.
26. Ibid., p. 210; Ferro, *Great War*, p. 41.
27. T. Wolff, *Vorspiel*, p. 276.
28. Mommsen, 'Domestic Factors in German Foreign Policy', p. 34.
29. Brock, 'Britain Enters the War', p. 146; Barnett, *Collapse of British Power*, p. 55.
30. Shannon, *Crisis of Imperialism*, p. 458.
31. A. Gregory, 'British Public Opinion', p. 15.
32. Carsten, *War against War*, p. 24; Koss, *Gardiner*, pp. 148ff.; Marquis, 'Words as Weapons', p. 468.
33. Lloyd George, *War Memoirs*, vol. I, p. 41.
34. Marwick, *Deluge*, p. 72.
35. Marquis, 'Words as Weapons', p. 469.
36. Esposito, 'Public Opinion', p. 17.
37. Ibid., p. 33.
38. Ibid., p. 40.
39. Pogge von Strandmann, 'Historians', p. 7.
40. Morris, *Scaremongers*, p. 359.
41. T. Clarke, *My Northcliffe Diary*, p. 63.
42. Ibid., pp. 58f.
43. Bogacz, 'Tyranny of Words', p. 643.
44. T. Clarke, *My Northcliffe Diary*, pp. 65–7.
45. Bogacz, 'Tyranny of Words', p. 651 and n.
46. Esposito, 'Public Opinion', p. 27.
47. A. Gregory, 'British Public Opinion', p. 8.
48. Ibid., p. 10.
49. Gebele, *Die Probleme*, p. 20.
50. Ibid., p. 24.
51. Ibid., p. 23.
52. See, e.g., Saad El-Din, *Modern Egyptian Press*, p. 13.
53. Marquis, 'Words as Weapons', p. 478.
54. Livois, *Histoire de la presse*, pp. 399–402.
55. Bellanger *et al.*, *Histoire générale*, pp. 32, 409.
56. Becker, *Great War*, pp. 47, 53.
57. Marquis, 'Words as Weapons', pp. 471, 481.
58. H.-D. Fischer, *Pressekonzentration*, pp. 226f.; Koszyk, *Deutsche Presse*, pp. 14ff. See in general Koszyk, *Deutsche Pressepolitik*.
59. Morgenbrod, *Wiener Grossbürgertum*, p. 92.
60. Dresler, *Geschichte*, p. 53.
61. Becker, *Great War*, p. 50.
62. Manevy, *La Presse*, p. 150; Livois, *Histoire de la presse*, p. 402; Bellanger *et al.*, *Histoire générale*, p. 417.
63. Manevy, *La Presse*, p. 149n.
64. PRO KV 1/46, MI5 G-Branch Report, Annexe, ff. 75–6. See also Gebele, *Die Probleme*, p. 435.
65. Hynes, *War Imagined*, pp. 80f., 232f.
66. Gebele, *Die Probleme*, p. 20n.
67. Ibid., p. 21.
68. Bellanger *et al.*, *Histoire générale*, p. 32.
69. Ibid., p. 440.
70. Koszyk, *Zwischen Kaiserreich und Diktatur*, pp. 40–111.
71. Welch, 'Cinema and Society', p. 33.

72. Marquis, 'Words as Weapons', pp. 471, 481–5.

73. T. Wolff, *Der Marsch*, p. 274.

74. Livois, *Histoire de la presse*, p. 402.

75. Ibid., pp. 407f.; Bellanger *et al.*, *Histoire générale*, p. 439.

76. Koszyk, *Deutsche Presse*, pp. 19, 21.

77. Nägler, 'Pandora's Box', p. 4.

78. Ibid., p. 27.

79. Marquis, 'Words as Weapons', p. 473.

80. Gebele, *Die Probleme*, pp. 23f.

81. Ibid., pp. 36ff.

82. Ibid., p. 20.

83. Bruntz, *Allied Propaganda*, p. 23.

84. Gebele, *Die Probleme*, pp. 37f. Details in A. J. P. Taylor, *Beaverbrook*, pp. 137ff.

85. A. J. P. Taylor, *Beaverbrook*, pp. 146–53. Taylor's verdict on his hero's achievements as Minister for Information is conspicuously tepid, p. 156.

86. Gebele, *Die Probleme*, pp. 33f.

87. Bruntz, *Allied Propaganda*, pp. 8f., 13ff.; Albert, *Histoire de la presse*, p. 77; Bellanger *et al.*, *Histoire générale*, pp. 420–27.

88. Koszyk, *Deutsche Presse*, p. 20.

89. Ibid., p. 18. Cf. Marquis, 'Words as Weapons', p. 475; Prakke, Lerg and Schmolke, *Handbuch*, p. 105.

90. Morgenbrod, *Wiener Grossbürgertum*, p. 92.

91. Bruntz, *Allied Propaganda*, pp. 31ff.

92. Hiley, 'British Army Film', pp. 172ff.

93. Feldman, *Great Disorder*, p. 48.

94. Nägler, 'Pandora's Box', p. 15.

95. Bruntz, *Allied Propaganda*, p. 75.

96. Gebele, *Die Probleme*, pp. 39n., 40n., for details of the similar but unsung efforts of MI7(b). See in general Bruntz, *Allied Propaganda*, pp. 52, 85–129, 188–216; Fyfe, *Northcliffe*, pp. 236–53.

97. Manevy, *La Presse*, pp. 53f.; Bellanger *et al.*, *Histoire générale*, pp. 432f., 439ff.

98. On the British case see the biographical studies in Messinger, *British Propaganda*.

99. Hiley, 'British Army Film', pp. 169ff.

100. Ibid., pp. 166ff.

101. Reeves, 'Film Propaganda', pp. 466ff. Other documentaries in the same vein included *The King Visits His Armies in the Great Advance* and *The Battle of the Ancre and the Advance of the Tanks*.

102. Welch, 'Cinema and Society', p. 33.

103. Ibid., pp. 38f., 41ff.

104. Nägler, 'Pandora's Box', p. 15.

105. D. Wright, 'Great War', p. 78; Gebele, *Die Probleme*, p. 35. The last-named was set up by G. W. Prothero, editor of the *Quarterly Review*, and Harry Crust, editor of the *Pall Mall Gazette*, with party leaders as figureheads.

106. Nägler, 'Pandora's Box', pp. 17ff.

107. Hynes, *War Imagined*, p. 70.

108. D. Wright, 'Great War', p. 70.

109. Ibid., p. 72; Hynes, *War Imagined*, pp. 26f.

110. Pogge von Strandmann, 'Historians', p. 16.

111. Ibid., p. 26.

112. D. Wright, 'Great War', pp. 82f.

113. Ibid., p. 86.

114. Colin and Becker, 'Les Écrivains', pp. 425–42.

115. Bogacz, 'Tyranny of Words', p. 647 and n.

116. Hynes, *War Imagined*, pp. 217ff.

117. See Audoin-Rouzeau, *La Guerre des enfants*.

118. Mosse, *Fallen Soldiers*, pp. 128, 140f.

119. Koszyk, *Deutsche Presse*, p. 16.

120. Hynes, *War Imagined*, p. 221.

121. W. S. Churchill, *World Crisis*, vol. III, p. 246; Woodward, *Great Britain*, p. 48.

122. Details in W. S. Churchill, *World Crisis*, vol. III, pp. 244–51; Woodward, *Great Britain*, pp. 80f.; T. Clarke, *My Northcliffe Diary*, pp. 74–106; A. J. P. Taylor, *Beaverbrook*, pp. 101–27. In fact, it was the resig-

nation of Fisher which did the real damage. Apart from Repington's devastating despatch in *The Times*, blaming military reverses on lack of shells, and the leader which accompanied it, most of the press campaign came after 20 May, by which time the coalition had not only been agreed but announced in Parliament.

123. T. Clarke, *My Northcliffe Diary*, p. 107.
124. Fyfe, *Northcliffe*, pp. 221–35.
125. Squires, *British Propaganda*, p. 63n.
126. Gebele, *Die Probleme*, p. 67.
127. Ibid., pp. 61f.
128. Fussell, *Great War*, pp. 21f.
129. D. Wright, 'Great War', p. 75.
130. Bogacz, 'Tyranny of Words', p. 662.
131. Ibid., p. 663.
132. Hynes, *War Imagined*, pp. 69, 111. Cf. Marwick, *Deluge*, p. 85.
133. Bogacz, 'Tyranny of Words', pp. 664f.
134. D. Wright, 'Great War', p. 72.
135. Marwick, *Deluge*, pp. 85f.
136. Bentley, *Liberal Mind*, pp. 19f.
137. D. Wright, 'Great War', p. 75.
138. Marwick, *Deluge*, p. 73.
139. Ibid., pp. 70, 73.
140. Marquis, 'Words as Weapons', p. 487. Ponsonby's example was in fact a German fabrication.
141. T. Wilson, 'Lord Bryce's Investigation', p. 374. Bryce made no serious attempt to verify the statements from 'witnesses' which his committee received; indeed, he managed to outdo the Belgians' own official reports into the atrocities (which tended to concentrate on requisitioned goods).
142. Gullace, 'Sexual Violence', pp. 714ff., 725ff., 734–9, 744ff.
143. D. Wright, 'Great War', p. 72.
144. Ibid., p. 92.
145. Barnett, *Collapse of British Power*, p. 57; Marwick, *Deluge*, p. 88.
146. Esposito, 'Public Opinion', p. 46.
147. Barnett, *Collapse of British Power*, p. 57.
148. Hynes, *War Imagined*, p. 71.
149. Ibid., p. 73.
150. Esposito, 'Public Opinion', p. 35.
151. Mann, *Betrachtungen eines Unpolitischen, passim.*
152. Bogacz, 'Tyranny of Words', p. 655 and n.
153. Hynes, *War Imagined*, pp. 12, 62f.
154. Mosse, *Fallen Soldiers*, pp. 132–6.
155. Hynes, *War Imagined*, p. 118; Fussell, *Great War*, p. 26; Mosse, *Fallen Soldiers*, pp. 61, 142.
156. Hynes, *War Imagined*, p. 117; Fussell, *Great War*, pp. 87f.
157. Becker, *Great War*, pp. 31, 37f., 164. Quotations from the *Petit Parisien* and the *Petit Journal*.
158. Marwick, *Deluge*, p. 89.
159. Pogge von Strandmann, 'Historians', esp. pp. 31ff, 38f.
160. D. Wright, 'Great War', pp. 77, 83.
161. Hiley, 'British Army Film', p. 177.
162. Gebele, *Die Probleme*, p. 34.
163. Hiley, 'Kitchener Wants You'.
164. Hiley, 'British Army Film', p. 173.
165. D. Wright, 'Great War', p. 89.
166. Reeves, 'Film Propaganda', pp. 468ff. As receipts declined in 1917–18, films were also shown in areas without cinemas using 'cinemotors', which brought weekly audiences for war documentaries up to 163,000.
167. Ibid., p. 485.
168. Ibid., p. 479.
169. Ibid., p. 486.
170. Welch, 'Cinema and Society', pp. 41–5.
171. Mosse, *Fallen Soldiers*, p. 147–9.
172. Gombrich, *Aby Warburg*, p. 206.
173. Squires, *British Propaganda*, pp. 64–8.
174. Cassimatis, *American Influence*, pp. 15–28; Leontaritis, *Greece and the First World War*, esp. p. 102.

175. Bruntz, *Allied Propaganda*, p. 147.

176. Fussell, *Great War*, pp. 65ff.

177. J. Winter, *Great War*, pp. 287f.

178. Fussell, *Great War*, p. 87.

179. Becker, *Great War*, pp. 43f.

180. Ashworth, *Trench Warfare*, p. 35.

181. Fuller, *Troop Morale*.

182. Bertrand, *La Presse francophone*, esp. pp. 90f.

183. Bellanger *et al.*, *Histoire générale*, p. 439; Livois, *Histoire de la presse*, pp. 407f. On the other French trench newspapers, see pp. 419–27 (essay by General Weygand).

184. Eksteins, *Rites of Spring*, pp. xv, 196.

185. Welch, 'Cinema and Society', p. 40.

186. Kraus, *Die letzten Tage*, pp. 404ff.

187. Reeves, 'Film Propaganda', pp. 481, 486.

188. Timms, *Karl Kraus*, p. 276.

189. Kraus, *Die letzten Tage*, pp. 50, 74ff., 148f., 154–9, 188f., 241–4, 256–61, 292, 304–7, 458f., 491.

190. Kraus, *In These Great Times*, p. 75.

191. Sösemann, *Theodor Wolff: Tagebücher*, vol. I, p. 39.

192. Heenemann, 'Die Auflagenböhe', pp. 70–86.

193. Cattani, *Albert Meyer*, p. 48; Berger, *Story of the New York Times*.

194. Welch, 'Cinema and Society', p. 43.

195. See e.g. Becker, *Great War*, p. 71.

196. Gebele, *Die Probleme*, p. 27; T. Clarke, *My Northcliffe Diary*, p. 67.

197. Bellanger *et al.*, *Histoire générale*, pp. 408, 411.

198. Marquis, 'Words as Weapons', p. 484. See also Stummvoll, *Tagespresse und Technik*, pp. 48ff.

199. Bellanger *et al.*, *Histoire générale*, p. 450; Innis, *Press*, p. 8.

200. Koszyk, *Zwischen Kaissereich und Diktatur*, p. 33.

201. T. Clarke, *My Northcliffe Diary*, p. 112; Koss, *Gardiner*, p. 153.

202. Bellanger *et al.*, *Histoire générale*, p. 412.

203. Koszyk, *Deutsche Presse*, p. 23.

204. Huber, *Geschichte*, pp. 36, 46f.

205. Bellanger *et al.*, *Histoire générale*, p. 43.

206. Manevy, *La Presse*, p. 148; Bellanger *et al.*, *Histoire générale*, p. 408.

207. Koszyk, *Deutsche Pressepolitik*, p. 250.

208. Ibid.

209. Koszyk, *Deutsche Presse*, p. 24; Prakke, Lerg and Schmolke, *Handbuch*, p. 107. See esp. H.-D. Fischer, *Handbuch*, p. 229.

210. J. Horne and Kramer, 'German "Atrocities"', pp. 1–33; J. Horne and Kramer, 'War between Soldiers and Enemy Civilians'. Collective reprisals were, however, prohibited.

211. R. Harris, 'Child of the Barbarian', pp. 170–206.

212. Gullace, 'Sexual Violence', pp. 731ff.

213. J. Horne and Kramer, 'German "Atrocities"', pp. 15–23.

214. J. Horne and Kramer, 'War between Soldiers and Enemy Civilians', pp. 8ff.

9. Economic Capability

1. Kennedy, *Rise and Fall of the Great Powers*, pp. 314, 333ff. Cf. Bairoch, 'Europe's Gross National Product', pp. 281, 303.

2. J. M. Hobson, 'Military-Extraction Gap', pp. 464f.

3. Witt, 'Finanzpolitik und sozialer Wandel im Krieg', p. 425.

4. Wagenführ, 'Die Industriewirtschaft', p. 23.

5. Mitchell, *European Historical Statistics*, pp. 186ff., 199ff., 225ff., 290f.; Hardach, *First World War*, p. 91.

6. Godfrey, *Capitalism at War*, p. 47; Kemp, *French Economy*, p. 31n.

7. Burchardt, 'Impact of the War Economy', p. 45.

8. Kennedy, *Rise and Fall of the Great Powers*, p. 350.

9. Glaser, 'American War Effort', p. 22.

10. Wagenführ, 'Die Industriewirtschaft', p. 23; Hardach, *First World War*, p. 45.

11. Calculated from Hoffman, Grumbach and Hesse, *Wachstum*, pp. 358f., 383ff., 390–93; Wagenführ, 'Die Industriewirtschaft', pp. 23ff.; Feldman, *Iron and Steel*, pp. 474f.; Mitchell, *European Historical Statistics*, pp. 141ff. The increase in wine production (something also achieved in Hungary and Bulgaria) represented import substitution. Italian and French production declined slightly.

12. Burchard, 'Impact of the War Economy', pp. 42, 47. Cf. Bertold, 'Die Entwicklung'.

13. J. Lee, 'Administrators and Agriculture', pp. 232ff.

14. Mitchell, *European Historical Statistics*, pp. 285f.

15. J. Lee, 'Administrators and Agriculture', p. 235.

16. *Hansard*, 1 August 1914.

17. Offer, *First World War*, pp. 300–309; Hardach, *First World War*, pp. 11–19. Cf. Vincent, *Politics of Hunger*.

18. Tirpitz, *Deutsche Ohnmachtspolitik*, p. 68.

19. Hardach, *First World War*, p. 19.

20. M. Farrar, 'Preclusive Purchases', pp. 117–33.

21. Hardach, *First World War*, p. 30.

22. Burk, *Britain, America and the Sinews of War*, pp. 41, 80.

23. Hardach, *First World War*, p. 124.

24. Liddell Hart, *British Way*, p. 29. Cf. Ferguson, 'Food and the First World War', pp. 188–95.

25. Hardach, *First World War*, p. 33.

26. See the various estimates in Keynes, *Economic Consequences*, pp. 161, 165 (pre-war German estimates); *Economist*, 'Reparations Supplement', 31 May 1924, p. 6 (the McKenna Committee's estimate); Hoffmann, Grumbach and Hesse, *Wachstum*, p. 262; Kindleberger, *Financial History*, p. 225.

27. Bundesarchiv [formerly Potsdam], Reichswirtschafts ministerium, 764/268–301, 'Verluste der deutschen Handelsflotte'.

28. Eichengreen, *Golden Fetters*, pp. 82ff. For details on the German balance of payments, see Bresciani-Turroni, *Economics of Inflation*, pp. 83–93; on the British, E. Morgan, *Studies in British Financial Policy*, p. 341.

29. Zunkel, *Industrie*; Ehlert, *Die wirtschaftliche Zentralbehörde*; Feldman, 'Der deutsche organisierte Kapitalismus', pp. 150–71.

30. The classic study remains Feldman, *Army, Industry and Labour*. For echoes, see e.g. W. Fischer, 'Die deutsche Wirtschaft'; Bessel, 'Mobilising German Society'.

31. D. French, *British Economic and Strategic Planning*, pp. 6–27; Marwick, *Deluge*, p. 79.

32. Adams, *Arms and the Wizard*; Wrigley, 'Ministry of Munitions', pp. 32–56; Beveridge, *Power and Influence*, p 117. Cf. Dewey, 'New Warfare'; Chickering, 'World War'.

33. Hurwitz, *State Intervention*, p. 62. Cf. McNeill, *Pursuit of Power*, p. 327.

34. Reid, 'Dilution', p. 61.

35. Kemp, *French Economy*, pp. 28–57; Godfrey, *Capitalism at War*, pp. 64, 104f., 289–96.

36. J. Winter, 'Public Health', pp. 170ff.

37. J. Winter, *Great War*, pp. 279ff., 305.

38. J. Winter, *Capital Cities*, pp. 10f. See also Offer, *First World War, passim*.

39. L. Cecil, *Albert Ballin*, pp. 212f.

40. Warburg, *Aus meinen Aufzeichnungen*, pp. 34f.

41. Ferguson, *Paper and Iron*, p. 146.

42. Pogge von Strandmann, *Walther Rathenau*, p. 189.

43. Ibid., p. 200.

44. Feldman, 'War Aims', pp. 22f.

45. Ibid., p. 145.

46. Feldman, *Iron and Steel*, p. 80.

47. Moeller, 'Dimensions of Social Conflict', pp. 142–68.

48. Ferguson, *Paper and Iron*, p. 105.

49. Crow, *Man of Push and Go*, pp. 69–85.

50. Dewey, 'New Warfare', pp. 78f.

51. D. French, *British Economic and Strategic Planning*, pp. 11–25; Adams, *Arms and the Wizard*, pp. 14–69, 83, 90, 164–79; T. Wilson, *Myriad Faces*, pp. 217–36; Wrigley, 'Ministry of Munitions', pp. 34–8, 43–9; Wrigley, *David Lloyd George*, pp. 83–4; Crow, *Man of Push and Go*, pp. 86–92; Beveridge, *Power and Influence*, pp. 124ff. Cf. Marwick, *Deluge*, p. 99. On Russia, Stone, *Eastern Front*, pp. 196f. On France, Godfrey, *Capitalism at War*, pp. 45–8, 107, 184–210, 259f.

52. T. Wilson, *Myriad Faces*, p. 237; Wrigley, *David Lloyd George*, pp. 85–9.

53. Godfrey, *Capitalism at War*, pp. 186, 261–84.

54. McNeill, *Pursuit of Power*, p. 340.

55. Warburg, *Aus meinen Aufzeichnungen*, pp. 92, 100.
56. Hardach, *First World War*, pp. 58–61; Feldman, *Iron and Steel*, pp. 67f.; Feldman, *Great Disorder*, pp. 52ff.
57. J. Harris, *William Beveridge*, p. 235.
58. Kemp, *French Economy*, p. 45; Godfrey, *Capitalism at War*, pp. 49f.; McNeill, *Pursuit of Power*, p. 320.
59. Godrey, *Capitalism at War*, pp. 197f.
60. Ibid., pp. 107–22.
61. Boswell and John, 'Patriots or Profiteers', pp. 427–34; Alford, 'Lost Opportunities', pp. 222f. Cf. Wrigley, 'Ministry of Munitions', pp. 42f.
62. Boswell and John, 'Patriots or Profiteers', pp. 435f.; Hurwitz, *State Intervention*, pp. 174–9. Cf. G. Holmes, 'First World War', pp. 212–14.
63. Hurwitz, *State Intervention*, p. 179.
64. See Rubin, *War, Law and Labour*.
65. Glaser, 'American War Effort', p. 16.
66. Stone, *Eastern Front*, pp. 197–209.
67. Ibid., pp. 210f.
68. Hardach, *First World War*, p. 106.
69. Ferguson, *Paper and Iron*, pp. 105ff.
70. Feldman, *Iron and Steel*, pp. 11f.
71. Bresciani-Turroni, *Economics of Inflation*, p. 288.
72. Calculated from: *Vierteljahreshefte zur Statistik des Deutschen Reiches*, Ergänzungsheft II (1914), p. 11; (1915), p. 9; (1916), p. 9; (1917), p. 11; (1918), p. 11; (1920), p. 106.
73. Hardach, *First World War*, p. 106.
74. Boswell and John, 'Patriots or Profiteers', p. 443; Marwick, *Deluge*, p. 164; G. Holmes, 'First World War', p. 211; Alford, 'Lost Opportunities', pp. 210–18.
75. Lyashchenko, *History of the National Economy*, p. 751. See also Stone, *Eastern Front*.
76. Dewey, 'British Farming Profits', p. 378.
77. Kemp, *French Economy*, p. 54.
78. Graham, *Exchange*, p. 307f.; Petzina, Abelshauser and Foust, *Sozialgeschichtliches Arbeitsbuch*, vol. III, p. 82; Fontaine, *French Industry*, p. 455.
79. Stone, *Eastern Front*, pp. 205, 297ff.
80. Hurwitz, *State Intervention*, p. 72; Burk, *Britain, America and the Sinews of War*, pp. 24–38.
81. Godfrey, *Captalism at War*, pp. 69–74.
82. L. Cecil, *Albert Ballin*, p. 216; Warburg, *Aus meinen Aufzeichnungen*, pp. 34–7.
83. Feldman, *Iron and Steel*, pp. 72–7.
84. Burk, *Britain, America and the Sinews of War*, pp. 14–42. See also Burk, 'Mobilization of Anglo-American Finance', pp. 25–42.
85. Hurwitz, *State Intervention*, p. 173; G. Holmes, 'First World War', p. 208ff.; Godfrey, *Capitalism at War*, pp. 72–80, 94–101.
86. Godfrey, *Capitalism at War*, pp. 65–71.
87. Burk, *Britain, America and the Sinews of War*, pp. 45–8; Godfrey, *Capitalism at War*, p. 68; G. Owen, 'Dollar Diplomacy in Default', pp. 260–64; Crow, *Man of Push and Go*, p. 131, 143–7.
88. Bessel, *Germany*, pp. 5, 73, 79.
89. Ferguson, *Paper and Iron*, p. 124.
90. Bessel, 'Mobilising German Society', p. 10.
91. A. Gregory, 'Lost Generations', p. 71.
92. A. Jackson, 'Germany, the Home Front', p. 569; Petzina, Abelshauser and Foust, *Sozialgeschichtliches Arbeitsbuch*, vol. III, p. 27.
93. Henning, *Das industrialisierte Deutschland*, pp. 34f.
94. Dewey, 'Military Recruitment', pp. 204–21; Dewey, 'New Warfare', p. 75; Hurwitz, *State Intervention*, p. 135.
95. J. Horne, *Labour at War*, p. 401; Henning, *Das industrialisierte Deutschland*, p. 34.
96. Dewey, 'Military Recruitment', p. 204; Chickering, 'World War I', p. 13. Cf. Hurwitz, *State Intervention*, p. 169; McNeill, *Pursuit of Power*, p. 326; Marwick, *Deluge*, p. 96.
97. Adams, *Arms and the Wizard*, pp. 77, 93–7; Wrigley, *David Lloyd George*, pp. 13f., 169; J. Harris, *William Beveridge*, p. 210.
98. Wrigley, *David Lloyd George*, pp. 135f.
99. PRO CAB 37/141/38, Cabinet Committee on the co-ordination of military and financial effort, Jan. 1916.

100. Dewey, 'Military Recruitment', p. 215.
101. Wrigley, *David Lloyd George*, pp. 171–89. Cf. Waites, 'Effect', pp. 36f.
102. Wrigley, *David Lloyd George*, p. 226; Marwick, *Deluge*, p. 249; Grieves, 'Lloyd George'.
103. Lowe, 'Ministry of Labour', pp. 108–34.
104. J. Winter, *Great War*, pp. 43f.
105. Wrigley, *David Lloyd George*, p. 228.
106. Leunig, 'Lancashire', pp. 36–43; Zeitlin, 'Labour Strategies', pp. 35–40.
107. Greasley and Oxley, 'Discontinuities', pp. 82–100. I am grateful to Glen O'Hara for this point.
108. A. Gregory, 'Lost Generations', pp. 83f.
109. P. Parker, *Old Lie*, p. 16.
110. Angell, *Great Illusion*, p. 174.
111. J. Horne, *"L'Impôt du sang"*, pp. 201–23. See also Godfrey, *Capitalism at War*, p. 49; Kemp, *French Economy*, pp. 38–43; Becker, *Great War*, pp. 26f., 126, 202.
112. McNeill, *Pursuit of Power*, p. 321n.; Godfrey, *Capitalism at War*, p. 257.
113. Bieber, 'Die Entwicklung', pp. 77–153. The threat of conscription was used by British employers too: Rubin, *War, Law and Labour*, pp. 221, 225.
114. Ullrich, 'Massenbewegung', pp. 407–18.
115. Hardach, *First World War*, pp. 63–9, 179f.
116. Ullrich, 'Der Januarstreik 1918', pp. 45–74.
117. Manning, 'Wages', pp. 225–85.
118. Ferguson, *Paper and Iron*, p. 126. Cf. Kocka, *Facing Total War*, pp. 17–22; Burchardt, 'Impact of the War Economy', pp. 54f.
119. See in general Zimmermann, Günther and Meerwarth, *Die Einwirkung*.
120. Manning, 'Wages', pp. 276f.
121. J. Winter, *Great War*, pp. 232ff.; Manning, 'Wages', pp. 261–76. See also Phillips, 'Social Impact', pp. 118f.
122. In addition to the works already cited, see Harrison, 'War Emergency Workers' Committee'; J. Horne, *Labour at War*.
123. Wrigley, *David Lloyd George*, pp. 119f.; J. Harris, *William Beveridge*, pp. 208f.; Beveridge, *Power and Influence*, p. 132. In more than a quarter of cases when workers appealed to the Glasgow tribunal for certificates which their employers had refused them, the employers were overruled: Rubin, *War, Law and Labour*, p. 203.
124. J. Winter, *Great War*, p. 232.
125. Gerber, 'Corporatism', pp. 93–127.
126. Ibid., pp. 35, 41f., 73–6, 110–15, 187f., 208–11, 235f.; J. Harris, *William Beveridge*, p. 218; Wrigley, *David Lloyd George*, pp. 141f. See also Reid, 'Dilution', pp. 51, 57.
127. Wrigley, *David Lloyd George*, pp. 122–8; Beveridge, *Power and Influence*, p. 29; J. Holmes, 'First World War', p. 213.
128. T. Wilson, *Myriad Faces*, p. 228.
129. Wrigley, *David Lloyd George*, pp. 155–63; J. Harris, *William Beveridge*, pp. 219–26. See also Rubin, *War, Law and Labour*, pp. 47f., 96–101, 106f., 131f.; Reid, 'Dilution', p. 53. In many ways the whole issue of dilution was overdone. Not many women ended up working in the engineering industry; mostly they went into the service sector, taking the places of clerks: J. Winter, *Great War*, p. 46.
130. Wrigley, *David Lloyd George*, p. 147 (Asquith's phrase).
131. Beveridge, *Power and Influence*, p. 129. Cf. Marwick, *Deluge*, p. 246.
132. Lowe, 'Ministry of Labour', p. 116.
133. Bailey, 'Berlin Strike', pp. 158–74.
134. Wrigley, *David Lloyd George*, p. 137.
135. Ferro, *Great War*, pp. 178f.
136. Becker, *Great War*, pp. 203–19.
137. Ibid., pp. 144, 253–9, 298–301, 313f.
138. Burchardt, 'Impact of the War Economy'; Offer, *First World War, passim*. Cf. A. Jackson, 'Germany, the Home Front', pp. 563–76.
139. Witt, 'Finanzpolitik und sozialer Wandel im Krieg', pp. 424f.; Bry, *Wages in Germany*, pp. 233, 422–9, 440–45; Holtfrerich, *German Inflation*, p. 255.
140. Burchardt, 'Impact of the War Economy', pp. 41f.; Moeller, 'Dimensions of Social Conflict', pp. 147f.; A. Jackson, 'Germany, the Home Front', p. 567.
141. Holtfrerich, *German Inflation*, p. 255.

142. Beveridge, *Power and Influence*, pp. 143f.; D. French, *British Economic and Strategic Planning*, pp. 19f.; J. Harris, *William Beveridge*, pp. 234–41; Wrigley, *David Lloyd George*, pp. 180, 218; Dewey, 'British Farming Profits', pp. 373, 381; Marwick, *Deluge*, pp. 231–40.

143. Godfrey, *Capitalism at War*, pp. 61, 66f., 79, 83f., 129ff.

144. Becker, *Great War*, pp. 132–7, 145, 206–18, 233, 303.

145. Offer, *First World War*, p. 33.

146. Blackbourn, *Fontana History*, p. 475. Cf. A. Jackson, 'Germany, the Home Front', p. 575. For Kraus, the figure is 800,000 and the source is a 'Madman': Kraus, *Die letzten Tage*, p. 439. For an entertaining parody of *ersatz* product names, see ibid., pp. 398f.

147. Offer, *First World War*, p. 35.

148. Burleigh, *Death and Deliverance*, p. 11.

149. Offer, *First World War*, pp. 32f., 155.

150. J. Winter and Cole, 'Fluctuations', p. 243.

151. Voth, 'Civilian Health', p. 291.

152. The thesis was first advanced in his *Great War*, esp. pp. 105–15, 140, 148, 187f., and defended in 'Public Health', pp. 163–73; for two critiques see Bryder, 'First World War', pp. 141–57; and Voth, 'Civilian Health'. See also Marwick, *Deluge*, pp. 64f.

153. Kocka, *Facing Total War*.

154. Hoffmann, Grumbach and Hesse, *Wachstum*, p. 515. The coefficient is a crude measure of income equality.

155. Feldman, *Army, Industry and Labour*, pp. 97–117, 471f.; Hardach, *First World War*, pp. 115, 129.

156. See Kraus, *Die letzten Tage*, pp. 334f., for a wonderful scene in which a shopkeeper objects to being prosecuted for breaching price regulations on the grounds that he has subscribed to war loans and paid his taxes.

157. Ferguson, *Paper and Iron*, p. 132.

158. Moeller, 'Dimensions of Social Conflict', pp. 157f.

159. Offer, *First World War*, pp. 56f.

160. Ferguson, *Paper and Iron*, pp. 134f.

161. Petzina, Abelshauser and Faust, *Sozialgeschichtliches Arbeitsbuch*, vol. III, p. 124.

162. Lyth, *Inflation*, p. 158.

163. J. Winter, *Great War*, pp. 229, 242ff.; Marwick, *Deluge*, pp. 167, 243f.; Harrison, 'War Emergency Workers' Committee', p. 233.

164. For similar laments in Britain, see Waites, 'Effect', p. 51.

165. See Kocka, 'First World War'. Cf. Günther, *Die Folgen*.

166. Schramm, *Neun Generationen*, vol. II, p. 495.

167. Ibid., p. 501.

168. Becker, *Great War*, p. 226–31.

10. Strategy, Tactics and the Net Body Count

1. Herwig, 'How "Total" was Germany's U-Boat Campaign', *passim*.

2. Herwig, 'Dynamics of Necessity', p. 104.

3. Kennedy, 'Britain in the First World War', pp. 48, 54, 57f., 60f.; Herwig, 'Dynamics of Necessity', pp. 90f., 98.

4. Ferguson, *Paper and Iron*, p. 138.

5. Haupts, *Deutsche Friedenspolitik*, p. 119.

6. Ferguson, *Paper and Iron*, p. 139.

7. Offer, *First World War*, pp. 15–18. Cf. Simon, 'Alternative Visions of Rationality', pp. 189–204.

8. Herwig, 'Dynamics of Necessity', p. 89.

9. Ibid., pp. 93f.

10. See most recently, Herwig, *First World War, passim*.

11. Herwig, 'Dynamics of Necessity', p. 95. Altogether 65 French divisions fought at Verdun, compared with 47 German divisions, so that French casualties were more widely spread. The average German division was 'bled' whiter. See also Millett *et al.*, 'Effectiveness', p. 12.

12. Deist, 'Military Collapse', pp. 186–207.

13. Ibid., p. 197.

14. Ibid., p. 190.

15. Johnson, *1918*, pp. 141, 145.

16. Maier, 'Wargames', pp. 266f.

17. Ferguson, *Paper and Iron*, p. 138.

18. Herwig, 'Admirals *versus* Generals', pp. 212–5, 219, 224, 228. One of Holtzendorff's more picturesque suggestions was that Belgium be partitioned between the Hohenzollerns and the Bourbons, whom he envisaged restoring to the French throne.

19. In addition to Fischer, *Germany's War Aims*, see Gatzke, *Germany's Drive to the West*, and the definitive Soutou, *L'Or et le sang*.

20. L. Cecil, *Albert Ballin*, pp. 261–6, 269f.; Schramm, *Neun Generationen*, vol. II, p. 491.

21. Herwig, 'Admirals *versus* Generals', p. 219.

22. Warburg, *Aus meinen Aufzeichnungen*, p. 58.

23. Feldman, 'War Aims', pp. 5–12, 18.

24. Herwig, 'Admirals *versus* Generals', p. 231.

25. Kersten, 'Kriegsziele', *passim*.

26. Herwig, 'Admirals *versus* Generals', pp. 215ff.

27. Kitchen, *Silent Dictatorship, passim*.

28. Wehler, *German Empire*, pp. 215ff.; Stegmann, *Erben Bismarcks*, pp. 497–519.

29. Deist, 'Military Collapse', p. 194.

30. Trumpener, 'Road to Ypres', pp. 460–80. See also H. Harris, 'To Serve Mankind', pp. 31f.

31. Herwig, 'Dynamics of Necessity', p. 96.

32. Ferro, *Great War*, pp. 93f.; Banks, *Military Atlas*, pp. 281–301. Bombing raids by Zeppelins and bombers killed 1,413 Britons and injured 3,409; German casualties due to aerial bombing were 740 killed and 1,900 wounded.

33. Herwig, 'Dynamics of Necessity', pp. 85, 94.

34. Andrew, *Secret Service*, pp. 139–94.

35. For the view that Britain got her strategy right, see Kennedy, 'Britain in the First World War', pp. 37–49; Kennedy, 'Military Effectiveness', esp. pp. 344f.

36. Liddell Hart, *British Way*, pp. 12f., 29f.

37. Clark, *Donkeys, passim*.

38. See Terraine, *Douglas Haig;* Terraine, *Western Front;* Terraine, *Road to Passchendaele;* Terraine, *To Win a War;* Terraine, *Smoke and the Fire;* Terraine, *First World War.*

39. Barnett, *Swordbearers*.

40. Howard, 'British Grand Strategy', p. 36.

41. D. French, 'Meaning of Attrition', pp. 385–405.

42. Edmonds, *Short History*, p. 94.

43. D. French, 'Meaning of Attrition', p. 403.

44. Terraine, *First World War*, p. 122.

45. T. Wilson, *Myriad Faces*, p. 331.

46. Terraine, *First World War*, p. 172.

47. Guinn, *British Strategy*, p. 230; Woodward, *Great Britain*, pp. 276ff.

48. J. Gooch, *Plans of War*, p. 31.

49. T. Wilson, *Myriad Faces*, p. 441.

50. Ibid., p. 547.

51. Edmonds, *Short History*, p. 335. The words of Lieutenant-General Godley, commander of the 21st Corps.

52. G. Parker, *Times Atlas of World History*, pp. 248f.; Bullock, *Hitler and Stalin*, Appendix II; Davies, *Europe*, p. 1328.

53. Coker, *War and the Twentieth Century*, p. 93.

54. War Office, *Statistics of the Military Effort*, p. 246. Cf. T. Wilson, *Myriad Faces*, p. 559.

55. Howard, *Crisis of the Anglo-German Antagonism*, p. 14.

56. Stone, *Eastern Front*, p. 266.

57. Nägler, 'Pandora's Box', p. 14.

58. Dupuy, *Genius for War*, esp. pp. 328–32.

59. Simpson, 'Officers', pp. 63–98; Strachan, 'Morale', p. 389.

60. D. French, 'Meaning of Attrition', p. 386.

61. Cruttwell, *History of the Great War*, p. 627.

62. T. E. Lawrence, *Seven Pillars*, p. 395.

63. Terraine, *Smoke and the Fire*, p. 171.

64. Laffin, *British Butchers, passim.*
65. Bidwell and Graham, *Fire-Power*, pp. 2f.
66. See esp. Travers, *Killing Ground*, esp. pp. 66, 250.
67. Terraine, *White Heat*, p. 93.
68. Fuller, *Conduct of War*, p. 161.
69. Terraine, *Smoke and the Fire*, p. 179.
70. Edmonds, *Official History: Military Operations*, vol. I, p. 355; Terraine, *Smoke and the Fire*, p. 118.
71. Terraine, *White Heat*, p. 148.
72. Holmes, 'Last Hurrah', p. 284.
73. Maier, 'Wargames', p. 267.
74. R. Williams, 'Lord Kitchener', p. 118.
75. Ibid., p. 122. Cf. Terraine, *Douglas Haig*, p. 154; Philpott, *Anglo-French Relations, passim.*
76. Edmonds, *Short History*, p. 89.
77. Maier, 'Wargames', p. 269.
78. Philpott, *Anglo-French Relations*, pp. 163f.
79. Trask, *AEF and Coalition Warmaking, passim.*
80. Hussey, 'Without an Army', pp. 76, 81.
81. Edmonds, *Official History: Military Operations*, vol. I, p. 7.
82. Terraine, 'British Military Leadership', p. 48.
83. Travers, *Killing Ground*, pp. xx, 23.
84. T. Wilson, *Myriad Faces*, p. 309.
85. Prior and Wilson, *Command on the Western Front*, pp. 150f.
86. Bourne, *Britain and the Great War*, p. 171.
87. Travers, *Killing Ground*, pp. 5f.
88. Ibid., p. 49.
89. Creveld, *Command in War*, pp. 156f.
90. Ibid., p. 186; also p. 262.
91. D. Graham, 'Sans Doctrine', pp. 75f.
92. Bidwell and Graham, *Fire-Power*, p. 3.
93. Ibid., p. 27.
94. Travers, *Killing Ground*, p. 73; see also pp. 62, 75.
95. Travers, *How the War Was Won*, pp. 175–80. Cf. Travers, *Killing Ground*, p. 111.
96. Griffith, *British Fighting Methods*, p. 6.
97. Terraine, 'Substance of the War', p. 8.
98. Edmonds, *Official History: Military Operations*, vol. I, p. 313.
99. Kennedy, 'Britain in the First World War', p. 50.
100. Prior and Wilson, *Command*, pp. 153, 163–6. Sulzbach, *With the German Guns*, shows that only late in the war did Sulzbach begin to feel vulnerable to the other side's counter-battery fire.
101. Cf. Farndale, *History of the Royal Regiment of Artillery*, p. 178.
102. Geyer, 'German Strategy', p. 541.
103. Strachan, 'Morale', p. 383.
104. Herwig, 'Dynamics of Necessity', p. 95.
105. See esp. Griffith, *Forward into Battle*, p. 78.
106. The classic, if romanticized, account is Jünger, *Storm of Steel.*
107. Wynne, *If Germany Attacks*, p. 5.
108. Travers, *How the War Was Won*, p. 176.
109. Dupuy, *Genius for War*, p. 5.
110. Samuels, *Command or Control?*, p. 3.
111. Ibid., p. 5.
112. See in general Samuels, *Doctrine and Dogma*, p. 175.
113. Gudmunsson, *Stormtroop Tactics*, pp. 172ff.
114. Bessel, 'Great War', p. 21.
115. Griffith, 'Tactical Problem', p. 71.
116. Farndale, *History of the Royal Regiment of Artillery*, p. 158.
117. Bailey, 'First World War and the Birth of the Modern Style of Warfare', p. 3.
118. Griffith, *British Fighting Methods*, p. xii. Cf. Griffith, *Battle Tactics.*
119. Prior and Wilson, *Command*, p. 339.

120. Wawro, 'Morale in the Austro-Hungarian Army', p. 409.
121. Rawling, *Surviving Trench Warfare*, p. 221.
122. Trask, *AEF and Coalition Warmaking*, pp. 171–4.
123. Maier, 'Wargames', p. 273.
124. Johnson, *1918*, p. 166.
125. Ibid., p. 167.
126. Ibid., p. 94.
127. Ibid., p. 109.
128. Ibid., p. 112.
129. Strachan, 'Morale', p. 391.
130. Bickersteth, *Bickersteth Diaries*, p. 295.
131. Coker, *War and the Twentieth Century*, p. 120.
132. J. Johnson, *1918*, p. 189.
133. Ibid., pp. 189f.
134. See Förster, 'Dreams and Nightmares'.
135. Kennedy, 'Military Effectiveness', p. 343.
136. Edmonds, *Short History*, p. 281.
137. Herwig, 'Dynamics of Necessity', p. 102.
138. Howard, *Crisis of the Anglo-German Antagonism*, p. 17.
139. Prete, 'French Military War Aims', pp. 888–98.

11. 'Maximum Slaughter at Minimum Expense'

1. Harvey, *Collision of Empires*, p. 279.
2. Crow, *Man of Push and Go*, p. 69.
3. Harvey, *Collision of Empires*, p. 279.
4. Seligmann, 'Germany and the Origins', pp. 321f.
5. D. French, 'Meaning of Attrition', pp. 387f.
6. See e.g. Berghahn, *Modern Germany*, p. 48; Manning, 'Wages and Purchasing Power', pp. 260, 284f. For an overview, Zeidler, 'Deutsche Kriegsfinanzierung', pp. 415–34.
7. See, e.g., Kindleberger, *Financial History*, pp. 291f.; Holtfrerich, *German Inflation*, pp. 118ff.
8. Balderston, 'War Finance', pp. 222–44.
9. Witt, 'Finanzpolitik und sozialer Wandel im Krieg', p. 425. See also Lotz, *Die deutsche Staatsfinanzwirtschaft*, p. 104; Roesler, *Finanzpolitik*, pp. 197ff.; Bresciani-Turroni, *Economics of Inflation*, p. 47; F. Graham, *Exchange*, p. 7.
10. Roesler, *Finanzpolitik*, pp. 196–201; Hardach, *First World War*, pp. 157f.
11. Roesler, *Finanzpolitik*, pp. 206f.; Holtfrerich, *German Inflation*, p. 117.
12. Feldman, *Great Disorder*, pp. 26–51.
13. Roesler, *Finanzpolitik*, pp. 208ff., 216; F. Graham, *Exchange*, p. 216.
14. Feldman, *Army, Industry and Labour*, pp. 97–117, 471f.
15. Roesler, *Finanzpolitik*, pp. 225–7; Bresciani-Turroni, *Economics of Inflation*, p. 442.
16. Holtfrerich, *German Inflation*, pp. 79–94.
17. Gullace, 'Sexual Violence', p. 722.
18. Adams, *Arms and the Wizard*, p. 17n.
19. Skidelsky, *John Maynard Keynes*, vol. II, p. 302.
20. Hardach, *First World War*, p. 153.
21. Bankers Trust Company, *French Public Finance*, p. 11.
22. Calculated from figures in Balderston, 'War Finance', p. 225.
23. Knauss, *Die deutsche, englische und französische Kriegsfinanzierung*. Cf. Eichengreen, *Golden Fetters*, pp. 75ff.
24. Balderston, 'War Finance', pp. 225, 230–37. Cf. Kirkaldy, *British Finance;* Mallet and George, *British Budgets;* Grady, *British War Finance;* Stamp, *Taxation during the War;* E. Morgan, *Studies in British Financial Policy.*
25. Calculated from figures in Roesler, *Finanzpolitik*, pp. 196, 201; E. Morgan, *Studies in British Financial Policy*, p. 41; Balderston, 'War Finance', p. 225. A wealth of detail on British wartime taxation in Mallet and George, *British Budgets*, pp. 94–407.

26. Kemp, *French Economy*, pp. 46f. Cf. Truchy, *Finances de guerre*; Jèze, *Dépenses de guerre*.

27. Godfrey, *Capitalism at War*, pp. 215f.

28. Bankers Trust Company, *French Public Finance*, pp. 120, 187. On Italian war finance see Fausto, 'Politica fiscale', pp. 4–138.

29. Stone, *Eastern Front*, pp. 289f. See also Lyashchenko, *History of the National Economy*, pp. 768f.

30. Hardach, *First World War*, p. 167. Cf. Carr, *Bolshevik Revolution*, vol. III, pp. 144f.

31. Hiley, 'British War Film', p. 175.

32. Nägler, 'Pandora's Box', p. 14.

33. Details in Kirkaldy, *British Finance*, pp. 125–49.

34. Bankers Trust Company, *French Public Finance*, p. 18.

35. Apostol, Bernatzky and Michelson, *Russian Public Finance*, pp. 249, 252, 263.

36. Details in Roesler, *Finanzpolitik*, pp. 206.

37. Becker, *Great War*, pp. 147f. (citing the example of the Le Creuset works).

38. Stone, *Eastern Front*, pp. 290f.

39. Kemp, *French Economy*, p. 47.

40. Calculated from figures in Bankers Trust Company, *French Public Finance*, pp. 138f.; Balderston, 'War Finance', p. 227.

41. E. Morgan, *Studies in British Financial Policy*, p. 140. Cf. Bankers Trust Company, *English Public Finance*, p. 30.

42. Hardach, *First World War*, p. 162; Bankers Trust Company, *French Public Finance*, p. 18; Schremmer, 'Taxation and Public Finance', p. 398.

43. Apostol, Bernatzky and Michelson, *Russian Public Finance*, p. 282.

44. Hardach, *First World War*, pp. 167ff.

45. See e.g. Burk, *Britain, America and the Sinews of War*. See also Burk, 'Mobilization of Anglo-American Finance', pp. 25–42.

46. Moggridge, *Maynard Keynes*, plate 9. Between 1906 and 1915 Keynes kept a tally of his sexual encounters, recording the number of c's, a's and w's he managed each quarter. Characteristically, he also had a points system, in order to calculate a weighted index of his sexual gratification. The year August 1914–August 1915 was markedly worse than any previous year, and 14 per cent down on the previous four quarters.

47. Burk, *Britain, America and the Sinews of War*, p. 80.

48. Skidelsky, *John Maynard Keynes*, vol. II, pp. 314f.

49. Burk, *Britain, America and the Sinews of War*, pp. 83ff.

50. Ibid., p. 88.

51. Skidelsky, *John Maynard Keynes*, vol. II, p. 340. See also Burk, *Britain, America and the Sinews of War*, p. 203.

52. Burk, 'Mobilization of Anglo-American Finance', p. 37.

53. Burk, *Britain, America and the Sinews of War*, p. 64.

54. E. Morgan, *Studies in British Financial Policy*, pp. 317, 320f. Cf. Kirkaldy, *British Finance*, pp. 175–83; Mallet and George, *British Budgets*, table XVIII.

55. Bankers Trust Company, *French Public Finance*; Hardach, *First World War*, p. 148; Eichengreen, *Golden Fetters*, pp. 72f., 84f.

56. Eichengreen, *Golden Fetters*, p. 84.

57. Born, *International Banking*, p. 203.

58. Apostol, Bernatzky and Michelson, *Russian Public Finance*, pp. 320ff.

59. Crow, *Man of Push and Go*, pp. 121f. Details of sales and deposits of securities in Kirkaldy, *British Finance*, pp. 183–97.

60. Crow, *Man of Push and Go*, p. 149.

61. See e.g. Burk, *Britain, America and the Sinews of War*, pp. 198f.

62. Burk, 'Mobilization of Anglo-American Finance', p. 37.

63. Eichengreen, *Golden Fetters*, pp. 68–71; Hardach, *First World War*, p. 140.

64. Hynes, *War Imagined*, p. 289.

65. Details in Kirkaldy, *British Finance*, p. 176; Burk, *Britain, America and the Sinews of War*, pp. 74f.

66. E. Morgan, *Studies in British Financial Policy*, p. 152.

67. Becker, *Great War*, pp. 224ff.

68. Bogart, *Direct and Indirect Costs*. Cf. the discussion in Milward, *Economic Effects*, pp. 12f.

69. Skidelsky, *John Maynard Keynes*, vol. I, p. 348.

70. The figures are as follows (for sources see Figure 12 and Table 36):

	Ratio of British to German soldiers permanently incapacitated in British sector of Western Front	Ratio of British to German total public expenditure in dollars
1915	1.39	1.23
1916	1.44	1.84
1917	1.09	1.48
1918	0.73	1.34

12. The Death Instinct

1. Quoted in Fuller, *Troop Morale*, p. 30.

2. Ibid.

3. Even so convinced a believer in 'machine war' as Pétain reverted to the primacy of morale by December 1917: Strachan, 'Morale', p. 385.

4. Hynes, *War Imagined*, p. 106.

5. Audoin-Rouzeau, 'French Soldier', p. 225.

6. Ashworth, *Trench Warfare*, pp. 57f., 116.

7. Hynes, *Soldier's Tale*, p. 95.

8. D. Winter, *Death's Men*, pp. 92ff.; Fuller, *Troop Morale*, p. 65. Cf. Axelrod, *Evolution*, pp. 82f.

9. Audoin-Rouzeau, 'French Soldier', pp. 222f.

10. Jünger, *Storm of Steel*, pp. 81, 179f.

11. Ibid., pp. 92ff., 106f.

12. Ibid., p. 244.

13. Englander and Osborne, 'Jack, Tommy and Henry Dubb', p. 599; E. Brown, 'Between Cowardice and Insanity', pp. 323–45; Bogacz, 'War Neurosis', pp. 227–56; Talbott, 'Soldiers', pp. 437–54.

14. Leese, 'Problems Returning Home', pp. 1055–67.

15. Eckart, 'Most Extensive Experiment'.

16. Hynes, *War Imagined*, p. 176.

17. T. Wilson, *Myriad Faces*, p. 56; D. Winter, *Death's Men*, p. 42; Hynes, *War Imagined*, p. 204.

18. Jünger, *Storm of Steel*, pp. 6–9, 60.

19. Barnett, 'Military Historian's View'. See also Bourne, 'British Working Man in Arms', pp. 341f.: 'In a sense the soldier of 1918 even dressed like a factory worker . . .'

20. Audouin-Rouzeau, 'French Soldier', p. 224.

21. Jünger, *Storm of Steel*, p. 182.

22. Dallas and Gill, *Unknown Army*, p. 30.

23. Reichswehrministerium, *Sanitätsbericht*, pp. 140–43.

24. Cooke, 'American Soldier', p. 250.

25. Englander and Osborne, 'Jack, Tommy and Henry Dubb', p. 601; Fuller, *Troop Morale*, p. 76; K. Simpson, 'Officers', p. 77.

26. Coppard, *With a Machine Gun*, pp. 17f., 24, 77, 134f.

27. Englander, 'French Soldier', pp. 57f.

28. M. Brown and Seaton, *Christmas Truce*; Ashworth, *Trench Warfare*, p. 32; D. Winter, *Death's Men*, pp. 220f.

29. Jünger, *Storm of Steel*, p. 63; 'When it came to explosives, the retaliation was always at least in the ratio of two to one' (9 April 1916).

30. Ashworth, *Trench Warfare*, esp. pp. 19, 24–48, 99–115.

31. Axelrod, *Evolution*, pp. 73–86.

32. Dawkins, *Selfish Gene*, pp. 225–8.

33. In the simplest version of the Prisoner's Dilemma, two prisoners held separately have to decide whether to co-operate with one another by denying their guilt or to defect by betraying the other in return for immunity from prosecution. If both co-operate, they get the best collective result. But if one defects and the other does not, the defector does even better than he would if he stuck to co-operating. That constitutes the incentive to defect. But if *both* defect, both lose: that is the worst possible result. That is the incentive to co-operate. In the classic version described by Axelrod (*Evolution*), the game became more like a card game,

with a banker paying $300 to both players if they played the co-operate cards; $500 to the defector and –$100 to the 'sucker' if only one defected; and –$10 each if both defect. Axelrod described a series of iterated prisoner's dilemma-style 'tournaments' staged between competing computer programmes. The programme which did best was called TIT FOR TAT (TT). It never defected first, only doing so when it had been betrayed, and then only to the same extent, thereafter reverting to co-operation. In a simple 200-move game (with three points as the pay-off for co-operation), TT scored an average of 504 and topped the poll of the programmes; the top eight were all programmes which did not defect first. TT won five out of six of the tournaments which Axelrod conducted, with its combination of 'being nice, retaliatory, forgiving and clear'. In economics this line of reasoning has spawned the theory of rational choice and the Nash equilibrium (as opposed to the Pareto equilibrium of classical economics with its selfish, profit-maximizing individuals): Coleman, 'Rational Choice Perspective', pp. 166–80.

34. This apparent 'irrationality' is not unique to the First World War. One study conducted among economics students at Cornell University showed that 58 per cent of them would defect in the Prisoners' Dilemma even if they knew *for certain* that their fellow players were going to co-operate: Frank, Gilovich and Regan, 'Does Studying Economics', pp. 159–71.

35. Spiers, 'Scottish Soldier', p. 326.

36. Kershaw, *Hitler*, p. 93.

37. Jünger, *Storm of Steel*, pp. 51–4.

38. Ashworth, *Trench Warfare*, pp. 90, 105; Fuller, *Troop Morale*, p. 64.

39. Coppard, *With a Machine Gun*, pp. 108f.

40. Deist, 'Military Collapse', pp. 195, 201; Strachan, 'Morale', p. 394.

41. Englander and Osborne, 'Jack, Tommy and Henry Dubb', p. 595; Simkins, 'Everyman at War', p. 300.

42. Englander, 'French Soldier', p. 54.

43. Stone, *Eastern Front*, pp. 240f.

44. Englander, 'French Soldier', pp. 53ff. The classic study is Pedroncini, *Les Mutineries.*

45. Westbrook, 'Potential for Military Disintegration', pp. 244f.; Strachan, 'Morale', p. 387.

46. Dallas and Gill, *Unknown Army*, pp. 67–76; Fuller, *Troop Morale*, pp. 1f., 161f.

47. Hughes, 'New Armies', pp. 108f.

48. Englander and Osborne, 'Jack, Tommy and Henry Dubb', p. 604.

49. Fuller, *Troop Morale*, pp. 24, 51f.

50. Ibid., p. 67.

51. Carsten, *War against War*, p. 205.

52. Hynes, *War Imagined*, p. 214; Englander, 'French Soldier', p. 54. Around 10 per cent of all British soldiers shot were convicted of murder.

53. Hynes, *War Imagined*, p. 465; Hynes, *Soldier's Tale*, p. 18.

54. Englander and Osborne, 'Jack, Tommy and Henry Dubb', p. 595.

55. K. Simpson, 'Officers', p. 87.

56. D. Winter, *Death's Men*, p. 44.

57. T. Wilson, *Myriad Faces*, p. 60.

58. D. Winter, *Death's Men*, p. 40; Englander and Osborne, 'Jack, Tommy and Henry Dubb', p. 227.

59. Simkins, 'Everyman at War', p. 299.

60. Davies, *Europe*, p. 911.

61. Figes, *People's Tragedy*, pp. 264f.

62. Englander, 'French Soldier', pp. 55, 59, 67.

63. Deist, 'Military Collapse', pp. 192f.

64. K. Simpson, 'Officers', pp. 71, 81; Sheffield, 'Officer-Man Relations', p. 416.

65. Beckett, 'Nation in Arms', p. 21.

66. Strachan, 'Morale', p. 389.

67. Ibid., p. 414.

68. P. Parker, *Old Lie*, p. 172; Fussell, *Great War*, p. 165.

69. Hynes, *War Imagined*, p. 186.

70. T. E. Lawrence, *Seven Pillars*, p. 28.

71. Hynes, *War Imagined*, pp. 225, 366.

72. Coppard, *With a Machine Gun*, p. 69.

73. Spiers, 'Scottish Soldier', p. 320; K. Simpson, 'Officers', p. 85; Sheffield, 'Officer-Man Relations', p. 418.

74. Bourne, 'British Working Man in Arms', p. 345.

75. Fuller, *Troop Morale*, pp. 54f.

76. Ibid., p. 55.

77. Westbrook, 'Potential for Military Disintegration', pp. 244–78.

78. Becker, *Great War*, p. 159; Marwick, *Deluge*, p. 78.

79. Spiers, 'Scottish Soldier', pp. 317f.

80. Coppard, *With a Machine Gun*, pp. 83–7.

81. Numerous photographs and memoirs testify to the German enthusiasm for defecation: see e.g. Remarque, *All Quiet*, pp. 6f. The British regarded this as proof that the Germans were 'a dirty lot of bastards': Coppard, *With a Machine Gun*, pp. 90f.

82. D. Winter, *Death's Men*, p. 56. Cf. Jünger, *Storm of Steel*, pp. 8f., 14; Ashworth, *Trench Warfare*, p. 25; Englander and Osborne, 'Jack, Tommy and Henry Dubb', p. 600; Fuller, *Troop Morale*, pp. 59ff., 81f.

83. Jünger, *Storm of Steel*, p. 239; Strachan, 'Morale', p. 391.

84. Englander, 'French Soldier', p. 56.

85. Finch, 'Diary', 31 July 1917.

86. Fussell, *Great War*, pp. 46f.

87. Spiers, 'Scottish Soldier', p. 321. See also Hughes, 'New Armies', p. 104.

88. Coppard, *With a Machine Gun*, pp. 55, 78; Englander, 'French Soldier', p. 56.

89. Fuller, *Troop Morale*, p. 75.

90. Jünger, *Storm of Steel*, pp. 112f., 140, 227–33.

91. Fuller, *Troop Morale*, pp. 6, 58; Bond, 'British 'Anti-War' Writers', pp. 824f.

92. Finch, 'Diary', 30 June 1916.

93. D. Winter, *Death's Men*, p. 81.

94. Ibid., p. 82.

95. Dallas and Gill, *Unknown Army*, p. 63.

96. Fuller, *Troop Morale*, pp. 47f., 77f.; Bourne, 'British Working Man in Arms', p. 345; Englander and Osborne, 'Jack, Tommy and Henry Dubb', p. 598.

97. Deist, 'Military Collapse', p. 204.

98. Fuller, *Troop Morale*, pp. 64, 144–53.

99. Fussell, *Great War*, pp. 178f. Cf. Coppard, *With a Machine Gun*, p. 62, on the importance of risqué jokes.

100. Fussell, *Great War*, pp. 159, 162ff.

101. Coppard, *With a Machine Gun*, p. 88.

102. Simkins, 'Everyman at War', pp. 301f.; Fuller, *Troop Morale*, pp. 95–8.

103. Fuller, *Troop Morale*, pp. 110–13.

104. Englander and Osborne, 'Jack, Tommy and Henry Dubb', p. 595; Fuller, *Troop Morale*, pp. 85–93; Dallas and Gill, *Unknown Army*, p. 20.

105. Coppard, *With a Machine Gun*, p. 56.

106. Buckley, 'Failure to Resolve', pp. 71ff. Cf. Beckett, 'Nation in Arms', p. 19; Cooke, 'American Soldier', pp. 247f.; D. Winter, *Death's Men*, p. 99; Hynes, *War Imagined*, p. 371.

107. Becker, *Great War*, p. 155; Audouin-Rouzeau, 'French Soldier', p. 226; Englander, 'French Soldier', pp. 63f.

108. Englander, 'French Soldier', p. 57.

109. Fuller, *Troop Morale*, p. 72.

110. Ibid., p. 23.

111. Fussell, *Great War*, p. 170. See also P. Parker, *Old Lie*, p. 197; Hynes, *War Imagined*, pp. 116f., 206; J. Winter, *Great War*, pp. 293ff.

112. Hynes, *War Imagined*, p. 117.

113. Schneider, 'British Red Cross', pp. 296–315.

114. Remarque, *All Quiet*, pp. 114–33; Strachan, 'Morale', pp. 387, 393.

115. D. Winter, *Death's Men*, pp. 55–7. For a few of the many other examples see Spiers, 'Scottish Soldier', p. 318; P. Parker, *Old Lie*, p. 177; J. Winter, *Great War*, p. 299.

116. Fuller, *Troop Morale*, pp. 22f.

117. Coker, *War and the Twentieth Century*, p. 156.

118. Janowitz and Shils, 'Cohesion and Disintegration'. For a critical discussion, see Westbrook, 'Potential for Military Disintegration', pp. 251–60.

119. Fuller, *Troop Morale*, pp. 45, 70. Cf. Dallas and Gill, *Unknown Army*, pp. 39f.; Cooke, 'American Soldier', p. 246.

120. Westbrook, 'Potential for Military Disintegration', pp. 254ff.

121. Audoin-Rouzeau, 'French Soldier', p. 228.

122. Fuller, *Troop Morale*, pp. 35ff.

123. Spiers, 'Scottish Soldier', p. 323.

124. Perry, 'Maintaining Regimental Identity', pp. 5–11. See Kipling, *Irish Guards*.

125. Fuller, *Troop Morale*, pp. 23, 50, 171; Englander and Osborne, 'Jack, Tommy and Henry Dubb', p. 601; Dallas and Gill, *Unknown Army*, p. 31; Simkins, 'Everyman at War', pp. 306ff. Forty-two per cent of Canadian troops and around 18 per cent of Australians were British-born. As L. L. Robson has shown, the biggest social group in the AIF were in fact industrial workers; the 'digger' image was to some extent an invention.

126. Englander, 'French Soldier', p. 55.

127. J. Winter, *Sites of Memory*, pp. 64–9, 91f., 127ff., 206.

128. Fussell, *Great War*, pp. 40f., 116f., 131f., 137f. See also Mosse, *Fallen Soldiers*, pp. 74f.

129. Robbins, *First World War*, pp. 155ff. Cf. Moynihan, *God on Our Side*.

130. Fuller, *Troop Morale*, p. 156.

131. Kellet, *Combat Motivation*, p. 194.

132. Freud, 'Thoughts', pp. 1–25.

133. Freud, 'Civilization', pp. 26–81. See also his 'Why War', pp. 82–97.

134. Hynes, *War Remembered*, pp. 8f.

135. Fussell, *Great War*, pp. 19, 27.

136. Graves, *Goodbye*, p. 151.

137. J. Winter, *Great War*, p. 292.

138. P. Parker, *Old Lie*, p. 199.

139. Audoin-Rouzeau, 'French Soldier', p. 225.

140. Jünger, *Storm of Steel*, p. 18.

141. Ibid., pp. 22f.

142. J. Winter, *Great War*, p. 296; Hynes, *War Imagined*, p. 201.

143. Ellis, *Eye-Deep in Hell*, p. 167.

144. Coker, *War in the Twentieth Century*, p. 67.

145. Ibid., p. 34.

146. Creveld, *Transformation of War*, pp. 218–33.

147. T. Wilson, *Myriad Faces*, p. 10; Hynes, *Soldier's Tale*, p. 39.

148. Fussell, *Great War*, pp. 168f.

149. Ibid., p. 27.

150. Hynes, *Soldier's Tale*, p. 38. See also p. 33 for Major General M. F. Rimington's pre-war comment that 'the hunting breed of man' made a good cavalry officer because 'he goes into danger for the love of it'.

151. D. Winter, *Death's Men*, p. 91.

152. Jünger, *Storm of Steel*, p. 276.

153. Ellis, *Eye-Deep in Hell*, p. 168.

154. Macdonald, *They Called It Passchendaele*, p. xiii.

155. J. Winter, *Great War*, p. 292; Bond, 'British "Anti-War" Writers', p. 826.

156. Coker, *War in the Twentieth Century*, p. 162.

157. Jünger, *Storm of Steel*, pp. xii, 41, 43, 91, 209.

158. S. Gilbert, 'Soldier's Heart', p. 216ff.

159. T. Wilson, *Myriad Faces*, pp. 57–64.

160. D. Winter, *Death's Men*, p. 210.

161. Audoin-Rouzeau, 'French Soldier', p. 227.

162. Jünger, *Storm of Steel*, pp. 48f., 258ff.

163. Hynes, *Soldier's Tale*, p. 40.

164. Gammage, *Broken Years*, p. 90.

165. A. Simpson, *Hot Blood*, p. 168.

166. D. Winter, *Death's Men*, p. 211.

167. Broch, *Sleepwalkers*, pp. 444f.

168. Audoin-Rouzeau, 'French Soldier', p. 222.

169. Fussell, *Great War*, p. 171.

170. Jünger, *Storm of Steel*, pp. 55f., 171f., 207, 244.

171. Ellis, *Eye-Deep in Hell*, p. 100.

172. Hynes, *Soldier's Tale*, pp. 56f.

173. Ibid., p. 294; D. Winter, *Death's Men*, pp. 82f.; Audoin-Rouzeau, 'French Soldier', p. 223.

174. Freud, 'Thoughts', p. 22.

175. Becker, *Great War*, pp. 107–11.

176. Fussell, *Great War*, pp. 71–4.

177. Audoin-Rouzeau, 'French Soldier', p. 222.
178. Ellis, *Eye-Deep in Hell*, pp. 98–101.

13. The Captor's Dilemma

1. Hynes, *Soldier's Tale*, p. 48.
2. Reeves, 'Film Propaganda', p. 469.
3. Welch, 'Cinema and Society', pp. 34, 39.
4. Deist, 'Military Collapse', p. 203.
5. Sheffield, *Redcaps*, p. 56.
6. War Office, *Statistics of the Military Effort*, pp. 358–62.
7. Hussey, 'Kiggell and the Prisoners', p. 46.
8. Scott, 'Captive Labour', pp. 44–52.
9. R. Jackson, *Prisoners*, pp. 77–82.
10. Ibid., pp. 78f.
11. Ibid., p. 48.
12. Dungan, *They Shall Not Grow Old*, p. 137.
13. Noble, 'Raising the White Flag', p. 75.
14. Fussell, *Great War*, p. 177.
15. Keegan, *Face of Battle*, pp. 48ff.
16. Hussey, 'Kiggell and the Prisoners', p. 47; Sheffield, *Redcaps*, p. 56.
17. Hussey, 'Kiggell and the Prisoners', p. 48. These were explicitly incorporated in the British *Manual of Military Law*.
18. J. Horne and Kramer, 'German "Atrocities"', pp. 8, 26.
19. Ibid., pp. 28, 32f.
20. Jünger, *Storm of Steel*, pp. 262f.
21. Kraus, *Die letzten Tage*, pp. 579–82.
22. Gallinger, *Countercharge*.
23. Ibid., p. 40.
24. Ibid., p. 39.
25. Ibid., p. 42.
26. Ibid., p. 40.
27. Ibid., p. 48.
28. Ibid., p. 39.
29. Ibid., p. 38.
30. Ibid., p. 38.
31. Ibid., p. 39.
32. Ibid., pp. 29, 41f., 45f.
33. Ibid., p. 49.
34. Ibid., p. 48.
35. Ibid., p. 48.
36. Ibid., pp. 48f.
37. Ibid., p. 49.
38. Ibid., pp. 26ff.
39. Ibid., p. 49.
40. Ibid., p. 47.
41. Ibid., p. 47.
42. Ibid., p. 48.
43. Monash, *Australian Victories*, pp. 209–13.
44. Gallinger, *Countercharge*, p. 45.
45. Ibid., pp. 46f. Cf. Gibbs, *Realities*, p. 79.
46. Ibid., p. 37.
47. Hussey, 'Kiggell and the Prisoners', p. 47.
48. M. Brown, *Imperial War Museum Book of the Western Front*, p. 176.
49. Ibid., pp. 177f.
50. Maugham, *Writer's Notebook*, p. 86.
51. Graves, *Goodbye*, p. 112.
52. Ibid., p. 153.

53. M. Brown, *Imperial War Museum Book of the Western Front*, p. 31.
54. Sulzbach, *With the German Guns*, p. 187.
55. Finch, 'Diary', 31 July 1917.
56. Keegan, *Face of Battle*, p. 49. Cf. Bean, *Australian Imperial Force*, p. 772.
57. Keegan, *Face of Battle*, pp. 49f. Cf. A. Simpson, *Hot Blood*, p. 169.
58. Kellett, *Combat Motivation*, p. 190.
59. Ibid., p. 104.
60. Dungan, *They Shall Not Grow Old*, p. 137.
61. Remarque, *All Quiet*, p. 83.
62. Jünger, *Storm of Steel*, p. 263.
63. Ibid., pp. 218f.
64. Liddle, *1916 Battle*, p. 42.
65. D. Winter, *Death's Men*, p. 214.
66. Graves, *Goodbye*, p. 153.
67. M. Brown, *Imperial War Museum Book of the Western Front*, pp. 178f.
68. Ibid., p. 178.
69. Dungan, *They Shall Not Grow Old*, p. 136.
70. Coppard, *With a Machine Gun*, p. 71.
71. Ibid., pp. 106f. My emphasis.
72. D. Winter, *Death's Men*, p. 210.
73. Macdonald, *Somme*, p. 290.
74. Keegan and Holmes, *Soldiers*, p. 267.
75. Ashworth, *Trench Warfare*, p. 93.
76. Spiers, 'Scottish Soldier', p. 326.
77. Hussey, 'Kiggell and the Prisoners', p. 47.
78. Griffith, *Battle Tactics*, p. 72.
79. Ibid.
80. M. Brown, *Imperial War Museum Book of the Somme*, p. 220.
81. Griffith, *Battle Tactics*, p. 72.
82. A. Simpson, *Hot Blood*, p. 168.
83. Ibid.
84. Dungan, *They Shall Not Grow Old*, p. 137.
85. Ibid., p. 136.
86. As implied by Macdonald, *Somme*, pp. 228f.
87. Hussey, 'Kiggell and the Prisoners', p. 46.
88. D. Winter, *Death's Men*, p. 215.
89. Remarque, *All Quiet*, pp. 136ff.
90. Maugham, *Writer's Notebook*, p. 87.
91. Deist, 'Military Collapse'.
92. Mackin, *Suddenly*, p. 246.
93. Trask, *AEF and Coalition Warmaking*, p. 177.
94. Mackin, *Suddenly*, pp. 227f.
95. Ibid., pp. 201f.
96. D. Winter, *Death's Men*, p. 212.
97. M. Gilbert, *First World War*, p. 526.
98. Nicholls, *Cheerful Sacrifice*, p. 101.
99. Kraus, *Die letzten Tage*, p. 207.
100. Hynes, *War Imagined*, p. 266.
101. Coker, *War and the Twentieth Century*, p. 11.
102. Misogyny was only one of the *Freikorps'* nasty traits: see Theweleit, *Male Fantasies*.
103. Bessel, *Germany*, pp. 81, 261.
104. Mack Smith, *Italy*, pp. 333–72.
105. Malcolm, *Bosnia*, p. 162.
106. Fromkin, *Peace to End All Peace*, p. 393.
107. Foster, *Modern Ireland*, p. 512, cites a figure of 800 dead on the Free State side and 'far more republicans'. Not many people had been involved in the war against 'the British' either: Irish Republican Army 'active service' members numbered around 5,000 in 1920–21; the total numbers of police, including Royal Irish Constabulary and Black and Tans, was 17,000: ibid., p. 502.
108. Fromkin, *Peace to End All Peace*, pp. 415ff.

109. L. James, *Rise and Fall of the British Empire*, pp. 389, 400.
110. Ibid., p. 417.
111. Rummel, *Lethal Politics*, p. 39.
112. Ibid., p. 41.
113. Figes, *People's Tragedy*, p. 679.
114. Rummel, *Lethal Politics*, p. 47.
115. Figes, *People's Tragedy*, pp. 563f.
116. Volkogonov, *Lenin*, p. 103.
117. Figes, *People's Tragedy*, pp. 599f.
118. Krovosheev, *Soviet Casualties*, pp. 24f.
119. Volkogonov, *Trotsky*, p. 181.
120. Ibid., pp. 175f.
121. Ibid., pp. 178ff.
122. Volkogonov, *Lenin*, pp. 201f.
123. Ibid., pp. 68f.
124. Volkogonov, *Trotsky*, p. 185.
125. Pipes, *Russia*, p. 86. See also pp. 134f.
126. Figes, *People's Tragedy*, plate opposite p. 579.

14. How (not) to Pay for the War

1. Hynes, *War Imagined*, pp. 319f.
2. Ibid., pp. 359f. In reality, it was the rich (those with wealth above £100,000 and incomes above £3,000), not the broader middle class, who suffered a relative decline in their share of national income: Milward, *Economic Effects*, pp. 34, 42; Phillips, 'Social Impact', p. 112.
3. Waites, 'Class and Status', p. 52. See in general Middlemas, *Politics*, pp. 371–6, and the critique in Nottingham, 'Recasting Bourgeois Britain', pp. 227–47.
4. Foster, *Modern Ireland*, pp. 477–554.
5. Dowie, '1919–20', pp. 429–50.
6. With two differences: all men over twenty-one got the vote, but also all men of any age in the armed services, and all women over thirty who, under the old system of property qualification, were already local government electors or the wives of local government electors. The Germans meanwhile went further by giving all adult women the vote in 1919.
7. Bresciani-Turroni, *Economics of Inflation*, pp. 23f., 161–5.
8. T. Weber, 'Stormy Romance', pp. 24f.
9. See in general Bunselmeyer, *Cost of the War*; Kent, *Spoils of War*; Dockrill and Gould, *Peace without Promise;* Trachtenberg, 'Reparation at the Paris Peace Conference', pp. 24–55.
10. Keynes, *Collected Writings*, vol. XVI, pp. 338–43. For the sake of clarity, all figures relating to reparations are quoted in 'goldmarks', i.e. 1913 marks (20.43 goldmarks [equals] £1.00).
11. Ibid., p. 382n. Cf. Moggridge, *Maynard Keynes*, pp. 291ff.
12. Moggridge, *Maynard Keynes*, p. 293.
13. Keynes, *Collected Writings*, vol. XVI, p. 379.
14. Harrod, *Life of John Maynard Keynes*, pp. 231–4, 315, 394; Skidelsky, *John Maynard Keynes*, vol. I, pp. 358–63; Moggridge, *Maynard Keynes*, p. 301.
15. Keynes, 'Dr. Melchior', p. 415.
16. Haupts, *Deutsche Friedenspolitik*, p. 340.
17. Keynes, *Collected Writings*, vol. XVII, p. 119.
18. Text in Luckau, *German Peace Delegation*, pp. 306–406.
19. Ibid., pp. 319, 377–91; Burnett, *Reparation at the Paris Peace Conference*, vol. II, pp. 78–94.
20. Luckau, *German Peace Delegation*, p. 384. Emphasis in original.
21. Ibid., pp. 388f.
22. Ibid., pp. 389f.
23. Haupts, *Deutsche Friedenspolitik*, pp. 15f.
24. Keynes, 'Dr. Melchior', p. 428; Harrod, *Life of John Maynard Keynes*, p. 238; Moggridge, *Maynard Keynes*, pp. 308, 311. Revealingly, he wrote to Duncan Grant on May 14: 'Certainly, if I was in the German place, I'd rather die than sign such a Peace.'
25. Luckau, *German Peace Delegation*, p. 492.

26. Moggridge, *Maynard Keynes*, pp. 308f.

27. Ferguson, *Paper and Iron*, pp. 225ff.

28. Ibid., p. 225.

29. Keynes, *Collected Writings*, vol. XVII, pp. 3–23.

30. Keynes, *Economic Consequences*, p. 3: 'Those connected with the Supreme Economic Council [had] . . . learnt from the lips of the financial representatives of Germany and Austria unanswerable evidence of the terrible exhaustion of their countries'.

31. Ibid., pp. 25, 204.

32. Ibid., p. 51.

33. Ibid., pp. 102–200, 249f.

34. Ibid., pp. 209, 212, 251.

35. Ibid., pp. 270–76. Strikingly, Keynes positively advocated a German eastward orientation, arguing that only 'German enterprise and organisation' could reconstruct Russia: Germany's 'place in Europe' was 'as a creator and organizer of wealth for her Eastern and Southern neighbours'.

36. Maier, *Recasting Bourgeois Europe*, pp. 241f.; Kent, *Spoils of War*, pp. 132–8; Marks, 'Reparations Reconsidered', pp. 356f. The 12 billion goldmarks still outstanding from the 20 billion goldmarks demanded at Versailles was tacitly included in this total, while sums due to Belgium were not, so that the final sum outstanding was between 123 and 126.5 billion goldmarks. Webb suggests that 4 billion goldmarks was the real annual burden because of occupation costs and 'clearing' payments: *Hyperinflation*, pp. 104f.

37. Keynes, *Collected Writings*, vol. XVII, pp. 242–9.

38. Keynes, *Revision of the Treaty*.

39. Keynes, *Collected Writings*, vol. XVII, pp. 398–401; vol. XVIII, pp. 12–31, 32–43.

40. Ibid., vol. XVII, pp. 282f.

41. Ibid., vol. XVII, pp. 207–13, 234, 249–56.

42. Ferguson, *Paper and Iron*, pp. 358ff.

43. Keynes, *Collected Writings*, vol. XVIII, pp. 18–26. My emphasis.

44. The significance of this speech is not appreciated by Keynes's biographers: see Harrod, *Life of John Maynard Keynes*, pp. 316, 325; Skidelsky, *John Maynard Keynes*, vol. II, p. 115.

45. Ferguson, *Paper and Iron*, p. 359.

46. Ibid., pp. 357f.

47. Rupieper, *Cuno Government*, pp. 13f.; Maier, *Recasting Bourgeois Europe*, pp. 300f.

48. Skidelsky, *John Maynard Keynes*, vol. II, pp. 121f. Cf. Bravo, 'In the Name', pp. 147–68.

49. Ferguson, *Paper and Iron*, p. 369; Keynes, *Collected Writings*, vol. XVIII, pp. 119f.

50. Keynes, *Collected Writings*, vol. XVIII, pp. 134–41; Skidelsky, *John Maynard Keynes*, vol. II, pp. 121–5.

51. See Feldman, *Great Disorder*, pp. 695ff., 720–50, 823–35.

52. Keynes, *Tract on Monetary Reform*, p. 51n.

53. Keynes, *Collected Writings*, vol. XI, p. 365.

54. Ibid., vol. XXI, pp. 47f.

55. Ibid., vol. X, pp. 427f.

56. Haller, 'Rolle der Staatsfinanzen', pp. 137f. See also Holtfrerich, *German Inflation*, pp. 137–55; Webb, *Hyperinflation*, pp. 54, 104, 107.

57. F. Graham, *Exchange*, pp. 134, 117–49, 153–73.

58. Eichengreen, *Golden Fetters*, p. 141.

59. F. Graham, *Exchange*, pp. 4, 7–9, 11, 30–35, 248, 321.

60. Ibid., pp. 174–97, 209, 214–38, 248.

61. Holtfrerich, 'Die deutsche Inflation', p. 327.

62. Schuker, 'American "Reparations" to Germany', pp. 335–83.

63. Feldman, *Great Disorder*, pp. 255–72.

64. Seligmann, 'Germany and the Origins', p. 327.

65. Kindleberger, *Financial History*, pp. 292f.

66. Ferguson, *Paper and Iron*, p. 148.

67. Wheeler-Bennett, *Brest-Litovsk*, pp. 345ff., 439ff.

68. Ibid., pp. 325f.

69. Herwig, *First World War*, pp. 382ff.

70. Posen and West Prussia to Poland, along with part of Upper Silesia after a plebiscite; Danzig, which became a 'free city'; Memel, claimed by Lithuania; Hultschin to Czechoslovakia; North Schleswig to Denmark; Alsace-Lorraine to France; and Eupen-Malmédy to Belgium. In addition, the Rhineland was to be occupied

militarily for fifteen years and the Saar entrusted to the League of Nations for the same period, after which a plebiscite was to be held.

71. Warburg, *Aus meinen Aufzeichnungen*, p. 64.

72. Schwabe, *Deutsche Revolution und Wilson-Frieden*, p. 526; Krüger, *Reparationen*, pp. 82, 119; Haupts, *Deutsche Friedenspolitik*, p. 341.

73. Krüger, 'Rolle der Banken', p. 577.

74. Warburg, *Aufzeichnungen*, p. 75; Krüger, 'Rolle der Banken', p. 577; Krüger, *Deutschland und die Reparationen*, p. 119.

75. Haupts, *Deutsche Friedenspolitik*, pp. 337–40; Krüger, *Deutschland und die Reparationen*, pp. 128f.

76. Ferguson, *Paper and Iron*, p. 210.

77. Ibid., p. 225.

78. Ibid., pp. 347ff.

79. Webb, *Hyperinflation*, pp. 33f.

80. Witt, 'Tax Policies'.

81. Specht, *Politische und wirtschaftliche Hintergründe*, p. 75.

82. Ibid., pp. 69–71.

83. Bresciani-Turroni, *Economics of Inflation*, pp. 57ff.

84. Ferguson, *Paper and Iron*, p. 320.

85. Calculated from Webb, *Hyperinflation*, pp. 33, 37, and Witt, 'Finanzpolitik und sozialer Wandel im Krieg', pp. 425f.

86. Keynes, *Collected Writings*, vol. XVIII, p. 10.

87. D'Abernon, *Ambassador of Peace*, vol. I, pp. 193f.

88. Matthews, 'Continuity of Social Democratic Economic Policy', pp. 485–512.

89. Webb, *Hyperinflation*, p. 91.

90. Specht, *Politische und wirtschaftliche Hintegründe*, pp. 30, 43n.

91. Webb, *Hyperinflation*, p. 31.

92. Ferguson, *Paper and Iron*, p. 310.

93. Henning, *Das industrialisierte Deutschland*, p. 45.

94. Witt, 'Finanzpolitik und sozialer Wandel im Krieg', p. 424.

95. Calculated from Wagenführ, 'Die Industriewirtschaft', pp. 23–8; Bresciani-Turroni, *Economics of Inflation*, pp. 193f.; F. Graham, *Exchange*, pp. 287, 292; Hoffmann, Grumbach and Hesse, *Wachstum*, pp. 358f., 383–5, 388, 390–93.

96. Holtfrerich, *German Inflation*, p. 288.

97. Webb, *Hyperinflation*, p. 57.

98. Keynes, *Collected Writings*, vol. XVII, pp. 130f., 176.

99. Bresciani-Turroni, *Economics of Inflation*, pp. 200, 248, 446f.

100. Feldman, 'Political Economy', pp. 180–206.

101. Keynes, *Collected Writings*, vol. XVII, p. 131; Harrod, *Life of John Maynard Keynes*, pp. 288–95; Skidelsky, *John Maynard Keynes*, vol. II, p. 41.

102. Keynes, *Collected Writings*, vol. XVIII, p. 48.

103. Eichengreen, *Golden Fetters*, pp. 100–124.

104. Marks, 'Reparations Reconsidered', *passim;* Maier, *Recasting Bourgeois, Europe*, pp. 241f.

105. Holtfrerich, *German Inflation*, pp. 148f.; Webb, *Hyperinflation*, pp. 54, 104; Eichengreen, *Golden Fetters*, pp. 129f. Cf. Maier, 'Truth about the Treaties', pp. 56–67.

106. Webb, *Hyperinflation*, p. 107.

107. See for more detail on this point Ferguson, 'Balance of Payments Question'.

108. PRO CAB 37/141/15, Granville to Grey, 14 Sept. 1915; PRO CAB 37/141/15, Bertie to Grey, 15 Jan. 1916. See also PRO CAB 37/141/15, Sir John Pilter [Hon. Pres. of British Chamber of Commerce, Paris]: 'An after the war scheme for a customs union', 1 Sept. 1915.

109. PRO BT 55/1 (ACCI 5), British trade after the war: report of a sub-committee of the advisory committee to the Board of Trade on commercial intelligence with respect to measures for securing the position, after the war, of certain branches of British industry, 28 Jan. 1916. See also PRO BT 55/32 (FFT 2), Financial Facilities for Trade Committee: notes on post-bellum trade policy, with special reference to the penalization of German trade, undated, 1916; PRO RECO 1/356, Ministry of Blockade memorandum on 'trade war', 27 June 1917.

110. Bunselmeyer, *Cost of the War*, pp. 39–43.

111. PRO RECO 1/260, Final Report of the committee on commercial and industrial policy after the war [Balfour of Burleigh committee], 3 Dec. 1917.

112. Balderston, *German Economic Crisis*, pp. 82ff.

113. Schuker, 'American "Reparations" to Germany'.

114. Figures from Bresciani-Turroni, *Economics of Inflation*, pp. 194, 235; Wagenführ, 'Die Industriewirtschaft', p. 26.

115. F. Graham, *Exchange*, pp. 214–38, 261.

116. Ferguson, *Paper and Iron*, pp. 325ff.

117. Data on the structure of trade in Hentschel, 'Zahlen und Anmerkungen', p. 96; Laursen and Pedersen, *German Inflation*, pp. 99–107; Bresciani-Turroni, *Economics of Inflation*, p. 194.

118. Feldman, *Great Disorder*, pp. 484f. and n.

119. Bresciani-Turroni, *Economics of Inflation*, pp. 83–92, 100–154.

120. Holtfrerich, *German Inflation*, pp. 213f.

121. Ibid., pp. 206–20. Holtfrerich estimates that, if Germany had adopted deflationary policies, imports from the US would have been reduced by 60 per cent, and imports from the UK by 44 per cent.

122. This had been predicted by the socialist Rudolf Hilferding: 'With the increase of the issues [of notes] the balance of trade necessarily becomes passive. In effect, the issues increased internal prices, and that stimulated imports and impeded exports'; Bresciani-Turroni, *Economics of Inflation*, p. 44n; Maier, *Recasting Bourgeois Europe*, p. 251.

123. See the estimates in Bresciani-Turroni, *Economics of Inflation*, pp. 437f.; F. Graham, *Exchange*, pp. 44f.; Holtfrerich, *German Inflation*, p. 148.

124. Calculated from figures in Webb, *Hyperinflation*, p. 37; Witt, 'Finanzpolitik und sozialer Wandel im Krieg', pp. 425f.

125. Feldman, *Great Disorder*, pp. 214–39.

126. Bessel, *Germany*, pp. 73, 79.

127. Paddags, 'Weimar Inflation', pp. 20–24. See also Bresciani-Turroni, *Economics of Inflation*, p. 71n.; Webb, *Hyperinflation*, pp. 33, 37.

128. Paddags, 'Weimar Inflation', p. 38.

129. Figures in *Deutschlands Wirtschaft, Währung und Finanzen*, pp. 107–10.

130. See Ferguson, *Paper and Iron*, pp. 28off.

131. PRO RECO 1/775, Addison paper, Reconstruction finance, 10 Feb. 1918.

132. Calculated from figures from Hoffmann, Grumbach and Hesse, *Wachstum*, pp. 789f.; Mitchell and Deane, *British Historical Statistics*, pp. 401f.

133. Feldman, *Great Disorder*, pp. 46f., 816–19.

134. Keynes, *Tract on Monetary Reform*, pp. 3, 29, 36.

135. F. Graham, *Exchange*, esp. pp. 321, 324.

136. Laursen and Pedersen, *German Inflation*, pp. 95–8, 124ff.

137. Graham, *Exchange*, pp. 278f., 317f.; Laursen and Pedersen, *German Inflation*, pp. 77, 123.

138. Graham, *Exchange*, pp. 289; 318–21.

139. See e.g. Henning, *Das industrialisierte Deutschland*, pp. 63–83.

140. McKibbin, 'Class and Conventional Wisdom', pp. 259–48.

141. Holtfrerich, *German Inflation*, pp. 227–62.

142. Maier, *Recasting Bourgeois Europe*, pp. 114, 228–31.

143. Holtfrerich, *German Inflation*, pp. 265–78.

144. Haller, 'Rolle der Staatsfinanzen', p. 151.

145. Ferguson, *Paper and Iron*, p. 8. Cf. Feldman, *Great Disorder*, pp. 447ff.

146. H. James, *German Slump*, p. 42.

147. Ferguson, *Paper and Iron*, p. 8.

148. Ibid.

149. Ibid., pp. 8f.

150. Ibid., p. 9.

151. Feldman, *Great Disorder*, pp. 249, 253.

152. Bresciani-Turroni, *Economics of Inflation*, pp. 183, 215, 261f., 275, 286, 314f., 330ff., 404.

153. Keynes, *Economic Consequences*, pp. 220–33.

154. Lindenlaub, *Maschinebauunternehmen, passim*.

155. Balderston, *German Economic Crisis, passim*.

156. Roesler, *Finanzpolitik*, p. 207.

157. E. Morgan, *Studies in British Financial Policy*, p. 136.

158. Balderston, 'War Finance', p. 236.

159. Moeller, 'Winners as Losers', pp. 263–75.

160. Feldman, *Great Disorder,* p. 813.

161. See in general L. Jones, 'Dying Middle'; L. Jones, 'Inflation'; L. Jones, *German Liberalism, passim.*

162. Feldman, *Great Disorder,* pp. 574f., 855; H. James, *German Slump,* p. 353.

163. Diehl, 'Victors or Victims', pp. 705–36.

164. The Reich League of War Wounded, War Veterans and War Survivors, which had 830,000 members in 1922: Bessel, *Germany,* pp. 257f.

165. Cf. Aldcroft, *Twenties,* pp. 126f., 145–9.

166. Ferguson, 'Constraints and Room for Manoeuvre', pp. 653–66.

167. Webb, *Hyperinflation,* pp. 52ff. See also Eichengreen, *Golden Fetters,* pp. 139–42.

168. Figures calculated from Witt, 'Tax Policies', pp. 156f. Pre-war figures in Witt, *Finanzpolitik,* p. 379.

169. Calculated from Holtfrerich, *German Inflation,* pp. 50f.

170. Ibid., pp. 67f.

171. Interest rates for the years 1919, 1920 and 1921 in Holtfrerich, *German Inflation,* p. 73; Petzina, Abelshauser and Foust, *Sozialgeschichtliches Arbeitsbuch,* vol. III, p. 71.

172. Specht, *Politische und Wirtschaftliche Hintergründe,* p. 28, 51f.; Holtfrerich, *German Inflation,* p. 165; Feldman, *Great Disorder,* pp. 158f.

173. Graham, *Exchange,* p. 64.

174. Holtfrerich, *German Inflation,* p. 50; Bresciani-Turroni, *Economics of Inflation,* p. 448; Kroboth, *Finanzpolitik,* p. 494.

175. See in general Krohn, *Wirtschaftstheorien als politische Interessen.*

176. Paddags, 'Weimar Inflation', p. 45.

177. F. Graham, *Exchange,* p. 280; Webb, *Hyperinflation,* p. 99.

178. Keynes, *How to Pay for the War.*

Conclusion

1. Dostoevsky, *Crime and Punishment,* pp. 555f.

2. M. Gilbert, *First World War,* p. 509.

3. See Goldstein, *Winning the Peace.*

4. M. Gilbert, *First World War,* pp. 528, 530. As Gilbert rightly says, no people suffered more in the First World War than the Armenians: between 800,000 and 1.3 million were massacred by Ottoman forces in the first year of the war. Attempted genocide was not unique to the Second World War.

5. Hobsbawm, *Age of Extremes,* pp. 65f.

6. Cannadine, 'War and Death', p. 197.

7. Bogart, *Direct and Indirect Costs.*

8. Cannadine, 'War and Death', p. 200.

9. Petzina, Abelshauser and Foust, *Sozialgeschichtliches Arbeitsbuch,* vol. III, p. 28.

10. Mitchell, *European Historical Statistics,* p. 62.

11. Bessel, *Germany,* pp. 5, 73, 79. Cf. Whalen, *Bitter Wounds.*

12. See his *Pragerstrasse:* Cork, *Bitter Truth,* p. 252.

13. Kemp, *French Economy,* p. 59.

14. Bourke, *Dismembering the Male,* p. 33.

15. J. Winter, *Sites of Memory, passim.* For an illuminating critique, see Thomas Laqueur's review, 'The Past's Past', *London Review of Books,* 19 Sept. 1996, pp. 3ff. See also Mosse, *Fallen Soldiers.*

16. Cannadine, 'War and Death', pp. 212–17.

17. Kipling, *Irish Guards,* esp. vol. II, p. 28: '2nd Lieutenants Clifford and Kipling were missing . . . It was a fair average for the day of debut, and taught them somewhat for future guidance'.

18. M. Gilbert, *First World War,* p. 249.

19. Eichengreen, *Golden Fetters, passim.*

20. Knock, *To End All Wars,* p. 35.

21. Ibid., p. 77.

22. Ibid., p. 113.

23. Ibid., pp. 143ff.

24. Ibid., p. 152.

25. Hynes, *War Imagined,* p. 291.

26. Mazower, *Dark Continent,* p. 61.

27. Petzina, Abelhauser and Foust, *Sozialgeschichtliches Arbeitsbuch,* vol. III, p. 23.

28. Hobsbawm, *Age of Extremes*, p. 51.

29. Ferguson, *Paper and Iron*, p. 137.

30. W. Owen, *Poems*.

31. Sassoon, *War Poems*, p. 29.

32. The events are described in Sassoon, *Complete Memoirs*, pp. 471–557.

33. Willett, *New Sobriety*, p. 30.

34. Silkin, *Penguin Book of First World War Poetry*, pp. 265–8.

35. Coker, *War and the Twentieth Century*, pp. 58ff.

36. *1914* had gone through twenty-eight impressions by 1920, the *Collected Poems* sixteen impressions by 1928: Hynes, *War Imagined*, p. 300.

37. Bogacz, 'Tyranny of Words', p. 647n.

38. H. Cecil, 'British War Novelists', p. 801. Cf. Roucoux, *English Literature of the Great War*.

39. Grieves, 'Montague', p. 55.

40. H. Cecil, 'British War Novelists', pp. 811, 813.

41. Hynes, *War Imagined*, pp. 332ff.

42. Ibid., pp. 331f.

43. Cecil, 'British War Novelists', p. 810.

44. Graves, *Goodbye*, pp. 112f.

45. Ibid., pp. 78, 116. Also p. 152.

46. Ibid., p. 94.

47. Blunden, *Undertones*, pp. 56, 218.

48. Sassoon, *Memoirs of a Fox-Hunting Man*, p. 304.

49. Sassoon, *Memoirs of an Infantry Officer*, pp. 134, 139.

50. Sassoon, *Complete Memoirs*, p. 559.

51. Remarque, *All Quiet, passim*.

52. H. Cecil, 'British War Novelists', p. 803.

53. Ibid., p. 804.

54. Bond, 'British "Anti-War" Writers', pp. 817–30.

55. Hynes, *War Imagined*, pp. 450ff.

56. Bond, 'British "Anti-War" Writers', p. 826.

57. P. Parker, *Old Lie*, p. 27. See also Mosse, *Fallen Soldiers*, p. 68; Simkins 'Everyman at War', pp. 311f.

58. Barnett, 'Military Historian's View', pp. 8ff.

59. Coppard, *With a Machine Gun*, pp. 26, 44, 48.

60. Hašek, *Good Soldier Švejk*.

61. Jünger, *Storm of Steel*.

62. Craig, *Germany*, pp. 492f.

63. Theweleit, *Male Fantasies*, vol. 1.

64. See Pertile, 'Fascism and Literature', pp. 162–84.

65. Barnett, 'Military Historian's View', p. 6; Hynes, *War Imagined*, pp. 441f.; Bond, 'British "Anti-War" Writers', p. 822.

66. Holroyd, *Bernard Shaw*, vol. II, pp. 341–82; Hynes, *War Imagined*, pp. 142f., 393.

67. Hynes, *War Imagined*, pp. 243, 275.

68. Ibid., pp. 443–9.

69. Cork, *Bitter Truth*, pp. 76, 128, 189ff.

70. In fairness, Huelsenbeck had been given permission to study medicine in Zurich by the army, and Hans Richter had been wounded on the Eastern Front and was in Zurich for medical treatment. Tristan Tzara, who became the Dada movement's leading spokesman, was a Swiss Jew (his real name was Sami Rosenstock): Willett, *New Sobriety*, p. 27.

71. Kranzfelder, *George Grosz*, pp. 9–24; Schuster, *George Grosz*, esp. pp. 325, 452–87; Willett, *New Sobriety*, p. 24. Cf. Cork, *Bitter Truth*, p. 100.

72. Gough, 'Experience of British Artists', p. 852. (My emphasis.)

73. Cork, *Bitter Truth*, p. 163.

74. Willett, *New Sobriety*, p. 31.

75. Marwick, 'War and the Arts'. Cf. Cork, *Bitter Truth*, p. 165.

76. Willett, *New Sobriety*, p. 30.

77. B. Taylor, *Art and Literature*, pp. 14, 19.

78. J. Winter, *Sites of Memory*, pp. 159–63; J. Winter, 'Painting Armageddon', p. 875n. Cf. Eberle, *World War I and the Weimar Artists*.

79. Whitford, 'Revolutionary Reactionary', pp. 16ff.; O'Brien Twohig, 'Dix and Nietzsche', pp. 40–48.

80. Hitler, *Aquarelle:* see especially 'Fromelles, Verbandstelle 1915'.

81. Hynes, *War Imagined,* p. 462. Cf. J. Winter, 'Painting Armageddon', pp. 867f.

82. Gough, 'Experience of British Artists', p. 842.

83. J. Winter, 'Painting Armageddon', pp. 868ff.

84. Squire, *If It Had Happened Otherwise,* pp. 76f.

85. Ibid., p. 195.

86. Ibid., pp. 244, 248.

87. Ibid., pp. 110ff.

88. Guinn, *British Strategy,* pp. 122, 171, 238; J. Gooch, *Plans of War,* pp. 30, 35, 278. It is important to note that a German victory over France would *not*—as is often assumed—have shifted German politics to the Right. The Pan-Germans and the Kaiser may have thought so; but, as we have seen, Bülow and Bethmann knew well that the price of a war, whether victorious or not, would be a further move in the direction of parliamentary democracy.

89. Woodward, *Great Britain,* pp. 227f. Robertson was no less suspicious of Italian and French ambitions.

90. K. Wilson, *Policy of the Entente,* p. 79.

91. Geiss, 'German Version of Imperialism', pp. 114f.

Bibliography

Adams, R. J. Q., *Arms and the Wizard: Lloyd George and the Ministry of Munitions, 1915–1916* (London, 1978)

Afflerbach, Holger, *Falkenhayn: Politisches Denken und Handeln im Kaiserreich* (Munich, 1994)

Albert, Pierre, *Histoire de la presse* (Paris, 1990)

Albertini, Luigi, *The Origins of the War of 1914*, 3 vols. (Oxford, 1953)

Aldcroft, D. H., *The Twenties: From Versailles to Wall Street, 1919–1929* (Harmondsworth, 1987)

Alford, B. W. E., 'Lost Opportunities: British Business and Businessmen during the First World War', in N. McKendrick (ed.), *Business Life and Public Policy: Essays in Honour of D. C. Coleman* (Cambridge, 1986)

Amery, J. L., *The Life of Joseph Chamberlain*, vol. IV: *1901–1903* (London, 1951)

Andic, S., and J. Veverka, 'The Growth of Government Expenditure in Germany since the Unification', *Finanzarchiv* (1964)

Andrew, Christopher, 'The Entente Cordiale from its Origins to 1914', in N. Waites (ed.), *Troubled Neighbours: Franco-British Relations in the Twentieth Century* (London, 1971)

———, 'Secret Intelligence and British Foreign Policy 1900–1939', in C. Andrew and J. Noakes (eds.), *Intelligence and International Relations, 1900–1945* (Exeter, 1987)

———, *Secret Service: The Making of the British Intelligence Community* (London, 1985)

Angell, Norman, *The Great Illusion: A Study of the Relation of Military Power to National Advantage* (London, 1913 edn.)

Anonymous (ed.), *Documents diplomatiques secrets russes, 1914–1917: D'après les archives du Ministère des Affaires étrangères à Petrograd* (Paris, 1926)

Apostol, P. N., M. W. Bernatzky and A. M. Michelson, *Russian Public Finances during the War* (New Haven, 1928)

Armstrong, Elizabeth, *The Crisis of Quebec* (New York, 1937)

Ashworth, T., *Trench Warfare 1914–18: The Live and Let Live System* (London, 1980)

Aspinall-Oglander, C. F. (ed.), *Gallipoli*, 2 vols. (London, 1929–32)

Asquith, H. M., *The Genesis of the War* (London, 1923)

———, *Memories and Reflections, 1852–1927* (London, 1928)

Audoin-Rouzeau, Stéphane, 'The French soldier in the trenches', in H. Cecil and Liddle (eds.), *Facing Armageddon*

———, *La Guerre des enfants (1914–1918): Essai d'histoire culturelle* (Paris, 1993)

———, and Annette Becker, 'Vers une histoire culturelle de la Première Guerre mondiale', *XXe. Siècle* (1994)

Auswärtiges Amt, *German White Book Concerning the Responsibility of the Authors of the War* (New York, 1924)

Axelrod, R., *The Evolution of Co-operation* (London, 1984)

Bailey, J. B. A., *Field Artillery and Firepower* (Oxford, 1989)

———, 'The First World War and the Birth of the Modern Style of Warfare', *Strategic and Combat Studies Institute* (1996)

Bailey, Stephen, 'The Berlin Strike of 1918', *Central European History* (1980)

Bairoch, Paul, 'Europe's Gross National Product: 1800–1975', *Journal of European Economic History* (1976)

Balcon, Jill (ed.), *The Pity of War: Poems of the First World War* (Walwyn, 1985)

Balderston, Theo, *The German Economic Crisis, 1923–1932* (Berlin, 1993)
——, 'War Finance and Inflation in Britain and Germany, 1914–1918', *Economic History Review* (1989)
Bankers Trust Company, *English Public Finance* (New York, 1920)
——, *French Public Finance* (New York, 1920)
Banks, Arthur, *A Military Atlas of the First World War* (London, 1989)
Barker, Pat, *The Ghost Road* (London, 1995)
Barnes, Harry E., *The Genesis of the World War* (New York, 1925)
Barnett, C., *The Collapse of British Power* (London, 1973)
——, 'A Military Historian's View of the Great War', *Transactions of the Royal Historical Society* (1970)
——, *The Swordbearers* (London, 1963)
Barraclough, G., *From Agadir to Armageddon: Anatomy of a Crisis* (London, 1982)
Barth, Boris, *Die deutsche Hochfinanz und die Imperialismen: Banken und Aussenpolitik vor 1914* (Stuttgart, 1995)
Bean, C. E. W., *The Australian Imperial Force in France 1917* (Sydney, 1933)
Beaverbrook, Lord, *Men and Power, 1917–1918* (London, 1956)
——, *Politicians and the War*, 2 vols. (1928–n.d.)
Becker, Jean-Jacques, *The Great War and the French People* (Leamington Spa, 1985)
——, *1914: Comment les Français sont entrés dans la guerre* (Paris, 1977)
——, '"That's the death knell of our boys . . .'", in P. Fridenson (ed.), *The French Home Front* (Oxford, 1992)
——, and Stéphanie Audoin-Rouzeau (eds.), *Les Sociétés européennes et la Guerre de 1914–1918* (Paris, 1990)
——, *et al.* (eds.), *Guerre et Cultures, 1914–1918* (Paris, 1994)
Beckett, I., 'The Nation in Arms, 1914–1918', in I. Beckett and K. Simpson (eds.), *A Nation in Arms: A Social Study of the British Army in the First World War* (Manchester, 1985)
Bellanger, Claude, *et al.* (eds.), *Histoire générale de la presse française*, vol. III: *De 1871 à 1940* (Paris, 1972)
Bentley, Michael, *The Liberal Mind, 1914–29* (Cambridge, 1977)
Berger, Meyer, *The Story of the New York Times, 1851–1951* (New York, 1951)
Berghahn, V. R., *Germany and the Approach of War in 1914* (London, 1973)
——, 'Das Kaiserreich in der Sackgasse', *Neue Politische Literatur* (1971)
——, *Militarism: The History of an International Debate, 1861–1979* (Leamington Spa, 1981)
——, *Modern Germany: Society, Economics and Politics in the Twentieth Century* (Cambridge, 1982)
——, 'Politik und Gesellschaft im wilhelminischen Deutschland', *Neue Politische Literatur* (1979)
Bernhardi, General Friedrich von, *Germany and the Next War* (London, 1912)
Bernstein, G. L., *Liberalism and Liberal Politics in Edwardian England* (London 1986)
Bertold, R., 'Die Entwicklung der deutschen Agrarproduktion und der Ernährungswirtschaft zwischen 1907 und 1925', *Jahrbuch für Wirtschaftsgeschichte* (1974)
Bertrand, F., *La Presse francophone de tranchée au front belge, 1914–1918* (Brussels, 1971)
Bessel, Richard, *Germany after the First World War* (Oxford, 1993)
——, 'The Great War in German Memory: The Soldiers of the First World War, Demobilization and Weimar Politics Culture', *German History* (1988)
——, 'Mobilising German Society for War', paper delivered at the Münchenwiler conference on total war (1997)
Bethmann Hollweg, Theobald von, *Betrachtungen zum Weltkrieg*, 2 vols. (Berlin, 1919–21), trans. as *Reflections on the World War* (London, 1920)
Beveridge, W. H., *British Food Control* (London, 1928)
——, *Power and Influence* (London, 1953)
Bickersteth, John, *The Bickersteth Diaries, 1914–1918* (London, 1995)
Bidwell, S., and D. Graham, *Fire-Power* (London, 1982)
Bieber, H.-J., 'Die Entwicklung der Arbeitsbeziehungen auf den Hamburger Grosswerften (Blohm & Voss, Vulcanswerft) zwischen Hilfsdienstgesetz und Betriebsrätegesetz', in G. Mai (ed.), *Arbeiterschaft in Deutschland 1914–1918: Studien zu Arbeitskampf und Arbeitsmarkt im Ersten Weltkrieg* (Düsseldorf, 1985)
Bittner, Ludwig, and Hans Übersberger (eds.), *Österreich-Ungarns Aussenpolitik von der bosnischen Krise 1908 bis zum Kriegsausbruch 1914*, 9 vols. (Vienna, 1930)
Blackbourn, David, *Class, Religion and Local Politics in Wilhelmine Germany: The Centre Party in Württemberg before 1914* (New Haven/London, 1980)
——, *The Fontana History of Germany, 1780–1918: The Long Nineteenth Century* (London, 1997)

——, and Geoff Eley, *The Peculiarities of German History: Bourgeois Society and Politics in Nineteenth-Century Germany* (Oxford, 1984)

Bloch, Ivan S., *Is War Now Impossible? Being an Abridgment of 'The War of the Future in its Technical, Economic and Political Relations'* (London, 1899)

Blunden, Edmunds, *Undertones of War* (London, 1982)

Bogacz, Ted, '"A Tyranny of Words": Language, Poetry, and Antimodernism in England in the First World War', *Journal of Modern History* (1986)

——, 'War Neurosis and Cultural Change in England, 1914–1922', *Journal of Contemporary History* (1989)

Bogart, E. L., *Direct and Indirect Costs of the Great World War* (Oxford, 1920)

Boghitchevitch, M. (ed.), *Die auswärtige Politik Serbiens, 1903–14*, 3 vols. (Berlin, 1928–31)

Bond, Brian, 'British "Anti-War" Writers and their Critics', in H. Cecil and Liddle (eds.), *Facing Armageddon*

——, 'Editor's Introduction', in B. Bond (ed.), *The First World War and British Military History* (Oxford, 1991)

——, *War and Society in Europe, 1870–1970* (London, 1984)

Bordes, W. de, *The Austrian Crown: Its Depreciation and Stabilisation* (London, 1924)

Born, Karl Erich, *International Banking in the Nineteenth and Twentieth Centuries* (Leamington Spa, 1983)

Boswell, J., and B. John, 'Patriots or Profiteers? British Businessmen and the First World War', *Journal of European Economic History* (1982)

Bosworth, R. J. B., *Italy and the Approach of the First World War* (London, 1983)

Bourke, Joanna, *Dismembering the Male: Men's Bodies, Britain and the Great War* (London, 1996)

Bourne, J. M., *Britain and the Great War, 1914–1918* (London, 1989)

——, 'The British Working Man in Arms', in H. Cecil and Liddle (eds.), *Facing Armageddon*

Bravo, G. F., '"In the Name of our Mutual friend": The Keynes-Cuno Affair', *Journal of Contemporary History* (1989)

Bresciani-Turroni, Costantino, *The Economics of Inflation: A Study of Currency Depreciation in Post-War Germany* (London, 1937)

Broch, Hermann, *The Sleepwalkers* (London, 1986)

Brock, M., 'Britain Enters the War', in R. J. W. Evans and H. Pogge von Strandmann (eds.), *The Coming of the First World War* (Oxford, 1988)

——, and Eleanor Brock (eds.), *H. H. Asquith, Letters to Venetia Stanley* (Oxford, 1982)

Brooke, Rupert, *Poetical Works* (London, 1946)

Brown, Edward D., 'Between Cowardice and Insanity: Shell Shock and the Legitimation of the Neuroses in Great Britain', in E. Mendelsohn, M. R. Smith and P. Weingart (eds.), *Science, Technology and the Military* (New York, 1988)

Brown, Gordon, *Maxton* (Edinburgh, 1986)

Brown, Malcolm, *The Imperial War Museum Book of the Somme* (London, 1996)

——, *The Imperial War Museum Book of the Western Front* (London, 1993)

——, and Shirley Seaton, *Christmas Truce: The Western Front, December 1914* (London, 1984)

Bruch, R. vom, 'Krieg und Frieden: Zur Frage der Militarisierung deutscher Hochschullehrer und Universitäten im späten Kaiserreich', in Jost Dülffer and Karl Holl (eds.), *Bereit zum Krieg: Kriegsmentalität im wilhelminischen Deutschland 1890–1914. Beiträge zur historischen Friedensforschung* (Göttingen, 1986)

Bruntz, George G., *Allied Propaganda and the Collapse of the German Empire in 1918* (Stanford/Oxford, 1938)

Bry, G., *Wages in Germany, 1871–1945* (Princeton, 1960)

Bryder, L., 'The First World War: Healthy or Hungry?', *History Workshop Journal* (1987)

Buchan, John, *A Prince of the Captivity* (Edinburgh, 1996 edn.)

Buchheim, C., 'Aspects of Nineteenth-Century Anglo-German Trade Policy Reconsidered', *Journal of European Economic History* (1981)

Bucholz, Arden, *Moltke, Schlieffen and Prussian War Planning* (New York/Oxford, 1991)

Buckley, Suzann, 'The Failure to Resolve the Problem of Venereal Disease among the Troops of Britain during World War I', in *War and Society* (1977)

Bullock, Alan, *Hitler and Stalin: Parallel Lives* (London, 1994)

Bülow, Prince von, *Memoirs, 1903–1909* (London, 1931)

Bunselmeyer, R., *The Cost of the War, 1914–1918: British Economic War Aims and the Origins of Reparations* (Hamden, Conn., 1975)

Burchardt, L., 'The Impact of the War Economy on the Civilian Population of Germany during the First and Second World Wars', in W. Deist (ed.), *The German Military in the Age of Total War* (Leamington Spa, 1985)

Burk, K., *Britain, America and the Sinews of War, 1914–1918* (London, 1985)

——, 'John Maynard Keynes and the Exchange Rate Crisis of July 1917', *Economic History Review* (1979)

——, 'The Mobilisation of Anglo-American Finance during World War I', in N. F. Dreisziger (ed.), *Mobilization for Total War: The Canadian, American and British Experience, 1914–1918, 1939–1945* (Waterloo, Ontario, 1981)

——, 'The Treasury: From Impotence to Power', in K. Burk (ed.), *War and the State* (London, 1982)

Burleigh, Michael, *Death and Deliverance: Euthanasia in Germany, c. 1900–1945* (Cambridge, 1994)

Burnett, P. M., *Reparation at the Paris Peace Conference*, 2 vols. (New York, 1940)

Buse, D. K., 'Ebert and the Coming of World War I: A Month from his Diary', *Central European History* (1968)

Butler, David, and Gareth Butler, *British Political Facts, 1900–1994* (London, 1994)

Butterfield, Herbert, 'Sir Edward Grey in July 1914', *Historical Studies* (1965)

Cain, P. J., *Economic Foundations of British Overseas Expansion, 1815–1914* (London, 1980)

——, and A. G. Hopkins, *British Imperialism*, vol. I: *Innovation and Expansion, 1688–1914* (London, 1993)

Calleo, David, *The German Problem Reconsidered: Germany and the World Order, 1870 to the Present* (Cambridge, 1978)

Cammaerts, Emile, *The Keystone of Europe: History of the Belgian Dynasty* (London, 1939)

Canetti, Elias, *Crowds and Power* (London, 1962)

——, *The Tongue Set Free* (London, 1989)

Cannadine, David, *G. M. Trevelyan: A Life in History* (London, 1992)

——, 'War and Death, Grief and Mourning in Modern Britain', in J. Whaley (ed.), *Mirrors of Mortality: Studies in the Social History of Death* (London, 1981)

Capie, F., and A. Webber, *A Survey of Estimates of UK Money Supply and Components: 1870–1982* (London, 1984)

Carr, E. H., *The Bolshevik Revolution*, vol. III (London, 1983)

Carsten, F. L., *War against War: British and German Radical Movements in the First World War* (London, 1982)

Cassimatis, Louis P., *American Influence in Greece, 1917–1929* (Kent, Ohio, 1988)

Cattani, Alfred, *Albert Meyer: Chefredaktor der Neuen Zürcher Zeitung von 1915 bis 1930, Bundesrat von 1930 bis 1938* (Zurich, 1992)

Cecil, Hugh, 'British War Novelists', in H. Cecil and Liddle (eds.), *Facing Armageddon*

——, and Peter H. Liddle (eds.), *Facing Armageddon: The First World War Experienced* (London, 1996)

Cecil, L., *Albert Ballin: Business and Politics in Imperial Germany* (Princeton, 1967)

Céline, Louis-Ferdinand, *Voyage au bout de la nuit* (Paris, 1932)

Challener, R. D., *The French Theory of the Nation in Arms* (London, 1955)

Chickering, Roger, 'Die Alldeutschen erwarten den Krieg', in Jost Dülffer and Karl Holl (eds.), *Bereit zum Krieg: Kriegsmentalität im wilhelminischen Deutschland 1890–1914. Beiträge zur historischen Friedensforschung* (Göttingen, 1986)

——, *Imperial Germany and a World without War* (Princeton, 1975)

——, *Imperial Germany and the Great War, 1914–1918* (Cambridge, 1998)

——, *We Men Who Feel Most German: A Cultural Study of the Pan-German League, 1886–1914* (London, 1984)

——, 'World War I and the Theory of Total War: Reflections on the British and German Cases, 1914–1915', paper delivered at the Münchenwiler conference on total war (1997)

Childers, Erskine, *The Riddle of the Sands* (1903; repr. London, 1984)

Churchill, R. S., *Winston S. Churchill*, vol. II: *Companion*, part III: *1911–1914* (London, 1969)

Churchill, Winston S., *The World Crisis, 1911–1918*, 5 vols. (London, 1923–9)

Clark, Alan, *The Donkeys* (London, 1961)

Clarke, I. F. (ed.), *The Great War with Germany, 1890–1914* (Liverpool, 1997)

—— (ed.), *The Tale of the Next Great War, 1871–1914* (Liverpool, 1995)

——, *Voices Prophesying War, 1763–1984* (London/New York, 1992)

Clarke, Tom, *My Northcliffe Diary* (London, 1931)

Clausewitz, Carl von, *On War*, ed. Anatol Rapaport (London, 1968)

Cline, D., 'Winding Down the State', in K. Burk (ed.), *War and the State* (London, 1982)

Coetzee, M. S., *The German Army League: Popular Nationalism in Wilhelmine Germany* (Oxford/New York, 1990)

Coker, Christopher, *War and the Twentieth Century: The Impact of War on Modern Consciousness* (London/Washington, 1994)

Coleman, James S., 'A Rational Choice Perspective on Economic Sociology', in N. Smelser and P. Swedberg, *The Handbook of Economic Sociology* (Princeton, 1994)

Colin, G., and J-J. Becker, 'Les Écrivains, la guerre de 1914 et l'opinion publique', *Rélations Internationales* (1980)

Collier, B., *Brasshat: A Biography of Field Marshal Sir Henry Wilson* (London, 1961)

Commission de publication des documents relatifs aux origines de la guerre de 1914, *Documents diplomatiques français, 1871–1914*, 41 vols. (Paris, 1929–59)

Cook, Chris, and John Paxton, *European Political Facts, 1900–1996* (London, 1998)

Cooke, J., 'The American Soldier in France, 1917–1919', in H. Cecil and Liddle (eds.), *Facing Armageddon*

Coppard, George, *With a Machine Gun to Cambrai: The Tale of a Young Tommy in Kitchener's Army, 1914–1918* (London, 1969)

Corbett, Sir Julian, and Sir Henry Newbolt (eds.), *Naval Operations*, 5 vols. (London, 1920–31)

Cork, Richard, *A Bitter Truth: Avant-Garde Art and the Great War* (New Haven/London, 1994)

Craig, G. A., *Germany, 1866–1945* (Oxford, 1981 edn.)

———, *The Politics of the Prussian Army, 1640–1945* (Oxford, 1955)

Creveld, Martin van, *Command in War* (Cambridge, Mass., 1985)

———, *Supplying War: Logistics from Wallenstein to Patton* (London, 1977)

———, *The Transformation of War* (New York, 1991)

Crothers, C. G., *The German Elections of 1907* (New York, 1941)

Crow, D., *A Man of Push and Go: The Life of George Macaulay Booth* (London, 1965)

Cruttwell, C. R. M. F., *A History of the Great War, 1914–18* (Oxford, 1964)

Cunningham, Hugh, 'The Language of Patriotism, 1750–1914', *History Workshop Journal* (1981)

D'Abernon, Viscount, *An Ambassador of Peace*, 2 vols. (London, 1929)

Dahlmann, Dieter, 'Russia at the Outbreak of the First World War', in Becker and Audoin-Rouzeau (eds.), *Les Sociétés européennes et la Guerre*

Dallas, G., and D. Gill, *The Unknown Army* (London, 1985)

Danchev, A., 'Bunking and Debunking: The Controversies of the 1960s', in B. Bond (ed.), *The First World War and British Military History* (Oxford, 1991)

Dangerfield, George, *The Strange Death of Liberal England* (London, 1935)

Davidson, R., 'The Board of Trade and Industrial Relations', *Historical Journal* (1978)

Davies, Norman, *Europe: A History* (Oxford, 1996)

Davis, L. E., and R. A. Huttenback, *Mammon and the Pursuit of Empire: The Political Economy of British Imperialism, 1860–1912* (Cambridge, 1986)

Davis, Richard, *The English Rothschilds* (London, 1983)

Dawkins, Richard, *The Selfish Gene* (Oxford, 1989 edn.)

DeGroot, Gerard, J., *Blighty: British Society in the Era of the Great War* (London/New York, 1996)

Deist, Wilhelm, 'The Military Collapse of the German Empire: The Reality behind the Stab-in-the-Back Myth', *War in History* (1996)

Delarme, R., and C. André, *L'État et l'économie: Un Essai d'explication de l'évolution des dépenses publiques en France* (Seuil, 1983)

Demeter, K., *Das deutsche Offizierkorps in Gesellschaft und Staat 1650–1945* (Frankfurt am Main, 1965)

Deutschlands Wirtschaft, Währung und Finanzen (Berlin, 1924)

Dewey, P., 'British Farming Profits and Government Policy during the First World War', *Economic History Review* (1984)

———, 'Military Recruitment and the British Labour Force during the First World War', *Historical Journal* (1984)

———, 'The New Warfare and Economic Mobilisation', in J. Turner (ed.), *Britain and the First World War* (London, 1988)

Diehl, James M., 'Victors or Victims? Disabled Veterans in the Third Reich', *Journal of Modern History* (1987)

Dockrill M. L., and J. D. Gould, *Peace without Promise: Britain and the Peace Conference, 1919–1923* (London, 1981) d'Ombrain, N., *War Machinery and High Policy: Defence Administration in Peacetime Britain* (Oxford, 1973)

Dostoevsky, Fyodor, *Crime and Punishment,* trans. David Magarshack (London, 1978)

Dowie, J. A., '1919–20 is in Need of Attention', *Economic History Review* (1975)

Dresler, Adolf, *Geschichte der italienischen Presse,* vol. III: *Von 1900 bis 1935* (Munich, 1934)

Droz, J., *Les Causes de la première guerre mondiale: Essai d'historiographie* (Paris, 1973)

Düding, D., 'Die Kriegsvereine im wilhelminischen Reich und ihr Beitrag zur Militarisierung der deutschen Gesellschaft', in Jost Dülffer and Karl Holl (eds.), *Bereit zum Krieg: Kriegsmentalität im wilhelminischen Deutschland 1890–1914. Beiträge zur historischen Friedensforschung* (Göttingen, 1986)

Dugdale, Blanche E. C., *Arthur James Balfour, 1st Earl of Balfour, 1906–1930,* 2 vols. (London, 1936)

Dugdale, E. T. S. (ed.), *German Diplomatic Documents, 1871–1914,* 4 vols. (London, 1928)

Dukes, J. R., 'Militarism and Arms Policy Revisited: The Origins of the German Army Law of 1913', in Dukes and J. Remak (eds.), *Another Germany: A Reconsideration of the Imperial Era* (Boulder, 1988)

——, and J. Remak (eds.), *Another Germany: A Reconsideration of the Imperial Era* (Boulder, 1988)

Dungan, Myles, *They Shall Not Grow Old: Irish Soldiers and the Great War* (Dublin, 1997)

Dupuy, T. N., *A Genius for War: The German Army and Staff, 1807–1945* (London, 1977)

Eberle, M., *World War I and the Weimar Artists: Dix, Grosz, Beckmann, Schlemmer* (New Haven, 1985)

Eckardstein, Freiherr von, *Lebenserinnerungen,* 3 vols. (Leipzig, 1919–20)

Eckart, Wolfgang U., '"The Most Extensive Experiment That Imagination Can Produce": Violence of War, Emotional Stress and German Medicine, 1914–1918', paper delivered at the Münchenwiler conference on total war (1997)

Economist, The, Britain in Figures, 1997 (London, 1997)

——, *Economic Statistics, 1900–1983* (London, 1981)

Edelstein, M., *Overseas Investment in the Age of High Imperialism* (London, 1982)

Edmonds, Sir James (ed.), *Official History: Military Operations, France and Belgium,* 14 vols. (London, 1922–48)

——, *A Short History of World War I* (London, 1951)

Egremont, Max, *Balfour* (London, 1980)

Ehlert, H. G., *Die wirtschaftlichen Zentralbehörde des Deutschen Reiches, 1914–1919: Das Problem der Gemeinwirtschaft in Krieg und Frieden* (Wiesbaden, 1982)

Eichengreen, Barry, *Golden Fetters: The Gold Standard and the Great Depression, 1919–1939* (New York/Oxford, 1992)

——, and Marc Flandreau, 'The Geography of the Gold Standard', *International Macroeconomics* (October 1994)

Eksteins, Modris, *Rites of Spring: The Great War and the Modern Age* (London, 1989)

Eley, Geoff, 'Army, State and Civil Society: Revisiting the Problem of German Militarism', in Eley, *From Unification to Nazism: Reinterpreting the German Past* (Boston, 1986)

——, 'Conservatives and Radical Nationalists in Germany: The Production of Fascist Potentials, 1912–28', in M. Blinkhorn (ed.), *Fascists and Conservatives* (London, 1990)

——, *Reshaping the German Right: Radical Nationalism and Political Change after Bismarck* (New Haven, 1979)

——, '*Sammlungspolitik,* Social Imperialism and the German Navy Law of 1898', *Militärgeschichtliche Mitteilungen* (1974)

——, 'The Wilhelmine Right: How It Changed', in R. J. Evans (ed.), *Society and Politics in Wilhelmine Germany* (New York, 1978)

Ellis, J., *Eye-Deep in Hell* (London, 1976)

Englander, D., 'The French Soldier, 1914–18', *French History* (1987)

——, and J. Osborne, 'Jack, Tommy and Henry Dubb: The Armed Forces and the UK', *Historical Journal* (1978)

Erdmann, K. D., 'Hat Deutschland auch den Ersten Weltkrieg entfesselt? Kontroversen zur Politik der Mächte im Juli 1914', in Erdmann and E. Zechlin (eds.), *Politik und Geschichte: Europa 1914—Krieg oder Frieden?* (Kiel, 1985)

——, 'War Guilt 1914 Reconsidered: A Balance of New Research', in H. W. Koch (ed.), *The Origins of the First World War* (London, 1984)

——, 'Zur Beurteilung Bethmann Hollwegs', *Geschichte in Wissenschaft und Unterricht* (1964)

Esposito, Patrick, 'Public Opinion and the Outbreak of the First World War: Germany, Austria-Hungary and the War in the Newspapers of Northern England', unpublished master of studies thesis (Oxford, 1997)

Falkenhayn, Erich von, *Die oberste Heeresleitung 1914–1916* (Berlin, 1920)

Farndale, M., *History of the Royal Regiment of Artillery: Western Front, 1914–18* (London, 1986)

Farrar, L. L., *The Short-War Illusion: German Policy, Strategy and Domestic Affairs, August-December 1914* (Oxford, 1973)

Farrar, M. M., 'Preclusive Purchases: Politics and Economic Warfare in France during the First World War', *Economic History Review* (1973)

Faulks, Sebastian, *Birdsong* (London, 1994)

Fausto, Domenicantonio, 'La politica fiscale dalla prima guerra mondiale al regime fascista', *Ricerche per la Storia della Banca d'Italia*, vol. II (Rome, 1993)

Fay, Sidney B., *The Origins of the World War*, 2 vols. (New York, 1930 edn.)

Feldman, G. D., *Army, Industry and Labour in Germany, 1914–1918* (Princeton, 1966)

———, 'The Deutsche Bank from World War to World Economic Crisis, 1914–1933', in Gall *et al.*, *The Deutsche Bank, 1870–1995* (London, 1995)

———, 'Der deutsche organisierte Kapitalismus während der Kriegs- und Inflationsjahre 1914–1923', in H. A. Winkler (ed.), *Organisierter Kapitalismus* (Göttingen, 1974)

———, *The Great Disorder: Politics, Economics and Society in the German Inflation* (New York/Oxford, 1993)

———, *Iron and Steel in the German Inflation, 1916–1923* (Princeton, 1977)

———, 'The Political Economy of Germany's Relative Stabilisation during the 1920/21 Depression', in Feldman, *et al.* (eds.), *Die deutsche Inflation: Eine Zwischenbilanz* (Berlin/New York, 1982)

———, 'War Aims, State Intervention and Business Leadership in Germany: The Case of Hugo Stinnes', paper delivered at the Münchenwiler conference on total war (1997)

Ferguson, Niall, 'The Balance of Payments Question: Versailles and After', *Centre for German and European Studies Working Paper* (Berkeley, 1994)

———, 'Constraints and Room for Manoeuvre in the German Inflation of the Early 1920s', *Economic History Review* (1996)

———, 'Food and the First World War', *Twentieth Century British History* (1991)

———, 'Germany and the Origins of the First World War: New Perspectives', *Historical Journal* (1992)

———, 'The Kaiser's European Union: What If Britain Had Stood Aside in August 1914?', in Ferguson (ed.), *Virtual History*

———, 'Keynes and the German Inflation', *English Historical Review* (1995)

———, *Paper and Iron: Hamburg Business and German Politics in the Era of Inflation, 1897–1927* (Cambridge, 1995)

———, 'Public Finance and National Security: The Domestic Origins of the First World War Revisited', *Past and Present* (1994)

——— (ed.), *Virtual History: Alternatives and Counterfactuals* (London, 1997)

———, *The World's Banker: A History of the House of Rothschild* (London, 1998)

Ferro, Marc, *The Great War, 1914–1918* (London, 1973)

Field, Frank, 'The French War Novel: The Case of Louis-Ferdinand Céline', in H. Cecil and Liddle (eds.), *Facing Armageddon*

Figes, Orlando, *A People's Tragedy: The Russian Revolution, 1891–1924* (London, 1996)

Finch, A. H., 'A Diary of the Great War', MS, private possession

Fischer, E., W. Bloch and A. Philipp (eds.), *Das Werk des Untersuchungsausschusses der Verfassungsgebenden Deutschen Nationalversammlung und des Deutschen Reichstages 1919–28: Die Ursachen des deutschen Zusammenbruches im Jahre 1918*, 8 vols. (Berlin, 1928)

Fischer, Fritz, *Bündnis der Eliten: Zur Kontinuität der Machtstrukturen in Deutschland, 1871–1945* (Düsseldorf, 1979), trans. *From Kaiserreich to Third Reich: Elements of Continuity in German History, 1871–1945* (London, 1986)

———, 'The Foreign Policy of Imperial Germany and the Outbreak of the First World War', in Schöllgen (ed.), *Escape into War? The Foreign Policy of Imperial Germany* (Oxford/New York/Munich, 1990)

———, *Germany's Aims in the First World War* (London, 1967)

———, *Griff nach der Weltmacht: Die Kriegszielpolitik des kaiserlichen Deutschlands 1914–1918* (Dusseldorf, 1961), trans. *Germany's Aims*

———, 'Kontinuität des Irrtums: Zum Problem der deutschen Kriegszielpolitik im Ersten Weltkrieg', *Historische Zeitschrift* (1960)

———, *War of Illusions: German Policies from 1911 to 1914* (London/New York, 1975)

———, *Weltmacht oder Niedergang* (Frankfurt, 1965), trans. *World Power or Decline* (New York, 1974)

Fischer, Heinz-Dietrich (ed.), *Handbuch der politischen Presse in Deutschland, 1480–1980: Synopse rechtlicher, struktureller und wirtschaftlicher Grundlagen der Tendenzpublizistik im Kommunikationsfeld* (Düsseldorf, 1981)

———, *Pressekonzentration und Zensurpraxis im Ersten Weltkrieg: Texte und Quellen* (Berlin, 1973)

Fischer, Wolfram, 'Die deutsche Wirtschaft im Ersten Weltkrieg', in N. Walter (ed.), *Deutschland: Porträt einer Nation*, vol III: *Wirtschaft* (Gütersloh, 1985)

Floud, R. C., 'Britain 1860–1914: A Survey', in Floud and D. McCloskey (eds.), *The Economic History of Britain since 1700, vol. II* (Cambridge, 1981)

Fontaine, A., *French Industry during the War* (New Haven, 1926)

Forester, C. S., *The General* (London, 1936)

Förster, Stig, 'Alter und neuer Militarismus im Kaiserreich: Heeresrüstungspolitik und Dispositionen zum Kreig zwischen Status-quo-Sicherung und imperialistischer Expansion, 1890–1913', in Jost Dülffer and Karl Holl (eds.), *Bereit zum Krieg: Kriegsmentalität im wilhelminischen Deutschland 1890–1914*. Beiträge zur historischen Friedensforschung (Göttingen, 1986)

———, 'Der deutsche Generalstab und die Illusion des kurzen Krieges, 1871–1914. Metakritik eines Mythos', *Militärgeschichtliche Mitteilungen* (1995)

———, *Der doppelte Militarismus: Die deutsche Heeresrüstungspolitik zwischen Status-quo-Sicherung und Aggression, 1890–1913* (Stuttgart, 1985)

———, 'Dreams and Nightmares: German Military Leadership and the Images of Future Warfare, 1871–1914', unpublished paper delivered at the Augsburg conference (1994)

———, 'Facing "People's War": Moltke the Elder and Germany's Military Options after 1871', *Journal of Strategic Studies* (1987)

Foster, Roy, *Modern Ireland, 1600–1972* (Oxford, 1988)

Frank, Robert, Thomas Gilovich and Dennis Regan, 'Does Studying Economics Inhibit Co-operation?', *Journal of Economic Perspectives* (1993)

French, David, *British Economic and Strategic Planning, 1905–1915* (London, 1982)

———, 'The Edwardian Crisis and the Origins of the First World War', *International History Review* (1982)

———, 'The Meaning of Attrition', *English Historical Review* (1986)

———, 'The Rise and Fall of "Business as Usual"', in K. Burk (ed.), *War and the State* (London, 1982)

———, 'Spy Fever in Britain, 1900–1915', *Historical Journal* (1978)

French, Sir John, *1914* (London, 1919)

Freud, Sigmund, 'Civilization and its discontents', in John Rickman (ed.), *Civilization, War and Death* (London, 1939)

———, 'Thoughts for the time on War and Death', in John Rickman (ed.), *Civilization, War and Death* (London, 1939)

———, 'Why War?', in John Rickman (ed.), *Civilization, War and Death* (London, 1939)

Friedberg, A. L., *The Weary Titan: Britain and the Experience of Relative Decline, 1895–1905* (Princeton, 1988)

Fromkin, David, *A Peace to End All Peace: Creating the Modern Middle East, 1914–1922* (London, 1991)

Fuller, J. F. C., *The Conduct of War* (London, 1972)

Fuller, J. G., *Troop Morale and Popular Culture in the British and Dominion Armies, 1914–1918* (Oxford, 1990)

Fussell, Paul, *The Great War and Modern Memory* (Oxford, 1975)

Fyfe, Henry Hamilton, *Northcliffe: An Intimate Biography* (London, n.d. [c. 1930])

Galet, E. J., *Albert King of the Belgians in the Great War: His Military Activities and Experiences Set Down with his Approval* (London, 1931)

Gall, Lothar, *Bismarck: The White Revolutionary*, 2 vols. (London, 1986)

———, 'The Deutsche Bank from its Founding to the Great War, 1870–1914', in Gall *et al.*, *The Deutsche Bank, 1870–1995* (London, 1995)

Gallinger, August, *The Countercharge: The Matter of War Criminals from the German Side* (Munich, 1922)

Gammage, B., *The Broken Years: Australian Soldiers in the Great War* (Canberra, 1974)

Garvin, J. L., *The Life of Joseph Chamberlain*, vol. III: *1895–1900* (London, 1934)

Gatrell, P., *Government, Industry and Rearmament, 1900–1914: The Last Argument of Tsarism* (Cambridge, 1994)

———, *The Tsarist Economy, 1850–1917* (London, 1986)

Gatzke, Hans, *German's Drive to the West: A Study of Germany's Western War Aims during the First World War* (Baltimore, 1966)

Gebele, Hubert, *Die Probleme von Krieg und Frieden in Großbritannien während des Ersten Weltkrieges: Regierung, Parteien und öffentliche Meinung in der Auseinandersetzung über Kriegs- und Friedensziele* (Frankfurt am Main, 1987)

Geiss, Immanuel, *Das Deutsche Reich und der erste Weltkrieg* (Munich, 1985)

——, *Das Deutsche Reich und die Vorgeschichte des Ersten Weltkrieges* (Munich, 1978)

——, 'The German Version of Imperialism: *Weltpolitik*', in Schöllgen (ed.), *Escape into War? The Foreign Policy of Imperial Germany* (Oxford/New York/Munich, 1990)

——, *July 1914: The Outbreak of the First World War—Selected Documents* (London, 1967)

——, *Der lange Weg in die Katastrophe: Die Vorgeschichte des Ersten Weltkrieges, 1815–1914* (Munich/Zürich, 1990)

Gerber, L.-G., 'Corporatism in Comparative Perspective: The Impact of the First World War on American and British Labour Relations', *Business History Review* (1988)

Geyer, Michael, 'German Strategy in the Age of Machine Warfare, 1914–1945', in P. Paret (ed.), *Makers of Modern Strategy from Machiavelli to the Nuclear Age* (Oxford, 1986)

Gibbon, Lewis Grassic, *A Scots Quair* (London, 1986 edn.)

Gibbs, Philip, *Realities of War* (London, 1929)

Gilbert, B. B., *David Lloyd George: A Political life—Organiser of Victory, 1912–16* (London, 1992)

Gilbert, Martin, *First World War* (London, 1994)

Gilbert, Sandra M., 'Soldier's Heart: Literary Men, Literary Women and the Great War', in M. Higgonet (ed.), *Behind the Lines* (New Haven, 1987)

Girault, René, *Emprunts russes et investissements français en Russie* (Paris, 1973)

Glaser, Elisabeth, 'The American War Effort: Money and Material Aid, 1917–1918', paper delivered at the Münchenwiler conference on total war (1997)

Godfrey, John F., *Capitalism at War: Industrial Policy and Bureaucracy in France, 1914–1918* (Leamington Spa, 1987)

Goldstein, Erik, *Winning the Peace: British Diplomatic Strategy, Peace Planning and the Paris Peace Conference, 1916–1920* (Oxford, 1991)

Gombrich, E. H., *Aby Warburg: An Intellectual Biography* (Oxford, 1970)

Gooch, G. P. and Harold Temperley (eds.), *British Documents on the Origins of the War, 1898–1914*, 11 vols. (London, 1926–38)

Gooch, J., *The Plans of War: The General Staff and British Military Strategy, c. 1900–1916* (London, 1974)

——, 'Soldiers, Strategy and War Aims in Britain, 1914–1918', in B. Hunt and A. Preston (eds.), *War Aims and Strategic Policy in the Great War* (London, 1977)

Gordon, M. R., 'Domestic Conflict and the Origins of the First World War: The British and German Cases', *Journal of Modern History* (1974)

Gough, Paul, 'The experience of British Artists in the Great War', in H. Cecil and Liddle (eds.), *Facing Armageddon*

Grady, H. F., *British War Finance, 1914–1919* (New York, 1968 edn.)

Graham, Dominic, 'Sans Doctrine: British Army Tactics in the First World War', in T. Travers and C. Archer (eds.), *Men At War: Politics, Technology and Innovation in the Twentieth Century* (Chicago, 1982)

Graham, F. D., *Exchange, Prices and Production in Hyperinflation Germany, 1920–1923* (Princeton, 1930)

Graves, Robert, *Goodbye to All That* (London, 1960)

Greasley, D., and L. Oxley, 'Discontinuities in Competitiveness: The Impact of the First World War on British Industry', *Economic History Review*

Gregory, A., 'British Public Opinion and the Descent into War', unpublished manuscript

——, 'Lost Generations: The Impact of Military Casualties on Paris, London and Berlin', in J. Winter (ed.), *Capital Cities*

Gregory, P. R., *Russian National Income, 1885–1913* (Cambridge, 1982)

Greschat, M., 'Krieg und Kriegsbereitschaft im deutschen Protestantismus', in Jost Dülffer and Karl Holl (eds.), *Bereit zum Krieg: Kriegsmentalität im wilhelminischen Deutschland 1890–1914. Beiträge zur historischen Friedensforschung* (Göttingen, 1986)

Grey of Falloden, Viscount, *Fly Fishing* (Stocksfield, 1990)

——, *Twenty-Five Years*, 2 vols. (London, 1925)

Grieves, Keith, 'C. E. Montague and the Making of *Disenchantment*, 1914–1921', *War in History* (1997)

——, 'Lloyd George and the Management of the British War Economy', paper delivered at the Münchenwiler conference on total war (1997)

Griffith, Paddy, *Battle Tactics of the Western Front: The British Army's Art of Attack, 1916–18* (New Haven/London, 1994)

——— (ed.), *British Fighting Methods in the Great War* (London, 1996)

———, *Forward into Battle: Fighting Tactics from Waterloo to Vietnam* (Chichester, 1981)

———, 'The Tactical Problem: Infantry, Artillery and the Salient', in P. Liddle (ed.), *Passchendaele in Perspective: The Third Battle of Ypres* (London, 1997)

Groh, D., "'Je eher, desto besser!" Innenpolitische Faktoren für die Präventivkriegsbereitschaft des Deutschen Reiches 1913/14', in *Politische Vierteljahresschrift* (1972)

———, *Negative Integration und revolutionärer Attentismus, 1909–1914* (Frankfurt, 1973)

Grünbeck, Max, *Die Presse Grossbritanniens, ihr geistiger und wirtschaftlicher Aufbau: Wesen und Wirkungen der Publizistik—Arbeiten über die Volksbeeinflussung und geistige Volksführung aller Zeiten und Völker* (Leipzig, 1936)

Gudmundsson, Bruce I., *Stormtroop Tactics: Innovation in the German Army, 1914–18* (Westport, Conn., 1995)

Guinard, Pierre, *Inventaire sommaire des archives de la guerre, Série N, 1872–1919* (Troyes, 1975)

Guinn, P., *British Strategy and Politics, 1914–18* (Oxford, 1965)

Gullace, Nicoletta F., 'Sexual Violence and Family Honor: British Propaganda and International Law during the First World War', *American Historical Review* (1997)

Günther, A., *Die Folgen des Krieges für Einkommen und Lebenshaltung der mittleren Volksschichten Deutschlands* (Stuttgart/Berlin/Leipzig, 1932)

Gutsche, W., 'The Foreign Policy of Imperial Germany and the Outbreak of the War in the Historiography of the GDR', in Gregor Schöllgen (ed.), *Escape into War? The Foreign Policy of Imperial Germany* (Oxford/New York/Munich, 1990)

Haller, H., 'Die Rolle der Staatsfinanzen für den Inflationsprozess', in Deutsche Bundesbank (ed.), *Währung und Wirtschaft in Deutschland, 1876–1975* (Frankfurt am Main, 1976)

Hamilton, Sir Ian, *Gallipoli Diary*, 2 vols. (London, 1920)

Hamilton, K. A., 'Great Britain and France, 1911–1914', in F. Hinsley (ed.), *British Foreign Policy under Sir Edward Grey* (Cambridge, 1977)

Hankey, Baron, *The Supreme Command, 1914–18*, 2 vols. (London, 1961)

Hansard, The Parliamentary Debates (Authorized Edition), 4th series (1892–1908) and 5th series (1909–1980)

Hansen, Ferdinand, *The Unrepentant Northcliffe: A Reply to the London 'Times' of October 19, 1920* (Hamburg, 1921)

Hardach, Gerd, *The First World War, 1914–1918* (Harmondsworth, 1987)

Harris, Henry '"To Serve Mankind in Peace and the Fatherland at War": The Case of Fritz Haber', *German History* (1992)

Harris, J., *William Beveridge: A Biography* (Oxford, 1977)

Harris, Ruth, 'The "Child of the Barbarian": Rape, Race and Nationalism in France during the First World War', *Past and Present* (1993)

Harrison, R., 'The War Emergency Workers' Committee', in A. Briggs and J. Saville (eds.), *Essays in Labour History* (London, 1971)

Harrod, R. F., *The Life of John Maynard Keynes* (London, 1951)

Harvey, A. D., *Collision of Empires: Britain in Three World Wars, 1792–1945* (London, 1992)

Harvie, Christopher, *No Gods and Precious Few Heroes: Scotland, 1914–1980* (London, 1981)

Hašek, Jaroslav, *The Good Soldier Švejk and his Fortunes in the Great War*, trans. Cecil Parrott (Harmondsworth, 1974)

———, 'A Sporting Story', in Hašek, *The Bachura Scandal and Other Stories and Sketches*, trans. Alan Menhennet (London, 1991)

Hatton, R. H. S., 'Britain and Germany in 1914: The July Crisis and War Aims', *Past and Present* (1967)

Haupts, L., *Deutsche Friedenspolitik: Eine Alternative zur Machtpolitik des Ersten Weltkrieges* (Düsseldorf, 1976)

Hazlehurst, Cameron, *Politicians at War, July 1914 to May 1915: A Prologue to the Triumph of Lloyd George* (London, 1971)

Heenemann, Horst, 'Die Auflagenhöhe der deutschen Zeitungen: Ihre Entwicklung und ihre Probleme', unpublished D.Phil. thesis (Leipzig, 1929)

Hendley, Matthew, '"Help us to secure a strong, healthy, prosperous and peaceful Britain": The Social Arguments of the Campaign for Compulsory Military Service in Britain, 1899–1914', *Canadian Journal of History* (1995)

Henig, Ruth, *The Origins of the First World War* (London, 1989)

Henning, F.-W., *Das industrialisierte Deutschland, 1914 bis 1972* (Paderborn, 1974)

Hentschel, V., 'German Economic and Social Policy, 1815–1939', in P. Mathias and S. Pollard (eds.), *The Cambridge Economic History of Europe*, vol. VIII: *The Industrial Economies: The Development of Economic and Social Policies* (Cambridge, 1989)

——, *Wirtschaft und Wirtschaftspolitik im wilhelminischen Deutschland: Organisierter Kapitalismus und Interventionsstaat?* (Stuttgart, 1978)

——, 'Zahlen und Anmerkungen zum deutschen Außenhandel zwischen dem Ersten Weltkrieg und der Weltwirtschaftskrise', *Zeitschrift für Unternehmensgeschichte* (1986)

Herbert, A. P., *The Secret Battle* (London, 1976 edn.)

Herrmann, David G., *The Arming of Europe and the Making of the First World War* (Princeton, 1996)

Herwig, Holger H., 'Admirals *versus* Generals: The War Aims of the Imperial German Navy, 1914–1918', *Central European History* (1972)

——, 'The Dynamics of Necessity: German Military Policy during the First World War', in Williamson Murray and Allan R. Millett (eds.), *Military Effectiveness* (Winchester, Mass., 1988)

——, *The First World War: Germany and Austria-Hungary* (London, 1997)

——, 'How "Total" Was Germany's U-Boat Campaign in the Great War?', paper delivered at the Münchenwiler conference on total war (1997)

Hibberd, D. and J. Onions (eds.), *Poetry of the Great War: An Anthology* (London, 1986)

Hildebrand, K., *Deutsche Aussenpolitik, 1871–1918* (Munich, 1989)

——, 'Julikrise 1914: Das europäische Sicherheitsdilemma. Betrachtungen über den Ausbruch des Ersten Weltkrieges', *Geschichte in Wissenschaft und Unterricht* (1985)

——, 'Opportunities and Limits of German Foreign Policy in the Bismarckian Era, 1871–1890: "A system of stopgaps"?', in Schöllgen (ed.), *Escape into War? The Foreign Policy of Imperial Germany* (Oxford/New York/Munich, 1990)

——, *Das vergangene Reich: Deutsche Außenpolitik von Bismarck bis Hitler, 1871–1945* (Stuttgart, 1995)

Hiley, N., '"The British Army Film", "You!" and "For the Empire": Reconstructed Propaganda Films, 1914–1916', *Historical Journal of Film, Radio and Television* (1985)

——, 'Counter-Espionage and Security in Great Britain during the First World War', *English Historical Review* (1986)

——, 'The Failure of British Counter-Espionage against Germany, 1907–1914', *Historical Journal* (1983)

——, 'Introduction', in Le Queux, *Spies of the Kaiser*

——, '"Kitchener Wants You' and "Daddy, what did you do in the war?": The Myth of British Recruiting Posters', *Imperial War Museum Review* (1997)

Hillgruber, A., 'The Historical Significance of the First World War: A Seminal Catastrophe', in Schöllgen (ed.), *Escape into War? The Foreign Policy of Imperial Germany* (Oxford/New York/Munich, 1990)

Hirschfeld, Gerhard, Gerd Krumeich and Irina Den (eds.), *Keiner fühlt sich mehr als Mensch: Erlebnis und Wirkung des Ersten Weltkriegs* (Essen, 1993)

Hitler, Adolf, *Aquarelle* (Berlin, 1935)

——, *Mein Kampf*, trans. Ralph Manheim (London, 1992)

Hobsbawm, Eric, *The Age of Empire, 1875–1914* (London, 1987)

——, *The Age of Extremes: The Short Twentieth Century, 1914–1991* (London, 1994)

Hobson, J. A., *Imperialism: A Study* (1902; London, 1988)

Hobson, J. M., 'The Military-Extraction Gap and the Wary Titan: The Fiscal Sociology of British Defence Policy 1870–1913', *Journal of European Economic History* (1993)

Hodgson, Geoffrey, *People's Century: From the Dawn of the Century to the Start of the Cold War* (London, 1995)

Hoetzsch, Otto (ed.), *Die internationalen Beziehungen im Zeitalter des Imperialismus: Dokumente aus der Archiven der Zarischen und der Provisorischen Regierung*, 5 vols. (Berlin, 1931)

Hoffmann, W. G., F. Grumbach and H. Hesse, *Das Wachstum der deutschen Wirtschaft seit der Mitte des 19. Jahrhunderts* (Berlin, 1965)

Holmes, G., 'The First World War and Government Coal Control", In C. Barber and L. J. Williams (eds.), *Modern South Wales: Essays in Economic History* (Cardiff, 1986)

Holmes, Richard, 'The Last Hurrah: Cavalry on the Western Front, August September 1914', in H. Cecil and Liddle (eds.), *Facing Armageddon*

——, *War Walks from Agincourt to Normandy* (London, 1996)

Holroyd, Michael, *Bernard Shaw*, vol. II: *The Pursuit of Power* (London, 1989)

Holt, Tonie, and Valmahai, *Battlefields of the First World War: A Traveller's Guide* (London, 1995)

Holtfrerich, C.-L., 'Die deutsche Inflation 1918 bis 1923 in internationaler Perspektive. Entscheidungsrahmen und Verteilungsfolgen', in O. Büsch and G. D. Feldman (eds.), *Historische Prozesse der deutschen Inflation, 1914 bis 1923: Ein Tagungsbericht* (Berlin, 1978)

——, *The German Inflation, 1914–1923* (Berlin/New York, 1986)

Hoover, A. J., *God, Germany and Britain in the Great War: A Study in Clerical Nationalism* (New York, 1989)

Horne, Alistair, *The Price of Glory* (London, 1962)

Horne, John, '"*L'Impôt du sang*": Republican Rhetoric and Industrial Warfare in France, 1914–18', *Social History* (1989)

——, *Labour at War: France and Britain, 1914–1918* (Oxford, 1991)

——, and Alan Kramer, 'German "Atrocities" and Franco-German Opinion, 1914: The Evidence of German Soldiers' Diaries', *Journal of Modern History* (1994)

——, and A. Kramer, 'War between Soldiers and Enemy Civilians, 1914–15', paper delivered at the Münchenwiler conference on total war (1997)

Howard, Michael, 'British Grand Strategy in World War I', in P. Kennedy (ed.), *Grand Strategies in War and Peace* (New Haven/London, 1991)

——, *The Continental Commitment* (London, 1972)

——, *The Crisis of the Anglo-German Antagonism, 1916–17* (London, 1996)

——, 'The Edwardian Arms Race', in Howard, *The Lessons of History* (Oxford, 1993)

——, 'Europe on the Eve of World War I' in *Howard, The Lessons of History* (Oxford, 1993)

Huber, Max, *Geschichte der politischen Presse im Kanton Luzern 1914–1945* (Luzern, 1989)

Hughes, C., 'The New Armies', in I. Beckett and K. Simpson (eds.), *A Nation in Arms: A Social Study of the British Army in the First World War* (Manchester, 1985)

Hurwitz, S. J., *State Intervention in Great Britain: A Study of Economic Control and Social Response, 1914–1918* (New York, 1949)

Hussey, John, 'Kiggell and the Prisoners: Was He Guilty of a War Crime?', *British Army Review* (1993)

——, '"Without an Army, and Without Any Preparation to Equip One": The Financial and Industrial Background to 1914', *British Army Review* (1995)

Hynes, Samuel, *The Soldier's Tale: Bearing Witness to Modern War* (London, 1998)

——, *A War Imagined: The First World War and English Culture* (London, 1990)

Inglis, K., 'The Homecoming: The War Memorial Movement in Cambridge, England', *Journal of Contemporary History* (1992)

Innis, H. A., *The Press: A Neglected Factor in the Economic History of the Twentieth Century* (Oxford, 1949)

International Institute of Strategic Studies, *The Military Balance 1992–1993* (London, 1992)

Jackson, A., 'Germany, the Home Front: Blockade, Government and Revolution', in H. Cecil and Liddle (eds.), *Facing Armageddon*

Jackson, Alvin, 'British Ireland: "What If Home Rule Had Been Enacted in 1912?"', in Ferguson (ed.), *Virtual History*

Jackson, Robert, *The Prisoners, 1914–1918* (London/New York, 1989)

Jäger, Wolfgang, *Historische Forschung und politische Kultur in Deutschland: Die Debatte 1914–1980 über den Ausbruch des Ersten Weltkrieges* (Göttingen, 1984)

James, Harold, *The German Slump: Politics and Economics, 1924–1936* (Oxford, 1986)

James, Lawrence, *The Rise and Fall of the British Empire* (London, 1994)

Janowitz, M., and E. A. Shils, 'Cohesion and Disintegration in the Wehrmacht in World War Two', in Janowitz (ed.), *Military Conflict: Essays in the Institutional Analysis of War and Peace* (Los Angeles, 1975)

Jarausch, Konrad H., *The Enigmatic Chancellor: Bethmann Hollweg and the Hubris of Imperial Germany* (New Haven/London, 1973)

——, 'The Illusion of Limited War: Chancellor Bethmann Hollweg's Calculated Risk, July 1914', *Central European History* (1969)

Jay, Richard, *Joseph Chamberlain: A Political Study* (Oxford, 1981)

Jeze, G., *Les Dépenses de guerre de la France* (Paris, 1926)

Johansson, Rune, *Small State in Boundary Conflict: Belgium and the Belgian-German Border, 1914–1919* (Lund, 1988)

Johnson, J. H., *1918: The Unexpected Victory* (London, 1997)

Johnson, Paul, *The Offshore Islanders* (London, 1972)

Joll, James, *Europe since 1870: An International History* (London, 1973)

———, *The Origins of the First World War* (London/New York, 1984)

———, *The Second International, 1889–1914* (London, 1955)

Jones, Larry E., '"The Dying Middle": Weimar Germany and the Fragmentation of Bourgeois Politics', *Central European History* (1972)

———, *German Liberalism and the Dissolution of the Weimar Party System, 1918–1933* (Chapel Hill/London, 1988)

———, 'Inflation, Revaluation and the Crisis of Middle Class Politics: A Study of the Dissolution of the German Party System, 1923–1928', *Central European History* (1979)

Jones, Maldwyn A., *The Limits of Liberty: American History, 1607–1980* (Oxford, 1993)

Junger, Ernst, *The Storm of Steel: From the Diary of a German Storm-Troop Officer on the Western Front*, trans. Basil Creighton (London, 1929)

Kahan, A., 'Government Policies and the Industrialization of Russia', *Journal of Economic History* (1967)

Kahn, Elizabeth Louise, 'Art from the Front, Death Imagined and the Neglected Majority', *Art History* (1985)

Kaiser, David E., 'Germany and the Origins of the First World War', *Journal of Modern History* (1983)

Keegan, John, *The Face of Battle* (London, 1993)

———, and R. Holmes, *Soldiers: A History of Men in Battle* (London, 1985)

Kehr, Eckart, 'Klassenkämpfe und Rüstungspolitik im kaiserlichen Deutschland', in Kehr, *Der Primat der Innenpolitik: Gesammelte Aufsätze zur preußisch-deutschen Sozialgeschichte im 19. und 20. Jahrhundert*, ed. Hans-Ulrich Wehler (Berlin, 1970)

Keiger, J. F. V., *France and the Origins of the First World War* (London, 1983)

Kellett, A., *Combat Motivation: The Behaviour of Soldiers in Battle* (Boston, 1982)

Kemp, T., *The French Economy 1913–1939* (London, 1972)

Kennan, George F., *The Decline of Bismarck's European Order: Franco-Russian Relations 1875–1890* (Princeton, 1974)

———, *The Fateful Alliance: France, Russia, and the Coming of the First World War* (Manchester, 1984)

Kennedy, P. M., 'Britain in the First World War', in Williamson Murray and Allan R. Millett (eds.), *Military Effectiveness* (Winchester, Mass., 1988)

———, 'The First World War and the International Power System', *International Security* (1984–5)

———, 'German World Policy and the Alliance Negotiations with England 1897–1900', *Journal of Modern History* (1973)

———, 'Military Effectiveness and the First World War', in Williamson Murray and Allan R. Millett (eds.), *Military Effectiveness* (Winchester, Mass., 1988)

———, *The Rise and Fall of the Great Powers: Economic Change and Military Conflict from 1500 to 2000* (London, 1988)

———, *The Rise of the Anglo-German Antagonism, 1860–1914* (London, 1980)

———, 'Strategy Versus Finance in Twentieth Century Britain', *International History Review* (1981)

———, and P. K. O'Brien, 'Debate: The Costs and Benefits of British Imperialism, 1846–1914', *Past and Present* (1989)

Kent, Bruce, *The Spoils of War: The Politics, Economics and Diplomacy of Reparations, 1918–1932* (Oxford, 1989)

Kershaw, Ian, *Hitler*, vol. I: *Hubris* (London, 1998)

Kersten, D., 'Die Kriegsziele der Hamburger Kaufmannschaft im Ersten Weltkrieg, 1914–1918', unpublished thesis (Hamburg, 1962)

Keynes, J. M., *The Collected Writings of John Maynard Keynes*, vol. XI: *Economic Articles and Correspondence*, ed. D. Moggridge (London, 1972)

———, *The Collected Writings of John Maynard Keynes*, vol. XVI: *Activities 1914–19, The Treasury and Versailles*, ed. E. Johnson (London, 1977)

———, *The Collected Writings of John Maynard Keynes*, vol. XVII: *Activities, 1920–22, Treaty Revision and Reconstruction*, ed. E. Johnson (London, 1977)

———, *The Collected Writings of John Maynard Keynes*, vol. XVIII: *Activities, 1922–32, The End of Reparations*, ed. E. Johnson (London, 1977)

———, *The Collected Writings of John Maynard Keynes*, vol. XXI: *Activities, 1931–39, World Crises and Policies in Britain and America*, ed. D. Moggridge (London, 1982)

———, 'Dr Melchior: A Defeated Enemy', in *Two Memoirs* (London, 1949), reprinted in *Collected Writings*, vol. X: *Essays in Biography*, ed. A. Robinson and D. Moggridge (London, 1972)

———, *The Economic Consequences of the Peace* (London, 1919)

———, *How to Pay for the War* (London, 1940)

———, *A Revision of the Treaty* (London, 1921)

———, *A Tract on Monetary Reform* (London, 1923), reprinted in *Collected Writings*, vol. IV (Cambridge, 1971)

Kiernan, T. J., *British War Finance and the Consequences* (London, 1920)

Kindleberger, Charles P., *A Financial History of Western Europe* (London, 1984)

Kipling, Rudyard, *The Irish Guards in the Great War*, vol. I: *The First Battalion* (Staplehurst, 1997); vol. II: *The Second Battalion* (Staplehurst, 1997)

Kirkaldy, A. W., *British Finance during and after the War* (London, 1921)

Kitchen, M., *The German Officer Corps 1890–1914* (Oxford, 1968)

———, 'Ludendorff and Germany's Defeat', in H. Cecil and Liddle (eds.), *Facing Armageddon*

———, *The Silent Dictatorship: The Politics of the German High Command under Hindenburg and Ludendorff, 1916–1918* (New York, 1976)

Klemperer, Victor, *I Shall Bear Witness: The Diaries of Victor Klemperer, 1933–41* (London, 1998)

Knauss, R., *Die deutsche, englische und französische Kriegsfinanzierung* (Berlin/Leipzig, 1923)

Knightley, P., *The First Casualty: The War Correspondent as a Hero, Protagonist and Mythmaker from the Crimea to Vietnam* (London, 1975)

Knock, Thomas J., *To End All Wars: Woodrow Wilson and the Quest for a New World Order* (New York/Oxford, 1992)

Koch, H. W., 'The Anglo-German Alliance Negotiations: Missed Opportunity or Myth?', *History* (1968)

Kocka, Jürgen, *Facing Total War: German Society, 1914–1918* (Leamington Spa, 1984)

———, 'The First World War and the *Mittelstand*: German Artisans and White Collar Workers', *Journal of Contemporary History* (1973)

Komlos, J., *The Habsburg Monarchy as a Customs Union: Economic Development in Austria-Hungary in the Nineteenth Century* (Princeton, 1983)

Koss, Stephen, *Fleet Street Radical: A. G. Gardiner and the Daily News* (London, 1973)

———, *The Rise and Fall of the Political Press in Britain*, vol. II: *The Twentieth Century* (Chapel Hill/London, 1984)

Kossmann, E. H., *The Low Countries, 1780–1940* (Oxford, 1978)

Koszyk, Kurt, *Deutsche Presse, 1914–1945: Geschichte der deutschen Presse*, vol. III: *Abhandlungen und Materialien zur Publizistik* (Berlin, 1972)

———, *Deutsche Pressepolitik im Ersten Weltkrieg* (Düsseldorf, 1968)

———, *Zwischen Kaiserreich und Diktatur: Die sozialdemokratische Presse von 1914 bis 1933* (Heidelberg, 1958)

Kranzfelder, Ivo, *George Grosz, 1893–1959* (Cologne, 1994)

Kraus, Karl, *In These Great Times: A Karl Kraus Reader*, ed. Harry Zorn (Manchester, 1984)

———, *Die letzten Tage der Menschheit: Tragödie in fünf Atken mit Vorspiel und Epilog* (Frankfurt am Main, 1986)

Krivosheev, Colonel-General G. F. (ed.), *Soviet Casualties and Combat Losses in the Twentieth Century* (London/Mechanicsburg, Penn., 1997)

Kroboth, R., *Die Finanzpolitik des Deutschen Reiches während der Reichskanzlerschaft Bethmann Hollwegs und die Geld- und Kapitalmarktverhältnisse (1909–1913/14)* (Frankfurt am Main, 1986)

Krohn, C.-D., *Wirtschaftstheorien als politische Interessen: Die akademische Nationalökonomie in Deutschland, 1918–1933* (Frankfurt am Main, 1981)

Kruedener, J. Baron von, 'The Franckenstein Paradox in the Intergovernmental Fiscal Relations of Imperial Germany', in P.-C. Witt (ed.), *Wealth and Taxation in Central Europe: The History and Sociology of Public Finance* (Leamington Spa, 1987)

Krüger, P., *Deutschland und die Reparationen 1918/19: Die Genesis des Reparationsproblems in Deutschland zwischen Waffenstillstand und Versailler Friedensschluss* (Stuttgart, 1973)

———, 'Die Rolle der Banken und der Industrie in den deutschen reparationspolitischen Entscheidungen nach dem Ersten Weltkrieg', in H. Mommsen *et al.* (eds.), *Industrielles System und politische Entwicklung in der Weimarer Republik*, vol. II (Düsseldorf, 1977)

Krumeich, Gerd, 'L'Entrée en guerre en Allemagne', in Becker and S. Audoin-Rouzeau (eds.), *Les Sociétés européennes et la Guerre de 1914–1918* (Paris, 1990)

Kynaston, David, *The City of London*, vol. I: *A World of Its Own, 1815–90* (London, 1994)

———, *The City of London*, vol. II: *Golden Years, 1890–1914* (London, 1996)

Laffin, John, *British Butchers and Bunglers of World War One* (London, 1988)

Lammers, D., 'Arno Mayer and the British Decision for War in 1914', *Journal of British Studies* (1973)

Langhorne, R. T. B., 'Anglo-German Negotiations Concerning the Future of the Portuguese Colonies, 1911–1914', *Historical Journal* (1973)

———, *The Collapse of the Concert of Europe: International Politics, 1890–1914* (London, 1981)

———, 'Great Britain and Germany, 1911–1914', in F. Hinsley (ed.), *British Foreign Policy under Sir Edward Grey* (Cambridge, 1977)

Lasswell, H. D., *Propaganda Technique in the World War* (London, 1927)

Laursen, K. and J. Pedersen, *The German Inflation, 1918–1923* (Amsterdam, 1964)

Lawrence, J., M. Dean and J.-L. Robert, 'The Outbreak of War and the Urban Economy: Paris, Berlin and London in 1914', *Economic History Review* (1992)

Lawrence, T. E., *Seven Pillars of Wisdom* (Harmondsworth, 1962 edn.)

League of Nations, *Memorandum on Production and Trade, 1923–1926* (Geneva, 1928)

Lee, D. E., *Europe's Crucial Years: The Diplomatic Background of World War I, 1902–1914* (Hanover, New Hampshire, 1974)

Lee, Joe, 'Administrators and Agriculture: Aspects of German Agricultural Policy in the First World War', in J. Winter (ed.), *War and Economic Development* (Cambridge, 1975)

Leese, P., 'Problems Returning Home: The British Psychological Casualties of the Great War', *Historical Journal* (1997)

Lenin, V. I., *Imperialism: The Highest Stage of Capitalism—A Popular Outline* (London, 1934 edn.)

Leontaritis, George B., *Greece and the First World War, 1917–1918* (New York, 1990)

Lepsius, J., A. Mendelssohn-Bartholdy and F. W. K. Thimme (eds.), *Die grosse Politik der europäischen Kabinette, 1871–1914: Sammlung der diplomatischen Akten des Auswärtigen Amtes*, 40 vols (Berlin, 1922–7)

Le Queux, William, *Spies of the Kaiser: Plotting the Downfall of England*, ed. Nicholas Hiley (London, 1996)

Leslie, John, 'The Antecedents of Austria—Hungary's War Aims: Politics and Policy-Makers in Vienna and Budapest before and during 1914', in Elisabeth Springer and Leopold Kammerhofer (eds.), *Archiv und Forschung: Das Haus-, Hof- und Staatsarchiv in seiner Bedeutung für die Geschichte Österreichs und Europas* (Vienna/Munich, 1993)

Leugers, A.-H., 'Einstellungen zu Krieg und Frieden im deutschen Katholizismus vor 1914', in Jost Dülffer and Karl Holl (eds.), *Bereit zum Krieg: Kriegsmentalität im wilhelminischen Deutschland 1890–1914. Beiträge zur historischen Friedensforschung* (Göttingen, 1986)

Leunig, T., 'Lancashire at its Zenith: Transport Costs and the Slow Adoption of Ring Spinning in the Lancashire Cotton Industry, 1900–13', in I. Blanchard (ed.), *New Directions in Economic and Social History* (Edinburgh, 1995)

Lévy-Leboyer, M., and F. Bourgignon, *L'Économie française au XIXe. siècle: Analyse macro-économique* (Paris, 1985)

Liddell Hart, Basil, *The British Way in Warfare* (London, 1942)

Liddle, Peter H., *The 1916 Battle of the Somme* (London, 1992)

——— (ed.), *Home Fires and Foreign Fields* (London, 1985)

Liebknecht, Karl, *Militarism and Anti-Militarism* (London, 1973)

Lieven, D., *Russia and the Origins of the First World War* (London, 1983)

Lindenlaub, D., *Machinebauunternehmen in der Inflation 1919 bis 1923: Unternehmenshistorische Untersuchungen zu einigen Inflationstheorien* (Berlin/New York, 1985)

Lipman, Edward, 'The City and the "People's Budget"', unpublished MS (1995)

Livois, René de, *Histoire de la presse française*, vol. II: *De 1881 à nos jours* (Lausanne, 1965)

Lloyd George, David, *War Memoirs*, 6 vols. (London, 1933–6)

Loewenberg, P., 'Arno Mayer's "Internal Causes and Purposes of War in Europe, 1870–1956": An Inadequate Model of Human Behaviour, National Conflict, and Historical Change', *Journal of Modern History* (1970)

Lotz, W., *Die deutsche Staatsfinanzwirtschaft im Kriege* (Stuttgart, 1927)

Lowe, R., 'The Ministry of Labour, 1916–1919: A Still, Small Voice?', in K. Burk (ed.), *War and the State* (London, 1982)

———, 'Welfare Legislation and the Unions during and after the First World War', *Historical Journal* (1982)

Luckau, A., *The German Peace Delegation at the Paris Peace Conference* (New York, 1941)

Ludendorff, E. von, *The General Staff and Its Problems: The History of the Relations between the High Command and the Imperial Government as Revealed by Official Documents*, 2 vols. (London, 1920)

———, *Meine Kriegserinnerungen* (Berlin, 1920), trans. as *My War Memories, 1914–18*, 2 vols. (London, 1923)

Lyashchenko, P. L., *History of the National Economy of Russia to the 1917 Revolution* (New York, 1949)

Lyth, Peter J., *Inflation and the Merchant Economy: The Hamburg Mittelstand, 1914–1924* (New York/ Oxford/Munich, 1990)

McDermott, J., 'The Revolution in British Military Thinking, from the Boer War to the Moroccan Crisis', *Canadian Journal of History* (1974)
MacDonald, Lyn, *1914: The Dawn of Hope* (London, 1987)
——, *1914–1918: Voices and Images of the Great War* (London, 1988)
——, *1915: The Death of Innocence* (London, 1993)
——, *The Roses of No Man's Land* (London, 1980)
——, *Somme* (London, 1983)
——, *They Called It Passchendaele: The Story of Ypres and of the Men Who Fought in It* (London, 1978)
McEwen, John M., 'The National Press during the First World War: Ownership and Circulation', *Journal of Contemporary History* (1982)
Mack Smith, Dennis, *Italy: A Modern History* (Ann Arbor, 1959)
Mackay, R. F., *Fisher of Kilverstone* (Oxford, 1973)
Mackenzie, Norman, and Jeanne Mackenzie (eds.), *The Diary of Beatrice Webb*, vol. III, *1905–1924: The Power to Alter Things* (London, 1984)
McKeown, T. J., 'The Foreign Policy of a Declining Power', *International Organisation* (1991)
McKibbin, Ross, 'Class and Conventional Wisdom: The Conservative Party and the "Public" in Inter-war Britain', in McKibbin, *The Ideologies of Class: Social Relations in Britain, 1880–1950* (Oxford, 1990)
Mackin, Elton E., *Suddenly We Didn't Want to Die: Memoirs of a World War I Marine* (Novato, California, 1993)
Mackintosh, 'The Role of the Committee of Imperial Defence before 1914', *English Historical Review* (1962)
McNeill, W. H., *The Pursuit of Power: Technology, Armed Force and Society since AD 1000* (London, 1982)
Maddison, Angus, *Phases of Capitalist Development* (Oxford, 1982)
Maier, Charles S., *Recasting Bourgeois Europe: Stabilisation in France, Germany and Italy in the Decade after World War I* (Princeton, 1975)
——, 'The Truth about the Treaties', *Journal of Modern History* (1979)
——, 'Wargames: 1914–1919', in Robert I. Rotberg and Theodore K. Rabb (eds.), *The Origin and Prevention of Major Wars* (Cambridge, 1989)
Malcolm, Noel, *Bosnia: A Short History* (London, 1994)
Mallet, B., and C. O. George, *British Budgets*, 2nd series: *1913/14* to *1920/21* (London, 1929)
Manevy, Raymond, *La Presse de la IIIe. République* (Paris, 1955)
Mann, Thomas, *Betrachtungen eines Unpolitischen* (Berlin, 1918)
Manning, J., 'Wages and Purchasing Power', in J. Winter (ed.), *Capital Cities*
Marchand, R. (ed), *Un Livre noir: Diplomatie d'avant-guerre et de guerre d'après les documents des archives russes, 1910–1917*, 3 vols. (Paris, 1922)
Marder, A. J., *British Naval Policy, 1880–1905: The Anatomy of British Sea Power* (London, 1964)
Marks, Sally, 'Reparations Reconsidered: A Reminder', *Central European History* (1969)
Marquand, David, *Ramsay MacDonald* (London, 1997)
Marquis, Alice Goldfarb, 'Words as Weapons: Propaganda in Britain and Germany during the First World War', *Journal of Contemporary History* (1978)
Marsland, Elizabeth, *The Nation's Cause: French, English and German Poetry of the First World War* (London, 1991)
Martel, Gordon, *The Origins of the First World War* (London, 1987)
Martin, Gregory, 'German Strategy and Military Assessments of the American Expeditionary Force (AEF), 1917–18', *War in History* (1994)
Marwick, Arthur, *The Deluge: British Society and the First World War* (London, 1991 edn.)
——, 'War and the Arts', paper delivered at the Münchenwiler conference on total war (1997)
März, E., *Austrian Banking and Financial Policy: Creditanstalt at a Turning Point, 1913–1923* (London, 1984)
Matthews, W. C., 'The Continuity of Social Democratic Economic Policy, 1919 to 1920: The Bauer-Schmidt Policy', in G. Feldman *et al.* (eds.), *Die Anpassung an die Inflation* (Berlin/New York, 1986)
Maugham, W. Somerset, *A Writer's Notebook* (London, 1978)
Mayer, A. J., 'Domestic Causes of the First World War', in L. Krieger and F. Stern (eds.), *The Responsibility of Power: Historical Essays in Honour of Hajo Holborn* (New York, 1967)
——, *The Persistence of the Old Regime* (New York, 1971)

Mayeur, Jean-Marie, 'Le Catholicisme français et la première guerre mondiale', *Francia* (1974)

Mazower, Mark, *Dark Continent: Europe's Twentieth Century* (London, 1998)

Meinecke, Friedrich, *Die deutsche Erhebung von 1914* (Stuttgart, 1914)

———, *Die deutsche Katastrophe* (Wiesbaden, 1946)

———, *Die Geschichte des deutsche-englischen Bündnisproblems* (Munich, 1927)

Messinger, Gary S., *British Propaganda and the State in the First World War* (Manchester, 1992)

Mews, Stuart, 'Spiritual Mobilisation in the First World War', *Theology* (1971)

Meyer, H. C., *Mitteleuropa in German Thought and Action, 1815–1945* (The Hague, 1955)

Michalka, Wolfgang (ed.), *Der Erste Weltkrieg: Wirkung, Wahrnehmung, Analyse* (Munich, 1994)

Middlemas, Keith, *Politics in Industrial Society* (London, 1979)

Miller, S., *Burgfrieden und Klassenkampf: Die deutsche Sozialdemokratie im Ersten Weltkrieg* (Düsseldorf, 1974)

Millett, Allan R., Williamson Murray and Kenneth Watman, 'The Effectiveness of Military Organizations', in Williamson Murray and Millett (eds.), *Military Effectiveness* (Winchester, Mass., 1988)

Milward, Alan S., *The Economic Effects of the Two World Wars on Britain* (London, 1984)

Ministère des Affaires Étrangères [Belgium], *Correspondance Diplomatique relative à la Guerre de 1914* (Paris, 1915)

Ministerium des k. und k. Hauses und des Äussern, *Diplomatische Aktenstücke zur Vorgeschichte des Krieges 1914*, 3 vols. (London, 1920)

Mitchell, B. R., *European Historical Statistics, 1750–1975* (London, 1981)

———, and P. Deane, *Abstract of British Historical Statistics* (Cambridge, 1976)

Moeller, Robert G., 'Dimensions of Social Conflict in the Great War: The View from the German Country-side', *Central European History* (1981)

———, 'Winners as Losers in the German Inflation: Peasant Protest over the Controlled Economy', in G. Feldman *et al.* (eds.), *Die deutsche Inflation. Eine Zwischenbilanz* (Berlin/New York, 1982)

Moggridge, D. E., *Maynard Keynes: An Economist's Biography* (London, 1992)

Moltke, E. von, *Generaloberst Helmuth von Moltke: Erinnerungen, Briefe, Dokumente 1877–1916* (Stuttgart, 1922)

Mommsen, W. J., 'Domestic Factors in German Foreign Policy before 1914', *Central European History* (1973)

——— (ed.), *Kultur und Krieg: Die Rolle der Intellektuellen, Künstler und Schriftsteller im Ersten Weltkrieg* (Munich, 1996)

———, 'Die latente Krise des Deutschen Reiches', *Militärgeschichtliche Mitteilungen* (1974)

———, *Max Weber and German Politics, 1890–1920* (Chicago, 1984)

———, 'Public Opinion and Foreign Policy in Wilhelmian Germany, 1897–1914', *Central European History* (1991)

———, 'The Topos of Inevitable War in Germany in the Decade before 1914', in V. R. Berghahn and M. Kitchen (eds.), *Germany in the Age of Total War* (London, 1981)

Monash, Sir John, *The Australian Victories in France in 1918* (London, 1920)

Monger, G. W., *The End of Isolation: British Foreign Policy, 1900–1907* (London, 1963)

Monk, Ray, *Wittgenstein: The Duty of Genius* (London, 1990)

Montgelas, M. and W. Schücking (eds.), *The Outbreak of the World War: German Documents Collected by Karl Kautsky* (New York, 1924)

Morgan, E. V., *Studies in British Financial Policy, 1914–1925* (London, 1952)

———, and W. A. Thomas, *The Stock Exchange* (London, 1962)

Morgan, K. O. (ed.), *Lloyd George Family Letters, 1885–1936* (Oxford, 1973)

Morgenbrod, Birgitt, *Wiener Grossbürgertum im Ersten Weltkrieg: Die Geschichte der 'Österreichischen Politischen Gesellschaft' (1916–1918)* (Wien, 1994)

Morley, Viscount, *Memorandum on Resignation* (London, 1928)

Morris, A. J. A., *The Scaremongers: The Advocacy of War and Rearmament, 1896–1914* (London/Boston/Melbourne/Henley, 1984)

Morton, Frederick, *Thunder at Twilight: Vienna 1913–1914* (London, 1991)

Moses, J. A., *The Politics of Illusion: The Fischer Controversy in German Historiography* (London, 1975)

Mosse, G., *Fallen Soldiers: Reshaping the Memory of the World Wars* (Oxford, 1990)

Moyer, Laurence V., *Victory Must Be Ours: Germany in the Great War, 1914–1918* (London, 1995)

Moynihan, M. (ed.), *God on Our Side: The British Padres in World War One* (London, 1983)

Murray, B. K., *The People's Budget, 1909–10: Lloyd George and Liberal Politics* (Oxford, 1980)

Nägler, Jörg, 'Pandora's Box: Propaganda and War Hysteria in the United States during the First World War', paper delivered at the Münchenwiler conference on total war (1997)

Nicholls, A. J., and P. M. Kennedy, (eds.), *Nationalist and Racialist Movements in Britain and Germany before 1914* (London/Oxford, 1981)

Nicholls, Jonathan, *Cheerful Sacrifice: The Battle of Arras, 1917* (London, 1990)

Nicolson, C., 'Edwardian England and the Coming of the First World War', in A. O'Day (ed.), *The Edwardian Age: Conflict and Stability, 1902–1914* (London, 1979)

Noble, Roger, 'Raising the White Flag: The Surrender of Australian Soldiers on the Western Front', *Revue Internationale d'Histoire Militaire* (1990)

Nottingham, Christopher J., 'Recasting Bourgeois Britain: The British State in the Years Which Followed the First World War', *International Review of Social History* (1986)

O'Brien, P. K., 'The Costs and Benefits of British Imperialism, 1846–1914', *Past and Present* (1988)

——, 'Power with Profit: The State and the Economy, 1688–1815', inaugural lecture, University of London (1991)

O'Brien Twohig, Sara, 'Dix and Nietzsche', in Tate Gallery, *Otto Dix, 1891–1961* (London, 1992)

Offer, Avner, 'The British Empire, 1870–1914: A Waste of Money?', *Economic History Review* (1993)

——, *The First World War: An Agrarian Interpretation* (Oxford, 1989)

——, 'Going to War in 1914: A matter of Honour?', *Politics and Society* (1995)

O'Hara, Glen, 'Britain's War of Illusions: Sir Edward Grey and the Crisis of Liberal Diplomacy', unpublished B.A. thesis (Oxford, 1995)

Oncken, H., *Das Deutsche Reich und die Vorgeschichte des Weltkriegs*, 2 vols. (Berlin, 1933)

O'Shea, Stephen, *Back to the Front: An Accidental Historian Walks the Trenches of World War I* (London, 1997)

Österreichisches Bundesministerium für Heereswesen und Kriegsarchiv (ed.), *Österreich-Ungarns letzter Krieg, 1914–1918*, 7 vols. (Vienna 1930–38)

Overy, Richard, *Why the Allies Won* (London, 1995)

Owen, G., 'Dollar Diplomacy in Default: The Economics of Russian-American Relations, 1910–1917', *Historical Journal* (1970)

Owen, Wilfred, *The Poems of Wilfred Owen*, ed. Jon Stallworthy (London, 1990)

Pachnicke, Peter, and Klaus Honnef (eds.), *John Heartfield* (New York, 1991)

Paddags, Norbert, 'The Weimar Inflation: Possibilities of Stabilisation before 1923?', unpublished M.Sc. dissertation (Oxford, 1995)

Parker, Geoffrey (ed.), *The Times Atlas of World History* (London, 1993 edn.)

Parker, P., *The Old Lie: The Great War and the Public School Ethos* (London, 1987)

Paulinyi, A., 'Die sogenannte gemeinsame Wirtschaftspolitik Österreich-Ungarns', in A. Wandruszka and P. Urbanitsch (eds.), *Die Habsburgermonarchie, 1848–1918*, vol. I (Vienna, 1973)

Peacock, A. T. and J. Wiseman, *The Growth of Public Expenditure in the United Kingdom* (Princeton, 1961)

Pedroncini, G., *Les Mutineries de 1917* (Paris, 1967)

Perry, Nicholas, 'Maintaining Regimental Identity in the Great War: The Case of the Irish Infantry Regiments', in *Stand To* (1998)

Pertile, Lino, 'Fascism and Literature', in David Forgacs (ed.), *Rethinking Italian Fascism* (London, 1986)

Petzina, D., W. Abelshauser and A. Foust (eds.), *Sozialgeschichtliches Arbeitsbuch*, vol. III: *Materialen zur Statistik des Deutschen Reiches, 1914–1945* (Munich, 1978)

Phillips, G., 'The Social Impact', in S. Constantine, M. W. Kirby and M. Rose (eds.), *The First World War in British History* (1995)

Philpott, W. J., *Anglo-French Relations and Strategy on the Western Front* (London, 1996)

Pipes, Richard, *Russia under the Bolshevik Regime, 1919–24* (London, 1994)

——, *The Russian Revolution 1899–1919* (London, 1990)

Pogge von Strandmann, H. (ed.), 'Germany and the Coming of War', in Pogge von Strandmann and R. J. W. Evans (eds.), *The Coming of the First World War* (Oxford, 1988)

——, 'Historians, Nationalism and War: The Mobilisation of Public Opinion in Britain and Germany', unpublished MS (1998)

——, *Walther Rathenau: Industrialist, Banker, Intellectual, and Politician: Notes and Diaries, 1907–1922* (Oxford, 1985)

Pohl, M., *Hamburger Bankengeschichte* (Mainz, 1986)

Poidevin, Raymond, *Les Relations économiques et financières entre la France et l'Allemagne de 1898 à 1914* (Paris, 1969)

Pollard, Sidney, *Britain's Prime and Britain's Decline: The British Economy, 1870–1914* (London, 1989)
——, 'Capital Exports, 1870–1914: Harmful or Beneficial?', *Economic History Review* (1985)
Porch, D., 'The French Army and the Spirit of the Offensive, 1900–1914', in *War and Society* (1976)
Pottle, Mark (ed.), *Champion Redoubtable: The Diaries and Letters of Violet Bonham Carter, 1914–1945* (London, 1998)
Prakke, Henk, Wilfried B. Lerg and Michael Schmolke, *Handbuch der Weltpresse* (Cologne, 1970)
Prete, Roy A., 'French Military War Aims, 1914–1916', *Historical Journal* (1985)
Price, Richard, *An Imperial War and the British Working Class* (London, 1972)
Prior, R., and Trevor Wilson, *Command on the Western Front* (Oxford, 1992)
Prost, Antoine, 'Les Monuments aux Morts: Culte républicain? Culte civique? Culte patriotique?', in P. Nora (ed.), *Les Lieux de mémoire*, vol. 1: *La République* (Paris, 1984)
Public Record Office, *M.I.5: The First Ten Years, 1909–1919* (Kew, 1997)

Raleigh, Sir Walter, and H. A. Jones (eds.), *The War in the Air*, 6 vols. (London, 1922–37)
Rathenau, Walther, *Briefe*, 2 vols. (Dresden, 1926)
Rauh, M., *Föderalismus und Parlamentarismus im wilhelminischen Reich* (Düsseldorf, 1972)
——, *Die Parlamentarisierung des Deutschen Reiches* (Düsseldorf, 1977)
Rawling, B., *Surviving Trench Warfare: Technology and the Canadian Corps, 1914–18* (Toronto, 1992)
Reader, W. J., *At Duty's Call: A Study in Obsolete Patriotism* (Manchester, 1988)
Reeves, Nicholas, 'Film Propaganda and Its Audience: The Example of Britain's Official Films during the First World War', *Journal of Contemporary History* (1983)
Reichsarchiv, *Der Weltkrieg 1914 bis 1918*, 14 vols. (Berlin/Coblenz, 1925–56)
Reichswehrministerium, *Sanitätsbericht über das Deutsche Heer (deutsches Feld- und Besatzungsheer) im Weltkriege 1914–1918 (Deutscher Kriegssanitätsbericht, 1914–18)*, 4 vols. (Berlin, 1934, 1938)
Reid, A., 'Dilution, Trade Unionism and the State in Britain during the First World War', in S. Tolliday and J. Zeitlin (eds.), *Shop Floor Bargaining and the State: Historical and Comparative Perspectives* (Cambridge, 1985)
Remak, J. '1914—the Third Balkan War: Origins Reconsidered', *Journal of Modern History* (1971)
Remarque, Erich Maria, *All Quiet on the Western Front*, trans. Brian Murdoch (London, 1996)
Renzi, W. A., 'Great Britain, Russia and the Straits, 1914–1915', *Journal of Modern History* (1970)
Rezzori, Gregor von, *The Snows of Yesteryear: Portraits for an Autobiography* (London, 1991)
Rich, N., and M. H. Fisher (eds.), *The Holstein Papers: The Memoirs, Diaries and Correspondence of Friedrich von Holstein, 1837–1909*, vol. IV: *Correspondence, 1897–1909* (Cambridge, 1961)
Richardson, L. F., *Arms and Insecurity* (London, 1960)
Riegel, L., *Guerre et littérature: Le Bouleversement des consciences dans la littérature romanesque inspirée par la Grande Guerre* (Paris, 1978)
Ritter, G., *Der Schlieffenplan: Kritik eines Mythos* (Munich, 1956), trans. *The Schlieffen Plan: Critique of a Myth* (London, 1958)
——, *Staatskunst und Kriegshandwerk: Das Problem des 'Militarismus' in Deutschland*, 4 vols. (Munich, 1965–8), trans. *Sword and the Sceptre*
——, *The Sword and the Sceptre: The Problem of Militarism in Germany*, vol. II: *The European Powers and the Wilhelminian Empire 1890–1914* (Coral Gables, 1970)
Robbins, K., *The First World War* (Oxford, 1984)
——, *Sir Edward Grey: A Biography of Grey of Falloden* (London, 1971)
Robert, Daniel, 'Les Protestants français et la guerre de 1914–1918', *Francia* (1974)
Robertson, Sir William, *Soldiers and Statesmen*, 2 vols. (London, 1926)
Roesler, K., *Die Finanzpolitik des Deutschen Reiches im Ersten Weltkrieg* (Berlin, 1967)
Ropponen, R., *Die russische Gefahr: Das Verhalten der öffentlichen Meinung Deutschlands und Österreich-Ungarns gegenüber der Aussenpolitik Russlands in der Zeit zwischen dem Frieden von Portsmouth und dem Ausbruch des Ersten Weltkrieges* (Helsinki, 1976)
Rosenbaum, E., and A. J. Sherman, *M.M. Warburg & Co., 1798–1938: Merchant Bankers of Hamburg* (London, 1979)
Rothenberg, G. E., *The Army of Francis Joseph* (West Lafayette, 1976)
——, 'Moltke, Schlieffen and the Doctrine of Strategic Envelopment', in Peter Paret (ed.), *Makers of Modern Strategy from Machiavelli to the Nuclear Age* (Princeton, 1986)
Roucoux, Michel (ed.), *English Literature of the Great War Revisited* (Picardie, 1988)
Rowland, P., *The Last Liberal Governments*, vol. II: *Unfinished Business, 1911–1914* (London, 1971)

Rubin, G. R., *War, Law and Labour: The Munitions Acts, State Regulation and the Unions 1915–1921* (Oxford, 1987)

Rummel, R. J., *Lethal Politics: Soviet Genocide and Mass Murder since 1917* (New Brunswick, 1990)

Rupieper, H. J., *The Cuno Government and Reparations, 1922–1923: Politics and Economics* (The Hague/London/Boston, 1976)

Russell, Bertrand, *Portraits from Memory* (London, 1958)

Rutherford, W., *The Russian Army in World War I* (London, 1975)

Ryan, Alan, *Bertrand Russell: A Political Life* (London, 1988)

Saad El-Din, *The Modern Egyptian Press* (London, n.d.)

Saki, *When William Came: A Story of London under the Hohenzollerns*, reprinted in *The Complete Works of Saki* (London/Sydney/Toronto, 1980)

Samuels, M., *Command or Control? Command, Training and Tactics in the British and German Armies, 1888–1918* (London, 1995)

——, *Doctrine and Dogma: German and British Infantry Tactics in the First World War* (New York, 1992)

Sassoon, Seigfried, *The Complete Memoirs of George Sherston* (London, 1972)

——, *Memoirs of a Fox-Hunting Man* (London, 1978)

——, *Memoirs of an Infantry Officer* (London, 1997)

——, *The War Poems*, ed. Rupert Hart-Davis (London/Boston, 1983)

Sazonov, S., *Fateful Years, 1909–1916: The Reminiscences of Count Sazonov* (London, 1928)

Schmidt, G., 'Contradictory Postures and Conflicting Objectives: The July Crisis', in Schöllgen (ed.), *Escape into War? The Foreign Policy of Imperial Germany* (Oxford/New York/Munich, 1990)

——, 'Innenpolitische Blockbildungen in Deutschland am Vorabend des Ersten Weltkrieges', *Aus Politik und Zeitgeschichte* (1972)

Schneider, Eric, 'The British Red Cross Wounded and Missing Enquiry Bureau: A Case of Truth-Telling in the Great War', *War in History* (1997)

Schöllgen, Gregor, 'Germany's Foreign Policy in the Age of Imperialism: A Vicious Circle', in Schöllgen (ed.), *Escape into War? The Foreign Policy of Imperial Germany* (Oxford/New York/Munich, 1990)

——, *Imperialismus und Gleichgewicht: Deutschland, England und die orientalische Frage, 1871–1914* (Munich, 1984)

——, 'Introduction: The Theme Reflected in Recent German Research', Schöllgen (ed.), *Escape into War? The Foreign Policy of Imperial Germany* (Oxford/New York/Munich, 1990)

Schramm, Percy Ernst, *Neun Generationen: 300 Jahre deutscher 'Kulturgeschichte' im Lichte der Schicksale einer hamburger Bürgerfamilie*, 2 vols. (Göttingen, 1963–5)

Schremmer, D. E., 'Taxation and Public Finance: Britain, France and Germany', in P. Mathias and S. Pollard (eds.), *The Cambridge Economic History of Europe*, vol. VIII: *The Industrial Economies: The Development of Economic and Social Policies* (Cambridge, 1989)

Schuker, S., 'American "Reparations" to Germany, 1919–1933', in G. Feldman and E. Möller-Luckner (eds.), *Die Nachwirkungen der Inflation auf die deutsche Geschichte, 1924–1933* (Munich, 1985)

Schulte, B. F., *Europäische Krise und Erster Weltkrieg: Beiträge zur Militärpolitik des Kaiserreichs, 1871–1914* (Frankfurt, 1983)

——, *Vor dem Kriegsausbruch 1914: Deutschland, die Türkei und der Balkan* (Düsseldorf, 1980)

Schuster, Peter-Klaus, *George Grosz: Berlin–New York* (Berlin, 1994)

Schwabe, K., *Deutsche Revolution und Wilson-Frieden: Die amerikanische und deutsche Friedensstrategie zwischen Ideologie und Machtpolitik, 1918/19* (Düsseldorf, 1971)

Scott, Peter T., 'Captive Labour: The German Companies of the BEF', *The Great War: The Illustrated Journal of First World War History* (1991)

Searle, G. R., 'Critics of Edwardian Society: The Case of the Radical Right', in A. O'Day (ed.), *The Edwardian Age: Conflict and Stability, 1902–1914* (London, 1979)

——, *The Quest for National Efficiency* (Oxford, 1971)

Seligmann, Matthew, 'Germany and the Origins of the First World War', *German History* (1997)

Semmel, B., *Imperialism and Social Reform: English Social-Imperial Thought, 1895–1914* (London, 1960)

Shand, James D., "Doves among the Eagles", German Pacifists and their Government during World War I', *Journal of Contemporary History* (1975)

Shannon, R., *The Crisis of Imperialism 1865–1915* (London, 1974)

Sheffield, Gary, 'Officer-Man Relations, Discipline and Morale in the British Army of the Great War', in H. Cecil and Liddle (eds.), *Facing Armageddon*

——, *The Redcaps: A History of the Royal Military Police and Its Antecedents from the Middle Ages to the Gulf War* (London/New York, 1994)

Showalter, D., 'Army, State and Society in Germany, 1871–1914: An Interpretation', in Dukes and Remak (eds.), *Another Germany*

Silkin, Jon (ed.), *The Penguin Book of First World War Poetry* (London, 1996)

Simkins, P., 'Everyman at War: Recent Interpretations of the Front Line Experience', in B. Bond (ed.), *The First World War and British Military History* (Oxford, 1991)

——, *Kitchener's Army: The Raising of the New Armies, 1914–16* (Manchester, 1988)

Simon, Herbert A., 'Alternative Visions of Rationality', in Paul K. Moser (ed.), *Rationality in Action: Contemporary Approaches* (Cambridge, 1990)

Simpson, A., *Hot Blood and Cold Steel: Life and Death in the Trenches of the First World War* (London, 1993)

Simpson, K., 'The Officers', in I. Beckett and K. Simpson (eds.), *A Nation in Arms: A Social Study of the British Army in the First World War* (Manchester, 1985)

——, 'The Reputation of Sir Douglas Haig', in B. Bond (ed.), *The First World War and British Military History* (Oxford, 1991)

Skidelsky, R., *John Maynard Keynes*, vol. I: *Hopes Betrayed 1883–1920* (London, 1983)

——, *John Maynard Keynes*, vol. II: *The Economist as Saviour, 1920–1937* (London, 1992)

Snyder, J., *The Ideology of the Offensive: Military Decision-Making and the Disasters of 1914* (Ithaca/London, 1984)

Sommariva, A., and G. Tullio, *German Macroeconomic History 1880–1979: A Study of the Effects of Economic Policy on Inflation, Currency Depreciation and Growth* (London, 1986)

Sösemann, Bernd, 'Medien und Öffentlichkeit in der Julikrise 1914', in Stephan Kronenburg and Horst Schichtel (eds.), *Die Aktualität der Geschichte: Historische Orientierung in der Mediengesellschaft—Siegfried Quandt zum 60 Geburtstag* (Giessen, 1996)

—— (ed.), *Theodor Wolff: Tagebücher, 1914–1919*, 2 vols. (Boppard am Rhein, 1984)

Soutou, Georges-Henri, *L'Or et le sang; Les Buts de guerre économiques de la Première Guerre mondiale* (Paris, 1989)

Specht, A. von, *Politische und wirtschaftliche Hintergründe der deutschen Inflation, 1918–1923* (Frankfurt am Main, 1982)

Spiers, E., 'The Scottish Soldier at War', in H. Cecil and Liddle (eds.), *Facing Armageddon*

Squire, J. C. (ed.), *If It Happened Otherwise: Lapses into Imaginary History* (London/New York/Toronto, 1932)

Squires, James Duane, *British Propaganda at Home and in the United States from 1914 to 1917* (Cambridge, Mass., 1935)

Stamp, J., *Taxation during the War* (London, 1932)

Stargardt, Nicholas, *The German Idea of Militarism: Radical and Socialist Critiques, 1886–1914* (Cambridge, 1994)

Statistiches Jahrbuch für das Deutsche Reich (Berlin, 1914)

Statistisches Reichsamt (ed.), *Zahlen zur Geldentwertung in Deutschland 1914 bis 1924, Sonderhefte zu Wirtschaft und Statistik*, 5. Jg., 1 (Berlin, 1925)

Steed, Henry Wickham, *Through Thirty Years, 1892–1922*, 2 vols. (London, 1924)

Stegmann, D., *Die Erben Bismarcks: Parteien und Verbände in der Spätphase des wilhelminischen Deutschlands—Sammlungspolitik, 1897–1918* (Cologne, 1970)

——, 'Wirtschaft und Politik nach Bismarcks Sturz: Zur Genesis der Miquelschen Sammlungspolitik 1890–1897', in I. Geiss and B. J. Wendt (eds.), *Deutschland in der Weltpolitik des 19. und 20. Jahrhunderts: Fritz Fischer zum 65. Geburtstag* (Düsseldorf, 1973)

Steinberg, Jonathan, 'The Copenhagen complex', *Journal of Contemporary History* (1966)

——, 'Diplomatie als Wille und Vorstellung: Die Berliner Mission Lord Haldanes im Februar 1912', in H. Schottelius and W. Deist (eds.), *Marine und Marinepolitik im kaiserlichen Deutschland* (Düsseldorf, 1972)

Steiner, Zara S., *Britain and the Origins of the First World War* (London, 1977)

——, *The Foreign Office and Foreign Policy, 1898–1914* (Cambridge, 1969)

Stern, Fritz, 'Bethmann Hollweg and the War: The Bounds of Responsibility', in Stern, *The Failure of Illiberalism* (New York, 1971)

——, *Gold and Iron: Bismarck, Bleichröder and the Building of the German Empire* (Harmondsworth, 1987)

Stevenson, David, *Armaments and the Coming of War: Europe 1904–1914* (Oxford, 1996)

Stockholm International Peace Research Institute, *Yearbook 1992: World Armaments and Disarmament* (Oxford, 1992)

Stone, Norman, *The Eastern Front 1914–1917* (London, 1975)

——, *Europe Transformed, 1878–1919* (London, 1983)

——, 'Moltke and Conrad: Relations between the Austro-Hungarian and German General Staffs, 1909–1914', in P. Kennedy (ed.), *The War Plans of the Great Powers* (London, 1979)

Strachan, H., 'The Morale of the German Army 1917–1918', in H. Cecil and Liddle (eds.), *Facing Armageddon*

Straus, A., 'Le Financement des dépenses publiques dans l'entre-deux-guerres', in Straus and P. Fridenson (eds.), *Le Capitalisme français au 19e et 20e siècle: Blocage et dynamismes d'une croissance* (Paris, 1987)

Stuebel, H., *Das Verhältnis zwischen Staat und Banken auf dem Gebiet des preussischen Anleihewesens von 1871 bis 1913* (Berlin, 1935)

Stummvoll, Josef, *Tagespresse und Technik: Die technische Berichterstattung der deutschen Tageszeitung mit besonderer Berücksichtigung der technischen Beilagen* (Dresden, 1935)

Sulzbach, Herbert, *With the German Guns: Four Years on the Western Front*, trans. Richard Thonger (Barnsley, 1998)

Sumler, David E., 'Domestic Influences on the Nationalist Revival in France, 1909–1914', *French Historical Studies* (1970)

Summers, A., 'Militarism in Britain before the Great War', *History Workshop* (1976)

Sweet, D. W., 'Great Britain and Germany, 1905–1911', in F. H. Hinsley (ed.), *British Foreign Policy under Sir Edward Grey* (Cambridge, 1977)

——, and R. T. B. Langhorne, 'Great Britain and Russia, 1907–1914', in F. H. Hinsley (ed.), *British Foreign Policy under Sir Edward Grey* (Cambridge, 1977)

Talbott, John E., 'Soldiers, Psychiatrists and Combat Trauma', *Journal of Interdisciplinary History* (1997)

Tawney, R. H., 'The Abolition of Economic Controls, 1918–1921', *Economic History Review* (1943)

Taylor, A. J. P., *Beaverbrook* (London, 1972)

——, *English History, 1914–1945* (Oxford, 1975)

——, *The First World War* (Harmondsworth, 1966 edn.)

——, *The Struggle for Mastery in Europe, 1848–1918* (Oxford, 1954)

——, *War by Timetable: How the First World War Began* (London, 1969)

Taylor, Brandon, *Art and Literature under the Bolsheviks*, vol. II: *Authority and Revolution, 1924–1932* (London/Boulder, Colorado, 1992)

Taylor, Sally, *The Great Outsiders: Northcliffe, Rothermere and the Daily Mail* (London, 1996)

Terhalle, E., 'Geschichte der deutschen Finanzwirtschaft vom Beginn des 19. Jahrhunderts bis zum Schluss des zweiten Weltkrieges', in W. Gerloff and F. Neumark (eds.), *Handbuch der Finanzwissenschaft* (Tübingen, 1952)

Terraine, John, 'British Military Leadership in the First World War', in Liddle (ed.), *Home Fires*

——, *Douglas Haig: The Educated Soldier* (London, 1963)

——, *The First World War* (London, 1983)

——, *The Road to Passchendaele* (London, 1977)

——, *The Smoke and the Fire* (London, 1980)

——, 'The Substance of the War', in H. Cecil and Liddle (eds.), *Facing Armageddon*

——, *The Western Front* (London, 1964)

——, *White Heat: The New Warfare, 1914–18* (London, 1982)

——, *To Win a War* (London, 1978)

Theweleit, Klaus, *Male Fantasies*, vol. I: *Women, Floods, Bodies, History* (Minneapolis, 1987)

Thomas, Daniel H., *The Guarantee of Belgian Independence and Neutrality in European Diplomacy from the 1830s to the 1930s* (Kingston, 1983)

Thompson, J. M., *Europe since Napoleon* (London, 1957)

Times, The, The History of The Times, vol. IV: *The 150th Anniversary and Beyond, 1912–1948* (London, 1952)

Timm, H., 'Das Gesetz der wachsenden Staatsausgaben', *Finanzarchiv* (1961)

Timms, Edward, *Karl Kraus: Apocalyptic Satirist* (New Haven/London, 1986)

Tirpitz, A. von, *Deutsche Ohnmachtspolitik im Weltkriege* (Hamburg/Berlin, 1926)

——, *Erinnerungen* (Leipzig, 1919)

Trachtenberg, Marc, 'Reparation at the Paris Peace Conference', *Journal of Modern History* (1979)

Trask, David F., *The AEF and Coalition Warmaking, 1917–18* (Lawrence, Kansas, 1993)

Travers, T. H. E., *How the War Was Won* (London, 1992)
——, *The Killing Ground: Command and Technology on the Western Front, 1900–18* (London, 1990)
——, 'The Offensive and the Problem of Innovation in British Military Thought', *Journal of Contemporary History* (1978)
——, 'Technology, Tactics and Morale: Jean de Bloch, the Boer War and British Military Theory, 1900–1914', *Journal of Modern History* (1979)
Trebilcock, Clive, 'War and the Failure of Industrial Mobilisation: 1899 and 1914', in J. Winter (ed.), *War and Economic Development* (Cambridge, 1975)
Trevelyan, G. M., *Grey of Falloden* (London, 1937)
Truchy, H., *Les Finances de guerre de la France* (Paris, 1926)
Trumpener, Ulrich, 'Junkers and Others: The Rise of Commoners in the Prussian Army, 1871–1914', *Canadian Journal of History* (1979)
——, 'The Road to Ypres: The Beginnings of Gas Warfare in World War I', *Central European History* (1975)
——, 'War Premeditated? German Intelligence Operations in July 1914', *Central European History* (1976)
Tuchman, Barbara, *August 1914* (London, 1962)
Turner, L. C. F., *Origins of the First World War* (New York, 1970)
——, 'The Russian Mobilisation in 1914', in P. Kennedy (ed.), *The War Plans of the Great Powers, 1880–1914* (London, 1979)
——, 'The Significance of the Schlieffen Plan', in P. Kennedy (ed.), *The War Plans of the Great Powers, 1880–1914* (London, 1979)

Ullrich, V., 'Der Januarstreik 1918 in Hamburg, Kiel und Bremen: Eine vergleichende Studie zur Geschichte der Streikbewegung im Ersten Weltkrieg', *Zeitschrift des Vereins für hamburgische Geschichte* (1985)
——, *Kriegsalltag: Hamburg im Ersten Weltkrieg* (Cologne, 1982)
——, 'Massenbewegung in der Hamburger Arbeiterschaft im Ersten Weltkrieg', in A. Herzig, D. Langewiesche and A. Sywottek (eds.), *Arbeiter in Hamburg: Unterschichten, Arbeiter und Arbeiterbewegung seit dem ausgehenden 18. Jahrhundert* (Hamburg, 1982)

Vagts, Alfred, *A History of Militarism: Civilian and Military* (New York, 1959)
Vierteljahreshefte zur Statistik des Deutschen Reiches (1914–20)
Vincent, C. P., *The Politics of Hunger: The Allied Blockade of Germany, 1915–1919* (Athens, Ohio, 1985)
Vincent-Smith, J. D., 'Anglo-German Negotiations over the Portuguese Colonies in Africa 1911–1914', *Historical Journal* (1974)
Volkogonov, Dmitri, *Lenin: Life and Legacy* (London, 1994)
——, *Trotsky: The Eternal Revolutionary* (London, 1996)
Vondung, V., 'Deutsche Apokalypse 1914', in Vondung, *Das wilhelminischen Bildungsbürgertum* (Göttingen, 1976)
Voth, H.-J., 'Civilian Health during World War One and the Causes of German Defeat: A Re-examination of the Winter Hypothesis', *Annales de Demographie Historique* (1995)

Wagenführ, R., 'Die Industriewirtschaft: Entwicklungstendenzen der deutschen und internationalen Industrieproduktion, 1860–1932', *Vierteljahreshefte zur Konjunkturforschung*, Sonderheft 31 (1933)
Wagner, A., *Grundlegung der politischen Ökonomie* (Leipzig, 1893)
Waites, B., *A Class Society at War: England, 1914–18* (Leamington Spa, 1987)
——, 'The Effect of the First World War on Class and Status in England, 1910–20', *Journal of Contemporary History* (1976)
Wake, Jehanne, *Kleinwort Benson: The History of Two Families in Banking* (Oxford, 1997)
Wallace, Stuart, *War and the Image of Germany: British Academics, 1914–1918* (Edinburgh, 1988)
War Office, *Statistics of the Military Effort of the British Empire during the Great War, 1914–20* (London, 1922)
Warburg, Max M., *Aus meinen Aufzeichnungen* (printed privately, n.d.)
Warner, Philip, *World War One* (London, 1995)
Wawro, Geoffrey, 'Morale in the Austro-Hungarian Army: The Evidence of Habsburg Army Campaign Reports and Allied Intelligence Officers', in H. Cecil and Liddle (eds.), *Facing Armageddon*
Webb, S. B., *Hyperinflation and Stabilisation in Weimar Germany* (New York/Oxford, 1989)
Weber, Eugen, *The Hollow Years: France in the 1930s* (London, 1995)
——, *The Nationalist Revival in France* (Berkeley, 1959)

Weber, Thomas, 'A Stormy Romance: Germans at Oxford between 1900 and 1938', unpubl. master of studies thesis (Oxford 1998)

Wehler, Hans-Ulrich, *The German Empire, 1871–1918* (Leamington Spa, 1985)

Weinroth, H., 'The British Radicals and the Balance of Power, 1902–1914', *Historical Journal* (1970)

Weiss, Linda, and John M. Hobson, *States and Economic Development: A Comparative Economic Analysis* (Cambridge, 1995)

Welch, David, 'Cinema and Society in Imperial Germany, 1905–1918', *German History* (1990)

Westbrook, S. D., 'The Potential for Military Disintegration', in S. C. Sarkesian (ed.), *Combat Effectiveness* (Los Angeles, 1980)

Whalen, Robert Weldon, *Bitter Wounds: German Victims of the Great War, 1914–1939* (Ithaca/London, 1984)

Wheeler-Bennett, J. W., *Brest-Litovsk: The Forgotten Peace* (London, 1956)

Whiteside, N., 'Industrial Labour and Welfare Legislation after the First World War: A Reply', *Historical Journal* (1982)

——, 'Welfare Legislation and the Unions during the First World War', *Historical Journal* (1982)

Whitford, Frank, 'The Revolutionary Reactionary', in Tate Gallery, *Otto Dix, 1891–1961* (London, 1992)

Willett, John, *The New Sobriety, 1917–1933: Art and Politics in the Weimar Period* (London, 1978)

William II, *Ereignisse und Gestalten aus den Jahren 1878–1918* (Leipzig/Berlin, 1922), trans. *My Memoirs, 1878–1918* (London, 1922)

Williams, B., 'The Strategic Background to the Anglo-Russian Entente of 1907', *Historical Journal* (1966)

Williams, R., *Defending the Empire: The Conservative Party and British Defence Policy, 1899–1915* (London, 1991)

——, 'Lord Kitchener and the Battle of Loos: French Politics and British Strategy in the Summer of 1915' in L. Freedman, P. Hayes and R. O'Neill (eds.), *War, Strategy and International Politics* (Oxford, 1992)

Williamson, John G., *Karl Helfferich, 1872–1924: Economist, Financier, Politician* (Princeton, 1971)

Williamson, S. R., Jr., *Austria-Hungary and the Coming of the First World War* (London, 1990)

Wilson, K. M., 'The British Cabinet's Decision for War, 2 August 1914', *British Journal of International Studies* (1975)

——, 'The Foreign Office and the "Education" of Public Opinion before the First World War', *Historical Journal* (1983)

——, 'Grey', in K. Wilson (ed.), *British Foreign Secretaries and Foreign Policy from the Crimean War to the First World War* (London, 1987)

——, 'In Pursuit of the Editorship of *British Documents on the Origins of the War, 1898–1914*: J. W. Headlam-Morley before Gooch and Temperley', *Archives* (1995)

——, *The Policy of the Entente: Essays on the Determinants of British Foreign Policy* (Cambridge, 1985)

Wilson, Trevor, 'Britain's "Moral Commitment" to France in July 1914', *History* (1979)

——, 'Lord Bryce's Investigation into Alleged German Atrocities in Belgium, 1914–15', *Journal of Contemporary History* (1979)

——, *The Myriad Faces of War: Britain and the Great War, 1914–1918* (Cambridge, 1986)

Winter, Denis, *Death's Men: Soldiers of the Great War* (London, 1978)

Winter, J. M., (ed.), *Capital Cities at War: Paris, London, Berlin, 1914–1919* (Cambridge, 1997)

——, *The Great War and the British People* (London, 1985)

——, 'Oxford and the First World War', in Brian Harrison (ed.), *The History of the University of Oxford*, vol. VIII: *The Twentieth Century* (Oxford, 1994)

——, 'Painting Armageddon: Some Aspects of the Apocalyptic Imagination in Art: From Anticipation to Allegory', H. Cecil and Liddle (eds.), *Facing Armageddon*

——, 'Public Health and the Political Economy of War, 1914–1918', *History Workshop Journal* (1988)

——, *Sites of Memory, Sites of Mourning: The Great War in European Cultural History* (Cambridge, 1995)

——, and Blaine Baggett, *1914–1918: The Great War and the Shaping of the 20th Century* (London, 1996)

——, and Joshua Cole, 'Fluctuations in Infant Mortality Rates in Berlin during and after the First World War', *European Journal of Population* (1993)

Winzen, P., 'Der Krieg in Bülow's Kalkül. Katastrophe der Diplomatie oder Chance zur Machtexpansion', in Jost Dülffer and Karl Holl (eds.), *Bereit zum Krieg: Kriegsmentalität im wilhelminischen Deutschland 1890–1914. Beiträge zur historischen Friedensforschung* (Göttingen, 1986)

Witt, Peter-Christian, *Die Finanzpolitik des Deutschen Reichs, 1903–1913* (Lübeck, 1970)

——, 'Finanzpolitik und sozialer Wandel im Krieg und Inflation 1918–1924 in H. Mommsen *et al.* (eds.), *Industrielles System und politische Entwicklung in der Weimarer Republik*, vol. I (Düsseldorf, 1977)

——, 'Finanzpolitik und sozialer Wandel: Wachstum und Funktionswandel der Staatsausgaben in Deutschland, 1871–1933', in H.-U. Wehler (ed.), *Sozialgeschichte heute: Festschrift für Hans Rosenberg* (Göttingen, 1974)

——, 'Innenpolitik und Imperialismus in der Vorgeschichte des Ersten Weltkrieges', in Karl Holl and G. List (eds.), *Liberalismus und imperialistischer Staat* (Göttingen, 1975)

——, 'Reichsfinanzen und Rüstungspolitik', in H. Schottelius und W. Deist (eds.), *Marine und Marinepolitik im kaiserlichen Deutschland 1871–1914* (Düsseldorf, 1981)

——, 'Tax Policies, Tax Assessment and Inflation: Towards a Sociology of Public Finances in the German Inflation, 1914 to 1923', in Witt (ed.), *Wealth and Taxation in Central Europe: The History and Sociology of Public Finance* (Leamington Spa/Hamburg/New York, 1987)

Wohl, Robert, *The Generation of 1914* (London, 1980)

Wolff, Leon, *In Flanders Fields* (London, 1959)

Wolff, Theodor, *The Eve of 1914* (London, 1935)

——, *Der Marsch durch zwei Jahrzehnte* (Amsterdam, 1936)

——, *Das Vorspiel* (Munich, 1924)

Woodward, Sir Llewellyn, *Great Britain and the War of 1914–1918* (London, 1967)

Wright, D. G., 'The Great War, Government Propaganda and English "Men of Letters"', *Literature and History* (1978)

Wright, Q., *A Study of War* (Chicago, 1942)

Wrigley, C., *David Lloyd George and the British Labour Movement* (London, 1976)

——, 'The Ministry of Munitions: An Innovatory Department', in K. Burk (ed.), *War and the State* (London, 1982)

Wynne, G. C., *If Germany Attacks* (London, 1940)

Wysocki, J., 'Die österreichische Finanzpolitik', in A. Wandruszka and P. Urbanitsch (eds.), *Die Habsburgermonarchie, 1848–1918*, vol. I (Vienna, 1973)

Zechlin, E., 'Deutschland zwischen Kabinettskrieg und Wirtschaftskrieg: Politik und Kriegsführung in den ersten Monaten des Weltkrieges 1914', *Historische Zeitschrift* (1964)

——, 'Julikrise und Kriegsausbruch 1914', in K. D. Erdmann and E. Zechlin (eds.), *Politik und Geschichte: Europa 1914—Krieg oder Frieden?* (Kiel, 1985)

——, 'July 1914: Reply to a Polemic', in H. W. Koch (ed.), *The Origins of the First World War* (London, 1984)

——, *Krieg und Kriegsrisiko: Zur deutschen Politik im Ersten Weltkrieg* (Düsseldorf, 1979)

Zeidler, Manfred, 'Die deutsche Kriegsfinanzierung 1914 bis 1918 und ihre Folgen', in Wolfgang Michalka (ed.), *Der Erste Weltkrieg: Wirkung, Wahrnehmung, Analyse* (Munich, 1994)

Zeitlin, J., 'The Labour Strategies of British Engineering Employers, 1890–1922', in H. Gospel and C. Littler (eds.), *Managerial Strategies and Industrial Relations: An Historical and Comparative Study* (London, 1983)

Zilch, R., *Die Reichsbank und die finanzielle Kriegsvorbereitungen von 1907 bis 1914* (Berlin, 1987)

Zimmermann, W., A. Günther and R. Meerwarth, *Die Einwirkung des Krieges auf Bevölkerungsbewegung, Einkommen und Lebenshaltung in Deutschland* (Stuttgart/Berlin/Leipzig, 1932)

Zunkel, F., *Industrie und Staatssozialismus: Der Kampf um die Wirtschaftsordnung in Deutschland, 1914–1918* (Düsseldorf, 1974)

Index

Notes: **Bold** page numbers refer to Tables and Figures. The Notes have been indexed only where significant further information can be found.

Abyssinia, Italian invasion of 42
Addison, Christopher 262, 421
Admiralty
    plans for naval blockade of Germany 62, 66, 86, 161
    rivalry with War Office 103
    see also Churchill; Committee of Imperial Defence; Fisher; Royal Navy
Aehrenthal, Alois Baron Lexa von, Austrian foreign minister 147
Afghanistan 41, 54, 60
Africa
    German colonial claims in 46–7, 50, 68–9, 169, 171, 444
    redistribution of colonies 434
Agrarian League (Germany) 28
agriculture
    and food production 276
    Germany 251–2, 252, 413
air power 163, 290, 304, 522n
Aitken, Max *see* Beaverbrook
Albania 147, 148, 390
alcohol, army rations 351–2
Aldington, Richard, poet xxvi, xxix
Algeciras Act (1906) 69
All Quiet on the Western Front (Remarque) xxiii, xxx, 381, 386, 449, 450
    film version xxiii, 453
Allatini, Rose, writer xxviii, 221
Allenby, General E. 305
Alsace-Lorraine 96, 434
    German population in 440
Amalgamated Society of Engineers (ASE), strike 274–5
Amiens 307, 311, 312, 313
Angell, Norman 21–3
British Neutrality League 181
    on German military strength 93

on military spending 114, 135, 190, 195
    The Great Illusion 7, 21, 22–3
Anglo-French *Entente Cordiale* (1904) 53–4, 80
    becomes defensive alliance 64
    effect on Anglo-Russian relations 54
    see also Grey
Annesley, Arthur 359
anti-militarism 20–30, 29
    influence on historical analysis 26
    at outbreak of war 178, 179–80, 181–4
    see also pacifism
Antwerp
    fall of 168
    importance of 67, 502n
Apis, Colonel, Serbian Military Intelligence 146
Apollinaire, Guillaume, poetry xxvii, 448–9
aristocracy
    Anglo-German links 25
    army officers 89, 202, 305–6
Arlen, Michael, *The Green Hat* xxviii
Armenia 210, 434, 542n
armies
    available manpower 9, 297–8, 297, 299
    logistics of mobilization 93, 95–7
    see also casualties; defence expenditure; soldiers; strategy; technology, military
arms industry
    benefits of war 32, 261–2, 263–5
    munitions production 259–60, 260, 263
arms race
    cost of 105–11
    as explanation for war 82–3, 442
    naval 83–7
    and proposed naval limitation agreement 70–72
Army League (Germany) 15, 18, 19, 28, 472nn
    and defence expenditure 136
Arras offensive 293

artillery 93, 96, 303–4, 306–8, 310–11
artists
    British 456–7
    Dadaism 454, 544n
    German 454–5, 456
    portrayal of horrors of war xxx–xxxi, 454–5
    Russian 456
    Vorticist 454, 455
Asquith, H. H.
    on 1914 bank crisis 192, 195
    and Conservative opposition 59, 165
    and decision for war 160, 161, 162, 164
    and evidence of foreign espionage 14
    and expectation of Franco-German war 65
    expectation of short war 319
    memoirs xxxvi, xxxix
    and nature of commitment to France 76–7, 78
    on naval arms race 87
    Northcliffe's campaign against 230
    and plans for Expeditionary Force 66
    as Prime Minister, silence on foreign policy 58
    six principles for intervention 163
    and taxation 119
    see also Grey; Liberal Party; Lloyd George
Asquith, Margot 165–6
Asquith, Violet 177
Astor, Waldorf 214
attrition, strategy of xliii, 209, 292–4, 297, 300–303
Australian soldiers 199, 355, 363, 531n
    casualty rate 299
Austria xxx, 409, 434
    economy 44, 118, 249
    fiscal system 125
    franchise 29
    money supply 330, 331
    POWs 368
    Vienna stock exchange 191
    see also Austria-Hungary
Austria-Hungary
    annexation of Bosnia 61, 118, 146, 147
    and Balkans 143
    censorship 220
    collapse of 434
    economy
        cost of living 331; defence expenditure 106, 107,
        108–9, 110, 111, 125; dualist financial system
        117–18, 125; financial weakness 135;
        government bonds 130; public borrowing
        130
    Navy 85
    official propaganda 225
    pre-emptive war mentality 100, 148
    press 215
    relations with Russia 99
    relations with Serbia 99, 147–8
    reprisals against Serbia 147, 154–5
    Ultimatum to Serbia 156–7
    see also Austria; Hungary

Austro-Hungarian Army
    casualties 295, 299
    collapse 312
    military potential 93
    military strength 91, 92, 93
    POWs 369
    war costs per death 337

Baghdad railway see railways
balance of power, concept of 144
Balfour, A. J. 56
    'active defence' policy 292
    policy towards Germany 49, 51, 164
Balkan War, First (1912–13) 147
Balkan War, Second (1913) 148
Balkans 143, 147
    German view of 25
    Russian interests in 41, 61
    Slav nationalism 61, 99, 100
    see also Bosnia; Greece; Serbia
Ball, Hugo, artist 454
Ballin, Albert, German shipowner 191, 197, 252
    advice against war 33
    need for fiscal reform 137
    opposes annexation 287, 498n
    and proposed naval agreement 70–71
    on war economy 252, 257–8
Bank of England 128, 197, 321
    and international monetary system 37–8
banks and bankers
    Anglo-German co-operation in China 47–8
    opposition to war 32–3, 192–3, 195, 197
    see also Bank of England; City of London;
        Reichsbank; Rothschilds
Barbusse, Henri, Le Feu xxx, 236
Barker, Ernest, Why We Are At War 228
Barker, Pat, Regeneration xxxi
Baruch, Bernard M., US banker 263
Bassermann, Ernst, National Liberal leader 19,
    98
Bassermann-Erzberger resolution (1913) 123
Baumgarten, Otto 208
Beauchamp, Earl 160, 161, 162
Beaverbrook, Lord xxxvi, 230
    war propaganda 213–14, 223
Bebel, August, German Social Democrat 140
Beckmann, Max xxx
Beerman, August 388
Begbie, Harold, journalist xxviii, 396
Behncke, Admiral Paul 287
Békássy, Ferenc 184
Belgian Congo 42
Belgian neutrality xxxix, 201, 444
    British pre-war view of 62–3, 67, 443
    German view of 150–51
    relative unimportance in British decision 161–2,
        163–4
    violation of 162–3, 231–2

Belgium 144, 158, 317, 433–4
 anti-militarism 30
 casualties 299
 franchise 29
 German ambitions in 169, 170–71
 German annexation plans 287–8, 317, 502–311
 German atrocities in xl, 232, 246–7
 industrial production 251
 military potential 93
 military strength 92, 101–2
 POWs 369
 see also Schlieffen Plan
Belgrade 156, 157
Bell, Clive xxvii, 181
Belloc, Hilaire 32, 238
 imaginary history 458
Bellows, George, artist 454
Benedict XV, Pope 356
Benedikt, Moritz 241
Bennett, Arnold 228, 229, 236
Berchtold, Count Leopold, Austrian foreign
 minister 147, 148, 151
Beresford, Admiral Lord Charles 11
Bergmann, Carl, German Foreign Office 409
Berlin-Baghdad railway 51, 69
Berliner Tageblatt 215, 216, 222, 243, 244
Bernhardi, General Friedrich von 92
 Germany and the Next War 15, 136
Bertie, Francis 53, 69
 ambassador in Berlin 63, 69, 167, 177
Bethmann Hollweg, Theobald von, Chancellor
 xxxvi, xxxviii–xxxix, 24, 459
 and annexations 287
 and co-operation with Britain 68, 69, 70–71
 declining influence 288
 and defence expenditure 111–12, 123
 hope of British neutrality 68, 71–2, 158–9,
 170–71, 173
 and invasion of Belgium 162–3
 and need for military service 91
 pessimism of 98–9, 177
 and Prussian franchise 289
 and Rathenau 33
 on Russian threat 98–9, 149
 and Sazonov's offer of talks 156–7
 'September Programme' (war aims) 169, 171–2,
 173
 on timing of war 148, 152
 war and social revolution connection 28
Beumelburg, Werner, memoirs 452
Beveridge, William 176, 184, 206
 on war economy 261, 276
Bickersteth, Revd Julian 314
Binding, Rudolf, memoirs 452
Bismarck, Count Otto von 43, 46, 143
 and federal system 115, 116, 117, 121
black market 279, 280, 320, 321
Black Sea Straits 51, 54, 60, 143

Blaker, Richard, writer xxx
Bleibtreu, Karl, Offensive Invasion against
 England 7, 173
Bloch, Ivan Stanislavovich 189, 190
 on economic consequences 189, 190, 192
 Is War Now Impossible 9–11
Bloch, Marc 354
Blohm & Voss (Hamburg shipbuilders) 32, 263–4,
 267, 270–71, 272
Bloomsbury group xxviii–xxix, 181, 327
 see also Bell, Clive; Keynes, John Maynard
Blunden, Edmund xxvi, xxix
 Undertones of War 450–51
Boer War 15, 16, 103
 and Anglo-German relations 51
 cost of 115, 119, 127
 and Francophobia 5
Böhm, John 375
Bolshevism, fear of 400, 410, 436
Bonar Law, Andrew 165, 166
Booth, George 259, 262, 329
Bosnia-Hercegovina 146, 390
 annexed by Austria 61, 118, 146
 Yugoslav state 434
Bottomley, Horatio 209, 219, 243
Bowman, Lt 372
Boxer Rising (China) 48
Boy Scout Movement 15, 102, 469n
Boys' Brigade 102
Brailsford, Henry Noel, The War of Steel and Gold
 23
Braun, Otto, German Social Democrat 178
Brennan, Anthony 385
Brentano, Lujo 228
Bresciani-Turroni, Constantino 425
Brest-Litovsk, Treaty of 285, 286, 408
Brian, Havergal, opera 453
Briand, Aristide 317
Bridges, Lt Col 67
Bridges, Robert 209
Briey (France), iron producing area 96, 287, 502n
British Army 15
 casualties 293, 294, 300
 casualty statistics 295, 296, 299, 301, 302
 chaplains 356–7
 deficiencies of 102–3, 305–6
 discipline 345, 346–8
 enlistment 198–9, 200, 201–7
 generals' difficulties 303–5
 killing of prisoners 375–82
 military efficiency 337–8
 military strength 92, 94
 officers 103, 202, 300, 305–6, 347
 POWs 369
 regimental identity 354, 446
 relations with Allies 304–5
 strategy 292–4, 297, 300, 310–11
 structure 102–3, 305–6, 310

use of armaments 306–7, 310–11
see also British Expeditionary Force;
    Committee of Imperial Defence;
    conscription; soldiers; Territorial Army; War
    Office
British Empire 37, 38, 434
    Angell's defence of 22–3
    casualties 295, 299, 369
    and defence expenditure 110, 491n
    financial limits of 37, 328–9
    war costs per death 337
British Expeditionary Force (BEF)
    deployment of 167–8
    early plans in event of Franco-German war 62,
        63–4
    German perception of 103
    see also British Army
British Guiana 54
British National Factories 260
British Neutrality Committee 181, 182
British Neutrality League 181
Brittain, Vera, Testament of Youth xxiii, 362
Brockdorff-Rantzau, Count Ulrich von, German
    foreign minister 409
Brockway, Fenner, playwright 23, 221
    The Devil's Business 23
Brooke, Rupert 184–5
Bruchmüller, Col Georg 309
Brusilov, General Alexei 204
Bryan, Jack 376
Bryce, Lord 101, 232, 513n
Buchan, John
    novels xxix
    propagandist 213, 224, 237
Bulgakov, Mikhail, The White Guard 453
Bulgaria 147, 434
    casualties 295, 299
    national debt 324
    POWs 369
    request for armistice 285
    Russian intervention in 41, 144, 148
    war costs per death 337
Bölow, Prince Bernhard Heinrich von, Chancellor
    25, 27, 132, 172
    on French influence 39
    German fears of encirclement 68
    and naval rivalry 84, 85
    and possible Anglo-German alliance 49, 50
    and Reich finance 122, 135, 136
Burns, John 160, 165
Buxton, Noel 77

Cabinet
    divisions within 56, 58, 160–61, 486n
    ignorance of French negotiations 76–7
    opposition to Grey 77–9
    persuaded by violation of Belgian neutrality
        161–4

support for neutrality 160–61
Caillaux, Joseph, French finance minister 16, 29
Caine, Hall, King Albert's Book 231
Callwell, Sir Charles 292
Cambon, Jules, French ambassador in Berlin 177
Cambon, Paul, French ambassador in London 76,
    79, 80, 156, 191, 195
Cambrai, battle of 308, 333
Cambridge University 24, 182
Campbell, Col Ronald 377
Campbell-Bannerman, Sir Henry, Prime Minister
    56, 58, 63, 76
Canadian Army Corps 199, 355, 376, 379
    casualty rate 299, 312
Canetti, Elias 176, 294
capital, British export of 35, 36–7
capitalism xxxviii
    and Marxist theory of war 31–2
Caprivi, General Leo von, Chancellor (from 1890)
    43, 89, 147
Carrington, Guy 352
Carson, Sir Edward 224
cartoons 5–6
Cassel, Sir Ernest 51, 70–71
Castelnau, General de 167
casualties xliii–xliv
    aerial bombing 522n
    British 293, 294, 340
    cost per death 331, 336–8, 337
    demographic effects of 436–7
    Dupuy's study 298–9
    French 293, 294, 316, 340, 512n
    German 293–4, 311, 340
    and morale 312–13, 339
    permanently disabled 437, 527n
    statistics 295, 296, 299
    Western Front 298–300, 301, 302
    wounded 294–6
    see also prisoners-of-war
Catholic church
    France 208
    Germany 18, 208
Céline, Louis-Ferdinand, Journey to the End of
    Night xxx
cemeteries, war xxxiii
censorship xliii, 220, 221, 235
    British 211, 219–20
    DORA 186, 219, 220, 221
    France 220–21, 222
    Germany 220, 221, 222
    postal 186
    United States 222–3
Central Asia, Russian interests in 41
Central Powers (Germany, Austria-Hungary)
    economic efficiency 318, 336, 444
    economic inferiority 248–9
    military effectiveness 248–9, 318, 336, 445
    naval inferiority 85

population 248, 249, 297–8
trade control 266
war costs per death 337, 445
war expenditure 322, 323
see also Austria-Hungary; Germany
Centre Party (Germany) 123, 289
Chamberlain, Austen 165, 312
Chamberlain, Joseph 49, 50, 52
  tariff reform 39, 118
Chamberlain, Neville 165
Chapman, Guy 348, 361
Charteris, Brig Gen Sir John 292–3, 305
Chemin des Dames offensive 285
Chesterton, G.K. 228, 231
Childers, Erskine, The Riddle of the Sands 1
children, influenced by propaganda 239
China
  Anglo-German co-operation on 47–9
  Russian influence in 47–8
Churchill, Lord Randolph 111
Churchill, W.S.
  1909 report of German fiscal weakness 75,
    137–8, 140
  'active defence' policy 292
  on Belgian and Dutch neutrality 66–7
  on danger of German aggression xxxix, 75, 140
  enthusiasm for war 160, 166, 177–8
  and foreign espionage 14
  on French military strength 66
  on German colonial expansion 68–9
  imaginary history 457
  limited naval preparations 159, 160
  naval estimates (1913) 113, 114
  and naval presence in Mediterranean 67–8,
    78–9
  necessity of navy 75, 86–7
  need for conscription 104
  on Providence 209
  The World Crisis xxxvi
  on treatment of prisoners 388
cinema see films
City of London
  and 1914 financial crisis 192–3, 194, 195, 196,
    197
  see also Bank of England
class see aristocracy; middle classes; working class
Class, Heinrich, Pan-German League 18, 20
Clausewitz, Karl von 354–5
Clemenceau, Georges 266
Clémentel, Etienne 255, 262, 266
coal production 33, 250–51, 262
Cocteau, Jean 212
Cole, G. D. H. 23
Cole, R. W., The Death Trap 2
Committee of Imperial Defence (CID) 14, 103
  August 1911 meeting 65–6
  December 1912 meeting 66–7
  expectation of Franco-German war 65

and Germany as 'Napoleonic' threat 74–5
nature of commitment to France 76–7
support for Expeditionary Force policy 64
Whitehall Gardens conference 62
see also Admiralty; War Office
communications
  battlefield 304
  telegraph 130
  see also railways
Communist Party (Germany) 389
comradeship 206, 354, 446, 451
Conan Doyle, Sir Arthur 228
Conrad von Hötzendorf see Hötzendorf
conscientious objectors 181, 186
conscription in Britain 15, 21–2, 102, 103–4
  introduced (1916) 198
  see also enlistment; military service
Conservative Party
  approval of Grey's policy 58–9, 164–5
  and Ireland 164–5
  support for intervention 165
  see also Balfour
Constantinople 148
  Russian ambitions for 42, 61, 460
Coppard, George 203, 343, 344, 346, 349, 382–3,
  452
counter-factual options xlv
  alternative British strategies 290–91, 459
  alternative German strategies 315–17
  British limited involvement or neutrality 168–9,
    170–72, 458–60
  consequences of German victory 460–61, 545n
  delay in sending BEF 167–8, 457
  European Customs Union 457, 458, 460–61
  German expansive monetary policy 141–2
  J. C. Squire's 1932 collection 457–8
  Liberal defeat on eve of war 166–7
  naval war 459
  Russia and 460–61
  stabilization of German mark 428–32
Courland 286, 409, 441
cowardice, executions for xxxiii, 346
Crewe, Marquess of 160
Crimean War 143, 144
Croatia 390
Crowe, Eyre 14, 102, 155, 461
  appeasement of Russia 60, 80
  fear of German 'Napoleonic' threat 74, 75
  and Grey's pro-French policy 63
culture, patriotic denigrations of 233–4
Cummings, E. E. xxix
Cuno, Wilhelm, German Chancellor 406
Curties, Captain, When England Slept 2
Czechoslovakia 434
Czechs 145

Daily Mail 11, 22, 217–18
  circulation 241, 242, 243

Daily News 216–17, 243
Dalziel, Henry 214
D'Annunzio, Gabriele 390, 452
Davenport, Lord 276
David, Eduard, SPD deputy 178
Davis, H. W. C., *Why We Are At War* 228
Dawes Scheme 407
Dawson, A. J. 2, 206
  debt and credit risk 132, 333, 336
  defaults on 397
  effect of hyperinflation on German 421–2
  German post-war 414
  government bonds 127–32, 131, 133–4, 135
  international xliii, 126–35
  national 126, 127–8, 127, 129–30, 320–21, 324–6, 324, 325
  trade deficits 253–4, 254
  war bonds 225, 324–6
  war debts (in 1931) 419
  yields 130–31, 131, 135, 333, 334–5, 336
  see also finance; reparations; taxation
defence expenditure 105–7, 106, 108–9
  and German Army Bill (1913) 122–3, 138, 139–40, 141
  as percentage of net national product 110–11, 110
  political factors in 111–12, 114, 120, 136–7, 141–2
  see also debt; taxation
Defence of the Realm Act (DORA) 186, 219, 220, 221
Dehmel, Richard, poet 234
Delbrück, Hans 50, 97, 172
Delcassé, Théophile, French politician 16, 42
  relations with Britain 53, 54
democracy
  extension of franchise 28–9, 29, 289
  middle classes and 427–8
  in Reichstag 116–17
Department of Information 224
desertion 344–5, 367
  Bolsheviks 393
Deutsch, Felix, AEG 412
Deutsch-Asiatische Bank 47, 48
Dilke, Sir Charles 45
diplomacy
  German risks 285–9
  and Germany's pre-emptive war option 99–100, 443
Directorate of Military Operations
  early plans for BEF 62–3
  Foreign Section (MO₅) 12–13
Dix, Otto, artist 238, 454, 455, 456
Dominican Republic 55
Donald, Robert 214, 224
Dornan, Louis 372
Dostoevsky, Fyodor, *Crime and Punishment* 433
Doughty, Charles, poetry 2

drama xxiii–xxiv, xxx, 2–3, 23
  war-inspired 453
  see also Kraus
Drewenick, Sgt 376
du Cane, Sir John 315
du Maurier, Guy, *An Englishman's Home* 2–3, 14
Dyer, Brig Gen Reginald 391

Eastern Front
  German strategy 285, 286
  refugees from 186–8
  surrenders on 368
Eastern Rumelia 41, 144
Ebert, Friedrich
  German Social Democrat 31, 176, 178–9, 310
  Reich President 410
Eckardstein, Baron Hermann von 49, 50
economic efficiency xliii, xliv
  Central Powers 318, 336, 444–5
  war economies 254–5, 256–9, 261, 262–3, 264–5, 267, 280
  see also military effectiveness
economic revisionism, German policy of 407, 417–18
economics
  as decisive factor in war 9, 190–91
  effect of outbreak of war 189, 190–91
  effect of war on global 438–9
  fiscal systems 113, 114–16
  political factors in 111–13, 114, 120
  post-war boom 412–13
  pre-war growth 44
  public expenditure 111–113, 112, 115
  role in origins of war 33–9
  theory of rational choice 528–9n
  see also debt; defence expenditure; finance; inflation; taxation
Edmonds, Charles xxix, 451
Edmonds, Sir James, historian xxxv, 12
Edward VII, King 50, 166
  and invasion theory 13–14
  and Serbian crisis 155
Egypt 390
  British occupation (1882) 41, 107
  relations with France over 41, 53
Einem, Karl von, Prussian War Minister 89
Einem, Col Gen von 351
Einstein, Albert 182
Einstein, Lewis 319
Eisenhart, Karl, *The Reckoning with England* 3
Elgar, Edward 24
emigration
  from Britain 37, 38
  from Germany 38
employers, appeals for recruits 207
employment *see* labour supply; unemployment
Engels, Friedrich 8
enlistment 198–9, 200, 268, 444
  patriotic motives 201–3

other motives 205–7
see also conscription; military service
Erzberger, Mathias, German finance minister 410, 429, 494n
Esher, Viscount, member of CID 23, 64, 292, 319
and Germany as 'Napoleonic' threat 75
espionage
British 12–13, 290
code-breaking 13
German 12, 14–15, 150
and immigration restrictions 11–12
novels of 1, 2, 5–6
Estonia 145, 409, 434
ethnic minorities 145
and self-determination 439–41
Europe, latent German hegemony 34, 74–5, 461
European Customs Union
as counter-factual possibility 457, 458, 460–61
German ambitions for 171, 172–3, 287, 444
Mitteleuropa concept 19, 288
Ewart, John Spencer, Director of Military Operations 63
Ewart, Wilfred, *Way of Revelation* 450
Expressionism xxvi, 454

Fabian Society 23–4
Fahlenstein, soldier 373
Falkenhausen, Ludwig von 172
Falkenhayn, Erich von xxxv, 98, 287
and Verdun 285, 316
Falls, Cyril, military historian 451
Farr, Pte Harry 347
Fascism 460
in Italy 390
Fashoda incident (1895) 41–2
fatalism
among German leaders (1914) 97–9
among soldiers 364–5
Fatherland Party 227, 289, 389
Faulks, Sebastian, *Birdsong* xxxii
Fay, Sidney, American historian xxxviii
Fehrenbach, Konstantin, German Chancellor 430, 432
Feilgenhauer, Sgt 375
Ferguson, John Gilmour xix–xxi
Fiedler, H. G. 183
films
anti-war 453
censorship of 222, 223
newsreels 226, 227, 243, 513n
propaganda 225, 226–7, 236–7
romantic 453–4
The Battle of the Somme 226, 236–7, 367–8
finance
1914 crisis 191–194, 196, 319, 444
foreign investment 35–7, 36, 129
Franco-Russian 43–4
German weakness 75, 135–41

power of British xliii, 35–8, 321–2, 326
see also finance, war
finance, war 318–19
British 321–2
cost per death 331, 336–8, 337
dollar exchange rates 332
German 320–21
war bonds 225, 324–6
Finch, Harry 175, 203, 351, 352, 379–80
Finland 145, 286, 409, 434
First World War
academic studies of xxiv–xxv, xxxiii–xxxv
accurate forecasts of 8–11
continuing influence of xxiii, xxxii–xxxiii
first media war 212, 444
as greatest error of history 461–2
historical interpretations of xxxvii–xlii
military and political memoirs xxxv–vi
official histories and documents xxxiv–xxv, 466n
see also counter-factual options
Fischer, David, German state secretary 411
Fischer, Fritz, historian
on German war aims 169–70
Griff nach der Weltmacht xl–xli, 27
Fisher, Admiral Sir John 23
naval reforms 84
naval strategy 11, 63, 64, 86
Fitzmaurice, Lord 217
Fitzpatrick, Sir Percy, two minutes' silence 437–8
Foakes-Jackson, F. J. 182
Foch, Marshal Ferdinand 305
food
imports 276
price controls 278–9
production 251–2, 252, 515n
rationing 276–7
soldiers' rations 350–51
supplies xliii, 277
Ford, Ford Madox xxvii, 24, 340, 449
Parade's End xxviii
foreign investment *see* finance
Foreign Office, British
acceptance of invasion theory 14
and exaggeration of German threat 75–6
Forester, C. S., *The General* xxix
Foulds, John, *World Requiem* 453
France xxxv, 16, 88
alliance with Russia 42–5, 87, 150
and Britain; British obligation to xxxix, 73, 103, 156, 158; and *Entente Cordiale* (1904) 53–4, 80; and Grey's defensive alliance 62, 63–4, 66; rivalry 4–5, 39, 40, 41–2, 45
and Anglo-French shipping 266–7
anti-Semitism in 460
anti-war novels xxx
censorship 220–21, 222
colonial empire 69, 434

democratisation in 28–9, **29**
economy
cost of living 331; defence expenditure 106, 107, 108–9, 110, 110, 111, 114; economic growth 44; fiscal system 114, 120–21; foreign investment 35, 36; government bonds (*rentes perpétuelles*) 128, 131, 132, 134; industrial production 250, 251; loans to Russia 43–4; money supply 330, **330**; national debt **126**, **127**, 128, 324, **324**, **325**, 326, **422**; National Defence Loans 325; post-war economic policies 415, 423, 431; public borrowing 126; trade deficit **254**; war debts **419**; war · economy 255, 325
German aims in 171
German annexation plans 287, 502nn
international influence 39
labour; strikes 275; supply 268, 270; trade unions 273–4, **274**, wage differentials 273
mortality rates 277
occupation of Ruhr 397, 403, 405–6, 419–20
procurement system 260, 261–2, 264–5, 266–7
propaganda 224, 234
reaction to outbreak of war 176, 179, 182, 187
reclaimed Alsace and Lorraine 434
relations with Germany 16, 73, 103, 156
religious fervour 208
and reparations proposals 402–3
war aims 317
war costs per death **337**
war memorials xlii
see also French Army; French Navy; Morocco
franchise
extension of 29, 396, 536n
in Germany 117
Francis Ferdinand, Archduke 146, 148, 496, 507n
Franco-Prussian War (1870–71) 46
Franco-Russian alliance 42–5, 87
Francophobia 4–5
Frankau, Gilbert, memoirs 451
Frankfurter Zeitung 216, 225
Frederick Augustus, of Saxony 123–4
free trade 20, 36, 118
and 'imperial preference' 39
see also tariffs; trade
Freikorps units 389, 452, 535n
French Army
bizarre strategy 96, 167, 292
casualties **295**, **296**, 298, **299**, **302**
and German offensive 167–8
killing of prisoners 374–5, 386
military potential **93**
military strength 65, 91, 92, **92**, **93**, **94**
mutinies 345
patriotism 355
POWs **369**
relations with allies 304–5, 315

trench newspapers 238
use of gas 290
French Congo 69
French Navy 67–8, 85
French, Sir John xxxv, 202, 219, 304–5, 308
doubts about Belgian neutrality 67
Freud, Sigmund 182, 357–9, 362, 365, 447
Furse, Michael, Bishop of Pretoria 209

Galician offensive, Russian 285
Gallinger, August, on taking no prisoners 374–6, 377, 378–9
Gallipoli 290, 291
Gallipoli (film) xxxii
Galsworthy, John 228, 229, 231–2
Gance, Abel, *J'Accuse* 453
Garbutt, Lt W. D. 383
Gardiner, A. G. 216
on Grey 56–7
Garvin, J. L. 38, 210
Garwood, Maj F. S. 379
Gebsattel, Konstantin von, Pan-Germanist 289
Geiss, Immanuel, historian xli, 71
Genoa Conference (1922) 410
genocide, in Armenia 210, 542n
geopolitics, in German universities 18
Georgia **286**
Gerloff, Wilhelm 136
German Army 1913 Army Bill 122–3, 138, 139–40
casualty statistics **295**, **296**, **297**, 299, **301**, **302**
crisis of morale 312, 313–14, 317
effect of disarmament on 439
food shortages 350–51
increasing power of 257–9, 282, 286, 288–9
indifference to BEF 103, 154
inferiority to French 88, 91–2
killing efficiency 289, 294, 300–303
logic of pre-emptive strike 151–2, 153–4, 443
military potential **93**
military service 89, 91–2
Military Transport Plan 93, 95
mutinies 345
and national identity 355
officers 89, 91, 309
operational proficiency 308–10, 315, 316
perception of Russian military 151–2
pessimism in 97–8, 151
POWs 369, 371–2, **371**
pressures to enlarge 15, 89–91
and Schlieffen Plan 88–9, 96–7, 284–5
and Spring Offensive 285, 293–4, 316, 386–7, 448
strength 89, **90**, **94**
structure of 89, 91, 92, 309–10
taking no prisoners 373–5
see also Ludendorff
German colonies
British tolerance of 68–9, 70

claims in Africa 46–7, 50, 68–9
confiscated 409
German diaspora 440–41, **440**
German invasion
    English novels of 1–2, 3, 6, 8
    German novels of 3–4, 7
    official British view of 13–15, 87
German Navy 12, **84**, 85, 288
    effectiveness of blockade 252–3, 276, 445
    and submarine campaign 230, 282–4
    Tirpitz's expansion programme 32, 70, 71, 83–7
Germanophilia, in England 24–5
Germans in England
    banking families 25
    spies xxx, 12, 14–15
    at universities 24–5
Germany
    1913 Army Bill 122–3, 138, 139–40
    annexations 286, 287–8, 502–3nn
    anti-militarism in 25–7, 28, 30
    anti-war elements banned 185–6
    anti-war novels xxx
    censorship 220, 221, 222
    Dammtor war memorial xlii
    dream of European customs union 19, 171,
      172–3
    economy 44, 249; and banking crisis (1914)
      191–2, 197; defence expenditure 106, 107,
      108–9, 110–11, 110, 123–5, 135–7, 141–2,
      443; economic expansion theory 33, 34–5;
      export growth 34–5, 38–9; federal fiscal
      system 115–17, 121–5, 135, 492n, 493–4nn;
      financial weakness 75, 135–41, 443; foreign
      investment 35, 36; government bonds 129,
      131, 132, 134, 135, 324–5; industrial growth
      34, **35**; industrial production **250**, 250, 251;
      national debt **126**, **127**; public borrowing
      126, 129, 320–21; public expenditure **112**,
      115–16, 141–2, 492n; trade deficit 253–4,
      254; *see also war economy* (below)
    fatalism on eve of war 97–9
    food shortage 276, 277
    foreign policy 27–8; ambitions in France 170–71,
      287, 498n, 502nn; annexations 286, 287–8,
      502–3nn; attempts at entente with Britain
      45–52; diplomatic risks 285–9; dream of
      European customs union 19, 171, 172–3; fear
      of Russia 43, 96, 98–100, 171–2; fears of
      encirclement 68, 152; and fragility of
      European alliances 150; and France 16, 73,
      103, 156; hopes of British neutrality xl–xli,
      150, 156, 162; and Morocco 52, 69; as
      'Napoleonic' threat 74–5, 170, 172;
      overestimate of enemies' strength 96, 443;
      pre-emptive war option 33, 99–100, 151–2,
      153–4, 284, 443; pre-war objectives 169–73;
      recognition of British naval power 70–72, 85;
      relations with Austria-Hungary 147, 148,

      149, 284–5; and Turkey 69; view of Serbia
      148, 149
    franchise **29**
    historians xxxviii, xl–xlii
    labour; strikes 271, 275, **275**; supply 191, 267–8;
      trade unions 273–4, **274**; wages and
      productivity 271, **272**
    official histories and documents xxxv
    political parties 122–4
    political structure (federal) 34, 145, 257–8,
      288–9
    population and manpower available **297**, **299**
    press comment 215–16
    propaganda 224–6, 227, 228, 237
    prophetic literature 3–4, 5, 6–7, 173
    radical Right (nationalist) 16–20
    reaction to Russian mobilization 147, 149–50,
      157–8, 497n
    rebuttal of atrocity allegations 237
    religious fervour 208
    response to mobilization 198
    social inequality 278–80
    socialist vote **29**
    war aims 169–72, 286, 288–9
    war costs per death 337
    war economy; corporatism 254–5, 256–9, 261,
      444; cost of living 331; money supply
      329–30, 330; national debt 320–21, 324, **324**,
      325, 326; procurement system 259, 260–1,
      263–4, 265–6; war loans 326, 426
    see also counter-factual options; German Army;
      Germany, post-war; Reichstag; Triple
      Alliance
Germany, post-war
    capability for paying reparations 414–19, 416,
      537n
    defaults on reparations 397, 417, 418–19, **419**
    economic policy to avoid paying reparations
      411–12
    economy 407–8, 423–5
    employment levels 420, 423–4
    expectation of tough peace conditions 408–10
    foreign investment 413
    foreign loans 401, 404, 409, 413, 417
    hyperinflation 397, 398, 406–7, 540n
    monetary policy 429
    options for financing reparations 401–2, 403–4
    public spending 420–21, 432
    tax reforms 410–11, 429
    territorial losses 409, 434, 538–9n
    trade deficit 413, 417–18, 540n
    violence 389–90
Gibbon, Lewis Grassic, *A Scots Quair* xxix
Gibbs, Philip, journalist xxviii, 377
Gillespie, Alexander 360
Gilman, Charlotte Perkins 210
Gladden, Norman 364, 378
Gladstone, W. E. 20–21, 111

globalization 38, 438–9
gold standard 38, 127, 439
Goltz, Colmar von der 88
Goschen, Sir William 119
  as ambassador in Berlin 61, 70, 72, 138
  on German domination of Europe 74, 75
Gosse, Edmund 234
Göttsche, NCO 373
Gough, Gen Sir Hubert 346
Graham, Stephen, on killing of prisoners
  376–7
Grant, Duncan 181, 184
Grauthoff, Ferdinand, *The Collapse of the Old
  World* 7, 173
Graves, Robert xxix, 24, 348, 353, 359
  Goodbye to All That xxiii, 379, 450
Great Britain
  anti-war literature xxvii–xxx
  decision for war 160–2, 163–4, 168–9, 173, 177,
    443–4
    see also Grey
  diplomatic documents xxxv
  economy; consols (government bonds) 127, 131,
    132, 133, 333; cost of living 331, 396; defence
    expenditure 105–7, 106, 108, 110–11, 110,
    113, 114, 491n; economic decline theory 34;
    economic growth 44; external debt (post-
    war) 396; financial power of xliii, 35–8, 248;
    foreign investment 35–7, 36; money supply
    329, 330; national debt 126, 127–8, 127, 324,
    324, 325, 326, 421–2, 422; post-war
    deflationary policies 421; public borrowing
    126, 127; rising public spending 113, 114; tax
    system 118–19, 248, 322–3; trade deficit 253,
    254; and US finance 327–9; *see also war
    economy* (below)
  effect of intervention on German war aims
    170–72
  expectation of German post-war competition
    415
  foreign policy; appeasement of powers which
    posed threats 52–5; dangers of Franco-
    Russian alliance for 40, 42–5; defensive
    alliance with Japan 54; and German colonial
    claims in Africa 46–7, 68–9; global
    dominance of 37–8, 39; perception of
    German world ambitions xxxix, xli, 74–6,
    164, 443; perception of threat xlii, 443; and
    proposed naval limitation agreement 70–72;
    rapprochement with Germany 45–52, 69–70,
    87; relations with France 39, 40, 41–2, 53–4;
    relations with Russia 39, 40, 41, 42–3, 54, 79;
    relations with USA 54–5; and strategic
    importance of France 163–4; trade controls
    265–7; unimportance of Germany to 53, 442;
    see also Grey
  franchise 29
  histories of war xxxiii–xxxv, 466n

justifications for intervention in memoirs
  xxxix–xl
labour; labour supply 268–70; strikes 274–5,
  275; trade unions 273–4, 274; wages and
  productivity 271, 272
military potential 95
naval supremacy 70–72, 84–5, 163–4
post-war conditions 395–6
propaganda *see* propaganda and propagandists
prophetic war novels 1–3, 4–7
use of DORA 186
war costs per death 337
war economy 255–6, 444–5; food rationing
  276–7; procurement system 259–60, 260,
  261, 262, 264–5, 266–7; war debts 327–9,
  419; War Loans 325, 426
see also Asquith; British Army; British Empire;
  counter-factual options; Lloyd George;
  Royal Navy
Greece 51, 390, 441
  casualties 295, 299
  expansionism 144
  First Balkan War 147
  national debt 324
  POWs 369
Grenfell, Francis 202, 360–61
Grenfell, Julian 360, 363, 449
Grew, Joseph, American diplomat 100
Grey, Sir Edward (Lord Grey of Falloden) xxxvi,
  xxxix, 56–60, 180
  acceptance of invasion theory 14
  and Belgian neutrality 159
  and decision for war 160–2, 168–9, 173, 177,
    443–4
  defensive alliance with France 62, 63–4, 66,
    72–3
  doubts German attack on Russia 100–101
  and Fashoda incident 42
  and four-power conference (July crisis) 154–5,
    156, 159, 192–3
German financial weakness 138
Germanophobia 57–8, 72, 73
  level of defence expenditure 82, 105, 191
  and logic of German pre-emptive war 152
  and nature of commitment to France 77–80,
    149, 158–9, 163–4, 443
  passion for fishing 59–60
  and plans for Expeditionary Force 63, 66
  policy on Russia 60–62, 72–3, 79
  and public opinion 177
  rapprochement with Germany 69–70, 71–2
  warnings to Lichnowsky 149, 154–5, 158, 159,
    161, 499–500n
grief 437–8
Grierson, Lt Gen James, Director of Military
  Operations 62
Groener, Lt Col Wilhelm, German army
  technocrat 95, 96, 153

Grosz, George, artist xxx–xxxi, 454
Gurner, Ronald, memoirs 451
Gurney, Ivor 349, 365, 437
Gwinner, Arthur von 51

Haber, Fritz 228
Hague Convention (1899) 246, 371, 372–3
Hague Peace Conferences (1907) 10, 86
Hahn, Kurt 183
Haig, Field Marshal Earl 209, 305–6, 357
   'active defence' policy 293
   prospect of armistice 312–13, 314
Haldane, Gen Sir Aylmer 390
Haldane, Richard, War Minister
   on German threat 14, 68, 86
   mission to Berlin (1912) 70–71
   and Territorial Army 102
   unhappy at commitment to France 76, 160
Hall, Radclyffe 362
Hamburg bourse, crisis 191–2, 197
Hamilton, Agnes, writer xxviii
Hamilton, Edward, Treasury official 127
Hamilton, Sir Ian, memoirs xxxv
Hankey, Sir Maurice, Secretary of CID 14, 66, 315
Hanotaux, Gabriel, French Foreign Minister 42
Hansemann, Adolph, German banker 47, 48
Harcourt, Lewis, Colonial Secretary 71, 79
   and Belgian neutrality 162, 163
   opposition to Grey 77, 160, 161
Harcourt, Sir William 119
Hardie, Keir 23, 179
Hardinge, Sir Charles 14, 70, 73, 76
Hardman, Freddie 184
Hardy, Thomas 24, 228, 232, 233, 449
Harmsworth family see Northcliffe; Rothermere
Hart, Sir Robert, in Hong Kong 47
Hašek, Jaroslav, The Good Soldier Švejk 203–4, 452
Hassall, John, artist 454
Hatzfeldt, Paul von, German ambassador 47, 49
Hauptmann, Gerhard 228
Havenstein, Rudolf, Reichsbank president 32, 33, 136
Hay, Ian, The First Hundred Thousand 449
Hay-Pauncefote Treaty (1901) 55
health
   and food supplies 277–8
   illness in trenches 343
Heeringen, Josias von 91
Heeringen, Vice-Admiral Moritz von 24
Heinrich, Crown Prince 155–6
Heinrichka, Max, Germany's Future 4
Helfferich, Karl, German finance minister 33, 408
Hemingway, Ernest, A Farewell to Arms xxiii
Henderson, Arthur 179
Herbert, A. P. xxix, 359
Herbert-Spottiswood, John, British spy 13
Hill, Headon, The Spies of Wight 1
Hindenburg, General Paul von 258, 288

Hirst, F. W., editor of Economist 77
Hitler, Adolf 428, 456, 460
   enthusiasm for war 174–5, 204
   Mein Kampf xxxvii, 175–6
   on propaganda 213, 247
Hobhouse, C. 160
Hobson, J. A. xxxviii, 21, 181
Hocking, Joseph, novel 449
Hohenlohe, Prince, at Oxford 24
Holstein, Friedrich von 47, 50
Holtzendorff, Admiral Henning von 287, 521n
homosexuality 348–9
   Keynes's 327, 526n
Hong Kong & Shanghai Banking Corporation 47, 48
Hope, Anthony 233
Hötzendorf, Baron Franz Conrad von, Austrian
   CIGS xxxvii–xxxviii, 92, 98, 100, 148
House, Colonel Edward, US envoy 150, 152–3, 287
housing, Germany 279
Huelsenbeck, Richard, artist 454, 544n
Hugenberg, Alfred, Krupp director 33, 245–6
Huguet, French military attaché 62
Hungary 145
   economy 118, 125, 324
   franchise 29
   loss of territory 409, 434
   see also Austria-Hungary
Huth family 25

imagery, of outbreak of war xxxvi–xxxvii
immigration restrictions, and espionage 11–12
Imperial Ottoman Baghdad Railway 51
Imperial War Graves Commission 436
imperialism xxxviii, 27, 31–2, 434
   American 54–5
   and economic globalization 38, 39
   liberal 22–3
Independent Labour Party (ILP) 179, 186
Independent Socialist Party (Germany) 289
India 170
   Amritsar massacre 391
Indian Army 102, 299
industrial production 34, 35, 250–51, 250, 413
   cartels 261
   coal 250–51, 262
   German iron and steel 33, 250, 263, 264
   labour supply 267–75
   profits 263–4, 265, 320
   and wages 271–2, 272
   see also arms industry
industrialization, Russia 44–5
inflation
   1921 deflation 413–14, 431
   cost of living 330–31, 331, 396
   costs of 425–6
   effect on bond price/yield 130–31, 131
   effect on German debt 421–2

effect of reparations on 407–8
Germany 320, 329
hyperinflation in Germany 397, 398, 406–7
money supply 329–30, 330
and newspaper prices 244–5
post-war 397
social costs of 426–8
intelligence service, British 12–13, 75
see also espionage
international relations, in preceding century 39, 40,
41–5
Iraq 390, 434
Ireland 199, 221
civil war 390, 396, 535n
Home Rule bill 164
Partition 396, 434
Irish Nationalists 20
iron and steel production
France 96, 287, 502n
Germany 33, 250, 263, 264
Italian Army 99, 312
casualties 295, 299
desertion 345
POWs 368, 369
Italy 42, 267, 333
acquisition of territory 434
censorship 220
creation of state 144, 145
economy; defence expenditure 106, 110, 111;
economic growth 44, 250; government
bonds 135; industrial
production 250, 250; money
supply 330; national debt 324,
324, 325, 422; post-war policies
423; trade deficit 254
franchise 29
post-war violence 390
strikes 275
war costs per death 337
war literature 452
Izvolsky, Alexander, Russian Foreign Minister
147

J'Accuse (Gance), film 453
Jackson, Henry 182
Jacob, Gen Sir Claud 384
Jagow, Gottlieb von, German foreign minister 100,
150–52, 156, 162, 177, 286
James, L., The Boy Galloper 1
Japan 47, 434
defensive alliance with Britain 54
war with Russia 54, 495n
Jardine, Matheson & Co. 47
Jaurès, Jean, French socialist 29–30, 190, 193
Jerrold, Douglas, military historian 451
Jews
in Eastern Europe 441
pro-German 469n

Joffre, General Joseph 16, 150, 154, 317
attaque brusquée strategy 96, 488n
journalists
propagandists xxviii, 11–12
war correspondents 223, 224
see also writers
July Crisis
assassinations in Sarajevo 146, 204, 496
Austrian ultimatum 156–7
German business and 32–3
German reaction 147–9
Grey's four-power conference 154–5, 156, 159,
192–3
Russian mobilization 149–50
Jung, Franz 455
Jünger, Ernst
on killing of prisoners 373, 381
refusal to surrender 387–8
war diaries and novels 340, 341, 344, 350, 359,
361–3, 364, 452
Jutland, battle of 283

Kahn, André 365
Kamenev, Gen S. S., Red Army 394
Kapp, Wolfgang
Fatherland Party 289
Nationalist Circles 229–30
Kautsky, Karl, German Social Democrat xxxv,
xxxviii
Kehr, Eckart, historian xl, 27, 89, 125
Keim, August, German Army League 15, 19, 136
Kell, Captain Vernon 12, 14
Kemal, Mustapha (Ataturk) 390
Kemp, Lucy, artist 454
Kennedy, Paul, on role of economics 33–4
Kennedy, Revd G. A. Studdert 356
Kershaw, Kenneth 202
Kessler, Count Harry, German Liberal 24
Keynes, John Maynard xxii, 319, 327, 526n
and 1914 financial crisis 192, 195, 321
advocates German eastward orientation 537n
counter-inflationary advice 406
Economic Consequences 399, 402, 407, 414,
425–6
opposition to reparations 399–400, 402–3, 414
opposition to war 184, 327
support for inflationary policies 405, 406–7,
422–3
Tract on Monetary Reform 406, 422–3
Keynes, Neville 182
Kiderlen-Wächter, Alfred von, German foreign
minister 28, 147
Kiggell, Lt Gen Sir Lancelot 385–6
Kipling, Rudyard 228, 231, 438, 449
Kitchener, Earl, Secretary of State for War 167, 198,
319
policy of attrition 292
Kleinwort family 25

Klemm, Wilhelm, poetry xxvi
Koester, Admiral von 70
Köpke, Major General 88
Kosovo 147
Kraus, Karl, *The Last Days of Mankind* (play)
 xxiii–xxiv, xxx, 176, 208, 214, 374
  on power of press 239–41
  on returning soldiers 388–9
Krenek, Ernst, opera 453
Krupp A. G. 263
Kühlmann, Richard von 287

La Rochelle, Drieu, writer 176
Labour Party (British) 20, 23
  reaction to outbreak of war 178, 179, 180–81
labour supply xliii, 244, 445
  and enlistment 206, 268–9, 508n
  German labour exchanges 191
  in industry 267–75
  mobility 270–71
  reserved occupations 269, 508n
  skilled and unskilled 269–7, 271–2, 273
  women 267, 268
  see also strikes; unemployment; wages
Lammasch, Heinrich 25
Langlois, Hippolyte, French artillery expert 96
Lansdowne, Marquess of, Foreign Secretary 52,
 53–4, 60, 86, 165
Latvia 145, 286, 434, 441
Latzko, Andreas, *People at War* xxx
Lawrence, D. H. xxviii, 449
Lawrence, T. E. 204, 303
 Seven Pillars of Wisdom xxix, 348–9
Le Cateau 168
Le Queux, William 2, 5–6
  as propagandist 11–12, 14, 232
  The Invasion of 1910 1–2, 4, 11
League of Nations 402, 434, 439
Lebanon 434
Leete, Alfred, Kitchener poster 236
Léger, Fernand, artist 454, 455
Leishman, John, American diplomat 139–40
Lenin, V. I. 31–2, 460
  military ruthlessness of 392–4
Leroux, George, artist xxxi
Lersner, Kurt von, German Foreign Office 400
Lever, Sir William 201
Levetzow, Captain von 288
Lewis, Wyndham, Vorticist artist 358–9,
 454, 455
Liberal League (imperialist) 56
Liberal Party (British)
  fiscal policy 119–20
  Francophile policy 62
  imperialism of 22–3
  and Ireland 164–5
  landslide election victory (1906) 56
  opposition to intervention 77, 160

and pacifism 20–21
  see also Asquith; Cabinet; Grey; Lloyd George
Lichnowsky, Prince, German ambassador to
 Britain 24, 162
  Grey's warnings to 149, 154–5, 158, 159, 161,
 499–500n
Lichtenstein, Alfred, 'Prayer before Battle'
 xxvi–xxvii
Liebknecht, Karl 26, 178, 179
Liman von Sanders affair 69, 148
literature *see* drama; novels; poetry
Lithuania 145, 286, 409, 434
Littlejohn, W. S. 359–60
Livonia 409
Lloyd George, David 57, 59, 176
  and 1914 bank crisis 197
  and Bank of England 321–2
  on Belgian and Dutch neutrality 66–7
  budgets 119, 321
  and coalition 166, 396
  on conscription 103–4
  and decision for war 160, 161–2, 313,
 444
  on generals 293, 303
  importance of navy 75, 87, 114
  on improved Anglo-German relations 70,
 87
  and labour supply 268, 269, 273, 274
  Mansion House speech (1911) 69, 77, 499n
  social policy 114, 235
  use of propaganda 213, 214, 220, 223–4
  and war economy 262
  War Memoirs xxxvi, xxxix
Locke, William J., novels 449
Lockwood, Col Mark 5
Logan, William Barnet, memoirs 451
London, crowds 189
London School of Economics 182
London Ultimatum (1921) 403–4, 414
Long, Walter 165
Loos, battle of 307
Loreburn, Earl, Lord Chancellor 77, 102
Loucheur, Louis, Minister of Armaments 262
Lowe, Charles, on Le Queux 5
Lucy, John 342, 347, 362
Ludendorff, Erich xxxv, 105, 258
  admission of defeat 313–14, 315
  army reforms (1916) 308
  Great Memorandum (1912) 91, 141
  military dictatorship 288
  Operation Michael (spring offensive 1918) 285,
 293–4, 316, 386–7, 448
  pessimism of 97
  on propaganda 212
Ludwig, Emil, imaginary history 457
Lusitania, sinking of 247, 282–3
Luther, Hans, German finance minister 422
Lutyens, Sir Edwin xxxiii

Luxembourg 146, 171, 502n
Lyttleton, Neville, CIGS 76

McAdoo, William Gibbs, UU Treasury 325
McCrae, John 449
MacDonald, Ramsay 23, 164, 180–81, 229
Macedonia 144, 147, 148, 441
McGill, Patrick 365
McKenna, Reginald 66, 160, 327, 487n
Mackin, Elton, US Army 387
Mackintosh, Lt Ewart, poem 438
Majority Social Democrats (Germany) 289, 389
Mallet, L., Foreign Office 72, 73, 80
Manchester Guardian 216
Manchuria, Russia and 48, 54
Mann, Heinrich, *Man of Straw* 17
Mann, Thomas 19, 233
Manning, Frederic xxix, xxx
Marinetti, Filippo, Futurist artist 455
Marlowe, Thomas, editor of *Daily Mail* 217–18
Marne, Battle of the 168
Martin du Gard, Roger, *The Summer of 1914*
    xxx
Martin, Rudolf 5, 6
Marxist-Leninist theory
    on German militarism 26–7
    imperial origins of war 31–2
Masefield, John 228, 236
Massingham, H. W. 21
Masterman, Charles 223, 233, 396
Maurice, Brig Frederick 292
Maurois, André, imaginary history 457
Maurras, Charles 317
Maxim-Nordenfelt company 32
Maxton, James, ILP leader 179, 186
Maxwell, Col Frank, VC 384
May, Lt A. G. 378
Mayer, Arno, historian xxxviii
medals, war xx–xxi
Mediterranean, Anglo-French plans for naval
    defence 67–8, 78–9
Medley, D. J. 228
Meinecke, Friedrich 19, 175, 228
Melchior, Carl
    on inflation 424
    influence on reparations policy 400, 403, 410,
        411–12
memoirs
    German military 452
    political and military xxix, xxxv–xxxvi, 450–51,
        466n
Mensdorff, Count, Austrian
    Ambassador 191
Messines, attack at 293, 305
Messter, Oskar, film maker 227, 237
Metternich, Count, German ambassador 63, 138
Meynell, Francis xxvii
Michaelis, Georg, Chancellor 289

middle classes
    effect of war on 395–6
    impoverishment 278–80, 536n
    and parliamentary politics 427–8
    patriotism 189, 280
    and post-war economic policies 423–4, 426–8
    support for German nationalism 16–17, 19–20
    as volunteers 199
militarism xxxviii, 1, 28
    and anti-militarism 20–30, 29, 442
    in Britain 15–16
    church 208–9
    in decline 28–30
    and disarmament 439
    in France 16
    German 26–7
    Navy League (Germany) 16, 17, 18
    see also arms race; Army League (Germany);
        radical nationalism
military effectiveness xliv
    Central Powers 248–9, 294, 300, 318, 336, 445
    Triple Entente 294, 300, 337–8, 445
    see also economic efficiency
military service
    Belgium 101–2
    France 16, 92, 93
    in Germany 89
    and mobilization 197–8
    Russia 92
    see also conscription; enlistment
Milne, A. A., lampoon 5–6
Milner, Lord 315
Miquel, Johannes, Prussian finance minister 27
Mitteis, Ludwig 24
Mitteleuropa
    concept 19, 288
    see also European Customs Union
Mlada Bosna student terrorists 146
MO5 *see* Directorate of Military Operations
Moltke, Helmuth, Count von (Elder) 8, 88,
    99–100
Moltke, Helmuth von (Younger) 18, 19, 85, 170,
    209
    on Balkans 147
    financial constraints 137, 140
    and invasion of Belgium 162, 502n
    pessimism of 92, 97–9, 177
    and pre-emptive war option 100, 151, 153
    and Schlieffen Plan 96–7
monarchy
    European links 25, 435
    fall of Romanovs, Habsburgs and
        Hohenzollerns 434–5
    in new nation states 144, 409
Mond, Alfred 262
Mons, retreat from 168, 202
Montagu, Edwin 434
Montague, C. E., journalist xxix, 451

Montenegro
First Balkan War 147
military strength and potential 92, 93
morale 237, 280, 354-5
British Army 346
collapse of German 312, 317, 354, 386-7, 448
and discipline 346-9, 446
French 333
see also surrender
Morgan, J. H. 232
Morgan, J. P. (New York bankers) 266, 328, 329
Morley, John, Viscount, Lord President 57, 78
and decision for war 160, 161, 164
Morocco 52
first crisis (1905-6) 54-5, 63, 69
second crisis (1911) 14, 15, 28, 69, 139
mortality rates 277
Mosse, Rudolf 246
Mottram, R. H. xxix
Mozambique 51
Muir, Ramsay 228
Müller, Admiral Georg von 18-19, 83, 85
Müller, Gustav 172
Munitions of War Act (1915) 273, 274
Munro-Ferguson, Ronald 58
Murray, Gilbert 228, 229, 231, 233, 236
Murray, Sir Archibald 319
music
popularity of German composers 24
war-inspired 453
mutinies 345, 367

Nash, Paul, artist xxx, 454
Nation (Liberal journal) 77, 100, 221
National Liberal Party (Germany) 19-20, 26, 123, 494n
National Service League 15
National Socialism (Nazism) 16, 17, 428
and German diaspora 440
National War Aims Committee 224, 236
nationalism xxxviii, 355
Balkan 143-4
France 16
German radical 16-20, 28
and nation states 144-6
Slav 61, 99, 100
see also patriotism
naval blockade of Germany
Admiralty plans for 62, 66, 86, 161
effectiveness of 252-3, 276, 445
German fears of 84
see also Royal Navy
Navy League (Germany) 16, 17, 18
Netherlands 67, 101
German aims for 171, 502n
Schlieffen Plan and 88
Neue Freie Presse 241
Neuhof, Capt Kurt 154

neutrals
propaganda aimed at 215, 223, 224, 236-7, 243
trade with 252-3
treatment of 247
see also Belgian neutrality
Nevill, Capt W. P. 360
New Fatherland League (Germany) 181, 185, 227
New Zealand forces, casualty rate 299
Newbolt, Sir Henry, poet 58, 201, 231
newspapers 11, 77, 185, 243
bellicosity xliii, 217
British 241, 242, 243-6, 243
circulation 241, 242, 243-6, 243, 244
criticism of decision for war 215-17
economic problems for 244-5, 444
French 243, 244, 245
German 243, 244-6, 244
for propaganda 212-14, 230
trench 238
see also Northcliffe; press; Times
Nicholas II, Tsar of Russia
and agreement to mobilize 157-8
murder of 435
reading of Bloch 10, 470n
Nichols, Robert, 'The Assault' 361
Nicholson, Field Marshal Sir William, CIGS 66
Nicolai, Georg Friedrich 182
Nicolai, Major, German intelligence 153-4
Nicolson, Sir Arthur, Under-Secretary of State 60-61, 72, 74, 80, 139
Niemann, August, World War—German Dreams 3
Nivelle, General Robert 209, 224
Nivelle offensive 293
No-Conscription Fellowship 181, 182, 186, 346
non-conformism (British) 20
Northcliffe, Lord
Daily Mail 11, 22, 310
influence of 217-18, 230, 509n
and Rothschild 195, 217
war propaganda 212-13, 214, 234
Norway 144
novels
anti-war xxx, 449
French anti-war xxx
German anti-war xxx
German prophetic 3-4
patriotic war fiction 449-50
post-war xxviii-xxx
prophetic 1-7
see also All Quiet . . . ; poetry
Noyes, Alfred 231

o'Flaherty, Liam, writer xxx
Oh! What a Lovely War xxiii, xxiv, xxxii
Oldmeadow, Ernest, North Sea Bubble 3
Oliver, Frederick 165
Ollivant, Maj A. H. 167
Omdurman, battle of 42

Oncken, Hermann 228
O'Neill, Pte 182
Oppenheim, E. Phillips, *A Maker of History* 2, 12
Ostaufmarsch option (attack on Russia) 315
Osten-Sacken, Ottomar, Baron von der 137
Ostend 168
Ottley, Sir Charles, secretary of CID 86
Ottoman Empire
  Anglo-German interests in 50–51, 69
  decline of 143–5, 147
  Sultan deposed 434, 435
  see also Turkey
Owen, Wilfred 205, 348, 359, 447, 462
  poetry xxiii, xxvi, 448
Oxford University
  Germanophilia 24–5
  opposition to war 183
  Red Book 228, 211, 235–6

pacifism 20, 181, 146
  conscientious objectors 181, 186
  in Germany 25, 181, 182
Pacifist Society (Germany) 181
Page, Walter, American ambassador 140
Paléologue, Maurice, French
  ambassador to Russia 150
Palestine 390, 414
Pall Mall Gazette 218–19
'Pals' Battalions 206
Pan-German League 17, 18, 19, 289
Panama Canal crisis (1893) 43, 55
Paris, mass exodus 186, 189
Parliamentary Recruiting Committee 205, 226, 211
Partridge, Eric 367
patriotism 16, 189, 227
  among soldiers 354–5
  motive for enlistment 201–3
peace
  disenchantment with xliv, 451
  see also reparations
Peace Society (Germany) 185
Pease, Joseph 160, 161, 162, 165, 177, 501n
Pemberton, Max, *Pro Patria* 5
Pershing, Gen John 305
Persia, Russian interests in 54, 60
Pétain, Marshal Philippe 285, 308, 527n
Petrov-Vodkin, K., artist 456
Philippines 54
Piedmont, and Italian state 144
Pimenov, Y., artist 456
Planck, Max 228
Plowman, Max, writer xxix, 346
poetry
  anti-war xxvi–xxvii, 448, 449
  defence of war 448–9
  German 449
  by non-combatants 449

patriotic 229, 231, 449
  prophetic 2
  see also Ford; Graves; Lichtenstein; Owen;
    Sassoon etc.
Pohl, Admiral von 154
Poincaré, Raymond, French President 16, 29, 121, 147, 154
  and reparations 405–6
Poland 169, 172, 286, 397, 538n
  independence 409, 434
Ponsonby, Arthur 77, 232
population
  and available manpower 297–8, 297, 299
  Central Powers 248, 249
  effect of war dead on 436–7
  and German casualties 297
  German growth rate 35, 38, 92, 436
  and proportion of military personnel 95
  Triple Entente 248, 249
population transfers, in post-war Europe 441
Port Arthur, dispute with Russia 48
Portugal 38
  African colonies 50, 51, 68–9
  casualties 295, 299
  POWs 369
Pound, Ezra 449
Powell, E. C. 176
press
  British provincial 217, 218
  diversity of opinion 215–19
  government control 219–20
  power and cynicism of 239–41
  proprietors 214, 245–6
  see also censorship; films;
    newspapers
price controls 278–9, 320, 321
Princip, Gavrilo 146
Prisoner's Dilemma 344, 528–9nn
prisoners-of-war 294, 296, 368, 369, 370, 445
  captor's dilemma 372–3
  as hostages 371–2
  killing of 373–84, 447–8
  in labour force 267, 371
  orders for taking 384–6
  propaganda value 372
  tortured in Russian Civil War 394
  see also surrender
procurement systems 259–67
  integrated Entente 266–7
Progressive Party (Germany) 123, 289
propaganda and propagandists 14, 183, 223–4
  autonomous 183, 226–30
  effectiveness of 235–9, 444
  German 15, 213
  government use of 214, 223–5
  Le Queux 11–12
  leaflets 225
  to raise money 225, 324–6

slogans 234
style and content 231–5
use of atrocity stories 232, 237, 246–7, 444
see also films; newspapers
Protestantism
and attrition 209
and German radical nationalism 18
Prussia 137, 144, 323
public opinion
and decision for war 161, 162, 176, 177, 189
fear of war 186–7
support for war xliii, 174–7
and willingness to fight 197–9, 200, 201–5
see also patriotism; propaganda
Punch 5–6

Quade, Julius 375
Quidde, Ludwig 185
Quigley, Hugh 385
Quiller-Couch, Sir Arthur 233
Quirnheim, Col Mertz von 289

racial theories, in German universities 18–19
Rade, Martin 208
radical nationalism, Germany 16–20, 28
Radical Party (France) 121
Radicalism, in British Liberal party 56, 57, 77
railways 48, 265
and army mobilization 93, 96, 101
Berlin-Baghdad 33, 51, 61, 69
German state subsidies 420, 424–5
Russian 96, 151, 265
Trans-Siberian 48
Ranke, Leopold von, balance of power 144
Rapallo, Treaty of (1922) 410
Rathenau, Walther, AEG 389, 404, 424
and war economy 257–8
Rawlinson, Sir Henry 292, 305–6
Raymond, Ernest, novelist 359, 450
Read, Herbert xxix, 348
'Other Ranks' Letter Home 201
Rebmann, Edmund, National
Liberal 19–20
Redlich, Josef 176
refugees
from Eastern Front 186–8
from Paris 186
repatriation of 441
Reichsbank, monetary policy 141
Reichstag
democratic nature of 116–17
power over budgets 116
public borrowing 129
taxes 115–16, 121–2, 124–5,
493–4nn
Reims offensive 285
religion
among soldiers 355–7, 446

Armageddon 210–11
influence of 207–11
see also Catholic church; Protestantism
Remarque, Erich Maria, All Quiet on the Western
Front xxx, 381, 451
Renn, Ludwig, Krieg xxx
Renoir, Jean, La Grande Illusion 453
reparations
Allied failure to enforce 419–21
Dawes Scheme 407, 414
French influence on 402–3
German ability to pay 414–19, 416, 537n
German options for financing 401–2, 403–4
Keynes's criticism of 399–400, 402–3, 404
London Ultimatum schedule 403–4, 414
outstanding liabilities (1931) 418–19, 419, 537n
owed to US 412
Repington, Charles à Court 220, 230, 331, 333,
463n, 512n
Representation of the People Act (1918) 396
republicanism, in Europe 145, 434–5, 436
Revelstoke, Lord 51
revolution
and Bolshevism 333, 400, 410, 436
as likely outcome of war 10, 28, 31–2
Rhineland
French plans for 317
occupation 539n
Richert, Dominik 373
Richter, Max Emil 375
Riddell, Sir George 214, 217
Riezler, Kurt, secretary to Bethmann Hollweg 18,
98, 151, 173
on growth of armaments 82, 83
Rilke, Rainer Maria, poet 449
Rivers, W. H., psychologist xxxi, xxxii
Roanne, French state arsenal 260, 261–2
Roberts, Field Marshal Lord 87
national service scheme 11, 102
Robertson, Col William, later Field Marshal Sir
William xxxv, 75, 292, 460
Germany as main threat 60, 63
and invasion theory 13, 87
attrition policy 293
Robertson, Sir John 339
Robinson, Heath 6
Rolland, Romain 182
Roosevelt, Theodore, US President 55, 72
Rosebery, Earl of 41, 42, 230
pessimism of 56, 478n
Rosenberg, Alfred 213
Roth, Joseph 360
Rothermere, Lord (Harold Harmsworth) 214, 509n
Rothschild, Alfred de 197
Rothschild family 25, 32
efforts to avert war 32
Rothschild, Lord
and 1914 banking crisis 192, 193, 195

on financial relations with Germany 70
on German financial weakness 139
Rothschilds' bank 32
Paris branch loans to Russia 43, 193
Rouault, Georges, artist 456–7
Rowntree, Arnold 77
royal families see monarchy
Royal Navy 10, 70, 75
dominance of 38, 70–2, 84–7
limited preparations 159, 160, 161
strategy 283–4
see also Admiralty; Churchill; naval blockade
Ruhr, French occupation of 397, 403, 405–6,
419–20
Rumania 251, 315, 434
creation of 144, 145
franchise 29
national debt 324
Rumanian Army 375
casualties 295, 299
POWs 369
Runciman, Sir Walter 77–8, 162, 165
Russell, Bertrand 57, 176, 182, 186, 318
Russia xxxv, 9–10, 29, 45
1905 revolution 28
and Armenia 434
and Balkans 61, 143, 144, 147–8
Bolshevik Revolution 333
see also Russian Civil War; Union of Soviet
Socialist Republics
defeat of 285, 286, 315
economy; cost of living 331; defence expenditure
106, 107, 108–9, 110–11, 110, 114–15;
economic growth 44, 44, 249, 250; financial
weakness 135, 328; fiscal system 114–15, 121,
323; French loans to 43–4, 48; government
bonds 128, 131, 132, 134; industrial
production 44–5, 250, 250, 251, 265; money
supply 329, 330, 331; national debt 126, 127,
324, 324, 326; post-war 397, 408; public
borrowing 126; trade deficit 254; war
economy 263, 264–5, 267, 280; War Loans 325
February Revolution (1917) 289
franchise 29
and Franco-Russian alliance 42–5
Galician offensive 285
Grey's appeasement of 60–62
illiberal reputation 61–2, 185
influence in Far East 47–8
loss of territory 409, 434
mobilization 30, 149–50, 157–8, 198, 204, 497n
reaction to Austrian reprisals on Serbia 154–5,
156–7
relations with Austria-Hungary 99, 147
relations with Britain 39, 40, 41, 42–3, 45, 73
relations with Germany 61, 73
strikes (1914) 30
war costs per death 337

Russian Army 345, 355
casualties 295, 298, 299
military potential 93
mobilization 30, 96, 149–50, 157–8, 198, 204,
497n
peacetime/war strength 91, 92, 92, 94
POWs 368, 369
Russian Civil War (1918–22) 391–4, 391, 436, 441,
448
Russian Navy 68, 79, 85, 143
Russo-Chinese alliance (1896) 48
Russo-Japanese war 88, 115

Saki (Hector Hugh Monro) 3
Salisbury, Marquess of 46, 48, 53, 105
and relations with Germany 49, 50
Samoa 50, 55
Samuel, H. 160, 165
Sanderson, Sir Thomas, Foreign Office 63, 76
Sandzak of Novi Pazar 147
Sarajevo
assassination in 146, 204, 496
see also July Crisis
Sassoon, Siegfried xxix, xxx, xxxi, 24, 201, 202, 348,
353, 363
Memoirs of a Hunting Man xxiii, 451
poetry xxvi, 238, 342, 448
Saxe-Coburg-Gotha, Duke of 24–5
Sazonov, Sergei, Russian foreign minister 61, 79,
147–8
offer of talks 156–7
Schäfer, Dietrich, Pan-Germanist 18
Scherl, August 245
Schiffer, Eugen, German finance minister 409
Schlemmer, Oscar, artist 454
Schlieffen, Count Alfred von 18, 92, 97, 99–100, 209
formulates Grosse Denkschrift 88–9
Schlieffen Plan 95–7, 99, 163, 315–16
economic factors for 190
flaws in 167–8, 284–5
Schmidt, Robert, German economics minister 412
Schmidt-Gibichenfels, Otto 19
Schmoller, Gustav 228
Scholars' Protest 182, 183
schools 3
patriotic culture in 201–2
Schramm family 280
Schramm, Percy 198, 207–8, 210
Schröder family 25
Schücking, Walther 182, 186–7
Schultz, Max, British spy 13
Schumacher, Hermann 287
Scotland, volunteers from 199
Scots
casualty rate 298, 299, 339, 507n
national identity 145, 355
Scott, C. P., editor of Manchester Guardian 73, 213,
216

Seaman, Owen 228
Second International 178
 Stuttgart (1907) 31
Seeburg, Reinhold 208
Seely, J. E. B. 300
Selborne, Earl of, First Sea Lord 45, 53, 55, 83
self-determination, principle of 286, 439–41
Serbia 25, 99, 247, 315
 Austrian ultimatum to 156–7
 expansionist nationalism 144, 146–7, 390
 franchise 29
 Yugoslav state 434
 see also Slav nationalism
Serbian Army 92, 93, 295, 299
 POWs 369
Seton Hutchison, Lt Col Graham 372
Shaw, George Bernard 23–4, 181, 453
 Common Sense about the War xxvii, 236
Shee, George, National Service League 15
shelling and shell-shock 340–2, 437
Sherriff, R. C., Journey's End 453
shipping, merchant
 post-war 412, 420
 wartime 265–6, 412
shipyards, German 32, 263–4
 see also Blohm & Voss
Siam 41, 54
Siemens, Georg von 51
Simon, Sir John 160, 161, 162, 165
Sinclair, May 362
Sisson, Edgar 214
Siwinna, Carl, Guide for Fantasy Strategists 6
Slav nationalism 61, 99, 100
 see also Serbia
Slevogt, Max, artist xxxi
Slovaks 145
Smith, F. E. 166, 223
Smith-Cumming, Cdr Mansfield, British spy 12–13
Social Democratic Party (SPD) (Germany) 17, 124
 anti-militarism 23, 25–6, 122
 and military spending 122, 123, 493n, 494n
 reaction to outbreak of war 178–9
 social inequality 278–9
 socialist parties
 in France 29–30
 pre-war electoral successes 28, 29
 see also Labour Party; Social Democratic Party
soldiers
 collective identity 354–5, 446
 comforts and discomforts 350–54, 446
 desertion 344–5, 367
 discipline and punishments 346–8, 446
 distortion of time 365–6
 excitement of fighting 360–63, 446–7
 informal truces 343–4
 killing of prisoners 373–84
 leave 353–4
 leisure and humour 352

motivations xliv, 201–3, 205–7, 446–7
 mutinies 345, 367
 natural aggression 357–60, 447
 pay 343
 permanently crippled (pensioners) 437, 527n
 and post-war violence 388–91
 propaganda directed at 225, 238, 355, 444
 religion among 355–7, 446
 revenge 382–3, 447
 risks and fatalism 363–5, 447, 450, 452
 shell-shock 341–2
 see also casualties; morale; surrender; trench
  warfare
Somerset Maugham, W. 378–9, 386
Somme offensive 292, 305
Sophie, Duchess of Hohenberg 146, 507n
Sorley, Charles Hamilton, poet 448
South Africa 51–2
 casualty rate 299
 see also Boer War
South-West Africa, German colony in 47
Spain 52, 54
Spencer, Harold 231
Spencer, Stanley, artist 456
spiritualism 356
Spring offensive (1918) 285, 293–4, 316, 386–7, 448
Springs, Elliott White, American writer xxx
Squire, J. C. 179–80
Stamforth, Lt John 382
Steed, Henry Wickham, foreign editor of Times 32,
  195, 217
Steiner, Rudolf, theosophist 18
Steinhauer, Gustav, German spy 12
Stevenson, Frances 164
Stewart, Maj John 384
Stinnes, Hugo 33, 259, 263, 424
 on annexation plans 287–8
Stone, Capt Christopher 385
Stop the War Committee 181, 186
strategy xliii, 88, 445
 attrition 292–4, 297, 300–304
 British navalist 291–2
 defence in depth 309
 French 96, 167, 285
 German 282–5, 308–9, 315–16
 see also Schlieffen Plan
Strauss, Richard, Oxford honorary doctorate 24
Stravinsky, Igor 453
strikes 23, 271, 274–5
 Britain 274–5, 396, 445
 Germany 271, 275, 275, 445
 in Russia (1914) 30
Strong, T. B. 183
Stuart Jones, H. 183
Stücklein, Daniel 136
submarine warfare 230, 282–4
 effect on trade 253
Sudan, Anglo-French antagonism over 41–2

suffragettes 205
suicide 367
Sukhomlinov, General V. A. 263
Sulzbach, Herbert 198, 379, 389, 523n
Summerall, Maj Gen Charles P., US Army 387
surrender
    dangers of 368–9, 371, 447
    by German soldiers 300, 311, 312, 368, 386–8,
       447
    rationale of 367–73
    see also prisoners-of-war
Sutherland, Pte David 438
Swinton, Maj Ernest 223
Switzerland 101, 146
Symbolism, in poetry xxvi
Syria 434
Szögyéni-Marich, Count Ladislaus 148, 151

Tames, Charles 378
tanks 260, 290, 307
tariff reform, Britain 39
tariffs
    France 120
    on German imports 417
    Germany (Reich) 122
    see also free trade; taxation
Tawney, R. H. 353–4
taxation
    direct 115–16, 118, 119, 120–21
    to finance war 322–4
    German post-war reforms 410–11
    indirect 115–16, 118, 121, 122, 125, 320
    to service national debt 426–7
    of war profits 323
Taylor, A. J. P. xxxviii
    The First World War xxxiii–xxxiv
technology, military xxxviii, 9, 93, 310
    air power 290, 310
    artillery 93, 96, 303, 307–8, 310–11
    tanks 260, 290, 307
Teilhard de Chardin, Pierre 361
telegraph, effect on money markets 130
television
    1914–1918 documentary xxxii
    Testament of Youth xxiii
    The Great War documentary xxxii
Territorial Army 14, 102
    enlistment 200
Thiepval, war memorial xlii, 437
Thomas, Albert, French minister 260, 261–2
Thomas, D. A. (Lord Rhondda) 262
    Minister of Food 276
Thomas, Edward, poet 449
Thomas, W. Beach 234
Thompson, D. C., Weekly News 11
Thompson, Edward, memoirs 451
Thomson, J. J. 182
Thurstan, Violetta 362

Tibet, Russian interests in 54
time, distorted in battle 365–6
Times, The
    bellicosity 217–18
    censorship 220
    circulation 243, 243, 244, 245
    'Declaration by Authors' 228
Tirpitz, Grand Admiral Alfred von xxxv, 97, 154
    naval programme 32, 70, 71, 83–4, 486n
    strategy 283, 287
Tonkin (Indo-China), French expedition 41
Toynbee, Arnold 232
toys, patriotic 229
Tracy, Louis, novelist 4–5
trade
    British capital exports 35, 36–7
    controls 265–7
    deficits 253–4, 254
    disruption of 9, 195, 250, 276
    German exports 34–5, 38–9
    German post-war deficits 413, 417–18, 540n
    post-war recovery 412
    see also free trade
trade unions 178, 273–4, 274, 346, 445
    Germany 273–4, 274, 445
trench warfare
    Christmas truces 343–4
    effect on nature of war 88, 303
    horrors of 340–4
    newspapers 238, 352
    standard of trenches 350
Trevelyan, Charles 161, 162, 165
Trevelyan, G. M. 182, 228
Triple Alliance (Germany, Austria and Italy) 46,
    150
    military spending 106, 107, 108–9, 111
    see also Central Powers; individual countries
Triple Entente (Britain, France and Russia) 150
    available manpower 298
    economic superiority 444–5
    killing efficiency 294, 300, 445
    military spending 106, 107, 108–9, 111
    moral superiority on neutrals 247
    naval superiority 85
    population 248, 249
    trade controls 266–7
    war costs per death 337, 445
    war expenditure 322, 323
    see also individual countries
Triple Entente (Britain, Italy and Austria) (secret)
    46
Tripoli, Italian invasion (1911) 99
Trotsky, Leon, ruthlessness of 392–4
Turkey 291, 390
    and Armenia 210, 434, 542n
    casualties 295, 299
    German interests in 69, 143, 148
    loss of territory 409, 434

POWs 369
  war costs per death 337
Tweedmouth, Lord, First Lord of Admiralty 63, 70
Tyrrell, William, Grey's PPS 71–2, 74

Ukraine 145, 286, 409, 434
Ullstein, Leopold 246
Ulster Volunteer Force 164
Umbreit, Paul, on German post-war economy 425
unemployment 188, 189, 206
  effect of deflationary policies on 431–2
  labour market inflexibility 439
  see also labour supply; trade unions
Ungaretti, Giuseppe, poet xxvii, 449
uniforms and clothing 350
Union of Democratic Control (UDC) 182
Union of Soviet Socialist Republics (USSR) 436,
    440, 452–3
United States of America xxx, 54–5, 145, 434
  Allied trade controls 266–7
  American Expeditionary Force 312, 343, 387
  casualties 295, 299, 312
  censorship 222–3
  cost of living 331
  enters war 209, 284
  finance for Britain 327–9, 396, 418
  foreign investment 36
  industrial production 251
  loans to Central Powers 328
  national debt 324, 324, 325–6, 325, 421, 422
  New York finance markets 328, 329, 333, 336
  POWs 369
  propaganda 214, 225, 227
  relations with Britain 54–5
  Senate repudiation of Versailles 439
  trade with neutrals 253
  war costs per death 337
  war debts 419
  war economy 262–3, 444–5
  war loans 325–6
universities
  academic denigration 233
  apologetics for war 228–9
  German 18–19, 25, 228, 233
  opposition to war 182–3
  see also Oxford

Van Creveld, Martin 360, 362
Vaughan, Edwin Campion 340
Venezuela 50, 54
Verdun 285, 316, 437, 521n
Versailles, Treaty of xliv, 412
  as economic disaster 397
  Keynes's criticism of 399–400, 407
  see also reparations
veterans' associations xxii, 17
Vickers Brothers 32
Victoria, Queen, German connections 25

violence
  continuing post-war 388–91, 452–3
  indulgence in 358–9, 362–3, 379–80, 382–3
  in Russian Civil War 392–4
Viviani, René, French premier 29
Volunteer Force 15
Vondung, Klaus 210
Vring, Georg von der 452

wages
  differentials 271–3
  and productivity 271
Wagner, Siegfried (son of Richard) 24
Waldersee, Alfred Count von 88, 89, 99
Waldersee, Georg Count von 151, 153–4
Wallas, George 182
Wandel, General Franz von, on Ludendorff's plans
    91 war
  expectation of protracted struggle 88, 97–8,
    319–20
  sells newspapers 11, 212, 241, 242, 243–6, 243,
    244
  see also armies; trench warfare
War Council (British), despatch of BEF 167
war memorials xlii, 437–8
  cemeteries xxxiii
  Glasgow Academy xxi–xxii
  two minutes' silence 438
War Office (British) 74, 103
  and plans for Expeditionary Force 62
  propaganda films 226
  see also Committee of Imperial Defence;
    Haldane; Robertson
War Press Office (Germany) 220
War Raw Materials Office (KRA) (Germany) 258,
    261
Warburg, Aby 237
Warburg, Max, banker
  and 1914 bank crisis 191–2, 197
  advice to Kaiser against war 33, 100
  on economic strategy on reparations 412
  and German bond yields 135
  German financial weakness 137, 139
  on hyperinflation 425
  relations with Rothschilds 70
  and reparations proposals 400, 401, 406, 409
  restrictions on submarines 284
  suggestion of Baltic colonies 441
  talks in Belgium 287
  and war economy 257
Warburg (M. M.) & Co. bank 69, 139, 400
Warburg, Paul 402
Ware, Sir Fabian 436
Webb, Sidney and Beatrice 23, 319
Weber, Max, National Liberalism 19
Weill, George 215
Weisbuch, Friedrich 376
Wells, H. G. 210, 228, 229

Mr Britling Sees It Through xxviii, 236
War in the Air 6–7
Weltpolitik, German xli, 19, 68, 83
Wermuth, Adolf, German Treasury secretary 135
Westarp, Kuno Count von 124
Western Front
    British strategy 291
    German strategy 284–5
    see also Schlieffen Plan
Whitehall Gardens conference 62–3
William II, Kaiser xxxvi, 25, 191, 288, 289, 499n
    ambitions 169, 170
    calls for naval agreement 70–71
    exile 435
    financial constraints on military 137
    suggests pre-emptive war 33, 100, 152
    'war council' of 1912 65, 68, 85, 91
Williamson, Henry xxx
Wilson, Arthur, First Sea Lord 66
Wilson, Charles Rivers 342
Wilson, H. W., on Angell's *The Great Illusion* 23
Wilson, Sir Henry, Director of Military Operations
    69, 105, 313, 315
    and deployment of BEF 167
    prediction of Franco-German war 65–6, 103
    and use of Territorials 102
Wilson, Woodrow, US President xxxviii, 20, 55, 329
    and British finance 327–8
    Fourteen Points 214, 317
    and League of Nations 434
    and self-determination 286, 439
Winnington-Ingram, A. F., Bishop of London
    208–9
Wirth, Joseph, German Chancellor 411
Wittgenstein, Ludwig 207
Witthoefft, Franz 410
Wodehouse, P. G., *The Swoop!* 6
Wolff, Theodor, journalist 151
women
    excitement of war 362
    in labour force 267, 268, 519n
    pressure on men to enlist 205–6
Wood, Walter, *The Enemy in our Midst* 2
Woolf, Virginia xxviii–xxix, 181, 322
working class
    German anti-militarist 25–6
    as recruits 199, 206–7
    unemployment 189
    see also socialist parties; trade unions
writers
    academic 228–9, 231
    ex-soldiers' memoirs xxix
    German origins of British 24
    historians xxxiii–xxxv, xxxix–xlii
    modern fiction xxxi
    non-combatant xxvii–xxix
    pessimistic 6–11
    political and military memoirs xxxv–xxxvi
    popular 228, 229, 231
    'prophetic' novelists 1–2
    see also journalists; novels; poetry; propaganda

Yanushkevich, General Nikolai, Russian CGS
    157–8
York Liberal Association 77
Yorkshire Post 218
Young Committee recommendations (1929) 415
Younghusband, Sir Francis 227
Ypres
    first battle 168
    third battle 293, 305
    Wipers Times 238

Zanzibar 47
Zenhoff, Hugo am, Prussian minister 428
Zimmermann, Arthur, Foreign minister 286
Zimmermann, Hugo 376
Zuckmayer, Carl, poetry xxvi, xxvii
Zweig, Arnold, *The Case of Sergeant Grischa* xxx
Zweig, Stefan 176